TALL SHIPS
AND
TANKERS

THE HISTORY OF THE DAVIE SHIPBUILDERS

Eileen Reid Marcil

Copyright © 1997 by Davie Industries Inc.

All rights reserved. The use of any part of this publication reproduced, transmitted in any form or by any means, electronic, mechanical, photocopying, recording, or otherwise, or stored in a retrieval system, without the prior written consent of the publisher – or, in case of photocopying or other reprographic copying, a licence from the Canadian Copyright Licensing Agency – is an infringement of the copyright law.

Canadian Cataloguing in Publication Data

Marcil, Eileen
    Tall ships and tankers : the history of the Davie shipbuilders

Issued also in French under title: Au rythme des marées.
Include bibliographical references and index.
ISBN 0-7710-5666-4

1. Davie Industries - History. 2. Shipbuilding - Quebec (Province) - Lévis - History. 3. Shipyards - Quebec (Province) - Lévis - History. I. Title.

VM301.D38M37 1997   338.7623830971459   C97-931733-9

Every reasonable effort has been made to give appropriate credit for copyright material that appears in this book. The publisher apologizes for any inadvertent error or omission.

The publishers acknowledge the support of the Canada Council and the Ontario Arts Council for their publishing program.

Set in Minion by M&S, Toronto
Printed and bound in Canada

McClelland & Stewart Inc.
The Canadian Publishers
481 University Avenue
Toronto, Ontario
M5G 2E9

1 2 3 4 5   01 00 99 98 97

TABLE OF CONTENTS

Foreword — v
Preface — ix

Introduction — 1

Part 1: Quebec
1. George Taylor 1811-17 — 19
2. Allison Davie 1821-31 — 27

Part 2: Levis
3. Levis 1831-36 — 41
4. Elizabeth Davie 1836-50 — 53
5. George T. Davie 1850-62 — 67
6. New Interests 1863-82 — 77

Part 3: Lauzon
7. Lauzon 1882-97 — 97
8. George T. Davie & Sons 1897-1907 — 111
9. The Pre-War Years 1907-14 — 127
10. George Duncan Davie 1914-19 — 143

Part 4: The Struggle to Survive
11. Canada Steamship Lines (1) 1920-25 — 167
12. Canada Steamship Lines (2) 1925-39 — 187

Part 5: Naval and Wartime Shipbuilding
13. At Last, A Home-Built Navy 1910-45 — 217
14. The Ships 1939-45 — 225
15. Workers and Workplace 1939-45 — 245

Part 6: Post War

16 Transition to Peacetime Production 1945-51   267

Part 7: The Golden Years

17 The McLagan-Lowery Team 1951-58   291
18 The St. Lawrence Seaway 1959-68   319
19 Takis Veliotis 1959-68   347

Part 8: New Challenges

20 Power Corporation 1968-76   375
21 Head Office, Lauzon 1976-81   403
22 Dome and Versatile Davie 1981-87   425
23 MIL – Donald Challinor 1987-89   443
24 MIL – Guy Véronneau 1989-96   457
25 Looking Ahead 1991-96   475

Epilogue   493

Appendices

Appendix A: South Shore Jurisdiction   505
Appendix B: Davie Family Genealogy   506
Appendix C: Davie Shipyard Presidents   508
Appendix D: Presidents of the Shipyard Workers' Union 1949-97 509
Appendix E: Yard Lists   510

Abbreviations Used in Notes and Bibliography   535

Notes   536

Bibliography   569

Glossary of Shipbuilding and Nautical Terms   578

Index of Ships   581
General Index   588

FOREWORD

It is with a great deal of pride that we have undertaken to introduce this story of over 170 years of human endeavour, a history that predates Canada. It is also particularly gratifying that we can publish this work in 1997 – the centenary of the first ship built by Davie on the present site and, at the same time, the 350th anniversary of the founding of Levis.

As the new owner of Davie, we are very conscious that we are following in the footsteps of some great men and women, people who have dedicated their lives, and those of their families, to the complex, arduous, and often dangerous task of building and repairing ships and other industrial work.

Without question, Davie is a family story, full of happy times and successes as well as disappointments and failures. It is also a story that reflects a wider sphere of interests: the development of the South Shore communities; the maturing of a nation at war and at peace; the dramatic changes of its marine industries as they went from wood to steel and from sail to steam and then to diesel; the growth of a trading nation. As we tour the yard and the ships under construction, we are also struck by the advanced computer technologies employed by Davie both in its construction processes and in the ships' own equipment and systems. Far from being part of a sunset industry of yesteryear as so many people believe, we see a vibrant spirit fighting to survive in what has become a worldwide industry dominated by low-cost, high-tech but subsidized players.

Despite all these changes, it is clear that many of the challenges that face us today are little different from those that were faced by Allison,

FOREWORD

George T., George D., and Charlie. The uncertainties of Canada's maritime policies, the absence of a strong merchant marine, the ever-present need for capital investment, the extreme business cycles that can quickly lead from a boom to a bust with the attendant misery that unemployment brings to its family of workers, as well as the ever-present challenge of taming the Quebec winters, these are situations that always seem to have been with us.

But, notwithstanding all the difficulties and the frustrations, shipbuilding at Lauzon and Levis has always been a colourful and challenging business, a glorious story that deserves to be told and to be shared with all those with an interest in maritime affairs.

We are grateful to the past managements of Davie who had the foresight to see that this book had to be written. With the passage of time and the many rapid changes of ownership over the last twenty years, there was a great danger the history might be lost. That it has taken some eight years to gather together and to write is not surprising when one sees the depth of detail that has been incorporated. It is a fascinating story and Dr. Eileen Marcil is to be congratulated on a superb work.

It is also very fitting, we believe, that the task of completing the history and seeing it through to publication has fallen on us. Dominion Bridge itself was born in 1882, the same year that George Taylor Davie moved his yard from the small site near the ferry landing to a site adjacent to the Lorne Dry Dock. Dominion Bridge and Davie have always had a close relationship, whether as competitors or in various joint and co-operative ventures so that this joining of two prestigious Quebec-based Canadian companies provides a natural conclusion to the book while marking the beginning of a new chapter in both their histories.

It is a tribute to the dedication, skill, and determination of our predecessors that the company continues to forge ahead under the Davie name. We are proud to have been able to play our part in ensuring its continuance and to have helped in the telling of this glorious history. We also hope that,

FOREWORD

in its telling, it will rekindle the belief in Canadian skills and workmanship and will inspire future generations to reach for the sky.

The Board of Directors

Left: *Michel Marangère, chairman and* CEO *of Dominion Bridge Corporation.*
Middle: *Nicolas Matossian, president and* COO *of Dominion Bridge Corporation.* Right: *J.-Arthur Gélinas, vice-president of Dominion Bridge Corporation, president and* CEO *of Industries Davie Inc.*

Michel L. Marengère   Nicolas Matossian   J. Arthur Gélinas

PREFACE

When Michael Ayre and I met at the wedding of the daughter of a mutual friend, we immediately found a subject of common interest. Mike, a vice-president of the MIL Davie shipyard in Lauzon, was convinced that the shipyard's long history was worth telling. I had just completed a study of the construction of wooden square riggers at Quebec and shared his opinion. Fortunately, Davie's president, Don Challinor, did, too. Since then, the Davie shipyard has changed owner, and I am particularly grateful to the Dominion Bridge Corporation for consenting to the completion and publication of the history, and for the strong support that it has given the project.

It was to be a factual account written primarily for the shipyard's past and present employees and their families, and it was to cover the entire Davie story from the arrival of the first Quebec shipbuilder in the family in 1811 until the present day. The wealth of nineteenth-century documents at the Archives nationales de Quebec would provide the main sources for the first part of the history. The problem would be the first decades of the twentieth century. But I was fortunate, as the prompt action of Daniel Johnson and Pierre Préfontaine led to many documents giving insight to that period literally being snatched from the incinerator, and the history was saved. To them both, my sincere thanks.

As to the more recent history, much has depended on the willingness of individuals to be interviewed. I would like to thank: Wilbrod Bherer, Gordon Black, Louis Desmarais, Paul Gourdeau, Marcel Lafrance, Richard Lowery, Paul Martin, Robert McGilvray, Arthur Nightingale, Maurice

PREFACE

Provencher, Louis Rochette, Ladrière Samson, John Stubbs, Edward White, and Ken Wood, all of whom passed on information that I particularly needed, or helped me obtain it, and were more than generous with their time. I offer special thanks to Louis Rochette, who read the manuscript and clarified a number of points.

I spoke also to many other Davie employees and retirees, and people who had a different connection with the yard. Some meetings helped fill in a large section of the jigsaw puzzle, while others produced only a small missing piece. But regardless of how much of the interviews actually went into the book – the space being limited – the time that each person gave me was invaluable in that it helped me to understand the yard better, and though I cannot mention each of them by name, I thank each and every one of those to whom I have spoken.

And I thank also the members of the Davie family who shared the family history they knew: Lynne Brodie; Anne Mimi Garneau; James and Derek Hannaford; Fleur Whitworth; and Brenda Wilson.

In Quebec and elsewhere, I have benefited from the patience and kindness of archivists and librarians, among them many members of the staff of the Archives nationales du Québec à Québec, in particular Yves Robert, Marie-Jeanne Rochette, Denis Giguère, Pierre-Louis Lapointe, Renald Lessard, Jacques Morin, Marjolaine Thibault, and Celine Villeneuve. My thanks also to Patricia Kennedy, Steve Salmon, and Eva Marotte, at the National Archives, Ottawa; and Glenn Wright, formerly of the Public Records Office, all of whom have never failed to respond. Monique Mailloux of the Laval University library and M. Lepine of the Bibliothèque nationale in Montreal were most helpful, as were also Graham Gavert at Elco and Anita Diamant at the Alcan Archives.

I am indebted also to: Maurice Smith and Earl Morehead of the Marine Museum of the Great Lakes at Kingston, whose fine CSL and German and Milne collections helped greatly in the writing of this book; Sonia Chassé and Alain Franck of the Musée Maritime Bernier; Mme. Gosselin, archivist at the Société du Port de Québec; Michael Moir at the Toronto Harbour

PREFACE

Commission; the staff of the Baldwin Room at the Metropolitan Toronto Library; and Nora Hague at the McCord Museum, Montreal.

The photographs in the history come mainly from Davie's own photographic archives. I am indebted, however, to Christine, Margot, and Rolande Gagnon for allowing us to choose freely from their collection; to Paul Gourdeau for allowing us access to his; and to Robert Aspinall of the Museum in Docklands, London; Lynne Brodie; William Campbell; Calista Cave; Gustave Charland; Michel Lessard; James Morton; Robert I. Perrault; Mildred Payson; Tony Price; the Maritime Museum of British Columbia; Brenda Wilson; and the many Davie employees who submitted photos enabling a wide choice to be made.

Members of Mike Ayre's department deserve special mention: Steve Kack, who was given the task of finding answers to my queries and threw in photographic services; Gina Perreault, public relations officer, who was always willing to search for missing information; and Maryse Prince, who helped in a great many ways – including dealing with my computer glitches. David Christopher, Michael Donnison, Gisèle Giguère, and Charles Méthot were all very helpful. Nor do I forget the varied help I received from Lise Cardinal, Ken Childs, Farhad Cohensedgh, John Cook, Paul Crandall, Alec Douglas, Max Dunbar, Pierre Gaudet, Frank Rowan, Duncan Stacey, Bill Swanson, and Roland Webb, who all helped in various ways.

Lastly, writing this history and getting to know something about the Davie shipyard has been a privilege, and I thank Mike Ayre for giving me that opportunity, and I thank him for his patience in reading and re-reading the manuscript and for his many suggestions.

And finally, I am fortunate to have had Jonathan Webb as my editor at McClelland & Stewart. I greatly appreciate his most efficient editing and knowledgeable suggestions, and thank him also for remaining cheerful and supportive throughout.

What writer does not owe a debt of gratitude to his family? I thank each and everyone.

Master Shipbuilder George Taylor (1782-1861). "The Founder." Oil painting by an unidentified artist. Courtesy Anne Mimi Garneau.

INTRODUCTION

Platers and welders have largely taken the place of the ship carpenter, and engineers have supplanted the sailmaker and his ally, the wind, but pride in building a good ship is as strong today as it was a hundred years ago, and nowhere is that more evident than at the launching of a ship at the Davie shipyard in Lauzon. The chapters that follow tell the story of George Taylor and of Allison and Elizabeth Davie, and their descendants; of the shipyards that they established where close to a thousand ships have been built; of the generations of skilled craftsmen who spent their working lives in those yards and the people who work there today. But first a short introduction to the South Shore opposite Quebec City, where Allison Davie established his shipyard more than 160 years ago.

In 1628, a large tract of land across the St. Lawrence River from Quebec was given the name "Pointe Lévy" by the explorer Samuel de Champlain in honour of Henry de Lévy, Duke of Ventadour and Vice-Roy of New France. In 1636, it became the lower half of Sieur Jean de Lauson's Seigneury of Lauson,[1] and eleven years later the first two concessions were granted to François Byssot (or Bissot) de la Rivière and Guillaume Couture respectively who thus became the seigneury's first *censitaires*.[2] Bissot, the son of a bourgeois, would hold several official positions in the seigneury and colony,

INTRODUCTION

The waterfront at Pointe Lévy. Old engraving.
P-600-6 /PN-276/3, ANQ.

including those of seigneurial attorney and provost judge, while at the same time undertaking various industrial and commercial activities. Couture, though a timber-framer by trade, would be better known as a Jesuit layman (*donné*), Indian interpreter, explorer, ambassador, farmer, and judge, and even as an alternative member of the Governor's Conseil Souverain.[3]

Both would exert considerable influence in the early days of the seigneury, but it is Bissot the manufacturer who concerns us here. After building a flour mill on the banks of the brook that separated their properties, and ensuring its success by having it named the "*moulin banal*" or common mill to which the *censitaires* were obliged to take their grain to be ground, he turned next to establishing the first tannery in New France. Soon the prepared hides of cattle, deer, seal, and porpoise were being delivered to Quebec's shoemakers who made it up into footgear and muffs, chests and trunks. Within a few years, and because the intendant Jean Talon insisted that the army wear shoes made in the colony, enough leather was being tanned to make 8,000 pairs of shoes a year.[4] Of all the industries that Talon set up in the colony, the tannery was probably the most successful. It was also the first important industry in the Seigneury of Lauson.

Gradually, new settlers arrived on the South Shore. They cleared the land and tilled and sowed their fields. They hunted and fished, and maintained harmonious relations with the native Algonquians who spent the summers on the riverbanks. They witnessed the growth and development of the town of Quebec on the other side of the river. They saw the arrival of the spring fleet each year, bringing new colonists and supplies, and the departure of the last ships at the end of the season, before the river froze over. They watched with pride as the first merchant ships were launched from the Intendant's shipyard at the mouth of the St-Charles River in 1666, and with disappointment when the yard ground to a standstill a few years later.[5]

In 1675, when the increase in the population on the South Shore warranted the founding of a parish, a gift from King Louis XIV helped pay for the construction of the Church of Saint-Joseph-de-la-Pointe-Lévy on land donated by François Bissot adjoining his tannery and mill. The church would be restored and enlarged in 1721 by Guillaume Couture, son of the original settler, and rebuilt on the same site in 1830 after it burned down.[6]

In 1739, a royal naval dockyard was set up on the St. Charles River at Quebec to build warships for the French navy. Within a few years the dockyard had spilled into a second yard in the Lower Town, and a total of ten warships were built at the two yards between 1742 and 1756. It was an achievement of which René-Nicolas Levasseur, the French master builder, the craftsmen who came to the colony to oversee the program, and all the local workers who learned their trade from them could be proud.[7]

There was no counterpart to Quebec's development at Pointe Lévy, however, and the population there remained small. The St. Lawrence was a formidable barrier that, though it gave protection to the town of Quebec, effectively cut off the land opposite, leaving it vulnerable to attack. By the end of the French regime, the number of concessions that had been granted

INTRODUCTION

had increased, but few of the *censitaires* had made their home there.

Following the cession of New France to Britain in 1763, the Seigneury of Lauson was bought by General Murray who, on leaving the colony shortly after, leased it to Major Henry Caldwell before selling it to him outright.[8] Caldwell, who thus became its eleventh seigneur, was the first to make a special effort to develop the land.[9] Within months a large grist (coarse flour) mill had been built at the mouth of the Etchemin River. The timing was not propitious, however, for the following year, when American troops invaded Canada, they burned it down. Undeterred, Caldwell rebuilt the mill as soon as the conflict ended and pursued his goal, vigorously promoting both agriculture and industry in the seigneury. In 1803, he handed over the administration of the seigneury to his son John, and by 1804 the grist mill had grown into a huge complex of grist mills and sawmills with wharfing around them where twenty ships could

Saint-Joseph-de-la-Pointe-Lévy, 1838. Henry William Bernard, NA, C-11923.

INTRODUCTION

load.[10] John Caldwell was naturally receptive when timber contractors came to Canada with large orders to fill for the Admiralty. From 1809 on, the beaches on either side of his mill complex served as timber-forwarding coves. Those to the west of the mill property at New Liverpool were occupied by the Hamilton Brothers; those to the east at Hadlow Cove by Christopher Idle & Company.[11]

Caldwell's plans for the development of the seigneury called for the founding of a town on the heights opposite Quebec, but once again their implementation was delayed by circumstances outside his control – this time, the War of 1812. When it ended, he bought back enough of the conceded land to found his town. He set aside property for a church, a park, and a marketplace, and offered the rest for sale, subdivided into building lots. He called the new town Aubigny. To make it more accessible, he joined in partnership with the shipbuilder John Goudie and others for the construction of a steam ferryboat that would link Quebec and Pointe Lévy. The 86-foot side wheeler *Lauzon*, built by Goudie and put into operation on a fixed schedule in 1818, was the first steamboat built at Quebec and also the first steam ferry on the St. Lawrence River. In conjunction with the ferry service, a hotel was built at the South Shore landing place, which boasted stabling for 150 horses.

Local ferrymen, who were known for their resourcefulness and independence of spirit, and for the skill with which they carried man, beast, goods, and even conveyances across the river in open boats or canoes, reacted angrily to the paddle steamer *Lauzon*, the *chienne d'invention anglaise* that stole their trade. But the *Lauzon*'s first captain, Michel Lecours dit Barras, and other operators were hired from among them, and they realized the potential benefits the new technology offered. Soon, they became enthusiastic proponents of the use and advancement of mechanical invention, and in particular of steam. Within a few years several of the former canoe men were steamboat owners.

Meanwhile, in spite of the active shipping market and the expansion of shipbuilding in the port, the South Shore had not attracted a permanent

INTRODUCTION

Left: Agreement with the crew members of the tug Powerful. *Right: The timber drogher* Columbus, *3,690 tons. Built by Charles Wood in 1824 on the southeast tip of the Isle of Orleans, entirely of square timber, she was the largest vessel afloat at the time. Courtesy Musée du Québec.*

shipyard. A few large ships were built in the timber coves prior to the War of 1812, but in the record years 1825 and 1826, when eighty-eight large sailing ships (32,600 tons of shipping) were built in shipyards in the port of Quebec, not one was laid down on the South Shore. Even the well-situated property close to the ferry landing at Pointe Lévy offered for sale as "suitable for a shipbuilding yard" in 1824 did not tempt a builder.

Nevertheless, the people of the South Shore, like their neighbours opposite, were caught up in the excitement of the several maritime firsts that dazzled Quebeckers and visitors alike during the 1820s. In 1823, for instance, the first purpose-built towboat (tug) appeared in the harbour, and in the same year a huge, 3,690-ton timber carrier was laid down on the southwest tip of the Isle of Orleans. Attention was focused on the port of Quebec from as far away as London, as the Scottish naval architect Charles Wood successfully launched the *Columbus* despite the dire predictions of many sceptics. Before leaving for London aboard her, he laid down an even larger vessel, the 5,280-ton *Baron of Renfrew*.[12] Then in 1827 the first

INTRODUCTION

floating dry dock to be put into service in North America arrived at Quebec from the shipbuilder's yard in Montreal.

At last, in 1832, a shipbuilder by the name of Allison Davie realized the potential benefits of locating on the South Shore. He moved his shipyard across the river from Quebec to a site below the cliffs near the ferry landing and installed a patent slip, or marine railway, thus establishing the first real shipbuilding industry on the South Shore.

Before long James Tibbits, a New Brunswick merchant, joined him. In addition to setting up a timber-forwarding cove at the beach property he rented to the south of the ferry landing, Tibbits established a shipyard, a large foundry, and a machine shop, bringing over English and Scottish engineers and founders to work there while training local labourers. Benjamin Huot dit Saint Laurent and Zéphirin Leblanc are among those who profited from the training. Later, they would be largely responsible for the South Shore's rise to prominence as a marine engineering centre.[13]

Then in 1843, John Nicholson and his partner William G. Russell

INTRODUCTION

packed their shipyard on the Canoterie into the floating dock they had just built and towed it across the St. Lawrence to a new location immediately to the south of Tibbits's foundry, and another important South Shore shipbuilding enterprise was born. Though Nicholson died shortly after, the shipyard survived until early in the twentieth century, sending many a fine square-rigged sailing ship down the ways, and when there was no longer a demand for sailing ships, building an occasional steamboat to supplement the ship repairs. Other smaller shipyards were set up in the 1840s, but were short-lived. At William Benson's yard at New Liverpool, only two ships were laid down; at William Henry and Edmund Sewell's yard at the north end of Notre Dame des Victoires, only four.

The South Shore shipyards and timber coves attracted new settlers, who in turn needed homes and services. By the mid-nineteenth century, the population had grown considerably, and the Church of Saint-Joseph-de-la-Pointe-Lévy, although rebuilt and enlarged after it burned in 1830, was too small. As a result, in 1851 Aubigny and the area around it above and

The Church of Notre-Dame-de-la-Victoire, Levis, in 1870. Built in 1851 in what was known at the time as the Town of Aubigny (Levis) to accommodate the parishioners in that rapidly expanding area. P600-6/N-1075-35, ANQ.

INTRODUCTION

below the cliff were officially detached from the old parish to form the new Paroisse de Notre-Dame-de-la-Victoire-de-Lévis. At the same time, the area's municipal affairs were entrusted to the Corporation de la Paroisse de Notre Dame de la Victoire, which received its charter ten years later as the "Ville de Levis" or "Town of Levis."[14] According to the 1851 Canadian census, there were 4,415 souls in the new parish, while the mother church, which had already lost some of its territory to the breakaway Parish of Saint-Jean-Chrysostôme in 1828, was left with a vastly reduced membership of 1,535.[15]

The founding of the Parish of Notre-Dame-de-la-Victoire was the signal for the development for which both Henry and John Caldwell had striven so hard. In 1851, forty-two large sailing ships were built in the port of Quebec, but only one of the nineteen shipyards in which they were built was on the South Shore. By 1881, however, South Shore shipbuilders such as Pierre Brunelle, senior and junior, Guillaume (William) Charland, senior and junior, George T. Davie, Hyppolite Dubord, Thomas Dunn,

Guillaume Francoeur dit Charland (or William Charland Sr.). Charland began building sailing ships in 1848 and laid down the port of Quebec's last square rigger, the barquentine White Wings, *at his Lauzon shipyard (now part of the Davie shipyard) in 1893.*
Courtesy Gustave Charland.

INTRODUCTION

Charles Jobin, F.-X. Marquis, Etienne Samson, and Edmund Sewell[16] had between them built close to a hundred large sailing ships for the overseas market, some of them to order and others on speculation. They were good ships. William Coker, surveyor for Lloyd's Register of British and Foreign Shipping, described Brunelle's 688-ton ship *Anomia* of 1860 as "remarkably well put together," adding, "the workmanship throughout is excellent." He even went so far as to compare the work done in Brunelle's shipyard with that done in the Royal Dockyards in Britain. He wasn't the only one to appreciate Brunelle's skill. The 1,122-ton ship *Brunelle* of 1855 often logged 14 knots, making her, according to her master, Captain Orkney of Greenock, one of the fastest ships afloat.[17] Meanwhile, Charland's 1,259-ton ship *Lauderdale* of 1880 obtained a class of 11A, the highest given by Lloyd's to any sailing ship built in the port.

But the demand for wooden sailing ships was nearing its end as steel-hulled ships proved their superiority, and one after another Quebec shipyard closed down. The yards on the South Shore held out the longest. During the 1880s and 1890s, they launched eleven of the last fourteen sailing ships that were built in the port. After that, an occasional contract to build a steamboat came their way, but the Davie and Russell yards relied for their survival on salvage and repair work, which they often executed in the large wooden floating docks that had become such an important part of their yards.

Most of the large deep-water sailing ships built on the South Shore had been destined for overseas ownership, but many of the steamboats that were built there were for South Shore owners. It is not possible to list all those who became involved in building or sailing them, but their more easily identifiable owners, who were also sometimes their builders or captains, include Jean-Baptiste Beaulieu; Julien Chabot; Georges and Ignace Couture; Allison, George, Gershom, and William Davie; Jean Duclos; Jean-Baptiste Dussault; Théodule Foissy; Pierre Lecours dit Barras; James McKenzie; Jacques Normand; Louis Poiré; Robert Sample; Edmund Sewell; James Tibbits; and François and Édouard Verreault. Their faith in steam played a

INTRODUCTION

William Charland Sr.'s 356-ton barquentine White Wings, *seen here on the day of her launching.* Fonds Wurtele, G-7, ANQ.

The steam ferry Northern Light, *393 tons, built at Levis by Edmund Sewell in 1876. She was the first icebreaker to work in the Gulf of St. Lawrence and the Northumberland Strait for the Dominion government.* Fonds Initial, N1176-150, ANQ.

INTRODUCTION

large part in the development of a vigorous engineering trade on the South Shore in the last half of the nineteenth century.

More important still were the Carrier, Lainé Foundry and Machine Shops. Long before Tibbits built his foundry, the Caldwell mills, set up with the help of British and American millwrights and engineers, had been a showplace of marine technology. James Tibbits put engineering skills within the grasp of the local inhabitants and stimulated their interest in marine applications of steam. Benjamin Huot dit Saint Laurent carried on his work, training men such as Damase Lainé, who in 1864 sought the financial assistance of the local merchant Charles William Carrier to set up a foundry in Levis, and established the Fonderie canadienne, owned by D. Lainé et Cie. Five years later the foundry was moved to the waterfront,[18] and a new company, Carrier, Lainé et Cie, was formed. Soon it was unrivalled in the trade on either side of the river. Many of the steamboats owned in the port were engined there, and for several decades all the marine engineers hired by the Dominion government are said to have been Carrier, Lainé trainees. Constantly innovative and expanding, the

This advertisement in the Quebec Directory *for Carrier, Lainé et Cie, makers of engines and boiler makers for mills and ships, shows their works on the waterfront at Levis. Offered are ships' bridges, girders, and framing of wrought iron; flour mill and sawmill machinery; kitchen and other types of stoves; and a variety of cast-iron utensils and ornaments. "Repairs of all kinds quickly carried out at moderate prices."*

INTRODUCTION

The statue of the Curé Joseph-David Déziel by the sculptor Louis-Philippe Hébert, which was erected in front of the Church of Notre-Dame-de-la-Victoire in 1885. Unknown photographer. P600-6/N-85-0124, ANQ.

company moved gradually into the manufacture of stoves and other equipment on a factory basis, bringing foremen from France and Belgium to train the workers.

In 1880, Carrier, Lainé et Cie received a considerable vote of confidence, and their workers a great boost, when it was entrusted by the Dominion government with the contract for the machinery for the new Lorne Dry Dock at Saint-Joseph-de-la-Pointe-Lévy (Lauzon). It is said that when the time came to set the machinery in motion a hitch occurred, but the veteran Zéphirin Leblanc was there to supply the magic touch that was needed. While the dry-dock machinery was being built, a contract for the construction of 100 railway flatbeds for the Intercolonial Railway was undertaken by the firm, and the employees worked around the clock to meet the deadline. The firm's versatility was demonstrated again in 1884 when a fire engine was built there for the town of Levis.

INTRODUCTION

Levis grew to be a town of considerable size, due in large measure to the driving force of its *curé*, Joseph-David Déziel. Its citizens had a strong sense of community, and it was well-endowed with public buildings. In November 1851, for instance, even before the parish church had been completed, a college building was already taking shape beside it. It was followed by a hospice for retired clergy and, in 1864, by a convent for the education of girls, and then by an orphanage. The parishioners' love and appreciation of the *curé*, who has always been considered the founder of both the parish and the town of Levis, was given expression three years after his death in the fine statue sculpted by Louis-Philippe Hébert that was erected in front of the church.[19]

In the last half of the nineteenth century, the South Shore benefited not only from increased activity in the port, but also from the railways that connected it to the Maritimes, to Richmond, Quebec, and Portland, Maine, at a time when the railway had not yet come to the North Shore. The South Shore's isolation from Quebec, although diminished because of the steamboats, became something of an advantage, fostering a strong bond among the workers, and good relations between employees and their employers. It was reported, for instance, that when Etienne Samson and Alexander

An early illustration of the Collège de Levis, whose first students enrolled in 1853.
P600-6/PN-287/3, ANQ.

14

INTRODUCTION

From Allison (Foddie) Davie's collection of photographs on glass plates, the Hotel de Ville, Levis. It was built from 1884 to 1885, a period of rapid expansion of the town during which both the railway and the Lorne Dry Dock were introduced.

Russell returned from a business trip to Britain in 1876, employees of the Dunn and Samson shipyard lined the road from the ferry landing to the yard, which they had decorated with flags and bunting, and welcomed their employer with enthusiastic *vivats* and rounds of rifle- and gunfire. Similar stories are told of the relationship between the workers and their bosses at Carrier, Lainé et Cie, and of the respect that was accorded George T. Davie by his men. Thus Pointe Lévy, so underdeveloped at the beginning of the nineteenth century, began the twentieth with a fast-growing urban population that had a strong common interest in marine engineering.

Almost 100 years later, the shipbuilding industry is still the driving force on the South Shore. Rue George D. Davie, which traces what had been the common boundary between the properties of François Bissot and Guillaume Couture more than three centuries ago, leads today to a large industrial site, whose sheds and building slips and docks, and the slow-moving cranes circling high above them, reveal the modern Davie shipyard.

Part One

QUEBEC

A flotilla of vessels leaving Quebec sails along the south channel between the Isle of Orleans and the St. Lawrence River's south shore. Those in the distance to the right of the flagpole are abreast of St. Patrick's Hole, where George Taylor was employed as master shipbuilder from 1811 to 1812. Those closer to Quebec are rounding Pointe Lévy. On the other side of town, centre left, *is the mouth of the St. Charles River and, below the spired buildings and out of sight, the Canoterie.* W.H. Bartlett, View from the Citadel of Quebec. Engraved by R. Wallis for *Canadian Scenery Illustrated*, London, 1832.

1

GEORGE TAYLOR

1811-17

On May 27, 1811, the ship *Three Brothers* slipped from the North Sea port of North Shields, England, and set sail for Quebec. Britain and France were at war, and her master no doubt pointed her head northward, taking the long way around the British Isles to avoid the Channel and thus lessen the chances of encountering an enemy warship or privateer. It was six weeks before she reached the Newfoundland Banks, and another six before she finally dropped anchor at Quebec, where the master shipbuilder Captain George Taylor, his wife, and eight-year-old daughter, Elizabeth, stepped ashore. One can well imagine the feeling of relief with which Taylor later wrote in the family Bible, "Arrived at Quebec, 19th August, after a fine passage. Thank God."

George Taylor's journey to Quebec, like that of many other shipwrights, was the result of Britain's dependence on imported timber. This dependence had begun two centuries earlier when charcoal-burning blast furnaces required for iron smelting began to proliferate, resulting in the depletion of domestic woodlands. In order to meet her normal cooking, heating, and building requirements, Britain was soon obliged to import timber, and the first shipments from the Baltic were unloaded in her ports. The huge quantities that were needed to rebuild London following the

Great Fire of 1666 further aggravated the shortage, and the situation worsened when extensive naval shipbuilding programs were begun in 1676. With one seventy-four–gun ship requiring the equivalent of 3,700 mature trees, the consumption of the Royal Dockyards alone grew from an average of less than 10,000 one-ton loads between 1688 and 1697 to five times that amount between 1760 and 1788.[1] When large quantities also had to be provided for the repair and replacement of the heavy shipping casualties of the Napoleonic Wars, more than a million loads of timber were imported annually.

In 1806, British timber merchants, who had built up a substantial trade shipping timber across the North Sea in protected convoys, found their supplies abruptly cut off as a result of Napoleon's blockade of the Baltic ports. With no stocks at home to fall back on, they began importing North American wood.[2] Admiralty contractors, who were similarly obliged to transfer their timber-harvesting operations to North America, and thus incurred heavier freight charges, were awarded a premium on their orders. And British shipwrights from naval dockyards were made available to help them both with the selection and cut of shipbuilding timber, and with the construction of the extra transports that were needed to carry it.

Soon the forests of Lake Ontario, Lake Champlain, and the Ottawa valley resounded to the woodsman's axe. On the water's edge, the fallen timber was built into rafts for its voyage to Quebec, where it was sorted and inspected by the cullers, ready for loading. A seemingly endless stretch of timber coves lay along the riverbanks above and below Quebec. The timber rafts came sweeping down the river and spilled their huge cargoes on to the beaches, while a forest of tall ships moored three or four deep waited for their holds to be filled.

But despite the large number of ships that were sent over for the timber, still more were required. Local shipyards were working to capacity, so ships were also laid down in the timber merchants' coves. Shipbuilders and timber merchants vied for the services of shipwrights. They hunted, sometimes in vain, for the seasoned shipbuilding timber they needed. They

Timber ship discharging at the Commercial Docks in the Port of London 1827, where many of Quebec's timber ships unloaded their cargoes. Engraving. Port of London Authority. Courtesy The Museum of London Museum in Docklands Project.

despaired over cargoes of iron, copper, sails, and rigging that had fallen prey to the enemy or the elements and would never reach them. But somehow the ships were built, and they sailed for Britain with their holds, and sometimes their decks, piled high with timber.

All the while, rising American anger at the frequency with which her supposedly neutral vessels were being searched for deserters by the British Navy increased the likelihood of a retaliatory invasion of Canada. Shipwrights' contracts stipulated that in the event of hostilities, they were to report immediately to one of the naval dockyards on the Great Lakes.[3]

George Taylor had been appointed by the merchants Patterson, Dyke and Company to supervise the construction of vessels in their timber cove at St. Patrick's Hole on the Isle of Orleans. He wasted no time in settling into his new job.[4] Before the year had ended, not only had contracts for the construction of three large ships, the 366-ton *Mary*, the 363-ton *Wolfe's Cove*, and the 407-ton *Thomas Henry*, been awarded by Patterson, Dyke, who agreed to "furnish a spot of ground sufficient for the building," but all had been laid down.⁵ The builders were mostly former Royal Dockyard employees, shipwrights such as William Gilley and John Ray, who undertook to build the entire hull, or subcontracted to plank the port or starboard side, or both, or to caulk or do the joinery, and so on, and hired their own gang to work with them. But as the ships took shape, the likelihood of an American invasion increased, and on June 18, 1812, likelihood became certainty: America declared war on Britain and her army advanced into Upper Canada. When the three ships under construction on the Isle of Orleans were completed,⁶ Taylor left for the Great Lakes at the head of a party of 120 shipwrights and 30 seamen.

Canada was far from prepared for the invasion. Its population was a bare 300,000, which, with its native allies and British soldiers (but with Britain an ocean away), faced an 8-million-strong America across an unprotected frontier. There were severe British losses on Lake Erie and on Lake Huron in the early stages of the war, but after York (Toronto) fell, the invading forces halted while they waited for their fleet on Lake Ontario to be strengthened, thus giving the battered Canadian colony a respite. There

---

TO SHIP CARPENTERS.
WANTED.

TWO or THREE MEN to undertake making the Masts, Spars, Yards, caps, tops and Tressel Trees, for a vessel now building at New-Liverpool, to whom liberal Wages will be given by the day; or, if prefered, a sum for making the whole complete.—Caulkers are also wanted to commence on the 1st day of March, either by the foot or by the day, inquire at the Subscribers' Office. GEO & WM HAMILTON.
Quebec, 18th January, 1814

Shipyard workers were in great demand during the War of 1812 when George and William Hamilton advertised for carpenters and caulkers.
Quebec Gazette, January 18, 1814.

then began the "Shipbuilders' War," as both countries called on their leading shipbuilders to out-build the other and gain control of the Great Lakes. Fortunately, the arrival at Kingston of several Quebec shipbuilders, with a large contingent of their workers, at a time when the regular dockyard staff was badly disorganized, tipped the scales in Canada's favour. Under the dynamic Quebec master shipbuilder John Goudie, several vessels were armed and others built. They included two frigates, the 60-gun *Prince Regent* and the 44-gun *Princess Charlotte*, and the 112-gun ship *St. Lawrence*, a ship the size of Nelson's *Victory* and the largest ship that would be built on the Great Lakes during the war. To have been given the contract to build this 2,000-ton three-decked warship at Kingston speaks of the respect in which Goudie's competence was held. Only the timber was available locally. The rest of the material and equipment, as well as the shipbuilders and workers, had first to be found and then transported by steamboat and bateau with frequent portages all the way from Quebec. Unfortunately, unlike the part that Goudie played in the war, George Taylor's contribution is not known to us. We know only that his reputation as an excellent shipbuilder was in no way diminished by it.

The war came to an end late in 1814. Naval contracts were cancelled or cut back and soon the workers had begun to return to private shipyards. Although the exceptional demand for new tonnage of all kinds evaporated with the signing of the peace treaty, there was still an occasional contract for a merchantman to be had. There were also surveys and repairs to be carried out, and many overtaxed shipyard facilities required attention.

George Taylor now set out to establish his own yard, and his first concern was either to find a partner or to obtain the services of a first-class foreman. Shipowners were wary of investing in the construction of a ship when the investment might be jeopardized by the death or incapacity of a shipbuilder who had no competent person to replace him. When Taylor visited his home town in England, his brother-in-law and cousin, (Simon) Temple Taylor, both a shipwright and block-maker by trade, agreed to join him in Quebec. Grandson of the important master shipbuilder Simon

Sir James Yeo's flagship St. Lawrence, *built by Quebec shipwrights at Kingston during the War of 1812. Her 157-foot keel was 4 feet longer than that of Nelson's* Victory, *her 52-foot beam, 1 foot wider. Her depth of hold was 3 feet less. She measured 2,300 tons to* Victory's *2,162. John Goudie was the naval contractor in charge.* Charles H.J. Snider, Watercolour, T 15243, Baldwin Room, Metropolitan Toronto Library.

Temple of Shields and son of the shipwright Edward Taylor, Temple Taylor would be invaluable in helping to maintain a high standard in the new yard.

On his return to Quebec, Taylor looked around for a suitable spot for his shipyard. There was little river frontage available at the town itself, but in 1817, the year Temple Taylor arrived with his family, a small shipyard belonging to the estate of the wine merchant Peter Brehaut fell vacant. It straddled St. Charles Street immediately to the west of St. Thomas Street on the Canoterie. George Taylor signed the lease on October 10, 1817, for a one-storey dwelling house with a room fitted out as a forge at its west end, a steam house, and a wharf on which there was a stone hangar 70 feet long and 32 feet wide.[7] He no doubt hoped that the shipyard he was about to establish would survive him, perhaps to be run by his descendants, but he could scarcely have imagined the great twentieth-century Davie shipyard at Lauzon of which it was destined to be the forerunner.

Captain Allison Davie (1799–1836), who bought the land at Levis and operated the highly successful patent slip from 1832 until his death by drowning four years later.
Courtesy Anne Mimi Garneau.

2

ALLISON DAVIE

1821-31

Despite the fury of the winter storm, the brig *Findlay* finally made Quebec, her rudder broken, her stem and her deck badly damaged, and parts of her bulwarks, timber heads, chain plates, rails, and stanchions carried away. The shipment of rum she was carrying was quickly unloaded and arrangements were made for her to winter at Bell's shipyard on the St. Charles. Seventy-five days of battling one Atlantic storm after another must have taken its toll on the crew, and its members were no doubt soon putting thoughts of their ordeal aside in one of the many taverns in the port.[1]

Later that week, accompanied by three members of the crew, Captain Allison Davie, the *Findlay*'s master, took the customary precaution of calling on a notary to make a deposition, or protest, regarding the voyage. Their ship, notary Lauchlan McPherson recorded, "had experienced extraordinary rough and tempestuous weather and [had been] overtaken by a succession of violent storms, tempests and gales of wind. . . ." It was only "with the greatest difficulty and exertion they succeeded in getting her to [Quebec]." Moreover, the deponents declared, they had "used their utmost endeavours and exertions to preserve the . . . vessel and her cargo from damage." "Whatever losses, injuries and damages might have

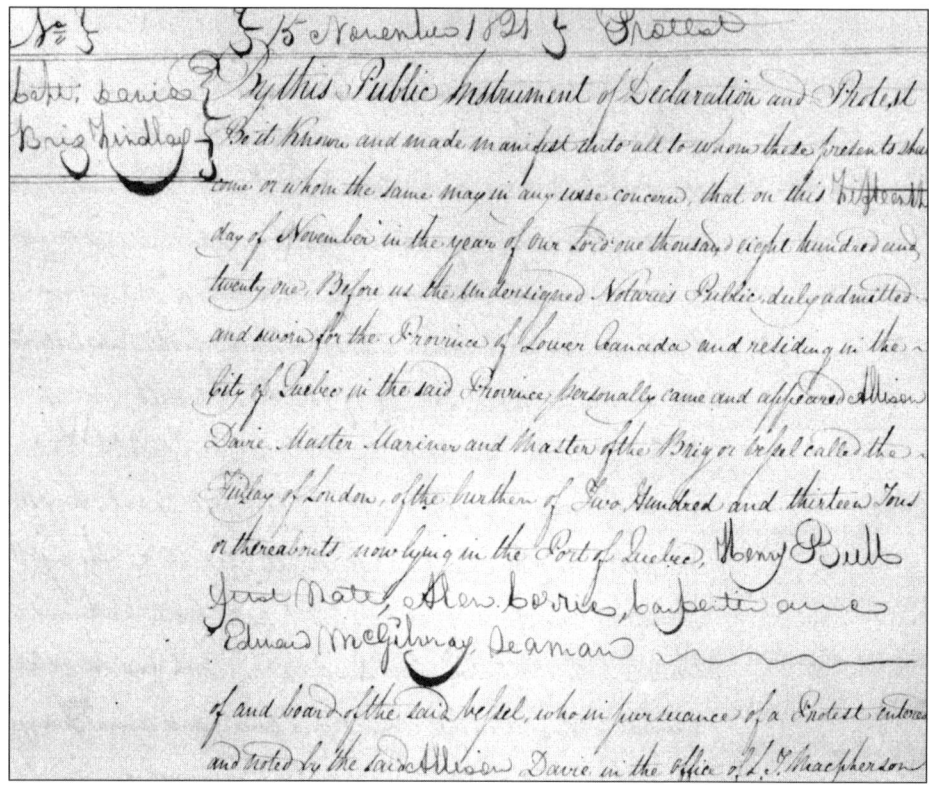

Protest against the weather, signed on November 15, 1821, by Allison Davie, master mariner; Henry Bull, first mate; Allen Corrie, carpenter; and Edward McGilvray, seaman.
Gr L. McPherson, ANQ.

happened to the cargo," they protested, "were in no way occasioned by any unseamanship, mismanagement or neglect of any of them, or the rest of the crew."[2] Then, having reported back to Archibald Findlay, of Yarmouth, England, the owner of the brig, Captain Allison Davie settled down to wait for his reply.[3]

In spite of the cold and frequent snowfalls, a new brig was taking shape beside the *Findlay*,[4] but apart from the activity at Bell's shipyard, and at two or three others,[5] the waterfront was quiet. Christmas came and went, and the river froze over. The cold penetrated deeper and deeper yet, almost imperceptibly, the days were growing longer and eventually April arrived.

By the third week of April most of the ice had left the river and its shores had taken on their spring appearance. The snowbanks disappeared and the first swallow was seen. Several small sailboats from La Malbaie and the Ile aux Coudres landed welcome cargoes of cattle and provisions for the local markets. The first deep-sea vessel made port from St. Vincent's, and a boat that brought fresh fish from Sorel and news of a clear channel through Lac Saint-Pierre was followed two days later by the first two river steamboats of the season. Overhauled and freshly painted, they were ready to initiate the season's Quebec–Montreal run. It remained only for the spring fleet to make its appearance. On May 15, sails were sighted and in the course of the next forty-eight hours, twenty-three sailing ships rounded Pointe Lévy and made port. The summer season was suddenly well under way.[6]

A few days later, the new brig at Bell's shipyard was ready to take the water. It was the first launch of the season, and a large crowd gathered to watch as the 281-ton *St. Charles* slid down the ways.[7] We can be sure that Captain Allison Davie had watched every stage of the construction with the greatest interest and that he attended both the launching and the traditional breakfast that followed, and that Lauchlan McPherson, who served as notary to both Bell and Davie, as well as Bell's neighbours, George Taylor and his wife and daughter, were also among the guests.

McPherson and Davie saw each other again the following day, when the notary went aboard the *Findlay* to read a protest he had been asked to deliver. The charter party between Thomas and William King of London and the brig's owner Archibald Findlay required that after unloading her consignment for Quebec, the *Findlay* be made ready to receive a cargo of wood, staves, fish, and other goods that, with a deck load of lumber or horses, were to be carried to Demerara together with the 20,000 bricks taken on in London. Nothing had yet been done to repair the damage the *Findlay* had suffered on her voyage to Quebec. The charterers were anxious to load their outward cargo and demanded that Captain Davie have the vessel put in seaworthy condition immediately. "What have you to say?" McPherson inquired.

"I am waiting for instructions from my owner how to act and which I daily expect to receive," was Allison's reply.[8] In fact, it suited him well to spend some time in Quebec.

A resident of North Yarmouth, England, though of Scottish origin, Allison Davie had followed in his father's footsteps and gone to sea at a tender age, and the sea had become his life. He had served in ships chartered to the East India Company for the transport of troops and supplies in the Mediterranean during the Napoleonic Wars and, following the war, had become a shipmaster on the Atlantic run.[9] At Quebec, he had found the woman he wanted to marry, but Elizabeth Johnson Taylor was the only child of the master shipbuilder George Taylor, and it was well-known that, before Taylor would grant his daughter's hand, he required that two conditions be met. Because he had no son to inherit his shipyard, the man who married his daughter must agree both to become his partner in the business and to perpetuate the Taylor name by giving it to the children of the marriage, as well as his own.

Taylor had left for Britain in search of business in the summer of 1821 and his return had been delayed until the following May. Concerned that he might not come back and pay his overdue rent, his landlord took legal action against him and advertised his shipyard for rent. His doubts were shared by Temple Taylor who, with a young family to feed, moved to the other side of town in search of work. When George Taylor arrived back, he was just in time to renew his lease and retain the yard, but he brought no contracts with him. And once again he was on his own.

Nevertheless, things began to look up. The end of the Napoleonic Wars in 1815 had raised fears among timber merchants that the duty on Baltic timber might be rescinded with serious consequences to the economy of the port of Quebec. However, intense lobbying in Westminster had resulted in the passage of the Timber Act of 1821 whose protectionist duties continued to favour the importation of Canadian timber. This was good news for Canadian shipbuilders, as well as for the timber merchants, because increased exports of timber meant more ships arriving at Quebec

Report of the valuation of the brig Henderson *of Workington, which was calculated by George Taylor of the City of Quebec, master shipbuilder, and William Fisher, master mariner and master of the ship* Margaret. *The* Henderson *was valued at £1,000 British Sterling.* June 8, 1823, greffe of the notary E.B. Lindsay, ANQ.

to load, and each was a potential customer for maintenance or repairs. The builders could also look forward to the day when extra wartime tonnage had been absorbed and they would build new ships on speculation, ships that they would load with an initial cargo of timber and send over to Britain, where both vessel and cargo would be sold. That day, moreover, was not far away.

From 1823 to 1826, Quebec shipyards seethed with activity. Vessels were laid down on beaches where the chirp of a caulker's mallet had never been heard before. From an average of fewer than five ships a year from

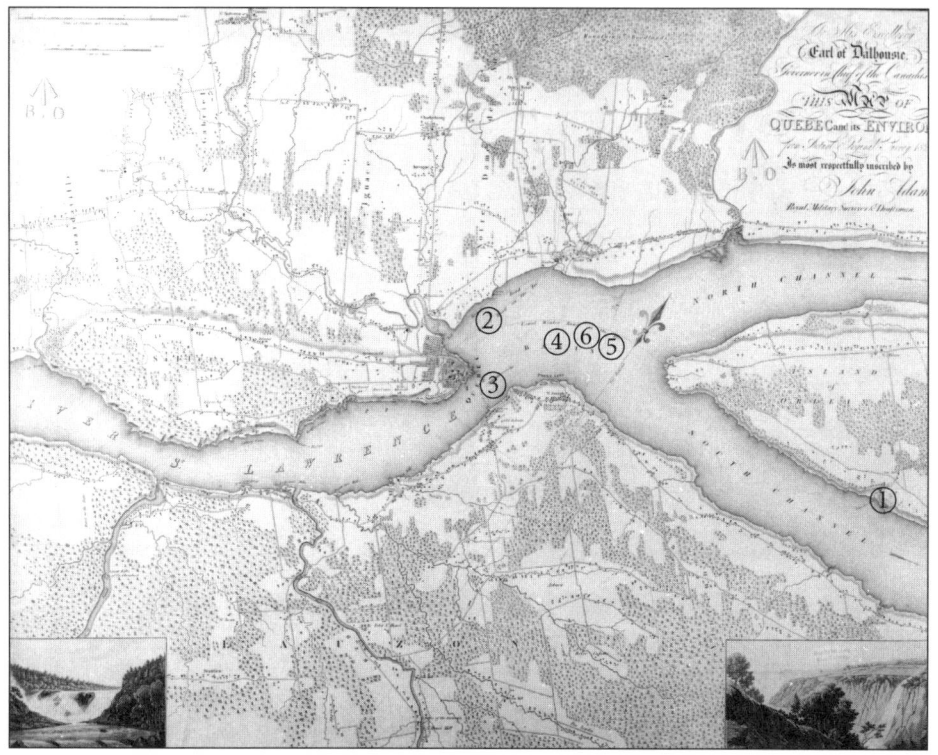

Where George Taylor, Allison Davie, and their descendants carried on their trade – (1) Saint Patrick's Hole, Isle of Orleans, (2) the Canoterie, (3) Levis, (4) the "Lower Yard," and (5) and (6), Lauzon (St. Joseph). Detail from John Adams' Map of Quebec and its Environs 1822.

1815 to 1823, production in the port rose to fifteen in 1824 and forty-three and forty-five respectively in 1825 and 1826. The number of shipyard workers grew from fifty-five in 1818 to more than three thousand in 1826.

Allison had not immediately been willing to accept Taylor's terms and leave the sea in order to marry Elizabeth, and he continued to sail backwards and forwards across the Atlantic. He left Quebec late in September 1823 to deliver the recently completed barque *Constantia* to William Acraman in Bristol,[10] and on his return voyage in May he was shipwrecked off the Cape Breton coast. The experience may well have helped him to make up his mind. When he sailed for Liverpool a year later as master of

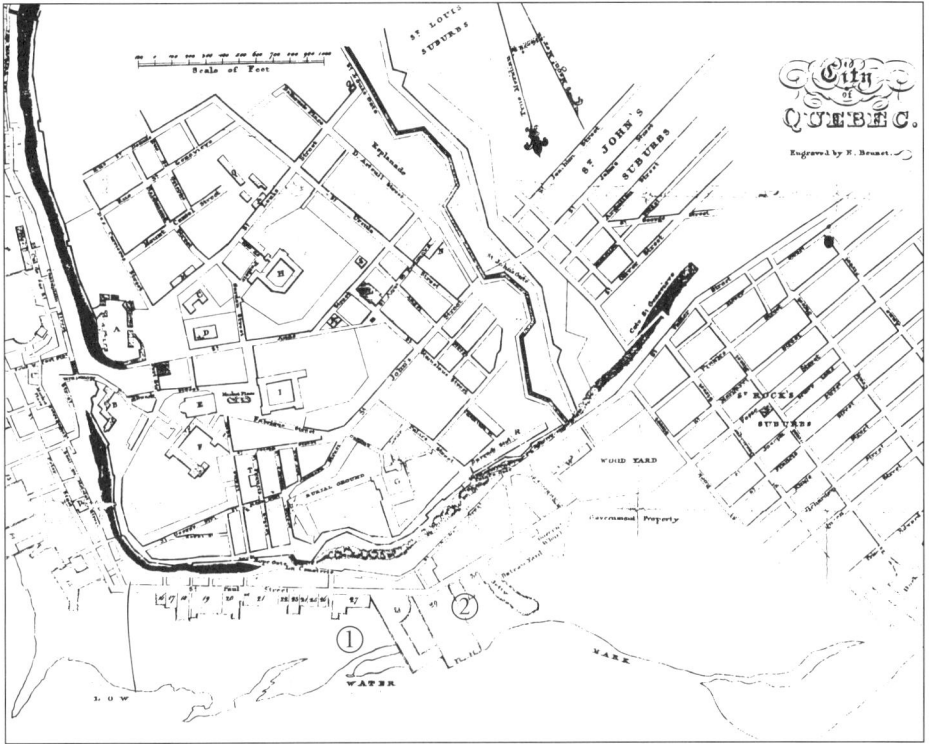

Plan of the City of Quebec in 1822. The shipyards identified include George Taylor's (1) and John Bell's (2). Engraved by E. Bennet, Quebec Directory for 1822. *T.H. Neilson, Quebec, Gleason & Cowan, 1822.*

the barque *Sir Watkin*, it was understood that Elizabeth would become his wife the following spring.

The marriage ceremony was conducted by the Reverend Doctor Harkness of the barque *Scotland* on April 16, 1825, at St. Andrew's Church, Quebec, and on the same day the partnership between Allison and his father-in-law came into force.[11] Allison left for London later that year to deliver the first vessel built under the partnership, the 424-ton ship *George Canning*, and we may surmise that Elizabeth accompanied him on a honeymoon trip.

During the first years of their marriage, Allison and Elizabeth Davie lived at the Canoterie shipyard, and it was there that their first child, Elizabeth

Taylor Davie, was born in 1826.[12] If there was any misgiving at the birth of a daughter, it was soon forgotten with the arrival of a son two years later, who was followed at yearly intervals by two more boys. As Allison had promised, the first was named for his grandfather, George Taylor, while the second took his father's name, Allison, and the old family name, Gershom, was revived for the third.[13] What pleasure the christening of his first grandson and namesake must have given the old shipbuilder, and what satisfaction when two brothers arrived to back him up. His daughter had married the right man!

The Taylor–Davie partnership also flourished. Between 1825 and 1831, four fully-rigged ships of more than 400 tons and four smaller ones were laid down.[14] Among them was the 221-ton brig *Kingfisher*, the first vessel built at Quebec for British naval service. It was undoubtedly a feather in the cap of the two builders: the yard was awarded the contract because of its reputation for high-class work. The attendance of the governor-general and the Countess Dalhousie at the launching ceremony on May 14, 1827, underlined the occasion. With the 79th Highlanders providing a band and a guard of honour, the *Kingfisher* glided into the water to the strains of "Rule Britannia," following which a salute was fired from the twenty-one guns put on board for the occasion. She was pierced for eighteen guns and carried a likeness of a unicorn as a figurehead, while her quarter badges bore the Dalhousie arms.[15] An old tradition which required that the shipwright of a naval vessel be given a piece of plate at her launching was observed in the presentation by Lord Dalhousie to Taylor of a commemorative silver cup, engraved with the Dalhousie arms and ornamented with a raised unicorn on its lid.[16] The cup has a prominent place in the portrait of George Taylor that was painted to mark the occasion. Handed down in the Davie family from oldest son to oldest son or daughter, it has been a source of great pride to the family.

Another small vessel laid down in the yard was the 126-ton schooner *Union* of 1828, built for the local association of pilots.[17] This, too, was a significant indication of the quality of work at the yard, for pilots, who often sailed with their apprentices to meet ships in the Gulf of St. Lawrence

Entitled "Quebec from Davy's shepyard [sic] Feb. 24th 1830," this watercolour by James Cockburn was painted at the Taylor-Davie shipyard on the Canoterie. At that time, however, George Taylor was ill and Allison Davie was building the brig Grenada, *which he launched on April 24.* Watercolour, NA.

in dreadful weather conditions, were careful in their choice of shipyard. But, unfortunately, contracts such as these were few and far between. The exceptional demand for new vessels for the overseas market had led to heavy overproduction and a depressed market which lasted until 1828.

Fortunately, there had been some ship repairs, or "old work." And, like other master shipbuilders in the port, Taylor undertook ship surveys. There was a constant demand for this service, as it was customary for all vessels requiring major repairs to be surveyed by disinterested parties. Moreover, expert opinions were required to settle a wide variety of legal and insurance shipping claims. Because the surveying team was generally made up of three men, of whom two were master shipbuilders and the third a ship's officer, harbour official, or some other competent person, and because the number of master shipbuilders in the port was limited, Taylor's services were frequently solicited.[18]

Davie came to realize that the shipyard's success did not lie in occasional small, though prestigious, contracts for new construction, or even in the general shipping market, whose cyclical fluctuations made shipbuilding a business of such high risk. Nor was steamboat construction a safe alternative – it was a new trade, one in which engineers still had many

Specifications for the Trinity House schooner *Union* built by George Taylor and Allison Davie in 1828. Gr. E.B. Lindsay, February 7, 1828.

problems to resolve, and just as uncertain. But with hundreds of ships arriving at the port each year to fetch timber – no fewer than 714 in the 1826 season – there was another possibility that appeared to lead to a more secure future: the business of ship repairs. With frequent bad weather and as yet few aids to navigation, the St. Lawrence could be depended on to inflict a certain amount of damage on maritime traffic. Moreover, an increasing number of wrecks was sold by order of the underwriters, many of them to the shipbuilders for salvage, repair, and resale.

There was no dry dock at Quebec; consequently, ships requiring repairs had to be worked on between tides. Some were shored up on a hard beach ("on the hard"), others on a gridiron (a wooden grill on the beach), while still others were simply careened on the beaches, allowing only one side to be worked on at a time. In 1827, however, a large box-like structure, along both of whose sides was painted, in large letters, "CANADA FLOATING DOCK," arrived at the Campbell and Black shipyard at Cape Cove from its building yard in Montreal, in the tow of the paddle steamer *Hercules*.[19] It was not only the first floating dry dock in British North America, but also the first to be put into commercial operation successfully in all North America. There can be little doubt that Black's dock was the envy of every other Quebec shipbuilder, including Allison Davie.

Part Two

LEVIS

The Algonquian Indians who camped at Pointe Lévy each year provided a ferry service to Quebec by canoe and, following the construction of the patent slip, delighted in manning its capstan. Later, it was converted to run with steam. R.A. Sproule, Quebec. Lower Canada. View of Quebec from Point Levi—1832. *Lithograph by W. Walton, printed by C. Hullmandel, London, 1832.*

3

LEVIS

1831-36

Allison Davie was quick to see that Black's floating dock was highly profitable, and recognizing that there was room for another dry-docking facility in the port, he decided that he too would have one. His, however, would be a marine railway or "patent slip." Unlike the floating dock, a patent slip would allow him to haul three vessels out of the river one after another and work on all three at the same time. Eventually, he would build a horizontal plane beside the slip and, with the help of transfer trucks, repair or winter many more. Allison shouldered the full responsibility for this decision, for in 1828 George Taylor had become seriously ill, and Temple Taylor, who had moved away from the shipyard in 1821 and might have joined him in the venture, had passed away that same year.[1] In 1828 also, George Taylor had lost his wife. Thus Allison and Elizabeth began their new venture with their little family and the added responsibility of her father's care.

In 1829, Allison bought a river-front property in the Parish of Pointe Lévy opposite Quebec, which, together with the adjoining lot that he purchased the following year, gave him approximately 400 feet of frontage, the whole at a total cost of £385.[2] When Elizabeth signed the second deed of sale on his behalf in December 1830, Allison was already on a visit to

The whole of the river front facing Quebec was originally in the Parish of Saint-Joseph-de-la-Pointe-Lévy and was collectively known as Pointe-Lévy, or Point Levy. In 1861, the area in which the Davie shipyard was situated became part of the new Parish of Notre-Dame-de-Lévis, and soon after, the municipality took the name Levis, too. In this view across the river from Quebec, we see a sailing ship on the patent slip. Unsigned watercolour in the collection of the Musée du Quebec. 78.381.

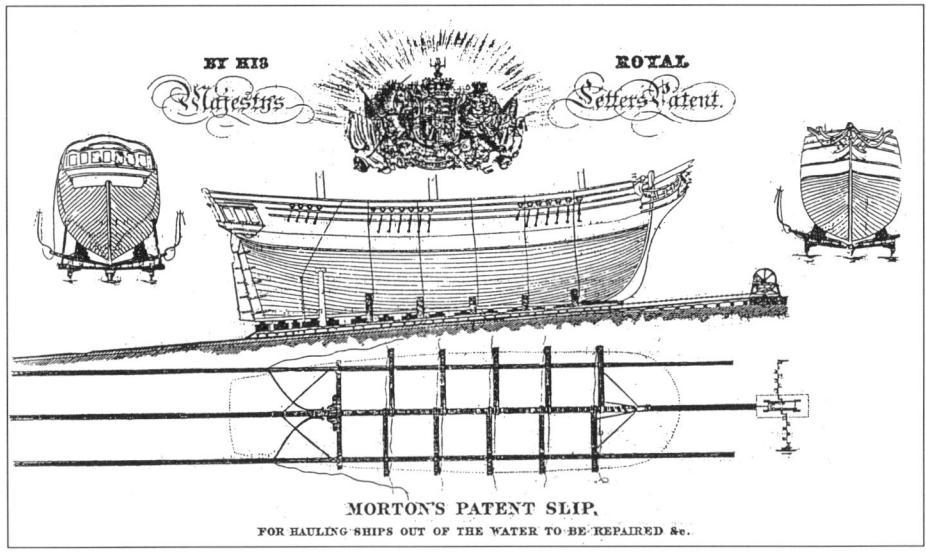

The original Morton Patent Slip, patented in 1819, as installed by Allison Davie at his shipyard at Levis. Courtesy Peabody & Essex Museum, Salem.

Thomas Morton in Leith, Scotland, acquiring the right to build one of his patent slips.

There were several reasons for buying the land at Pointe Lévy, not the least of which was its topography. It featured a solid ledge of rock whose natural slope was ideal for the 500-foot-long slip, and beyond the ledge was an abrupt drop into thirty or forty feet of water. The rock made a sound foundation on which wharves could be built at relatively little expense while large ships could be brought in close under their own sail. The fact that Quebec was a ferry ride away was both an advantage and a disadvantage. Though many supplies had to be carried across, and this entailed delays and additional expense, the relative isolation ensured that there was a pool of workers whose options were fewer and demands less onerous than those of their counterparts in Quebec. The site had the advantages also of a western exposure and a headland that protected the yard and the ships that would winter there from the northeast or "bad weather" winds.

On his return from Scotland, bringing the necessary plans, parts, and specifications for the patent slip, Allison petitioned the government for the water lot in front of his land, which was essential for its operation. He obtained the approval of the Board of Trinity House, which had jurisdiction over shoreline installations and considered that the proposed improvements would not constitute an obstacle to shipping.[3] He then oversaw completion of the construction of the last two vessels built at the Canoterie shipyard, the 198-ton brig *Corrib* and 224-ton *Grenada*, launching them in 1829 and 1830 respectively, before giving up the lease.[4]

Allison was then free to turn his full attention to the new shipyard at Levis, where work had begun on the wharfing and shipyard buildings. By the end of 1831 he could survey with pride the wharf he had had built. But the force with which the ice broke up in the spring of 1832 was far greater than expected and carried the whole structure away.[5] Disappointed but determined, he wasted no time in contracting with the wharf specialists Francis and James Wiseman to build another. The wharf is described in the specifications as a foundation for a 500-foot-long marine railway rising three-quarters of an inch per foot, to be built of wood filled with stone and to extend to "the very extremity of low water mark." From the lower end to a third of its length, it was to be 20 feet in width widening to 40 feet for the rest.[6] While it was under construction, the local founders and blacksmiths, Thomas Wildes, Thomas Tweddell, and Weston & Galbraith, were busy fulfilling their contracts for the considerable amount of foundry work that the railway required.[7]

On May 1, 1832, soon after the birth of their fourth son, William Edward, the family moved across the river from the crowded Canoterie to a house near the new shipyard and rented from the ferryman Jean-Baptiste Bégin.[8] Allison and Elizabeth were thus able to supervise the work on both the shipyard installations and the fine new home that Joseph Latouche was building for them. The move was timely, for it removed them from the ravages of the cholera epidemic that struck Quebec later that year, claiming more than 4,000 lives but leaving the Davie family unscathed, as would the second epidemic two years later. The house was completed that year, and the family moved in, naming it the "Homestead," the name by which it is still generally known today. The patent slip was ready for the first attempt to haul a vessel from the water in late October 1832, but rather than taking a chance with a sailing ship, a barge was hauled dry. The trial was satisfactory, and the finishing touches were made to the slip through the winter.[9]

With the arrival of spring, the 270-ton brig *Rosalind* reached Quebec from her forced wintering at Ile aux Coudres, and with her the opportunity for an appropriate test of the patent slip. On May 1, 1833, she was safely hauled out of the river for repair.[10] The work was completed one month later, and the *Quebec Gazette* was able to report that "on Saturday morning last, the beautiful Brig *Rosalind*, the first vessel repaired on Messrs Taylor and Davy's [sic] new Patent Slip was let down from her elevated situation, and returned to her native element, to the admiration of a vast concourse of persons who had assembled to witness the novel sight. . . ." An Algonquian band that camped in the vicinity each year – some of them worked at the shipyard – spiritedly appropriated the task of turning the capstan. The *Quebec Gazette* was correct in surmising that "the undertaking, which has not been completed without a heavy outlay of capital, will no doubt meet with that encouragement the industry and enterprise of Mr. Davy, the proprietor, so justly merits," for like the floating dock, the marine railway had no difficulty finding customers. We are told, in fact, that they waited their turn in the stream.[11]

Over the next three years, three daughters, Harriet, Isobel, and Clementine, were born to the Davies, but soon after Clementine's birth, in March of 1836, they experienced the loss of their four-year-old son, William Edward. An even greater tragedy awaited them: the death of Allison himself. On June 9, 1836, while returning from Quebec with his caulker, Joseph Mandeville, he was hailed by the captain of the brig *Venus*, who had brought him a letter from Britain. Wasting no time, Allison climbed aboard to fetch it and took the opportunity to fill his kerchief with the almonds he was offered for his family. The almonds cost him his life. He forgot the kerchief, and when it was thrown down to him as he sat waiting in his boat, it landed in the river. He leaned over the gunwales too far when he tried to retrieve it, lost his balance, and toppled in. Though he is said to have been a strong swimmer, he did not reappear. Ten days later his body was washed ashore on the Isle of Orleans, where it was found by the joiner Alexis Ferland, who made a temporary coffin in which to return it to the family.[12]

The funeral service was held on September 21, 1836, at St. Andrew's Presbyterian Church, Quebec, after which Allison Davie, only thirty-seven years old, was laid to rest by his family and friends in the English Burying Ground, beside St. Matthew's Church. Elizabeth, who was expecting another child three months later, was thus left alone to bring up their eight children.[13]

According to the custom of the province, an inventory, which fortunately has survived, was taken of Allison's belongings. In it is listed the movable and immovable property of the "community" that existed

> PROVINCE OF LOWER-CANADA, } **AN INQUISITION.**
> DISTRICT OF QUEBEC.
>
> indented, taken for our Sovereign Lord the King, at the Parish of *Quebec* in the County of *Quebec* in the District of Quebec, on the *twentieth* day of *June* in the *first* year of the reign of our Sovereign Lord WILLIAM the FOURTH, by the Grace of GOD, of the United Kingdom of Great Britain and Ireland King, Defender of the Faith, before *Bernard Antoine Panet* Esquire, Coroner of our said Lord the King, of and for the said District, on view of the body of *Allison Davie late of Quebec a Shipbuilder* then and there lying dead, upon the oath of *John Ted, Jean Olivier Brunet, Joseph Provost, Patrick O'Brien, William Baxter, Zaccheas Williams, William Wilson, Charles Vallé, Germain Laprise, John [...] and Peter Donaghue*

Coroner's report on Allison Davie's drowning, in which the jury found that "in over ritching [sic] the edge of the said Boat to pick up a certain bundle from the waters of the River Saint Lawrence which had been thrown to him the said Allison Davie accidentally, casually, by misfortune and against his will came to his death and not otherwise." ANQ.

between Allison and Elizabeth, as well as the property – the shipyard and stock-in-trade – that belonged to the shipbuilding partnership between Allison and his father-in-law that had remained in force in spite of George Taylor's absence due to illness.[14]

The Homestead that Allison Davie built under the cliff a short distance to the north of the ferry landing 165 years ago still stands today. Its red-painted, wood-shingled roof, which extends over the front gallery, is clearly distinguishable from across the river. It was built in the style of many of the tradesmen's homes of the time – blacksmiths, coopers, wheelwrights, and others – with the family quarters above the workshop. It is a fine, well-built house with carefully worked stone foundations and ornate brick chimneys, its doors and large casement windows framed by generous mouldings.

Because both the house and the inventory have survived, we are able to picture the Davie family in their comfortable surroundings: the carpeted parlour with mahogany loo (a card game) table and chest of drawers, the chimney ornaments and inevitable spyglass (telescope) trained downriver – inevitable, that is, in a shipbuilder's home – the mahogany-framed mirror and five large gilt-framed pictures of naval scenes on the walls, a work box, and six straw-bottomed chairs. The separate and well-appointed dining and drawing rooms, the master bedroom and dressing room, kitchen and out-kitchen, all on the main floor. Above, the bedrooms with sloped ceilings and gabled windows for the youngsters. The coach house and stable. The livestock: two horses, two cows, eight hens, and, adding an exotic note that lent a touch of colour to the yard, two peacocks.

The "Homestead," the family residence with office below, built by Allison Davie in 1832. It is still standing today and has been declared a historic site. George T. Davie's son, Allison Cufaude Davie, like his brothers and sisters, was born in this house, and he lived in it all his life. To the right, the gate to the garden. Studio Moderne.

This extra-large chair was built at the shipyard for George Taylor, who weighed more than 300 pounds. It is seen here under the portrait of his grandson and namesake, George Taylor Davie, at the Homestead. Studio Moderne.

On the riverside, the shipyard buildings comprised a blacksmith's forge, an engine house – steam power having taken the place of the Algonquian band – and a small building where steam was produced for bending planks. A large wharf or pier, to protect the patent slip, was under construction. (According to the inventory, £500 was to be spent to complete it before winter set in to avoid its destruction by ice.) In the yard were two working carts, a pair of teaming wheels and iron axle, and the usual shipyard paraphernalia: pitch kettles, tar barrels, wheelbarrows, and so on. Valuable stores crammed the cellar of the dwelling house. Those that had to be kept dry, such as sheathing paper and sails, were stacked in the attic of the engine house. Sixty-five thousand shingles piled in a corner of the steam house were destined no doubt to roof a projected building.

Sheets of copper, copper nails, and copper rings accounted for more than 40 per cent of the value of the inventory. They represented an important part of the work on the patent slip, that of copper sheathing. Not only was old sheathing replaced on damaged hulls, but newly launched vessels were also sheathed on the patent slip; if it were done on the building ways,

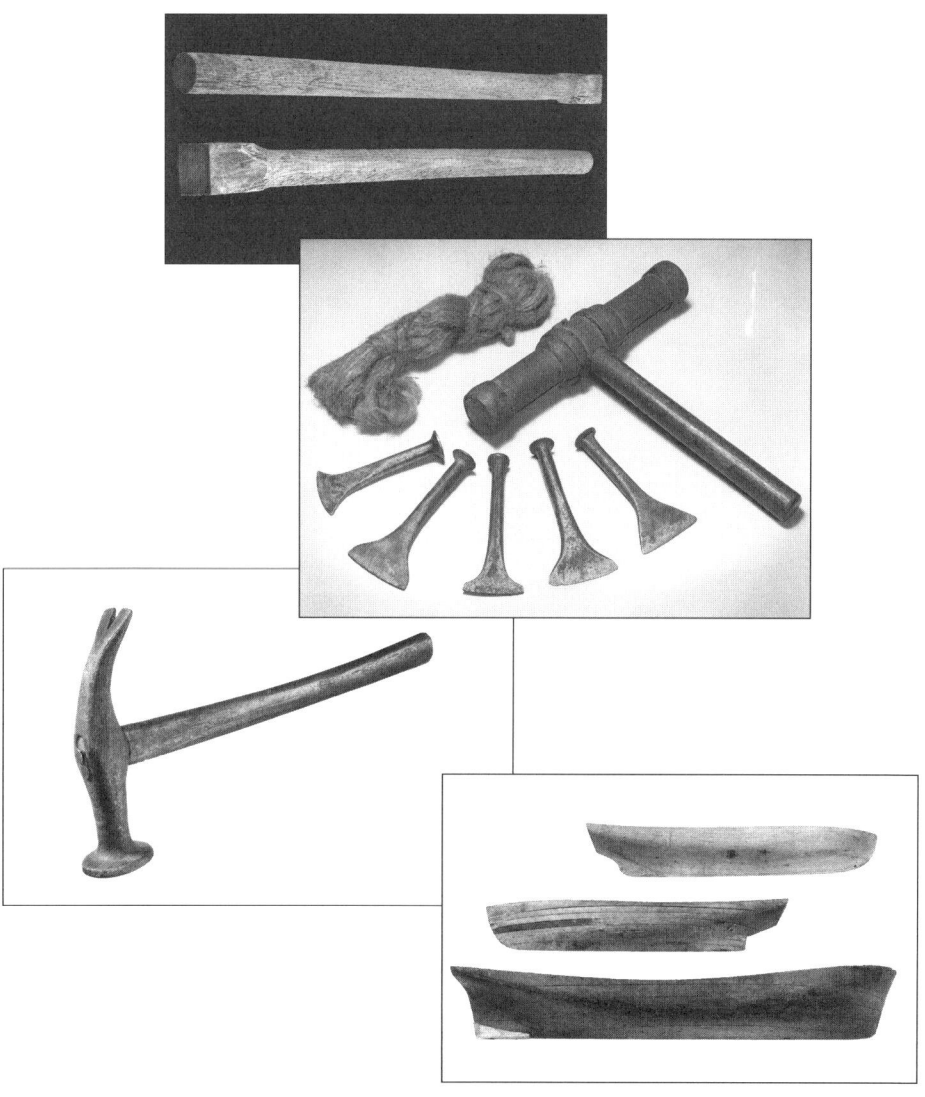

Tools used in building a wooden ship (top to bottom): *oak trunnels, which were used, as well as bolts, to fasten the planking to the frame of the ship; NMC, 16-77-7; caulking mallet and irons, and rove of oakum, forced between the planks and then covered with pitch, to render the ship watertight; NMC, 16-77-13; coppering hammer, from the original Davie shipyard in Lévis, used to apply copper sheathing; NMC, 16-77-20; wooden half-models which were used to project the lines of a vessel on the Mould Loft floor. They were used in Quebec shipyards to build large sailing ships in the mid-nineteenth century.*

～ BLACKSMITHS ～

IN THE DAYS of the sailing ship, the shipyard blacksmiths forged large quantities of bolts, spikes, and items such as shackles, gudgeons and pintles, chain-plates, mast-collars and caps. Though their work was greatly reduced with the arrival of the metal ship, some things were still forged. Davie's foreman blacksmith Lucien Laflamme was a first-class worker. In addition to putting in a day's work at the shipyard, he filled orders for small hardware such as door holdbacks and hooks, which he fashioned at home in his little forge with the help of his wife. He gave superb service, frequently making as many as two dozen pieces overnight. Today, forgings for the most part have been replaced by welded fabrications.

---

the metal might be damaged during the launching.

The majority of the stock of timber was either oak or elm, with white pine, which was used extensively for decking, a distant third. Birch knees and spruce futtocks, trunnels, props, and wedges made up the rest. The typical shipyard tools included a whip saw, gin and pair of trestles, the blacksmith's outfit, cramps, jack screws and crosscut saws, augers, and riming irons, and, more unusually, two hydraulic ship lifts and a copper puncher.

Though business had been brisk, the partnership debts, including a mortgage of £600 with Trinity House and £400 owed to William Price for copper, balanced the receivables. These debts, and the paltry ten shillings and fourpence in the Quebec Bank account, indicate that the shipyard was still in a precarious position, due presumably to the high cost of the installation.

Because Allison died intestate and was "in community of property" with his wife, Elizabeth was left with three-quarters of their personal property, while the remaining quarter went to their seven children in equal shares. Ownership of the shipyard was different, however. It had belonged to the two partners equally, so George Taylor retained possession of his half, while Elizabeth inherited half of Allison's share, or one-quarter, and her seven children an equal share of the remaining quarter. Between them, Elizabeth and her children owned only half of the shipyard. Due to her father's ill health, however, it was Elizabeth who would ensure the firm's survival until her sons were old enough to take over.

Elizabeth Johnson Davie (1803–60), wife of Allison Davie and daughter of the master shipbuilder George Taylor. Canada's first woman shipbuilder, who ran her late husband's shipyard until her sons were old enough to take over from her. Courtesy Anne Mimi Garneau.

4

ELIZABETH DAVIE

1836-50

Following allison's death, George Taylor took charge of the patent slip, leasing Allison's half of the yard from his estate for the yearly sum of £62 10s.[1] But Taylor was not well enough to manage alone. In spite of the many demands of her young family, and in particular the care of her last born, William Taylor, Elizabeth was obliged to replace her father for the long stretches when he was unable to work. She thus became competent in such matters as choosing suitable shipbuilding timber in the forest and learned to handle the workers with the same firmness with which she brought up her family. In particular, she kept a watchful eye on the apprentices, whose wages she is said to have sewn into their pockets with instructions that they "take them straight home to mother."[2] Soon after 1841, her father's health deteriorated further, and she took over alone.

There have not been many women shipbuilders in Canada, and Elizabeth may well have been the first one. We should not be too surprised that she took to the role so readily, for she had lived among shipbuilders all her life. Besides her husband and father, her maternal grandfather, Simon Temple, had been an important shipbuilder, while his son and namesake owned two shipyards at South Shields, England, each with a dry dock, the latest being described at its opening in 1798 as "the most complete in the

This view from Pointe Lévy offers a sample of the different craft that could be seen on the river at that time. The crew is busy hauling up the sails of the ship that has come to the end of her transatlantic voyage, while ahead of her, the twin-stacked paddle steamer not only is loaded to capacity, but has two barges in tow with additional passengers. Most of the timber rafts have been dropped off at the timber coves farther upstream, and the one we see will soon arrive at her destination, too. In general, the native Quebeckers were not seafaring people, but felt at home on the river and many kept their own small boats, as is shown here. Among those in the foreground are some of the Indians who camped at Pointe Lévy each year and a member of the garrison. B. Beaufoy, View of Quebec, On stone by T. Picken, lithograph by Day & Haghe, London, c.1840.

Kingdom." Included among Temple's customers were the East India Company and the Admiralty. It may well have been at Temple's yard that George Taylor learned the trade.[3]

Unfortunately, neither yard records nor any business or personal correspondence concerning the early days of the Levis shipyard have yet come to light from which we might learn firsthand of the problems that Elizabeth faced during the long years before her sons took over from her.

The work and worry entailed in running both home and shipyard were undoubtedly considerable. With as many as a thousand ships calling at the port annually, however, there was no shortage of work for the patent slip, and the yard survived.

An encouragement to Elizabeth and an important milestone for the business was the official award in 1838 of letters patent, or title, for the water lot in front of the shipyard, requested by Allison Davie in 1831 and asked for again by Elizabeth and her father in 1837.[4] The award legalized their position, for until then the patent slip had encroached on government property. The grant was a substantial one, covering an area of almost 72,000 square feet, with approximately 450 feet of frontage and 20 feet of water at its limit at low water, and allowing wharves and buildings on the property. In return, the Davies were required to build within three years a public wharf or wharves where vessels visiting the port could load and unload, and to provide moorage, wharfage, and the use of the shipyard cranes to anyone requesting them.

It was not expected that these services be given free, however. A reasonable amount could be charged following a tariff approved by the executive council of the province. The Davies were also required to permit free passage over the land at all times of the day or night to those engaged in towing boats, barges, rafts, scows, and other vessels up and down the river. Lastly, the government retained the right to build one or more batteries or other military defence works on the property, should the need ever arise. The grant was made in "free and common soccage," and was subject to an annual rent of £35 19s. 0½d., retroactive to 1831 and payable on the day of the Feast of St. John the Baptist. In fact, considerable tolerance was shown in its collection: it was not until 1882 that George T. Davie paid a lump sum of $2,397 to cover more than fifty years of rent![5]

Until mid-century, the yard was wholly taken up with repair work, with only one exception. In 1841, George Taylor received an order from his old and valued customer, Trinity House, for the construction of a 97-ton schooner, the *Union Yacht*.[6] She was to be 68 feet long, copper-fastened, and

The Davie shipyard at Levis at the time that it was run by Elizabeth Davie. The Homestead is at the foot of the cliff with the original stable and the well house, left. Along the road, from right to left, the shipyard buildings include a 90-foot tradesmen's shed with mould loft above, a smithy, steamhouse, and open storage shed, the backs of the buildings serving to cut down on fencing, and the deep water wharf or "block," centre. The finger piers of the marine railway, right, and a pair of sawyers at work, below, a typical sight in a shipyard of the time. This watercolour by George Seton is the earliest illustration so far uncovered in which the buildings of the Davie shipyard can be easily identified. A Panoramic View of Quebec from Point Levi, Quebec, September 17, 1847 to July 7, 1849. NA, Picture Division, Neg.C-96435.

built of oak and elm, and to be fitted with specially strong davits for handling the pilot boats. Although the "draught and sketch of the deck" prepared for the owner have not survived, the specifications have. This carefully written document ends with the admonition: "All iron to be of the best quality – and it must be expressly understood that the copper must be also of the best drawn copper – If any copper should be attempted to be drove that has passed through the fire with an intent to reduce it to the size mentioned in the agreement it will be rejected – and if any is found to be drove secretly either in the shape of nails or bolts the contract to be forfeited and the Penalty paid." The penalty of £500 did not come into play. The contract was successfully carried out, and in recording her launching, the *Quebec Mercury* commented that "her model and strength does great credit to the builder."[7] Undoubtedly this was true. Seven years later, the sturdy schooner crossed the Atlantic and was registered in Belfast by her new owner. She was the last vessel that George Taylor built.

But Elizabeth's most significant task during these years was probably the upbringing of the Davie boys, including George, who would one day take over the yard. We can only surmise that George's three younger brothers, after receiving some schooling, were given practical training. We know only that William, the youngest, who was born after his father's death, became a steamboat captain. George, however, was sent to Gale's boarding school at Saint-Augustin, where he remained until he was old enough to stand up to the rigours of shipyard life. He was then apprenticed to the master shipbuilder John Munn.[8] The choice was a happy one. Munn, who was born into a shipbuilding family in Irvine, Ayrshire, had come to Quebec to join his father when he was a young man and had inherited the yard when his father died shortly after.[9] He had become one of Quebec's most respected shipbuilders. In the rich tradition of apprenticeship, George lived at Munn's house at his shipyard in the suburb of St. Roch, where he was brought up as a son while learning the "mysteries" of the trade.[10] According to custom, he would have received board, lodging, and a clothing allowance during his apprenticeship and, though given some tools at the end of his term, would have been encouraged to make others.

He was privileged to have been accepted as an apprentice by Munn, for there were at the time two types of apprentice at the shipyards: the master's apprentices, such as George, of which each shipbuilder generally had no more than one or two; and the shipyard apprentices, of which there might be many. The shipyard apprentices, for whom the yard foreman was generally responsible, served an average of three or four years while living at their own homes and were paid on a small but increasing scale as they became more competent until they could take their place among the regular ship carpenters. It was a good system that allowed them to support themselves while they learned a trade that enabled them to escape from the ranks of unskilled labourers. It was good for the shipbuilders, too, not because the apprentices earned less than the regular ship carpenters, as some have suggested, since their term was relatively short, but because it built up a pool of skilled workers in the town.

The three-year apprenticeship agreement between eighteen-year-old Pierre Dorion and George Taylor, which was signed on March 23, 1825, before notary Campbell. During those years, Dorion was to earn nine shillings, ten shillings, and eleven shillings successively, and to receive £1 3s 4d in lieu of tools. ANQ.

The training of a master shipbuilder's apprentice was far more comprehensive than that for a ship carpenter, and as a rule lasted for seven years. The apprentice learned not only to build a ship, from the drafting and laying down to its outfitting, crewing, and delivery, but also many other aspects of the trade, including the selection, purchase, and handling of timber supplies and other materials and equipment, the management of the work force, all the financial aspects of building and selling ships, and the general care of a yard. As in all practical training, the manner in which each unexpected problem, incident, or accident was settled was a

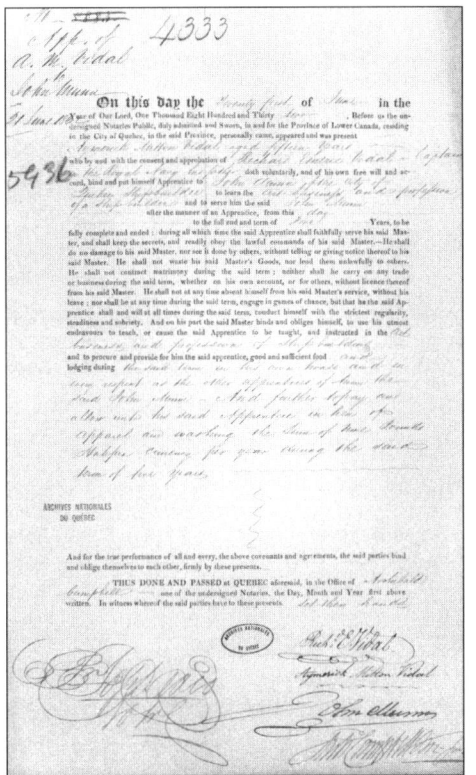

Apprenticeship Indenture of Aymerick Vidal to John Munn, in which Vidal binds and puts himself apprentice to learn the art, business, and profession of a shipbuilder and Munn agrees to teach him, and to procure and provide good and sufficient food in his own house, and in every respect as his other apprentices, and to allow him in lieu of apparel and washing the sum of £9 Halifax currency per year. In return the apprentice agreed not to contract matrimony, nor to carry on any other trade, to keep his master's secrets, not to engage in games of chance, and to conduct himself with strictest regularity, steadiness, and sobriety. Munn probably signed a similar contract with George T. Davie, which does not appear to have been registered. Gr Archibald Campbell, June 21, 1832.

lesson in itself. George learned firsthand, for instance, the importance of both fire prevention and the maintenance of a fire-fighting capability when a large part of St. Roch and many of her shipyards, including Munn's, were gutted in the conflagration in 1845. Later in life, he remembered that when Munn rebuilt his yard, he used stone and brick for the key buildings, not wood.

Finally, George would have learned much of a more abstract nature from his master. The young apprentice was fortunate to have as his model a man who had not only earned recognition in British shipping circles for his high shipbuilding standards, but also did not compromise his principles and for whom philanthropy was a way of life.

The exact period of George's apprenticeship is not known, as no indentures have been found and may well have been verbal, but it is likely that it began in 1841 or 1842 when shipbuilding in the port was on the increase and George was thirteen or fourteen years old. Munn himself was regularly launching four large sailing ships a year. In 1843, he would build the first Quebec ship to exceed a thousand tons, the 1,079-ton ship *Scotland*, and also lay down his first steamboat, the 222-ton side wheeler *Rowland Hill*.[11] Unfortunately, however, Munn's experience in steamboat construction was not a happy one.

Paddle steamers had become a significant presence on the St. Lawrence in the thirty years or so since 1809 when John Molson put the *Accommodation*, Canada's first steamboat, into service between Montreal and Quebec. Though St. Mary's current at Montreal proved too strong for her engines, she nevertheless showed the tremendous advantage of steam travel on the river. The *Accommodation* was broken up in 1811 and was followed by the *Swiftsure* and the *Malsham*,[12] both of which were used as troop transports during the War of 1812, and when the war ended they were joined by other steamboats, which together provided a regular and much appreciated service between Montreal and Quebec. Once travellers became accustomed to the clouds of soot they belched from their smokestacks, how could they not look kindly on this new form of travel that cut the sailing time between Quebec and Montreal from an average of seventeen to two and a half days? The warmth of public feeling towards them is evident from the tone of a report in the *Quebec Mercury* on May 4, 1821: "On Saturday last our harbour presented a gay and animated spectacle, in the arrival of none less a number than eight Steam Boats with flags flying and guns firing, from their wintering station in William Henry [Sorel] . . . *Swiftsure, Montreal, Lady Sherbrooke, Caledonia, Malsham, Quebec, Telegraph* and *Car of Commerce*. All handsome and newly painted."

And yet, the impact of steam on river transportation had only just begun, for a different kind of steamboat, the first of which was even then being built for John Torrance in Montreal, would revolutionize local shipping.[13] The *Hercules* was registered in 1823 as a "towboat" (the word "tug" had yet to be coined), and when she successfully towed her first customer,

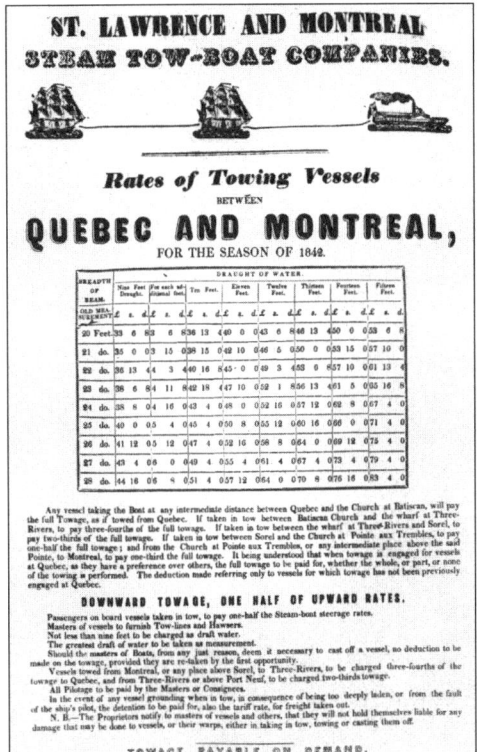

The tariff for tows between Montreal and Quebec in 1842.

the 200-ton *Margaret*, from Quebec to Montreal the following May, St. Lawrence River history was made. By the end of the season, the *Hercules* had made twenty-six round trips between the two towns and towed at least sixty vessels, including a line of three brigs and three schooners on one downward trip, while on another occasion she had towed the 3,690-ton timber drogher *Columbus*, the largest vessel afloat anywhere, a distance of 160 miles to Bic.[14]

Towboats made themselves indispensable in no time. Shipowners realized savings both in the time their vessels spent waiting for the wind to change and, if they had previously used ordinary steamboats for towing, in the new towboats' less expensive and more efficient service. As one merchant put it, "The Tow Boat . . . seems most perfectly to answer the purpose intended." Apart from towing big and small vessels of all kinds, masts and

Launching the Royal William, *Quebec, Lower Canada, April 29, 1831.* Watercolour, James Pattison Cockburn. Courtesy National Archives of Canada, C-12649.

rafts of timber were towed up- and downriver, and from one location to another in port. Moreover, the towboats were found by shipbuilders to be more satisfactory than the regular steamboats in restraining sailing ships at their launching.

In spite of a propensity to collisions, generally caused by excessive speed (cowboy captains showing off to their enthusiastic passengers), as well as to fires, the steamboats had the confidence of the shipbuilders. George Taylor and Allison Davie joined John Munn and others as founding members when the Quebec and Halifax Steam Navigation Company was incorporated in March of 1831 for the purpose of establishing steam navi-

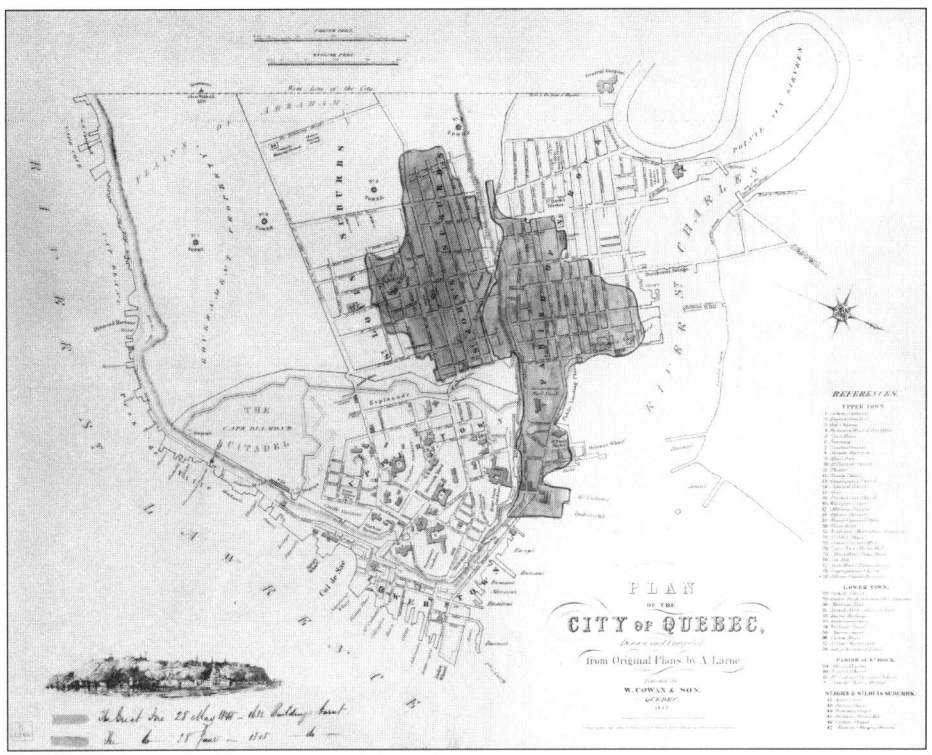

The limits of the fires of May and June 1845 that engulfed the Bell and former Taylor-Davie shipyard on the Canoterie, and also, extreme right, on the northeast corner of St. Roch, Munn's. Plan of the City of Quebec, *Drawn and compiled by A. Larue. Published by W. Cowan & Son, 1842.*

gation between Halifax and Quebec.[15] The company's first and only boat, the side wheeler *Royal William*, was built under the supervision of James Goudie at the Campbell and Black shipyard at Cape Cove, Quebec, and made three successful round trips to Halifax that year. In the wake of a futile second season, however, most of which she spent in quarantine because of the cholera epidemic, she was unable to meet her expenses and ended up in her creditors' hands. Sent to England, she was first chartered to the Portuguese, but finished her career in the Spanish navy under the name of *Isabela Segunda*. She bears the distinction of being the first steamboat to have fired a shot in anger.[16]

A non-contemporary drawing of the ss John Munn *of 1847, designed by Pierre Brunelle and built at John Munn's shipyard in St. Roch while George T. Davie was at the yard.* Charles H.J. Snider, Steamer 'John Munn', 1847-63, *Baldwin Room, Metropolitan Toronto Library.*

Although the *Royal William*'s career was hardly what her makers had intended, her successful crossing of the Atlantic has to be considered an important milestone in the advance of steam navigation. Thus John Munn had no reason to feel that he was taking an undue risk when he agreed to build steamboats for service on the St. Lawrence. Circumstances, however, would prove otherwise.

The 187-foot ps *Rowland Hill* was launched in 1845, and was followed in 1846 by the ps *John Munn*, which at 293 feet became the largest steamboat on the river. Both were designed by the local shipbuilder Pierre Brunelle and built in Munn's yard under Brunelle's superintendence for the People's Line of Steamers. Unfortunately, the People's Line had greatly overextended itself and its financial difficulties were Munn's undoing. Munn had guaranteed the bank loan not only for the construction of the two steamboats built in his yard, but also for a third built by George Black.

As a result of the failure of the company and, more particularly, of the merchant John Wilson, its principal owner, Munn had a bank debt of £44,000 to settle, and many of Wilson's other debts and commitments fell on his shoulders too. To satisfy his creditors, he sold off the steamboats, and when that was not enough, his properties went one by one, until eventually only his heavily mortgaged shipyard was left.

What a lesson George T. Davie learned in his last years at Munn's shipyard! His apprenticeship over, he had earned the coveted position of foreman, but was unable to enjoy the direction of the flourishing yard it had once been. Instead, he saw his master's hard-earned fortune vanish in the steamboat venture. It was undoubtedly a wise young man as well as a skilled shipbuilder who left for Levis in 1850 at twenty-two years of age.

Towards the Close of Day – The Canada Timber Docks, Liverpool. *As the timber trade increased, the docks at the south end of Liverpool no longer sufficed and these docks were built at the north end especially for that trade. It was said that their huge gates were so well-balanced that no more strength was required to open them than was required to strike the keys of a piano. Neatly stacked piles of Canadian lumber are waiting to be delivered to the purchasers.* Painted by Robert Dudley, exhibited at the Royal Academy Exhibition in 1872, and bought by Baron Albert Grant, of Liverpool. *The Graphic,* August 24, 1872.

5

GEORGE T. DAVIE

1850-62

From 1850 to 1856 George and his brother Allison, sometimes working in a formal partnership, shared the direction of the family yard. Like their father, they concentrated on dry-dock work, only occasionally undertaking the construction of a new steamboat or a square-rigged sailing ship. The volume of shipping on the river was still increasing and business was brisk. Whether they employed their two younger brothers at the yard, we do not know. Elizabeth's hands were full providing a comfortable home life for her grown-up children who, with the exception of Harriet, were in no hurry to leave home. She also retained her interest in the property and business and guided her sons in their financial affairs, keeping a tight rein on expenditures. Typically, it was she who handled a small rental property they owned. From the outset, agreements between members of the family were as strictly recorded as contracts with strangers, and thanks to these surviving documents we are able to piece together the history of the yard from 1850 on.

The brothers' first steamboat was built in 1851 in a joint venture with the merchant James Tibbits and a fourth party, whom they subsequently bought out.[1] It was at Tibbits's foundry and machine shop that the 50-h.p. engine for the proposed boat was to be built by James's brother Benjamin

Tibbets (the brothers adopted different spellings) and his partner, Thomas Morgan. Benjamin was a recognized designer and patentee of improvements on the compound engine in his native province, New Brunswick.[2] His engine was described as "a double or high low pressure engine of the oscillating kind, with slide valves, variable cut off and one starting bar." Together with its boiler and furnace, it was to be fixed to the hull of the steamboat under construction in the Davie yard by May 1, 1852. The price of £1,800 covered the right to run the engine under the "B.F. Tibbets Patent," and the engine builders were to receive an additional 5 per cent of the profits of the 1852 season, provided the boat matched the speed of any other twice her length on the St. Lawrence, and that her towing power exceeded that of John Molson's towboat *Lumber Merchant*. Built in Montreal in 1837, the *Lumber Merchant*'s strength had not yet been bettered.

But when delivery was made four months late, the engine was not yet in full working order and the boat had neither the power nor the speed specified. Certainly, there were extenuating circumstances. Thomas Morgan had died, and Benjamin, who had contracted tuberculosis, had less than a year to live. The Davies, however, could ill afford the loss of capital and expected revenue and were obliged to borrow £500 against the latest addition to their yard, a wooden floating dock.[3] Fortunately, James Tibbits, his brother's guarantor, honoured his commitment and took over the boat.[4]

Somewhat singed by their first experience in steamboat building, George and Allison must have been more than delighted in May 1853 when the timber merchant William Price agreed both to advance £3,000 towards the cost of building a fully rigged ship, and to handle her charter to Britain and subsequent sale. Price was an old business friend of their father's, and his charges were reasonable for the time: a commission of 5 per cent on the loan, a broker's fee of 2½ per cent on the charter, a further 2½ per cent for the collection of freight charges in Britain, and 4 per cent on the sale of the vessel by his agents there.[5]

Although the 680-ton ship *Daylesford* was small compared to the average ship of 1,000 to 1,500 tons laid down in the port that year, she was

William Price (1789–1867), prominent timber merchant. The Price and Davie families enjoyed a cordial two-way business relationship for close to a century. Courtesy Antony Price.

built on similar lines. Raised on an elm keel, she had futtocks (ribs) of oak and tamarack, and tamarack and spruce knees. Her planking from the keel upward was of elm, red pine, and tamarack, and she was covered with the customary yellow pine deck. The quality of her workmanship was described by Thomas Menzies, the local Lloyd's surveyor, as "very good," and a class of 7A1 was recommended, the highest that was then available for a Quebec ship.[6] A month after her October launching, she set sail for London, where her class was confirmed. Because she arrived at the height of the demand for ships to carry troops and supplies to the war in Crimea, she is likely to have fetched at least £12 to £14 per ton, or double the market price of the previous year – all in all, a profitable undertaking for the Davies that compensated, perhaps, for the disappointing outcome of their first steamboat venture.

At the beginning of the following season, in April 1854, George and Allison entered into a formal five-year shipbuilding and repairing partnership under the name "G. and A. Davie." The rent of the yard had risen over the years to reflect the improvements that had been made, including the

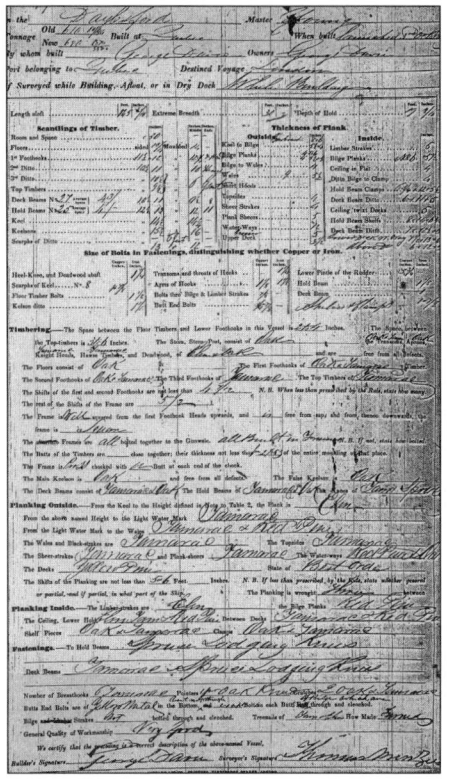

Lloyd's Survey Report of the 610-ton ship Daylesford. In summing up, the surveyor Thomas Menzies writes, "This ship is framed with single Floor and Cross Chocks Connecting heels of Lower Foothooks. The timber is good and free from Sap and well put together. The entire Plank from Keel to Bilge inclusive is Rock Elm all above is Tamarac excepting two planks in midships below Wales of Red Pine. It is well wrought and Treenails well driven. The Shelves, Clamps and Ceiling are well fayed and Seamed[?] bolted and Treenailed. The Beams good. Knees well fitted & Bolted, Is not bilge Bolted & there are no through butt Bolts excepting those in the Bilge. The General Workmanship is very good. When bolted as required by Rules and Knees and Riders fitted, I consider her entitled to be Classed 7 A1." Report No. 77, November 1853.

acquisition of the floating dock to augment the capacity of the patent slip for dry-dock work. The capital of £500 bearing interest of 6 per cent, supplied by George, was sufficient to cover the rent alone. Working capital had to be borrowed.[7]

In the strong market of the early 1850s, the majority of local shipbuilders stretched their operations to the limit and many were ruined when the market crashed. George and Allison, however, refrained from laying down another ship. Instead, they directed their efforts to the trade in which the Davie shipyard would excel, that of "wrecking" or salvaging wrecked vessels, and invested £120 in the purchase of the stranded barque *Elizabeth*.[8] She was lying on the treacherous White Island Reef, some ten to eleven miles to the south of the Saguenay River,[9] and her exceptionally low price suggests that she was badly damaged. What became of her we do not know. The Davie brothers were perhaps frustrated by the heavy cost of hiring a tug, for shortly after they decided to build their own and laid down the keel of a 116-foot side wheeler. Christened *Rambler* at her launching in 1855, she was sent to Montreal to be fitted with two 25-h.p. 8-foot stroke Gilbert engines. Her registration certificate states that she travelled at 11 to 15 mph with her 20-foot wheels reaching 30 revolutions per minute, and that she used two bushels of coal per hour of the nine hundred bushels (twenty-five chaldrons) she carried. She was the first of several salvage tugs owned by the Davies, most of which were built in their own yards, and her first captain was George T. Davie himself.[10]

The construction of the *Rambler* led to a contract to build the 259-ton paddle steamer *Lord Seaforth* for their neighbour, James McKenzie. McKenzie owned the large hotel at the ferry landing in Levis and, among other activities, ran a steamboat service. The *Lord Seaforth* would give good service on the river until she was sold to the U.S. government in 1865.[11] James McKenzie was not only a friend and an occasional customer of the shipyard; he, and later his estate, supplied some of the extra capital the shipyard needed over a period of thirty years, in amounts varying from £1,000 to £1,500.[12]

Presently, the Davies tried their hand at salvage again. The ship *Ethelred*[13] was wrecked in a violent storm at the mouth of the Chaudière River near New Liverpool and was put up for auction in July 1856. She was forty-six years old and might then have honourably ended her career, but she lay close to the yard, and the Davies made the high bid of £600 for her. After the necessary repairs had been carried out,[14] she was sent off under their ownership, but, unluckily, she was grounded and wrecked a second time on her outward journey. Her salvage was the last act of the brothers' formal partnership. Even before her repairs had been completed, the association was prematurely ended. According to the terms of the dissolution, dated August 1, 1856, George, who would continue to operate the shipyard on his own, wound up the partnership accounts and retained the stock-in-trade.[15]

The settlement of their father's estate a few months earlier may have influenced their decision to break up the partnership, though the connection between the events is not immediately apparent. At that time, Elizabeth acquired the share that each of her seven children had in the shipyard property in return for her expenses on their behalf during their upbringing and an amount of £156 which each received. Her full ownership of the yard was a temporary expedient, however, as her children were her joint heirs and on her death would inherit a larger share than they held before. A more probable reason for the dissolution of the partnership was that Allison and his younger brothers, Gershom and William, had already set their sights on the field of steam transportation and Allison did not want to be liable for any current or future debts of the yard, nor George for his.

The shipping market had now recovered from the crash of 1854, and a barque was laid down in October of 1856, followed by a fully rigged ship. These were the 337-ton *Comet*, launched in May 1857, and the 785-ton *Gananoque*, launched in October of the same year. In order to build these ships on speculation, George T. Davie obtained a loan from George Burns Symes, the Quebec agent for the Liverpool shipbrokers Holderness and Chilton, who financed many of the local builders. As Davie had to pay a commission to both the agent and his principals, the terms of the loan were far more onerous than those that he and his brother had obtained from Price.[16] To make matters worse, by the time the vessels reached the British market the prices had fallen, so they were built at a loss. Yet their records of service must have given George T. Davie some satisfaction. By 1866 the *Gananoque* had served at least seven years on the London-to-New Zealand run. The *Comet*, which was trading in the same period between London and Cape of Good Hope, was owned in Rangoon and was still sailing the high seas in 1901.[17] Fortunately, the weakness of the shipping market did not affect the volume of business of the patent slip and floating dock, both of which continued to bring in a steady revenue, while the *Rambler* more than earned her keep.[18]

In August 1860, George T. Davie's eldest sister, Elizabeth, married Captain George William Haws, who came from a seafaring and shipbuilding family like her own. His father, John Haws, had left Scotland to work in the naval dockyard at Halifax during the War of 1812 and was able to save enough money to set up a shipyard in New Brunswick, where he settled. George Haws went to sea on his father's ships at the age of fourteen or fifteen and obtained his master's certificate at the age of twenty-four. On his father's death, he bought out his brothers and sisters to become owner as well as master of the *Calista Haws*. He spent much of the first eight years of his marriage to Elizabeth at sea. Their two children were born at the Homestead.

Meanwhile, George T. Davie had succeeded in winning the hand of Mary Euphemia Patton, daughter of Lauzon timber merchant Duncan Patton; the two married on September 3, 1860.[19] She was a Catholic and he a Presbyterian, and, as was frequently the case at the time, it was agreed that the daughters of the marriage would be brought up in their mother's faith, while the sons would adhere to their father's religion. But good Catholic that she was, Mary took no chances and saw to the early baptism in the Roman Catholic church at Levis of their four sons, Charles McCarthy (1866), John Leavitt (1868), Allison Cufaude (1870), and George Duncan (1873), as well as of their two daughters, Anne (1864) and Mary Elizabeth (1875). Their father's absence from the ceremony was noted in the register in each case.[20] When the boys were older, however, they attended the Presbyterian church with their father.

On October 10, 1860, only a month after George and Mary's wedding, Elizabeth Johnson Davie died at her home in Levis.[21] The importance of her role in keeping the shipyard going for her sons and, as it turned out, for many generations of shipyard workers on the South Shore cannot be exaggerated. She died at the relatively early age of fifty-seven, but had the satisfaction of seeing her husband's shipyard solidly established as a result of her courageous effort. Though all her children inherited equally from her, three years later the four boys bought out their three surviving sisters

Top: *Elizabeth Taylor Davie (1826–1923), sister of George T. Davie and wife of George William Haws.* Ambrotype, courtesy McCord Museum. Bottom: *Captain George William Haws (1831–85). A member of the Liverpool and Saint John, New Brunswick, seafaring Haws family.* Ambrotype, courtesy McCord Museum.

(Isobel had died in 1841), who each accepted a mortgage on their share of the property in the amount of $4,800.[22]

George Taylor died soon after his daughter, on February 6, 1861.[23] He had wanted both his name and shipyard business to survive him, and both did. His grandson, George Taylor Davie, would do honour to his name, and though it was a new shipyard, which specialized in ship repairing rather than shipbuilding and which his son-in-law, Allison, had set up at Levis, its roots were on the Canoterie, and it is George Taylor who has always been remembered in the family as "the founder."

The Bratsberg *arrives safely at the Levis shipyard aboard a floating dry dock. Spectators watch from the smaller floating dock, bottom right.* Merrilees Collection, neg. PA 171090, NA.

6

NEW INTERESTS

1863-82

THE DAVIE BROTHERS became increasingly involved in the operation of steamboats. George T. Davie welcomed his brothers' interest in a field complementing that of the family shipyard and gave them his full support. It was clear to almost everyone that the future of shipping lay in steam propulsion: in the thirty-two years ending in 1849, just twenty-five steamboats had been built at Quebec. In just six more years, from 1849 to 1855, another twenty-five were built in the port. During the same period, an even larger number were built elsewhere on the St. Lawrence. Those who were not convinced by the figures had only to watch the river to see the proliferation of steamboats and steamboat lines.

But competition among the port's towboat operators became ruinous until the problem was resolved by amalgamation.[1] In 1863, the South Shore owners united, pooling ownership of their boats in exchange for shares to form the St. Lawrence Tow Boat Company.[2] A lease was taken on St. Andrew's Wharf in Lower Town Quebec. This, with "two double offices" in the brick building that stood there, became the company's Quebec terminal.[3] The company also acquired the shipyard in Glenburnie Cove, Lauzon, that Pierre Brunelle had set up only a few years earlier for

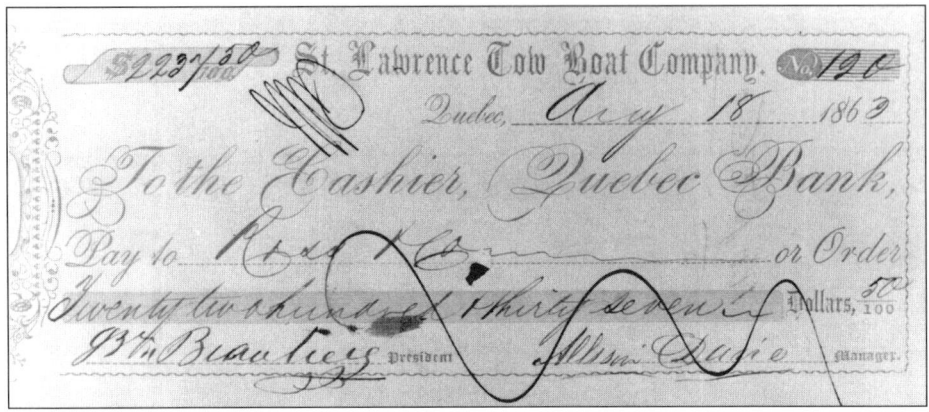

Cheque in the amount of $2,237.50, payment for the shipyard at Lauzon bought by the St. Lawrence Tow Boat Company. Made out to Ross & Co., it is signed by J.-B. Beaulieu, President, and Allison Davie, Manager. Included in Deed of Sale of land. Gr Sam Glackemeyer, August 18, 1863.

his short, unsuccessful venture into shipbuilding. At the same time, the large lot with approximately 575 feet of river frontage to the immediate southwest of the Tow Boat Company's new premises was purchased by the four Davie brothers and became what they referred to as their "lower yard."[4] In the absence of pertinent papers or records, we do not know what immediate purpose the yard served. It seems likely that it supplemented the busy towboat company's yard and was probably bought for either or both Allison and Gershom.

The St. Lawrence Tow Boat Company's first president was the local steamboat builder and owner Jean-Baptiste Beaulieu, while the first manager and secretary was Allison Davie, by then the owner or part owner of several steamboats. George and Gershom, who had also acquired interests in steamboats, were among the shareholders, while William, who had obtained his ticket as a steamboat captain, became the company's agent in Montreal in 1866. On Allison's death less than a year later, William replaced him as manager.[5]

Eight years later, in 1871, a different group of South Shore steamboat owners, including William, who had acquired thirty-two shares in the

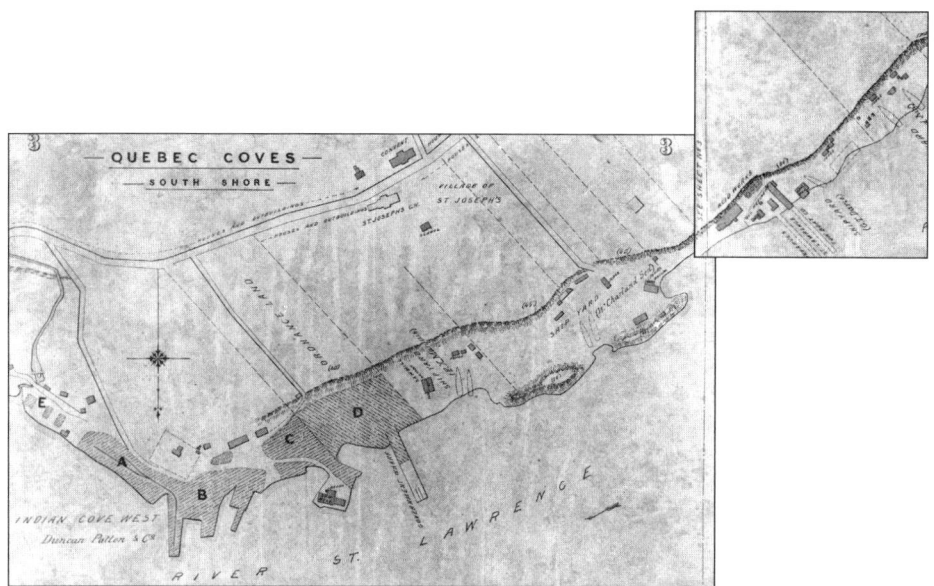

Pointe Lévy and Glenburnie Cove, showing the Lauzon shipyards in the 1870s. Left to right, shaded area B, *Duncan Patton's shipyard, where he had large sailing ships built in the 1860s by Pierre Brunelle and his son, the yards of F.-X. Marquis, William Charland Sr., St. Lawrence Towboat, Davie's "lower yard" William Charland Jr.'s yard. Atlas of Quebec Coves – South Shore – Sheets 3 and 4, 1876.* NC-83-9-7, ANQ.

Hector, joined together to form another towboat company, the Levis Towboat Company or Association des rémorqueurs de Levis.[6] Unlike the St. Lawrence Tow Boat Company, associates in the Lévis Tow-boat Company retained the ownership of their boats, but shared the contracts. By 1876, however, both the St. Lawrence Tow Boat Company and the Levis Tow-boat Company had been absorbed into the powerful St. Lawrence Steam Navigation Company.[7]

While his brothers became more and more involved in steamboat operations, George built up a long list of successful salvage operations. He also allowed himself to be tempted by the strong shipping market generated by the American Civil War and built two sailing ships. The 383-ton barque *Ondine*, laid down in September 1863 and launched in June 1864, was sold to Dundee, whence she traded with the West Indies, while the

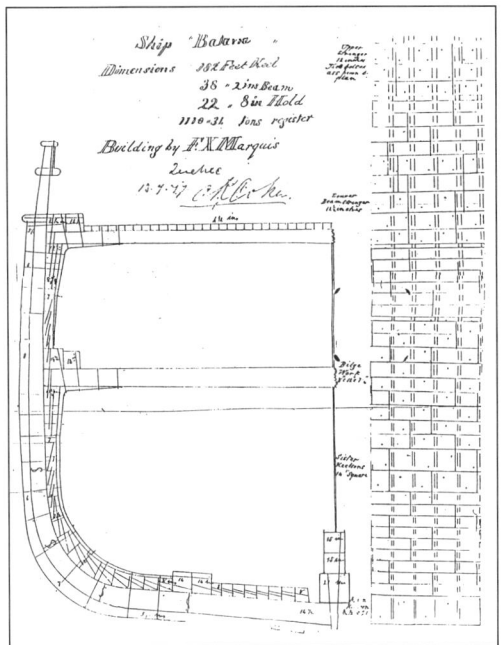

Midship plan of the fully rigged ship Batavia, *built in 1877 in F.-X. Marquis' shipyard in Lauzon, now the western part of the Davie shipyard, or Davie West.*

1,064-ton ship *Bonniton*, the last large sailing ship that George T. Davie built, was completed in 1865 and sold on the London market. The *Bonniton*'s construction was financed by the shipbroker James G. Ross to the amount of $20,000, and the timber merchant Charles Sharples bought a half-share in her before she left. She would serve her new owner on the Liverpool-to-India run and was reported to still be in service in 1891 as the Dutch barque *Nicolette*.[8]

On September 30, 1870, George bought out his two surviving brothers, Gershom and William, to become sole owner of both shipyards. In exchange for their share of the properties, Gershom and William were absolved of their responsibility for the payment of the mortgages on them, amounting to $29,770. In addition, William received $3,200 in notes, while the balance owed to Gershom was secured by a 7 per cent mortgage.[9] The whole transaction cost George approximately $37,000. The change of ownership, however, did not prevent either brother from working for or with George at various times in the future. In fact, Gershom kept accounts for

George Taylor Davie (1828–1907), left, *oldest son of Allison and Elizabeth, who bought out his brothers' and sisters' shares to become sole owner of his father's shipyard at Levis, and later founded the Lauzon shipyard.* Oil painting, unsigned. Courtesy Fleur Garneau Whitworth. *George T. Davie's, and later Foddie's, office,* below, *known as the "Patent Slip Office" on the lower floor of his house at Levis, with his massive desk and safe beyond. Photographed in the 1920s when Allison Davie was in charge there, it no doubt looked very much as it did in his father's day.*

the two shipyards, while William, who had qualified as a shipmaster, took charge later of the yard's salvage operations afloat.

George continued to enhance his reputation as a salvage expert, or "wrecker." He maintained a team of specialists, including engineers, ship carpenters, divers, and others, who were on call around the clock ready to assist any ship in distress. He worked in close co-operation with the neighbouring Carrier, Lainé Company, which undertook engine repairs, while Davie men mended the hulls.[10] Permanent hull repairs on wooden ships were carried out according to established shipbuilding practice. To repair metal hulls, however, often required considerable ingenuity because the Davie yard had not yet acquired a full complement of the appropriate tools. In some cases, a sheet of rubber sandwiched between a damaged plate and a piece of elm planking, and the whole bolted in place through the rivet holes, allowed a ship to get back to its home port for permanent repairs. A vessel with more serious damage might require "platforming," or the fixing of a temporary floor or platform in one or more of its holds. Each job was unique and helped to build up a pool of experience from which to draw. George Davie bought many condemned ships and, following their repair in his shipyard, sent them over to the shipowner Richard Haws, brother of Elizabeth Taylor Davie's husband, for sale on the Liverpool market. One such salvaged ship was the little barque *Strathardle*, which sailed for Liverpool in 1872.[11] By this time George William Haws had left the sea and had settled with his wife and children in their home on the bluff overlooking his brother-in-law's shipyard. George Haws worked in close collaboration with George Davie as Quebec agent for the shipping firm that he and his brother Richard had founded.

There was plenty of work to keep the shipyard busy. In November 1872, a second floating dock was added to its equipment, one that had been built by the shipbuilder Thomas H. Oliver in 1844 and had been operated by him at Pointe à Carcy, in Quebec's Lower Town. Known until then as the *East India Dock*, it measured 183 by 48 feet and could handle vessels of up to 190 feet in length drawing 12 to 15 feet.[12] It was rebuilt in 1877. Today,

Vessels wintering at the Levis shipyard, including the Lord Stanley, *which generally wintered at Indian Cove, Lauzon. The sign over the shed,* bottom left, *reminds the workers of the no-smoking rule that was enforced at all the shipyards. The chimney,* centre left, *identifies the Paradis sawmill.*

more than 100 years later, the remains of this dock are still visible at low tide in front of the shipyard at Levis and are the only known survivor of Quebec's early wooden floating docks.

Davie would have used the larger dock, however, for work on the London-based *Vindolana*. The 1,964-ton steamer lay stranded in the Traverse below the Isle of Orleans when, in 1878, George Davie contracted with her master, Robert Robertson Gillon, to raise, float, and bring her to Quebec.[13] He was to go down himself or to send his foreman with his salvage schooner and steamer, a barge, and five large steam pumps, taking two experienced divers together with divers' assistants, engineers, carpenters, and other workmen. His charges, as was frequently the case, would depend on whether he was successful. Certainly, Davie and his men stood to benefit considerably from a successful mission.

If successful, he could charge for the		*If unsuccessful*, only	
Use of largest pump	$60/day	Men's wages ea.	$1.00/day
Use of next largest	50/day	Divers' wages ea.	5.00/day
Use of third size	40/day	Engineers' wages ea.	2.00/day
Men's wages ea.	$1.70/day	Foreman's wages	4.00/day
Divers' wages ea.	$25/day		
+ all sums disbursed for materials and services		+ sums disbursed for materials and services[14]	

The *Vindolana* was safely brought back to the shipyard and repaired.

Besides being well-equipped with dry-docking facilities, the shipyard's floating equipment, too, was frequently upgraded. In 1875, George Davie bought the 12-h.p. paddle steamer *Cité*, which he kept until 1878, when he laid down his second *Rambler*. A screw-driven tug, much smaller than her predecessor, she had a 50-h.p. engine, compared to two 25-h.p. horizontal engines in the first, that allowed a reduction in the length of her engine room alone from 65.7 to 27 feet.[15] Two years later she was joined by the 23-

ton tug SS *Kate*. The first *Rambler* was sold in 1882 to a Montreal owner.[16] The 95-foot-long, 196-ton salvage schooner *G.T.D.* was laid down in the same year. Under her coat of white paint, the strongly built and specially equipped *G.T.D.* became a legend in the annals of wrecking history on the St. Lawrence.[17] All of these vessels were built for and laid down at the Levis yard.

In 1883, George T. Davie built his first steam ferryboat, for the Quebec and Levis Ferry Company. She was not entirely new, however, for she was rebuilt from the burned-out passenger ferry *Prince Edouard* to plans that were drawn up by Captain Robert Sample. Work began on Christmas Eve, and she left the yard renamed PS *Pilot* the following summer to be fitted out with two new high/low 75-h.p. engines by M. McDougall in Montreal. In 1910, when a new company won the contract for the Quebec-to-Levis service, she was moved downriver to serve between Rivière Ouelle and Murray Bay. Her days came to an end abruptly when she ran ashore on l'Ile Rouge in the winter of 1913–14.[18] The Davie yard also built the ferryboat *North*, sister to the *South* built by Russell. These were sturdy 289-ton paddle steamers, 132 feet long, with 30-h.p. low-pressure engines by P. Gilbert of Montreal. The *North*, which was delivered in 1886, ran for twenty-four

Left: *The salvage of the 1,964-ton SS* Vindolana *following her stranding in the Traverse, below the Isle of Orleans in 1878, with Davie's salvage schooner* G.T.D. *and tug* Rambler *in attendance. Three large pumps can be seen emptying the water from the hull on the starboard side, while two others are working on the port side.* Artist unknown. In the collection of the Musée maritime Bernier, neg. 87.03.38. Right: *The* Vindolana. In the foreground, *the bed on which she will be brought to rest.* Merrilees Collection, neg. 171783, NA.

years between Quebec and Levis until the contract for the service was obtained by a different company. And then, undaunted, her owners continued to operate her on an illegal run between Couture's Wharf, Levis, and Chouinard's in Quebec for another seventeen years. In all, she gave forty-one years of service, ending in August 1926, when she was beached at Patton's Cove to undergo the same fate as many of her contemporaries: her engine was removed and she was set on fire to salvage her iron.[19]

In 1886, Davie also replaced his second tug *Rambler* with a stronger boat, the 89-foot *Challenger*, which was fitted with an 86-h.p. compound engine installed at the neighbouring Carrier, Lainé works. She was built by and for William T. Davie, and though she was sold only two years later to the federal Department of Agriculture, when the Davies ordered a still

The ferry North *displays her fine panelling as she waits for her passengers alongside the Richelieu and Ontario Navigation Company (part of Canada Steamship Lines since 1913) wharf in front of the Finlay Market Hall. View,* Notman Photographic Archives, McCord Museum of Canadian History 2378.

The Levis waterfront, 1880, with the Davie shipyard, extreme left. In addition to the buildings shown on the Berlinguet plan, a large shed can be seen on the block. Detail from photo N87-0466, Collection initiale, ANQ.

more powerful boat, the *Challenger*, like other Davie vessels, would be long-lived, serving her new owners for twenty-six years before being transferred to the Compagnie Générale d'Entreprises Publiques. She was finally struck off the register in 1944 at the end of a fifty-eight-year career.[20]

By the 1880s, George T. Davie could look back with satisfaction on what he had achieved. He and Mary Euphemia had a large family, all of whom had so far survived. He had had the pleasure of carrying out his trade in his own well-appointed, efficient shipyard, which he had expanded through the acquisition of several small adjoining lots to cover approximately five acres, two of deep water, two and a half of beach, and another half above the high-water mark. Nine wharves, including the foundation for the patent slip, lined the waterfront. Among the buildings, most of which were built before 1864, there was a large wooden three-storey workshop 93 feet long, incorporating the mould loft, carpenters' and riggers' shops, and a small adjoining shed. There was also a long open shed 135 by 14 feet, a wooden shed 21 feet long, a store and steam-box house, a blacksmith's forge and shed, another wooden shed 70 feet long in which the salvage

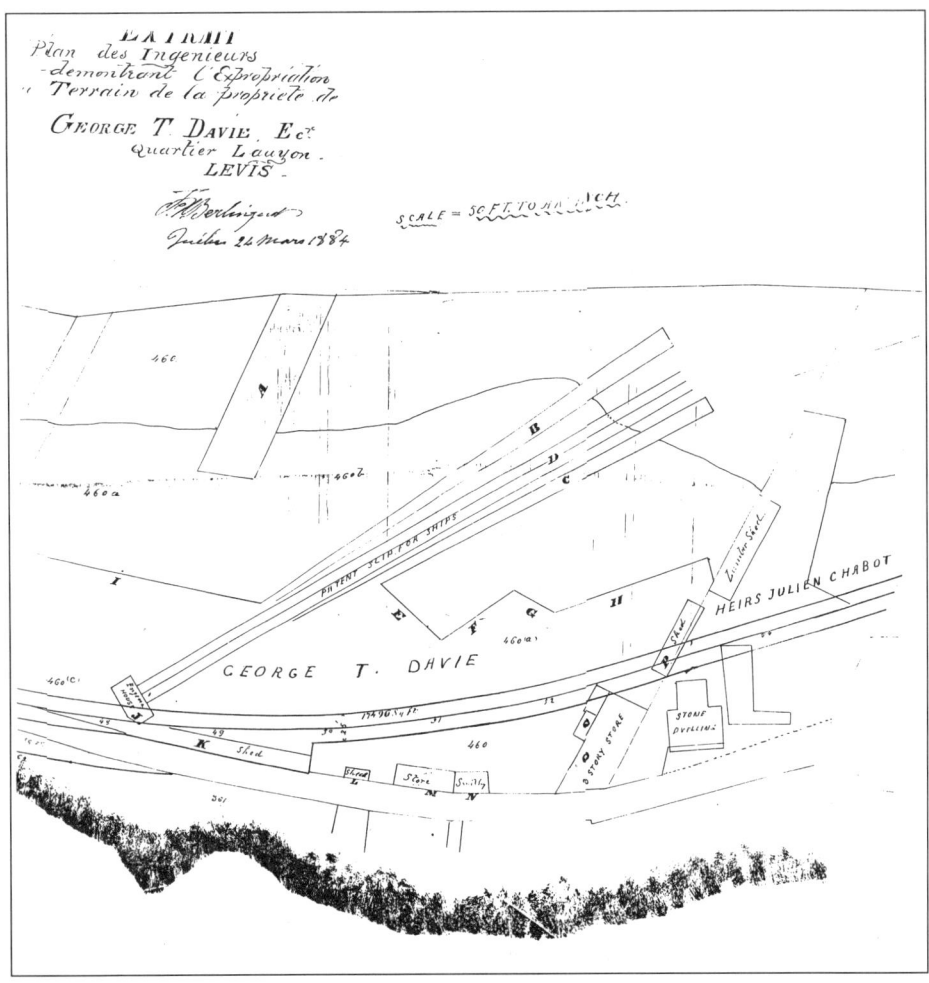

"Extrait Plan des Ingénieurs démontrant l'Expropriation. Terrain de la propriété de George T. Davie Ecr, Quartier Lauzon, Lévis." The shipyard at Levis at the time of the expropriation. (A) Deep water pier or "block," (B) and (C) finger piers of patent slip, (D) Marine Railway, (E) to (I) wharves, (J) engine house for slip, (K) open wooden shed, 135 by 14 feet, (L) wooden shed, 21 feet, (M) store and steam-box house, (N) blacksmiths' forge and shed, (O) large wooden workshop, three storeys high, 93 feet long, (P) shed for storing pumps, 70 feet long. A brick store which has already been taken down is not shown. The lower and upper floating dock beds are between (A) and (B), and (A) and (I). Compare watercolour of 1847 to 49, in which we see that the main elements of the yard were already there.

F. Berlinguet, Québec 24 mars 1884. NA.

pumps were stored, an engine house for the patent slip, and a new brick store. Supplementing the patent slip for dry-dock purposes were the two wooden floating docks 180 and 240 feet long respectively (the original small dock dating back to the early 1850s having been replaced by the larger one), each with its own "bed." Lastly, there were the tug *Kate* and schooner *G.T.D.*, which were indispensable for Davie's salvage operations and thus a very important part of the yard's equipment. The shipyard was surrounded by a high fence broached by a portcullis-type gate, both of which were painted red to match the shingled roof of the dwelling house. A bell hanging in the belfry at the south end of the engine house rang the work hours and served also to summon the men at night in emergencies. Allison Davie Haws, the son of George T. Davie's sister, Elizabeth Taylor Haws, and born in the Homestead, wrote, "They had a good outfit for shipbuilding . . . the big store for laying out rigging plans and all the other work required for shipbuilding." The path that had traversed the property had long since become a public road, the rue Commerciale, and beside the old family home there was now a brand-new brick stable.

But George T. Davie was to find out that he had built up the shipyard only to have it savaged to make way for the St. Charles branch of the Intercolonial Railway, for which a twenty-five-foot swath across the property was expropriated in 1882. Not only was the yard cut in two, but the brand-new brick building was taken down and several others were affected. Davie's request that the shipyard be bought outright was turned down. Instead, stipendiary evaluators, none of whom were knowledgeable about ships or shipyards, made an obvious undervaluation, estimating the yard's total worth at $50,000, on the basis of which they adjudged 50 per cent damages of $25,000. Their figures were immediately contested by Davie.

Testifying on Davie's behalf, the official valuator for the City of Quebec made an assessment of $325,000, slightly more than the $300,000 reckoned by the shipbuilder Narcisse Rosa, which in turn was rather higher than the $260,000 evaluation of William Simons, the Lloyd's agent and port warden, who had known the property for thirty years. Others judged its worth at

Left: *A flat-bottomed goelette shows off her distinctive flat bottom (with marker lantern attached) as she is towed back to the shipyard for repairs.* Below: *A schooner is hauled up the marine railway.* In the foreground, *the shipyard's tall fence and portcullis-style gate.*

from $100,000 to $200,000. As far as damages were concerned, the difference of opinion was even greater. One of the government's evaluators, a clerk in a hardware store in St-Sauveur, recommended no more than 4 per cent, while Arthur Tweddle, superintendent and engineer of the Quebec and Levis Ferry Company, suggested as much as two-thirds. Several shipbuilders, meanwhile, maintained that 50 to 60 per cent was the correct figure.[21] Evaluation would appear to have been a hit-and-miss proposition at the time.

In 1887, the government raised its offer to $50,000 in the face of Judge Taschereau's warning that if Davie were not awarded at least that much and decided to take the matter to the Supreme Court, the award might well be greater. George T. Davie accepted. With 6 per cent interest from 1882, it gave him a total of $64,000.[22]

It was fortunate, for our purposes, as well as Davie's, that the award on the Levis yard was contested, for the court documents contain many interesting details. For instance, we learn that the capital investment was calculated as $150,000 for the shipyard and marine railway, and $120,000 for the floating docks and marine pumps; that the difference between the amounts billed and the sum of the wages and materials for a one-year period amounted to $6,000 for the yard and railway, and $10,000 for the docks; that the thirty men who worked in the shipyard and on the marine railway earned an average of $300 per year, while a further seventy-five on the floating docks earned a little over 10 per cent more over all. Another fact, emerging from a statement made by Pierre Duclos, one of Davie's witnesses, is that he had been the yard foreman from the time that George T. Davie first took over the yard, a period of thirty-two years. The list of ships of all kinds and sizes that were tended to over a four-year period and the charges for work carried out are also of great interest and confirm that the yard was indeed a busy and successful one.

At the lower yard beside the towboat terminal, which at that time was generally leased to other shipbuilders, the improvements to the property consisted of a large cruciform shed on the beach, which measured 80 by 60

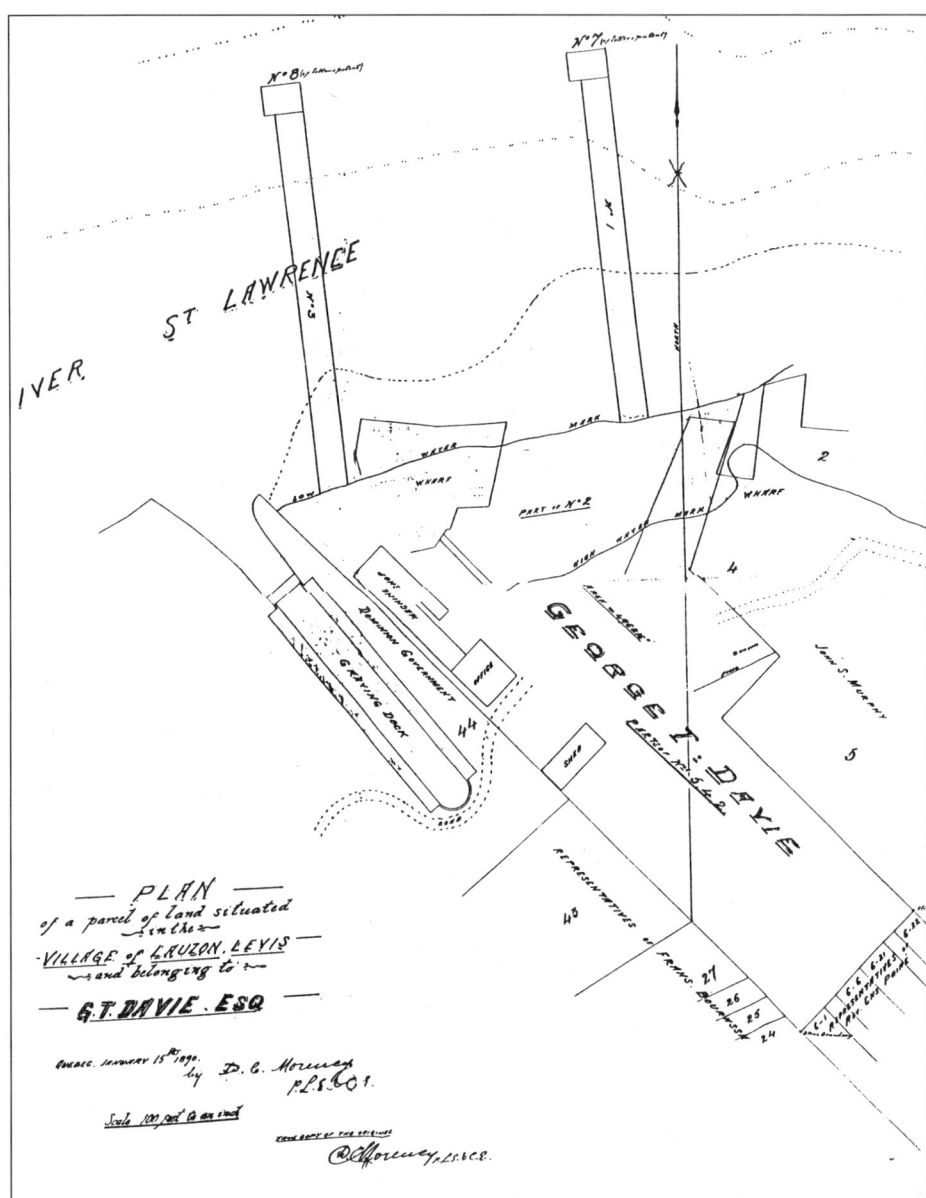

The shipyard property at Lauzon showing the part that George T. Davie kept when he sold to John S. Murphy the eastern end of the property that he had bought from Mary Hanbury. Survey by D. Morency, January 15, 1890. Plan accompanying the deed of sale before J. Auger, N.P., January 21, 1890.

feet, and below the cliff an office and blacksmith's shop and forge. There was never a possibility of moving the Levis shipyard to the lower yard, for it too was to be cut through for the railway. The expropriation award of almost $5,000 – in that case Davie's contestation was not admitted – gave him in all the tidy sum of $69,000.[23]

This sum allowed him finally to pay off the last of the mortgages on both shipyards, as well as on a new property in Lauzon, known as Indian Cove West, that he had bought in 1882 from his mother-in-law, Mary Hanbury, Duncan Patton's widow, for the sum of $25,000.[24] In the past, in order to expand and improve the business, he had frequent occasion to borrow money. He had turned at those times to James McKenzie and later to his heirs, to the Presbyterian church at Levis, the Breakey family of timber merchants at Breakeyville, not far from Levis, and to his sisters. His floating docks, as well as the properties, had served as the collateral. Now, for the first time since the yard was established, there were no creditors on the books. Even though the Levis shipyard, having been bisected by the railway, was no longer the yard it had been, George did not look back. He did not give up the original shipyard his father had founded at Levis. It continued to carry out its work on smaller wooden vessels. But he used the rest of the expropriation award to set up a shipyard on his new Lauzon property where repairs could be made to large metal-hulled ships, a shipyard whose location abutting the government dry dock already under construction could not have been better, a modern shipyard that he would be proud to leave to his sons.

Part Three

LAUZON

The Donaldson Line steamer Titania, *which ran aground on Anticosti Island, was the first ship docked in the Lorne Dry Dock. In the spirit of the occasion, some of the men have gone aloft for this inaugural picture taken in September 1886.* Andrew Merrilees Collection, NA/PA-171782.

7

LAUZON

1882-97

By the 1880s, it had become evident even to their most ardent detractors that steamships were taking the place of sailing ships and that metal hulls were replacing wooden ones. One after another, the Quebec shipyards, from which more than 1,600 square-rigged sailing ships had been launched in little over a century, fell silent. The last tall ship to be built on the St. Charles River, the 792-ton barque *Keewatin*, was launched from Peter Baldwin's shipyard in 1881, and after that only another eight square riggers were laid down in the port: three by William Charland, Sr., two by his son William Charland, Jr., and three by Etienne Samson, all of them on the South Shore.[1] The little 396-ton barquentine *White Wings*, which left William Charland, Sr.'s yard (now the western end of the Davie shipyard) in 1893, was the last.

There remained a large volume of shipping on the river, however, which allowed some of the yards in which salvage and repair work were carried out to remain open. That they were able to do their work successfully was largely due to the men's skill in handling the huge wooden floating docks with which the yards were equipped, docks that in some cases measured as much as 236 by 54 feet. But the metal-hulled ships were not restricted in length by the strength of the wood, as were their predecessors, and as time

The barque Wyle *careened for repairs.*
Andrew Merrilees Collection,
NA/PA-171091 or 2.

went by their numbers increased and their dimensions outgrew even the largest of the wooden docks.[2] Moreover, none of the existing shipyards in Quebec was equipped to handle permanent repairs to large metal-hulled ships. With many of the lucrative repair contracts necessarily going elsewhere, the pressure on the government finally led to action.

After years of argument as to whether the port of Quebec should be equipped with a graving dock and then as to whether it should be built on the Isle of Orleans, at the mouth of the St. Charles, in one of the coves at Sillery, or at Lauzon, the federal government decided to put an end to the local wrangling and chose the Lauzon site.[3] Plans for the dock were prepared by the engineers Knipple and Morris of England, and the firm of Larkin & Connolly, builder of the dry docks at Kingston, Ontario, and Esquimalt, British Columbia, was the successful bidder. Contracts were signed on August 17, 1878,[4] and work began immediately. Two hundred and twenty-five men were employed in the excavation, and when the governor-general of Canada, the Marquess of Lorne,[5] laid the cornerstone on June 17, 1880, the work was on schedule and 2,000 cubic yards had been dug.[6] The dock, which was blasted out of solid rock, was lined with blocks of Deschambault granite set in cement, filled in behind with concrete. The sides and landward end sloped outward with steps, or "altars," five feet high and one foot wide, while a single gate closed the entrance just beyond the deep 7-by-10-foot pump well. It measured 480 feet in length with 73 feet bottom width inside and a 62-foot opening. It had taken six years to complete, at a cost of $931,130. The inauguration of the dock took place on September 24, 1886, with Hector Langevin, Minister of Public Works of the Dominion, presiding.

Davie's new property lay immediately to the east of the Lorne Dry Dock and encompassed a little more than ninety-one acres of land fronted by another one and three-quarter acres of water lots. Duncan Patton, Davie's late father-in-law, had operated a timber cove there, and his widow sold it to Davie complete with the houses, stores, and steam sawmill that were on it, and the booms, anchors, and chains that had been used for restraining the stocks of floating timber. There were also several large wharves and piers, and two shipbuilding slips dating from the 1860s when Pierre Brunelle built sailing ships there for Patton.[7] The lease on the eastern section, known as Indian Cove West, which the merchant James McLaren had held since 1867,[8] was immediately surrendered, but Davie allowed his brother-in-law, William Patton, who had carried on his father's lumber business on the rest of the land, to retain his lease until 1884.[9] The sale price of the entire property was $25,000, or the amount of the mortgages that it had secured. In 1887, George T. Davie resold the greater part (on the eastern side) to the timber merchant John Simon Murphy, for $3,722 and the amount of the mortgages on it. A large part of Murphy's land, including all the beach between the high- and low-water mark, has been bought back by the shipyard since then,[10] yet the name Murphy is not forgotten. A wharf built in 1941–42 for the Crown and granted to Davie on March 3, 1947, was built by Patrick "Paddy" Murphy, his nephew, and still bears his name today.

The government dry dock was available to any shipbuilder who was willing to pay the docking fee of $200 plus five cents per ton per day, but Davie's purchase of the land beside it gave him a clear advantage over other builders, one that he wasted no time in exploiting. At that time there was a brisk cattle trade between Canada and Britain, and in November 1885 the Donaldson Line steamer and cattle boat *Titania* was stranded in a snowstorm on the north side of Anticosti Island on her return passage from Glasgow to Montreal. Although it was generally considered that

The Lorne Dry Dock seen from its southeastern end during excavation. PA 27544, NA.

there was little chance of getting her off at that late date, George T. Davie, who was in charge of the salvage operation, could not resist the challenge, but his attempt was foiled by bad weather and he had to postpone his efforts until the spring. He contented himself for the time being with the salvage of 100 tons of pig iron and some of her materials. In the spring, he bought the condemned vessel, which, with more of her cargo discharged, finally floated off on August 1 and was towed to Quebec. His divers then set to work recovering the jettisoned cargo off Anticosti Island. The *Titania* entered the Lorne Dry Dock on September 1, 1886, three weeks before the dock's official opening. Buying the ship was a bold move, for Davie had neither the experienced metalworkers nor the facilities he needed to repair her. It was to rectify this deficiency that he left in the

Workers pose on the steps of the Lorne Dry Dock. The three young men in the front row are believed to be Allison, John, and George D. Davie, left to right.

spring for Henderson's shipyard on the Clyde in Scotland, where the *Titania* had been built. There, he succeeded in persuading thirty-five-year-old James Lavery, the foreman for her construction, to come over to Lauzon with a number of skilled workers to put a new bottom on her. When the job was finished, most of the Scottish workers returned home, but some remained to form an experienced nucleus of metalworkers within the new shipyard's work force. Lavery, who brought over his wife and seven children, became the yard foreman. When the time came for the *Titania* to leave the dock, the government waived her docking fees in celebration of the fact that she was the first ship to occupy it. She left for Liverpool consigned to Richard Haws for sale and was bought soon after by John H. Rowe, a shipowner.

As the *Titania*'s repair neared completion, George T. Davie developed plans for his workshops. The drawings and specifications for a 412-foot-long building, which would incorporate the temporary shop set up for the repairs to the *Titania*, were drawn up by the architect Harry Staveley and were ready by the end of May 1887. The contract, signed on June 17, was carried out by Olivier Michaud, carpenter and joiner, and Joseph Couture, mason and bricklayer, both of Levis. It called for a new office, store, engine house, large workshop, forge, boiler house, and a safe with 16-inch brick walls, all under one roof. A new 70-foot-high square chimney for the boiler house was to be built and the existing furnace chimney was to be carried up to the same height. Construction, beginning at the south end, was not to interfere with the shipyard work.[11] The handsome red-brick workshop and office building took shape during the summer and fall of 1887.

The *Titania*'s place in the dock was taken by the 4,046-ton steamer *Lake Huron*, which was nearly three times her size. The *Lake Huron* had struck Madam Island on October 28, 1886, and been given a temporary repair outside the dock as her master had not wanted her to be frozen in for the winter at Quebec. She had left for Liverpool with three large pumps leased from Davie to keep her from foundering on the trip over, but their vibration had cracked the cement holding the temporary platform in her hold, and she had been obliged to return to Quebec after all. She entered the dock on May 9 and was there until August 31. In September and October, the steamers *Panama* and *Aviso Bouvet* were repaired. The docking of two dredges, two tugs, and four scows for the winter on November 29 brought an end to the first complete season of the dry dock – a satisfactory one for both George T. Davie, the amount of whose profits we do not know, and the dry dock, which made a profit of $12,000 on a revenue of $22,000.[12]

Only two vessels entered the dock in 1888, and on each there was only two weeks' work to be done, but the violent storms that introduced the season of 1889 helped keep all the repair yards in the port, as well as the dry dock, busy. First to be docked was the 3,983-ton steamer *Polynesian*, which had collided with the steamer *Cynthia* off Long Point on May 22 when

The Beaver Line 4,046-ton steamer Lake Huron *spent the summer months of 1888 in the Lorne Dry Dock after striking Madam Island the previous October.*
Andrew Merrilees Collection, NA/PA-171089.

outward-bound for Liverpool from Montreal. The smaller ship sank with the loss of eight men and was so damaged that the experienced diver who examined her declared that he would not attempt to raise her, even if he were offered $10,000. The *Polynesian*, with her bow cut down to the keel, and the stem, fore foot, and a large quantity of twisted and broken plating and frames of the *Cynthia* inside her, proceeded to Quebec, where she spent three months in the Lorne Dry Dock undergoing repairs. On her undocking, the tramp steamer *Deddington* took her place, followed by the 2,802-ton Moss Line steamer *Canopus* in October 1889. After her departure, the steamer *Quebec* was docked for the winter.

The year 1889, however, was exceptional, for it must be admitted that the Lorne Dry Dock was far from being the immediate runaway success that had been anticipated. Whenever possible, the Davies continued to use their wooden floating docks and thus avoided paying docking fees. In 1890, they went so far as to have the plans for a Crandall marine railway drawn up.[13] It had taken years of vigorous lobbying to have the dry dock built, yet

The Allan Line 3,983-ton steamer Polynesian *in dry dock in 1889 following her disastrous collision with the steamer* Cynthia *near Montreal. The* Polynesian *brought many immigrants to Canada; she was known to them, for reasons that are not difficult to imagine, as "Rolling Polly." In 1893, when she was fitted with triple-expansion engines her name was changed to* Laurentian, *but her nickname stuck.*

it was more frequently empty than occupied during the navigation season. Nevertheless, it was necessary, as were the stronger tugs that could handle the new and bigger ships. Without such facilities, marine insurance rates would have been far higher, which would have discouraged owners from using the St. Lawrence River ports.

The Davies upgraded their equipment accordingly. In 1888, William sold his tug *Challenger* to the government, while a far more powerful twin-screw tug was built to the Davies' specifications by the Henderson shipyard in Glasgow. George T. Davie himself went over to accept delivery

> ## ✦ TUGS ✦
>
> FOR 121 YEARS, Davie's tugs played their part in the everyday life of the port, answering the call of ships in distress and bringing them safely in, often at the completion of a spectacular salvage operation. They had towed sailing ships and barges, greatly reducing their time between the river ports. Under the direction of George D. Davie, they had helped carry the central span of the Quebec Bridge to the spot from which it was hoisted into its place. They had been on hand for every launching at each of the Davie shipyards, and at other yards in the port, restraining the vessels before nudging them back to their outfitting berths. They had towed giant oil rigs away from the shipyard, as well as the ships. Their whistles had screamed as they helped tug the *Franconia* off the rocks at the end of the Isle of Orleans before towing her safely to the Lorne Dry Dock for repairs. Nor was their work restricted to shipyard work; under the expert command of Captain John Stylidiadis, they had been on call around the clock to assist arrivals and departures from the port transporting the pilots to and from their charge.

and sail her home, arriving back on May 12, 1889, to find a large crowd waiting to welcome both him and the new tug. For good measure, the spectators that day were also able to take in the launching of the steamer *Marie Louise*, which had been rebuilt at the Davie yard and was waiting to be launched on his return.[14] Given the name *Lord Stanley*, Davie's new tug soon became a familiar sight on the St. Lawrence as, accompanied by the salvage schooner *G.T.D.*, she steamed to the assistance of stranded vessels. Her triple-expansion engines were a tremendous improvement over those

The Davies' two tugs: Challenger *of 1886, whose decoration reflected William T. Davie's pride of ownership, built at their Levis shipyard and fitted at Carrier, Lainé works with an 86-h.p. compound engine; and the* Lord Stanley *of 1889, built by D. & W. Henderson, South Shields, England, with 225 h.p. triple-expansion engines, but with less concern for ornamentation.*

of her predecessors: lighter, smaller, and more fuel-efficient, yet with a considerable increase in power, from 86 to 225 h.p.[15]

There were also official changes on the labour front during the 1880s. Following the legalization of the organization of labour in Canada in 1872, the first local assemblies of Knights of Labour were formed in 1882,[16] and in 1885 the Quebec Factory Act, the province's first labour legislation, was passed. In 1886, a royal commission was set up to report on the relations between capital and labour, and the same year the Knights split up into craft and industries unions, the craft unions forming the American Federation of Labour or AFL. Two years later, A.T. Lépine, a member of the

Left: *Chipping off the ice to facilitate removal of a propeller.* Right: *Twin-screw steamer ready to resume service after completion of repairs to her 6,360-pound propeller.*

Knights, became the first real labour representative in Parliament when he was elected MP for Montreal East.

However, labour did not wait for legislation to avail itself of the strike tool. The first strike by ship carpenters in the port of Quebec took place as early as 1840, and it had been followed by others, notably in 1857 and in 1867. The unions had encountered fierce opposition from merchants and industrialists, and when the Ship Carpenters' Society sought incorporation in 1850, its request was strongly contested by the Chamber of Commerce.

There was a profound difference in attitude, however, between the average Quebec worker and his counterpart in other provinces, and particularly the newly arrived workers from the British Isles. Besides being far more comfortable with a paternalistic employer, the Quebec worker was strongly bound to the teachings of the Catholic Church, which decried all union activity. Nevertheless, in 1890 a young union, perhaps influenced by the new workers from Glasgow, did try flexing its muscles at the shipyard, threatening to strike if George T. Davie did not fire four men who were late in paying their union dues. By way of answer, Davie locked out his 102 employees until the protest ended, saying that he would rather sell at a loss the ship that was under repair than bow to their threats.[17] But all the while the labour movement was growing stronger. In 1892, a Quebec Provincial

George Duncan Davie as a young officer serving under his uncle William aboard the Davie tugs. Ph. Gingras.

Executive Committee of the Trades & Labour Congress (TLC) of Canada was set up, and in 1897 a TL council was established at Montreal.

These important events in George T. Davie's life took place against a background of personal tragedy, for in 1885 in a shipyard accident, he lost his oldest son, Charles, who was serving an apprenticeship in the yard, and ten months later his brother Gershom died at fifty-six years of age.[18] Both were severe blows, for in each case he lost not only a close member of the family, but someone on whom he could rely in the business, too. Though Charles was only eighteen years old, as the shipbuilder's son he would already have had an extensive knowledge of the yard's affairs.

George could find some consolation, however, in the fact that he and Mary had been blessed with four sons, and he reacted to the deaths of Charles and Gershom by hastening the integration of the three who remained into the business. John Leavitt, or "Jack," now the oldest, entered the technical side of the shipyard as a draftsman in the drawing office. The second, Allison Cufaude, generally known as "Foddie," put his good business sense to use in the accountancy department, while acting also as secretary to his father. The youngest, George Duncan, was apprenticed at the Carrier, Lainé machine shop and foundry in Levis, the leading firm in its line in the port. Founded by Charles William Carrier, a former apprentice at the Tibbits works, the quality of the training there was as thorough as it had been at the Tibbits yard. On completing his term, George D. worked with his uncle William in the salvage end of the business and like him became a steamboat captain, at some time undergoing further training in Glasgow. He had a good teacher in his uncle William, who had become a highly respected authority on the floating-off of stranded vessels on the St. Lawrence route and off the shores of Newfoundland.

By 1897, George T. Davie felt that the time had come to hand over the business to his three sons, Jack, Foddie, and George, then twenty-nine, twenty-seven, and twenty-four years old respectively, and on April 4 of that year, the four men visited the notary to sign two deeds that had been prepared to give effect to his decision. First, a partnership agreement was signed between the sons for the purpose of carrying on the trade of shipbuilding and ship repairing under the name "George T. Davie & Sons." The capital was to be provided by each of them equally, and each was to devote his entire time to the business, for which he was entitled to draw no more than $25 per week, though at the end of each year he could draw his share of the year's profits. The second deed was a sale and conveyance from George T. Davie to the partnership of the three shipyard properties with buildings, improvements, and stock-in-trade, all of which remained mortgaged to the father, however, as security for an annuity of $8,000 per year that the partnership was to pay him.[19] It was a reasonable figure in view of the fact that he had spent $100,000 on the machinery for the Lauzon plant alone and that, in spite of his "retirement," he was still very much a part of the firm.

Hull Number 1, the paddle steamer Champion *of 1897. She had a 30-h.p. low-pressure engine. She was built for the Compagnie Maritime et Industrielle de Lévis for service between Québec and Berthier. She is seen here following her sale to the Thousand Island Navigation Company when she ran between Kingston, Ontario, and the United States. She ended her days at Hamilton in 1952 under the name* Hamiltonian, *at the venerable age of fifty-five.* Marine Museum of the Great Lakes at Kingston.

8

GEORGE T. DAVIE & SONS

1897-1907

It was under the new ownership of the firm that the 140-foot paddle steamer *Champion* was launched on May 1, 1897, and was designated Hull Number 1 on the Lauzon shipyard's yard list. She was clinker-built on an iron frame and was propelled by a 30-h.p. Rousseau and Tourig low-pressure engine. The Compagnie Maritime et Industrielle de Lévis, her owners, had ordered her for the short run downriver to Berthier. After serving in that and various other capacities over the years – she was used, for example, to ferry troops to transports waiting in the river during the Great War – she was transferred to the Thousand Island Navigation Company at Kingston in 1926,[1] eventually ending her days in 1952 in Hamilton as the *Hamiltonian*. It was a long and useful career for the new company's first ship. Hull Number 2, the *George T. Davie*, a large composite barge built for the Montreal Transportation Company to carry grain on the Upper Lakes, was launched in 1898.[2] But the Canadian shipbuilding industry was badly hurt by both British and American competition, and the construction of the two vessels did not herald a general improvement in the trade, any more than had the first steel ship built in Canada, the ss *Manitoba* of 1889.[3] In fact, no other new vessels were laid down at the Lauzon yard until 1909. In the intervening years, both management and

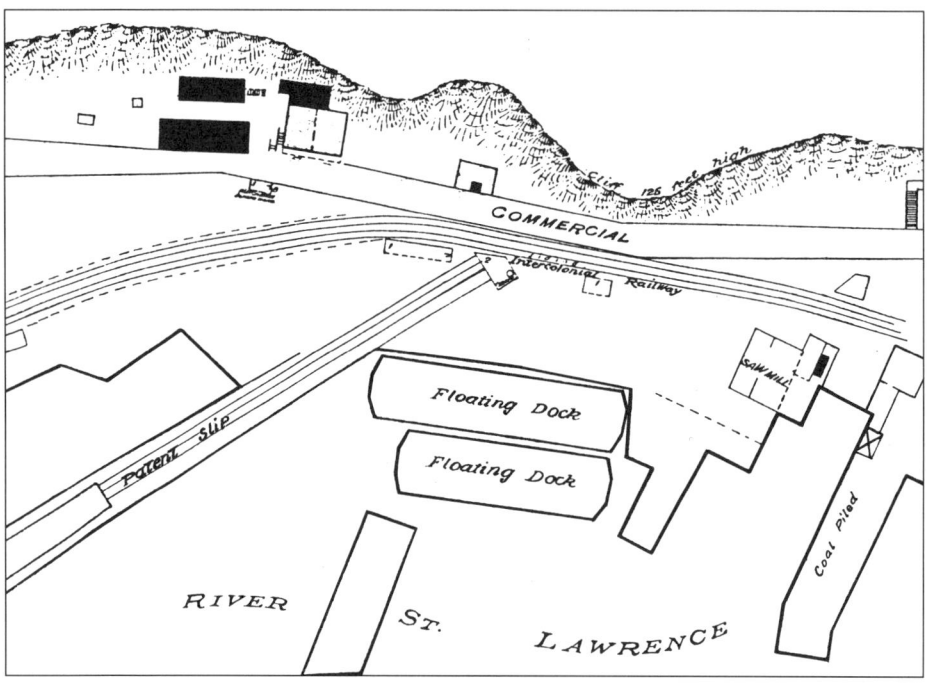

The Levis shipyard twenty years after the expropriation. The large three-storey shed to the east of the patent slip has disappeared, but the two wooden floating docks are there, a brick store has been built behind the stable and there is an annexe to the house. (The larger dock was sometimes employed at the Lauzon yard where it had a second bed.) Conveniently located to the west of the yard is the Paradis sawmill. Charles Goad, Atlas of 1909, C829-106, ANQ.

workers learned a great deal about the construction of metal ships in the course of the salvage and repair work that they engaged in.

Canadian shipbuilders considered that the government should subsidize the shipbuilding industry to allow it to turn to steel construction, but, in fact, government policy actually favoured foreign competition. British ships entered Canada duty free, while Canadian shipbuilders were required to pay duty on the materials and equipment they had to import in order to build ships to compete with them. Their complaints, however, fell on deaf ears, and British manufacturers retained their market advantage.⁴ Nor was competition confined to new construction. Some of the most lucrative repair contracts for the largest vessels continued to elude Quebec shipbuilders.

Ships were becoming larger all the time. By 1896, only nine years after the Lorne Dry Dock's inauguration, it was either too short, too narrow, or both too short and too narrow, to accommodate the largest of them. An attempt to dock the Quebec Steamship Company's ss *Carolina* that year, for instance, had to be aborted because of her width. In 1905, when the Allan Line's 10,387-ton steamer *Bavarian* was grounded and an attempt was made to dock her, the bulge that the accident had caused in her side prevented her entry, and she had to be beached instead. As a result of further damage caused by ice during the winter, she became a complete loss and, though only six years old, was sold for scrap. By 1912, there were twenty-five vessels sailing the St. Lawrence regularly that could not be accommodated in any dock anywhere on the river.

The lobby of shipbuilders, shipowners, and other interested parties who called for the dry dock to be enlarged had a powerful ally in the Harbour Commission. Eventually their voices were heard. A hail of falling rocks damaged several shipyard buildings during the blasting for the extension, and Davie's employees were more than a little relieved when the lengthened dock was ready for use at the beginning of the season of 1901.⁵ The extension allowed the dock to take vessels of up to 600 feet, or 610 feet with the stern overhanging the gates.⁶ Though a great improvement, the extra length did not help in the case of ships with wider beams, such as the *Carolina*, or the Canadian Pacific Railway's liners, *Empress of Britain* and *Empress of Ireland*.

In the meantime, the opportunity had presented itself to sell the *Lord Stanley* to the government for hydrographic service on Lake Superior, and the Davies had taken advantage of the offer to order a more powerful tug from Rennoldson and Sons of South Shields. She was built to George T. Davie's specifications with two sets of triple-expansion compound engines

The Lord Stanley *alongside the finger wharf below the patent slip. The collection of pumps on the quay were a familiar sight. They were kept there so that they could be loaded instantly in an emergency.*

and, like the *Lord Stanley*, was specially strengthened for working in ice conditions. At 160 feet, she was 20 feet longer than her predecessor and had 1,700-i.h.p. (indicated horsepower) propelling machinery, a powerful steam windlass, a steam winch forward for salvage work, and another aft for working the towing hawsers and special steering gear. Two marine boilers working at 180 pounds pressure supplied her steam. Her electrical installation included masthead lights and sidelights, and, it was reported, the captain could call any officer or wake up the watch below simply by touching a button, which appears to have been something of a novelty at the time, at least as far as tugs were concerned. She was built of steel under Lloyd's Special Survey and was classed 100 A1. William T. Davie stood by

The new Davie tug, Lord Strathcona, *(left) shows off her powerful propellers in the dry dock at South Shields in 1902. She would be by far the most powerful tug on the St. Lawrence. Her two sets of triple-compound engines were capable of producing 1,700 i.h.p. Right: The tug* Lord Strathcona *with her constant companion, the salvage schooner* G.T.D., *a familiar sight on the river for many seasons.*

while she was under construction, and his brother George T. and son, George W., travelled to South Shields for the trials. Given the name *Lord Strathcona*, she arrived in Quebec on May 4, 1902, with William and his son aboard and was immediately put into service.[7]

The same high performance that the Davies looked for in their tugs, they expected from their plant at Lauzon. This was described by reporters on both sides of the Atlantic as the best-equipped salvage yard in America, some even comparing it favourably to the best in Britain. Every effort was made to keep it up to date, and while the normal shipyard strength was about 50 men, as many as 300 were taken on at times to meet an emergency. In 1903, in order to repair the SS *Iberian* after it struck ground at Red Island, steel plates were brought over from Britain and a new set of plate rolls was installed that could roll a plate 30 feet long. At that time,

Left: *The iron barque* Sardhana *of Glasgow, which went ashore in dense fog on July 22, 1903, a mile and a half from the light station at Pointe des Monts on the North Shore of the St. Lawrence. She is seen here under repair in the Lorne Dry Dock.* P-546/G-34, ANQ. Right: ss Carolina *stranded on the shore of the Saguenay River at Passe Pierre in 1904, as Davie's salvage team approaches.*

Captain Farrington, master of the *Iberian*, was quoted as saying that it was "indeed satisfactory to shipping men generally to have such a thoroughly equipped dock and to also possess such men as Messrs. G.T. Davie & Co., together with the large contingent of skilled mechanics and others trained in the system of shipbuilding." This was by no means an isolated compliment. Many others, written by shipmasters and owners, were reported by the press. However, one can only presume that Farrington's reference to the "thoroughly equipped dock" referred to the Davie workshops, for the equipment of the dry dock itself was frequently criticized, especially its lack of steam cranes. One master in particular, from whose ship a considerable amount of cargo had to be unloaded, strongly protested the fact that the dock did not have the facilities that "comparable docks everywhere else provided."[8]

GEORGE T. DAVIE & SONS

Left: *Euphemia Patton (1832–1920), wife of George Taylor Davie and daughter of the timber merchant Duncan Patton, from whose estate George T. Davie bought the shipyard property at Lauzon.* Courtesy Anne Mimi Garneau. Right: *George Taylor Davie in his later years.* Courtesy Anne Mimi Garneau.

As far as the shipyard equipment was concerned, the workers had been quick to adapt to the pneumatic tools with which the drilling, riveting, chipping, and caulking were now done. These had been introduced into American yards as a solution to the freezing problem to which hydraulic tools were subject. Their design had subsequently been improved in Britain so that they were actually lighter and easier to handle than hydraulic tools. George D. Davie would later claim that they not only did a good job but were also the safest available, refuting the suggestion that pneumatic tools were dangerous, which appeared in the press when one of his workers lost an eye to a flying rivet.[9]

The shipyard's competence in dry-dock work was matched by its excellent salvage record. George T. Davie claimed that in its first fifty years of wrecking, his firm never lost a ship in an operation of which it had sole charge. He felt, however, that in order to survive, the yard should widen its field of operations. In 1901, he contracted with the Cleveland-based American Shipbuilding Company to join the halves of vessels they built. The strategy was necessary because the vessels the American company was building would be too long at finished length to pass through the locks to Montreal. The first of these, the ss *Minnetonka*, purchased by the Great Lakes and St. Lawrence Transportation Company for the grain trade, was towed to Quebec from Cleveland in May 1902. Settling the two sections down in their respective places in the Lorne Dry Dock ready for riveting together was expected to take a week, but the crowd that gathered to watch

The G.T.D. wrecking schooner lying in one of the floating docks at the Levis shipyard. Behind her to the left, *the engine house for the patent slip, its belfry at the far end housing the shipyard bell. The roof is split to accommodate the bowsprit of the lead ship on the patent slip.*

as the operation began was amazed to see it finished in a matter of minutes. Two hundred workmen, four times the usual shipyard strength, then set about the rest of the riveting, which was finished in little over a month. In September, the *Minnetonka*'s sister ship, the *Minnewaska*, was sent down in two sections and similarly joined.[10] Several more vessels were put together in this way, while others were cut in two so as to be able to make the journey in the opposite direction. Among the latter were the *Keewatin* and her sister, the *Assiniboia*, both of which were built in Govan, Scotland, in 1907 for the Canadian Pacific Railway Company. Their length, 336 feet, could not be accommodated by the canals to Lake Erie. The two ships would serve between Owen Sound, Port Arthur, and Fort William until 1965. Unlike her sister, the *Keewatin* then got a reprieve from the shipbreakers and does duty today as a popular museum and restaurant at Douglas, Michigan.

In April 1903, the salvage team lost its leader, William T. Davie, George's only surviving brother, who died at the age of sixty-seven. He had enjoyed his new command as captain of the *Lord Strathcona* for only one season.[11] His death was attributed to a beating he had received some years previously from a gang of "crimps," or waterfront criminals, who made a living in various nefarious ways, principally by supplying merchant vessels with sailors who had been encouraged by them to desert other ships. The attack is described by the mariner historian Frederick William Wallace, who no doubt heard the story from one of the Davies themselves:

> He [William] was alone in the cabin of his ship, which was lying close to the Davie's yard at Levis, when a party of crimps boarded the ship and invaded the cabin. Picking up an unloaded rifle, Davie used it as a club, but was soon overpowered. When the dockyard men arrived in force to rescue him, the crimps had their victim spread-eagled and were hauling him up and down the poop ladder. The steps wrecked his back and he never recovered. It was said that if he had only covered the gang with his rifle, instead of using it as a club, he might have held them off.[12]

William Taylor Davie (1836–1903), youngest son of Allison and Elizabeth Davie, steamboat captain and salvage expert. Courtesy Lynne Brodie.

William had worked closely and loyally with his brother as his salvage tug captain and expert for many years and had been an excellent teacher for his nephew George D. Davie. However, he had not been able to buy back his share in the Davie shipyards whose ownership George guarded jealously for his sons. William must have regretted selling it to him in 1870 and investing the money in a chandlery store business that he and his brother-in-law, Robert George Sample, set up in partnership in 1873. Although well located at 53 St. Peter Street, Quebec, in the former property of William Hunt, the sailmaker, the market was no longer what it had been, and the business failed five years later.[13] In a will written shortly before his brother's death, George had made it clear that William, who already "had profits from running the *Lord Stanley*," could not expect anything else. Though William's three sons worked at the shipyard, they had no part in its management nor any financial interest in it. George W. was a clerk, William (Willie) an engineer, and Oswald an electrician. They remained at the Levis yard until 1910 or 1911, and then one after the other moved away.[14]

Pierre Duclos (1822–1903), for many years foreman of the Davie shipyard, at Levis and later at Lauzon.

Within two months of William's death, George attended the funeral of Pierre Duclos, his former foreman and friend, who died at the age of eighty-one. He was one of the apprentices whose wages Elizabeth Davie had sewn into his pocket, and he had become George's right-hand man when George took over his father's yard in 1851. He took with him many shared memories of both good and bad times at the Levis and, later, the Lauzon yards. He was greatly respected not only in the shipyard, but also in the community, where he had served as a church warden for many years, and later had been elected mayor of the part of Levis known as Bienville.[15]

There were other trials during George T. Davie's last years, including the loss of the salvage schooner *G.T.D.*, of which he had been so proud. It was the nature of salvage work and the weather conditions in which the Davies' vessels were frequently obliged to sail that it was not uncommon for them to be damaged in some way or other. In November 1905, the *G.T.D.* caught fire and became a total loss while working to free the Allan Line steamer *Batavian* as she lay aground on the Wye Rock off St. Thomas Point, near Montmagny. The schooner had to be replaced quickly, and a stronger vessel, the 123-foot Nova Scotian-built schooner *Tyree*, with steam-operated winches and windlass, was bought and later renamed *G.T.D.* The new *G.T.D.* was equipped with six 15-inch pumps, three pulsometers (or vacuum pumps), and seven large boilers and carried a full set of spare parts for all of them, so that they could be repaired on the spot. Her interior was fitted out as a first-class machine shop. There was accommodation on board for sixty men who, when they were not engaged in salvage work, were employed in the yard or machine shop and responded to the whistle of the *Lord Strathcona* as firemen to a fire bell. Many of them were highly experienced in wrecking, having spent a great many years working for the Davies. Both vessels always kept up steam, so that they would be ready to sail at a moment's notice, and the two soon became as familiar a sight as the first *G.T.D.* and the *Lord Stanley* had been before.

A year later, a spark from an Intercolonial train caused a far more serious fire than any previous fire lit by sparks, and a number of properties surrounding the Levis shipyard, including the Paradis sawmill, the Globe Hotel, and at least ten houses, many of them occupied by several families, were burned to the ground.[16] Though the Davies themselves were fortunate that their home was spared, the ever-present threat of fire was hard on all those who lived close to the tracks, and the experience was undoubtedly frightening for them.

And now George T. Davie's own long and fruitful life was drawing to a close. When he died on September 1, 1907, at seventy-nine years of age, the South Shore mourned the loss of a man who had not only played a leading part in its shipbuilding tradition, but also had ensured its survival from the days of the carpenter to those of the engineer. During his fifty-year stewardship of the family business, he had shown both prudence and initiative. Although he had built the business up gradually, he had not lacked the courage to take decisive action and seized opportunities as they arose. He lived modestly and worked hard, setting an example to all those around

Left: *Dogcarts were a familiar sight at this time both in the towns and in the countryside. This one appears to have been pressed into service at the shipyard to carry some light timber.*
Right: *Bowler hats were* de rigueur *from an early age for the shipbuilder and his sons, as we see in this typical group around the office door.*

him as was in keeping with the times. He taught his sons to take pride in Davie workmanship, and at the end of the year he took pride in ensuring that no bill was left outstanding. Even if it meant taking out a mortgage, each New Year started with a clean slate.

The needy benefited over the years from his and his wife's anonymous and generous help, as did the whole community for a total of nearly ten years from his sound judgement as an elected councillor. "In spite of the many demands of his business," wrote Pierre-Georges Roy, the distinguished local historian, "Mr. Davie was always interested in the progress of the Town of Levis. In 1861, when the Town was incorporated, he agreed to represent the Lauzon ward on the Council. He was councillor for the same ward on two occasions, from 1875 to 1881, and from 1886 to 1889. He was above all a man of action. His speeches at the Council Meetings were never long and never spoken for the gallery. He gave his opinion on the business under consideration, and his colleagues who had confidence in his judgement and his business experience were quick to accept his point of view."[17]

George Taylor Davie. No longer at the helm of the shipyard, but still at the reins of his carriole.

Through his foresight in handing the reins of the business to his sons in 1897, the shipyard did not undergo the upheaval that might have resulted from his death. The team was not only in place, but had many years of experience working together. John managed the Lauzon shipyard, with James Lavery still in charge of all work done outside the shops, while George Duncan Davie had replaced his uncle William in charge of salvage operations, and Harry Lamontagne had succeeded Pierre Duclos as shop foreman. The position of master blacksmith was held by Hector Duchesneau, and that of master carpenter by Isaie Samson. The clerks, Thomas O'Neill, Edouard Samson, and Thomas Morritt, were also old employees, as were Achille Bissonet and Joseph Guérin, who looked after the security of the plant.

When his brothers and the shipyard's key employees moved to Saint-Joseph (Lauzon), around 1885, Allison (Foddie) had remained at the Homestead with his parents, where he continued to keep the books, served as his father's secretary, and kept an eye on the work at the old familiar yard in Levis. It had become his particular preserve and would remain so for the rest of his life. Though George T. Davie's counsel was undoubtedly missed on many an occasion, the old shipyard, too, did not falter with his passing.

The summer ferry Lauzon *of 1910, A. Angstrom of Toronto, naval architect, and Alfred Pérusse, mechanical superintendent, nears completion. A rare photograph that shows the horses, which had not yet been supplanted by mobile cranes. The* Lauzon *operated on the Quebec-to-Levis run for eighteen years, was then sold to the city of Three Rivers, and gave good service on the Three Rivers-to-Ste. Angèle crossing under the name* Cité des Trois Rivières.

9

THE PRE-WAR YEARS

1907-14

THE CONSTRUCTION OF the Lorne Dry Dock and the new Davie facility beside it had radically changed the distribution of ship-repair business at Quebec. Until then, the Davie yard had competed on a more or less equal footing with other yards. These included Henry Dinning's shipyard at Cape Cove and Alexander Russell's at Levis, both of which were equipped, like theirs, with two floating docks. There was also the former Gilmour yard at Wolfe's Cove, now owned by the timber merchant John Roche, in which there was a gridiron and a floating dock; and, in the 1880s, F.-X. Marquis's ship railway at Lauzon.[1] Davie's patent slip, two floating docks, and excellent reputation had attracted a large part, but by no means all, the business. But in setting up a new shipyard beside the new dry dock, George T. Davie had gained an overwhelming advantage, and one by one the other shipyards closed down. At the end of the century, the Russell and Davie yards were the only yards left in the port that could handle a 2,000-ton ship, but there was not enough work to keep them both busy. Competition between them became so intense that on at least one occasion, Davie's men, armed with rifles and axes, guarded their floating dock all night for fear that Russell's men would make good their threat to burn it. All this changed in 1906. Their sixty-year rivalry came to an end when Alexander Russell

Alexander Russell (1851–1926)
Courtesy Mildred Russell.

conveyed his shipyard to its mortgage holder and took a position in a shipping office in Quebec. In 1909, his considerable experience in maritime matters earned him the appointment of port warden.²

With the Russell shipyard no longer a competitor, Davie obtained the contracts from the Traverse de Lévis Limitée to replace the aging summer ferries *South* and *North*, which had operated between Quebec and Levis since 1885 and 1886 respectively. The plans for the new boats, Hulls Numbers 3 and 4 on the yard list, had been prepared by A. Angstrom of the Richelieu and Ontario Navigation Company. They were ready for launching within a few days of each other at the end of April 1910, and within a month had been fitted out and delivered to their owners. On the strength of its performance, the shipyard was then awarded the contract for the two new winter ferries, which were delivered in October and November respectively.

All four boats were clinker-built on steel frames, and their machinery was engineered at the former Carrier, Lainé machine shops, now known as the Canadian General and Shoe Machinery Company. The 133-foot, 280.7-ton summer ferries *Levis* and *Lauzon* had vertical-compound fore and aft engines, while the 121-foot, 338-ton winter boats *Colomb* and *Plessis*, were

Hulls 5 and 6, the winter ferries Plessis *and* Colomb, *October 1910. On account of their relatively narrow beam, these ferries are said to have been able to manoeuvre well and wiggle free when caught in the ice. Later ferries were wider and had more difficulty.*
P600-6/PN-276/2, ANQ.

fitted with inverted triple-expansion fore and aft engines. They were a far cry from the first regular winter steam ferry on the Quebec to Levis crossing, the 75-h.p., 104-ton steamer *Arctic*, built by James Tibbits in 1862–63, which had caused a furore when she broke up the ice bridge between the two shores. Prior to that date, the ice bridge had remained unbroken all winter to allow free passage over the river.

Thirteen years had elapsed since the last launching at the shipyard, and the early hour of the ceremonies did not deter the crowd of two to three thousand from attending. Some visitors from Quebec took the 11:30 p.m. ferry the night before so as not to miss the occasion. Others set out at 4:30 in the morning.[3] All the traditions were observed. The four sponsors were Marie Demers, daughter of the president of the ferry company; Alma Gosselin, daughter of one of its directors; a Mrs. Joseph Côté; and George D. Davie's daughter, Brenda (known as Kitty). Special visitors were invited to a reception at George D. Davie's home beside the shipyard afterwards. Many of them were no doubt curious to see the inside of the house that the famous Arctic explorer Joseph-Elzéar Bernier had built for himself when he was appointed superintendent of the dry dock in 1887.[4] It was an occasion for the people of the South Shore to be doubly proud because the ferry service itself was back in the hands of South Shore residents in a new company, La Traverse de Lévis, Limitée, after having been operated by the Quebec-owned Quebec and Levis Ferry Company since 1876.

But in spite of the enthusiasm generated by the launchings, the future of the Lauzon shipyard had become a matter of serious concern to the Davie brothers. The order book was empty. Competition from American shipyards for the salvage and repair trade, their bread and butter, was constantly increasing, and the Canadian government would do nothing to protect the Canadian yards. By 1912, the Davies were prepared to give up the shipyard if only the government would nationalize it, to prevent it from falling into the hands of the American Wrecking Trust. George D. Davie went so far as to meet with the Minister of Marine and Fisheries, but the government refused to intervene.

Meanwhile, across the Atlantic, Germany was steadily building up a fleet of warships, and in an effort to keep the upper hand, the British, too, had

The loaded floating dock alongside the wharf with gate open to allow the water to flow in, so that the vessel can be floated out.

embarked on a heavy and expensive naval shipbuilding program. Although Britain assumed the responsibility for the naval preparedness of the Empire, the competition was becoming a heavy burden to her taxpayers. The British government had been urging since 1887 that a larger proportion of the expenses be paid by taxpayers of the colonies and dominion.

At a series of colonial conferences at the turn of the century, Canadian delegates held the position that Canada was already making a considerable contribution in other ways. She had accepted the responsibility for fishery protection on her seas and lakes, had taken over the operation of the wireless stations and the hydrographic survey from the Admiralty, and was in the process of taking over the responsibility for the Esquimalt and Halifax naval bases. In addition, Canadians had paid for the construction of the Canadian Pacific Railway, which facilitated fast mail as well as passenger

The vessel on the left is in the submerged floating dock; the other is on the marine railway.

and goods services between Britain and Australia and the Far East, to the advantage of all parties. The prime minister, Wilfrid Laurier, declared that Canada was not prepared to make an annual contribution to help defray the expenses of the British Navy, regardless of the fact that Australia and New Zealand were doing so. He was nevertheless of the opinion that Canada should have her own navy, a navy run by a Canadian minister, manned by Canadians and built, if possible, in Canada, but which would be placed under Admiralty control in the event of war.

Although the Naval Bill Laurier introduced to implement this policy was eventually passed, it encountered strong opposition from Frederick Monk, the head of the provincial Conservatives, and from Henri Bourassa, the rebel Liberal, who campaigned actively against it. Bourassa maintained that Canada should not commit herself to fight in Britain's wars, and that a commitment for an annual expenditure of $3 million should not be made without a plebiscite. The Leader of the Opposition, Sir Robert Borden,

A square-rigged ship in the floating dock was at one time a common sight. Notman Archives, Courtesy Michel Lessard.

agreed with Laurier in principle, but preferred that the Canadian Navy be considered a unit of the British Navy. His amendments, like those put forward by Monk, were defeated, and in 1910 the Naval Service Act entered the statute book.[5]

The act provided for the setting up of a department of the naval service, and called for a Canadian navy modelled on the British Navy, a naval college, a naval reserve and a naval volunteer reserve to back up the regular force. In order to encourage the construction of dry docks, on the same day that the Naval Bill was passed in the House, assent was also given to the Dry Docks Subsidies Act, a bill that empowered the government to grant a subsidy in the amount of 3½ per cent annually of a dry dock's cost, for thirty-five years.

Neither Canadian shipbuilders nor the Canadian government had any illusion that they had the technical competence to build sophisticated warships. A call for tenders for the construction of four cruisers of the improved Bristol type and six improved River class destroyers, the second of two alternative programs the Admiralty had suggested, was directed of necessity to British shipbuilders who were willing to establish a shipyard in Canada. While it was reckoned that building the ships in Canada would cost one-third more than having them built in Britain, the benefits from introducing a significant program of naval construction into the country were expected to outweigh the cost.

Tenders ranging from $11,280,000 to $13,055,804 were received from seven British yards: Cammell Laird and Co., who were willing to open a yard at Saint John, New Brunswick; British and Canadian Shipbuilding and Dock Company, who cited a Sydney, New Brunswick, location; Vickers, Sons and Maxim, who would build "on the St. Lawrence River"; Sir W.G. Armstrong, Whitworth & Company, and Swan Hunter on the Tyne; William Beardmore of Glasgow; and Thames Ironworks, Shipbuilding & Engineering, who did not state the location for their intended operations, though apparently Swan Hunter, which went on to found the Halifax Shipbuilding Co. Ltd., had Halifax in mind.[6] Before a decision was taken, however, Robert Borden's Conservative government swept into office in the election of 1911 and immediately shelved Laurier's naval program.

In its place, Borden introduced his own naval aid bill in 1912, which authorized spending $35 million from the Consolidated Revenue Fund of Canada on battleships or cruisers for the British Navy. But Borden had badly misjudged the temper of the Canadian Parliament. Immediately, old flames were rekindled, and though the minority Liberals could not prevent the bill's passage through the House, they could use delaying tactics and did so through twenty-three weeks of debate until closure was applied. For Borden, it was a hollow victory, however, for the Conservatives did not have a majority in the Senate, where it took only nine days for the bill to be killed. Moreover, it was abundantly clear that any attempt to push it through the Upper House before Borden had the opportunity to appoint several more Conservative senators would fail.

While he was in office, Sir Wilfrid Laurier, using the anticipated naval contracts as a lure, had persuaded Vickers, Sons and Maxim (renamed Vickers Limited in 1911) to agree to establish a shipyard at the east end of Montreal. In 1910, the Montreal Harbour Commission, which was not averse to having a first-class facility installed in the port, gave Vickers a fifty-year lease on fifty acres of land in Maisonneuve. The commission agreed, moreover, to co-operate in reclaiming the site and to supervise the civil engineering work. The Vickers shipyard was also forgiven payment of land taxes for twenty years by the municipality of Maisonneuve with the sole condition that it encourage its employees to reside there.[7] Canadian Vickers Limited was incorporated in June 1911 and in 1912 brought over a large floating dock, the *Duke of Connaught Dry Dock*, which had been built for them in the Vickers shipyard at Barrow under the terms of the Canadian Dry Dock Act.[8]

The creation of the Vickers shipyard at Montreal, which now had no immediate prospect of naval work, was not what Davie needed. The other Montreal shipyards, like those in Sorel, had not threatened the Davies unduly. In fact, the McCarthys, who ran a successful shipyard at Sorel, were close enough friends to be godparents of some of their children.[9] The Collingwood Shipyard on Georgian Bay had been building steel lakers since 1901,[10] but the St. Lawrence shipyards could not compete on the Upper Lakes market as there was no passage for ships of that size. Competition from Vickers, with the weight of its parent company behind it, was another matter. Moreover, it came at a difficult time. John Davie, aged forty-four, was seriously ill and since 1909 had not been able to carry out his duties at Lauzon; Allison (Foddie) was fully occupied with the Levis yard; and George D., who since William's death in 1903, was in charge of the salvage business as well as the yard, was finding the double load far too heavy.

The cost of keeping constantly at the ready the salvage tug and schooner, equipment such as scows, divers' outfits and centrifugal pumps, and the personnel to operate them, had become prohibitive. The number of wrecks on the river was diminishing so there were fewer opportunities to earn salvage fees, and there were times when George Davie had contracted to send his tug to work elsewhere. This had helped him to meet expenses, but meant that the tug had not always been available in an emergency, which had led to complaints. In 1905, in order to secure a constant service on the river and in keeping with its new policy, the government awarded the Davie shipyard an annual subsidy of $10,000 to help defray the cost of the very efficient service it provided, on condition that the *Lord Strathcona* be on call at all times. Similar arrangements were made with the Dominion Coal Company in the Maritime provinces and the British Columbia Salvage Company. In 1912, however, the Davies decided that they no longer wanted to carry the burden of the wrecking business alone, and a new company, the Quebec Salvage and Wrecking Company was formed, which took over the business, complete with the *Lord Strathcona* and all the equipment and appliances. The contract with George T. Davie & Sons was terminated, and the government signed the next five-year contract with the new company at an increased annual subsidy of $25,000. In 1914, the Quebec Salvage and Wrecking Company was taken over by the Canadian Pacific Railway Company.[11]

> ### ⌒ DIVERS ⌒
>
> FOR ALMOST A century and a half divers have formed an important part of Davie crews that have engaged in salvage and repair work and helped in the docking of vessels. They are the underwater eyes of the shipbuilder and must have sufficient experience in ship construction to be able to report knowledgeably on the damage to a ship's hull, and even at times, to repair it themselves under water. Their work is most valuable, especially when it avoids the use of a dry dock.

Freed of the salvage operation, George was able to devote his attention to the regular repair work at the yard, and also to a contract for the construction of a 180-foot single-screw steel hopper barge for the government's River St. Lawrence Ship Channel Service. It was to be used for deepening the north channel of the St. Lawrence to the east of the Isle of Orleans. The barge, delivered in September 1913, was a breakthrough for the shipyard, because she was the first vessel built there entirely of steel.[12] Her machinery and boilers were built by the Canadian General and Shoe Machinery Company.[13] Following her delivery, she was manned by a crew of sixteen officers and men and was put to work with suction dredgers that pumped loads of nearly 1,000 tons into her, which she carried away, returning in a short time for reloading.[14] Davie also successfully negotiated with the Department of Public Works for the construction of six steel scows, all of which were built and delivered in May and June 1914.

The shipyard continued to depend on repair work, however, and managed to remain competitive despite the fact that so little had been done to equip the Lorne Dry Dock since its construction. There were still no travelling cranes, nor even capstans as late as 1913. Its pumps were so obsolete that they took a full fifteen hours to pump it out, five times longer than at any other dock along the Atlantic seaboard.[15] Nevertheless, in May that year, Davie beat out both Canadian Vickers at Montreal and a New York firm to win the contract to repair the 5,000-ton *Wabana* after it went on the rocks at Fame Point. In twenty-seven workdays, 100 badly buckled and broken plates, half of which had to be renewed, were fixed. Apparently, the skill, experience, and ingenuity of the Davie workmen helped compensate for the old-fashioned derricks and other equipment with which they worked.

If the pumps of the Lorne Dry Dock were antiquated, so was its size, particularly at a time when the British Admiralty was concerned with the possibility that naval vessels would have to be docked when on overseas duty. Members of the Canadian Shipping Federation, who had joined together to form a company to take advantage of the Dry Dock Act and build a larger dock, had been unable to raise more than $300,000, far from enough to undertake its construction. They were delighted in 1913 when the government agreed to take over the project. The question once again was where? In a memorial to Sir Robert Borden, dated March 23, 1912, the federation pointed out that neither the St. Charles River nor the St. Lawrence River sites proposed were suitable for a dry dock. Neither had a sufficient depth of water, and ice conditions at both were bad in winter so that either site would entail heavy dredging costs in order to connect the dock with the navigable part of the river. Moreover, there would be the added expense of hiring extra staff. Lauzon was the only place in the port of Quebec where it was possible to dock vessels during the winter months.[16] It would be less expensive to build the dock there because it could be quarried out of the natural rock. Large vessels would be able to enter the dock without the help of tugs, and as the prevailing winds were west and east, they would not interfere with the docking as they would at the other two sites.[17] George D. Davie was a member of the Canadian Shipping Federation, which may be why the added advantage, that it would be readily accessible to Davie's shops, was not mentioned. The views of the federation prevailed, and a site was chosen on Davie's eastern boundary.

Soon after, twenty-five and a half acres of land, including eleven and a half of reclaimed beach land, were expropriated for the purpose, and early in 1913 U. Valiquet, superintending engineer for the Department of Public Works, was instructed to prepare the plans and specifications on which tenders were called. The contract was signed with M.P. and J.T. Davis of Quebec, the lowest bidder, on October 7, and excavation began before the end of the year.

The new Champlain Dry Dock was 1,150 feet long, with a 120-foot-wide opening and 40-foot depth on the sill at high water. It could be divided into two compartments of 650 and 500 feet by a floating caisson. This caisson could also be used to replace the outer dock gate, a rolling caisson, when it required repairs. At high water in spring, the dock would contain 38 million gallons of water, but at other times the water level would be far lower, and its three horizontal centrifugal-type pumps, each with a capacity of 63,000 gallons a minute, were expected to empty the dock in about two and a half hours. Two auxiliary pumps were installed to take care of leakage and seepage. As well as a pump house, a power house was built to provide the 3,000 h.p. which might be required at any time of the day or night.[18]

With the new dry dock on its way to becoming a reality, the Davies were faced with an important decision. The dock would allow them to undertake work on larger vessels, but in order to do so and to discourage a competitor from settling on the other side of the dock, they would need to extend their facilities. Unfortunately, the pre-war years were lean ones, with the Vickers yard in Montreal competing for repair work and the lack of protection from American yards. They needed an injection of outside capital. The unsuccessful attempt to get the government to nationalize the shipyard in 1912 made them look elsewhere.

In March 1914, the newspapers carried rumours to the effect that the Davie yard had been sold to Vickers, and though George D. Davie admitted that it had been necessary to get new capital, he denied that Vickers had supplied it. There was, nevertheless, some truth to the story, for a great deal was going on behind the scenes. In April that year, Allison and George D. confronted the fact that John would not recover his health, and set in motion the legal procedures by which they took over full responsibility for the yard. The partnership between the three brothers was dissolved and John handed over his interest in both the Levis and the Lauzon shipyards to his brothers against a promise of one-third of the profits made by the company, and one-third of the sale price should it be sold. At the same time, Allison and George D. formed a new company with the same name, George T. Davie & Sons, for the operation of the two yards. A year later, when John L. Davie died, his brothers had already made an agreement to sell the "moveable and immoveable property of the business carried on under the name Geo. T. Davie & Sons at Lauzon," as a going concern.[19]

The purchaser was Charles A. Barnard, K.C., a Montreal lawyer who had allowed himself to neglect his profession in order to become an entrepreneur or businessman. In the years ahead, his ill-founded ventures would have disastrous consequences both for the Davie shipyard and for himself. It was to Barnard "in Trust" that George and Allison Davie had sold the Lauzon shipyard so that he might set it up as a limited company.[20] The sale to Barnard, at a price of $400,000, $50,000 down and the rest in the form of a mortgage payable in twenty years at 5 per cent, was ratified on April 29, 1914. A new company, the Davie Shipbuilding and Repairing Company with capital of $500,000, was incorporated on June 4, the same year, and that company bought the shipyard and its assets and liabilities from C.A. Barnard on October 26, giving him in exchange 4,000 "fully paid" $100 shares (its entire original share issue, with the exception of the five qualifying shares in the names of Allison Davie, George D. Davie, Thomas O'Neill, Joseph Gravel, and Andrew Thomson). Moreover, as part of the agreement, the Davie Shipbuilding and Repairing Company Limited (henceforth DSRCL) took over Barnard's $350,000 mortgage debt to the Davies. The stock book of the company shows that on the same day, Barnard transferred 3,200 of his shares to the British Maritime Trust Ltd. and 266 each to Claude Bryan and W. Grant Morden, all of London and all with close ties to Vickers and Canada Steamship Lines; he retained 263 shares himself.[21] These were the real owners for whom Barnard had bought the shipyard for an outlay of $50,000. The upshot of the deal was that the new company had neither working capital nor clear title to the yard, a heavy price to pay for its incorporation. In order to operate, a line of credit in the amount of $25,000 was arranged with the Merchant's Bank of Montreal. George D. Davie, who signed a three-year contract to manage the shipyard, was named president and the other directors were Allison Davie; Thomas A. O'Neill, the shipyard's senior accountant; Joseph P.A. Gravel; Andrew Thomson; and Charles Barnard.

The deals that were made in the course of these transactions may never come to light. Nor can we know the extent to which Allison and George D. Davie were aware of what was going on.[22] What is clear is that when the First World War broke out, John had died and the Davie's Lauzon shipyard, no longer a Canadian family business, was heavily mortgaged to the British Maritime Trust. Within three years, it was to all effects and purposes one more anonymous company under the heading "International Subsidiaries and Connected Companies" on the balance sheet of the great armaments conglomerate, Vickers Limited.[23] On the surface, however, the change was not apparent. Vickers kept a low profile, and George D. Davie continued as general manager of the firm.

Davie and Vickers were not the only Canadian shipyards under British ownership at this time. On the east coast, the board of the Tyne shipbuilders, Swan, Hunter & Wigham Richardson, which considered the operation of a floating dock at Sydney, Cape Breton, Nova Scotia, as early as 1903, authorized the purchase of land in Halifax two years later and subsequently set up the Halifax Shipbuilding Co. Ltd.[24] On the other side of the country, at Esquimalt, on the understanding that the employees and staff would be retained, the Bullen shipyard had been acquired by the Clyde shipbuilder Yarrows in 1913; the price: $300,000. Three-quarters of the shares of the new company, valued at $25,000, were issued in Sir Alfred Yarrow's name, the remainder in that of his son Norman. According to Sir Alfred, the idea was "to undertake repair to vessels and their machinery and be on the spot to build Canadian Navy vessels of the class we are familiar with."[25] Davie's new owners would undoubtedly have concurred with this brusque statement of intent.

George D. Davie poses with three of his senior employees, Warner, Neil Baker, and Harry Lamontagne. The schooner M.P. Connolly *is in the dry dock, 1918.*
Andrew Merrilees Collection, NA/PA-171076.

10

GEORGE DUNCAN DAVIE

1914-19

T HE TENSIONS THAT had been building in Europe came to a head on August 4, 1914, as German forces marched into Belgium. Britain immediately issued an ultimatum demanding that Belgian neutrality be respected, and when it expired, the British and German people found themselves at war. The war has been called the "war of the trenches," but it was also a war at sea, a war in which German submarines preyed relentlessly on the merchantmen that were Britain's life line. At first they encountered little opposition, for the Admiralty had badly underestimated the submarine threat, but the odds improved greatly in favour of the Allies when fast submarine-chasing motor launches began arriving in Britain from across the Atlantic. The speedy delivery by Davie of more than 300 of these motor launches was a significant contribution to the war effort.

At the outbreak of hostilities, two ferry boats were nearing their launching dates at the shipyard: the 127-foot paddle steamer *Le Progrès* for the Corporation of Three Rivers, and the 111-foot *Louis Philippe*, the first of the many vessels that the Davie shipyard would build for the Canada Steamship Lines fleet.[1] Both had left the yard by the end of September, yet no other vessel was laid down during the winter as Davie, like so many other shipyards in the British Empire, waited for an overall naval

Launch of the ferry Louis Philippe, *the first vessel built for Canada Steamship Lines in September 1914. A number of shipping lines had been amalgamated to form Canada Steamship Lines the previous year.*

shipbuilding plan to be put into effect. Materials and equipment were reserved for naval ships already under construction. Even the important Harland & Wolff shipyard at Belfast was obliged to lay off workers because it had no Admiralty work on hand.[2]

But in April 1915, the empty slips were forgotten when Davie secured a contract to assemble a trial run of forty 80-foot wooden submarine chasers for the Electric Launch Company, or Elco, a division of the Electric Boat Company, of Bayonne, New Jersey, with the prospect of an order for many more. Elco was well-known on both sides of the Atlantic for the design and quality of its powerboats. The American tycoon John Jacob Astor and the Grand Duke Alexander of Russia had been among their satisfied customers. A successful visit by Sir Trevor Dawson, Vickers' managing director, had led to the signing of a $22-million contract between Elco and the British Admiralty for 550 submarine chasers.[3]

The United States at this time was officially neutral. An order of this size would not have escaped detection and would have had serious legal and political ramifications. It may have been Dawson himself who proposed that Elco prepare the component parts and send them for assembly to two Canadian shipyards, Davie Shipbuilding and Repairing Company Limited and Canadian Vickers Limited in Montreal. Vickers Limited had worked closely with Elco on submarine construction in the past and was a major holder of its stock. It was also the majority stockholder in both the Davie Shipbuilding and Repairing Company (DSRCL) and Canadian Vickers. The whole matter was kept very much in the family.

Plans and patterns for the motor launches, or M.L.s, as they were known in the service, were finalized at the Elco plant, and the first fifty boats were assembled there. Measuring 75 by 12 by 4 feet 3 inches and displacing approximately 42 tons, they were driven by two 220-h.p. engines that produced a guaranteed maximum speed of 19 knots, and a cruising speed of 15, maintainable for four hours. A platform for a three-pounder gun was provided on their foredeck,[4] but the guns were not mounted when, disguised as pleasure boats, with a coat of white paint and appropriate temporary names such as *Betsy* and *Lillian*, they cruised north to Halifax. On their arrival, the masquerade ended and they were painted naval grey and shipped to Britain.

In the meantime, the Navy had realized that by adding an extra five feet to their length, it would be possible simultaneously to improve the boats' accommodation and to slightly enhance their performance. It was accordingly decided that the remaining boats would be 80 feet long. The formidable task of ordering, gathering, inspecting, and testing the component parts and equipment was carried out at Elco. It involved procuring an enormous quantity of wood: nearly 2 million feet of white oak for keels and frames, close to 2.25 million feet of yellow pine planking, and almost 4 million feet of ash, pine, and other wood for joiner work. In addition, the

Above: *Eleven of the three hundred and twenty submarine-chaser motor launches built for the Admiralty during the First World War, ready for sideways launching.* Andrew Merrilees Collection, NA/PA-171068. Left: *Submarine chasers in front of the Custom House at Quebec, 1916, await shipment across the Atlantic.* NA/PA-143243.

firm had to acquire and approve all the piping, electrical fittings, fastenings, paint, and other equipment and fittings that were necessary to complete the 550 boats. Everything was then sorted, individually numbered and crated, and shipped in a total of 1,144 railway cars to the Vickers' shipyard at Montreal and to Davie's at Lauzon.[5]

At Davie's, the call went out for extra workers, and old hands living at Cap Blanc who had worked on wooden ships in their youth found their way over to Lauzon to line up with local workers and offer their services. The old Charland shipyard to the west of the Lorne Dry Dock, where sailing ships had been built in the nineteenth century, was rented and readied for the job.[6] Buildings were erected, railway sidings laid down, and a railway engine acquired for the yard. These preparations meant that as many as eighty boats could be laid down and assembled at the same time on slips that now filled both the old and new yards. Some were even built

The Drawing Office in 1917. Alex Campbell, Davie's new naval architect, centre standing, with staff. Musée maritime Bernier, 87.02.216.

The staff pose outside the office in 1917. Musée maritime Bernier, 87.02.215.

Wartime permit to visit the United States, granted to George D. Davie in 1917.

side-by-side on a single slip, ready to be launched sideways one after another. At Vickers, where there were forty building ways for the motor launches, one batch of twenty-four boats was built in the dry dock and launched by flooding it. Elco kept rigorously abreast of the work carried out at both yards through reports and progress photographs. The American company also lent Davie their expert, John Guttridge, to supervise the construction of the first boats.[7]

Before long, Davie's initial contract for forty boats was increased to two hundred and ninety.[8] The first fifty were cradled and shipped to Britain in lots of four on the decks of transport ships. But when winter set in, closing navigation on the river, the Admiralty suggested that the balance be sent by rail to Halifax for despatch. A trial run was made in which a mockup of a motor launch was transported to Halifax to see that there were no obstructions along the line. It was not a wasted effort. Several semaphores and switch standards were moved after the test, and in some cases the track itself had to be shifted a few feet so that the boats would clear station platforms. With these precautions taken, eighty-four motor launches were sent by rail without mishap, each on a Northwest lumber car lengthened at both ends to take care of the overhang. Unfortunately, the flatcars were not always available, which made it difficult to schedule delivery. Consequently, their despatch by rail was discontinued in the spring of 1916. The rest left from Quebec on troop transports, the last ones in November that year.[9] The successful planning and execution of this extraordinary contract in just 488 days, two weeks ahead of an already tight schedule, has been cited as one of Elco's proudest achievements.[10] For Davie's management and workers, the same claim can be made.

In active service, many of the motor launches joined the patrols off the British coast where a large number of merchant vessels had fallen prey to marauding German submarines. Others served in the Mediterranean, the Dardanelles, the West Indies, and elsewhere. Sixty-two motor launches took part in the Zeebrugge and Ostend raids in April 1918, and though they were unable to carry out their entire mission, the courage of their crews served as an inspiration to all those around. Three M.L. captains received the Victoria Cross for bravery in evacuating the blockship crews under heavy enemy fire during one day's action, and many members of their crews were mentioned in despatches.[11]

The motor launches lived up to their description as submarine chasers. They are said to have been greatly feared by German seamen on account of their speed and the depth charges they carried. They also served as minesweepers, their shallow draft allowing them to pass through waters that would have been dangerous for deeper boats, and they assisted in escorting convoys of merchant ships. Their fine stems and flat transom sterns, however, were not ideal in heavy seas. They needed competent yachtsmen as their skippers, and it was fortunate that their well-trained crews included many experienced fishermen. Yet the boats were extremely seaworthy and often served for days on end as far as 150 miles offshore. The fact that there was a repeat order for thirty similar M.L.s from the Admiralty in 1917, and that the French, too, ordered twelve in 1918, speaks undeniably of their satisfactory performance.[12]

So crucial was the fight against submarines that, if Davie had done no more for the Allied cause during the war, it would still have been a significant contribution. However, the submarine-chaser program was followed by construction of fifty 125-foot steel barges that were laid down in the first nine months of 1917 to assist in the Royal Engineers' operations on the Nile. And then, as the barges began leaving the shipyard in May, the yard embarked on a program of naval trawler and drifter construction.

A few years before the war, the British Admiralty had decided to establish a trawler division of the Royal Naval Reserve, to be known as R.N.R.(T), because it felt that fishing boats would make good minesweepers. As it happened, the mine threat was less serious than expected, but almost 4,000 fishing vessels, close to the entire British fishing fleet, were eventually pressed into anti-submarine service. When the war spread to the Mediterranean, more boats were needed and Canada agreed to build some. A special branch of the Canadian Naval Service was set up to handle the

One of the fifty 125-foot steel barges built by Davie for the Imperial Royal Engineers mocked up in the mould loft. Musée maritime Bernier, 87.02.145.

The dumb (that is, without propulsion) barges were laid down wherever sufficient space could be found. Musée maritime Bernier, 87.02.166.

General view of the building berths in August 1917 (left) *showing some of the fifty steel barges built for the Royal Engineers for service on the Nile, under construction.* Andrew Merrilees Collection, NA/ PA-171109. *Mr. Baker with army officers* (right) *who visited the shipyard to inspect the dumb barges.*

program. Joseph W. Norcross, vice-president of Canada Steamship Lines, volunteered to take charge of it and was appointed director of shipbuilding. He took A.A. Wright as his assistant.[13] Canada Steamship Lines contributed the entire sixth floor of their head office building in Montreal, and the program got under way in February 1917. Thirteen shipyards across Canada participated, with Canadian Vickers acting as the lead yard, responsible for making and distributing the plans and ordering the material. All in all, one hundred 84-foot steam-driven wooden drifters and sixty 125-foot steam-driven steel trawlers were built under the program.[14]

Davie was fortunate to receive a contract for fifty of the drifters at a time when many other yards where wooden vessels were built were having to lay men off. They were typical Grimsby coal-burning herring drifters with accommodation for a crew of ten, some in the cabin aft and some in the forecastle. Norcross had no doubt learned from Elco's method of organizing the submarine-chaser program. A.A. Wright was sent to British Columbia to place orders for clear Douglas fir, which was to be sawn to specifications and delivered to the yards, and despite all the congestion on the railways, it began arriving within six weeks.

Davie also built eight of the forty-eight castle-class steel coal-burning trawlers. As the name "trawler" indicates, they were modelled on the sturdy and widely used North Sea fishing vessels, but without the fish ponds and fish-stowage arrangements.[15] They were driven by triple-expansion engines capable of developing about 500 i.h.p. with large three-furnace multi-tubular marine boilers, which produced a speed of 10 knots. There was accommodation on board for fourteen men.

In October 1917, to avoid their being iced in by the winter, hulls from Vickers and other inland shipyards were towed to the Louise Basin at Quebec where, at the auxiliary fitting-out basin set up by Davie at Shed 14, mechanics installed engines, boilers, gun pedestals, and guns.[16] Each week some twelve drifters were outfitted, given their trial under steam, and delivered.[17]

By the time the drifters and trawlers entered service, it was decided to use them on the anti-submarine Eastern Patrol that operated off the eastern coast of Canada and Newfoundland in 1917 and 1918. The drifters were fitted with six-pounder guns and the trawlers with twelve-pounders, and each was equipped with from two to six depth charges. When the first German submarines made their appearance off the east coast in the summer of 1918,[18] it was the first time in history that Canadian naval vessels built in Canada and crewed by Canadians were called upon to defend Canada's shores and shipping lanes.

After America entered the war in 1917, production suffered as material and equipment from the United States was diverted for the American war effort. As a result, the last six trawlers ordered from Davie (one of which was converted to a merchantman before completion), as well as the twelve French submarine chasers ordered in March 1918, were delivered after the Armistice had been signed. They would be the last naval vessels built at the Davie yard for more than twenty years.

We can only wonder how many of these sturdy trawlers and drifters have survived. They all were sold after the war and left to serve their new owners, some in European waters, some as far away as on the South China

Sea. Thanks to James Pottinger, who identified one of the drifters and wrote an article in *Shetland Life* about her,[19] we know that Hull 367, CD 10, served several decades as a fishing boat in Scandinavia and was still in good enough shape to be converted in 1983 for use as a charter sailing vessel for Dutch owners. Under the name *Knørrur* (big and mighty), she continues to offer sailing vacations out of Willemstad.

Despite naval appropriation of so much of Davie's shipbuilding capacity during the war, the yard also successfully carried out other work, including an important contract for a 2,382-ton twin-screw ferry awarded by Canadian Northern Steamships Limited, a subsidiary of the Canadian National Railway. She was modelled by the CNR's naval architect, A. Angstrom, on a ferry built by William Gardner & Co. in New York (their Hull Number 303) and was designed to carry twenty 40-foot freight cars on her main deck. The $368,000 contract for this ferry, the *Canora*, which was awarded to the yard in November 1915,[20] specified a John Inglis Company of Toronto 4-cylinder triple-expansion surface condensing engine with which she was to be capable of travelling fourteen statute miles per hour (12.15 knots) without forcing the engines, with a deck load of 1,336 tons. Completed shortly after her launching in June 1918, she operated for many years between Port Mann, British Columbia, on the south side of the Fraser River opposite New Westminster, and Patricia Bay, Vancouver Island. Eventually she was sold to the Union Steamship Company of New Zealand.

Another merchant vessel built at this time (which started out otherwise) was the 317-ton passenger and freight steamer *Labrador*, the first Canadian-built ship bought by John and George Clarke for their new shipping line. The Clarkes, who were owners of the *Encyclopædia Britannica*, had founded Clarke City in the wilderness of Labrador at the beginning of the century. By 1907 they had established a pulp mill there to ensure their supply of paper and had built a nine-mile railway to the coast. When they decided to operate their own shipping line, they arranged for one of the eight steel trawlers that was laid down at Davie's in 1917, *TR 45*, to be completed as a cargo vessel with accommodation for a few passengers.[21]

Steel trawler TR 35 *ready for launching, April 1918. Note the typical launching cradle.*

A special treat for the children, who were George Duncan Davie's guests at the launching of the trawler TR 36, *May 14, 1918.* Andrew Merrilees Collection, NA/PA-171075.

Two of the fifty wooden drifters built at the shipyard at the Champlain Dry Dock gates, 1917. Andrew Merrilees Collection, NA/PA-171102.

During the war, the British Merchant Shipbuilding Advisory Committee recommended that a large number of vessels be built to a standard design to help make up for the losses inflicted by German submarines. Contracts were given out by the Imperial Munitions Board to British, Canadian, Hong Kong, Shanghai, Japanese, but mostly American shipyards. The Cunard Steamship Company acted as intermediary in the United States as long as America held its neutral position in the war, while Furness Withy and the Federal S. N. Company acted as agents in Japan. These standardized ships, which all had the prefix "War" attached to their names, had priority in the shipyards over all other types of merchant ships under construction. Shipyards on the west coast, on the Great Lakes and at Montreal, Quebec, Sorel, and Nova Scotia shared the eighty-seven contracts given to Canadian yards. Because of the abundance of shipbuilding timber in Canada, forty-six of these were for wooden-hulled ships. The others had to take their turn waiting for steel, almost all of which had to be imported from the United States. The movement of huge quantities of

ss Canora *at Tilbury Dock, Vancouver, with tug number 2 and barge.*
Maritime Museum of British Columbia, P-3927.

munitions, food supplies, machinery, and so forth that the United States was producing slowed deliveries down considerably. All these standard ships were dry cargo ships, the wooden-hulled ships of 3,300 tdw; those with metal hulls, from 1,800 to 8,800 tdw.[22]

The Davie shipyard had been too busy with naval contracts to take part in this program, but there was a similar Canadian merchant-ship program from which George D. Davie thought the Lauzon yard should benefit. At a board meeting in April 1916, he advised the directors that if the company were to be in a position to take advantage of the Champlain Dry Dock (which had been hurried to completion during the war) or to extend its shipbuilding operations, it would have to build new workshops. Without them, the company would be unable to accept orders for vessels of the size now under construction in other Canadian shipyards. It took two years for the board to approve his plan, but the new shops were finally built. In addition, at about the same time, construction commenced on a concrete outfitting wharf to the northeast of the Lorne Dock.[23] By the end of 1919, over a million dollars had been spent on building and equipping three new buildings: number 7, a platers' shop with furnace and bending blocks at one end and an angle set shop, at the other; number 11, housing both a machine shop and a carpenters' shop, with a mould loft above; and number 12, an electric power plant and electricians' shop.[24] With these additions, the yard could compete on equal terms with other builders. Even before the work had been completed, the first two orders were in hand.

The shipyard seemed now to be on a solid footing. It had its new workshops in addition to the Champlain Dry Dock, which at 1,195 by 120 feet was twice the length and twice the breadth of the Lorne. It had experienced workers who had proved their mettle during the war. Many of the young men who were taken on in the war years remained at the shipyard for the next thirty or forty years. In 1917, for example, Johnny Boutin was given the job of driving the one and only shipyard truck and taking care of the horses. The eight horses – six that belonged to the shipyard and two others that were hired when needed – did all the handling of the heavy metal plates and bars. After five years' service, Boutin was promoted to foreman, and twenty years later he was still in charge of transportation, though by then only one horse remained, the rest having been replaced by trucks.

As to the boss, George D. Davie had shown through his drive and versatility that he was well able to fill his father's shoes. His stature as a shipping expert, already considerable when the war began, had grown. His leadership abilities had been amply demonstrated too. He had not allowed red tape to stand in his way. When he realized, for instance, that there would be a delay in getting the necessary authority to order rails for a railway spur that was needed to carry out the Elco contract, he assumed the responsibility himself. The spur was completed within the week allotted for the task, the boats laid down on time, and the inevitable arguments as to who had authorized delivery of the rails and who should pay for them were left to be fought out later.[25] The directors of Elco, impressed by the quality of his collaboration, presented him with a gold watch on completion of the contract.

The steamer Fremona *enters the dry dock in September 1916 after her stranding on Anticosti Island on July 31, while on her way from Montreal to Bordeaux with a cargo of horses, corn, and other general cargo.* Andrew Merrilees Collection, NA/PA-171103.

The Champlain, Lady Laurier, *and* Lady Grey *in the Lorne Dry Dock.*
Andrew Merrilees Collection, NA/PA-171095.

Under George D. Davie's direction, the Davie shipyard delivered 424 vessels in the space of four years. This was achieved in spite of chronic shortages of materials and supplies, especially the steel plates needed for both naval contracts and high-priority merchant ship construction. Moreover, the shortages were intensified in 1917 when the United States entered the war and its government immediately commandeered all shipbuilding supplies.

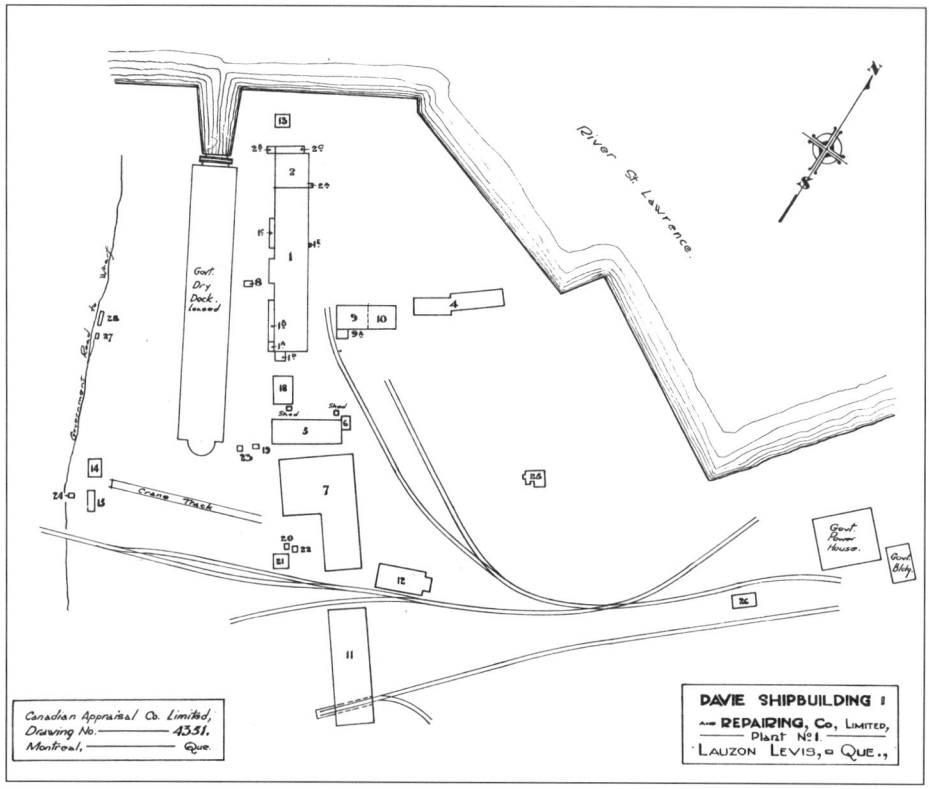

Davie Shipbuilding and Repairing Co. Ltd. at the end of 1919 showing the recently erected buildings. No. 7, a plater's shop; No. 11, a carpenters' and machine shop, with a mould loft above; and No. 12, an electric power plant and electrician's shop.

Unfortunately, George D. Davie's efficiency was in marked contrast to the way its president, Charles A. Barnard, managed the company's affairs. The Davie family business had been built up over more than eighty years by ploughing earnings back into it, holding a rein on expenses, and restricting borrowing to amounts that could be covered by reasonable mortgages. Barnard, however, had an extraordinary disregard for the basic maxims of borrowing. He operated on the one-jump-ahead principle. He became so embroiled in complex and questionable financial dealings that he was unwilling to show the company's books even to its directors. He himself would later admit he had run the DSRCL as if he owned it.[26]

*George D. Davie with Mr. Wooder at the Mathews Steamship Company Ltd. yard.
ss Steelton beyond. Andrew Merrilees Collection, NA/PA-171077.*

Back in 1914, when the partnership between the Davie brothers was dissolved and the new company took its place, George D. Davie had announced that he himself would continue to operate and control the shipyard.[27] He had discovered, however, that while he managed the shipyard, Barnard, as the representative of the powerful holders of all but the five qualifying shares in the company, ran its business affairs. Early in 1916, Davie's dissatisfaction with the situation led, at his request, to a new definition of their respective responsibilities. It was agreed at a subsequent meeting of the board that the "powers generally conferred on a President" were in future to be held by the chairman, while the president would have no other powers than those usually given to an honorary president. The new chairman was, of course, Charles Barnard. The fact that George D. Davie was still president, and his powers as general manager unchanged, was no doubt a face-saving move to reassure those doing business with the firm, while protecting George D. Davie from financial responsibility for any actions Barnard might take.

Before long, however, Barnard was again interfering in the operation of the shipyard itself. This was not appreciated by the man who was known to his employees and family alike as "Boss George."[28] In 1916, when Barnard took advantage of Davie's absence to come to an agreement with the shipyard's union, it was the last straw. Davie considered that the terms of the agreement were not in the best interests of the company and that he would lose control of his men. Accordingly, he resigned both the presidency and his directorship, retaining only the management of the shipyard for the duration of his contract (though later he agreed to prolong his position as general manager). In taking this action, he was merely formalizing the existing situation and avoiding further liability for Barnard's actions. Thomas Robb, another director of the company, also resigned at this time. He wrote that he had "no control whatsoever in the management of affairs, no proper access to its books, more particularly in connection with the workings of Department 3 [the leased area where the submarine chasers were built], nor over the transactions as recorded in the Minute Book, and therefore [could] . . . not accept liability for what . . . [had] been done." Shortly after these resignations, J.T. Boissinot, the secretary-treasurer of the company and a long-time Davie employee, asked to be relieved of the "responsibility in connection with signing cheques for Department 3."[29] The implications of his request are obvious.

However, discontent at the corporate level was not allowed to interfere with production. Davie had successfully met each of its wartime challenges, and the company had profited handsomely.[30] Barnard informed the directors on his return from a visit to England in January 1917 that the shareholders had agreed to his taking 12½ per cent of the net earnings of the company calculated back from the date of its incorporation. He was entitled to the fee, he maintained, because the whole responsibility for the affairs of the company rested on his shoulders causing him to be absent from his law office a great deal, and consequently he could not actively practise his profession. (In fact, Davie was only one of a large number of business ventures that kept him out of his office.) George D. Davie, who, in Barnard's own

The tug Belle *towing the steamer* Lauzon, *in First World War "dazzle paint," into the Champlain Dry Dock.* Andrew Merrilees Collection, NA/PA-171094.

words, had worked night and day under great pressure to complete the Elco contract was to receive 5 per cent, and fees for the five directors were to be doubled from $5,000 retroactively to December 1, 1915. Dividends of 7 per cent were declared again in 1916, 1917, and 1918 and one of 3½ per cent for 1919, as well as a special distribution of $132,000. Barnard continued to skim off 12½ per cent of net earnings in management fees, which represented annual amounts of about $76,000, while George D. Davie received $15,000 extra salary for both 1917 and 1918.

For George Davie, the reinvestment of wartime profits in the shipyard in preparation for the years ahead was in keeping with the principles that his family had always followed. However, when he let out the contracts for the improvements to the yard, he was probably unaware that, under Barnard's direction, a good part of the profits with which he expected to pay the bills had evaporated. The surplus of over $600,000 at the end of 1918 was in the process of becoming a deficit of almost $727,000 in 1919. Though he must have been familiar with Barnard's business methods, he cannot have guessed the extent of the damage he had done.

George D. Davie and his brothers, who had given up the family shipyard in order to ensure that it had the investment and working capital it needed, lost the shipyard without gaining the capital. Worse, they now discovered that much of the profit George and his men had worked so hard to make during the war had disappeared.

Part Four

THE STRUGGLE TO SURVIVE

Building the 3,610-ton ss Canadian Hunter *for the Canadian Merchant Marine.*

11

CANADA STEAMSHIP LINES (1)

1920-25

U NTIL THE END of 1919, the relationship between the Davie Shipbuilding and Repairing Company and Canada Steamship Lines was more than that of supplier and buyer. The two companies were financed by the British Maritime Trust and they had several common directors. Included among them were Colonel W. Grant Morden, of London, England, the man behind the amalgamation of various shipping companies to form Canada Steamship Lines in 1913, and three men who helped bring his plan to fruition: Captain Joseph W. Norcross, James Playfair, and Charles Barnard. Norcross, who was then vice-president of CSL and later became its president, was also a director of Vickers Limited of London. James Playfair of Midland, Ontario, an important figure in shipping on the Great Lakes, had helped Morden acquire the shares of both the Inland and the Northern Navigation companies for CSL. Barnard was counsel and vice-president of Canada Steamship Lines, president of Davie, and agent for its principal shareholders (including Morden) in the Vickers-controlled British Maritime Trust.[1] Further interlocking of directorships resulted from the trust being represented on both boards. On January 2, 1920, however, the relationship between the shipyard and the

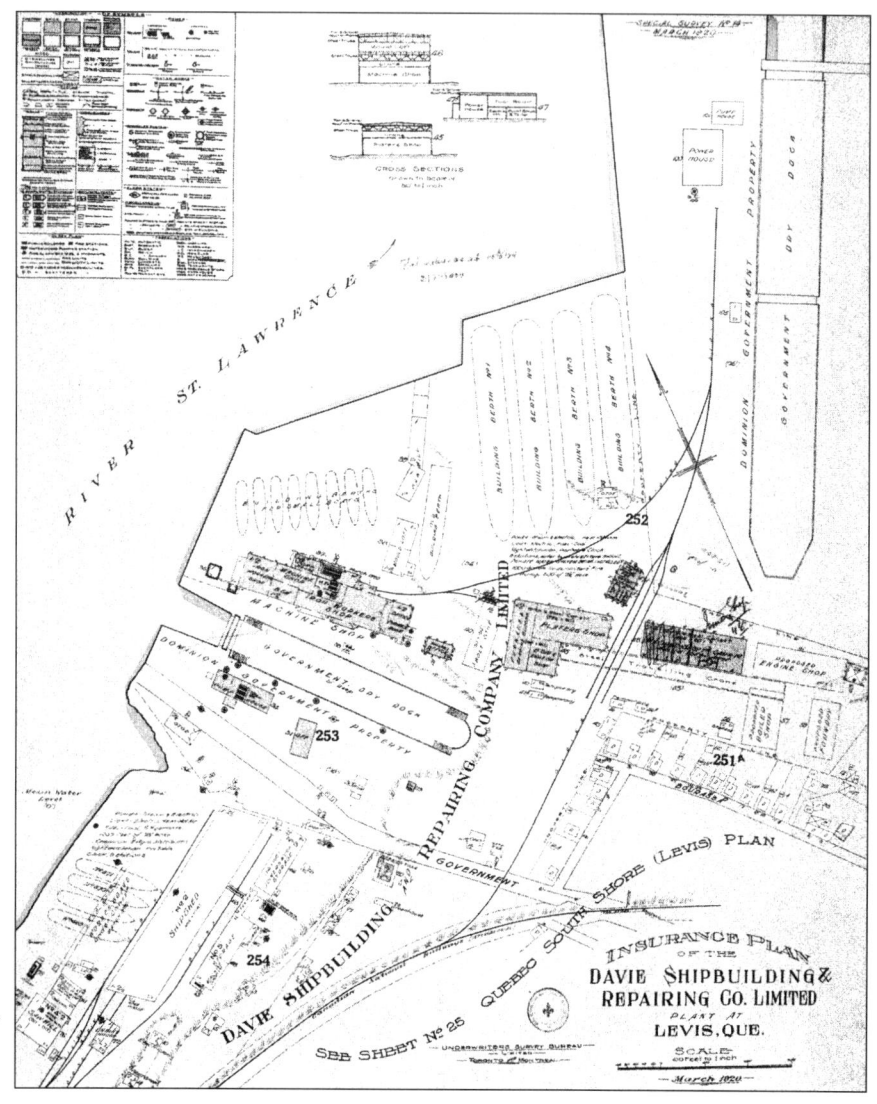

Combined plants Number 1 between the two government dry docks, with its new facilities for handling four large ships at a time and a number of smaller ones, and Number 4, to the southwest of the Lorne Dry Dock, where the last four of the French barges are shown under construction. George D. Davie's private property is the triangular area between the Government Road, the cliff, and the railway track. Insurance Plan of the Davie Shipbuilding & Repairing Co. Limited Plant at Levis, Que., March 1920, Underwriters Survey Bureau Limited, Toronto & Montreal. Bibliothèque nationale du Québec, Montreal.

shipping line assumed a very different character, for on that date the management of Davie was taken over by Canada Steamship Lines. This resulted ultimately in the outright acquisition of the Davie Shipbuilding and Repairing Company Limited by a newly structured Canada Steamship Lines in 1925.

Although it would later be shown that Barnard's mismanagement was largely, if not wholly, responsible for the financial difficulties that led to these changes, at the time blame was laid on two contracts that the shipyard had obtained in August 1918. The first was a plum $4-million order from the French government for twelve wooden twin-screw steam barges that were to transport coal between England and France. The second was for two 3,600-ton steel steamers, the *Canadian Trapper* and the *Canadian Hunter*, ordered by the Canadian government for the Canadian Government Merchant Marine, or CGMM.

The contract for the barges was obtained through the French government's agents, the Anderson Company of New York. The price of $215 per ton, according to Barnard, would net Davie not less than $195 per ton, "as a certain commission had to be paid to the Anderson Company and others in connection with securing the contract," but would leave "a good margin of profit" on the $165 per ton it would cost to build them.[2] Because Davie's main plant was reserved for steel shipbuilding, a new plant for the construction of the wooden barges, known as Plant Number 4, was set up on land to the west of the Lorne Dry Dock rented from the Charland estate, the site of the former wartime Plant Number 3.

The barges, designed by the naval architects Tams, Lemoine and Crane of New York, were to be 195 feet long with a deadweight carrying capacity of 1,500 long tons, and to be able to sustain a speed of at least 8 knots when fully loaded, or 9½ knots if they were light or half-loaded. Their 275-i.h.p. surface condensing engines and other machinery were subcontracted to the Tidewater Shipbuilders at Trois-Rivières, for whom Canada Steamship Lines, its parent company, acted as guarantor.[3] Contracts for fifty of these barges, representing the beginning of the rebuilding of the

French Merchant Marine following the war, were given to Canadian yards. Delivery of the twelve ordered from Davie was to take place between May 31 and August 20, 1919.[4]

Construction of the *Canadian Trapper* and *Canadian Hunter* was part of a Canadian government program to build up the country's exports and a merchant fleet to carry them. The idea had been advanced by the Honourable C.C. Ballantyne, Minister of the Marine, who reasoned that Canada's war effort had shown that she was no longer just an agricultural country and it was time that her industrial potential was developed. The country's extensive railway system linked to the steamers of the CGMM would span the globe, while the ships themselves would be built in Canada, with Canadian steel. The government named CSL president, J.W. Norcross, director of ship construction in charge of all shipbuilding for the CGMM.

The Canadian Trapper *– 331 feet by 46 feet 6 inches by 25 feet 6 inches, gross tonnage 3,599.94 – gets a coat of paint in the dry dock.*

His experience at CSL and as manager of the wartime fishing vessel program made him the natural candidate for the job.⁵

The program was tailored to suit the facilities of shipyards from Halifax to Vancouver. Vessels of three types in seven sizes from 2,800 to 10,500 tons were ordered. By the summer of 1919, forty-five were under construction.⁶ The first two ordered from Davie were single-deck 331-foot long ships of 5,100 tons, with poop, bridge, forecastle, and double bottom. Their triple-expansion surface condensing engines were to allow them to travel at 12 knots. Profits from the two ships ordered from Davie under this program, as well as from the French contract, were expected to pay for setting up the new Plant Number 4.⁷

But the contract for the French barges ran into difficulties. Three months after the contract was signed, the shipyard was advised that there

In 1918, Davie received an order for twelve 195-foot coal-burning twin-screw steam barges from the French government. Here we see the TSS *Mulhouse in yard Number 4, April 27, 1920. She was one of the last four to be launched.* Andrew Merrilees Collection, NA/PA-171073.

would be a change in the specifications, and all work on the vessels stopped pending a decision. George Davie warned that the requested boiler change would affect the performance of the barges unless the engines too were changed. His warning was ignored, however, and the change made. When it was shown during trials that George Davie was right, the customer responded by refusing to take delivery at the contract price. DSRCL, it argued, had not been relieved of its contractual responsibility with respect to the speed of the barges because of the change, but solely in regard to the delivery date.[8] Sued for $900,000, Davie countered with a $1-million claim.[9]

The case eventually was settled out of court, but the delay in the adjustment of accounts was unfortunate. Davie's financial position was already shaky. With the exception of the progress payments due at intervals on the two CGMM vessels, Davie had no other ready source of funds. The advantageous financial position in which the company had found itself after successfully carrying out its wartime shipbuilding program, which should have provided a cushion of working capital, had been undermined by Barnard's mismanagement. The cancellation of a contract to build a steamer – for Livanos, a Greek shipowner[10] – when the war ended added to the difficulties.

And so, at the end of 1919, Davie's account was overdrawn in the amount of $640,000, the bank refused further credit, and the wage bill for its 1,500 employees could not be met.[11] Apart from the shipyard's debts to its regular suppliers, a total of $250,000 was owed to various firms involved in construction of the new plant. The main creditor, however, was its subcontractor, Tidewater, to which $275,000 was already due for equipment installed in the first CGMM vessel, and another $360,000, payable as work on both ships advanced. Norcross, as president of Canada Steamship Lines, was gravely concerned about the situation at Davie. His company was another important creditor and guarantor. It had advanced $500,000 for work under way, including completion of the cancelled Greek ship which, it had been decided, was to join the CSL fleet. Norcross was concerned, too,

CANADA STEAMSHIP LINES (1)

J.W. Norcross (1872-1933). Former steamboat captain on the Great Lakes, president and managing director of Canada Steamship Lines, 1919-1922

about the contracts for the CGMM ships that he himself had awarded to Davie. When Tidewater had the first vessel seized pending settlement of its outstanding account, Norcross reacted by seizing the CGMM vessels, which were in danger of being seized by other creditors. With no new orders to keep the Davie shipyard going after the launchings the following April 1920, the shipyard faced closure.

When they were advised by Norcross of the situation, DSRCL's principal shareholders in Britain were surprised at the extent of Davie's financial problems and were angry that Tidewater, a company they also almost wholly owned through their interest in Canada Steamship Lines, had behaved in this way. In order to protect their "investment in the [Davie] shipyard," they acted on Norcross's recommendation that Canada Steamship Lines take over Davie's management. Though an auditor's report had shown that the shipyard's assets in the amount of $2.5 million were sufficient to meet its liabilities, Norcross insisted that in fairness to his (the CSL) shareholders, the Davie shareholders guarantee any liabilities in excess of that amount. Following a flurry of transatlantic cables and some hesitation, they agreed.

A management agreement incorporating the DSRCL shareholders' guarantee was signed between Canada Steamship Lines and the shareholders on January 2, 1920. On the same day, a trust deed securing an issue of debentures in the amount of $2.5 million, which was further secured by a mortgage of the shipyard movables and immovables, was executed by Davie Shipbuilding and Repairing Company Limited in favour of the Prudential Trust Company. Canada Steamship Lines was to take full control and direction of the shipyard for a term of one year, and in return to receive a commission of 2½ per cent of the amounts it paid or guaranteed on the shipyard's behalf, as well as a management fee whose amount would be decided when the contract came to an end. As far as CSL shareholders were concerned, Norcross's persistence with regard to the guarantee paid off: Davie shareholders soon found themselves obliged to honour it at a cost of $350,000 for the extra liabilities of the shipyard and a further £3,737 9s 10d for their part of an out-of-court settlement of the French government claim.[12]

Under the new management arrangement, the steamer laid down for Livanos took her place in the CSL fleet under the name *Mapledene*.[13] So did the *Maplecourt* (formerly *Northwest*), one of the ships bought by Barnard from the Northern Steamship Company and brought through the Welland Canal in two sections to be put together again at Davie's.[14] The two CGMM vessels, *Canadian Trapper* and *Canadian Hunter,* were delivered in the summer of 1920, the first sailing to Montreal to pick up a cargo for the United Kingdom, and the second proceeding to Sydney, Nova Scotia, to load for her maiden voyage to Liverpool. In the meantime, a contract for a third and larger vessel for the CGMM, a 5,400-ton (8,300 d.w.t.) ship to be named *Canadian Challenger* had been received at the end of 1919. She was 69 feet longer than the others, and there would not be a larger ship built at the yard until 1942. Her triple-expansion engines, which were capable of producing a speed of 11 3/4 knots, were supplied and fitted by Tidewater Shipbuilders. She was laid down in May 1920 and delivered in October 1921.[15]

Lloyd's Machinery Certificate for the wood screw steamer Mapledene *of 1920, which was completed for* CSL *following the cancellation of the contract given to Davie by Livanos.*

Another contract, for a 400-foot-long railway ferry, did not materialize. It's possible that the international unions, which had recently lost their attempt to take over the shipyard's work force, were able to make good their threat to prevent Davie from obtaining the necessary steel. Davie did build a new steel tug for the shipyard, the *Busy Bee*. A strong boat, though smaller than the other Davie tugs, she was the first to be built at the Lauzon yard and was a useful addition to its floating equipment. She can be picked out in many old Quebec waterfront and river photographs. She may still be posing for photographers: seventy years after her launching, she has taken on a new life as the houseboat *Exploreur II* in the Dominican Republic.[16]

Affiliations between shipyards and shipping companies are generally

THE STRUGGLE TO SURVIVE

Launching of the tug Busy Bee, *June 11, 1919.*
Andrew Merrilees Collection, NA/PA-171112.

The tug Busy Bee *picking up the tow line of the* Empress of France *in 1919.*
Andrew Merrilees Collection, NA/PA-171038.

profitable to both concerns, as overhauls and new construction can be scheduled to their mutual advantage. The peaks and troughs of the shipbuilding trade are eased, and the major expenses of the shipping company better rationalized. For Davie, however, the circumstances were different. Management by Canada Steamship Lines was intended to be a stop-gap measure. CSL was itself in an extremely precarious financial situation that prevented it from remedying one of Davie's main problems, the shortage of working capital.[17] Without it, Davie's hands were tied, as no bids could be made on contracts for large ships.

Moreover, it was an open secret that a merger between major Canadian and British steelmaking, shipping, and shipbuilding interests was being engineered. On the Canadian side, the Dominion Steel Corporation, the Nova Scotia Steel and Coal Co., the Steel Co. of Canada, Canada Steamship Lines, and the Davie, Halifax, and Collingwood shipyards were expected to join in, and on the British side and supplying the capital, there were the shipbuilders William Beardmore of Glasgow, Lord Furness of Furness Withy and Company, Sir Trevor Dawson of Vickers Limited, and others. Once again, Grant Morden was in the thick, if not at the bottom, of it, and Charles Barnard and Roy M. Wolvin were also involved. In April 1920, in a speech before the Empire Parliamentary Association in Ottawa, Morden described the merger as a great step towards the realization of "that beneficial Imperialism of which Cecil Rhodes was such a great exponent. Ore from Canadian mines, smelted by coke obtained from Canadian coal," he said, would be "turned into billets by Canadian labor. The billets and blooms in turn shipped to the great steel manufacturers in Great Britain, and thence distributed to all the countries of the Empire in the form of productive machinery." It would be, he claimed, "the greatest hope the shipbuilding industry in Canada has yet seen for the future. A company of the magnitude of the one projected will bring down the cost of raw material to the shipbuilder. It will require for its own business a good sized fleet, which conceivably would be built nowhere else than in Canada. By making available cheaper plates and shapes it will put the Canadian shipbuilder, and especially those on the Atlantic coast, in a position that will enable them to compete on equal terms with anyone."[18]

As matters turned out, the merger was far from being a great boon and hope for the future. The British Empire Steel Company (Besco), as the new concern was called, caused a great deal of grief to the employees at its works in Cape Breton, Nova Scotia, where management rode roughshod over the workers, while producing few of the projected benefits. Originally intended to be capitalized at $500 million, it had eventually been set up in 1919 in true Barnard form with $100 million of watered-down capital.[19] Norcross gave in to the persuasive powers of Morden, who had the full backing of CSL's London Advisory Committee, and agreed that CSL would join the merger. To his credit, however, he stipulated that the agreement would be subject to CSL's board being satisfied with the way Besco was organized. This proviso was subsequently invoked to break that agreement.[20] This let CSL off the hook, but left Davie in the same position – without working capital. To make matters worse, the United States Shipping Board was flooding the market with some 2,300 standard merchant ships and hundreds more that never would see service. Shipbuilding prospects were bleak.[21]

When a delegation of Canadian shipbuilders visited Ottawa to request that the government grant a bonus of $10 per h.p. on steel ships built in Canada for a period of ten years to prevent heavy unemployment in the shipyards and maintain the impetus the government shipbuilding program had created, their request was turned down. The government had received considerable criticism for the price of approximately $200 per ton that it had paid for the CGMM fleet and was not looking for more. As a consequence, after the delivery of the *Canadian Challenger* in October 1921, Davie's order book for new construction remained empty.

Nevertheless, government contracts for maintenance and repairs helped the shipyard eke out a precarious existence. In 1920, for instance, additional tween decks (interior decks) were built for four CGMM vessels. In 1921, the hull and engines of the *Cartier* and the *Arctic* were repaired in

ss Manola *in the Graving Dock with her newly constructed stern.* NA/PA-141501.

the Lorne Dry Dock.[22] Canada Steamship Lines, whose contract to run the Davie shipyard had been extended, was not in a position to award profitable contracts to the yard, but it arranged for Davie to overhaul the CSL steamships *Thunder Bay*, *Hamilton*, and *Narragansett* at cost in 1923. When doubt was cast on the ethical propriety of this arrangement in view of the overlapping directorships on the boards of the two companies, CSL consulted its lawyers, and they explained that it would keep skilled workers from leaving the shipyard and perhaps being unavailable should the shipping market improve.[23] A bow section was then built for Barnard's own ss *Manola* (ex *Frontenac*). He had purchased the vessel in two sections, and the original bow had been lost on the way from Erie, Pennsylvania, to Lauzon. The new bow was then joined to the stern section, which had made the trip safely from Buffalo, New York.

But many repair contracts that Canadian shipbuilders felt should have been theirs eluded them and once again shipbuilders pleaded for some kind of government protection from U.S. competition. In March 1921, George Davie testified before the royal commission investigating lake freight rates, that "after a ship is in our dry dock for repairs, we have competition from American concerns to do those repairs. They tender against us on nearly every repair job we have, but we are never asked to tender against the U.S. firms on repairing an American vessel." His plea fell on deaf ears. Moreover, struggling as it was to get outside contracts, Davie was also fighting a financial cancer from within. In November 1923 the worst occurred. This time there was no bailout by the shareholders. Three years after CSL took over its management, DSRCL went into liquidation.

Barnard, who had been sinking deeper and deeper into a financial morass of his own making, had been dragging Davie down with him. Shipyard profits had been siphoned off without explanation. The company's 1919 balance sheet, for instance, showed not only that Barnard owed it an amount of $66,753.77, but that the figure had been arrived at after some "extraordinary" amounts had been credited to his account.[24] In their report, the accountants noted that the amount of the management commission and the special distribution to shareholders had not been approved by the directors. Moreover the transfer to Barnard's account of the commission of $360,000 on the French barges should have been in the amount of $202,500, or 5 per cent.[25]

That Barnard was allowed to continue in a position of authority for so long is an indication of the hold he had established over Norcross. The CSL president later admitted that he had "known for some time that things were in a rather mixed up mess and had communicated [his] fears to Colonel Morden" when he visited Montreal in the summer of 1919.[26] Earlier in 1919, Barnard and his friend M.J. Haney had helped Norcross take the office of president of Canada Steamship Lines from its president, James Carruthers who, they complained, asked too many questions for their

Charles Barnard as he appeared in several editions of Who's Who in Canada *prior to the Home Bank scandal.*

liking, and they had been rewarded with appointments as vice-presidents of CSL. It was on a motion of Barnard's, seconded by Haney, that Norcross's salary had then been raised to $50,000.[27]

Typical of what Norcross referred to as Barnard's "mixed up messes" was his connection with the Continental Construction Company, Limited. According to the minutes of the DSRCL directors' meeting on December 20, 1917, at which the four directors present were Barnard, McKeown, Herdman, and Chart, Barnard reported that the lease by the DSRCL of the Charland property on behalf of the Electric Boat Company would expire the following February and that the rental for the following year would be double the current rental. Continental Construction Company, he went on to say, had offered to take on the lease and to acquire from the Electric Boat Company the buildings erected on the property by them and either carry on business jointly with the DSRCL or lease the whole to DSRCL under an agreement mutually agreed upon. It was accordingly agreed by the directors that Davie should transfer to the Continental Construction Company the right to remove the buildings or to collect their cost from the Charland estate. And what was the Continental Construction Company? A company set up in December 1916, whose incorporators included Lorne Clayton Herdman and George Edward Chart. Conflict of interest was far more common in the early decades of the century than it is today, but Barnard seems constantly to have been involved in deals that pushed it to the limit.

It was Barnard's record as a director of the Home Bank, however, an office he had held since 1916 despite strong resistance from its western Canadian branches and a record littered with irregular transactions, that eventually caught up with him. Over the years, he had distorted facts and used his position to obtain credit and "commissions" for a number of unsound business deals. Included among them was his personal speculation on the vessels *Vaudreuil* and *Papoonge*, whose purchase and repair he financed using the Davie shipyard's name, only to lose almost $1,410,000 on the two when the shipping market fell. When his ventures began to close in on him, he attempted to circumvent trouble by incorporating a holding or investment corporation, the British Dominions Holding and Investment Company, to take over his assets and indebtedness. G.T. Clarkson, the Home Bank's liquidator, later estimated that there would be a loss of $950,000 on the holding company's debt of $1,428,811.[28]

Barnard and other Home Bank directors and officials were brought to justice in Criminal Court in 1923.[29] In spite of the battery of lawyers who defended them, two officials and six directors of the bank were found guilty of filing false returns and received prison sentences. Barnard's was the heaviest – eighteen months in the Ontario Reformatory with a further indeterminate period of six months less one day. On appeal, all six managed to have their convictions quashed, and the charges of conspiracy filed against them dropped, along with those against M.J. Haney, a former Home Bank president.[30] Happily, however, "the Home Bank scandal" laid the facts bare and Barnard's ten-year association with the Davie shipyard came to an end.³¹

The Home Bank and DSRCL were not the only companies that suffered from their association with Barnard. Norcross, advised by Barnard, had got CSL itself into such a sorry state that he was unable to obtain financing from either his usual source, the London Committee, or the company's bankers in Montreal. In February 1922, the *Financial Post* began publishing a series of articles exposing the "mismanagement" of the company.³² In desperation, Norcross appealed to the investment firm of Kissel, Kennicot and Company in New York, to whom he had obtained an introduction from Montreal's Nesbitt, Thomson and Company. He was in no position to refuse their solution, which was that their own expert make a survey of the true state of affairs of the company, determine the policy that was needed, take over the presidency, and run the company accordingly. The man chosen for the job was William H. Coverdale of Coverdale and Colpitts, a management firm. Coverdale reported his findings to the CSL

William Coverdale (1871–1949), president of Canada Steamship Lines and of the Davie Shipbuilding and Repairing Company Limited, 1925–49.
Courtesy Marine Museum of the Great Lakes at Kingston.

annual general meeting on May 16, 1922, and then set in motion the process of reform.

For Davie, however, the provisions of the Bankruptcy Act moved forward relentlessly. The liquidator George W. Scott, of the firm P.S. Ross & Sons, received no bids when Davie's assets were first put up for auction in December 1923, and the shipyard was kept in operation while efforts to find a purchaser continued. In November 1924, the Department of Railways and Canals ordered a 77-foot steam tug, the *W. A. Bowden*, and Canada Steamship Lines had two steel pontoons built to replace the wooden ones at their Quebec terminal. In December, the Lachine Ferry Company Ltd. gave a contract for an oil-engined auto ferry with a thirty-five-car capacity, the *Jacques Cartier*, and the Brown Corporation ordered a steel scow.

When a second call for tenders for the purchase of the shipyard was made that month, William H. Coverdale submitted a bid on behalf of Canada Steamship Lines "in order to salvage Norcross's investment in the shipyard." The bid was simple. His company would honour the bonds in the amount of $325,000 still held by the Davie brothers, pay the expenses of liquidation, and take over the shipyard. No other tender was received, and the offer was accepted. Davie's creditors and shareholders were advised that they could not expect to receive any proceeds derived from the company's assets.[33]

On January 9, 1925, a new Davie Shipbuilding and Repairing Company Limited was incorporated. Ten thousand paid-up shares of capital stock without nominal or par value were issued to Canada Steamship Lines. The shipyard thus became a wholly owned subsidiary of CSL. As of May 28, 1925, the permanent officers of the new Davie Shipbuilding and Repairing Company Limited officially took over its affairs: W.H. Coverdale, as director and president; R.Brock Thomson, director and secretary; J.L. Hobson, director and treasurer; George D. Davie, director and general manager; J.

Thomas Boissinot, assistant treasurer; J. Tobin, assistant secretary. David Craig remained superintendent of the yard, and Alex C. Campbell, Davie's naval architect since 1917, chief draftsman.[34] Though it would not all be plain sailing, Davie had been given a new lease of life.

Launch of the Canada Steamship Lines passenger steamer St. Lawrence, *350 by 68.6 by 21 feet, gross tonnage 7,015.59. May 1928.* Andrew Merrilees Collection, NA/PA-171065.

12

CANADA STEAMSHIP LINES (2)

1925-39

During the last half of the 1920s, the DSRCL shipyard rebounded, building five freighters and three large passenger steamers for its parent company and fulfilling a number of orders for the government and private firms. The CSL contracts were prestigious, particularly those for the passenger ships, and made good publicity for the yard, but even orders for wood or steel pontoons or scows provided work for the expanding work force and were welcome.

The first contract, for two new tugs for the timber merchants Price Brothers, helped maintain the century-old business relationship between the Davie and Price families. The 100-foot *William Price* was built for towing booms of timber across Lake St. Jean, on the Saguenay River, and the 56-foot *Coosie*, a steel winding tug, was for inshore work. Because she was to serve on a landlocked lake, the *William Price* was a "knock-down" job. Built at the Lauzon shipyard, she was then taken apart and shipped to Roberval, where she was reassembled, riveted, launched, and finished. *Coosie*, on the other hand, was completed at the yard and then shipped to Roberval on a railway flatbed. Unfortunately, she fell off during the journey. She was, however, stoutly built and, having been lifted back on to the flatbed by crane, suffered no serious harm. Both tugs were designed by the Montreal naval architect Walter Lambert. While they were under construction, a 150-foot steel single-screw ferry steamer, *L'Ile d'Orléans* for La Traverse de l'Ile d'Orléans Limitée, was also on the ways. Delivered in July 1925, she became a familiar sight on the river ferrying islanders and excursioners between the island and the two riverbanks until the Isle of Orleans Bridge was completed in 1938, making her redundant. After her sale in 1944 to La Compagnie Traverse Rivière du Loup-Tadoussac Ltée, she was renamed *Rivière du Loup* and sailed between Rivière du Loup and Tadoussac, later Saint-Simeon, until 1965. She then served for another five years, from 1965 to 1970, under the name *Madelon II*.

Two sister package freighters for CSL's expanding Great Lakes fleet came next: the *City of Toronto* and the *City of Kingston*. Mary Coverdale, daughter of the president, was the sponsor. The freighters were each approximately 1,690 tons and measured 230 by 38 by 23 feet. Fill-in contracts included two 101-foot steel pontoons for the Levis ferry company; one for the Department of Public Works; and a wooden scow that was built for use as a service boat at the shipyard and given the name *Kitty*, the family nickname of George D. Davie's daughter Brenda.

In the meantime, on his appointment as president of Canada Steamship Lines, Coverdale had begun a drastic restructuring of the company. He began by removing from the board of directors the men who had been close to Norcross. Turning to the company's operations, he wrote off the whole of the company's unprofitable ocean fleet while streamlining and renovating its freshwater fleet.[1] Gradually, he achieved a turnaround. Though CSL's reported profits of $143,818 in 1924 were the lowest since 1915 and 70 per cent less than those of the previous year, by 1927 he could claim that the company, which had recently acquired the Great Lakes Transportation Company (together with its shipyard at Midland), was the largest freshwater transportation company in the world, owning and operating property worth upward of $44 million.

Canada Steamship Lines' well-being was also Davie's. This became evident during the next few years when CSL ordered three more passenger

Top: *Steel steam tug* William Price, *100 feet by 24 feet by 12 feet 6 inches, at Roberval. This tug was built at Lauzon and was then knocked down and taken to Pointe Bleue for assembly. She was used for towing booms of pulpwood across Lake St. John.*
Middle: *The ferry* Ile d'Orléans, *built at the Davie shipyard in 1925, leaving Saint Petronille for Quebec on a Sunday in August 1927, with a load of forty-seven cars. She measured 144 by 53 feet 6 inches by 16 feet, with a gross tonnage of 795.27. She was the last ferry built for the Isle of Orleans service, as the service was discontinued after the bridge to the mainland was completed in 1938.* Edgar Gariépy, N1176-151, ANQ.

The tug or winding boat Coosie, *47.54 gross tons, which was to work the booms on Lake St. John inshore. She measured 56 feet 3 inches by 12 feet 6 inches by 7 feet and is seen here waiting to be put back on the tracks following her mishap.*

The package freighter City of Kingston *of 1925. Launched November 24, 1925, for the* CSL *fleet, with Mary Coverdale, daughter of the president of* CSL, *as sponsor. The* City of Kingston *measured 230 feet by 38 feet by 23 feet, 1,689.81 gross tons. She was fitted with a triple-expansion 1,100-h.p. engine.*

steamers, the *St. Lawrence*, the *Tadoussac*, and the *Quebec*, from the yard. The 6,328-ton *St. Lawrence*, 329 feet long and 67 feet wide, ordered in June 1926, was launched in June 1927 and rushed to completion the same month, by which time her slightly larger sister ships, *Tadoussac* and *Quebec* had also been laid down. Completed the following winter, they offered cabin accommodation for 550 passengers and boasted dining rooms where 225 guests could be served at a sitting. Alex Campbell designed and supervised the building of these ships, as well as the extensive remodelling of the SS *Richelieu* (formerly *Narragansett*, built in Wilmington, Delaware, in 1913), which became the fourth ship of the fleet. According to William Campbell, Alex's son, his father looked on these jobs as the high point of his career.[2] The *Quebec* caught fire and sank at Tadoussac in 1950.[3] The remaining three ships of the "Great White Fleet" reigned as undisputed queens of the St. Lawrence and were the pride of Canada Steamship Lines, offering luxury cruises between Montreal, Quebec, and the Saguenay[4] until 1965, when less expensive holidays by automobile finally brought an end to their sailings.

In the winter of 1925–26, Davie laid down the sister package freighters *Winnipeg* and *Selkirk* of 2,385 tons for CSL, which gave work to about 300 men at a time when it was scarce. Both management and labour made sacrifices to obtain the orders. Canada Steamship Lines lost several thousand dollars by having the ships built in Canada, and the men, who were aware that Davie had lost the order for two boats for the Quebec-Levis ferry that year to a British yard, accepted a wage cut of 10 per cent.

Building contracts remained scarce. In order to provide work in the winter of 1928–29, CSL ordered a slightly smaller package freighter, the *City of Windsor* of 1,905 tons, and followed it in January with an order for a bulk freighter that was specially designed to carry 100,000 bushels of grain or other cargo between Port Colborne, at the eastern end of Lake Erie, and Montreal. In order to increase her carrying capacity while keeping her measurements to canal size, the *Grainmotor* was fitted with an 8-cylinder 800 b.h.p. Bessemer engine, and three auxiliary Bessemer engines, one of 25 h.p. and two of 50 h.p. to power the pumps, winches, windlass, and steering gear. Her machinery was lighter and occupied less space than a steam installation, which, added to the advantages of storing oil rather than coal, enabled her to carry 5,000 bushels of wheat more than any other ship on that run. And though the extra $250 profit on each run may not seem much by today's standards, at that time it sparked interest as far away as in Britain, where the *Liverpool Journal of Commerce* ran an article that described her machinery and stated that her performance would be closely watched.[5] The *Grainmotor* also enjoyed the distinction of being the first diesel-powered ship built at the Davie shipyard.

The following winter, work was provided by the Department of the Marine, which awarded Davie a contract for a 185-foot steel hopper barge, *Hopper Barge No. 5*, for its dredging fleet on the St. Lawrence. She was designed with her hopper amidships, her propelling machinery aft, and

Keel-laying ceremony for Hull Number 495, the Canada Steamship Lines passenger steamer St. Lawrence, *in June 1926. She would measure 329 by 67 by 20.3 feet, with 6,328 gross tonnage.*

Canada Steamship Lines passenger steamer Tadoussac *being fitted out in the Champlain Dry Dock in 1928. She measured 350 by 68.6 by 21 feet, gross tonnage 7,012.51. Andrew Merrilees Collection, NA/PA-171041.*

CANADA STEAMSHIP LINES (2)

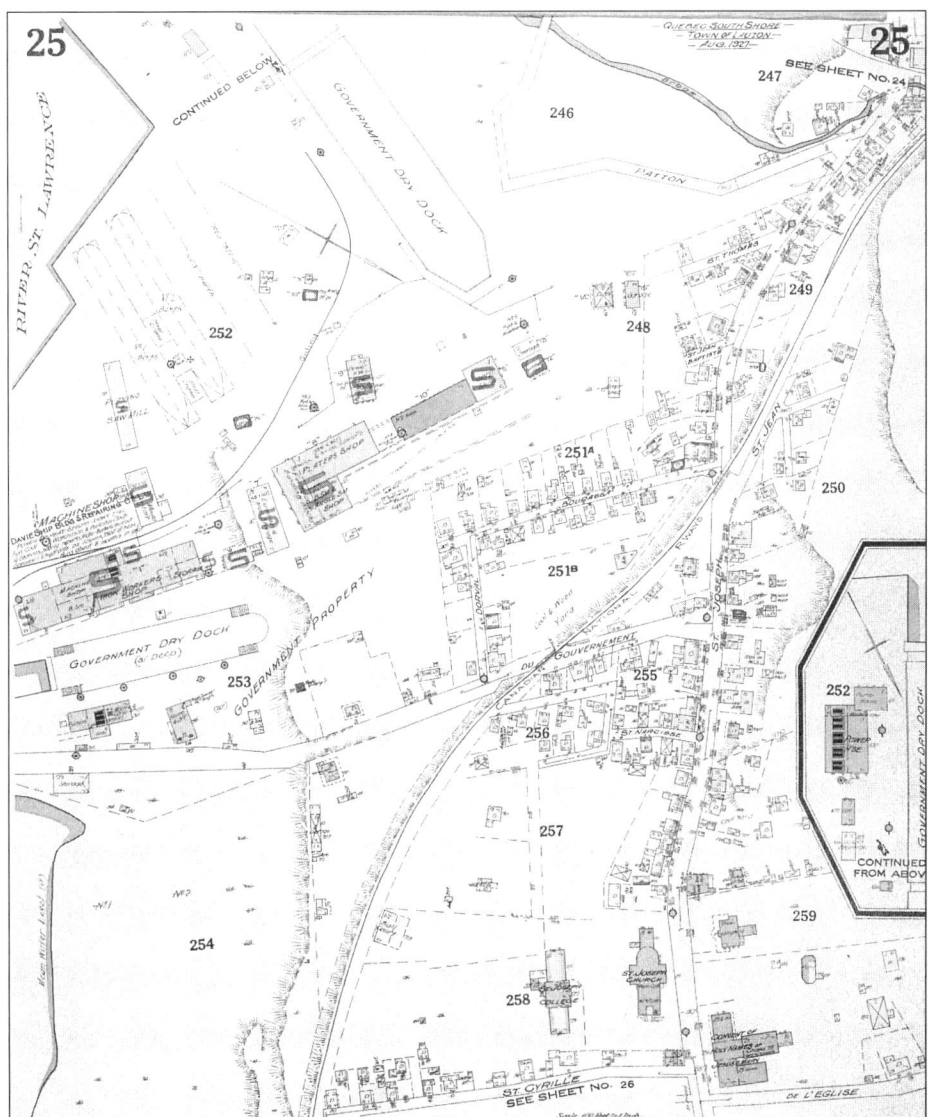

The shipyard in the last half of the 1920s. No major changes have been made, except that Plant Number 4 no longer forms part of the yard. The extension to the plate shop, marked "proposed" in the 1920 map, has been built and the tracks for the travelling crane behind the shop have been widened. The old building berth beside the sawmill has been removed, which has allowed the sawmill to be straightened out. Insurance Map. Sheet 25. Quebec South Shore — Town of Lauzon — August 1927. Bibliothèque nationale du Québec, Montreal.

THE STRUGGLE TO SURVIVE

accommodation for a crew of twenty-one forward, and was powered by John Inglis Company of Toronto engines that could maintain 750 i.h.p. on a six-hour trial. Her contract price was $224,900.[6] Launched in May, she was delivered in June. Times were hard and the contract was greatly appreciated.

Among the tugs that the company built at this time were the diesel tug *George M. McKee*, ordered by the Anticosti Corporation in 1927 for towing booms of pulpwood to Ellis Bay for shipment; the *Graham Bell*, delivered in the summer of 1929 to the Department of Railways and Canals; and

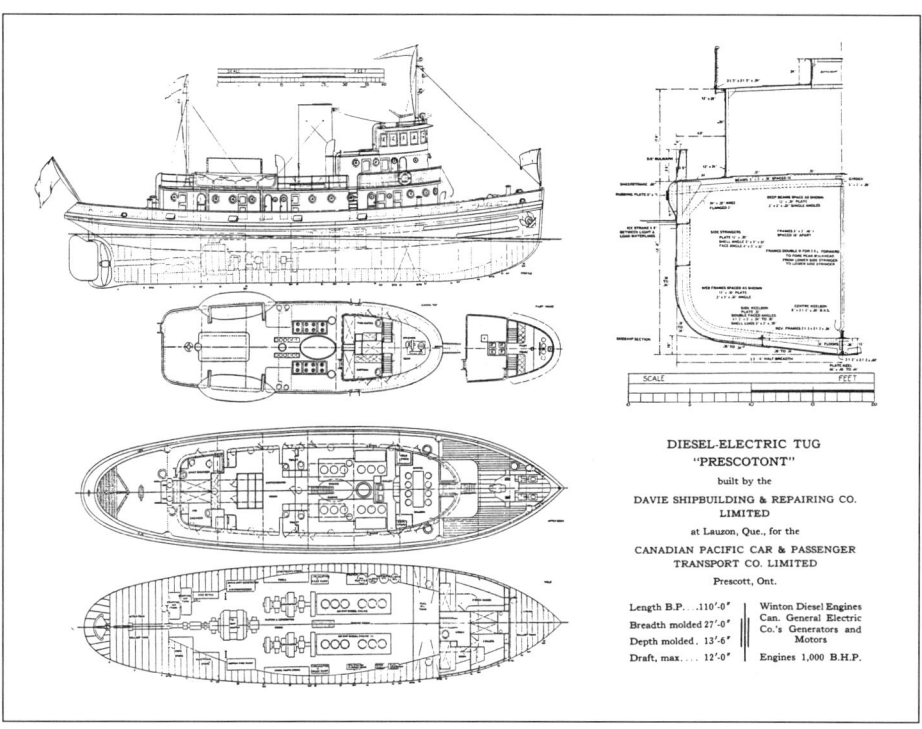

The diesel-electric tug Prescotont, *built by Davie in 1930 and one of Canada's earliest electrically driven tugs. She was designed to tow the 290 by 45-foot railway car float* Ogdensburg *between Prescott, Ontario, and Ogdensburg, New York State, linking the Canadian Pacific and the New York Central railway lines. Her extra-heavy construction allowed her to double as an icebreaker and ferry. Designed by the naval architects and marine surveyors, Lambert & German.*

Davie's own tug, *Manoir*, laid down in November 1929.⁷ They were followed in 1930 by the *Prescotont*, one of Canada's earliest electrically driven tugs, which was designed by the naval architects and marine surveyors Lambert & German.⁸ Owned by the Canadian Pacific Car and Passenger Transport Company,⁹ her extra-heavy construction allowed her to double as an icebreaker and ferry, as she towed the 290-by-45-foot railway car float *Ogdensburg*¹⁰ to link the Canadian Pacific and the New York Central railway lines. For forty years, the pair gave year-round service across Lake Ontario, between Prescott, Ontario, and Ogdensburg, New York. And then, on September 25, 1970, the Ogdensburg ferry slip burned down. Traffic was declining and the owners decided not to rebuild it. The two vessels were bought by the Detroit River Barge Line in 1972, and they began a second career transporting containers.¹¹

By the time the *Prescotont* had been laid down, the country was in the grip of the worldwide Depression. Straitened economic conditions would eventually close down all but twenty-four Canadian shipyards – there had been seventy-eight in 1919. The Davie shipyard was fortunate to have the orders for the four tugs, and even more fortunate to be awarded a $2-million contract by the Minister of Railways and Canals in April 1930 for the ferry *Charlottetown*. Canadian Vickers Limited,¹² which was to supply the Scotch boilers and 8,000-h.p. engines, and do the fine joiner work in the principal public rooms, would receive almost a third of the amount. The *Charlottetown* was designed to link Cape Tormentine, New Brunswick, and Port Borden, Prince Edward Island, carrying sixteen freight cars on three railway tracks on her main deck and forty automobiles on the mezzanine deck. Her public rooms provided seating for about 250 passengers and emergency sleeping accommodation for about a hundred. She also was designed by the naval architects Lambert & German, of Montreal, who claimed that she was the most powerful car ferry in the world. Her specifications greatly exceeded the requirements laid down by both the Board of Steamship Inspection and Lloyd's Register of Shipping because of

The tug Prescotont, *110 feet by 27 feet by 13 feet 6 inches, of 1930, ordered for the Prescott, Ontario, to Ogdensburg, New York, run by the Canadian Pacific Car and Passenger Transport Company Limited. Designed by Lambert & German, she was equipped with two 500-h.p. engines and was the first diesel-electric tug built in Canada.* NA/PA-171057.

the severity of the weather conditions under which she would operate. Under the command of Captain John Read, she eluded the German U-boats that threatened shipping off the Canadian east coast and, with the *Prince Edward Island*, kept the ferry route open to that island during the first years of the Second World War. But she met with disaster in 1941 off the Nova Scotia coast when she was wrecked on her way to a refit in Saint John after ten years of service.[13]

During the six years following the delivery of the *Charlottetown*, from July 1931 until July 1937, the Davie shipyard struggled for its existence, its building ways empty for all but eleven months. CSL, which had its own problems, was in no position to help. The addition of the ships of the Great Lakes Transportation Company, which Coverdale had bought on James Playfair's death in 1936 (Playfair was one of the men who helped found CSL), together with the new ships Coverdale had ordered, had resulted in a record increase of forty-seven vessels in the CSL fleet that year. That expansion exacted a heavy price, and CSL, too, might have foundered without the

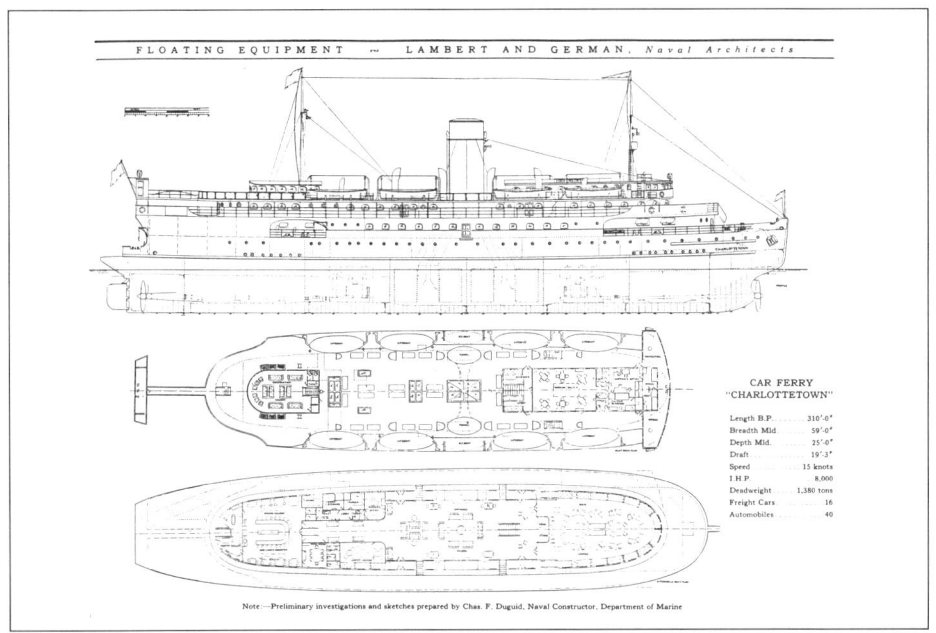

Preliminary sketches prepared by Charles Duguid, naval constructor, Department of Marine, for the car ferry Charlottetown *built by Davie in 1931 to link Cape Tormentine and Port Borden. She carried sixteen freight cars on three railway tracks on her main deck and forty automobiles on the mezzanine deck.* Lambert & German, Floating Equipment. Montreal, 1932.

understanding and co-operation of its senior shareholders.[14] Only two new vessels were laid down at Davie's. The first was the 180-foot steel single-screw tug and fire boat *Citadel*, which was ordered by the Department of the Marine and built between March and October 1932.[15] The *Citadel* worked in the port of Quebec for four years as a "Jack of all trades," towing, tending floating lights and buoys, and occasionally carrying out the work she was specially built for, that is, fighting a fire. She was then transformed for use as a pilot boat at Father's Point, Rimouski, where she replaced the less strongly built *Jalobert*.

Two years would elapse before the shipyard received the next order – a 125-foot steel ferry, the *Dartmouth*, for service between Halifax and Dartmouth. Between the construction of the *Citadel* and that of the

Left: *Stern and train gate of the ferry* Charlottetown, *which was built for Canadian National Railways in 1931. Andrew Merrilees Collection, NA/PA-171060.* Below: SS Charlottetown *under the builder's flag on the St. Lawrence. A combined icebreaker and ferry, she was built for year-round service between New Brunswick and Prince Edward Island and could carry up to sixteen railway cars, forty to fifty automobiles, and seven hundred and fifty passengers. Measuring 310 feet by 59 feet by 25 feet and of 1,380 tons, she was the heaviest ship that had yet been laid down at a Canadian shipyard. Courtesy R. Gagnon.*

Dartmouth, the shipyard saw some of its hardest days. They were reflected in an exchange of letters in March 1933 between T.R. Enderby, general manager of Canada Steamship Lines, and Davie's superintendent, David Craig. While acknowledging that substantial economies had been effected between 1932 and 1933, Enderby queried several charges related to a period in January and February 1933 when the plant was closed. Craig, defending them, pointed out that an amount of $1,349.75 was for the charwoman and foremen's half-salaries and had to be charged; that, contrary to Enderby's opinion, the coal consumption was as carefully watched as it could be; that the amount covering watchmen's salaries could not be cut any further because the five being paid were essential to satisfy the underwriters; and so on. Moreover, Craig wrote, unusual attention had been given to overhead expenses in the last two years and similar attention to work in the plant. Throwing the ball back into Canada Steamship Line's court, he countered, "If only we can have work, we should be in a position to show good results."

Though it was little consolation, Davie was not alone in its tribulations. Ship production worldwide dropped 70 per cent in three years, from 5 million tons in 1920 to 1.5 million in 1923, and the short recovery that followed had ended in the crash of the 1930s. As the main shipbuilding nation, Britain was particularly hard hit. In northeast England, unemployment reached as high as 70 per cent. This led to a rationalization in which the National Shipbuilders Security Limited bought out shipyards that were no longer viable, sold the properties for other uses, and exacted an undertaking that the affected areas would never again be used for shipbuilding.[16] In the United States, between 1920 and 1936, forty-nine shipyards with 300 launching ways equipped for steel-hull construction disappeared. That Davie's survived until business at last began to pick up in 1937 was due chiefly to its position on the river and the repair work that came its way.

In 1937, a 190-foot passenger and cargo vessel, the *North Gaspé*, was laid down for the Clarke Steamship Company. This was followed by the 130-foot patrol cruiser *French* for the RCMP. And that year also, the machinery was removed from the aging ferries that ran between Quebec

THE STRUGGLE TO SURVIVE

Some distress calls came from vessels far away, and two of the Davie shipyard divers are seen here with the pilot who took them to a stranded vessel, January 31, 1930. Andrew Merrilees Collection, NA/PA-171042.

and Levis, *Plessis* and *Colomb*, and installed in a new ferry, the *Louis Jolliet*, for the same service. As proof of the strength of her construction, sixty years later the *Louis Jolliet* can still be seen at her berth on the waterfront at Quebec, from which she regularly takes tourists on a trip downriver. In 1939, the Department of Transport awarded the shipyard the contract for the icebreaker *Ernest Lapointe*, which inaugurated a long association between Davie and the Marine Service (Canadian Coast Guard). This was to be the last vessel laid down at the yard before the outbreak of war.

And thus the 1930s came to an end. A sorry total of nine vessels was built by DSRCL in the whole decade, compared to forty-four in the 1920s. Figures reflecting the profits made during the twenties are not available, but Davie registered a loss on ship construction of $55,198 for the thirties, added to which there was an unabsorbed overhead of $615,750. Fortunately, a profit of $1,701,828 on repairs on a revenue of $4,037,780 allowed the yard to remain open, though the workforce was reduced to a mere 200 to 250 men.

George D. Davie was not at the shipyard throughout the thirties. No longer in robust health, he left following the delivery of the *Charlottetown* in 1931 and spent his last six years in retirement at Quebec.[17] How well he had accepted the ownership and direction of the company by Canada Steamship Lines is difficult to assess. He was undoubtedly grateful for the Lauzon shipyard's survival, but the Davies were accustomed to being their

George Duncan Davie (1873–1937), who in 1917, according to his own description, had blue eyes, balding fair hair, and a red moustache and beard. Five feet ten in height, he tipped the scales at 215 pounds. ANQ.

own masters. The fact that he took steps to ensure his son's independence is perhaps an indication of the constraints he himself had chafed under.

His son, Charles Gordon Davie, or "Charlie" as he was known to all, was the apple of his uncle's as well as his father's eye, and was the only great-great-grandson of the founder who followed the family trade. Born in Lauzon in 1902, he was brought up beside, and often in, the yard. He attended Quebec High School and completed his formal education at St. Alban's College, Brockville, and Bishop's College, Lennoxville. But shipbuilding was in his blood, and as soon as he was old enough, he embarked on an apprenticeship, moving from department to department at the Lauzon shipyard. His experience there was capped by a two-year training period at the Morse Dry Dock and Repair Company of New York, to which he was sent at the age of twenty-one, followed by a further three years at the American Ship Company of Lorain, Ohio. Soon after his return in 1927, he was appointed assistant general manager, reporting to his father at the DSRCL yard.

THE STRUGGLE TO SURVIVE

Above: *E. Walker, Charlie Davie, and E.D. Campbell, brother of the shipyard's naval architect, who was also employed at the Davie shipyard, at Pointe-Bleue in 1925.* Left: *Charles Davie leaves for his training at New York shipyards. A photo from his father's scrapbook.*

That same year, George D. Davie and his brother Allison bought the land immediately to the west of the Lorne Dry Dock, where the submarine chasers and later the French barges had been built, and set up a branch of the original family shipyard at Levis. The new yard was known as the George T. Davie and Sons' Lauzon yard and, like its parent yard at Levis, was primarily a repair yard. A Crandall marine railway for vessels up to 2,000 tons was ordered from Boston, and a 300-ton-capacity marine slipway and a gridiron for ships of up to 14-feet draft were built. The yard was advertised as being equipped with the best and latest tools, including portable electric welding machines, portable air compressors, and boring bars. Advertising boiler and engine repairs, steelwork, and tanks, as well as wintering facilities, the yard opened for business in May 1929 under Charlie's management and ownership, for his father and uncle had officially sold it to him for $195,859, payable on demand.[18] Both men would later forgive him the debt, his father in 1937 under the terms of his will, and his uncle as a gesture of affection two years later. The shipyard, which became known as "little Davie" or "Charlie's" ("le *petit* Davie" or "*chez* Charlie"), and later "Davie west," would be characterized by the fierce loyalty of its workers. We can only guess what Coverdale thought of his manager setting up this shipyard for his son beside the CSL yard, even though it was officially supposed to handle the smaller vessels that were not of interest to the CSL yard.

At the age of twenty-seven, therefore, Charlie settled down to run his own yard. He hired many of his father's old workers, most of them people with whom he had worked, who were willing to accept lower salaries than those paid at DSRCL and to work hard to make the yard a success. For the first four years, it remained a branch of the shipyard in Levis, but in 1933 the two yards were legally separated, and Charlie's yard retained the old name "George T. Davie and Sons," while the shipyard at Levis was given the new name "Davie Brothers" and remained under George and Allison's ownership.[19] In the winter of 1934–35, Charlie made a modest move to expand the business beyond repair work by embarking on the construction of a fleet of handsome, strongly built steel barges designed to carry rolls of newsprint along the Richelieu River to New York. They were fitted with Fairbanks Morse vertical diesel marine engines, and their hulls were specially designed for passage through the Champlain Locks. Hull Number 1, *Donpaco No. 4*, was the first of the seven identical 200-ton steel barges to be delivered. The others were the *Newscarrier, International No.1*, and *Kermic*, ordered by the Quebec Paper Sales and Transportation Company for the Donnacona Paper Company, and the *G.T.D.*, *A.C.D.*, and *G.D.D.*, built for the Davie Transportation Company, a company founded by George D., Allison, and Charlie Davie in 1933, with its head office at Charlie's shipyard. All were completed between 1935 and 1937. It speaks well for their construction that more than thirty-five years later in the early 1970s, five were bought by Verreault Navigation Limited and converted to dump barges, in which capacity they are still giving satisfaction.

In April 1937, George Duncan Davie died at his home overlooking the Plains of Abraham where he had spent his last years. The funeral service was held at the Chalmers-Wesley Church, Quebec, following which he was

Workers at the George T. Davie shipyard drop their tools while building the diesel barges Kermic *and* A.C.D. *in 1937 to pose for this souvenir photograph. Specially designed to carry newsprint, the 247-ton barges were 109 feet long.* Courtesy Dennis Rioux.

buried beside his father and other members of his family at the Mount Hermon Cemetery in Sillery. The messages of sympathy that poured in from far and wide testified to the high esteem in which he was held. Among the professional and philanthropic societies to which he had belonged were the Institution of Naval Architects of Great Britain, of which he became a member in 1917, the Royal Arcanum Society and, rather than the Masons to which his father and great-grandfather had been admitted, the Independent Order of Odd Fellows, a lesser-known friendly society founded in the eighteenth century.

Throughout his life George Duncan Davie had lived by the rhythm of the tides on the St. Lawrence River. He was the recognized authority on the river. When the Quebec Bridge was built, he was the natural choice to take charge of the tugs that towed the central span from its place of assembly on the beach at Sillery to the exact spot from which it was lifted into its place between the two waiting arms of the bridge. It was a difficult manoeuvre. A fleet of tugs had to steam to the centre of the river in perfect station and arrive at the precise place at the predetermined time according to the tide. And yet the operation was carried out perfectly on two occasions, in 1916

George D. Davie takes his daughter Brenda (Kitty) for a drive. Courtesy Brenda Wilson.

The central span of the Quebec Bridge lined up with the bridge for the final part of its voyage, September 17, 1917. Courtesy Gaetan Paquet.

The men responsible for delivering the centre span of the Quebec Bridge to the right place at the exact right time, George D. Davie and the tug captains.

and again in 1917. The first time, through no fault of Davie's, a piece of the structure gave way and the span fell into the river, but the second time the whole undertaking was completed successfully. On both occasions, huge crowds watched from the riverbanks, and it was reported that Davie's voice could be heard across the water as he directed the slightest of the tugs' movements with the precision of a gunnery officer.

Such exceptional skill, combined with his reputation as a shipbuilder, made him something of a legend on the St. Lawrence. He also gradually acquired a confidence that had not come naturally. Over the years, he became a very different man from the shy shipbuilder who replied awkwardly to the toasts when he launched his first four ferry boats in 1911.

His lack of fluency in French did not prevent him from forming a close bond with his employees. Even today, men who worked for him remember him with admiration and affection. We were like one big family, they say.

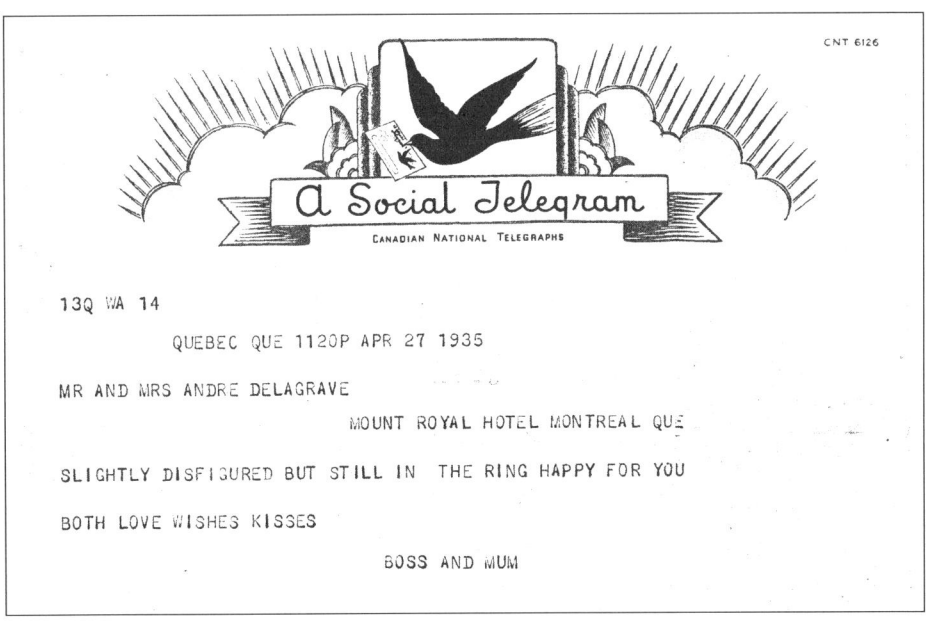

Telegram of good wishes from George D. Davie and his wife to their daughter Brenda and her husband, André Delagrave, signed "Boss and Mum." Courtesy Brenda Wilson.

Geo. T. Davie & Sons
Levis, Que.

112334

December 30th., 1916.

Sir Robert Borden, P. C.,
   Prime Minister of Canada,
      Ottawa.

Hon. Sir,-

    Mr. John Guttridge, who was our Superintendant last summer assembling the Submarine Chasers at our Ship Yard, Lauzon, and who is now in New York proposes taking a trip after New Year to England to visit relations there.

    I am sorry to trouble you in this matter, but, would consider it a personal favor, if you would kindly advise the necessary means to be taken to procure a passport there and return.

    Please accept my regrets at the loss your Government and especially the Province and District of Quebec has sustained by the death of the late Hon. T. C. Casgrain and who I also considered a personal friend of mine.

Yours respectfully,

George D. Davie

Letter from George D. Davie to Sir Robert Borden, then prime minister of Canada, requesting his advice in regard to a passport and offering his sympathy on the death of the Honourable T.C. Casgrain, a mutual friend. Borden papers, NA.

Pierre Beaulé, president of the shipyard's union in 1925, commented at the time that "Mr. Davie has always shown himself considerate with his men and in return the latter do their best to show their appreciation." George Davie continued the family tradition of taking an interest in the workers' personal lives and helping, sometimes anonymously, to make things easier for them. He was guided by compassion, not forced by legislation, to employ the handicapped. At least one paraplegic, Ovide Lévesque, a polio victim, was given free daily transportation to the shipyard to allow him to earn his living. Davie showed similar understanding when a workman, whom he had fired for stealing copper, was rehired a week later. The worker

Above: *George D. Davie's residence beside the shipyard in Lauzon, known as Villa Bernier, Lauzon. It was built by Captain Joseph Elzéar Bernier at the time that he was dockmaster of the Lorne Dry Dock.* N477-43-14, ANQ. Left: *Captain Joseph Elzéar Bernier, FRGS (1852–1934), mariner, Arctic explorer, and one-time shipyard superintendent, at the age of seventy-five.*

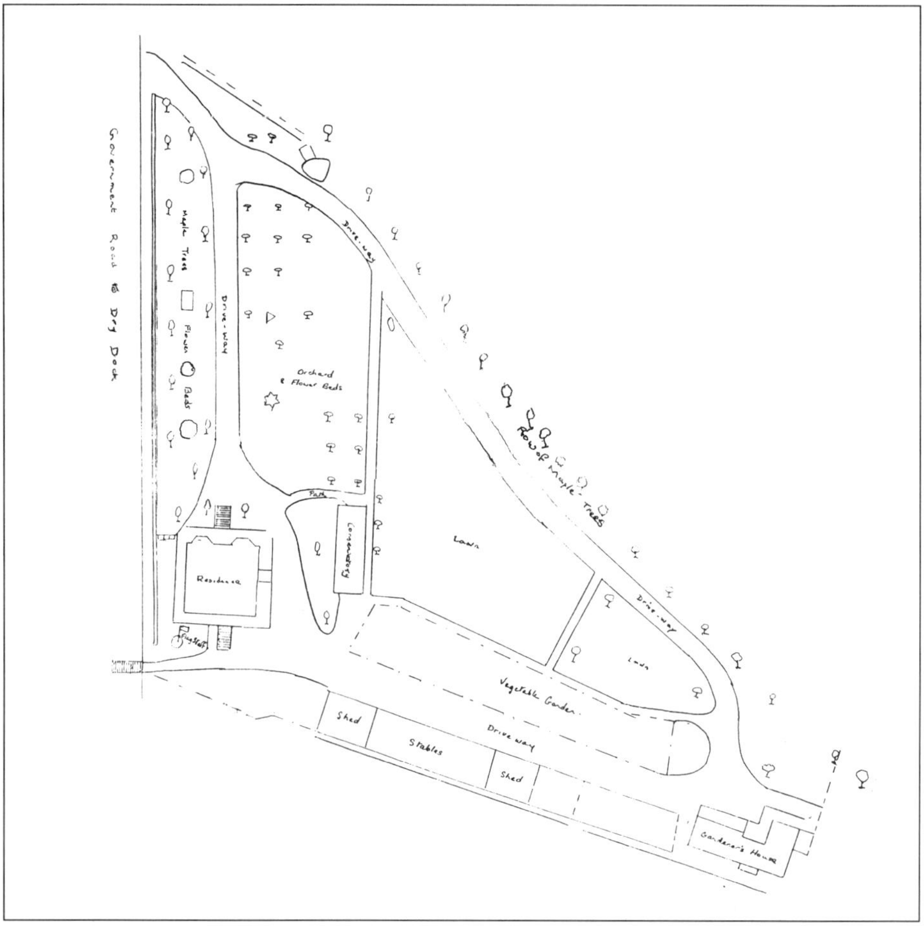

THE STRUGGLE TO SURVIVE

210

had a family, he told his foreman, and would have suffered enough and learned his lesson.

He was generous, too, with the use of his chauffeured car. It was not only on shipyard business that his employees or their families used it. Kathleen Hart, daughter of Thomas Hart, the shipyard's paymaster in the years following the war, remembers that George Davie would send her father to visit her every fortnight at the convent she attended, and that at times a group of the workers' children would be bundled into the car and taken to spend an afternoon on the beach at Gilmour Cove, nearby.

His pride in his shipyard was matched by his pride in his home on the bluff overlooking Charlie's shipyard. He had bought it from a good friend and a customer of the yard, the explorer Captain Joseph Elzéar Bernier who lived there from 1887 to 1890 when he was dockmaster of the Lorne Dry Dock.[20] During the years when George D. Davie owned and occupied it, the garden became a horticultural showplace with rows of elegant trees lining its walks, a profusion of blooms in the flower beds, fruit trees and bushes, and a kitchen garden that was a joy to the cook. A greenhouse lengthened the short Quebec growing season, and Davie was not averse to showing off

Top left: *"Plan of Grounds and Residence of George Duncan Davie, Esq., St. Joseph de Levis,"* G.K. Addey, Surv., 12 May 1915, CA1-62, 3188, ANQ. Bottom left: *A poignant reminder of "Boss George," who had died earlier that year, the G.D.D. is launched from the Marine Railway at the George T. Davie shipyard in October 1937.* Courtesy Lucien Godbout. Right: *Bicycles, which could easily be taken aboard the ferry, offered handy transportation to school in Quebec. Behind the boys, the well house. The trimmed grass and flower bed fronted the store facing the stable.*

in his lapel a bloom that had been grown there. He enjoyed having his children around him and received many of their friends on weekend visits. There are some who recall with fondness those faraway days when, springing onto their bicycles at Quebec when school was over on a Friday afternoon, they raced down Mountain Hill to catch the ferry, and once across the river, cycled over to a warm welcome at Lauzon. Monday morning would come too quickly and with it the prospect of wheeling their bicycles laboriously back up Mountain Hill to the school. Also fondly remembered by many is the fun of the gatherings for the launchings, which none of the family or circle of close friends would ever willingly miss.

This page from a publication of the naval architects Lambert & German is perhaps the most eloquent of tributes to George D. Davie. Among other prominent shipyard owners and managers, those featured include his son Charlie, his naval architect, Alex Campbell, and yard manager, David Craig.

How eloquent it is that in the photograph of Canadian shipbuilding personalities in the German & Milne publicity brochure of the 1930s, George D. Davie holds the centre position, and his son Charlie, his general manager, David Craig, and his naval architect, Alex Campbell, occupy three of the four corner spots. Surely, George D. Davie left his mark.

Part Five

NAVAL AND WARTIME SHIPBUILDING

HMCS Niobe. *The cruiser* HMCS Rainbow, *built in 1893 for the* RN, *was commissioned in the* RCN *in August 1910. One month later, she was joined by* Niobe, *which had been built that year and was the first ship in the* RCN *stationed on the east coast. They served in the* RCN *until 1920.* Courtesy David Christopher.

13

AT LAST, A HOME-BUILT NAVY

1918-45

THE CONTRIBUTION MADE by individual Canadians during the First World War changed the way Canadians thought of themselves and their country. It could hardly be otherwise. More than 400,000 Canadians stood shoulder to shoulder with Allied troops on the European battlefields; 22,000 Canadians served as members of the RAF; and nearly 10,000 served in the Canadian or British Navy. Through their sacrifice and service Canada came of age and her relationship with Britain was forever changed.

Prime Minister Borden had stood firm with the leaders of other former British colonies against the Admiralty proposal that their navies be integrated with the Royal Navy on a permanent basis, when the future defence of the Empire was discussed at the Impcrial Conference of 1918.[1] Indeed, he and the others made it clear that under no circumstances would they give up the peacetime control of their own navies. Britain had little choice but to acquiesce.

The member countries were not blind to the advantages of uniformity among the Empire's navies, however, and they requested that a qualified representative of the Admiralty advise them. To this the British government agreed. Lord Jellicoe toured Canada's naval facilities in November 1919, and at the end of the year he presented his recommendations to the gover-

Left: *Sir Wilfrid Laurier (1841–1919), Liberal prime minister of Canada from 1896 to 1911. Though he succeeded in getting his Naval Bill passed, he was thwarted by the electorate, for his plans for a Canadian Navy were set aside when the Conservatives came to power in 1911.* GH 772-68, ANQ. Right: *Sir Robert Borden (1854–1937), Conservative prime minister of Canada from 1911 to 1920. He was unable to get his Naval Aid Bill through the Liberal Senate.* P100054PB71, ANQ.

nor-general.[2] He proposed various options for the composition of the Canadian fleet that depended upon whether it was intended to defend Canada only or to take part in the defence of the seas generally. While his advice was heeded in some areas, there were more urgent demands on the Treasury and to the dismay of Canadian shipbuilders, no move was made to implement his proposals regarding the construction of a Canadian fleet.

Instead, the government availed itself of the offer of a gift of surplus British naval vessels, specifically asking for a cruiser and two newer destroyers to replace the worn-out cruisers HMCS *Rainbow* and *Niobe*. Chosen for the purpose were the RN cruiser *Aurora* and the destroyers *Patriot* and *Patrician*, all three of which were commissioned in the Canadian Navy in November 1920. *Aurora*'s career in the RCN would be a short one, however,

RCN *submarines* CC1 *and* CC2 *had been laid down in a Seattle shipyard for the Chilean Navy. Sir Richard McBride, premier of British Columbia, snapped them up for the Canadian Navy in 1914. They are seen here beside their mother ship at Esquimalt, August 5, 1914.* Courtesy Maritime Museum of British Columbia.

for the following year, when the new Liberal government under Mackenzie King cut naval estimates back by 40 per cent, it was decided to dispose of her along with the First World War submarines, *CC1* and *CC2*.[3]

By 1927, *Patriot* and *Patrician* were eleven years old and due to be replaced, and the government decided to order two new destroyers. The Yarrows shipyard at Esquimalt, British Columbia, was reportedly prepared to build them had more time been allowed, but once again an opportunity to encourage a domestic shipyard was missed, and Canadian shipbuilders could only shake their heads in frustration when the contract was awarded to John I. Thornycroft of Southampton, England. The two RN destroyers that were loaned to Canada to fill the gap while they were under construction[4] were commissioned in the Canadian Navy in 1928 under the names HMCS *Champlain* and HMCS *Vancouver*. And when the two new vessels HMCS *Saguenay* and *Skeena* were completed and delivered in June 1931, they crossed the Atlantic and joined them, as it had been decided to keep the old ones in commission for another five years.

In spite of these acquisitions, Commodore Walter Hose, head of the RCN, remained far from satisfied with the size of the fleet. Even if there were no war or if Canada were not involved in one, he wrote in 1930, at least one destroyer leader, five destroyers, and four twin-screw minesweepers were needed to protect the focal points of her overseas trade and carry out her obligations as a neutral country. He urged, therefore, that four modern minesweepers or "sloops" be built to replace the old ones, and that contracts for two of them be given at once.[5] In the face of the rapidly deteriorating economic situation, however, in each of the next four years not only were no new ships ordered, but naval estimates were cut back.

Walter Hose, RCN (1875 [at sea]–1965), director of Naval Service 1921–34. He wrote in 1930 that one destroyer leader, five destroyers, and four twin-screw minesweepers were needed to protect the focal points of Canada's overseas trade and to carry out her obligations as a neutral country, and that two minesweepers should be laid down at once, but he got nothing. Courtesy Maritime Museum of British Columbia.

Captain Percy Nelles succeeded Hose as chief of Naval Staff in 1934 and immediately took up the cause, proposing in a memorandum to his minister that as estimates did not allow the construction of the two destroyers, four minesweeping trawlers be laid down instead.[6] Nelles pointed out that, without minesweepers, the country might pay a heavy price in sunken merchantmen and disorganized traffic if war broke out. Moreover, he persisted, in the event of a conflict in which Canada remained neutral, the trawlers could serve both as coastal patrols and as tenders to air force bases, while in peacetime they could be used for training purposes with both the RCN and RCNVR. But even his argument that their construction would help relieve unemployment in the shipyards and other industries as 90 per cent of the total capital expenditure of $1 million would be spent on wages was to no avail.

Nelles persevered, however, pressing his case at every opportunity, stressing the need to assist the shipbuilding industry and urging not only the construction of four minesweepers, but also the replacement of all the older vessels belonging to government departments.[7] Eventually in 1937 his voice was heard. The purse strings of the defence budget were slightly slackened, and contracts for four minesweepers were awarded. Two of the contracts went to shipyards on the west coast, one to the Collingwood yard, and one to Quebec. The Quebec shipyard, however, was neither DSRCL nor George T. Davie, both of which already had some other small contracts on hand, but the up-and-coming Morton Engineering and Dry Dock Company, on the St. Charles River in Quebec's Lower Town.

The destroyers *Vancouver* and *Champlain* were due to be scrapped at the end of 1936, and the government had to give some attention to the question of their replacement. Instead of buying new ships, however, the RCN acquired the RN destroyers *Cygnet* and *Crescent* and arranged for the purchase of their sister ships *Crusader* and *Comet* in the course of the next two years. By 1938, therefore, the Navy had four new minesweepers and a flotilla of six destroyers. Hose's shopping list of 1930 was complete – except that the sixth destroyer was not a flotilla leader. But with the acquisition of the destroyers' former leader HMS *Kempenfelt* in August 1939 and her commissioning in the Canadian Navy as HMCS *Assiniboine* in November, the shortfall was overcome.[8]

In the meantime, however, the Canadian Navy had revised its list of minimum requirements upward to eighteen destroyers in 1936 and further increased it in January 1939 to include eight fast anti-submarine vessels, sixteen minesweepers, and eight motor torpedo vessels. The chief of Naval Staff recommended that two destroyers be laid down each year for six years, four anti-submarine vessels a year for two years, and four minesweepers for three years.[9] And yet, in spite of the steadily worsening political situation in Europe and the increasing likelihood of war, the government balked at ordering new vessels. Indeed, the amount needed to begin the building program was cut out of the 1939 naval estimates even before they were presented to Parliament.[10]

As a consequence, when Canada declared war on Germany on September 10, 1939, not a single ship was under construction for the Canadian Navy. Only four minesweepers had been built in Canada since the last war and no contracts for any other vessels were in the works. The Canadian Navy was made up of thirteen vessels, while a fourteenth, HMCS *Assiniboine*, was shortly to be delivered by a British yard.[11]

After the declaration of war, the government moved quickly, however, to put its contingency plan into effect. At an emergency session of Parliament held on December 12, an amount of $100 million was voted for national defence, and the interim War Supply Board was set up to replace the year-old Defence Purchasing Board. The immediate priority, as far as the Navy was concerned, was the protection of Canada's eastern and western harbour facilities. Accordingly, anti-submarine net booms were installed at Halifax and Esquimalt, while the Navy took control of all domestic and foreign ships in Canadian ports.[12] As in the First World War, the Minister of National Defence was granted the power to requisition Canadian vessels and a large number of fishing boats and pleasure craft were pressed into service for patrol and other duties. In addition, a number of American yachts were drawn into the net through a bold plan that circumvented their "neutral" status,[13] and arrangements were made for suitable merchantmen to be stiffened and armed.

Unlike the First World War, when shipyards were left idle while programs for construction were worked out, the government wasted no time in acting on the proposed naval shipbuilding program presented to the Cabinet by the chief of Naval Staff on September 18: it was approved within twenty-four hours. At the same time, formal authorization was given for the acquisition and conversion of private vessels and those belonging to government departments. At last, after many years of disappointment, the Canadian shipyards that had managed to weather the bad times were about to begin building naval ships, not only for the RCN but for the RN. Eventually, they would build them for the USN and other navies, too.

Bangor-type minesweepers HMCS Melville, Granby, Noranda, *and* Lachine, *diesel-engined, 153 feet 6 inches by 28 feet by 15 feet, and 566.5 tons, approach their launch dates in June 1941.*

14

THE SHIPS

1939-45

THE FIRST CANADIAN naval shipbuilding program of the Second World War called for the construction of 106 vessels: four destroyers, forty escort vessels (corvettes), twenty-eight minesweepers, thirty-two motor torpedo boats (MTBs), and two sloops.[1] In addition, three Canadian National Railway Prince ships (passenger liners) were to be converted to armed merchant cruisers. Because of the country's lack of experience in naval shipbuilding, however, the four destroyers would be built in Britain in exchange for Canadian-built corvettes in the ratio of five corvettes to each destroyer. This brought the number of corvettes to be built in Canada up to sixty, which was later revised to sixty-four. Twenty-eight of these were to be delivered in 1940, and the rest in 1941.[2] For a country whose naval shipbuilding had amounted to four minesweepers over the previous twenty years, the figures were both ambitious and optimistic. The Department of Munitions and Supply moved quickly, and in January 1940 awarded contracts for three or more corvettes to each of twelve shipyards across Canada. Davie was allocated ten.[3]

The lines of the corvette came from the drawing board of the naval architect William Reed, of Smith's Dock Company, South Shields, England. Smith's had specialized in supplying the whaling industry since 1910. In

1936, it had built the prototype for a new line of whaling ship, the *Southern Pride*. When the Admiralty considered the various proposals they received for coastal escort vessels in 1939, they chose Reed's adaptation of her design. The prototype of the corvette, the *Gladiolus*, was laid down in July 1939 and launched the following January.[4] By that time, however, the shortage of escort vessels had become critical, and before the month ended a large number had been ordered from British and Canadian yards. Originally known as "coastal escort vessels," or "patrol vessels, whaler type," it was not long before their cumbersome designation was changed to the more succinct "corvette." Their qualities included excellent seaworthiness and relative simplicity of construction. Winston Churchill, the First Lord of the Admiralty, was so impressed by them that, in spite of the large number of contracts that had already been given out, he insisted that the important Harland & Wolff shipyard at Belfast rearrange its building program and build them also.[5]

Corvettes were either of the "Flower class," or, later in the war, the much improved "Castle class." Modification of both also existed. Those built in Canada were all of the Flower or Revised Flower class,[6] but unlike the RN, which named its corvettes after flowers, the RCN gave theirs the familiar names of Canadian cities and towns – names such as *Vancouver*, *Lethbridge*, *Kitchener*, *Rimouski*, and *Summerside*. No wonder Canadians felt a special attachment to them.

They measured 205 feet 1 inch in length overall and 33 feet 1 inch in extreme breadth, with an 8-foot, 3-inch draft forward and 13-foot, 5-inch aft when fully loaded.[7] Generally speaking, the RCN ships had a displacement of 950 tons, slightly more than those of the RN, and were equipped with extra electrical equipment and steam heating.[8] All were propelled by single-screw reciprocating engines of 2,750 h.p. and were designed to travel at 16 knots. For armament, a 4-inch gun, 2-pounder pompom, machine guns, and standard depth charges were provided. Additional equipment varied. Minesweeping gear, for instance, which was fitted in the first program corvettes, was soon removed to make room for more depth charges aft.⁹ Over the years, many other improvements were made to their design and outfit. An important early change, the lengthening of the forecastle, served the double purpose of increasing the size of the crew's quarters and improving the vessel's seakeeping and habitability. Other noticeable changes included the disappearance of the mainmast; the relocation of the compass house aft before it too disappeared; changes to the bridge, including widening it; and the various locations of the radar hut.

The first four corvettes built by Davie, HMS *Hepatica*, *Snowberry*, *Spikenard*, and *Windflower*, were earmarked for the Royal Navy and were completed within ten months of the signing of the contracts. They sailed immediately for Halifax, where they were joined by eight others from various Quebec and Great Lakes shipyards. Because Davie was not the lead yard, it was a matter of special pride to the shipyard that HMS *Windflower*, commissioned on October 26, 1940, was the first corvette of the program to be delivered. Several that should have been handed over at the same

Hull 515, HMS Windflower, K 155, on sea trials, October 5, 1940. She was delivered November 5 and sailed from Halifax shortly after for the United Kingdom fitted with a dummy wooden gun to discourage U-boat attack. She was one of the first four Canadian-built warships to cross and measured 190 by 33 by 17 feet 6 inches at 728.11 gross tonnage.

time, including one each from the two other Quebec yards, Morton's and George T. Davie, were held up until spring, principally because of delayed deliveries of materials and equipment.[10] In fact, late consignments of additional equipment that was to have been installed in Halifax prevented most of the twelve corvettes that did get there on time from being sent on to Britain that year. *Windflower* was one of the four that made the trip. Manned by skeleton RCN crews, and with makeshift outfits, they left for the United Kingdom by the end of December. They carried dummy wooden guns meant to deceive U-boat crews, which caused both amazement and amusement to those who sailed in convoy with them.[11]

The first of the corvettes built for the Canadian Navy, HMCS *Collingwood*, had been commissioned in Collingwood on November 9,

The corvettes HMS Hepatica, Windflower, *and* Snowberry *fly the Union Jack to celebrate the launching of their sister* HMS Spikenard, *August 10, 1940. (K159, 155, 166 and 198).*
Courtesy R. Gagnon.

The corvette HMCS Shediac *undergoes sea trials shortly before her delivery, July 3, 1941. She served as an escort on the Newfoundland to Londonderry convoys and in various other theatres of war until she was paid off in 1945. One of only three corvettes that survived both the war and the shipbreakers' yards immediately after, the* Shediac *lived on as the Dutch whale catcher* Jooske W. Vinke *until 1965, when she was broken up in Santander, Spain.*

1940, and the remaining boats of the first program of corvettes were delivered by December 1941. Among them were Davie's HMCS *Rimouski*, *Pictou*, *Baddeck*, and *Buctouche*, launched at the end of 1940 and ready for commissioning in April and May 1941. The last two, *Shediac* and *Brandon*, took their place at the outfitting wharf in April 1941 and were delivered in July.

The Battle of the Atlantic was raging. The ships were urgently needed and warmly received, but little time could be allocated to the training of their crews. These sailors often found themselves at sea all too soon, with a great deal still to learn on the job.

Very soon, though, they were required to operate farther and farther out to sea. *Windflower* was among those on escort duty between Newfoundland and Iceland. She disappeared in December 1941 following a collision with the freighter *Zypenburg* in dense fog – the first Canadian corvette casualty.[12] Several of her sister ships became escorts on what were known as "mid-ocean" convoys, from Newfoundland to Londonderry, including *Hepatica*, who sailed in the inaugural "Newfie-Derry" convoy in January 1942, and *Spikenard*, who was lost on the same run a month later.[13] Others escorted Mediterranean convoys.

New tasks meant new requirements, and throughout the corvette building programs, in addition to the changes made to upgrade their equipment, changes were necessary to enable them to fulfil their extended roles. The new equipment took up extra space and required extra men to handle it, in turn imposing a need for extra accommodation. In some cases, the size of the original corvette crew of forty-two more than doubled, reaching in the extreme case an appallingly crowded ninety-three.[14] Despite these design changes, the corvettes remained highly manoeuvrable and extremely seaworthy. They were certainly not designed to give a smooth ride, however, especially since each new piece of equipment increased their top weight. They were there when the Battle of the Atlantic was at its worst, making the most of the very difficult conditions, and have remained the epitome of the Canadian fighting navy in the Second World War.

Few of Davie's surviving corvettes avoided being handed over to the shipbreakers at the end of the war. Among those that did, however, were HMCS *Pictou* and *Shediac*, which both became whale catchers, thus reverting to the purpose of the vessel on which their lines were based. *Pictou* sailed under the Honduran flag as the *Olympic Catcher* and later *Otori Maru*; *Shediac* as the Dutch *Jooske W. Vinke*. The *Baddeck*, the only other survivor, was sold in 1946 as the *Efthalia* and underwent several name changes in a varied career, which came to an end in 1966 when, under the Greek flag and bearing the name *Evi*, she went ashore near Jeddah.[15]

As soon as the last of the corvettes had been delivered, the shipyard turned to the Bangor-type minesweepers on order, HMCS *Melville*, *Granby*, *Noranda*, *Lachine*, *Digby*, and *Truro*. Their hulls were quickly assembled, the last of the six in the total Canadian program of 1940-41 being launched in June 1941, but their outfitting was delayed because of late delivery of their diesel engines. Measuring 162 by 28 by 8 feet 3 inches, they were armed with a 4-inch gun mounted forward, which would later be changed to a 12-pounder, a 2-pounder mounted aft,[16] and smaller ordnance on their bridge wings. For anti-submarine combat they were equipped with depth-charge throwers. Though four-fifths the size of corvettes, they had the same speed and offered drier conditions to their crew of six officers and seventy-seven other ranks. Built to clear the minefields that the Germans were expected to lay off the Canadian east coast, a contingency that did not materialize, they served mostly on convoy duty and were all paid off in July or August 1945. *Digby* and *Granby* were recommissioned in the RCN in 1953 and were based on the Great Lakes. *Digby* was then transferred to the west coast and spent her last two years there, from 1954 to 1956, while *Granby* was converted for duty as a deep-sea diving tender and continued in that capacity until 1966. *Brockville*, *Noranda*, and *Truro* joined the RCMP marine section temporarily under the respective names of *McLeod*, *Irvine*, and *Herchmer*. *Brockville* was subsequently recommissioned in the RCN; *Noranda* spent two years as the yacht *Miriana*; and *Truro* sailed under the name *Gulf Mariner* until she was broken up in 1964. And lastly, *Melville* was attached to the Department of Fisheries fleet under the name *Cygnus* in 1945 and was scrapped in 1961.[17]

In the fourteen months following the delivery of the minesweepers, Davie concentrated on merchant ship construction. The appalling Allied losses to U-boats from the very outset of the war had resulted in a British cargo shipbuilding mission being sent to North America in November 1940 with instructions to order as many standard merchant ships as possible. As none of the Canadian shipyards could handle the construction of the largest ships that were wanted, the Department of Munitions and Supply had been requested to have the Davie, Vickers, and Burrard Dry Dock Company plants upgraded as soon as the minesweepers were completed. They were then each to lay down two 10,000-ton standard cargo ships simultaneously and build six in all, each of which would be named after a Canadian fort. Orders for sixty similar North Sands-type ships (designed by J.L. Thompson of North Sands, Sunderland, England) were given to American yards.

By the time the standard ship program was under way, the Canadian government had decided to have a number of similar ships built on its own account to operate under the Canadian flag. A new Crown corporation, the Park Steamship Company, was given "the responsibility of their maintenance, and of chartering them and allocating them to the ocean routes where their services . . . [could] be best utilized in carrying munitions and supplies to the theatres of war."[18]

As a result of the two programs, Davie received contracts in January 1941 for six ships, of which the *Fort Tadoussac, Fort LaMaulne,* and *Fort Chambly* were ordered by War Supplies on behalf of the British government (but were in fact sold to the United States for Lend Lease to the United Kingdom), while the *Prince Albert Park, Gatineau Park,* and *Banff Park* were to be built for the Park Steamship Company. The number of different government departments that the program involved and, as a consequence, the endless instructions and regulations, and the number of different inspectors, sorely tried the patience of the shipyard staff. But C.D. Howe, the Minister of Munitions and Supply, was not unaware of the situation, and as other shipyards were drawn into the program, he set up another Crown corporation, Wartime Merchant Shipping Limited, "to supervise the performance of contracts for the construction and assembly of the merchant ships, and the construction and operation of shipyards and plants." Bringing the ships on order for Britain under one umbrella removed at least some of the irritants to which shipbuilders were subjected by the multiplication of jurisdictions with which they had to deal.

The Park and Fort vessels were designed to be built with the minimum of equipment. No extra-large shipyard cranes were needed to handle the parts, and all parts were supposedly interchangeable. The ships were registered as 424 feet 6 inches long by 57 feet 2 inches wide and 34 feet 9 inches deep, with a draft of 27.02 feet. The cargo space was divided into five holds, and two deep tanks were provided. They were fitted with single-screw reciprocating engines of 2,500 h.p. and three Scotch Marine Boilers and were designed to travel at 10.5 knots and consume 35.5 tons of coal per day.[19]

Smaller Canadian shipyards that took part in the program were given standard vessels of smaller tonnage to build – 7,500- and 4,700-ton cargo ships, 3,600-ton tankers, and 350- and 1,250-ton coasters. The overwhelming majority, however, were the 10,000-ton ships and of these, 349, including 13 tankers, were eventually built in Canada, mostly on the west coast.

Davie got six more orders in June 1941, for the *Fort Cataraqui*, *Fort Concord*, *Fort Saint-François*, which were also sold for Lend Lease, and the *Fort Mingan*, *Fort Carillon*, and *Jasper Park*. A last order for seven, the *Riverview Park*, *Fort Albany*, *High Park*, *Chippewa Park*, *Riverdale Park*, *Point Pleasant Park*, and *Fort Brunswick* was received in January 1942, making nineteen in all. They were launched at the rate of one a month, and by the time the last one was delivered in December 1943, their building time had been reduced to 107 days.

The unit price of $1,752,580 in the original contract was the price at which the British government had ordered the first six ships, and when the contract was taken over by the Canadian government, the same price was maintained for Davie. Similar agreements were made with Canadian Vickers and with Marine Industries, Sorel,[20] while other shipyards were given a management fee instead. In 1943, however, it was brought to the attention of C.D. Howe that the cost of building the standard ships was very much less than had been anticipated, and that Davie, for example, with firm price contracts for building nineteen 10,000-ton cargo ships, stood to make a total profit of between $8 and $10 million, or 36.4 per cent of cost. He immediately ordered that the price be renegotiated despite Canada Steamship Lines citing the sanctity of a contract and the fact that profits would be taken care of by the Excess Profits Act. Howe "saw no reason why East Coast shipyards should profit from taking twice as long to build the ships as those on the West Coast" and stood firm. The price was adjusted to allow a profit of $61,600 per ship, including $11,600 on the parts fabricated at the yard. The final price of the nineteen ships was a

Shipyard workers were proud of the rate at which they turned out the 10,000-ton cargo ships that were so greatly needed for carrying supplies to Europe. Nineteen were built in all, including the SS Jasper Park, *seen here. Of standard design, they measured 416 by 56 feet 10 inches by 37 feet 4 inches, approximately 7,132 tons.*

little over $28 million, an average of $1,475,501 per vessel, which was in line with the management fee of $50,000 that was being paid to west coast shipyards, but worked out a great deal higher than the management fee of $30,000 for the first ship and $25,000 thereafter paid to the government-owned yard in Montreal.[21]

Meanwhile the Navy chafed at the priority given to the construction of cargo ships, which prevented some of the shipyards from working on naval construction. The demand for merchant ships, it was argued, would always be in excess of supply. Moreover, shipyards could readily be occupied filling orders for merchant ships, but meeting the Navy's requirements was not nearly as simple. The point was driven home by Engineer Captain G.L. Stephens.

> Changes in war conditions, theatres of war and types of warfare involve changes in number and types of ship required, with multitudinous changes in design of hull, machinery and equipment

which cannot be forecast with any accuracy and, if guessed at, result in extravagant waste of money and materials. It is essential that some more flexible and workable arrangement than the present be adopted so that Naval requirements for ship construction can be made without competition and friction with Wartime Merchant shipping which results in such delay.[22]

As far as Davie was concerned, the Navy got its turn at the end of 1943 when the last standard merchant ships had been delivered, and the yard was awarded a contract for twelve of the twenty-nine frigates of the Navy's 1943–44 "Revised Frigate" building program. The rest were to be built at Yarrows and Canadian Vickers. Primarily intended as anti-submarine escort vessels, they incorporated the best anti-aircraft protection possible without prejudicing anti-submarine requirements or endurance. Though they were originally known as "twin-screw corvettes," or "super corvettes" (which is how many Davie retirees still refer to them) and they, too, were designed by William Reed, they actually bore no resemblance to corvettes. The first were laid down in Britain in 1941, and thirty-three had been built under Canada's 1942–43 naval shipbuilding program, thirteen by Yarrows in British Columbia, nine each by Canadian Vickers and Morton, and two at the Geo. T. Davie yard. Ten frigates of a slightly modified version had been built by Canadian Vickers,[23] and it was this version that the Combined Shipbuilding Committee at Washington was lobbying to have adopted as standard by the RN, USN, and RCN, so that shipyards could simplify production using prefabrication methods for large numbers of similar boats.

Frigates were primarily anti-submarine escort vessels, incorporating much improved anti-submarine capability, better anti-aircraft protection, and twice the endurance of a corvette. Measuring 301 feet 6 inches by 36 feet 7 inches by 12 feet 9 inches with a displacement of 2,216 tons, the frigates' speed was calculated at 20¼ knots standard displacement, and their endurance under trial conditions 7,000 miles at 15 knots, or 5,400 under operational conditions. Their anti-submarine equipment consisted of greatly improved asdic (submarine detection gear, later replaced by sonar), a gyro compass, a bottom log, an ARL plotting table, and dual-purpose echo-sounding gear. Their gun armament, which was far superior to that of the corvettes, included one twin 4-inch High Altitude/Low Altitude (HA/LA) gun forward on the forecastle deck level, one 12-pounder aft, Mark VIIP power-operated four-barrelled pompom – without any director (Twin Oerlikon to be fitted until 2-pounder available), two single Oerlikons on the wings of the bridge, and two Twin Oerlikons aft, and platforms for four extra Oerlikons were fitted. Anti-submarine armament was Hedgehog or "B" type "Squid" mortars on B Gun Deck level, and 150 to 200 depth charges. Layout and equipment of the bridges varied as they were constantly improved. Designed for both tropical and cold climate service, they provided accommodation for the commanding officer, four executive officers, an engineer officer, a secretary or medical officer, and 133 other ranks. Provision was made for refrigerated stores for fourteen days, with three months of stowage for dry provisions and canteen stores and twenty-one days for fresh vegetables. Sufficient stowage for four months was provided for naval stores.[24]

Plans for the frigates were provided by the British Admiralty, and J. Gilmore and Alex Campbell, the naval architects of Canadian Vickers and DSRCL respectively, were jointly responsible for preparing the working drawings and issuing the steel order sheets and other documents. In September 1943, four months after the contracts were awarded, Davie launched the first frigate, and four others followed by the end of the year. All twelve were completed and delivered in 1944. They were named:

HMCS *Toronto*	HMCS *Sea Cliff*
HMCS *Sainte-Thérèse*	HMCS *Penetang*
HMCS *Lasalle*	HMCS *Buckingham*
HMCS *Coaticook*	HMCS *Inch Arran*
HMCS *St. Pierre*	HMCS *Sussexvale*
HMCS *Prestonian*	HMCS *Carlplace*

THE SHIPS

They were commissioned into the RCN after the worst of the Battle of the Atlantic was over and were immediately detailed to join the escort groups operating out of Halifax and Londonderry. They were greatly appreciated by the men who served in them. Bill Macrae, of HMCS *Penetang*, for instance, described her as a good sea ship with great fighting ability, yet comfortable. But the frigates' war service was limited to a little over a year at most. VE-Day brought an end to the Atlantic war on May 8, 1945. Their crews were paid off in November or December 1945, some of them into the reserve.

In the years immediately following the war, three frigates were sold to foreign countries. *Carlplace* became the presidential yacht *Presidente*

Frigate HMCS Sea Cliff *K394 at her launching in July 1944.*

Trujillo in the Dominican Republic in 1946, where she was renamed *Hella* sixteen years later. *St. Pierre* joined the Peruvian Navy in 1947 under the name the *Teniente Palacios*, which was later abbreviated to *Palacios*, while *Sea Cliff* left for Chile in 1946 and finished her days in the Chilean Navy under the name *Covadonga*. Two frigates, *Coaticook* and *Lasalle*, suffered the ignominy of being sunk to form parts of a breakwater in British Columbia, although for a while *Coaticook* cheated the perpetrators, breaking free of her grave in 1961 and choosing her own burial place at Cape Race, where she was finally scuttled. The remaining seven were converted in the 1950s to Prestonian-class escorts, including of course, the name ship *Prestonian*, and served as training ships. Of these, *Penetang*, *Prestonian*, and *Toronto* were loaned to Norway in 1956 and were recommissioned in its Navy under the names, respectively, *Draug*, *Troll*, and *Garm*, and then were transferred outright to that Navy three years later. *Garm* became the torpedo boat depot ship *Valkyrien* in 1959, continuing to serve this way until 1977, while *Troll*, renamed *Horten*, began a new career as a submarine depot ship in 1965, which lasted until she was scrapped in 1972.[25] *Victoriaville*, one of the frigates built at the George T. Davie yard, served the longest in the RCN. Commissioned in June 1944, she too became a

Shipping wintering at the Davie Brothers shipyard at Levis during the Second World War. Vessels include SS *Saguenay Trader, Mechins, and* Maureen.

Prestonian class escort, but in 1966 took on the duties and name of HMCS *Granby* as a diving tender, finally being sold for scrap in 1974.

In 1944, as the war in Europe drew to its close, plans were made to transfer the whole weight of the war effort to the Pacific theatre. Canadian shipyards received orders for seventy-one 350-foot-long transport ferries, which had been designed by British naval architects for the express purpose of moving men and materials. They were larger than any of the other naval ships that had been laid down at the yard, 330 by 54 by 27 feet, and had steam-driven reciprocating engines of 5,500 i.h.p. and electrical generators. Davie, which was to build seventeen, delivered ten between May and November 1945, while an eleventh was towed to Sorel for completion. Contracts for the other six were cancelled when the war with Japan ended. The transport ferries were not given names, but were identified as HMLST 3507 to 3513 and HMLST 3522 to 3525. Built on a cost-plus basis of about $1.5 to $2 million with a maximum profit allowed of $135,000 per vessel,[26] they were the last naval ships that would be built at the yard during the war.

All in all, Davie's wartime production consisted of ten corvettes, six minesweepers, nineteen 10,000-ton cargo steamers, twelve frigates, eleven

Davie Brothers yard, busy with maintenance and repairs, including SS Daluarnic *and* MV De Vallier *on August 29, 1941.*

LST 3508, *330 by 54 by 27 feet, 4,290 gross tons, one of eleven that were built for the British Admiralty in 1945, in preparation for the transfer of the war effort to the Pacific. They were fitted with steam-driven reciprocating engines of 5,500 i.h.p. and electrical generators.*
Courtesy R. Gagnon.

transport ferries, and one 7,500-ton diesel cargo ship completed after the war had ended. To this total should be added more than 150 major repair jobs and many minor ones. In addition, the 172-foot icebreaker and service vessel *Ernest Lapointe*, for which Davie had signed a contract in May 1939 with delivery date a year later, was launched in November 1939, but had to wait on account of the priority accorded to the corvettes, to be completed finally in February 1941.[27] With a crew of thirty, she then left for the lower reaches of the St. Lawrence where her role, like that of the *Montmorency* and the *Montcalm*, was to clear ice jams to prevent flooding.

The war years were golden years for all Canadian shipbuilders. In the Quebec City area, four shipyards shared the bonanza with DSRCL. To the west of the Lorne Dry Dock, the George T. Davie & Sons shipyard (incorporated as George T. Davie & Sons, Ltd. in 1941) overcame a disadvantaged beginning with no drawing office and comparatively little equipment to build four corvettes, four trawlers, seven frigates, seven 4,700-ton cargo steamers, and five coasters, while the Morton shipyard, which did not survive for long in the postwar years,[28] nevertheless ended the war with an impressive total of twenty-one corvettes, eight frigates, four cargo vessels, and five coasters to its credit.

It should be pointed out, however, that these high production figures at two relatively small shipyards were made possible by their temporary amalgamation with a new Shipbuilding Division set up by the Anglo Pulp and Paper Mills, Limited, on the St. Charles River, where the hulls they built were finished and outfitted.[29] William E. Soles, the general manager of the division, had a staff of 150, including 12 draftsmen. Premises consisted of an office building and woodworking, machine, and pipe shops. There, 2,000 men, many of whom did not know port from starboard when they began, worked in three shifts a day to reduce the time between the arrival of the hull and the commissioning of the finished vessel from ten months in the case of the first, HMCS *Dunver*, to ten weeks for the last. Wilfrid Gagnon was comptroller and president of the umbrella company, Quebec Shipyards Limited.

Another small yard that was pressed into naval shipbuilding, the Chantier Maritime de St. Laurent, Limitée on the Isle of Orleans, built four minesweepers, a gate vessel for the Halifax barrier, and a tug, HMCS *Listowel*.[30] In Levis, the Davie Brothers shipyard, still under the direction of Allison Davie and his foreman Gérard Desprès, kept equally busy throughout the war building harbour craft and ship's boats for the navy, and carrying out repairs and maintenance to naval river patrol boats and whatever merchant ships the yard could handle.

Figures for the total war production of Canadian shipyards are impressive. Naval construction alone amounted to 224 ships, and 80 Fairmile "B" motor launches for the RCN,[31] 178 vessels for the Royal Navy, and 18 for the USN – 408 new naval vessels in all. No fewer than 456 merchantmen and

Paul Gourdeau examines one of the trim mahogany-planked ships' boats built at Davie Brothers, Levis, during the Second World War, with which the naval vessels built in the larger yards in the port, such as Davie's and Morton's, were equipped. Courtesy P. Gourdeau.

other civilian vessels were launched from Canadian yards also, including 349 10,000-ton ships and 18 tugs. In addition, of course, a great many conversions and modifications were undertaken, and innumerable repairs was carried out.

When the last naval vessels left the building slips at Davie's in 1945, their places were taken by merchantmen, the motor cargo vessel *Canadian Challenger* for the Canadian National Steamship Company, four steamers for the Chargeurs Réunis of France, and *Pontoon No. 5* for Canada Steamship Lines. History thus repeated itself, for at the end of the First World War, Davie was engaged in building another *Canadian Challenger* for an earlier Canadian government shipping corporation, as well as other cargo ships for France, while CSL would order a pontoon the following year.

But it was not the construction of these and similar vessels in other Canadian yards that held the greatest significance for Davie and other

Canadian shipbuilders in the aftermath of the war. Rather, it was the fact that the first four destroyers ever to have been laid down in Canada were nearing completion at the Halifax shipyard. This vote of confidence in the advances that had been made in Canadian shipbuilding in the course of the war augured well for the future of the industry.

Portrait of Philias Corriveau by the prominent Quebec artist Francesco Iacurto, RCA. Commissioned by the Davie Shipbuilding Company as a tribute to the wartime effort of its employees, it hangs in the president's office.

15

WORKERS AND WORKPLACE

1939-45

THE CONSTRUCTION PROGRAMS of the war years brought prosperity and optimism to the whole Canadian shipbuilding industry. At Davie alone, the work force increased from roughly 250 men to more than 4,300, while four new building slips, several new buildings, and greatly improved cranage transformed a yard which, like most Canadian shipyards, had seen little change since the end of the previous war. Wartime figures for two other shipyards in the port were equally impressive: the number of workers at the neighbouring George T. Davie yard rose from fewer than 100 to 2,000, while employment at Morton's peaked at 2,700 men.

Davie started the war with a skeleton but competent management team, headed by David Craig. A veteran shipbuilder, Craig began his career at seventeen years of age as a helper rigger at the Bertram Shipyard in Toronto. He subsequently worked at the Polson Iron Works, Owen Sound, and at Collingwood, before leaving to gain further experience at yards in Buffalo, New York; Detroit; and Ashtabula and Cleveland, Ohio. In 1909, he joined Davie as a loftsman, rose to the position of foreman of new construction and repairs, and was named assistant superintendent less than a year later. In 1926, he took over from Neil Baker as yard superintendent and chief estimator for ship repairs. When George D. Davie's health deteriorated, making

NAVAL AND WARTIME SHIPBUILDING

David Craig, a native of Winnipeg, who joined Davie in 1909. He was the yard manager for many years, and of him was written: "Much of the success in production [during the Second World War] has been due to his intelligent planning and the easy manner in which he handles labour." He retired in 1944.

it impossible for him to devote his energies to the yards, Craig became works manager. It was said that much of the success of Davie's production during the war years resulted from Craig's "intelligent planning and the easy manner in which he handled labour."[1] When he retired in 1944, he was replaced by Al Morley, an American.[2]

Charles (Charlie) Sauvageau was second in command. He had begun working at the Tidewater Shipyard in Trois-Rivières in 1909 when he was seventeen and continued to be employed by Canada Steamship Lines ever since, working in various locations and positions throughout his career. When the CSL hotel Manoir Richelieu burned to the ground in September 1928, Sauvageau oversaw its reconstruction, which he achieved in a matter of months.[3] He had been at the Davie shipyard since 1929 and was familiar with every facet of its operation. Not only was he assistant treasurer – the office of the treasurer, H.A. Cresswell, was in Montreal – but later on, he also handled estimates and the administration of ship repairs. R. Brock Thomson, who handled all dealings with the government from the CSL office in Montreal, could not have wished for a more faithful lieutenant. Every contract that Davie entered into was scrutinized by Charlie, who carefully spelled out changes that were in the best interest of the company.

His zealous efforts to keep shipyard expenses down were not always appreciated, however. A manager wanting a raise for one of his men needed Charlie Sauvageau's approval. Charlie would write the details on the back of a packet of cigarettes and then thrust it back in his shirt pocket saying, "I'll see what I can do." As often as not, it was only when he was warned that the man might move to another company that the raise would come through.[4] But no one doubted Charlie's loyalty to the company – the company's interests always came first.

He believed strongly in fostering a team spirit and could be relied on to support employee activities both inside and outside the shipyard. He was not only president of the office employees' bowling league organized by Charles Furois in 1943, but also one of its most enthusiastic players. He even donated a silver cup for the best team. He was equally generous with Davie's hockey team, of which he was the honorary treasurer: it was he who gave the cup that was awarded to the best player each year. A large contingent of workers demonstrated their respect and affection for him when his mother died in Montreal. They met the train that brought her back to Levis and accompanied her to her last resting place.[5]

The yard's technical team was headed by the naval architect Alex Campbell, another veteran. Following his apprenticeship in Britain, Campbell had worked at the Armstrong Whitworth shipyard in Newcastle, at Scotts of Greenock and Palmers in Jarrow, and for a short time at the Fore River Shipbuilding Company in Quincy, Massachusetts. He was hired by George D. Davie as chief draftsman in 1913. Except for a few months at a British shipyard during the First World War, he had remained at Davie's ever since. Sue Bjornstad, who took over from Campbell's daughter Kitty as his secretary in 1941, remembers him as a small, slight, quiet-spoken man with a heavy Scottish accent. Because he was shy, she says, he gave an impression of remoteness, but he was "by no means unkind," and they soon developed a good business relationship. He lived for his work, which was highly valued, and for his family. His only other strong interest was his cello. Six draftsmen worked under him in the drawing office: Mr. Weir, a

Alex Campbell (1888–1965). The naval architect at the Davie shipyard at Lauzon from 1917 to 1945, following which he set up an office in Montreal where he continued as consulting naval architect for Davie while at the same time carrying out work for other shipyards and shipping lines. Courtesy William Campbell.

tall jolly Scot; James Irving, his chief engineering draftsman, a relative newcomer who had joined Davie in 1940; Jim Pollock, an experienced hull draftsman; Paul Tremblay, a competent piping draftsman; and two electrical draftsmen, Kenneth King and Robert Guay.

K.M. (Ken) Wears was the yard superintendent. He was a true shipbuilder and an engineer with a thorough understanding and feel for machinery. He had learned the trade at Newcastle and was hampered only by his difficulty with the French language. His assistant, Jérémie Gagnon, had been at Davie's since 1916 and replaced him when Wears accepted a position at the Sorel shipyard in 1946. Gagnon was much closer to the men than Wears had been. He had become a father figure at the shipyard – no one had a bad word for Jerry. It was to him that workmen or widows appealed on behalf of their sons, and women on behalf of their sweethearts or husbands. They begged Jerry to hire their men so that they would not be sent to war, for though many French Canadians volunteered and served in the armed forces, many others were strongly opposed to Canada's participation in it. Many of them were taken on.

Wears and Gagnon were backed up by an experienced team of foremen, many of whom were engaged by George D. Davie himself. Some had been at the yard for more than fifty years. Hector Duchesneau, dean of the foremen, for example, began his five-year term as an apprentice blacksmith when the yard opened in 1886 and after twenty-one years as a journeyman became foreman blacksmith in 1912. He retired in 1944 when he was seventy-five. Léon Laflamme, known as "le Père Laflamme," who took over from him, may well have despaired of ever doing so, yet his own career lasted fifty years, and his two sons, Lucien and Jacques, each completed more than forty years of service. Among the others, Emile Samson, Philias Corriveau, and John Porter were already employed at the yard in 1905, and several more were taken on during the First World War.

The foremen of the Second World War were:

Blacksmith	Hector Duchesneau/ Léon Laflamme
Boiler makers & engineering	Joseph Hamelin
Bolters & steel platers	José Samson
Burners	Napoléon Morency
Carpenters, stagers, slingers	Willie Bilodeau
Cranemen	Ronaldo Ruel
Electricians	Edmond Jeune/ Alphonse Bolduc
Erectors	Évariste Ouellet
Foundry	P.G. Pérusse
Furnacemen	Lauréat Samson
Iron caulkers & chippers	Aurèle Robitaille/ A. Routhier
Joiner	Emile Samson / Emile Ringuet
Labourers	Adélard Latulippe
Loftsmen	Johnny Bernier
Machine shop	Joseph Lepage/A. Pérusse
Morton shop	Rosaire Leclerc /Roméo Vien
Painters	Joseph Lévesque

Pattern makers	Ernest Delisle
Pipefitters	Jack Tennet
Plate shop	Joseph Dumont
Plate shop night shift	Albert Corriveau
Policemen & watchmen	J.W. Scallen
Repairs	Émile Ringuet
Riggers	H. Morin
Riveters	Édouard Berrigan
Sam mill	Henri Bilodeau
Ship fitters	Omer Samson
Ship platers	Ronald [J.] Currie
Ship riggers	Henri Morin
Sprinklermen & firemen	A. Beaudoin
Steel yard	Jérôme Théberge
Storemen	Adolphe Huot
Tool room	Philias Corriveau
Tractors & trucks, horses	Johnny Boutin
Welder	Roméo O'Neil
Yard clerk	Nilus Tremblay
	John Porter
	Roméo Blais

They were responsible for training the vast majority of new employees taken on during the war, many of whom had not worked in a shipyard before, and integrating them with the more experienced work force.

Technical courses had been available to young men who worked at the yard since the nineteenth century. From 1873 on, for instance, ambitious Davie employees, along with apprentices from the Carrier, Lainé machine shops, had been encouraged to attend local evening courses sponsored by the Conseil des Arts et Manufacturiers. So popular did these courses become that by 1890 260 students attended them at the Institut des Ouvriers on Fraser Street in Levis. In 1922, when the Canadian government, urged by men such as Lomer Gouin, Minister of Public Works and Colonization, took on the responsibility for providing technical training, night courses in industrial design (*dessin mécanique*) were introduced, first at Levis, and the following year also at the Town Hall in Lauzon. In 1929, mechanics, under the direction of Ovide Brunet of Quebec's École technique, and joinery, at first under Davie's pattern shop foreman Ernest Delisle, and then under Dénary Hallé, were added to the curriculum.[6] In 1938, the school began giving daytime courses and its name was changed to the École des Arts et Métiers.[7]

Quebec City had an equivalent École technique, which was founded in 1911. It had reached an enrolment of 400 students by the time it expanded under the War Emergency Training Plan in 1939. Night courses in mechanics; joinery; and mechanical, electrical, automotive, and civil engineering were soon being given to over a thousand students, while Louis Letarte, head foreman of the platers' shop at Morton's, organized and directed the three-month Practical Course in Shipbuilding. The students learned bolting-up, punching, shearing, riveting, chipping, caulking, and oxyacetylene welding on a full-time or part-time basis. They were well taught. Steelworkers graduating from this course, including three-man riveting teams who were accustomed to working together, found jobs waiting for them, not only in the Quebec and Lauzon yards but as far away as Collingwood and Halifax.[8] As a result, students were quick to enrol when a second course, which trained loftsmen, markers-off, and draftsmen, was started in February 1942.

During the war, Davie needed far more men than the two technical schools could provide, however, and many of Davie's workers received all their training at the shipyard itself. New employees were hired as helpers and worked in this capacity during the day. After the day shift was over, they were allowed to do the job themselves under the guidance of their foreman or other experienced tradesman who were given special instruction in using shortcuts to passing on their skills. The system was highly successful. By February 1942, 1,700 men – riveters, welders, joiners, and others

– had been trained at the yard, and the shipyard work force numbered 2,500 men, more than ten times the pre-war figure. By 1944, the number had increased to 4,300.

The large increase in the work force led to a new Personnel Department being set up in 1941 with Peter Bartleman as manager. He was responsible for hiring personnel, handling their records, organizing employee health and safety, and looking into employee grievances. A hospital unit staffed by two nurses had evolved from the yard's small first-aid post, and it also came under Bartleman's control. He organized first-aid courses, introduced a group insurance plan, and sponsored safety measures in the shipyard. On-the-job safety was also stressed in the employees' monthly newspaper, *L'Écho Maritime*, which he ran.

Bartleman also ensured that there was adequate public transportation to carry the workers to and from the yard. Before the war, because old employees jealously guarded any new positions that became available for their sons and close relatives, men at both the Davie and the George T. Davie Lauzon shipyards had almost all come from local families. But the demand for new workers now greatly exceeded the local supply and many employees lived far from the yard, even across the river. Bartleman organized special trams that met the ferry from Quebec and whisked the workers to the yard. Other trams brought employees from Saint-Romuald and Charny, farther west.[9] At the end of the day's shift, the trams would be waiting in line for the men from the two shipyards, and there was a general rush and scramble to get on them. First stop was the ferry terminal. Men who lived closer to the yard had to find their own way home.

As the war progressed and the work force continued to increase, even the expanded tram service was no longer adequate. A fleet of eight new buses purchased by the Levis Tramway Company in 1944 and put into service from Charny and intermediate points to the shipyards handled some of the overflow. The fare was fifty cents return from Charny, forty cents from Saint-Romuald, or $2.25 and $1.50 respectively weekly. The Tramway company guaranteed that the buses would reach the shipyard in

> ## ⁂ WORKING CONDITIONS ⁂
>
> DURING THE YEARS following the Second World War, working conditions in the yard received attention. Roads within the yard were asphalted. Ventilation greatly improved the quality of the air in many of the shops. Gas masks became common where there were toxic fumes. In many instances, the newer technology itself made the work less dirty than it had been before. When oil burners replaced the coal burners on the cranes, for instance, the crane operators no longer resembled stokers at the end of their shifts. But yard work is not office work, and in spite of these and similar improvements, the hot showers that were provided to remove the grime at the end of the day were particularly welcome. Since then, conditions have constantly been upgraded – safety glasses, ear protectors, helmets, and metal-capped boots are used as a matter of course, and the shops have very efficient ventilation. Typical of the changes in working conditions is the banning of chipping with a pneumatic hammer, which has been replaced by arc-air gouging, and even this can only be done at specific times.

the morning in time to start the day's work.[10] At the beginning of the war, a very few workers owned an automobile and drove to the yard, often picking up fellow employees on the way. Thanks to the generous pay packets, however, the number of automobiles entering and leaving the shipyard each day increased steadily. Soon, partly to avoid accidents as workers in cars and on foot streamed through the gates, the first parking area for employees was set up.

Not all the workers came from locations that were within daily commuting distance, however. The luckier ones were able to relocate in the wartime housing development of about 150 homes a short distance to the

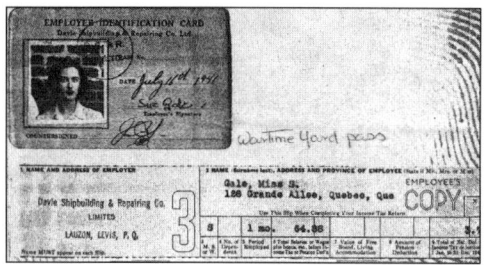

Wartime "Employee Identification Card" and pay slip. At $64.88 for one month's employment as secretary to the naval architect, it is not surprising that Sue Gale took the opportunity when it presented itself to move on to the Lloyd's office in Quebec.

east of the yard. Others knocked on doors in the vicinity asking for a room. Not a week went by without several such requests, remembers Mary Jane Perkins, who lived close by. Also vivid among her wartime memories is the crowd of perhaps 200 applicants, many of them farmers from the surrounding countryside, who gathered at the shipyard barrier each morning in the hope of finding work. She remembers especially the disappointed faces of those who were not picked.

Wartime security measures inevitably brought changes in the rather relaxed attitude that had previously prevailed at the yard. A worker accustomed to passing casually through the gates had now to line up at a booth where his entry and departure from the yard were scrupulously monitored. Children who once might have taken their father his lunch and played for a while in the shipyard yard could no longer do so. Such pleasant customs came to an end. Workers were out of luck if they forgot their lunches. Although lobbing a lunch pail over the shipyard fence out of sight of the guard was not unheard of, the chance that the pail would spring open, scattering its contents, discouraged the attempt. Gone, too, were Sunday visits to the yard. Before the war, shipyard workers often took their families and friends on tours of the yard, and George D. Davie had been happy to let them do so, but wartime security measures put an end to the custom.

Now all employees were given yard numbers and were assigned to one of five booths where they picked up their numbered identity badge at the beginning of each shift and left it when it was over. They picked up their pay – in cash – from the same booth at the end of the week. Preparing the payroll became a large-scale operation. Louis Godbout, who began work at the yard in 1942, was one of ten timekeepers at the booths. The men would fill in the hours they had worked on their work cards, he says, which were then checked by their foremen and handed to the timekeepers who made up the pay lists accordingly – so much at the regular rate, so much overtime (one and a half times the regular rate) and so much "dirty work" (one and an eighth). When the timekeepers had finished, the lists were checked by the paymaster, Emily Hamilton. The local bank with which the shipyard did business had to deal with a considerable increase in the cash it kept on hand, and the paymaster, Thomas Hart, who fetched the payroll in the company car, heaved a sigh of relief when he arrived safely back in the yard with his valuable load each week.

The workers were more than satisfied with the steady work and the wages they earned during the war. Government contracts during the first year of the war stipulated, as they had in the past, that rates of pay should be comparable to those paid for comparable private work. Since all shipyard work was now government work, however, there were no other yards on which to base the comparison, so a royal commission was set up to study the matter. The commission heard evidence from shipyard employers and employees or their representatives[11] and examined the situation in certain Quebec and Ontario shipyards, including the two Davie yards in Lauzon. The rates of pay for each trade, it concluded, should differ slightly according to the region, with Canadian Vickers at the top of the scale followed by the rural Ontario yards, then the two Lauzon yards, and finally Sorel.[12] The government cost of living bonus should be the same for all. A forty-eight-hour week with no more than 20 per cent overtime, unless circumstances were exceptional, was recommended. The commission also urged that advancement be on the basis of performance, not seniority, except in the case of apprentices; that a review of the classification and remuneration of each employee be made every three months; that a personnel and labour relations officer(s) be appointed in each yard; and that a grievance committee be established to promote good relations between employer and employees.

In Davie's case, the recommended minimum wage for the various trades varied from fifty-two cents an hour for a plater erector to seventy-five cents for a loftsman or pattern maker, with the majority of trades earning seventy cents. It was suggested that helpers and labourers receive between thirty and forty-eight cents an hour, and that apprentices begin at twenty-five cents an hour, with yearly increases of ten cents an hour to sixty-five cents in the fifth and final year. By the end of his fifth year, each apprentice should have worked 12,000 hours.

By 1942 a regular week at the Lauzon yards meant working from 7:00 to 12:00 and 1:00 to 6:00 on weekdays, and 7:00 to 12:00 and 1:00 to 4:30 on Saturdays. In effect, workers were putting in their forty-eight hours and 20 per cent overtime on a regular basis by working a fifty-eight-and-a-half-hour week. Many chose to work overtime far in excess of the recommended 20 per cent and were proud of the fact that the pay they earned enabled them to build and own their homes in record time. As to the suggested appointment of a personnel and labour relations officer, Davie already had one.

In addition to keeping the shipyard workers satisfied, the government had also to deal with the frustrations experienced by shipbuilders, who had to keep things going despite sometimes conflicting instructions from a succession of different government and other bodies. For instance, on the outbreak of war the year-old Defence Purchasing Board was replaced by the interim War Supply Board, which was given the responsibility for the purchase of war supplies and for the expansion of Canadian industry to meet war needs. Meanwhile the Department of Munitions and Supply was organized and took over in turn from the War Supply Board in April 1940. Within the department, a naval shipbuilding branch[13] was established, whose functions were to place contracts for naval vessels, advise on the financial terms of the contracts and their general interpretation, and control and co-ordinate the orders that were placed for steel and components.[14] In June 1944, after four and a half years of wartime building, this branch merged with Wartime Merchant Shipbuilding, which had had control of the

Tool room employees, including Philias Corriveau, third from left, pose outside their shop in 1944.

construction of merchant ships, to form Wartime Shipbuilding Limited.[15] When, finally, both naval and merchant construction came under the same jurisdiction, matters were simplified for all parties.

On the technical side, shipbuilders had to deal with both Canadian government inspectors and those of the British Admiralty Technical Mission (BATM), which was responsible for the design and inspection of naval construction, but delegated some of the work to Lloyd's Register of Shipping surveyors.[16] In view of the shipyards' lack of experience in building naval vessels, BATM's thorough attention to every facet of their construction was invaluable, if not always appreciated. Under BATM's supervision, staff and yard workers alike learned to work to the Admiralty's strict requirements. This proved to be an excellent preparation for the years ahead.

There were others whom the shipyards also strove to satisfy: the men who would operate and sail the ships in often perilous conditions, and who were surely entitled to their say. The officers who were to serve on the ship frequently stood by during her outfitting. Their preferences and idiosyncrasies were without official sanction, let alone a budget. In sympathy and friendship for the risks they were taking, the shipyard workers tried to stretch their resources to oblige. It gave workers at one shipyard great satisfaction to weld together a cot from "gash" (leftover) metal pieces and hinge it disguised to the bulkhead, for a chief petty officer who claimed he was unable to sleep in a hammock.

These are just a few of the aspects of day-to-day life in the shipyard during the Second World War. The full story would fill several volumes. The impression given by those who have spoken to the author about those years is that the many changes affecting the work force were fittingly exemplified by the strident new siren that was set up on the corner of the plate shed. It was intended to serve as a warning in case of enemy attack, but it was used also to signal the shift changes and, later, coffee breaks as well. It seemed to say, "This is an important fully fledged industry, and you, industrialized workers, must live by me."[17]

As to the changes in the plant itself, it was fortunate that Alex Campbell was there to handle them. Because of the shortage of work in the 1930s, Campbell had left Davie in 1938 to set up his own office in Montreal. He had continued, however, to act as the firm's naval architect, while carrying out similar duties for Canada Steamship Lines and the Marine Industries Shipyard at Sorel.[18] When Canada declared war, because of the resulting increase in construction, it was agreed that he would devote practically all his time to Davie.[19] His profound knowledge of the yard and its working conditions made him the ideal person to plan and supervise construction of the new facilities.

The first of the new buildings, a one-storey well-lighted mould loft with long windows on all four sides and the luxury of steam heating in the ceiling, began to take shape to the northeast of the plate shop in May 1940.

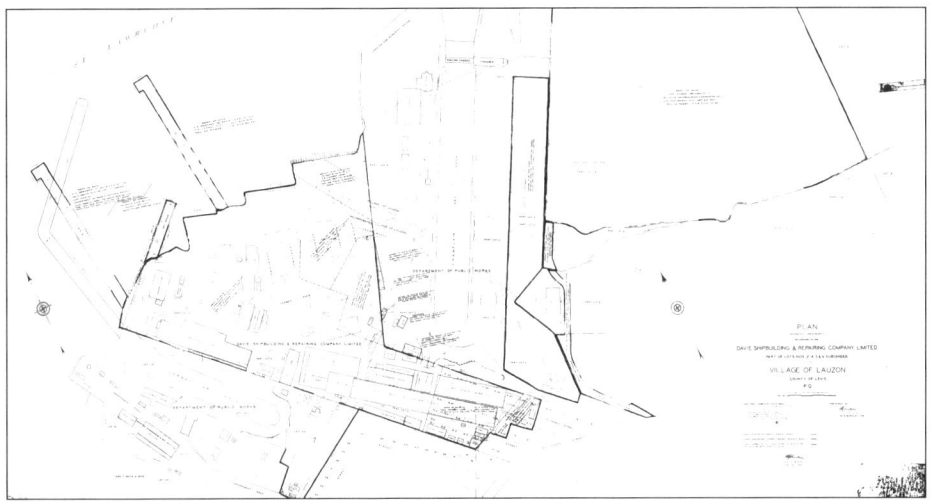

The DSRCL *shipyard as it was in February 1944, with the improvements made up to April 1955 added. Note the new mould loft at the head of the five building berths and, in the lower left-hand corner, the Morton shop that Davie leased.* "Plan showing property belonging to the DSRCL: Part of Lots Nos 2, 4, 5 and 6 sub-divided in the Village of Lauzon, County of Levis, P.Q." [1" = 200'] Prepared by Lindsay of M.D. Barclay, Inc., 26 February 1944, revised November 1944, March 1952 and April 1955.

In August, the riggers' shop received a face-lift, and a large extension was added to the back of the machine shop. The construction of a 624-foot-long enclosure for a 70-foot-span crane runway to facilitate the handling of steel followed in November, and in the spring of 1941, a matching brick extension was built on to the southeast end of the office building.[20]

Further improvements to the plant were carried out during the summer of 1942 in preparation for the frigate-building program, among them a new stores building, plate shop, and derrick towers; a roof over the crane runway; and new steel storage racks. To make way for the plate shop, the old stable, which had stood for half a century and whose twelve-inch-thick solid brick walls had not only sheltered the horses but provided a five-bedroom home for the watchman and his family on its second floor, had to go.[21] Then, in November 1942, a new garage, oxygen storage building, and cafeteria were built, and a freight elevator and new crane runway were

Every day during the war years thousands of workers streamed towards the time booths. Courtesy David Christopher.

installed.[22] The government paid for most of these improvements and for the purchase of new equipment worth $980,500. The government retained ownership of all but the roads and paving but gave Davie the right to purchase them later at a fair price. In 1942, also, when the government was to build an outfitting wharf at the shipyard, Davie sold back to the Crown the wharf lot immediately to the east of the entrance to the Lorne Dock, for which it held letters patent. An outfitting wharf was then built of a different configuration, which offered greater protection to the ships that were tied up there.[23]

Another facility that Davie exploited during the war was the machine shop known as the "Morton Shop." It had been set up by Morton shipbuilding in 1930 on a government-owned lot immediately to the south of the Lorne Dry Dock. It was meant to make it possible for the Quebec-based shipyard to take on repairs in the dry docks, but was rarely used until Davie leased it from Morton in 1940.[24] According to Rosaire Leclerc, the foreman and a former Morton employee, sixty-eight men were employed in the shop in 1944, including a blacksmith, two painters, and two loftsmen. They could make "all the small pieces" up to ten tons in size, such as the vehicle ramps for the barges, the rudders, skylights, ventilators, and so forth.

There was a general reorganization of the power supply to bring the shipyard up to date. This was particularly necessary to accommodate the change-over from riveting to welding.[25] In 1943, when two new building berths, 6 and 7, were prepared for the frigate program, receptacles and wiring were installed to cover welding requirements, as well as a general increase in the use of electricity. The following year, the other five berths were similarly upgraded.[26] As a result, the yard's consumption of electrical power, which had doubled from 300 h.p. in August 1939 to 700 h.p. in August 1940, jumped five-fold to 3,500 h.p. in 1943.[27]

The increasing reliance on electricity eventually led to the disappearance of the horses. From the shipyard's earliest days, horses helped with the heaviest work. When a steel stempost twelve inches wide and three inches thick had to be bent, for instance, shipyard horses were brought around to supply the requisite power. When an order of steel plates arrived by rail, a team of six or eight horses and a pair of wheels would be sent to the Grand Trunk Terminal to fetch them. Those days were now gone. The Davie shipyard was no longer an old-fashioned family operation. Thousands of newcomers had joined the payroll, most of whom were not descendants of Davie employees, as had been the custom before. Moreover, after close to forty years at Lauzon, in 1946 David Craig, the works manager since 1926, was retiring. So was Alex Campbell, who had been Davie's naval architect since 1913. The end of the war undoubtedly marked the end of an era.

Davie's status within CSL was also to end. Though Davie was well able

Riveter Alfred Garant worked on the four ferries built in 1910–11 and was still employed at the shipyard fifty years later when this photograph was taken. His son, Napoléon, began February 12, 1942, as a riveter's helper and worked for fifty-two years at Davie, retiring as a pipefitting foreman. NA PA 19746C.

Édouard Bélanger, Davie's champion riveter. A riveter was the king of a squad of five men. With strong support from his squad, Belanger beat the North American record set at a Vancouver shipyard, squeezing and finishing 2,100 rivets in a nine-hour shift in September 1941 – and even came up smiling. Riveters were not allowed to smoke on the job, but at least one riveter's helper would light his pipe for him so that he could take a few puffs through a rivet hole!

to build the lakers that CSL needed to renew her fleet on the Great Lakes, they would be too large to transit the locks at Montreal in order to get there. In 1945, on the death of its president and owner, Roy M. Wolvin, CSL bought Canadian Shipbuilding and Engineering Limited, thus acquiring the shipyards at Kingston, Collingwood, Midland, and Port Arthur. The purchase placed CSL in a position to construct and repair lakers both for its own fleet and for those of its competitors. Consequently, Davie lost the distinction of being the sole CSL "in-house" shipyard, though it remained the only one with a free run to the sea.[28]

To meet wartime needs and driven by government-financed investment, shipbuilding had become an important national industry. During the next half century, however, successive Canadian governments would try to deal with the industry's ever-shrinking role in changing world market conditions. For several decades, they were successful at supporting and encouraging the industry's continuing survival.

Part Six

POST WAR

CMS C.D. Howe *on patrol of the Eastern Arctic, at Pangnirtung, N.W.T., in 1951.*
W. Doucette. NA 59368/126558.

16

TRANSITION TO PEACETIME PRODUCTION

1945-51

JUST AS THE Canadian government had prepared long before the outbreak of the Second World War a war plan, parts of which were put into effect even before hostilities began, it also had a peace plan drawn up well ahead of time. In fact, only three months after war was declared, a committee was set up to consider the problems that veterans would face following their demobilization. The deliberations of the committee led to a number of wider studies, culminating in June 1944 in the formation of the Department of Reconstruction. It was the new department's mandate to find and implement solutions to a wide spectrum of postwar problems, among them the difficulties that shipyards and their suppliers would face in weathering the transition from wartime to peacetime production.[1] The department was instructed to keep the industry as nearly intact as possible and to keep unemployment down. Its priorities included the rapid removal and disposal of surplus naval and merchant ships and equipment, which would otherwise clutter the yards. Because it anticipated these problems, when the time came, it was able to act swiftly and decisively.

Quite apart from the considerable wartime increase in the size of many yards, the number of large or fairly large Canadian shipbuilding

POST WAR

Left: *Robert (Bert) Black (1903–1978), who replaced Alex Campbell as naval architect of the shipyard in 1945 and was general manager from 1952 to 1962. Canada Steamship Lines commissioned these three pastels from –Boudreault in 1963 as a tribute to the devoted service of the three men.* Right: *Charles (Charlie) Sauvageau (1896–1961). His devotion and skill as the firm's comptroller was greatly appreciated.*

yards had almost doubled from fourteen to twenty-five, while the number of smaller shipyards or boat yards had increased in even greater proportion, from fifteen to sixty-five. The work force, which had numbered 3,500 at the outset, had multiplied by a factor of nearly fourteen, to 48,000.[2] Though, inevitably, there were complaints that equipment and vessels were "given away," the department carried out its mandate effectively. Even as the yards were cleared of surplus naval equipment, supplies, and even some ships that were under construction, their order books were filled with contracts for merchant ships and their components.

The Quebec City area, especially the less industrialized South Shore, was considered particularly vulnerable to the effects of heavy unemployment, and a special effort was made to minimize the layoffs there.

Jérémie (Jerry) Gagnon (1897–1966). He began work as a "ship fitter" at Davie in 1916, took over from K.M. Wears as superintendent of the yard in 1946, and remained in charge until his retirement in 1963.

Consequently, the port's shipyards were soon building not only for Wartime Shipbuilding Limited, but also for Chinese and French merchant shipping lines to whom loans overseen by the Canadian Export Board were made available. Davie's share of thirteen cargo vessels for France – four lumber carriers, five colliers, a nickel carrier, and three wine carriers, in addition to the contract it had already been given for the *Canadian Challenger* – provided work that lasted until July 1949.

Nor were the shipyards neglected after these contracts had been fulfilled. In 1947, the Liberal government set up a body of experts in the maritime field, the Canadian Maritime Commission, to formulate a Canadian shipping policy that would protect both the shipping and the shipbuilding industries.[3] Their deliberations led to the Canadian Vessel Construction Assistance Act (CVCAA), later dubbed the "Hire Purchase" or "Angel" Plan, which took effect on January 1, 1949.[4] This act enabled an operator to buy a vessel through a tax write-off at perhaps 66 per cent of the original cost, provided it maintained its Canadian registry for five years. In addition to this initiative, as the last of the French vessels left the build-

Aerial view of Davie Shipbuilding and Repairing in 1946, showing the improvements made to the yard during the war, including the mould loft between the plate shop and the main building berths. Centre right, *the* Canadian Challenger. Top left, *beyond the Lorne Dry Dock, the George T. Davie shipyard.*

ing slips, a second program for the construction of Canadian government "civilian" ships had already begun.

The *Canadian Challenger* was completed in December 1946. A 7,500-d.w.t. single-screw diesel-powered passenger and cargo ship, she had been ordered by Wartime Shipbuilding and was purchased during construction by Canadian National Steamships for their West Indies fleet. Like her two sisters, laid down at Canadian Vickers and at Barrow, she was designed by Cox and Stevens of New York and was considered thoroughly up to date

The 7,500 d.w.t. single-screw diesel-powered MV Canadian Challenger *of 1946, the second Canadian Challenger to be built by Davie. Powered with a 6,000-h.p. Vickers-built Sun-Doxford motor, she had a range of 12,000 nautical miles with a sustained speed of 16 knots. In 1958, after twelve years' service in the Canadian National West Indies Steamship Line, she was sold to Cuba.*

both in her design and equipment, and in the comfort she offered. The lines of her bulbous and boldly raked bow and cruiser stern derived from careful research carried out at the National Research Laboratories in Ottawa and the naval tank in Washington. She was powered by a 6,000-h.p. Vickers-built diesel Sun-Doxford motor, and had a range of 12,000 nautical miles with a sustained speed of 16 knots.

After sailing for twelve years under the CN flag, the *Canadian Challenger* was sold to Cuba and continued in service under the name *Ciudad de Habana*.[5] She wasn't soon forgotten. According to Robert McGilvray, who joined the shipyard as a marine draftsman in 1945, her drawings remained a source of design data to which the technical staff frequently referred in the years following her delivery.

The first four ships for French owners were the 7,200-d.w.t. dry cargo carriers *Beyla*, *Bilma*, *Boffa*, and *Bouga*, powered by Sulzer Diesel motors

MV Beyla, *7,200 d.w.t., one of four cargo vessels built as lumber carriers for the Chargeurs Réunis, Paris, outfitting in the Champlain Dry Dock in 1947.* Photo Moderne, courtesy R. Gagnon.

and built to transport lumber from Indo-China and Africa to France. The contract with the Chargeurs Réunis of Paris for these four ships was signed in December 1945. Next off the ways were five colliers of 5,088 d.w.t.: the SS *Dakar, Phryne, Sna-1, Kaolack, Thesee*, followed by the nickel carrier, SS *Quebec*. All six were fitted with Canadian Skinner Uniflow engines. On their maiden voyages, they carried bauxite to France, after which they were put into service transporting coal between Milford Haven and France, except for the *Quebec*, whose run was to New Caledonia.

The last French ships, the 5,500-d.w.t. MV *Croisset, Canteleu*, and *Caumont*, were built for La Compagnie France Navigation's North African trade. They were of shelter-deck type, with powerful Sulzer-type engines manufactured in Le Havre that could develop 4,000 b.h.p. and produce a speed of 14 knots. Designed primarily for the transport of wine, they had twenty-two wine tanks with a carrying capacity for 305,862 gallons built into their lower holds. A team of French specialists was sent over to paint them on the inside with a special formula that gave them a brown porce-

The collier ss Kaolack, *5,088 d.w.t., delivered to the French government in 1948. She and her three sisters were to carry coal from Milford Haven to France.*
Photo Moderne, courtesy R. Gagnon.

lain-like finish. The pumping machinery for filling and emptying the tanks was also sent from France.[6] In each vessel, 220,602 cubic feet were allocated to general cargo with a further 64,000 cubic feet in two sets of refrigerated holds,[7] while a special hold in the stern was fitted with large hooks for the transport of horse meat. They each carried accommodation for a crew of forty-one.

The drawings for the French ships, through no fault of the designers, led to a considerable amount of unexpected extra work. There were two problems: the language and the metric measurements. The plans had been prepared by French naval architects during the German occupation. No doubt their interpretation and specifications were not expected to cause any difficulty to shipyards in Quebec. But the workers at Davie were not accustomed to French shipbuilding terms, and the conversion of measurements from metric to imperial was complicated. The metric sizes of the steel and other components that were asked for did not always correspond with those available in North America. Some items, including some steel bars, for example, were not manufactured in similar shapes.

POST WAR

Preparations are under way for the launching of La Compagnie France Navigation's wine carrier, Croisset, *5,500 d.w.t.* Photo Moderne, courtesy R. Gagnon.

The entire series of plans had therefore to be redrawn and new stability calculations made. All changes were made on the heavier and stronger side, and the resulting increase in tonnage was compensated for by the removal of weight in other areas. Fortunately, the ships were designed to be riveted, but were in fact welded, which in itself produced a certain reduction in weight. As each vessel was completed, still more calculations were necessary to reconvert all measurements to metric for the owners' "as-fitted" plans and tables of transposition.[8]

In order to handle these contracts, Davie had to take on extra technical staff. In the fall of 1945, William (Bill) White, a hull draftsman from the British Admiralty Technical Mission's Ottawa office,[9] and John O'Neill, a former naval architect in the RCN, were recruited.[10] Three employees on the staff of the ailing Morton Engineering and Dry Dock Company, Robert (Bob) W. McGilvray, a marine engineering draftsman, and Jean-Paul Zizka and Gustave Gosselin, both of whom were hull draftsmen, were only too happy to cross the river to work at Davie's. In addition, Ernest Gorman, a marine engineering draftsman from a consulting engineers company in Quebec City, John F. Robertson, an engineer from Toronto, and Ernest

Jean-Paul Zizka, a former Morton employee who joined Davie in 1945 and became senior chief draftsman.

Joyce, an engineering draftsman from the Canadian Department of Munitions and Supply, were hired. Within two years, Leonard (Len) A. Winslade, Pierre Turcotte, Robert Guay, Réal Tessier, Paul Premont, Bruce Morton (son of one of the founders of the Morton shipyard), Raymond Letarte, William Morris, and Hollis Morris had joined the staff. Most of these men would stay with Davie for many years.

While the French ships were still under construction, Davie obtained a contract for its first Canadian government Department of Transport postwar ship. This was the *C.D. Howe*, a one-of-a-kind multi-purpose vessel, designed primarily to inaugurate a new summer service known as the Eastern Arctic Patrol that would carry National Health and Welfare personnel, law-enforcement officials, Department of Northern Affairs and National Resources employees, and others to provide services for more than forty Inuit Arctic settlements. She was to be an icebreaker, weather patrol ship, lighthouse and buoy tender, as well as a floating hospital, cruise ship, and cargo carrier. The rest of the year she was to inspect and service lighthouses and buoys off Newfoundland, Labrador, and the Maritime provinces, except for a short period each spring when she would carry out the duties of an icebreaker and survey ship between the Strait of Belle Isle and Montreal.

POST WAR

Many hours of planning by the technical staff of the Department of Transport, the naval architects Milne, Gilmore & German, and the Davie shipyard staff resulted in a practical layout. An infirmary was included on the upper deck, along with the carpenters' shop, bakery, galley, and other facilities. The landing pad for her helicopter was located aft. Accommodation was provided for eighty-eight passengers and a crew of fifty-eight. She had a deadweight tonnage of 2,673 on an 18-foot 6-inch draft and was fitted with a twin-screw set of Skinner Uniflow 2,000-i.h.p. reciprocating engines with water tube boilers, giving her a speed of 13 1/2 knots and a radius of action of 10,000 nautical miles. She measured 276 by 50 by 26 feet.

The *C.D. Howe* was launched in September 1949 with Mrs. W.H. Howe, daughter-in-law of the Minister of Trade, as sponsor. Her commissioning in the Canadian Coast Guard followed in June, and she left shortly after on her first voyage. The careful planning and construction paid off: the *C.D. Howe* soon became the pride of the fleet. Towards the end of her twenty-one-year career, she served also for valuable oceanographic work. Then, following her decommissioning in 1970, she returned to Lauzon to be given

CMS ss C.D. Howe, *276 feet by 50 feet by 26 feet, 3,628 gross tonnage, built for the Eastern Arctic Patrol in 1950.* Courtesy R. Gagnon.

a special outfit for a new and different role. She had been bought by Vestgron Mines of Trail, British Columbia, who sent her to a fjord in Greenland to provide a snug berth for the workers engaged in their operations there. She changed flags in 1974 when she was sold to a Spanish citizen.[11]

The government used the occasion of the launching of the *C.D. Howe* to announce the imminent signing of two major contracts with Davie, one for the construction of an icebreaker, and the other appointing Davie the lead shipyard for a fleet of "Influence"-type minesweepers for the RCN. Canada had joined the North Atlantic Treaty Organization as a founding member earlier in 1949 and the minesweepers were to be built in consultation with her partners, Great Britain and the United States.

At about the same time, the yard obtained other contracts for the conversion or refit of frigates and minesweepers built during the war. In order to handle all the naval work without prejudicing its capacity for private construction, six experienced men were engaged. Among them were Tom Gibson, a Scottish senior naval architect who had spent many years working in Burma and Africa, and Warren Havens, an experienced hull outfit specialist.[12]

As lead yard for the minesweepers, Davie was responsible for producing the working plans and specifications, directing all experimentation, building the prototype, and organizing the procurement of any material not supplied by the government. This included examining tenders and obtaining government approval of those accepted. After ordering the material for the lead ship, Davie had then to send copies of the purchase orders to the "follow" shipyards for them to duplicate. Each yard was required to pay its own bills and recover the cost from the government. Construction of the minesweepers, together with the conversions and refits, was expected to provide the shipyard with work for some time. In fact, as far as the minesweepers were concerned, it provided rather more work than anticipated.

By November 1949, four designers, twelve senior draftsmen (including four lent by the Port Arthur, Victoria Machinery, and St. John shipyards) and fourteen intermediate draftsmen were working on the minesweeper plans at DSRCL. So that the boats would not be affected by magnetic mines, it had been decided that they would be of composite construction, with mahogany skin over aluminum frames and bulkheads, and that they would have an aluminum superstructure, furniture, and fittings. On March 21, 1950, work had advanced to the stage that Davie was asked to proceed with the construction of the first ship, HMCS *Gaspé*. Within a week, however, it was "back to the drawing board," because important changes in propeller arrangements were requested that rendered useless almost all the design and mould loft work that had already been done. This type of setback is to be expected when building a prototype, and invariably it triggers others further along the production planning line. But many of the problems that arose in the case of the minesweepers were of a technological nature and directly related to the decision to build the vessels of aluminum.

Aluminum companies had begun promoting the use of aluminum in marine construction in the 1930s until the war put a halt to experimentation. Following the war there were several instances where aluminum was used to reduce the weight of a superstructure, notably in the case of the SS *Redfern* in 1946, and her sister ship SS *Redriver*. On the west coast, a firefighting vessel in Vancouver Harbour was designed with deckhouses of aluminum to reduce her topside weight and lower the centre of gravity, while at Charlie's yard next door to Davie, five vessels with superstructures and minor bulkheads of aluminum were built for the Yangtze River trade.[13] But when it came to building a welded aluminum hull, there were still many problems that had not been solved. At the Navy's request, experiments were carried out at the McGill University laboratories to determine the most suitable aluminum alloys for the purpose, while joints of different kinds were prepared at the yard to be tested there for tensile strength, and experiments in bending, bevelling, and flanging were carried out in the shipyard's shops.

The plates, shapes, and rivets ordered from the Aluminum Company of Canada had in many cases to be custom made, so that deliveries tended to

TRANSITION TO PEACETIME PRODUCTION

be slow, and this sometimes led to structural changes and the revision of specifications. For the mahogany shell to be bolted on to the aluminum, special aluminum nuts and bolts had to be designed, as had the special manganese bronze pulleys, shaft brackets, and rudders. There were even problems in obtaining sufficient mahogany of the required quality. Of the load of mahogany deck planking received in December 1950, only 14 per cent was considered acceptable! Because of this, as well as the mahogany's exorbitant cost, B.C. fir was substituted.

As neither Davie nor the follow yards had previous experience in working in aluminum, they were able to get government assistance to equip themselves for the job. The government insisted, for instance, on a strict tally of the weight of the aluminum used, so appropriate scales headed the list. Tanks for pickling the aluminum as the work proceeded, one for plates and the other for shapes, were another requirement, as were a special Bull Yoke Riveter to drive aluminum rivets and an Argon arc welding machine. Even a covered slipway had to be built, as the Navy insisted that the vessels be assembled under cover.

After a great deal of research and development, the keel of the *Gaspé* was laid on March 15, 1951, and her launching took place in November. She then set out on her trials. Engineers were baffled when it was found that in the Arctic the aluminum attracted magnetic mines, and it was decided to do away with aluminum decks. As a result, the two Influence minesweepers, HMCS *Cowichan* and *Ungava*, that followed were given wooden ones. The minesweeper program was extremely costly because of the large amount of development that was required, but the Navy regarded it as an important introduction to the techniques with which it felt it should be familiar. It was not only the Navy that benefited. The techniques learned and the special equipment that the government paid for were of considerable advantage to the shipyards when they were put to use in merchant ship construction.[14]

Following the delivery of the *C.D. Howe* in June 1950, the diesel-powered steel tug *Otis Wack*, built to the design of the New York naval architect Robert W. Morrell, was completed for the Gypsum Packet Company of Windsor, Nova Scotia. There were no other orders for new merchant ships in the order book at the time, but plans for the new icebreaker, the 5,678-ton *d'Iberville*, were well advanced.

Thus the first five postwar years came to an end, and for Davie they were positive ones. Eleven merchant ships and a large icebreaker were delivered, and a healthy volume of repairs contributed on average 40 per cent of the gross profits of the shipyard. Profits from the operation of the shipyard's fleet of tugs reached $66,840 in 1950. And even if the yard's balance sheet was not what it had been during the war, it showed gross earnings for the five years of $2,388,822, and net earnings of $1,575,946 – a considerable improvement on pre-war days.

From the men's point of view, there was a radical change during these years, for they switched their union allegiance and joined the ranks of the Confédération des travailleurs catholiques du Canada (C.T.C.C.) under the name "Le Syndicat des Travailleurs des Chantiers Maritimes," on February 23, 1949. They had previously been represented by a number of international trades unions – the International Brotherhood of Electrical Workers, the International Moulders and Foundry Workers Union of North America, the United Association of Journeymen, and others – which had led to constant quarrelling.[15] There had been discontent with the autocratic and sometimes abusive rule of certain foremen, which was not unusual in the large industries of the day, and the men looked forward to the new union rectifying or at least improving the situation. They would not be disappointed. The new one-year collective agreement, which was signed within a week, took the first steps in the right direction. It was agreed that departmental seniority would prevail, and in order to determine the seniority rights of company employees in the case of layoffs, rehiring, promotion, and demotion, consideration would be given to seniority, ability, special qualifications, discipline, efficiency, and absenteeism. According to the new scale of wages, tradesmen were to be paid from 85 cents to $1.07, with the exception of rivet testers, pattern makers, loftsmen, and coppersmiths, who would earn a little more. The rate for labourers was fixed at sixty-nine cents, and for helpers, trainees, and youths under eighteen years of age, between sixty-one and seventy-nine cents. Night-shift workers would earn one and an eighth times the regular rate, and overtime in excess of fifteen minutes, one and a half times the rate. The rate would be doubled for work done on Sundays or on December 8, and the length of both the day and night shifts would be reduced eight and a half hours. Paid holidays were to be taken during the last and first weeks of the year. It was also agreed that a whistle would blow five minutes before starting time to enable the men to be at their jobs on time, and another ten minutes before the end of the shift to give them time to clean up. For the time being, there was no "closed shop."

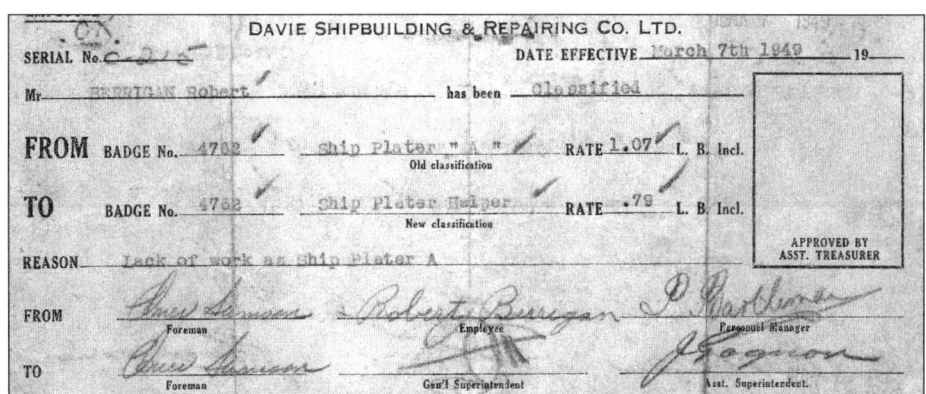

Berrigan father and son worked at the yard. When work was slack, Berrigan, Sr., took a pay decrease and worked as a helper so as to have a pay packet, though a reduced one, to take home. Courtesy R. Berrigan.

On a wider front, the political situation was far from encouraging. The postwar years saw the hopes of those who had lived through the "war to end wars" shattered. The Berlin blockade and the resulting airlift resulted in a stand-off between East and West. Then, in June 1950, North Korean forces invaded South Korea, and the UN Security Council responded with a vote in favour of military intervention. Canada provided eight RCN destroyers in relays of three as its naval contribution, the first three leaving Esquimalt for the war zone on July 5, 1950. They joined in the naval blockade, supported South Korean ground forces by bombarding North Korean positions, and served as escort vessels for amphibious forces and aircraft carriers, performing well and learning valuable lessons.[16] The experience would have an immediate and far-reaching effect on defence policy. The goal of the RCN became a 100-ship fleet equipped for coastal and harbour defence, and for anti-submarine warfare and convoy escort roles.[17] C.D. Howe was named minister of the new Department of Defence Production (DDP), and before long government contracts were accounting for half the work that was being carried out in Canadian shipyards.[18] Not only was the construction of a wide variety of ships, including anti-submarine warfare (ASW) frigates, escorts, minesweepers, gate vessels, and an arctic patrol vessel now on the books, but a great deal of overhauling, rearming, and refitting would also be required.

William Coverdale did not live to see the boom years that lay ahead for Canadian shipyards. In 1949, twenty-seven years after he took over the presidency of CSL, he died. As a young man, he had rescued both the CSL and Davie from the sorry state into which they had been driven. He managed their recovery decisively and successfully. As he grew older, he became more interested in the CSL luxury hotels and the antique Canadiana that he delighted in acquiring for them. As a result, the CSL group of companies gradually lost the bold leadership he had originally brought to it. A new broom was needed to sweep away the unproductive operations that had accumulated and to rationalize the rest with the same vigour that Coverdale himself had once displayed. For the time being, however, Colonel K.R. Marshall, a former director, was named president of the company, while R. Brock Thomson, the secretary of CSL, continued as president and CEO of DSRCL.

Colonel Marshall's presidency occurred during a difficult period in CSL's history. A power struggle developed between Sir James Dunn, president of the Algoma Steel Company, who was out to gain control, and those shareholders who opposed his bid. It was also during Marshall's term of office that the SS *Noronic* burned in Toronto Harbour in September 1949 with the tragic loss of 118 passengers. The commission that investigated the fire made such stringent recommendations that CSL would have had to put an immediate end to the entire Great White Fleet had they all been implemented. Though their severity was eventually reduced, it was decided to cancel plans to replace the *Kingston*, which ran between Toronto and Prescott, and simply to retire her and discontinue the run.[19] Then, only seven months later, the SS *Quebec* burned at Tadoussac, with a loss of seven lives. In both cases, arson was strongly suspected but never proved. Whatever the cause, it was the beginning of the end for the Great White Fleet, the pride of Canada Steamship Lines.[20]

After the war, both the George T. Davie yard at Lauzon and Morton's at Quebec also received a fair share of government contracts. The GTD shipyard built sixteen cargo vessels, including five for China, and five scows for the Department of Public Works. The Morton shipyard, which was sold to Hervé Baribeau in 1946 and became the St. Lawrence Metal & Marine Works Inc., had similar contracts, but would build its last ship in 1949.

George T. Davie, Ltd. had come through the war in excellent shape. The staff was still headed by Charlie Davie, and though he is generally remembered as having been "spoiled" as a young man, particularly by his uncle Foddie, and though he undoubtedly deserved his reputation as a bon vivant, he was serious about shipbuilding and ran an efficient yard. Maurice Paquet was his assistant manager and secretary-treasurer; J.B. Lemelin, the hull superintendent; J.A.D. Sampson, marine superintendent;

Maurice Paquet, long-time general manager of the George T. Davie shipyard at Lauzon. Courtesy Mme. Carmelle Paquet.

and Lorne Latremouille, purchasing agent. The staff of the drawing office, which came into being only in 1942, had proved itself to the extent that the yard was named lead yard for the construction of the RCN's new trawler-type gate vessels in 1949. There were now four building ways, one of which had been lengthened to 500 feet, with provision for its further extension to 700 feet at some future date should the need arise.

The shipyard itself gave the impression of quiet efficiency. Nothing was left lying around on the benches, floor, or other work areas. The men took a certain pride in the appearance of the yard. Even if it was busy, it seemed ready for captain's rounds. Although it was not able to compete with its far larger neighbour for the largest contracts, Charlie's yard could hold its own in the quality both of its building and its repairs. It got particularly high marks for the finishing work, its carpenters having an excellent reputation for the way they used every possible nook and cranny in a ship's interior to good effect.

In addition to a full order book of civilian construction, the shipyard now had the capacity to repair ocean-going ships of up to 12,000 tons and began to do so. A number of Park freighters were converted from coal to oil in the yard. And, in addition to the contract for the gate vessels, there were others from the Department of National Defence for a minesweeper, a loop layer, a Norten-type tug, and the conversion of two minesweepers and two frigates.

But tragedy was about to strike the Davie family once again. Since his father's death, Charlie had drawn even closer to his uncle Foddie, who was now getting on in years. On New Year's Eve 1946, Charlie started out from Quebec for the habitual exchange of New Year greetings at the Homestead, but on the way he lost control of his car, crashed into a bus, and died instantly. For many of his workers, Charlie was not only an employer but also a friend since childhood. His loss affected them personally. Uncle Foddie, all of whose aspirations had been directed towards Charlie, suffered a shock from which he would not recover. One hundred and ten years before, the first Allison Davie had met a violent death in the river. He had left four sons to carry on the family shipyard, and between them and their descendants they had founded three other shipyards, but the line of Davie shipbuilders had now come to an end, for though Charlie had been married for eighteen years, he had no children, and the rest of Allison and Elizabeth Davie's surviving descendants had other interests.

With a heavy heart, the men at the yard picked up their tools and carried on. Foddie Davie was elected interim president in Charlie's place, but handed the office over to Charlie's brother-in-law, André Delagrave, shortly after, retaining only the direction of the Levis yard himself. With the help of Maurice Paquet, who had served Charlie so well, as manager of the yard, and Lorne Latremouille, his assistant, Delagrave would succeed in keeping the Lauzon yard going, while maintaining the friendly atmosphere that it had enjoyed when Charlie was alive. Though he had no previous shipyard experience, Delagrave had a knack for knowing when to let things take care of themselves. When his men went on strike one time, he told them to let him know when they wanted to return to work, then left for Florida with his daughter, Brenda. After a while, two delegates from the shipyard turned up there, and he returned to reopen the yard. That was his style. He avoided confrontation. Above all, he had genuine affection for the

POST WAR

André Delagrave (1910–57), Charlie Davie's brother-in-law, who took over on his death as president of the George T. Davie shipyard. Courtesy Brenda Wilson.

workers and took delight at Christmas, for instance, in arranging for Santa Claus to arrive at the yard on a sleigh bringing a load of turkeys, which he handed out to the workers with obvious pleasure.

As was the case at most Canadian shipyards, one of Delagrave's constant problems was the difficulty of obtaining technical staff, for though there were always plenty of workers available when extra men were needed in the yard, there was no local training program that produced sufficiently qualified draftsmen. Work that the drawing office, under the naval architect Joseph Vallières, was unable to handle, was therefore farmed out to Alex Campbell, who still ran his office in Montreal. In 1950, Delagrave, who had decided to follow the practice of other Canadian shipyards, visited the United Kingdom to find some extra draftsmen. At a reception in Glasgow, he met a naval architect by the name of John Stubbs, hired him shortly after, and asked him to pick three draftsmen to bring to Canada. The choice was a good one. John Stubbs settled in well and was an excellent replacement for Vallières when he retired.[21]

Meanwhile, at the Levis yard, Foddie Davie's staff despaired of his shaking the trauma of his nephew's death. At seventy-seven years of age, his main interest in life had suddenly been snatched from him. No longer resilient, he preferred to run the shipyard at a loss than to take the risks that were always involved in shipbuilding. His employees, however, wanted to be as proud of their yard as the men at the Chantier Maritime de St. Laurent on the Isle of Orleans, the other small yard in the district, which had expanded during the war and was now flourishing under the presidency of Roméo Fillion. They tried to persuade their boss to start building instead of restricting the yard's activities to repairs and winterings but, always a retiring man, Allison Davie withdrew into himself and would not listen.

Part Seven

THE GOLDEN YEARS

Minesweeper HMCS Fundy MCB *159 shares the skyline with the Château Frontenac Hotel and other well-known Quebec landmarks following her commissioning in 1956.*

17

THE McLAGAN-LOWERY TEAM

1951-58

SIR JAMES DUNN, Q.C., president of the Algoma Steel Company, had been patiently buying up Canada Steamship Lines stock for a number of years, confident that one day he would be in a majority position and have the CSL fleet at Algoma's beck and call. In 1951, he further increased his CSL holdings, which, added to the support he obtained from other shareholders, gave him the control he sought. His first concern was to find the right man to run the shipping line and its subsidiaries, and he turned to C.D. Howe, who as minister of various industry-related portfolios had dealt with the top men in the field and was therefore well qualified to advise him. It was Howe who approached T. Rodgie McLagan, the general manager of Canadian Vickers Limited, on Dunn's behalf and succeeded in breaking down his initial resistance to the offer, thus preparing the way for an agreement between the two men.[1] An engineer with a dedication to efficiency, short and stocky of stature but long on determination and drive, Rodgie McLagan took over the duties of president and CEO of Canada Steamship Lines on August 1, 1951.

McLagan also temporarily assumed Brock Thomson's duties as head of Davie until he could find a suitable candidate to fill the post.[2] McLagan then endeavoured to persuade the man he had hired five years earlier as his

THE GOLDEN YEARS

Left: *T. Rodgie McLagan (1897–1972)* Right: *Lowery was Richard Lowery. president of all the Canada Steamship Lines shipyards from 1951 to 1971.*

naval architect and assistant manager at Vickers to join him at CSL, convinced that Richard Lowery had the requisite qualities and experience. Lowery had learned his trade on the Tyne where, as a student, he won scholarships in both Naval Architecture and Marine Engineering. He had spent five years as naval architect and assistant general manager of the Singapore Harbour Board, and after the fall of Singapore had built and managed shipyards in Australia for the Melbourne Harbour Trust. Following his repatriation to Britain at the end of the war, he joined Canadian Vickers. McLagan knew him to be both a first-class naval architect respected by government officials and civilian customers alike, and an executive who ran an efficient department and maintained a balanced relationship with his staff. He could also be counted on to deliver an excellent after-dinner speech. It is not surprising that McLagan was determined to have him "aboard."

The Davie shipyard was the bait. Though Vickers had five covered berths where work could be carried out during the winter months under optimum conditions, none was longer than 500 feet. Larger vessels had to be laid down and launched in two separate sections, which were then dry-docked and joined. The Davie shipyard had no such constraints. Conveniently located between the Lorne and Champlain dry docks, with ample space for the extension of its building slips and other facilities and an open run to the sea, it had far greater potential as a shipyard than had Vickers, and Lowery recognized that McLagan was offering him the opportunity to head what he felt could become a "world-class shipyard." Moreover, it was not only the presidency of Davie that he was being offered, but the presidency of all five CSL shipyards,[3] a prestigious position. He hesitated to leave his safe berth at Canadian Vickers, which he had hoped would lead him to the general managership of the firm, but he was finally won over. By October 1951, McLagan was able to announce that Richard Lowery had accepted his appointment as president of the CSL shipyards.

Once he had made up his mind, there was no damping Lowery's enthusiasm. This was fortunate – much had to be done during the next few years. For decades the Canadian government had sought the co-operation of the United States in building a seaway along the St. Lawrence to the Great Lakes, and constantly it had encountered opposition from Congress. Finally, the government of Louis St. Laurent had decided to go ahead with or without U.S. participation. The St. Lawrence Seaway Authority would be constituted by an Act of Parliament in December 1951 with a mandate to open up the Great Lakes to deep-sea vessels. As the shipbuilding boom that the seaway was expected to touch off was still several years away, the new team at CSL had the time it needed to make improvements to the shipyards and strengthen their staff so that they would be in a position to benefit from it.

In the spring of 1952, Al Morley, who had taken over from David Craig as general manager in 1944, left the shipyard and Robert (Bert) Black was appointed to take his place. Like Lowery, Black was well-known to

Part of the Drawing Office staff in 1951. Identified by number, they are: 1. Fernand Gaboury; 2. Robert Guay; 3. Laurent Cantin; 4. Gilles Fortin; 5. Marcel Pageau; 6. Madeleine Bureau; 7. Vera Small; 8. J. Harrington; 9. Fernand Mercure; 10. Paul Premont; 11. J.-Paul Zizka; 12. Eddie Lamb; 13. Rita Dugas; 14. Maurice Tremblay; 15. Georges Carrier; 16. Albert Caron; 17. Joe Gagnon; 18. Raymond Letarte; 19. Laurent Tremblay; 20. Gilles Beaudouin; 21. Gerry Hogan; 22. Warren Havens; 23. Donald O'Grady.

McLagan, having been his chief hull draftsman at Vickers before joining Davie. A hard worker with a quiet sense of humour, soft-spoken, and respected, he is remembered by old-time shipyard employees for his thick Scottish accent, which turned such simple phrases as "Beg your pardon?" into something quite unintelligible to the average Quebecker. Charlie Sauvageau became his assistant general manager, while keeping the office of comptroller, and Bill White his naval architect. Ian M. McGregor, the repairs manager; A. McLean (Archie) Kerr, production and construction manager; Bob McGilvray, chief engineer; and Jerry Gagnon, yard superintendent, made up the team.

It would not be plain sailing for Black. The new union, having consolidated its support, now felt sufficiently confident to make another more determined attempt to improve its members' working conditions. Among the changes it sought was a reduction in the work week from forty-eight to forty-five hours, and a wage increase of twenty-five cents an hour across the board. Negotiations came to an impasse and the work force went out on strike. The shipyard had several important contracts on hand. The two-month-long walkout that preceded renewal of the contract caused considerable upheaval to production schedules and prevented any deliveries being made in 1952. By the year's end, however, the workers had prevailed in reducing the foremen's domination of them and the yard had settled down.

A significant element in McLagan and Lowery's long-term plan for the shipyard was setting up a general engineering division, or Industrial Division, as it was first known, which would do engineering work unrelated to shipbuilding, using the skills and facilities available at the yard. This, they hoped, would break Davie's dependence on the notoriously unstable shipping market by providing employment for a core of valuable workers through the slumps, so that they would be available when times improved. In 1953, the original machine shop was extended to the southeast to accommodate the new Industrial Division, which opened for business in 1954 with Pat MacDonald as manager at the head of a team of five draftsmen. At first, simple engineering such as the manufacture of pressure vessels requiring a relatively low degree of measurement accuracy was undertaken. Gradually, as additional equipment was installed, the work diversified.

At the same time, other parts of the yard were being upgraded. In 1955, a badly needed modern pipe shop, 140 by 60 feet, took shape to the north of the Industrial Division building, which freed sufficient space in the old shop for a centralized modern store, improving the flow of ship-building operations. Gradually the yard was being updated when, on the evening of October 27, 1955, fate intervened to force a more drastic pace of change.

"We were playing cards at a charity event in the church hall," Roméo Bissonette, a former worker, recounts, "when we heard someone shout, 'The yard's on fire.' Jumping to our feet, we hesitated for a moment, staring at each other in disbelief, and then, scrambling for the door, rushed down there together." Held back at the barrier by security guards, the men watched in horror as teams of fire fighters battled the flames. Some of the older men wept openly at the destruction of the yard that meant so much to them. Those with homes close by trained hoses on them to protect them from flying sparks, while their families waited fully dressed in case they were ordered to abandon them. Others tore down the wooden fences along which the flames spread. But for most there was nothing to do but watch and wait for four long hours – until nothing was left of the principal shops but twisted girders. The foundry, plate shop, carpentry shop, prefabricating shops, garage, canteen, police and first-aid post and other stores, and all but the brick-built east end of the steel fabricating shop, were gone. Three of the workers' homes were burned to the ground as well, while several others were badly damaged. It was fortunate, indeed, that only a small night shift was working and there was no loss of life.

CONSTABLES AND FIREMEN

LIKE THE Plant Division, constables and firemen play an important role in keeping the shipyard running on a steady keel. Constables' responsibilities cover the overall security of the yard: they control the visitors; man the ambulance, co-operating with the first-aid staff; and report any incidents to management. Apart from working closely with the constables in cases of emergency, firemen are responsible for security against fire both of the plant and of any ships that may be berthed at the yard. To this end, they connect the safety systems of ships under construction and repair. They are in charge of the sprinkler system and do rounds each night. They man the fire post and answer calls, while ensuring good co-ordination with the local fire brigade.

THE McLAGAN-LOWERY TEAM

The destruction caused by the shipyard fire on October 27, 1955.

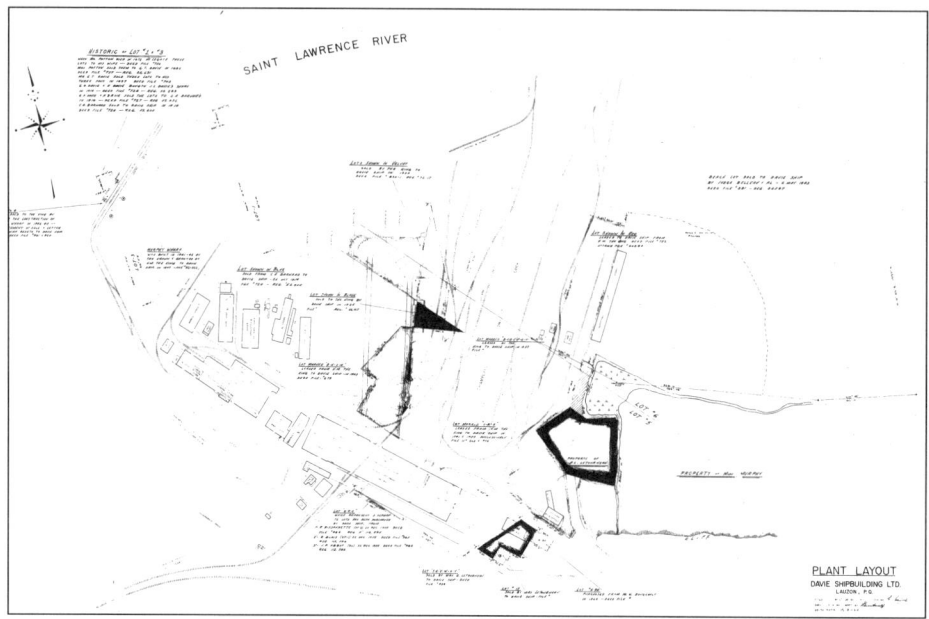

The rebuilt and re-structured Davie shipyard following the fire of 1955. "Plant Layout: DSRCL, Lauzon, P.Q." [1" = 200'] Checked by C. Gagne, app'd by MacDonald, 5-4-60, up-to-date 17 August 1960, showing road to be leased to DS.

Fortunately, the office building and drawing office with all the records and plans were spared. The Time Office building came through unscathed because those who had watched the fire from its roof extinguished the sparks as they landed on it. The naval store survived, and the three ships under construction, HMCS *Gatineau*, HMCS *Fundy*, and MV *Bluenose* also escaped unharmed.

Although many members of the staff had spent the whole night at the yard,[4] they were all back at their desks at eight the next morning, handling the many problems they had to confront. Reaction from head office was equally fast. Before the embers were cold, Richard Lowery arrived with a team of architects and builders to begin planning the reconstruction of the plant. Sir James Dunn, however, was not immediately of the same mind. When he toured the ruins with McLagan, his first reaction was to claim the insurance money and close the yard because, with four other yards, CSL did not need it. But when McLagan protested that it was impossible to close it, as there were ships under construction and others ordered, Sir James reluctantly concurred. "Oh well!" he reportedly said. "I guess we'll have to rebuild."

Unavoidably, there were layoffs, but the workers rose to the occasion and, in an all-out effort, completed the contracts that were under way with a minimum of delay. When the insurance money for the fire was collected in late December, Sir James Dunn ordered from his sickbed that the whole amount, nearly $2 million, be spent on rebuilding the yard.[5] It would be his last decision affecting Davie, for he died on the first day of the New Year and was thus denied the satisfaction of seeing the modern fabricating shop that was ready by the following spring.

Built of steel and aluminum, the shop was 613 feet long and 150 feet wide, with two 75-foot bays, one higher than the other for fabricating ship components. Two bridge cranes served the entire shop. The yard's new mould loft was built above the prefabricating shop's low bay, so that the area in front of the shop, where the old mould loft had been, would be available for lengthening the building slips. As a necessary complement to the new equipment, heavy lifting cranes were ordered for the fitting-out berths. The shipyard carpenters cannot have been altogether disappointed to leave their makeshift quarters behind the plate shop and move into a brand-new two-storey joiner shop. But the fast-growing needs of the prefabricating shop had been underestimated, and a year later when the builders returned to enlarge the main office building and put up a new garage, the low bay was lengthened by another 100 feet, and in 1957 the high bay was extended by an extra 200 feet, at which time it was equipped with three additional cranes.[6] In two years, the yard was entirely rebuilt. In the process, the previously scattered facilities of nineteen destroyed buildings were brought together under three roofs. With little strain on the company's finances, the yard had been radically improved. In fact, a brand-

Destroyer escort HMCS Gatineau DE *236 of 1959, 368 by 43 by 29 feet 3 inches.*

new yard was built almost on the proceeds from the insurance alone.

The McLagan–Lowery team took over at a time when DSRCL had a fair amount of government work in hand. Contracts for the Navy included the three minesweepers, which were in various stages of completion; a destroyer escort vessel, HMCS *Gatineau*, for which the contract had been signed in June; and the refits and conversions of the frigates *Jonquière* and *Cap de la Madeleine* and the Bangor minesweeper *Medicine Hat*, which were under way. At the end of 1953, following the delivery of the first two AMC minesweepers of the Influence Program, HMCS *Gaspé* and *Cowichan*, Davie was named lead yard for six MCB minesweepers of the F59 class. Only the prototype, however, was to be built at Davie. By this time, contracts from the private sector began to come in. The regular drawing office staff became so busy that in the summer of 1954 a second drawing office was set up under the direction of Tom Gibson to handle the preparation of plans and procurement of materials for the MCB program.[7]

As work on the new destroyer escort vessel and the MCBs progressed, contracts were signed for the refit and conversion of a third frigate, *La Hulloise*, while HMCS *Algonquin*[8] came in for refit and repairs following a collision. The Navy took delivery of MV *Fundy*, the lead boat of the MCB

Lieutenant Commander Ronald Hanlon, of the Principal Naval Overseer's staff; Tom Gibson, co-ordinator for Naval Programs; Lieutenant Commander Jim Smith, executive officer of the destroyer HMCS Algonquin; Commodore Ralph McClean, her first captain; Marc Levésque, superintendent of Electrical Installations, shortly before Hull 670 was accepted and commissioned in November 1973.

minesweepers, in 1956, and the launching of the destroyer escort HMCS *Gatineau* took place in June 1957. *Gatineau* would not be completed at the Davie yard, however: when a strike interrupted her outfitting, her lines were cut during the night and she sailed to Halifax, where the remainder of the work was done.

Meanwhile, Canada's Cold War commitments to NATO meant that naval contracts would continue to flow to her shipyards. Tom Gibson, who had administered the minesweeper contracts, was given the new post of co-ordinator for naval programs. He was responsible for all correspondence and contracts, for obtaining the drawings, and for seeing that all alterations were noted on the specifications and drawings. As the shipyard's representative with the Department of Defence Production, he also attended all bidders' conferences. These were often hectic meetings where he was kept very much on his toes, both to prevent other builders from gaining a bidding advantage, and to see that no unacceptable conditions were imposed by the government. He represented the yard at these conferences for twenty-five years, until 1982, though in the last three years following his official retirement at sixty-five years of age, he acted as a consultant.[9] Throughout his career, he was deeply respected for his intimate knowledge of the contracts and of government projects. He was always a major player behind the scenes in the financial and contractual successes of the company.

For years, naval contracts had required an inordinate amount of paper work. By 1956, it had become so excessive that a defence supply naval shipbuilding panel was set up to promote better understanding between the various government departments and to monitor the work of such organizations as the Naval Central Drawing Office[10] and the Naval Engineering Test Establishment. The panel was headed by Rear-Admiral (Ret'd) S. Mathwin Davis and included representatives of the RCN, of the deputy minister of the Department of National Defence, of the director of Shipbuilding Branch of the DDP, and of the Treasury Branch.[11] Its work led to the establishment in 1958 of the Naval Central Procurement Agency, which took over the entire responsibility for the purchase of all defensive and offensive armament and was also instrumental in transferring management of the Naval Central Drawing Office to the lead yard. The Naval Central Procurement Agency operated at a time when a large number of naval contracts were being given out. As cost-plus contracts gave way, first to incentive contracts and eventually to fixed prices, it helped make the transition easier. When its job was done, it faded away.[12]

The second important branch of government (besides the Navy) that called for the construction and maintenance of ships and other floating equipment was the Department of Transport. Its needs were handled by the Marine Superintendent's Branch. It was with the relatively small staff of this department that Davie dealt when building what were known then as Canadian Marine, but would later be known as Coast Guard, ships. Among those of unique design was the icebreaker *d'Iberville*, whose plans and specifications were prepared by Mathwin Davis of Milne, Gilmore & German, the naval architects for the *C.D. Howe*. These plans included a specially designed bow. Unlike the *C.D. Howe*, which was not a true icebreaker but a Special Arctic Service Vessel with a reinforced hull, the *d'Iberville* was not only an icebreaker but the first of Canada's "heavy" icebreakers. Her 2-inch-thick hull plating made her a difficult ship to build, but the problems were regarded as just another challenge by the technical staff and workers, who took pride in solving them. She was powered with two Vickers-Skinner Uniflow reciprocating steam engines of 5,400 h.p. each. She had a radius of action of 12,000 miles and carried two heli-

CGS d'Iberville

copters. Her double radar protection, depth indicators, and gyro compasses gave her the advantages of every known aid to navigation of that time. Designed to be operated by a crew of seventy-five, she had accommodation also for fifty passengers and could carry 350 tons of cargo.

Following completion of her trial trip in June 1953, the *d'Iberville* steamed on to Britain without returning to the shipyard. There she represented the Canadian civilian fleet at the Spithead Review celebrating the coronation of Queen Elizabeth II. The occasion would be remembered with particular pleasure not only by Richard Lowery and his wife, who made the trip as official guests, but also by some shipyard workers who made the trip because there was no time to "unload" them. On her return to regular duty, the *d'Iberville*'s first northern trip took her to Resolute Bay on Cornwallis Island and to Alexandria Fjord on Ellesmere Island. She helped in the establishment of a new RCMP station within 800 miles of the North Pole, a mission that proved her hull's resistance to the extra-thick ice. Its strength allowed her to penetrate farther north than any Canadian icebreaker had previously sailed. A side mission was also undertaken: the delivery of ballot boxes by helicopter to isolated settlements on the Labrador coast in preparation for the general election. This first tour quickly established confidence in the ship. In the years ahead, *d'Iberville* would prove herself over and over again.[13]

Other contracts signed with the Department of Transport in 1955 included one for a new lighthouse tender and buoy vessel, the MV *Montmorency* of 1,200 s.h.p., designed by Alex C. Campbell & Son of Montreal, and built for service at Parry Sound, Ontario; and another, for the medium-size MV *Montcalm* 4,000 i.h.p., to serve out of Quebec. The *Montcalm* proved herself when, on her way back to the shipyard following her trials, the captain signalled the engine room "full astern," but through a malfunction of the equipment, the engine room understood "full ahead." The ship hit the wharf at a 90-degree angle and climbed onto it a length of 100 feet. Louis Rochette, a member of the staff who was waiting on the wharf to hear how the trials went, claims that he actually ran away when he saw her coming. The ship's captain told him later that it was the best trial ever: "No damage at all after hitting that wharf at 6 knots." Needless to say, the wharf was not as fortunate.

Contracts for two more icebreakers were awarded in 1957. These were the 4,250-s.h.p. *Sir Humphrey Gilbert*, of similar hull design to two other DOT vessels, the *Montcalm* and the *Wolfe*,[14] but the only one of the three

CGS Sir John A. Macdonald, *triple-screw diesel icebreaker, of 1960.*

with diesel propulsion and, in a very different class, the powerful *John A. Macdonald*. The *Sir Humphrey Gilbert*, which was named for Newfoundland's first governor,[15] would be based at St. John's and serve both as an icebreaker and as a tender for navigation aids in the waters off Newfoundland and the Maritime provinces.

However, naval and Department of Transport construction accounted for only a part of the production of the yard. In fact, the first contracts signed by Lowery as president of the shipyard were not for the government vessels, but for two 28,000-ton commercial tankers. They were the first of a variety of merchant vessels that Davie built between 1951 and 1959, including tankers, freighters, bulk carriers, lake canallers, ferries, and tugs. Each of their launchings was regarded by McLagan and Lowery as an occasion to boost the image of both Canada Steamship Lines and Davie. Perhaps there was an element of competition with other Canadian yards, too, for launchings by other firms similarly were made the occasion for an elaborate celebration. The principal visitors were put up at the luxurious Château Frontenac Hotel in Quebec and driven to the shipyard in a cavalcade of Cadillacs with an escort of motorcycle police by way of the Quebec Bridge, or, if circumstances permitted and a ferryboat was available, were ferried directly across the river to the yard. When the launching ceremony ended, the guests were returned to the hotel for a reception and lavish banquet designed to affirm that Canada Steamship Lines' star was in the ascendant and all was well.[16]

In this typical fashion, in July 1953 the double ceremony of the launching of the 28,000-ton tanker *Andros Venture* and the keel-laying of her sister, the *Andros Fortune*, took place, with Maurice Duplessis, premier of the province, at the head of a list of several hundred guests.[17] The good publicity generated by the event would be followed by bad, however. A local newspaper reporter misunderstood the terms of the contract, which was for one vessel with an option for a second one, and wrote that Davie had been given a $6-million contract, but it had wound up costing $12 million! Nevertheless, in building these two ships, which were almost three times

THE GOLDEN YEARS

Oil tanker Andros Venture, *built for the Andros Shipping Co., Ltd., in 1953.*

the size of the *Canadian Challenger* or the 10,000-ton cargo ships built during the war, Davie once again had the distinction of building the biggest ships yet laid down in Canada.

Because of their considerable length, there was some concern about the effect of launching them stern-first (at Collingwood they were launched sideways). A test was set up to measure the flexibility of the first of the pair, the *Andros Venture*, from the time the bottle of champagne was broken and the vessel began to move. It showed that the maximum sag during launching had been three and a half to four inches and the hog only half of an inch, and that she had returned to her original form immediately. There had been no need for concern. She was completed in November that year and was the first ship delivered under the shipyard's new streamlined name, from November 3, Davie Shipbuilding Limited.[18]

The 12,400-ton freighter ss *Sunrip*, the largest ocean-going general cargo ship yet built in Canada and possibly the first in Canada with an all-aluminum superstructure, was another of Davie's landmark ships. The lessons learned in working aluminum during the construction of the naval minesweepers proved to be invaluable. The *Sunrip*'s lightweight superstructure made from 136 long tons of aluminum meant that she had 165 long tons' capacity greater than she would have had had she been of all-steel con-

The 12,400-ton freighter SS Sunrip *of 1954, 450 by 62 feet 6 inches by 31 feet three inches, the largest ocean-going general cargo ship yet built in Canada at that time, her aluminum superstructure gleaming in the sunshine.*

struction. Her aluminum lifeboats, hatch beams and boards, engine casings, furniture, stanchions, ladders, ballast and bilge piping, and funnel became a floating advertisement for her owner, Saguenay Shipping Limited, a subsidiary of Alcan.[19] Her special features included a system of centreline bulkheads, feeders, and trimming hatches similar to those found on grain vessels to prevent cargo from shifting. Her extra-large hatches were designed to provide digging space for equipment used to discharge bulk cargo. She was also the first ship in which the Davie team installed the shipyard's own patent feeders with key sections that could be folded away from the hatch, so that she could be converted to a general cargo carrier in a few hours.[20] Her main propulsion machinery was supplied by John Inglis of Toronto and consisted of one low-pressure and one high-pressure turbine, with a maximum combined rating of 5,500 s.h.p. at 118½ rpm. She was launched in June 1954 with Mrs. Powell, wife of the president of Saguenay Shipping Limited, R.E. (Rip) Powell, acting as sponsor, and left the shipyard in

November 1954 to begin her thirteen-year career carrying alumina between Port Esquivel, Jamaica, and the Alcan smelter at Kitimat, British Columbia.[21]

The ships built after the shipyard fire included the 259-foot lake canaller MV *Metis* for the CSL fleet. She returned to the yard on two occasions. The first time in 1959, she was lengthened to 331 feet, and the second time in the winter of 1965–66 she was converted to a self-unloading cement carrier.[22] In her original form, she served as a model for two ships that Davie built for the Hall Line: the 2,129-ton MV *Coniscliffe Hall* of 1957,[23] and her sister, MV *Rockcliffe Hall* of 1958.[24] The Hall Corporation, which had operated on the Great Lakes since 1880 and was now rapidly expanding, was a valuable new customer brought in by McLagan. McLagan's offer to finance the construction of the ships was more attractive to the corporation than the alternative of going to the banks. "It made sense," says Hall's former naval architect, Alec Pullin. "It was a very good shipyard and there were no problems with their ships." Davie would build a total of thirteen ships for the Hall Corporation over the years. Most of them were dry cargo ships, which were given names with the suffix *Hall*. Hall tankers were given the suffix *Transport*.

The shipyard was already prospering when the Suez Canal crisis precipitated a worldwide demand for large tankers to send around the Cape of Good Hope. A contract signed with the Federal Shipping Company on November 26, 1956, for a 40,000-ton tanker was duplicated the following January when the Montreal-based shipowner Phrixos Papachristidis ordered a sister to her, and once more the yard could claim to have the two largest-ever Canadian-built ships on its building ways. Meanwhile, thoroughly satisfied with the performance of the SS *Sunrip*, Saguenay Shipping ordered a slightly larger ocean-going freighter along the same lines. The 15,700-ton SS *Sunrhea*, named for Mrs. Rhea Davis, widow of Alcan's first president's son, was delivered at the end of 1958.

Among the ferries built during this period was the MV *Saguenay*, the Clarke Steamship Company's new car ferry for Saguenay River crossings at Tadoussac, which was delivered in May 1958. A double-ended vessel, which

Car and passenger ferry MV Saguenay, *136 by 37 by 14 feet 6 inches, built for Clarke Steamship Co. in 1959 for crossing the Saguenay River at Tadoussac.*

made it unnecessary to turn around between trips, she was the first of this design built at Davie. The *Saguenay* was also unusual in that she was privately owned, whereas most of the ferries built at the yard were for either the federal or provincial government.

The 6,419-ton ferry *Bluenose*, for example, was ordered by the federal Department of Transport for service between Bar Harbor, Maine, and Yarmouth, Nova Scotia. She had a carrying capacity of 600 passengers and 150 automobiles, and was expected to boost the economy at both ends of her run. Canadians hoped that she would encourage U.S. tourists to visit Canada, while the people of Bar Harbor looked to her to help overcome the lingering effect on the local economy of a devastating fire that had razed the surrounding forest and part of the town in 1947. Her facilities would include thirty private cabins, a cafeteria, newsstand, soda fountain, and nursery. She was to measure 320 by 65 by 32 feet and be powered by six 2,000-b.h.p. diesel engines. Though the experience of building the *Sunrip* helped solve some of the problems that arose in welding her 250-foot-long aluminum superstructure to her steel hull, it took the assistance of the engineering department of McGill University to solve them all. To the considerable satisfaction of those concerned, she was launched on May 25, 1955, and it was Madame Louis St. Laurent, wife of the prime minister, who named her *Bluenose*. Following the launching, a luncheon reception was held on the CSL's SS *Tadoussac*, which happened to be in the Lorne Dry Dock for an overhaul at the time. Completed later that year, the *Bluenose* sailed for Bar Harbor early in December under the command of Captain Kenneth Crump and arrived in Yarmouth on December 20.[25]

Bluenose was warmly welcomed on her first trip to Bar Harbor in January, and like Yarmouth the town decided to hold a special "Bluenose Day" in June. A crowd of vessels met and cheered her at each port in turn. And at each, she was escorted in for a day of flypasts, concerts, races, fireworks, dances, and other events, including an ox-pull and an "international" tug-of-war. It was just the beginning of a love affair that continued throughout her twenty-four years of service. In her first two decades, she steamed more than 700,000 miles and carried nearly 2 million passengers and 600,000 vehicles. By taking the ferry, motorists were saved 724 miles of driving on each trip. In addition, fish and other perishable products were carried from Nova Scotia to Boston in under six hours – a saving of sixteen hours over the land route. In 1980, *Bluenose* underwent a major refit, but her days were numbered. In her three final years in the Marine Atlantic fleet, she sailed only in summer, as she had since 1976. In 1983, the ferry *Stena Jutlandica* not only replaced her, but also assumed her name, and in the spring of 1984 she was sold under her new name *Marine Bluenose* to General Dynamics Corporation to serve as a floating storehouse and workshop at Quonset, Rhode Island.[26]

Finally, four tugs would be built in the McLagan–Lowery years, including two for the shipyard itself, for by 1954 Davie's own tugs *Manoir*, *Busy Bee*, and *Chateau* had completed a century of service between them and were nearing the end of their run. Besides working at the yard, the Davie tugs were on call generally in the port, and together they brought in a

The passenger and car ferry MV Bluenose, *320 by 65 by 32 feet. Built for the Department of Transport in 1955, she ran between Bar Harbor, Maine, and Yarmouth, Nova Scotia.*

steady though modest revenue. With the larger ships that they now had to handle, however, even the *Chateau*, known affectionately as "Le Coq" because of her superior strength, was becoming outdated. The first of Davie's new tugs, which was built in the summer of 1954, was named *Charlie S.* as a tribute to Charlie Sauvageau, beginning a tradition of naming the shipyard's tugs after Davie employees whose records of service merited special recognition. Bearing the shipyard's distinctive "D" on her funnel, she busied herself around the port for many years, until eventually she was acquired by McAllister Towing & Salvage Ltd. and left Quebec. Stationed now in Montreal harbour, she serves her new owner under the name *Cathy McAllister*. Davie's second new tug, built two years later, was the *Robert B. No. 1*, christened and proudly named by Mrs. R. Black in tribute to her husband. She has kept her original name but, following many years of service in the Davie fleet, belongs now to the CSL Group. When the *Robert B. No. 1* joined Davie's fleet of tugs, the *Busy Bee* departed, but there was still plenty of life left in her. She was sold by Sauvageau for the handsome sum of $60,000 – not bad for a vessel that had cost the shipyard $57,000 thirty years earlier! "Charlie Sauvageau was a great salesman," commented Louis Rochette, his assistant at the time. The two other new tugs, the *Foundation Victor* and *Foundation Valor*, were the first of several that

An unidentified cartoonist captured Bert Black and Charlie Sauvageau to the delight of their colleagues.

Davie built for the Foundation Maritime Company fleet, the same company that had bought the *Lord Strathcona* from the Quebec Salvage and Wrecking Co. in 1947.

These then were the main building contracts carried out by Davie. From time to time, smaller ones were fitted in among them. There was the 164-foot-long passenger car ferry MV *Radisson*, gross tonnage 1,183, for example, which was built in 1954 – in a record three months from contract signing to delivery – for the Sainte-Angèle to Trois-Rivières crossing. Seventeen barges were completed between April and August 1955 for the Department of Public Works.

Three years after the fire, every area of the shipyard was flourishing. The only shop that had not been rebuilt was the foundry. Though extremely useful in its time, the introduction of new building materials and techniques had lessened its importance. In the past, it had taken outside orders and more than paid for itself. But the need for foundry work had become sporadic. It was difficult to keep the foundry workers busy, a challenge made no easier by the increasingly restrictive clauses in the labour contract. It was therefore decided that all foundry work would be contracted out.

The Industrial Division, now known as the General Engineering Division (GED), meanwhile, rose from the flames and flourished. The man responsi-

Aerial view of rebuilt shipyard in 1958.

ble for its success was Takis Veliotis. A Greek, an engineer, and a naval officer, he was hired by Richard Lowery as a draftsman in the Marine Division in 1954. Rising quickly from the ranks, he obtained his first important promotion in September 1955 when he was named superintendent of the GED. It was he who supervised the installation of the division in its own bay in the new prefabricating shop following the fire, and he who pushed to obtain each of its subsequent extensions. It was Veliotis who built the strong technical team, including Fritz Tovar, a mechanical engineer who took over the managership in 1959,[27] and Tovar's successors, Bob Faulkner (1960–65) and John Gorman (1966–74). It was Veliotis, finally, who gradually enhanced the workshops' potential by acquiring new equipment and steadily upgraded the standard to which individual workers were qualified to work, which allowed the division to bid on increasingly sophisticated jobs.

Veliotis did not wait for contracts to turn up; he went looking for them. There were two main sources for contracts: the St. Lawrence Seaway, for which lock gates and other heavy equipment were required; and the Colombo Plan, brainchild of the Commonwealth foreign ministers' meeting in 1950, which encouraged developing nations to seek help in building up their industrial potential from their Commonwealth partners,

Canada among them.[28] Subcontracts for component parts of U.S. naval ships were another more lasting source of work, while the flow of orders for tank cars and tank-car tanks, which began in 1957 when the first contract was obtained from the Union Tank Car Corporation in Chicago, provided the division's bread and butter for a great many years.[29]

The floor had not yet been poured, nor the travelling crane installed, when the first important contract was carried out in the new shop – a 60-foot-diameter reactor hall for a Bombay nuclear power station built under the Colombo Plan for the Atomic Energy Commission of Canada. Shawinigan Engineering acted as consulting engineers. At the same time, for lack of space, a lighthouse base was under construction in the Champlain Dry Dock. In 1958, work began on the design and fabrication of six miles of high- and low-pressure piping for the Kundah Hydro-Electric project near Madras, India. Arthur Nightingale, a young marine engineer, previously assistant to Ian McGregor, the ship repair manager, joined the GED for the job. Nightingale's father had been a British Oil employee in India, and Arthur had grown up near Madras and spoke the local dialect fluently. This knowledge was expected, and proved, to be a tremendous asset at the site. Under his leadership, a team of Davie welders and one fitter, who were to teach local workers how to fit the steel, left for India in 1959 and spent two years there installing it. It was a prestigious job for Davie, which had pioneered the use of the newly invented high-tensile steel T1. In 1958 also, the division was awarded the contract to build a warehouse to store grain and a shipping wharf in Baie-Comeau for the Cargill Grain Company. From its inception, the GED showed a great deal of versatility and willingness to tackle unusual and difficult projects.

Sometimes the division made a profit; sometimes, because so much of its work was "one of a kind," it operated at a loss, but for the year 1958 Veliotis was able to claim that the GED had brought in more than the combined profits of the Shipbuilding and Repair divisions that year – $606,450. It should be pointed out, however, that production figures did not accurately reflect the situation of the Marine division as deliveries of ships were delayed by a nine-week strike. Nevertheless, there was reason for satisfaction with the General Engineering Division's figures.

The union claimed that the Davie men were the lowest paid and yet the best workers in any Canadian shipyard. The union's main objective, in addition to obtaining an increase in the rates of pay, however, was to put an end to a foremen's prerogative. Foremen decided who would be laid off and who re-called, a power that a few had shamefully abused. Such "protection" rackets, which were not uncommon in industries at the time, had become a prime source of worker discontent. The terms agreed to in the new contract included a reduced work week from 42½ to 40 hours; an increase in pay for labourers of 22 cents an hour from $1.28 to $1.50, and for tradesmen of 39 cents from $1.61 to $2, and the strict application of departmental seniority principles for layoffs. Greatly heartened by these improvements in their contract, the men returned to work with a will.

By 1958, the war had been over for twelve years, for seven of which Lowery had been at Davie's head. Under McLagan's and his direction, Canada Steamship Lines had taken full advantage of both the insurance settlement following the fire and generous government subsidies to make basic improvements to the yard. The plant renewal had helped productivity and enabled Davie to become more competitive. During the last seven years, the shipyard had delivered a total of forty-one vessels from 30-foot scows to 20,000-ton tankers, representing 84,000 gross tons of shipping, while both its Tug and its General Engineering divisions had flourished. The other CSL yards were also doing well. In 1958, the McLagan–Lowery team decided to introduce a corporate look: the trademark "Davieship" was adopted for Davie, and "Kingship," "Collship," and "Portship" for the others. (The Midland yard was closed in 1955.)

In 1951, Allison "Foddie" Davie died at eighty-one years of age. He had lived all his life at the Homestead and had managed the original Davie shipyard in Levis until the end, but he had not been the same man since Charlie's death four years before. The funeral service was held at the

THE GOLDEN YEARS

Spool-shaped caisson built to serve as a lighthouse base on Prince Shoal four miles off Tadoussac. The caisson was loaded with 8,000 tons of crushed rock at the site into which cement grout was pumped. It is not expected to move.

Presbyterian Church at Levis and then the last of the shipbuilding Davies was laid to rest. He himself had not married and his nephew Charlie had no children. He willed the Levis shipyard to his great-nephew Yvon Bossé, whom he had employed in his office. But Bossé was neither a Davie nor a shipbuilder, and for him the shipyard had no sentimental value. He immediately put it up for sale. The workers, however, could not bear the thought of the shipyard being sold to strangers, and Paul Gourdeau, Allison Davie's accountant and friend, managed to convince enough South Shore people to put up the total of $204,000 that was needed to buy it. Gourdeau would operate the little shipyard at Levis for the next thirty-five years.

The George T. Davie Lauzon shipyard was sold to Canadian Vickers of Montreal, which thus obtained not only a shipyard that was a going concern, but also one with easy access to the two well-disposed dry docks at Lauzon. André Delagrave was kept on as president, J. Edouard Labelle, Q.C., became chairman of the board, and Lewis J.-B. Forbes, vice-president. Maurice Paquet was named treasurer, and his brother J. Arthur Paquet, secretary. Apart from fulfilling contracts for a variety of small vessels, mostly from the Public Works Department, the yard concentrated at this time on ship repairs, using the Lorne Dry Dock as well as its own marine railway to work on their hulls. When the Davie Shipbuilding and Repairing Company dropped "and Repairing" from its corporate name – simply to shorten it – Delagrave was quick to notify his customers that although the neighbouring shipyard seemed to be going out of the ship-repairing business, his yard was not and offered even better service. Needless to say, the neighbouring yard had no intention of giving up the ship-repair business. In 1955, following the general shipyard trend to diversify, a subsidiary of Geo. T. Davie, Riverside Steel Works Limited, was incorporated.

The yard was enjoying buoyant times in 1957 when André Delagrave was struck down by a heart attack. He was only forty-seven. Even though it was known that he had a heart condition, his premature death shocked the shipbuilding community. His funeral was the occasion for a great outpouring of affection and esteem from a distinguished gathering, of whom none were more sincere in their grief than the large body of men who came from the shipyard to bury their chief. It was they who led the long funeral procession, and the more senior among them acted as his pallbearers.

Thus, in a period of ten years, Charlie Davie, Foddie Davie, and André Delagrave had all disappeared. With their passing, the last living ties of the South Shore's shipbuilding community to the Davie family were severed.

Meanwhile, following years of careful planning, the ground-breaking ceremonies for the new seaway had taken place on August 10, 1954, and in no time large tracts had become construction sites as work went ahead simultaneously on several fronts. In the five years that followed, 15,000 men excavated 200 million cubic feet of rock and soil; flooded nearly 40,000 acres – most of it Ontario and New York state farmland; erected the new Moses–Saunders bi-national hydro-electric station; built ten new lift bridges; raised the Jacques Cartier and Mercier bridges at Montreal to allow taller ships to sail under them; and built a canal along the south shore of the St. Lawrence to bypass the Lachine Rapids. Forty-one miles of Canadian National Railway main-line track, thirty-five miles of highway, and eight Ontario communities were relocated, and in the process 500 homes and 6,500 Canadians were moved.[30] One by one, each of the projects was completed, and when the last ships left the lakes at the close of the 1958 season, they brought an end to an era. From 1959 on, they would be sharing the seaway with larger vessels from all over the world.

Tug Jerry G. Courtesy R. Gagnon.

18

THE ST. LAWRENCE SEAWAY

1959-68

THE ST. LAWRENCE Seaway opened for business on the first day of the navigation season, April 29, 1959. Many of the merchantmen that passed through the locks at Montreal that day had special guests on board. With the Davie-built Coast Guard ships CMS *d'Iberville* and *Montcalm* leading the way, the vessels transited the St. Lambert lock, and then the CSL's veteran canaller *Simcoe*[1] took over at the head of those that continued the journey to the Upper Lakes. Fully conscious of the historic nature of the occasion, and proud of the leading role that CSL and its shipyards were playing, Rodgie McLagan and Richard Lowery entertained their guests aboard the *Simcoe*, savouring every moment.[2]

Two months later, Queen Elizabeth and Prince Philip were joined by U.S. President Eisenhower and Mrs. Eisenhower aboard the Royal Yacht *Britannia* for the official opening ceremony. As the *Britannia*'s bow broke the ribbon that had been stretched across the channel, the St. Lawrence Seaway was declared officially open and the royal couple's commemorative journey from Montreal to the head of the lakes began.[3]

At the end of the previous season, the maximum size of a St. Lawrence River and Great Lakes vessel, which had remained unchanged since the beginning of the century, was 259 feet in length by just under 44 feet in the beam. In a few months it had become 730 by 75 feet.[4] As a result, many deep-sea vessels that were previously too big to sail beyond Montreal were now able to proceed to the head of the Upper Lakes. Others that had been trapped in the lakes could transit the seven new St. Lawrence River locks on their way to Montreal and the sea. It was now possible for maximum-size bulk carriers to transport grain and other commodities from the Lakehead to ports on the Lower St. Lawrence without trans-shipment, and to return with a cargo of Labrador iron ore for the Great Lakes steel makers.

Canadian shipping companies had to keep their bulk canallers in service until the end of the 1958 season. They were therefore unable to revamp their fleets with fewer and larger vessels ahead of time. Faced with the heavy costs involved, they not unnaturally looked to Ottawa for assistance. The Liberal government, which had set the construction of the seaway in motion and was therefore responsible for their predicament, was no longer in power. But fortunately the shipbuilders could count on Leon Balcer, the Conservative Minister of Transport, who recognized that the Canadian inland merchant fleets would have to be modernized to remain competitive and made sure that the work went to Canadian shipyards. He introduced a generous 40 per cent subsidy (50 per cent for fishing trawlers) for Canadian-built ships that was to last from May 1, 1961, to March 1963, after which it would be reduced by 5 per cent. Shippers and shipbuilders were elated. The Conservative government was taking their welfare to heart.

Following their victory in the general election of April 1963, however, the Liberals made some changes in the program. Though the subsidy was to continue at 35 per cent until the end of 1965, it would then be reduced to 25 per cent, following which there would be a reduction of 2 per cent each year until it reached 17 per cent in 1970. In addition, some of the beneficial tax provisions granted to owners by the plan (generally known as the "Angel Plan") were removed. For example, they would no longer be exempt from their obligation to repay depreciation allowances when they disposed of ships built under the act. On the whole, however, the shipyards had reason to be thankful that they could look ahead to many years of full employment.

Not least among the beneficiaries was the Davie shipyard, which, between 1961 and 1969, delivered twelve maximum-size St. Lawrence/Great Lakes bulk freighters and two record-breaking tankers. The increased business represented a jump in the volume of the shipyard's production from 103,248 d.w.t. between 1949 and 1958, to 374,503 d.w.t. between 1959 and 1968, an increase of more than 250 per cent.

Davie's most important private customer during these years was its owner, Canada Steamship Lines. Like other shipping lines serving the St. Lawrence, CSL was in the throes of reorganizing its fleet to take maximum advantage of the enlarged seaway locks. It disposed of thirteen canallers in 1959 and replaced them with two full-size seaway bulk freighters, the *Murray Bay* built at Collingwood in 1959, and the *Whitefish Bay*, built by Davie. The latter would be stern-launched over the strong objections of Collingwood engineers, who were convinced that a laker of that length must be launched sideways to prevent the strain on her hull from being too great. Their fears proved groundless, however, and on her delivery in 1961, the *Whitefish Bay* became the new flagship of the CSL fleet.[5] Eleven other bulk freighters of full St. Lawrence/Great Lakes size followed her off the building ways in Lauzon, five of which joined the CSL house fleet. They were:

<u>Canada Steamship Lines</u>

1961	*Whitefish Bay*
1963	*Baie Saint Paul*
1964	*Saguenay*
1966	*Manitoulin*
1967	*Richelieu*
1968	*Frontenac*

<u>Nipigon Transport</u>

1968	*Lake Manitoba*

<u>Hall Corporation</u>

1963	*Frankcliffe Hall*
1965	*Lawrencecliffe Hall*
1966	*Beavercliffe Hall*
1969	*Ottercliffe Hall*

<u>Labrador Steamship</u>

1966	*A.S. Glossbrenner*

Though of similar hull shape, these lakers embodied a succession of improvements. *Whitefish Bay, Baie Saint Paul,* and *Frankcliffe Hall,* for instance, were driven by steam turbine engines, but the others, beginning with MV *Saguenay,* were diesel-propelled. *Saguenay's* four Fairbanks Morse engines were coupled to one propeller shaft and, like the CSL "fast Fort" package freighters, her variable-pitch propeller was designed to be operated by the captain from the bridge. In fact, the captain could control the entire ship from the bridge. Self-lubricating internal combustion engines did away with the need for oilers, and there was no longer a need for firemen in the crew of twenty-four. Moreover, by using high-tensile steel wherever practical and plastic ballast pipes instead of steel, a reduction in weight was achieved without a decrease in strength and a greater deadweight could be carried, which generated higher cargo revenues. Following her delivery on August 11, 1964, the *Saguenay* immediately began breaking records for carrying grain, ore, and coal. A considerable saving was also achieved in the number of man-hours needed for her construction.

First large bulk freighter built by Davie in 1961 was the SS Whitefish Bay. *Mrs. V.W. Scully, wife of the president of the Steel Company of Canada, was the sponsor. The* Whitefish Bay *under her captain, Commodore Andy Allan, became the flagship of the* CSL *fleet.*

Top: *The largest self-unloader* MV Manitoulin *(later* David K. Gardiner*), 27,000 short deadweight tons, built for Canada Steamship Lines in 1966. She was used almost exclusively in carrying metallurgical coal for the Steel Company of Canada.* Bottom: *Upper Laker bulk carrier* Frankcliffe Hall, *26000 d.w.t., (later* Halifax*) built for the Hall Corporation in 1963, at time of constant expansion of its fleet.*

The two large sister tankers were the 41,000-ton single-decked *Federal Monarch* of 1959 for Federal Petroleum Carriers Ltd., and Papachristidis Co. Ltd.'s *Emerillon* of 1960. Both were fitted with Westinghouse 17,600 s.h.p. cross-compound steam turbines, designed to produce 105.2 rpm. The cargo space was made up of twenty-seven tanks, with an approximate total capacity of 298,000 barrels of oil, and six water-ballast tanks. Their impressive size and handsome lines were greatly admired by the spectators at their launching. Each of these tankers in turn had the distinction of being the largest ship ever built at a Canadian shipyard, because Phrixos Papachristidis, knowing that the *Emerillon* would be delivered a year after the *Federal Monarch*, requested design changes that slightly increased her tonnage.[6] Following her registration in London, England, the *Federal*

Monarch had a fifteen-year charter to Imperial Oil lined up to carry crude oil to the Imperial Oil refineries in Halifax and Montreal. A similar long-term charter to Shell Oil awaited the ss *Emerillon*.

Purchasers of smaller vessels during the 1960s included Hall Corporation, which ordered four small tankers in addition to their four of maximum seaway size, while N.M. Paterson & Sons contracted for two 605-by-62-foot bulk freighters and four smaller ones. There were also two package freighters built for the Newfoundland service of Clarke's Gulf Ports Steamship Co., Ltd., the side loaders *Cabot* of 1965 and *Chimo* of 1967. Though their main features were similar to those of CSL's *Fort Saint Louis*, they carried in addition two 15-ton deck cranes. In view of their proposed winter service in the Gulf, they were constructed to Lloyd's Class I ice-strengthening regulations and were fitted with a higher standard of watertight doors, which completely eliminated the possibility of human error when they were being secured. Though popular with their owners, the two ships were highly unpopular among longshoremen, only 44 of whom were needed to unload them compared with 103 for comparable ships belonging to the company. Both were stretched in the 1980s. The

With the construction of the 41,245-ton bulk oil carrier ss Federal Monarch *built for the Federal Petroleum Carriers Limited of Halifax, Nova Scotia, Davie once again held the record for the largest ship yet built in Canada. Delivered in September 1959, she was a single-screw steam geared-turbine ship, with five-bladed, solid bronze propellers and electric-hydraulic steering gear. A fifteen-year charter to Imperial Oil lay ahead, during which she would carry crude oil to the Imperial Oil refineries in Halifax and Montreal.*

stern section of the *Cabot* was mated to the bow section of the *Northern Venture*, while the stern of the *Chimo* was mated with the *Hilda Marjanne*.

The future held a more unusual destiny for the *Menier Consol*, a 2,575-ton pulpwood carrier delivered to the Anticosti Shipping Company in 1962, which had the double distinction of being the first ship built by Davie under the new subsidy and the first to be built in the newly completed covered slip. The *Menier Consol* would be sold twenty-seven years later to Captain Norman Rogers of Toronto, who cut 60 feet off her bow and fitted gates across the opening to make a floating dry dock. She continues to serve that purpose in Toronto Harbour today, taking on ships of up to 200 feet in length.[7]

Apart from the general merchant ship building program, Quebec shipyards also benefited from the special effort made by the federal and provincial governments at this time to help the fishing industry through the renewal of the fishing fleet. As a result, many generously subsidized fishing boats were laid down, and though Davie usually left fishing boat

The first of the side loaders, the single-screw ocean-going, MV Cabot, *a multi-purpose package freighter built for Gulf Ports Steamship Co. (Clarke) for service between Montreal and Newfoundland, was sponsored by Mrs. J. R. Smallwood, wife of Newfoundland's premier. The* Cabot *had a Sulzer engine and could carry 7,900 tons of cargo, but was unpopular with dockworkers, because it took 44 men to unload her, as opposed to 103 in the case of conventional vessels like the* Gulfport *and* Highlander. *Special side port terminals were built to handle side loaders in Montreal and St. John's. In 1983 the* Cabot *was cut in two and her stern section was mated with the bow of the* Northern Venture *to become the Great Lakes bulk carrier* Canadian Explorer.

The bulk freighter MV Prindoc *and her sister,* MV Labradoc, *were named by two granddaughters of Senator Paterson at a double launching ceremony. Built to carry bulk cargo, especially Quebec newsprint, they were delivered to N.M. Paterson & Sons in 1966. All Paterson ships carried the suffix "doc" signifying the Dominion of Canada.*

The package freighter MV Fort Saint Louis *delivered to the Steel Company of Canada in August 1963. She had been christened by Mrs. Craig, wife of L.T. Craig, vice-president of the Steel Company of Canada in May. She was designed for the carriage of grain as well as package freight on the Great Lakes and of general cargo on international voyages. Two years later, however, she was acquired by* CSL *and in the summer she took part in a government experiment for helicopter delivery of cargo in remote places, whose success led to the establishment of a regular helicopter service.*

construction to smaller yards, she built three. They were the stern trawler MV *Acadia Albatross*, for the Acadia Fisheries Ltd. fleet, and two small diesel-powered refrigerated fish carriers for the Blue Peter Steamship Co.: *Blue Peter II*, the fourth vessel to carry that name in the fleet, and *Blue Cloud*. Innocent enough when she left Lauzon in 1964, *Blue Cloud* would achieve notoriety in 1982 when, having been sold to Miami interests and renamed *Biscayne Freeze*, she was confiscated by the Coast Guard Service at Boston for drug smuggling![8]

Inevitably, the sharp growth in the number and size of the vessels using the St. Lawrence Seaway led to a demand for more and stronger tugs, and in this area also, Davie, which had built and operated tugs since 1855, was not out-performed. In the early 1960s, Davie secured the Canadian patent for the new revolutionary "hydroconic" hull design that had been introduced by Seaworks Ltd. in Britain. This design was featured in all eight tugs built between 1960 and 1963. To further improve their performance, they were fitted with patented bulb-type rudders – a streamlined bulb post with a flat rudder – as well. Of the six harbour tugs and one ocean-going tug for Foundation Maritime, four were laid down in the covered berth and subsequently launched the same day. Canadian Fairbanks-Morse supplied the six-cylinder opposed piston engines of the smaller tugs, which developed 1,000 b.h.p. at 750 rpm, and the larger one was fitted with two five-cylinder similar engines developing 1,600 b.h.p. By June 1963, all the tugs – the *Foundation Vim*, *Foundation Viking*, *Foundation Viscount*, *Foundation Vigour*, *Foundation Viceroy*, *Foundation Vanguard*, and the larger *Foundation Valiant* – had left the yard.[9]

The eighth was the *Jerry G.*, named after the yard's superintendent, Jerry Gagnon. She was the third modern tug in Davie's own fleet and was slightly larger than the *Charlie S.* and the *Robert B. No. 1*. She replaced the *Chateau*, a veteran that had begun her varied career at the H. & C. Grayson shipyard near Liverpool in 1910. Originally named *Gopher*, the *Chateau* was requisitioned by the Admiralty at the beginning of the First World War, but was released soon after and in June 1914 arrived in Quebec, where she

The pulpwood carrier 2,575-ton MV Menier Consol, *built in 1962 for the Anticosti Shipping Company, in the covered slip. Twenty-seven years later she found a new vocation in Toronto when she was converted into a dry dock.*

Toronto Drydock, ex MV Menier Consol. *Courtesy Captain Norman Rogers.*

Blue Cloud, *frozen-fish carrier.*

carried out harbour duties for the Quebec Salvage & Wrecking Company. In 1923 the Saint John Dry Dock Co. bought her and named her *Ocean King*. Following her sinking with the loss of nine lives, while attending the berthing of the Canadian Pacific liner *Marloch* in Quebec harbour in June 1925, she was acquired by Davie. Her hull and superstructure were repaired and her machinery reconditioned. She was fitted with a new turbo generator in the engine room for salvage work and was equipped with powerful pumps that could discharge four jets of water simultaneously to give her a fire-fighting capability. She was sent back to Saint John for the winter, and on her return was named *Chateau*. She worked and sailed in the Davie fleet for thirty-four years. It was not without some feeling of loss that shipyard employees said farewell to the *Chateau* in 1960, when her fifty-year career came to an end.

Canada Steamship Lines had reason to be pleased with Davie's production of commercial ships during the 1960s and could be well satisfied also with the performance of the Repair Division. Under the shipyard's aggressive management, and despite strong competition from the George T. Davie yard next door, the division now had as many as a hundred ships passing through its hands in the course of a year. The volume of ships repaired during the winter had risen steeply with the introduction of steam to keep

Foundation Company of Canada tugs under construction in the covered slip in 1963.

the dry dock gates operational all year round, a change effected by the Canadian government's Department of Public Works, largely at Veliotis's insistence. Mainly because of the opening of the seaway, a number of transformations were carried out as well as the usual refits and modernizations. These generally involved "jumboizing" or stretching a vessel, though in at least one case a ship was deepened. The *Grainmotor*, which returned to the Davie shipyard after twenty-two years at sea, was given another five feet of depth, increasing her d.w.t. to 3,800 tons. She spent the next five years under the CSL flag before Bahamas Package Carriers bought her and changed her name to *Bulk Gold*. Other vessels were converted to self-unloaders.

But repair work was also often the result of accidents, rather than planning, and in that respect 1965 was a particularly good year for Davie, though not for the owners of two brand-new ships built by Davie. In November, the CSL's own six-month-old package freighter MV *Fort William* sank and overturned in Montreal harbour, after heeling over during cargo

Davie's tug Chateau, *ex* Ocean King, *ex* Gopher, *built in 1910 at the H. & C. Grayson shipyard at Garston, near Liverpool, and requisitioned by the Admiralty at the beginning of the First World War. In 1924, she was purchased by the St. John Dry Dock and Shipbuilding Co. and renamed* Ocean King. *Davie bought her after she sank in Quebec harbour in June 1925 and named her* Chateau. *Her hull and superstructure were repaired, her machinery was reconditioned, and a new turbo generator was fitted in the engine room for salvage work. She was also given a fire-fighting capability with four jets that discharged simultaneously.*

Davie's tug Chateau, *seen here on the brand-new Marine Railway Cradle at the George T. Davie shipyard, Lauzon, c.1928.* Courtesy Crandall Engineering.

operations and taking water through her side doors. She was subsequently righted and raised by the Foundation Co. of Canada and towed to Lauzon for repairs. The second ship, the Hall Corporation's bulk freighter *Lawrencecliffe Hall* (since renamed *David K. Gardiner*), loaded with iron ore, collided with the ocean freighter *Sunek* off the Isle of Orleans, right on Davie's doorstep. She was lying in 35 feet of water and was salvaged by Marine Industries Limited's salvage division under a "Lloyd's Open Form" "no cure, no pay" contract. After being refloated, she was towed to the Champlain Dry Dock to be repaired by Davie. In both cases, extensive repairs were required.[10]

Contracts for commercial ships, however, whether new work or repairs, by no means accounted for all of the shipyard's production during the 1960s. Davie, like many other Canadian yards, did not lack for government contracts from both the Canadian Marine Service (CMS) and the RCN. In 1959, Davie had contracts for three naval vessels on its books: two were for destroyer escorts (DDEs), the first "high-tech" warships to be built at the yard; and the third was for a 13,000-ton ocean-going replenishment vessel. The DDEs were designed to withstand "ugly" weapons. They could be sealed against contamination from atomic, biological, or chemical attack and had a first-class system of damage control. They were powered by steam turbines and fitted with extensive, complex electric and electronic systems that controlled every part of their equipment. Especially equipped for anti-submarine warfare (ASW), they carried, over and above the customary weaponry, such anti-submarine weapons as electronically controlled mortars and homing torpedoes. Innovations in the living quarters of their complement of 12 officers and 234 men reflected a changed attitude towards the importance of crew comfort. Each bunk was fitted with a foam rubber mattress and reading light. Mirrors and electric shaving outlets, aluminum clothes lockers and drawers, all were provided, as was a separate area designed for relaxation. These facilities were a far cry from the traditional combined sleeping and living quarters considered adequate in the past. HMCS *Gatineau* of the Restigouche class, under Captain H.L. Quinn,

SHIPBUILDING IN THE 1950s AND 1960s

CLOCKWISE FROM upper left: First the concept is transformed into plans in the Davie Drawing Offices. Next, after the lines of the ship have been projected full-size to the mould loft floor, the loftsmen make wooden templates from them. The metal frames are bent to conform to the templates, and then the individual components are assembled to make a ship on the building berth.

Destroyer escort HMCS Qu'Appelle *DDE264 of 1963, 356 by 42 by 28 feet 6 inches. She was to serve on the Pacific Coast under Commander J.M. Bishop.*

DSC, RCN, was delivered from Lauzon in February 1959, and her Mackenzie class sister HMCS *Qu'Appelle* under Commander A.G. Kilpatrick, CD, RCN, followed in 1963. *Qu'Appelle* was the fourth of the class to be commissioned and the last of the DDEs to be built by Davie, though Marine Industries, Halifax Shipyards, Canadian Vickers, Victoria Machinery, and Burrard's at Vancouver would share contracts for another sixteen, making a class of twenty in all.

In sharp contrast to the two destroyers, the 13,000-ton ocean-going replenishment vessel HMCS *Provider*, was unique – the only one of her class in the fleet. She was also a special challenge to Davie's technical staff, who developed the working drawings according to Lloyd's commercial classification standards from the design drawings produced at Naval Headquarters. In addition to carrying supplies of food, arms, and munitions, *Provider* was to serve as a refuelling and repair tanker, thus providing all of a ship's support requirements "at one stop." Transfer arrangements consisted of three fuelling beam rigs, a stern fuelling position, and four rigs

HMCS Provider *508, fleet supply ship of 1963.*

for solid supplies, while for personnel there were light jackstay fittings. The forward and after magazines were reached by elevators that were serviced by three forklift trucks and two pallet transporters, all electrically operated and spark-proof. There were twenty-six cargo tanks, with a capacity of 12,000 tons of diesel and aviation fuel, and cargo magazines for the transport of torpedoes, anti-submarine projectiles, general ammunition, and, if required, guided missiles. Special self-tensioning equipment, which automatically picked up the slack, was designed to prevent spills of oil or anything else during transfers. *Provider*'s unique design features included the central machinery control room and completely automated combustion control system. Once her speed was set, a computer system handled the response from her engines. As in the case of the destroyers, special consideration was given to the comfort of the crew, and all accommodation was air-conditioned. The *Provider* was equipped to carry six helicopters and was the largest ship to have been built in Canada for the RCN. This novel supply ship and tanker was launched by Mrs. R. Wright, wife of Rear Admiral R. Wright, a former comptroller of the RCN, in July 1962. She was commissioned on September 28 the following year, under the command of Captain Thomas C. Pullen, RCN, who would later earn fame for his work to safeguard the Arctic environment.[11]

Following *Provider*'s departure in 1963, Davie had no new naval ships on order for the first time since 1949, a situation that was of serious concern because, without naval work, the shipyard could not justify keeping intact its well-knit team of engineers and technicians. Fortunately, it still had on hand a number of contracts for refits and conversions. The Second World War destroyers HMCS *Huron* and *Sioux* were modernized at Davie's in 1960 and 1961 respectively so they could serve a few last years as training ships until the new generation of ships was ready to take their place.[12] The eight-year-old destroyer escort HMCS *Skeena*[13] underwent a far more fundamental transformation to a helicopter-carrying DDH in order to be able to do precisely the same thing.[14] The main operational improvements to *Skeena* comprised the Variable Depth Sonar (VDS), the activated fin stabilizers that made her more stable for landing the Sea King helicopters she was to carry, and the Sea King helicopters themselves. At the same time, the crew benefited from the enlargement and improvement of their mess decks and recreation areas. *Skeena* was recommissioned August 14, 1965, with Commander C.J. Mair, RCN, as her new captain.

When the Liberal government took over in 1963, it immediately instituted plans for a less costly and more efficient Navy. The annual defence budget was frozen at $1.53 billion, and it was not long before Paul Hellyer, the new Defence Minister, set in motion his highly unpopular plan for the unification of the three services, maintaining that the money thereby saved would be better spent on the purchase of improved fighting equipment.[15] Fourteen older RCN ships were retired, not to be replaced, and the building program for eight general-purpose frigates was cancelled. A new program was introduced for the construction of four DDE or Tribal 280 class destroyer escorts, two support ships, and one submarine.

At the beginning of 1966, Davie was awarded a contract for the refit of Canada's only aircraft carrier, HMCS *Bonaventure*, a twelve-year-old RN vessel purchased by the Canadian government in 1957. Davie's bid for the refit was $4,914,000 for specified work, plus an estimated $855,141 of labour for 200,000 hours of unknown work, the precise nature of which could be determined only after she had been opened up. Canadian Vickers' bid was $94,659 higher, while St. John Shipbuilding quoted $8,572,928. The

Aircraft carrier HMCS Bonaventure *in dry dock at Lauzon for an extensive refit in 1966.*

final cost was to include another $2,230,000 for equipment supplied by the government, as well as that of the cost of equipment and materials for the unknown work. When the *Bonaventure* was opened up in April 1966, she was found to be in worse condition than had been anticipated, and extras snowballed.[16] Nevertheless, work went ahead rapidly, and she was recommissioned in November 1966 under Captain R.H. Falls, RCN.[17]

Though not for "new" work, these naval contracts were largely responsible for maintaining the general high quality of construction at the Davie shipyard, which was widely considered to be the top Canadian yard at the time. Not only did the rest of Davie's production benefit from the technologically advanced equipment that was acquired for the purpose, but it benefited also from the effect of the higher naval finishing standard. The Canadian Marine Service also demanded high standards, and it was rare that there was not at least one CMS ship either building or repairing. The most challenging of these was the large icebreaker ordered in 1957 and delivered in 1960.

Built to maintain a supply route through the Northwest Passage during the open season with the help of smaller icebreakers, and to increase Canada's knowledge of the Arctic, the CMS *John A. Macdonald* would be the third most powerful in the world, following the U.S.S.R.'s nuclear-powered *Lenin* and the United States' *Glacier*.[18] Her extra-strong frame and shell were matched by a rugged shafting system with triple screws and four-bladed nickel vanadium steel propellers. Her special features included an enclosed crow's nest, large enough to hold two men, which was reached by a ladder fixed to the inside of her hollow foremast. She had a cruising range of 20,000 miles at 15,000 s.h.p. and accommodation for 106 passengers and crew, and could take on sufficient supplies to remain at sea without replenishment throughout an Arctic season. Her three helicopters, two motorboats, and four diesel-powered barges would enable her to perform a wide variety of missions.

She was christened by Olive Diefenbaker, the wife of the prime minister, in a spectacular launching ceremony on an October evening in 1959, when an early snowstorm added an unusual touch to the scene. According to Bill McCloy of the Canadian Coast Guard, her relatively uneventful construction was in itself a feather in the cap of the builders in view of her many special features. The launching of *John A. Macdonald* was a turning point, he says, in the service's operations. Her superior strength enabled her to penetrate farther north and do far more than any of her predecessors. Following her commissioning in September 1960, she left Lauzon to begin her career at sea under the command of Captain James L. Cuthbert.

In her first season, the *John A.*, as she was commonly known, sailed as far north as Sherwood Head on the northern tip of Axel Heiberg Island, helping in the establishment of the world's first isotope-powered automatic weather-recording station by a joint Canada–United States team. The

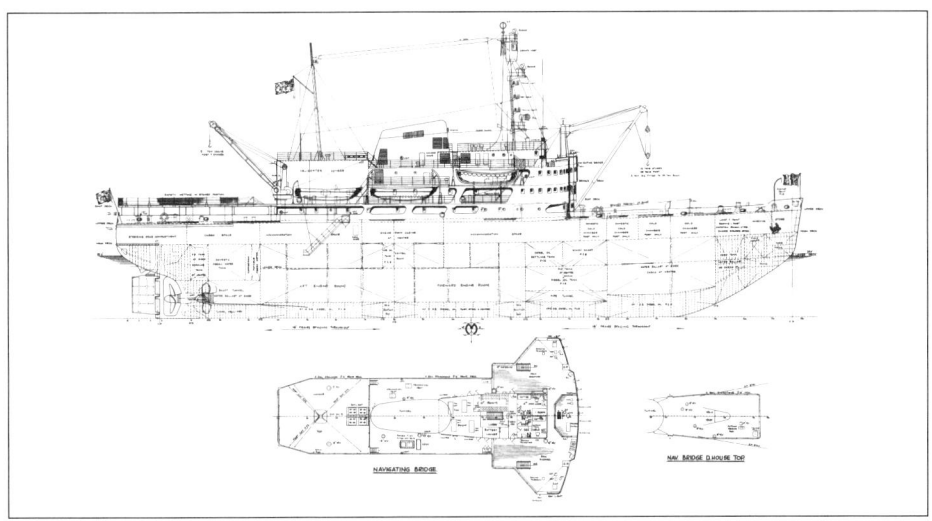

General arrangement profile and navigation bridge deck of CMS John A. Macdonald, *built for the Coast Guard in 1960 to maintain a supply route through the Northwest Passage during the open season with the help of smaller icebreakers. Design by Gilmore, German & Milne.*

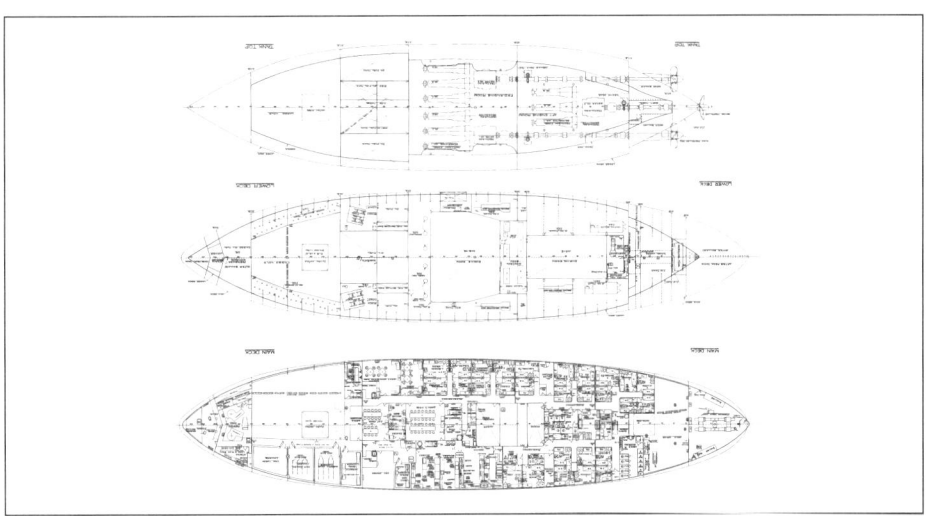

General arrangement profiles of the main and lower decks, and the tank top of CMS John A. Macdonald. *She had accommodation for 106 passengers and crew, and could take on sufficient supplies to remain at sea without replenishment throughout an Arctic season.*

scientific work that followed would take her to places unvisited by any explorer for a hundred years. Like the *d'Iberville* and other vessels built for the CMS by Davie, the *John A.* returned periodically to the shipyard for refits. She lived up to the expectations of her designers and builders by giving excellent service in the Coast Guard until December 1991. By that time, her yearly maintenance and repair bill had become too heavy, and in a moving ceremony she was formally decommissioned at Dartmouth, Nova Scotia, following a sail past in Bedford Basin.[19]

Though she was commissioned in the CMS fleet, whose ships were painted yellow, white, and black, for most of her life she had sailed under the distinctive colours of the Canadian Coast Guard Service, which took over the duties of the Canadian Marine Service on January 26, 1962. Marking the transfer, the black paint of the CMS fleet's hulls was covered with bright red; the superstructures remained gleaming white; and the white funnels emblazoned with a distinctive large red maple leaf made the new CCG fleet far more easily identified by returning helicopters, other ships, and the public at large.

In 1962, the Coast Guard Fleet was made up of sixty-one vessels, including ten full icebreakers – of which Davie had built five – sixteen light icebreakers or other types of ships for northern service, and twenty-eight others whose duties related in one way or another to navigational safety.[20] One hundred and thirty small steel craft landed supplies wherever they were needed. Together, the Coast Guard's Arctic and Sub-Arctic Fleet now transported more than 100,000 tons of cargo annually to close to 100 outposts.

An early innovation of the new CCG was the introduction of a search and rescue service. This fleet of fast cutters, based in Halifax, Vancouver, and Trenton, Ontario, was a boon both to fishermen and to recreational operators of small boats. Davie built one of the first cutters, the 95-foot CCGS *Rally*. Her 2,400-s.h.p. engines were designed along the lines of an American Coast Guard vessel and gave her a cruising range of 1,050 nautical miles. Gilles Fortin, a former Davie employee, has not forgotten their first aborted installation. He was watching the second engine being lowered into her hold when he was galvanized into action by a foreman's remark – "Don't you find that engine looks rather large?" "I stopped the crane immediately," Fortin recalls, "and when we checked, sure enough, the engine was too large to fit in without causing considerable damage." The consulting naval architects had changed the design of the hull but forgot to alter the engine arrangement. Thanks to the foreman's experienced eye and Fortin's quick reaction, a potentially costly mistake was minimized. The *Rally* was christened by Mrs. W.J. Manning, wife of the director of the Marine Works Branch of the Department of Transport, on April 19, 1963.

The CCGS *Alert* was also a search and rescue vessel, but because she was designed for ocean work, she was far heavier and more powerful. Her four diesel engines produced 9,716 i.h.p., with a 6,000-nautical mile range, and a capability of 18.75 mph, making her the fastest ship in the Department of Transport fleet. Headlines were made during her construction on

The CCGS *Alert, delivered in 1969, had a 6,000-nautical mile range and, at 18.75 knots, the highest maximum speed in the fleet. She had a crew of thirty-eight and was stationed at Dartmouth, Nova Scotia.*

THE GOLDEN YEARS

account of the new building methods that were employed by Davie. An early example of the benefits of modular construction, she was put together in the covered slip from twelve prefabricated units in thirteen days from her keel-laying to ready-for-launch.[21] Unfortunately, however, the delivery of the government-supplied main engines was delayed so, after the hull was built and outfitted as far as possible, Veliotis (now assistant general manager) ordered the covered slip to be closed until the work could be completed several months later. Both the *Rally* and the *Alert* were stationed at Dartmouth, Nova Scotia.

The last CCGS ship of this period was the 231-foot *J.E. Bernier*, a medium icebreaker of 4,250 s.h.p., named – no doubt popularly – for J.E. Bernier (1852–1934), a South Shore man, famed Arctic explorer,[22] and good friend of the Davie family. On her delivery in 1967, she had only to cross the river to reach the Quebec Coast Guard base on Champlain Boulevard from which she would carry out her duties. She replaced both

CCGS J.E. Bernier *christened on November 28, 1967, by Mrs. Jean Marchand, wife of the former president of the labour union to which Davie's yard workers belonged, and at that time Federal Minister of Manpower.*

the veteran icebreaker *Saurel*, which was retired, and the buoy tender *Chesterfield*.

And finally, although she belonged neither to the Coast Guard Service, nor the Department of Transport, it seems more fitting than not to mention the coaster MV *Eskimo* among the CCGS vessels. She was unusual in that she was designed and built for Canada Steamship Lines by Davie at the suggestion of the Department of Transport. Her intended use, for which her hull was strengthened, was to service outports along the Distant Early Warning (DEW) line in the far north.

She was delivered in May 1959, and her owners were highly pleased with her when, after carrying out her summer duties, she broke two winter navigation records in her first winter season, docking at Trois-Rivières on January 4, 1960, and then at Montreal on March 21, following a return trip to Europe. Her master, Captain Cowie, was presented with a silver tray by the Port Authorities at Trois-Rivières and received the traditional gold-headed cane from the Montreal Harbour Board commissioners. But the new government refused to honour their predecessor's promise to renew the contract at the end of the five-year term, giving it instead to Papachristidis Shipping, who employed instead a Liberty ship that sailed under the Greek flag.[23] This almost put an end to the *Eskimo*'s career in the CSL fleet. Rodgie McLagan was so annoyed that his first thought was to get rid of her. Good sense prevailed, however, and she was converted into a lake package freighter instead.[24]

Among other vessels ordered by the Department of Transport for public service was the 13,500-s.h.p. railway car and transport ferry MV *Frederick Carter* delivered in 1968. This was one of many vessels that were built over the years to fulfil Canada's commitment to maintain reliable and up-to-date ferry services between Newfoundland and the other Atlantic provinces. Named after a former prime minister and chief justice of Newfoundland, she was built for the run from North Sydney, Nova Scotia, to Port aux Basques, Newfoundland, and could carry up to twenty-nine railway freight cars on five lines of track and twelve transport-trailer

Train and truck ferry Frederick Carter, *built for the Department of Transport in 1968 to run between North Sydney, Nova Scotia, and Porte aux Basques, Newfoundland.*

trucks.[25] She measured 487 by 69 feet, had a total displacement of 10,875 tons, and like the icebreakers was specially strengthened to navigate in ice. She was christened by Mrs. C.A. Pippy, of St. John's, and when completed sailed for the Gulf under the command of Captain Edward Mulrooney.

Rounding off the roster of ships built for the government between 1959 and 1968, and showing the versatility of the yard, were a number of smaller vessels. Among them were the 60-foot sound sweeping barge, S.L.S. *No. 3*,[26] for the seaway, and the 164-foot bait-boat CGS *Arctica*, which replaced the Department of Fisheries' *Illex* that had serviced the Newfoundland fisheries for twenty-five years. The *Arctica* could freeze and store nearly 180 tons of bait-fish and carry it from areas where it was plentiful to where it was in short supply. In addition, she was fitted with communications and navigational devices that allowed her to undertake search and rescue missions. Designed by Alex C. Campbell & Sons, she was 150 feet long (between perpendiculars) and had a deadweight above draft of 340 tons and 1,280-b.h.p. diesel engines.[27] She could comfortably accommodate a crew of eighteen.

This account of the ships that were built and repaired at the Davie shipyard at Lauzon during the 1960s leaves no doubt as to what a glorious decade it was for Canadian shipbuilding. It might easily have been a disastrous decade, as Japanese and Swedish shipbuilders were introducing new, sophisticated building techniques. But the Canadian Vessel Capital

Assistance plan, the opening of the seaway, and increasing demand for tonnage that was a result of strong growth in the country's GNP, combined to produce a bonanza.[28] Moreover, McLagan's wise policy of building ships for competitors on the same terms as those built for the CSL fleet, and incorporating all their improvements, paid off handsomely. In the climate of trust that it created, Davie occupied the number-one position among domestic shipyards. Davie served its clients well by offering improved design and, due to the large scale of its operations, highly competitive prices. Government contracts, both for the RCN and for the Canadian Marine Service, gave the workers precious experience in extra-high-quality work. Consequently, the government remained a strong supporter of the Canadian shipbuilding industry for another decade. Davie Shipbuilding took full advantage of what was offered, producing fifty-one new vessels between 1959 and 1968 – three for the RCN, seven for other government service, and forty-one for private accounts.[29]

Tank cars under construction in the upper steel yard behind the plate shop.

19

TAKIS VELIOTIS

1959-68

THE 1960s SAW changes in staff and plant no less significant than the changes in shipping operations that occurred in the same period, as Davie's management was restructured in preparation for the expected shipbuilding boom. Bert Black remained in charge, while Takis Veliotis, whose vigorous management of the General Engineering Division had greatly impressed McLagan and Lowery, was appointed assistant general manager. Bill White, the shipyard's naval architect who, until he relinquished it to Veliotis, held the additional position of assistant manager, was named technical manager. Finally, at the end of the season, Donald Page was brought in from the Port Arthur shipyard to fill the new position of production manager. Because CSL had decided that all building contracts would thenceforth be given to the Davie and Collingwood shipyards, and that the Port Arthur yard would be used solely for repairs, Page's exceptional knowledge of ships would be of far greater value at Lauzon.

These changes were not without consequences, however. Bill White left Davie the following year (1960), and within two years relations between Black and Veliotis were so strained that McLagan was obliged to choose between them, and chose Veliotis. His way of handling the matter was to appoint Black vice-president of the four CSL shipyards reporting to Lowery,

THE GOLDEN YEARS

Takis Veliotis

leaving the position of general manager open for Veliotis.[1] Only nine years had elapsed since Veliotis first entered the shipyard as a draftsman.

Trouble now came to a head in another quarter. In 1961, Charlie Sauvageau, the shipyard's comptroller, died suddenly at the age of sixty-eight, shortly before he was due to retire. He had been with CSL since 1909, and with Davie since 1929. His death meant the loss both of an esteemed colleague or superior, and of a vibrant connection with the early days of the yard. He had prepared for his departure, however, and Louis Rochette, whom he had hired as his assistant in 1955, was well-qualified to step into his shoes. Rochette, who had graduated as a chartered and industrial accountant at Laval University, and had completed his studies after serving as a heavy bomber pilot during the war, had been the provincial government's chief auditor for retail sales tax before joining the staff at Davie. Unfortunately, Veliotis's business approach was very different from Rochette's, and when Veliotis took over as general manager, it soon became apparent that they would not be able to work together. In 1964, Rochette told McLagan that he could no longer accept the situation. Unwilling to give up either the shipyard manager in whose ability he had so much confidence or Rochette, McLagan tried to ease the tension by appointing

Left: *Sonny Craig, second from left, presenting trophies to the winners in the intra-mural bowling tournament at the end of the season.* Right: *Jerry Gagnon handing his son, Jerry Gagnon Jr., his gold watch for twenty-five years of service.*

Rochette acting treasurer for CSL at headquarters in Montreal. Rochette, however, remained dissatisfied and, as soon as he found a suitable position, resigned.[2] Within two years, Rochette would move up to become vice-president and general manager of Marine Industries Limited's shipyard at Tracy, Quebec.

In the meantime, another long-familiar face was missed in the yard. After forty-seven years of service, Jerry (Jérémie) Gagnon retired in March 1963. He had been taken on at Davie's as a young man in 1916, had served his first years under George D. Davie himself, and had worked his way up from the ranks. There was little about the yard and its workers that Gagnon did not know. A born leader, he had been at the forefront on every company occasion – a keel-laying or a baseball game, a launching or a social gathering. At the reception given to mark his retirement, he was presented with a gold chain for the watch he had received in 1952, but sadly, did not have long to wear it. He died three years later, in February 1966. His death was widely felt, not only on the South Shore, where he had been an important figure in the lives of those who had worked for and with him, but also in Cap Blanc, Quebec's Champlain Ward, where he lived and took such an active part in local affairs that he had come to be regarded as its

Don Page 1915–1993

unofficial mayor. As has generally been the custom with Davie's employees, he was not the only member of his family to work at the yard. Two of his sons would complete more than seventy years of service at the yard between them. Jérémie Jr. started working at the yard at the age of nineteen in 1939 and left because of ill health in 1974; Joseph died as he was about to take early retirement in 1985.

David Craig's son, Cyril (Sonny), had started working at Davie's as a water-boy in 1930 at the age of thirteen and, as soon as he was old enough, had trained as a welder. He was certainly one of the youngest employees – if not *the* youngest – to receive his gold watch for twenty-five years of service. It was he who replaced Jerry Gagnon in 1963. But Sonny was yet another veteran who would disappear suddenly, his career brought to an end in 1964 when he was taken ill. He died shortly after, only a year after he replaced Gagnon. Joseph (Joe) Lennox was appointed in his place.

With Sonny's untimely departure, none of the old guard who had been at the shipyard through the Second World War were left on the management team. Even Don Page, who was promoted to assistant general manager in 1967, was a relative newcomer at Davie, though a veteran of CSL's Kingston and Port Arthur yards. The rest of the top staff consisted of Jacques Regnaud, who had replaced Rochette as treasurer; Leonard Winslade, manager of Ship Repairs; John Gorman, manager of the General

Engineering Division; and Jimmy Fulcher, superintendent of Technical Services. Fulcher, who had come from Vickers-Armstrong's Naval Yard in Newcastle a few years earlier, headed up the most experienced technical team in Canada. It included Bob McGilvray, chief engineer, who had been with Davie since 1945; Bill Farish, naval architect; and Jean-Paul Zizka, senior chief draftsman. Two others who would play a long part in Davie's history joined Fulcher's team from the Naval Yard: Michael Ayre joined as assistant superintendent, Technical Services, in 1967 and Mike Donnison as a designer in 1966. On the production side, Joe Lennox was joined by Jimmy Gilliland as chief engineer (Production) and R.D. (Bob) Coleman as superintendent of Outfitting, while Peter Gwyn moved from personal secretary to the manager to Personnel manager, and Gus Gosselin, a long-time Drawing Office employee, joined the newly formed Planning Department combining with Charles Guay in Cost Control.

Richard Lowery continued to head the team from his office in Montreal. Indeed, the shipyard was fortunate to have as president a talented shipbuilder. Although he was also president of CSL's other four shipyards, he found time to spend with both the technical and the administrative staff. He understood the problems involved in building ships, as well as sailing them, and constantly sought improvements to both. His consideration for the crews led him to introduce changes to better their working and living conditions. He was frequently to be seen in the Drawing Office in Lauzon leaning over the plans of a ship with members of the technical staff worrying out a particular detail, and when the time came for trials, as likely as not he was there to see the results for himself.

Because McLagan was an efficiency expert, it was natural that efficiency would preoccupy Lowery too. Lowery made a special effort to improve productivity throughout construction. He stressed the importance of accurate cost accounting and control at the planning stage. And he tackled problems such as the inordinate amount of time that the men spent "wandering" around the yard. He solved this particular problem simply by setting up a

≈ DRAWING OFFICE ≈

AT FIRST WE mostly made corrections to plans that were sent to us. We had a copy made of the plan, drew the corrections and stuck them on, or else did them in yellow or white chalk on blue prints or in red ink on white. When the acetones began, we had to redo the plans completely to make alterations. *Jacqueline Blais*

WHEN WE ARRIVED in 1966, Quebec was in the midst of a heatwave. It was 92 degrees Fahrenheit with 99 per cent humidity. We had come from the north of England where the temperature if it was 75 degrees was headline news, and humidity never reached anything near that, except when it was raining. There was no air-conditioning then in the Drawing Office and I used to dress like an Apache with a piece of rag around my forehead and something around my chin because of the perspiration. We worked on the old-style linen, real linen covered with a waxy substance, and if it got wet in any way it affected the surface and left a smudge when it was blue-printed. In spite of the fact that I spent the time drying myself, my hand print is still on the first plan I worked on.

Mike Donnison

Mike Donnison. Things have changed a great deal in the thirty years Mike has been at the shipyard. Today he is more likely to be found at his computer.

ship-to-shop telephone and messenger service. Good results were also obtained by fostering a team spirit between the Drawing Office and the Production Control Department and proving to those concerned that pulling together was to their mutual advantage. His constant aim was to make Davie the greatest shipyard in Canada, and whether it was or not, he did his best to make sure the men felt it was. Among the measures he took to instil company pride was a "news service" through which information about the whereabouts and operations of Davie-built ships was sent on to the yard. The staff responded positively to his style of leadership. One of his most treasured possessions today is a beer tankard they gave him on which the names of the twelve ships delivered by the yard in the bumper year 1963 are inscribed. It was not only the number of vessels that was remarkable, he points out with pride, but also the fact that they required eight separate sets of designs and drawings to build them.

Dick Lowery's contribution to Canadian shipbuilding, however, went far beyond his accomplishments at Canadian Vickers and the CSL shipyards. He strove constantly for the general improvement of the industry. Convinced that co-operation among shipbuilders would be beneficial to all, he founded and was an active member of the Canadian Shipbuilding and Ship Repairing Association. He was also a founding member and the first president of the Eastern Canadian Section of the Society of Naval Architects and Marine Engineers, whose first official meeting was held at the Mount Stephen Club in Montreal in October 1952.

As an industry leader, he was among those whose advice on shipbuilding was sought by both Conservative and Liberal governments – nor did he shrink from offering unsolicited advice, if circumstances warranted it. In 1985, he was created an Officer of the Order of Canada in acknowledgement of the importance of his contribution to the Canadian shipping industries. Twenty-one years earlier, he had been the first Canadian to be awarded the prestigious Admiral Jerry Land Gold Medal by the Society of Naval Architects and Marine Engineers, of the United States, for "Outstanding Accomplishments in the Marine Field." Later, he became an

THE GOLDEN YEARS

Seven of thirteen hopper cars ordered by CP Rail, waiting to be picked up.

Pressure vessel for Union Carbide.

honorary vice-president of that society and also of the Royal Institution of Naval Architects, London.

Although every inch a shipbuilder, Lowery wholeheartedly supported Veliotis's efforts to develop the General Engineering Division, recognizing that the day might come when it would keep the shipyard afloat. Even when ship construction and ship repair were both doing well, he encouraged the division to accept contracts to build equipment for hydro-electric projects, petro-chemical processing, mining, transportation, and other industries. No one was more surprised than the workers themselves at the diversity of their production. The manufacture of pressure vessels led to that of tank cars and tank-car tanks, of which more than a thousand were completed by the end of 1964. Hydro-electric equipment, made from 1958 on, included hydraulic gates, penstocks, and pipelines, and was followed by heat exchangers, rotary kilns and dryers, autoclaves, bulk storage tanks, dredge pipes, silos, grading and sorting machinery, and other equipment.[3]

Most contracts called for the GED to install the equipment it fabricated. Georges Berberi, the erection manager for Canadian Projects from 1958 to 1964, headed the shipyard's field teams that travelled to every Canadian province except Prince Edward Island, from British Columbia to

Spillway gates and penstock for Manic II project.

THE GOLDEN YEARS

Scroll case for Manic II.

Newfoundland. Major equipment built, and in some cases designed, for hydro-electric companies included sluice gates, lifts, and towers for the Annapolis River Dam; a fixed roller-type gate and electrically powered gate hoist, several draft tube gates, and a gantry crane for Hydro-Quebec's Bersimis projects; eight giant penstocks and five spillway gates, each weighing 85 tons, for the Manic II development; an 8.5-ton capacity gantry crane and fourteen smaller 45-ton gates for the Pointe des Cascades power project above Montreal; eight intake gates for the Manitoba Hydro Grant Rapids project; and a penstock for Calgary Power. Other contracts included the fabrication and erection of the structural steel work for Warehouse Number 1 of a huge grain terminal at Baie-Comeau, for the Cargill Grain Company;[4] a decompression chamber for the navy; a 42-foot diameter fan intake section for the largest supersonic wind tunnel in Canada for the National Research Council; and a ladle built for the Steel Company of Canada plant in Hamilton. The GED manufactured loading ramps for CSL docks at Montreal, Etobicoke, and Hamilton, and produced deck-travelling hatch-cover lifting cranes that were designed in the GED drawing office, for both CSL's and its competitors' Upper Lakes bulk freighters.

Local contracts included the construction and delivery of an oil-storage tank, which was dispatched across the river aboard MV *Eskimo* to be set up at the Imperial Oil depot at Wolfe's Cove, and several contracts that were obtained by Takis Veliotis from the Canadian Army Research and

Gerald Bull's 120-foot gun on its testing site in Barbados.

Emile Robinson emerges from the barrel of the gun from which he has ground away the imperfections for a distance of 60 feet, the other 60 feet having been done from the other end by a fellow worker. He was lying on a dolly, he says, a great improvement from elbowing his way along as he did on earlier occasions. Courtesy E. Robinson.

Development Establishment (CARDE) at Valcartier, just outside Quebec. In some cases, CARDE's own machine shop was not large enough to handle them, and in others it did not have a sufficiently sophisticated welding capability.

GED installation teams, generally headed by John Gorman, travelled to the United States, West Indies, and South and Central America setting up equipment. It was Gorman who was in charge of the team that handled a special contract obtained from Gerald Bull, a former scientist at CARDE who later achieved fame as an aero-physicist, a contract that would have extraordinary international ramifications. Bull was determined to prove that a satellite could be launched into space from a gun. When he left CARDE, he continued to work on his High Altitude Research Project (HARP) under the aegis of McGill University's space research program (now Space Research Institute Incorporated). He obtained some old 16-inch naval guns of First World War vintage on which he planned to have extensions welded and, remembering the precision machining and skilled welding of Davie's General Engineering Division, gave it the contract for the work. The 120-foot gun was mounted on a railway bogies, so that when it was fired, the recoil was absorbed as it moved backward up an inclined plane. Bull succeeded in firing 5-foot shells at 6,200 feet per second, ninety-five miles into the atmosphere.

Emile Robinson, a veteran Davie employee, was a member of the team that carried out the tests in the Barbados on six occasions. When the gun barrel's inside wall became striated after a number of firings, he recalls, he was one of the few who was willing to be lowered with his arms above his head into the narrow upright barrel. Once inside, he had to weld the little grooves using small electrode sticks, and then grind the surface with special machinery designed and built in the GED machine shop. Other Davie welders who took part in the tests include Fernand Cliche, Norman Huot, Roger Gaumont, Raymond Brer, and Lambert Peltier.

Although these experiments were reported by the media at the time, it was not until much later that their greater significance became known.

Bull was determined to produce the gun. When his idea was rejected by the Canadian and American governments, he took his invention elsewhere. Iraq, which welcomed him with open arms, succeeded in importing British-built components for the gun shipped in violation of a ban on arms sales by describing them as parts for a pipeline.[5] Shipments were halted when the deception was revealed in the press. The story became headline news when Gerald Bull was murdered by hands unknown in 1990.

By building up the General Engineering Division, Veliotis was leading the shipyard along the same path as other important Canadian shipyards such as Canadian Vickers, Burrard Dry Dock, Canadian Shipbuilding and Engineering, the Kingston, Collingwood and Halifax shipyards, and Marine Industries Limited, all of which were engaged in general engineering by 1963. The availability in the shipyard of engineers and draftsmen, and a large force of metal workers, made heavy industrial fabrication an obvious line of work when these companies decided to diversify. Veliotis was never content to let Davie's GED merely coast along. He encouraged his staff to tender on projects that required technologies that the division had not yet acquired, looking upon such jobs as opportunities to upgrade skills and facilities. Land the job, he would say, and I will get you what you need to carry it out. When the six miles of high- and low-pressure piping for the Kundah hydro-electric project near Madras in India[6] were fabricated, for instance, it was the first time that the new quenching temper steel T1 made by US Steel had been successfully welded. The techniques used there were developed at a new welding department of the GED set up by John Gorman.[7] Many of the welders trained in this department commonly reached a higher standard than those in the shipbuilding division. They obtained certification by the Canadian Welding Bureau and the American Welding Bureau when required, and even met the very strict American Society of Mechanical Engineers (ASME) code. The department was so successful that the division soon won certification to operate its own radiography department using gamma rays and cobalt sources.[8]

How much resistance Veliotis encountered in persuading CSL to purchase sophisticated equipment we do not know. We do know that McLagan was willing to make a greater investment in the Davie yard than other CSL yards because its location below the seaway locks allowed both ocean-going ships and lake vessels to be built there. The high performance of the GED must also have been a factor. In any event, an extension was built on to the pipe shop in 1959, and the following year the outfitting wharf was completely rebuilt.

When the possibility of building submarines for the Canadian Navy was under discussion, CSL decided to bring the Davie shipyard up to the necessary standard so that it could tender for them when the time came. Plans were drawn up for a maximum security plant, the focal point of which was a covered berth. This was designed to be built in sections. The first section, which was 90 by 75 feet, had steel walls and aluminum sandwich encasing fibreglass insulation and was completed early in 1961. The section's two 50-ton overhead cranes were built by the GED. The whole installation cost $100,834 and in view of the buoyant shipbuilding market it was decided to go ahead immediately with a 255-foot extension at a cost of $288,611. There was no risk in building the berth ahead of the submarine program (which never did come about) because it could also be used to build small ships or for industrial work, and could be lengthened later if required. It was ready that July. Aside from the Foundation tugs and the *Alert*, few ships have been launched from it; almost all of its life it has served as an assembly or module shop.

Meanwhile, because the office building was increasingly crowded, a third floor was added in 1962 to be used as drawing offices. Also, to meet the busy construction program, a 102-by-80-by-43-foot-9-inch high extension was built on to the machine shop in October the following year. In 1964, the prefabrication shop was lengthened by 160 feet, thus increasing its size to 960 by 150 feet, and by the end of the year, a cafeteria for the staff had been built and was in operation. Before that there had been a dining room. Also in 1964, the offices came in for a much-needed remodelling, in the course of which a yard list of all the ships that had been built at the yard was prepared and hung in the hall. From then on, many an argument regarding tonnage or delivery date has been settled by a quick trip to the vestibule followed by an "I told you so."

By this time Davie was firmly committed to modular methods of prefabrication. With ship sections of up to 80 tons being built in the shop, it was necessary to get heavier cranes to handle them at the building berths, and a new crane was ordered from Butters in Scotland. It arrived in October 1968 packed in almost a hundred crates. The GED under Georges Berberi made short work of assembling it, and it was operational the next month. Not only was the purchase justified by the man-hours it saved, but, far more important, it also put an end to the risks that the crane operators had been taking by using two light cranes to lift the loads the new crane could lift on its own. Also ended were the constant repairs to the smaller cranes resulting from the overly heavy loads.

As these improvements were being made to the yard, others were suggested. Don Page received a polite reprimand from head office when he recommended transferring the tinsmiths to the "North Pole." The entire shipyard referred to the remaining part of the original machine shop that way, but head office either disapproved of such levity or the dig itself in official correspondence. Page also proposed that the electricians be relocated to the machine shop mezzanine and drew attention to the fact that the Navy and plant stores building, housed in an old sawmill that was one of the few original yard buildings, was a fire hazard. He succeeded in having the building razed and the site used for a multi-floored central stores building 80 by 100 feet.

The perimeter lighting of the yard was improved and the office workers' cafeteria completely modernized and renovated. When, in 1966, Davie was awarded the contract to refit the aircraft carrier *Bonaventure*, which would involve the temporary storage of parts and furnishings of the ship, a new stores building, a Butler building 200 by 100 feet wide, was erected where Don Page had suggested it go two years earlier. Towards the end of the year, work began on the final 105-foot extension to the covered berth, which increased its total length to 405 feet.

The general manager did not confine himself to his office building but, like the Davies before him, took considerable pleasure in doing the rounds of the shipyard – *his* shipyard – for that was very much the way he thought of it. As he strode around the shops, many of the workers would greet him by name. To their "*Bonjour*, Takis!" he would respond with an enquiry about their families, often surprising them by his ability to recall previous conversations about their wives and children. He seemed to take a genuine interest in their activities and well-being. He would question them about the work they were doing, listen to their suggestions, and make his own, keeping abreast of operations generally.

He made it his business to keep informed about the personal lives of his staff and their families. They knew that they could take a serious problem to him and that he would listen sympathetically and offer advice and help. He was quick to send flowers to a wife in hospital, for example, and to allow time off to visit her. But Veliotis's charisma was only one side of his person; there was another that many feared. In the words of one of his staunchest supporters, who also described him as a "fantastic guy," he could be "hard, even ruthless." Yet some will not agree, describing his outbursts as his way to let off steam. At least one employee, still a member of the management team, seems to have known how to handle their relationship. "I couldn't tell you how many times he fired me," he told me. "I just turned up the next day and nothing was said. He was like a father to me, and I took it like a scolding from a father."

Many stories are told about Veliotis. He could not stand to see a man with long hair. He once set up a barber in his office and then walked through the building picking out those whom he thought needed a haircut. Once he came across an old stove in one of the shops. Thinking that the workers had set it up to toast their sandwiches, a pet peeve of his, he set to smashing it with a sledgehammer, only to be told, when it lay in pieces, that it was used to heat electrodes for welding.

There were only two categories of employee for Veliotis: those from whom he expected and got unquestioning loyalty, who were on his team, and those who did not respond wholeheartedly, and were not. Members of the team found him an exciting man to work for. He kept them constantly on their toes, was always ready to protect and help them, and, so I have been told, even today remains loyal to them. They recognized the part he played in building up the yard following the fire in 1955 and applauded his unending efforts to upgrade the shipbuilding facilities while making the GED a top-rate engineering works. His success in obtaining work around the world was a source of pride to them.

By contrast, his dictatorial manner was not conducive to the maintenance of good relations with the union. According to Louis Desmarais, president of CSL, Veliotis had little regard for the workers' demands and needs. As a result, the labour situation was far worse at Davie than at other yards.[9] Clement Fleury, the union president at the time, states that in order to stand up to Veliotis, he formed a team of eighty stalwarts ("*poteaux*") who tried to keep control of the yard.

Whoever was responsible for this unhealthy situation, it did not help that the average worker saw the lavish launching parties hosted at the Château Frontenac as an indication of CSL's prosperity rather than as the public relations effort they were. The men simply did not believe management's argument that productivity had to improve for the shipyard to survive. The apparent financial strength of the parent company undoubtedly contributed to the many slowdowns and strikes that occurred in these and later years. This was also a time when the shipbuilding business was booming, a time when the union ranks might naturally increase.

Government officials learned the hard way that Takis Veliotis was not to be taken lightly. Under the smooth manner, there was a careful, thorough, and extremely determined man. This was never more evident than at the Commons Public Accounts Committee Inquiry into the refit and improvement of HMCS *Bonaventure* in 1969. An internal Davie document purportedly proving that the government had been grossly overcharged for the *Bonaventure* refit had been made public. The accusation led to such a hubbub in the media that the government bowed to Opposition demands and set up the enquiry. Both Richard Lowery and Takis Veliotis testified and Davie's books were subjected to a government audit.

Although at first it appeared that the prices were inflated – more than $500, for example, for the replacement of a bathroom cabinet – Veliotis showed that the job list in the possession of the M.P. had been wrongly interpreted. Far from giving a full description of work done, each item on the list was a heading under which related jobs were grouped. To complicate matters further, cabin numbers had been changed in the course of the contract, so that some of the charges under dispute referred to work in other cabins. By drawing on two moving vans of filing cabinets and the necessary staff to pull documents from them, all of which Lowery sent to Ottawa from the shipyard, Veliotis was able to justify the amounts charged for every job. As a result, Davie was completely exonerated, and its management praised for the efficient way that records were kept at the yard. By proving that in each case, orders for extra work had been signed by the government team in charge, Veliotis succeeded in getting the shipyard cleared of wrongdoing. The two government departments that handled the contract, however, were censured for poor contract administration.

Over the years "Big Davie" and the other CSL shipyards acquired an enviable reputation within the shipping industry. Working conditions and facilities had been steadily upgraded and the companies had taken on a certain *style*, the Canada Steamship Lines style, one that befitted a large shipping conglomerate that covered the operation of both cruise ships and merchantmen, a hotel chain, and other subsidiaries. The perquisites that the staff and their families enjoyed included weekend trips to Murray Bay on the CSL cruise ships. There they were given free accommodation and were required to pay only fifty cents for their full-course meals at the Manoir Richelieu. The staff of the Davie shipyard were proud to be a part of an organization that treated them with consideration, one that was respected throughout the country, and they were generally proud of the

Saguenay cruise boat.

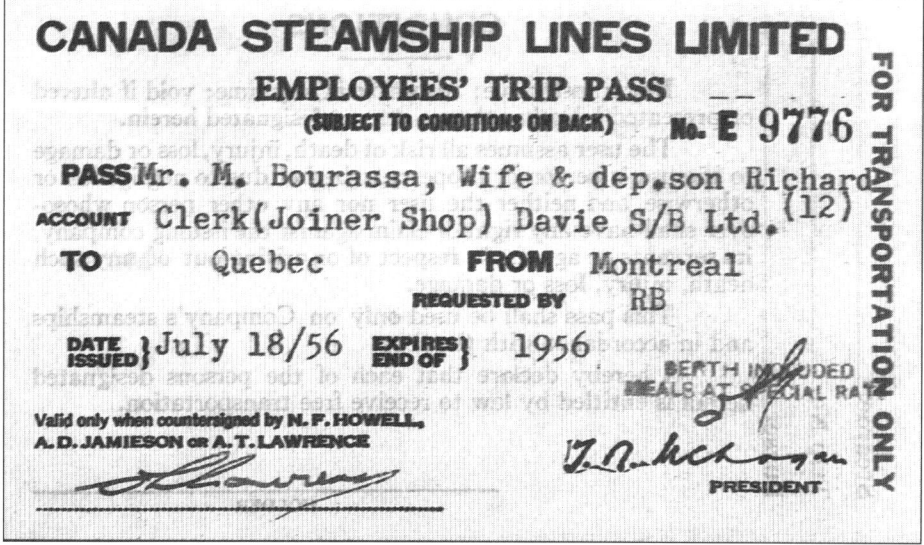

Employee's trip pass for M. Bourassa, wife, and son.

flair with which Takis Veliotis represented the yard. So was McLagan. He described Veliotis as a good business getter and excellent general manager. Richard Lowery agreed, finding him personable, very technically well-educated, and with a talent for leadership – one of the best shipbuilding executives he had ever known.[10] The fact that Veliotis was trilingual, speaking his native Greek and fluent English and French, and that he possessed some knowledge of other languages, was an additional asset. And, certainly, he had impressive physical attributes. Six foot four in height, he towered over most other men and exuded self-confidence. McLagan believed in rewarding excellence and in 1966 appointed him vice-president of Davie Shipbuilding.

While Canada Steamship Lines' shipyards were performing well, its cruise ships were not, and by the mid-1960s the halcyon days of CSL's glamorous *Great White Fleet* had come to an end. Gone were the games of quoits and shuffleboard on the deck, the lazy afternoons spent watching the majestic St. Lawrence coastline slip by, the flutter on the miniature horse race in the lounge, the singsongs, the elegant dining and dancing, the pizzazz of a swing orchestra against the throb of the engines. The jet plane had put a worldwide choice of holidays within reach of its former clientele, and the CSL's ships, as well as its hotels, were losing money. In 1965, CSL decided to discontinue the Saguenay River excursions, citing the risk of fire or other accident aboard the aging *Richelieu*, *Tadoussac*, and *St. Lawrence*. The truth was that there had been no more than thirty paying customers on some cruises in 1964. Nevertheless, for many of the public, the retirement of the Saguenay cruise ships meant both the severing of a personal link with the past and the disappearance of the most familiar ships on the St. Lawrence River. The three veterans were towed to a shipbreaker's yard in Antwerp where the career of the *Richelieu* and *St. Lawrence* came to an end. The *Tadoussac*, however, won a reprieve. Renamed *St. Lawrence*, she became a floating hotel. For a while she was berthed at Copenhagen and then, following an extravagant refurbishing, she lowered her welcoming gangplanks to the first of her visitors at Jedda.

Last launch from the George T. Davie yard at Lauzon. The staff gather round the president, Ken Wood, in light-coloured coat.

In CSL, too, there were changes, for Rodgie McLagan was making plans for his eventual retirement. He began by appointing John McGiffin vice-president and assistant general manager of CSL, and a year later, feeling comfortable with his choice, handed him his position as general manager as well. By 1966, McLagan, then in his seventieth year, was ready to resign as president and CEO of CSL "in the best interest of the shareholders," and at the Directors' Meeting in April, John McGiffin took his place as president, and McLagan became chairman of the board.

McLagan could look back on the decade that had just ended with considerable satisfaction. It had been one with plenty of work for Davie employees. The CSL fleet had been successfully restructured following the opening of the seaway. CSL shipyards had built ships not only for the CSL fleet but for the fleets of its competitors. The shipyards had shaken free from their heavy dependence on government contracts – thirty-five of the forty-five vessels delivered by Davie between 1959 and 1968, for example, were commercial vessels – and during those years several shipbuilding records had been broken. Moreover, McLagan had confidence in the men he was leaving in charge, and in none more than in Takis Veliotis.

The 1960s were also years when competition with the George T. Davie shipyard to the west of the Lorne Dry Dock kept both yards on their toes. Under Ken Wood's direction, production at the George T. Davie yard had amounted to thirty-five new vessels. In addition, three half-vessels, or bow sections, were built at the George T. Davie yard and joined in the Lorne Dry Dock to stern sections built at the Canadian Vickers shipyard in Montreal. The smaller yard also carried out a large amount of repair work. But the rivalry of the two yards was about to end, for Canadian Vickers decided that there was neither enough new work nor enough repair work to warrant the continued existence of two yards at Lauzon. In December 1967, the company announced that the assets of the George T. Davie shipyard had been sold to Davie Shipbuilding and that the Vickers shipyard in Lauzon would close down the following summer when the work on hand had been completed.[11] The men heard the news in shocked disbelief. They felt that they had almost literally been sold down the river. Their yard and livelihood had been taken from them, not because they had done a poor job – they knew they had not – but because the parent company in Montreal had incurred heavy losses on projects such as the construction of the government icebreaker *Louis Saint Laurent*, in which they had no part.

The George T. Davie shipyard had come through the war as a family yard, and in spite of its sale to Canadian Vickers, much of the family spirit had remained. Vickers tried to get the best deal possible for those of its employees who were taken on next door, but the Davie workers, influenced

Village de la réouverture

by an increasingly militant union, strongly resented the idea that former rivals should retain their seniority and better pension terms when the merger occurred. Knowing they were unwelcome, many of the more than 800 workers simply did not apply. During the six months in which the shipyard completed the work on hand, they were given time off to look for other work. They left one by one. On July 12, 1968, following the delivery of the fishing trawler *Triano*, the remaining George T. Davie employees were finally obliged to put down their tools. They made one last stand. They set up a tent village, which they called "Le village de la réouverture" (Village of the Reopening), hoping to get some reaction from the Canadian or Quebec governments. The attempt was in vain. Within a week the wall that had divided the two yards had been torn down.

Meanwhile, Davie Brothers at Levis had not been experiencing the same buoyant times as the Lauzon yards. Production had tumbled from the peak years 1958 and 1959 during both of which thirteen vessels were delivered, to an average of three 30- to 87-foot boats annually from 1964 to 1968. Once more, the yard had to rely to a great extent on maintenance and wintering for its bread and butter.

Built at the Davie Brothers shipyard in Levis for the Canadian Department of Northern Affairs and Natural Resources as a centennial project, the replica of Cartier's Grande Hermine *visited Expo 67 at Montreal before returning to Quebec and a permanent berth at Parc Brébeuf.*

An unexpected bonus came with Canada's centennial world fair, Expo 67, when the Department of Northern Affairs and Natural Resources decided to build a replica of Cartier's *Grande Hermine* as one of its centennial projects, and Davie Brothers was given the contract. Loads of Douglas fir, oak, and yellow cedar were delivered to the yard, ship carpenters from Ile aux Coudres joined the regular workers, and in the fall of 1966 the 79-foot galleon stood ready for launching. Mrs. Jean Marchand, wife of Canada's Minister of Manpower, christened her *Grande Hermine*, breaking the traditional bottle of champagne on her bows as she slid into the St.

Lawrence.[12] The *Grande Hermine* was sent to Expo 67 at Montreal and, when it ended, was returned to Quebec to be permanently berthed at the Cartier Brébeuf National Historic Park.

The year 1966 also marked a new departure for Davie Brothers, for the yacht *Intrépide*, which followed the *Grande Hermine* down the ways, was the first steel-hulled vessel to be built at the shipyard. The change was not a drastic one. Both wooden and steel-hulled boats continued to be built at the yard until 1981, when the last wooden vessel, the 60-foot crabbing boat MV *Frederic C.*, was delivered.[13]

Part Eight

NEW CHALLENGES

Sonar domes ready for export to the U.S. yard of Ingalls Shipbuilding.

20

POWER CORPORATION

1968-76

RODGIE McLAGAN HAD heard, in 1963, that Power Corporation had acquired a substantial block of Canada Steamship Lines stock and had felt uneasy, concerned that the Montreal-based company might be planning a takeover. Before long, Paul Desmarais, Power's president, requested representation on the CSL board, confirming McLagan's fears. By the end of 1968, the corporation had increased its holdings to 42 per cent of CSL common shares and 51.2 per cent of preferred, and thus it obtained control of the company and its subsidiaries, including the shipyards.[1] Davie had been a fully owned subsidiary of Canada Steamship Lines for forty-three years, and in that respect its status did not change, but the status of Canada Steamship Lines did.

At the time of McLagan's retirement in 1966, Canada Steamship Lines was operating smoothly under McGiffin's presidency, and when Power took over, no immediate shake-up of the officers and staff occurred. Within two years, however, Paul Desmarais replaced McGiffin with Desmarais's brother, Louis, and named McGiffin chairman of the board. Louis Desmarais was a newcomer to CSL, and his appointment came as a blow to Veliotis, who had looked forward to becoming president himself one day. Adding to Veliotis's bitterness was the knowledge that Louis Desmarais, to whom he now reported, was neither a shipbuilder nor even a man with experience in running a shipping line. A gulf of dislike and distrust soon opened between the two men, in marked contrast to the bond of respect and affection that had existed between Veliotis and McLagan.

Veliotis had other problems, too. He had enjoyed McLagan and Lowery's full backing through the golden years of shipbuilding, and under his management Davie had responded with a first-class performance. But the unprecedented demand for shipping and large hydro-electric and other installations, for which the new seaway had been largely responsible, was all but over, and the shipyards now had to find new markets. In 1966, at the launching of the *Maplecliffe Hall* at Canadian Vickers in Montreal, C.M. Drury, the Minister of Industry, declared that the Canadian shipbuilding industry was in "full health" and that the government had instigated several measures to support it,[2] but long-term orders for new merchant ships belied his optimism, and as each ship was completed and delivered, concern grew in the shipyard. Would there be another contract, or was this important side of the Canadian shipbuilding business about to disappear? The delivery by Davie in 1968 of two maximum seaway-size heavy diesel bulk carriers, CSL's *Frontenac* and the *Lake Manitoba* to Nipigon Transport,[3] left only four vessels to be completed. Three of these were for Hall Corporation, the 17,907-ton Great Lakes bulk carrier *Ottercliffe Hall* and the two smaller 4,981-ton tankers *Chemical Transport* and *Industrial Transport*. The other, the 14,000-ton tanker *Imperial Bedford*, was on order for Imperial Oil.[4] All would be delivered by August 1969 and what then?

Fortunately, Davie was able to win some government contracts from the new Department of Supply and Services, which combined the roles of the former Department of Defence Production, the Shipbuilding Branch of the Department of Transport, and others.[5] In addition, tenders that Davie submitted in December 1967, both for "lead" and "follow" yard status for the four-ship DDH-destroyer program, resulted in 1968 in the award to the Davie shipyard of the contracts for the construction of two destroyers as follow yard. The lead yard responsibility, including management of the

Hall Corporation oil tankers Chemical Transport *and* Industrial Transport *of 1969.*

The 14,000-ton oil tanker SS Imperial Bedford *built for Imperial Oil in 1969. A fifteen-year charter carrying crude oil to the Imperial Oil refineries in Halifax and Montreal awaited her.*

design through the Naval Central Drawing Office (NCDO), situated at the Canadian Vickers plant in Montreal, and the construction of the lead and one other destroyer, had gone to Marine Industries, Sorel.[6]

The helicopter-carrying destroyers (DDH), or "Tribals," as they would more generally be known, were multi-purpose warships of unique Canadian design that were considered by many to be among the most manoeuvrable and efficient vessels of their class. At 423 by 48 feet, with a displacement of 3,800 tons (deep draft displacement of 4,485 tons), they were bigger than the *Annapolis* class of helicopter destroyer and carried a double hangar to house two *Sea King* helicopters. Especially equipped for anti-submarine warfare, their sleek hulls and streamlined superstructures were tightly packed with the latest in anti-submarine and close-range anti-missile and anti-aircraft systems. Almost all the equipment could be controlled by the computers on the bridge, as could their twin propellers powered by four powerful gas turbine engines of Pratt & Whitney of Saint Lambert, Montreal, manufacture. The accommodation for 280 officers and men was both functional and attractive. In a break with tradition, the standard bunk length was increased to six feet six inches, and bunk areas, including those of the thirty training billets, were partitioned off from the rest of the living space to provide more restful sleeping conditions.

Because the ships were of modular construction, each module weighing at least 60 tons, and the technology had been so recently adopted, a great deal of extra planning was required. Consequently, it was not until February 1970 that the keels of both destroyers were laid.[7] Unlike Marine Industries, where the modules were built in smaller units and upside-down, Davie chose to build them right-side up and in units weighing more than 60 tons.[8]

The difference in building strategy necessitated extensive redrawing at NCDO, which had been a condition of Davie's bid, and it led also to contract adjustments and delays. Nevertheless, Davie succeeded in keeping up with the lead yard. The official ceremony for the launching of the lead destroyer *Iroquois* took place at Sorel on November 28, 1970, amid pomp and ceremony, and perhaps a little ribbing from those members of Davie's

Aerial view of the shipyard in 1969.

staff who attended, because Davie, as follow yard, had launched the sister ship, *Athabaskan*, a day earlier! In the neck-and-neck outfitting race that followed, delivery dates of government-supplied equipment became critical. Veliotis threatened to "hijack" the first Oto Melara five-inch gun on its way from Italy, as the ship transporting it passed Lauzon on the way to Sorel. This would have created an embarrassing situation, had a follow ship really become the lead. Needless to say, the threat was not carried out, but the fact that the thought even occurred to Veliotis indicates the intensity of the program. Following her trials, Commander R.D. Yanow took delivery of HMCS *Athabaskan*, and commissioned her into the Canadian Navy on September 30, 1972.

Other naval contracts at this time included a major refit of the Canadian naval escort maintenance ship HMCS *Cape Scott*[9] and the conversion to a DDH destroyer of the St. Laurent class Destroyer Escort HMCS *Margaree*, in 1965.[10] Over and above the Canadian military program, which

HMCS Athabaskan *DDH 282, delivered in September 1972, third of the* Athabaskans *in the Canadian Navy. She belonged to the first class of Canadian destroyers that were built as helicopter destroyers.*

provided a great deal of work for the yard, Davie also contracted to build parts of the hull of a large submarine support vessel in 50-ton units for a U.S. shipyard.

Non-naval government contracts during this period included the light icebreaker CCGS *Griffon* for Coast Guard service on the lakes. The *Griffon* was similar in size to the *J.E. Bernier*, though slightly longer and of shallower draft. And then, in its last days of office in 1970, the Union nationale provincial government ordered two new year-round ferries, each to carry 700 passengers and sixty-five vehicles, for the Quebec-to-Levis run.

These ferries were to be fitted with two engines, only one of which would be run in summer, when the channel was open, and both of which would be used in winter, when there was ice to contend with. This strategy eliminated the need for separate winter and summer ferries. Because the boats were much larger than their predecessors, the ferry company also had to face up to significant wharf and terminal improvements it had not counted on. Twenty-five years later, however, the ferries continue to ply the

Left: CCGS Griffon *built for the Department of Transport in 1970, and stationed on Lake Ontario.* Right: CCGS Griffon *laying a buoy.* Courtesy Ted Van Gaalen.

river bearing the names of the prominent Quebeckers they honour, *Lomer Gouin* and *Alphonse Desjardins*. Lomer Gouin, an eminent jurist who became premier and later lieutenant-governor of the province, was a strong promoter of classical colleges, and more exceptionally, technical and commercial schools. Alphonse Desjardins founded the caisses populaires, the popular savings banks now located throughout Quebec. Davie's steel stockyard manager, Desjardins's grandson Alphonse Desjardins, whose career at the shipyard lasted thirty-two years, stood proudly beside his daughter at the ferry's launching.

While the shipyard kept busy, mainly with government work, the Repair Department, whose job figures had tumbled from ninety vessels to sixty-six in 1967, rebounded following the closing of the George T. Davie yard in 1968 with a spectacular increase to 141 repairs. It was reckoned that Davie had obtained $591,000 of extra business due to its neighbour's closing, and it had brought in additional welcome profits of $173,000 that would otherwise have gone "next door."

The uncertainties of the shipping market did not prevent Davie from pressing on in 1968 with its five-year modernization program – quite the contrary. European and Far East shipyards were enhancing their performance with improved production facilities, better pre-planning, and the use of new technology. So dramatic and rapid were these improvements,

Left: *Standing, left to right: Jean-Paul Zizka, Ernest Gorman, Gus Gosselin. Seated: Robert McGilvray, Leonard Windslade, Bill White. Photo taken in the early 1950s.* Right: *Ferry M.V. Alphonse Desjardins, built in 1971 for the crossing between Quebec and Levis, and still on the job with her sister ship, M.V. Lomer Gouin.*

particularly in Japan, that Canadian yards, whose relatively lower productivity levels, higher labour costs, and combination of out-of-date shipbuilding methods and restrictive labour practices had until then been partly offset by generous government subsidies, could no longer ignore them if they were to survive. Davie began a series of radical changes. A new 440-by-120-by-45-foot-high plate storage shop was erected with a concrete floor, railway tracks, and a 15-ton overhead magnetic crane. An addition to the steel-handling shop was rushed to completion, allowing the inventory of steel plates to be housed indoors and stored flat, and a new magnetic overhead crane was installed to handle them, while new machines that shot-blasted the plates and primed them with a protective undercoat did away with a great deal of time-consuming and dirty work. After receiving their undercoat, the plates were ready to pass under one of the two automatic cutting machines that optically scanned the one-tenth-scale drawings to guide the cutting shape. The traditional wooden template now was used only for the shaped sections of the bow and stern. An American Tool Works lathe with 21-foot centres was installed in the machine shop, and a 200-ton bending machine in the prefabricating shop. At the end of the decade, not only had all the main buildings in the Davie shipyard been

The combined Davie Shipbuilding and George T. Davie shipyards seen from the west in 1971. The GTD yard is now known as Davie West.

modernized and many of them enlarged, but the equipment had also been made more efficient, so that prefabricated sections that were twice as heavy could be handled and larger ships could be built.

Yet, as 1969 drew to a close, only 850 out of 2,200 union members were actually employed, and international competition continued to threaten Davie's future. The union organized a "last chance" effort, supported by federal and provincial Members of Parliament, members of the Chamber of Commerce, and religious figures, including the well-known activist and parish priest of Saint-Roch, Quebec, Mgr. Raymond Lavoie. Mgr. Lavoie told a reporter for the Montreal newspaper *La Presse* he doubted that a capitalist company such as Davie could be interested, even for one minute, in the fate of the shipyard workers, and that while he was in favour of dialogue, he believed that it was time for revolutionary formulas!

> ## ⇌ PLANT ENGINEERING ⇋
>
> ON VISITING A shipyard, one tends to look at the ships under construction or repair on the waterfront, and then, perhaps, to visit the sheds to see the various shipbuilding tradesmen at work. But behind each plater deftly fitting the steel in place, or welder fastening the plates together in a shower of sparks in the shops, behind each department head and secretary in the drawing and other offices, there is another group of workers who make it possible for them to do their jobs efficiently. Not only do the men of the Plant Engineering Division look after every aspect of the plant itself, but they are also responsible for installing the services on the ships under construction or repair. Jean-Guy L'Hébreux, the director of the Plant Engineering Division, joined Davie as a draftsman on qualifying as an engineer at Laval University in 1969 and has been the Davie shipyard's "husband" since 1980. All building and repair work of the plant, all maintenance, from the most complicated piece of machinery down to the office stapler, and all purchases of stores and equipment are handled by him. He gets a great deal of satisfaction from doing his job well, and the appearance of the shipyard speaks of his efficiency.

Fortunately, whatever he had in mind was not acted on. By the following year, the world shipping market was on the rise again and both the federal and provincial governments were making determined efforts to improve the industrial performance and international competitiveness of Canadian manufacturing companies. Davie benefited from a number of federal programs. It qualified both for the Department of Industry, Trade and Commerce[11] program designed to foster export development, and that of the Department of Regional Economic Expansion Industrial Incentives

Branch, because employment and income on the South Shore lagged behind other parts of Canada.[12] In addition, the provincial Department of Industry and Commerce offered a program for new plants and another for existing facilities, the latter giving tax credits on all investments.

The strong upswing in the worldwide demand for shipping gave Davie, along with other Canadian shipyards, an opportunity to overcome its short-term, and even, it was hoped, longer-term problems. Between September and December 1970, the company received no fewer than ninety enquiries for vessels, most for tankers and bulk carriers of 80,000 tons or more. Another fifty-four enquiries followed in 1971.[13] The unusually high number partly reflected the exceptionally high freight rates for oil, and partly Davie's ability to offer more competitive delivery dates than its foreign competitors, as it was able to complete vessels for 1972. With so many potential contracts to choose from came the problem of deciding which would make the fullest possible use of the different trades and available facilities, and so achieve the maximum productivity of the yard.[14]

Davie decided to go after a contract from the Varnima group of Piræus, Greece. Valued at $53 million,[15] it represented almost half of the $108-million-worth of contracts held by Canadian shipyards in April 1971. The design for the three vessels was to be purchased from the Aker Group of Norway. It was then to be modified partly to shorten the length of the original design, in order to fit on Davie's building berths, and partly to suit Varnima needs. Even with these modifications, the vessels were much larger than any previously built by a Canadian shipyard. It was a daring decision to take on the contract, especially in view of the large choice of other contracts that were available at the time.[16]

Many problems would have to be solved before and during construction. Each tanker occupied two berths, so that two ships side by side took up all the berths in the main yard. They were so long that they extended from well below the high-water mark to just a few feet from the front of the main assembly shop, and the bow had to be erected at the last minute in order to avoid blocking access to the main shipyard. In order to support the heavy loads during construction and, more particularly, the tremendous 4,000-ton momentary load – one-quarter the weight of the ship, which would be borne by the forward poppet at the moment of stern lift – reinforced concrete slabs were poured both under and across the full length of both slipways. Because the ship was partly in water during construction, large weights were placed on the engine-room tank top[17] to prevent the hulls from floating away. Yet, in spite of these efforts to anticipate problems, the building of the Varnima tankers took Davie into a new, unknown, and therefore risky region.

Though the Varnima ships occupied all the main berths at Davie, two berths at Davie West (the former George T. Davie shipyard) were available, of which no use had been made since its acquisition. On these berths, medium-sized vessels of up to 350 feet overall could be built, giving Davie a little freedom to manoeuvre. As to assembly shop space, some was made available when the Industrial Division gave up the high and low bays to the Shipbuilding Division and concentrated its work in the shops of the Davie West yard.

By taking on the contracts for these enormous vessels, Davie entered what amounted to a new field. This enabled the company to further upgrade the plant through the Program for the Advancement of Industrial Technology (PAIT). A machine was developed at the yard and installed in the covered slip that automatically lifted the 4-ton stiffeners on to the steel side panel plates and held them firmly in place while they were being welded there, after which the rest of the prefabrication was carried out. And a 140-ton Kamag transporter was acquired to carry the 80-ton sections – far heavier than those the yard had previously built – from shop to shop and on to the building berth.

The General Engineering Division had become very robust in its fifteen years thanks to Veliotis's tireless efforts and McLagan's financial backing. There was continuing demand for increasingly advanced technology that the Industrial Division and Davie would be well-positioned to exploit.

In May 1969, a mobile offshore jack-up drilling rig, the *Kenting No. 1* was built under licence from Marathon-Letourneau in Mississippi, for Petrolia Oil Well Drilling Ltd. at Lake Erie. The owners provided the drawings and specifications,[18] and General Engineering built the spud legs and yokes for Davie's Marine Division.[19] It was the first Canadian-built oil rig, and though there were no follow-up orders at the time, the contract was a portent of things to come.

Two wind tunnels were built and delivered, one to the National Research Board in Ottawa and the other to a Romanian customer. A huge $4-million magnet for the cyclotron of the joint University of British Columbia–University of Alberta research particle accelerator (TRIUMF) was also constructed, which required the manufacture of laminated plates from 3 to 10 inches thick. Its six sections, each weighing 700 tons, built in the plate shop and assembled in the machine shop, were then broken down into 50- to 95-ton segments for shipment by rail. Building control gates for the Hydro-Quebec's Manicouagan-Outardes was another project of the Industrial Division. Not all developments were to Davie's advantage, however. In manufacturing tank cars, which had been a regular line, the Industrial Division was now encountering stiff competition from Dosco, and the number of orders declined.[20]

Fortunately, the Industrial Division had a far more important product with which to replace them, and one for which it has continued to receive contracts to this day: sonar domes. The GED first outbid Canadian Vickers to build thirty sonar domes for the U.S. Navy in 1971. In the course of the twenty-five years that have since elapsed, it has built them for the three main U.S. warship construction programs at the Ingalls and Bath shipyards: US-DD963 to 997 of the Spruance Class Destroyers; CG47 to 73 of the Aegis Class Cruisers; and DDG51 to 81 of the Arleigh Burke Class Destroyers. So completely satisfied have the Navy and the U.S. builders been with Davie's Quality Program, that they no longer consider close supervision of their construction necessary. The original resident inspector sent from the United States was soon replaced by occasional inspections, and now only a visual inspection on delivery is made since the quality

NEW CHALLENGES

Magnet for the cyclotron at the Tri-University Meson Facility (TRIUMF), University of British Columbia, which provides world-leading facilities for experiments in subatomic research. Eight Canadian universities are now involved.

is so high and Davie's own QA records are so complete and trustworthy.

Weighing in at about 100 tons, the dome is probably one of the most complex pieces of steel fabrication undertaken anywhere in the world, due to its complicated shape and the extremely severe tolerances demanded for perfect sonar performance. Initially, Davie engineers and managers had to work closely with the U.S. shipyards, Navy, and other subcontractors, particularly to perfect the accuracy needed in the castings, for which Lynn McLeod of Thetford Mines became Davie's specialist source. As a result of Davie's high standard of work, dependable deliveries, and the satisfaction given to its clients, it has effectively become the sole source for this product. The company has also obtained a separate spares support contract with the U.S. Navy for the fabrication of the complicated bead seat castings that support the rubber sonar window. Workers in the General Engineering Division are proud of the fact that all the sonar domes of the U.S. ships that took part in the Gulf War of 1990 were built by Davie.

The bonanza of foreign shipping orders tailed off sharply in the second half of 1971 when there was a slump in the oil market. Canadian demand was also reduced as major projects in the Great Lakes, such as International Nickel's sulphuric acid plant at Sudbury, Canadian International Paper's plant at Bancroft and Stelco's new complex on Lake Erie, were cancelled or

Right: *Sonar dome being loaded to ship for transport to Bath Iron Works.* Below: *The destroyer* USS Vincennes, *one of the ships fitted with a Davie-built sonar dome.*

put on hold. Veliotis felt that the downturn was only temporary, however, and proposed that the division add another string to its bow by undertaking the manufacture of turbines and generators. His proposal received a favourable evaluation from the Montreal firm of consulting engineers, Asselin, Benoit, Boucher, Ducharme, Lapointe, and their report of January 1972 led to an agreement with the Vevey Engineering Works of Vevey, Switzerland, to build hydro-electric turbines to its designs, and subsequently to the purchase of a half-million-dollar Berthier vertical milling machine with a 35-foot arm.

On the labour front, a new collective agreement was signed in the spring of 1970, retroactive to January of that year, which gave the men a rise of approximately 8 3/4 per cent in 1970, 5 3/4 per cent in 1971, and 6 per cent in 1972. In 1972, for example, a labourer earned $3.30 an hour, a steel plater $3.89, and a loftsman $4.43. But, in spite of management's concerted efforts, the union refused to give ground on trade demarcation, or the division of labour into narrow and inviolable categories. Consequently, the shipyard was obliged to employ many more men than were necessary to carry out even the simplest operations. Such practices increased membership in the union, thus giving it extra strength, but also increased the number affected by temporary layoffs. At a time when the yard was very busy, a union study showed that each of its 1,500 members had been laid off an average of 2.02 times a year over a period of five years. Had strict demarcation not existed, employment might have been far steadier. Trade demarcation remained a thorn in management's side and a major impediment to improved productivity, and, though more workers were on the payroll, many of them paid a price for it.

At the end of 1971, after twenty years in the prestigious position of president of the CSL shipyards, Richard Lowery, who was sixty-two years old and had enjoyed the worldwide respect and goodwill that his skill as a naval architect and his good nature commanded, elected early retirement. He had built up a strong and successful shipbuilding and industrial group, whose dynamism had led to many firsts over the years, but one cannot help

Top: *Air lock for nuclear power station at Point Le Preau, New Brunswick.* Bottom: *Aluminum platform, elevator for the Nimitz Class aircraft carrier CVN-70* Carl Vinson, *made completely of aluminum plate up to 2 inches thick.*

wondering if he realized, as he handed over the presidency of DSL to Takis Veliotis on January 1, 1972, that it was the end of a golden era. Certainly, he could not have imagined how turbulent a period the shipyard was entering both in regard to management and to ownership.

The death of T. Rodgie McLagan in 1972 was the signal for the trouble that had been brewing for the last two years between Veliotis and Louis Desmarais to come to a head. On the one hand, Veliotis continued to resent having to answer to a man who was not a shipbuilder, a man he claimed had the job that he, Veliotis, had been promised; on the other, Desmarais had no faith in Veliotis's management of the yard, especially the way he handled labour and even, at times, customer relations. More particularly, Desmarais was concerned with what he considered mismanagement of the Greek contract, whose overrun was in the millions, and for which he, Desmarais, ultimately bore the responsibility.[21]

Dissatisfied with the answers he was receiving from Veliotis, Louis Desmarais sent his own men to the yard to investigate. This infuriated Veliotis. What transpired between the two men is not generally known, but the sequence of events was as follows: Desmarais announced that Veliotis was to move his office to CSL headquarters in Montreal; Veliotis refused to do so, and then requested the opportunity to discuss the situation. Then, on November 14, Veliotis announced that he and three senior members of Davie's staff were leaving the shipyard immediately. Veliotis, it would appear, had obtained the position of manager of the important General Dynamics Quincy shipyard in Massachusetts. Leaving with him from Davie's staff were Peter Gwyn, assistant general manager; Joe Lennox, shipyard superintendent; and Jimmy Gilliland, chief engineer, Production. Veliotis had been Davie's general manager for ten years. Besides holding the office of president and general manager of Canada's most prestigious shipyard, he was also the current president of the Canadian Shipbuilding and Ship Repairing Association. As might be expected, news of his defection sent shock waves beyond the Canadian marine world.

Following Veliotis's departure, head office discovered that the cost overruns on the Varnima ships were far greater than had been previously reported. Gordon Black, vice-president, Finance, for CSL, found that the ships were 20 per cent rather than 35 per cent built. The 15 per cent difference, shown as revenue in the shipyard statements, had not yet been earned. By hiding this fact, and knowing that it would eventually come to light, Veliotis had bought time in which to leave on his own terms, and when he did so, he caught head office by surprise.[22] To make matters worse, in May that year, a lawsuit had been filed by Varnima's three subsidiaries that owned the ships, because of alleged failure to comply with contractual obligations and delays in construction. The suit was now under arbitration.[23] CSL might have won the case through *force majeure* in the courts, but three of the main witnesses were now in the United States, and even if they had been subpoenaed, they would undoubtedly have been hostile witnesses. Moreover, Davie could not spare those other members of its staff who might have testified and who were now overburdened with work because of the departure of the four, so the matter was settled out of court. This added considerably to the overrun.

It was necessary to make immediate arrangements for the management of the shipyard, while acting quickly to recruit men to replace Veliotis and those he took with him. George Cole, a retired CSL vice-president for Water Transportation, agreed to fill the gap until a new manager was found, and Leonard Winslade, who had served the company in several capacities, was named his assistant manager. Together they succeeded in maintaining calm management during a very difficult time. The first of the three 80,000-ton tankers, the *Kriti Star*, was completed and delivered in January 1973. And as work continued on the other two, head office scrambled to land the new contracts that were essential for the shipyard's future. At a time when both contracts and government subsidies were readily available, Davie should have been making money, but was instead facing an enormous loss. It was not surprising that in April 1973 the Registrar of Shipping at Quebec received a $20 cheque with a request that the name of the tug *Takis V.* be changed to *Donald P.*, as a tribute to Don Page.

NEW CHALLENGES

Left: *Arthur Nightingale, vice-president of Shipbuilding at* CSL, *became president of the Davie shipyard in 1972.* Right: *John Shepherd, vice-president and general manager of Davieship.*

Early in 1973 Arthur Nightingale, vice-president of shipbuilding at CSL, formerly with the General Engineering Division and an assistant superintendent of ship repairs at Davie, was appointed president of the Davie shipyard and set up his office in Montreal. Jacques Regnaud, who had held the positions of assistant general manager, treasurer, and comptroller of Davie Shipbuilding Ltd., was appointed vice-president of the company, and John Shepherd, shipyard manager at St. John Shipbuilding and Dry Dock Co. Ltd., joined Davie as general manager, and in August 1973 became vice-president as well. Leonard A. Winslade was also named a vice-president of the company.[24] Other appointments included that of Tom Pickersgill, who was brought back to the yard by Shepherd in June 1973 to become project manager,[25] and four months later was named director of Production, and Mike Ayre, who was mandated to create a completely new planning and control system intended to prevent the repetition of past mistakes. In 1975, Pickersgill and Ayre were both named assistant general managers, responsible for Production and Technical Services respectively.

Kriti Star, *one of the 80,000 d.w.t. tankers, being towed to the outfitting wharf following the launch.*

Eight new ships were delivered in 1973, including the *Kriti Star* and the *Kriti Land*, 785 feet 10 inches long by 127 feet 9½ inches (and to this day the largest ships ever built in Canada); four midwater stern fishing trawlers, the GC *Bassin, Fatima, Grande Entrée,* and *Grosse Ile* built for General Mills of Canada; and a fourth new tug for Davie's fleet, the *Leonard W.*, named for Leonard Winslade. On the military side, HMCS *Algonquin* was delivered to the Navy.

Because of a shortage of space in the main shipyard, the tug and two of the trawlers were laid down in the Champlain Dry Dock, while the other two trawlers were built on the berths at the former George T. Davie yard. They were built under the supervision of the Industrial Division's management due to the stretched resources of the Marine Division. It is sad to note that these two trawlers were the last ships built in the yard once affectionately known as "Little Davie," and now known as "Davie West," in what had been Canada's premier yard for the construction of fishing trawlers.

NEW CHALLENGES

At the launching of the Kriti Wave, *Arthur Nightingale, president of the* CSL *shipyards and Mrs. Nightingale, and Louis Desmarais, president of* CSL, *and Mrs. Desmarais.* Courtesy L. Desmarais.

Launched in November 1973, the 785-foot Kriti Wave *remains, with her two sisters, the largest vessel ever built in Canada. Her 800-ton Sulzer 8-cylinder diesel engine, the largest single engine ever installed in a vessel built in North America, was capable of delivering 23,200 b.h.p. Her cargo space was divided into twelve tanks, ten that held oil and two for ballast.*

At the main yard, the end of 1973 also saw the launching of the final *Kriti*, the *Kriti Wave*. Launchings have often been occasions when pride has been mixed with concern, and it was a relief when the last of the three large vessels was safely afloat. The construction of the *Kriti Star* had almost ended in disaster. One spring morning as she lay at the outfitting wharf, a mass of shore ice that extended from the ferry terminal to Pointe Lévy broke away. The ice travelled down the river, severed the ship's mooring lines, and carried her away. Fortunately Don Page, the production manager, was on board and able to take charge. As she bore down on the rocks at the southern end of the Isle of Orleans, he thundered out the order to put an axe through the restraining cable of her jury-rigged anchor. The gigantic ship's momentum was halted, and what might have been an extremely expensive accident was averted. Good fortune was smiling on the shipyard when this incident occurred: ten minutes later, Don and everyone else would have been off at lunch.

In spite of the many problems associated with the project, the contract for the construction of the *Kriti*s was prestigious and remembered with pride by those who had a part in their construction. The fact that these were also the first new ships in what has since become the large Varnima fleet, and that they are still in service more than twenty years later, is a tribute to their quality. But the price paid for the experience was heavy. Opinion is still divided on issues such as whether the 700 tons of steel a week that the shipyard was expected to handle was realistic, and whether the yard's berths and cranage were too small. It is generally admitted that the contract stretched the capabilities of the shipyard to its limit. Depending on the method of accounting, the three ships were built at a loss of $11 million or perhaps more.

As a result of all the unpleasantness, which had taken on the proportions of a "Greek feud," inspections and relationships during the construction of the *Kriti*s were difficult. Part of Nightingale's mandate was to restore good relations. As a broker in London, Nightingale had developed strong relations with Greek owners and was consequently considered the ideal man for the job!

Vigorous efforts were made by the new management team to find work for the yard. Four contracts were signed in 1973 for product carriers of approximately 39,000 deadweight capacity, two each for the Cunard Steamship Company of Great Britain and Ogden Marine of New York. They were based on a design by Norman Laskey of Camat Transportation Consultants. A week into 1974 an order for two similar ships for the Athel Line of London brought the number on order up to six and the value of work on hand to $160 million.

It had been decided that Davie would concentrate on the construction of large tankers, and Shepherd had been able to convince Nightingale and the board to take advantage of the government's program of industry modernization, under which the yard was able to obtain capital assistance in the form of grants and interest-free loans towards a three-phase five-year plan of improvements to help it maintain its competitive position in the export market. The two main objectives of the plan were to double the shipyard's steel-handling potential from 25,000 to 50,000 tons per year, and to reduce the fifty-two man-hours per ton needed to build ocean-going vessels to forty. Accordingly, provision was made for the construction of larger prefabricated units: in the first phase of modernization, the company added crane runways outside the two main building berths and acquired two electric berth cranes of 39 and 44 tons respectively and a 200-ton Kamag transporter. The shop doors were enlarged to accommodate the bigger units. A 320-foot extension to the panel shop was built with a new panel line facility.[26] The Norwegian computerized design and drafting (Autokon) software was introduced into the Drawing Office, and the Logatome burning machine controls were converted from one-tenth-scale drawings to computer numerical tapes.

The second phase of planned improvements, in 1975, included the purchase of two mobile cranes, of 200 and 75 tons, and of a Norwegian arc-welding ESAB machine, which could turn out a completely stiffened ship hull section every two hours. Using this machine, plates were automatically welded together by the submerged-arc process, and then stiffeners were welded to the panel at the rate of 225 linear feet every sixty minutes. The third and final phase of the five-year plan, which called for the modernization of the Murphy Wharf and the reclamation of the adjoining land in 1978, was not implemented until 1988.[27]

In 1974 Nightingale felt confident. The company, he announced, had never faced a rosier future. The shipbuilding market had turned around, and if it were not for rampant material and labour costs, he could easily book orders through to 1980. But Canadian steel mills would not quote prices in advance, and the workers' union refused to sign more than a three-year agreement. The company was in no position to sign contracts in direct competition with the world's great shipyards while these two important factors were unknown.[28] A third factor may have weighed even more heavily: following the heavy losses incurred by Davie in building the three *Kritis*, the banks and insurance companies refused to issue performance bonding guarantees at a competitive rate without a guarantee from both CSL and Power Corporation. As might be expected, Power Corporation would not agree to their conditions due to the uncertainty of costing.

Meanwhile, in 1974 Louis Desmarais had been appointed chairman and CEO of CSL and the office of president had been passed on to Paul Martin. (Desmarais would give up both appointments two years later, while Martin would buy CSL in 1981.[29]) It was Louis Desmarais's opinion that if Davie wanted to seek orders in the world's markets, but lacked the backing of its parent companies, its position would have to be strengthened in other ways. The answer, he felt, lay in a merger of Marine Industries Limited, Davie Shipbuilding Limited, and Canadian Shipbuilding and Engineering Limited, to form a single strong entity. By concentrating all shipbuilding on the St. Lawrence at Davie, and all general engineering at the MIL facilities at Tracy (Sorel), both companies would gain through the decrease in competition. A report prepared by the Montreal consultants, Asselin, Benoit, Boucher, Ducharme, Lapointe, favoured the merger, though it expressed concern about how the cyclical shipbuilding market would affect Davie if the shipyard no longer undertook general engineering.[30] In fact, the proposal found little support, and the matter gradually died. Later developments would show that Louis Desmarais had been ahead of his time.

Louis Desmarais continued to look for ways to enhance the company's performance. At the launching of Cunard's 600-foot-long 39,000-ton oil tanker *Lucellum* in December 1974, he appealed to all Canadian shipyard workers to join with owners of the yards in a climate of mutual trust and confidence and with a common objective of ensuring Canada's industrial competitiveness. Failure to do so, he said, would jeopardize the very existence of communities like Lauzon and companies such as Davie Shipbuilding. The Canadian government's new subsidy program, he said, cut shipbuilding subsidies from 17 to 14 per cent, which would be further reduced over the next six years to a maximum of 8 per cent in 1981, a clear message that productivity must be increased. Moreover, the government offered an incentive, according to which 3 per cent of every contract would be allocated as a grant to shipyards to invest in facility and productivity improvements, providing the shipyards agreed to match the investment dollar for dollar. Pointing to the newly installed $1.3-million heating and ventilation system in the assembly shops that afforded Davie's workers an environment unequalled through North American heavy industry as a benefit of this policy, he asked for their co-operation. But the order book was full, and the union was not yet ready to listen.

At the beginning of 1976, the second two 39,000-ton tankers, the *Ogden Saguenay* and the *Ogden Ottawa*, were in the final stages of completion. The keels of the last pair had been laid for the Athel Line. Plans were also being made for a new self-unloader for Canada Steamship Lines. Louis Desmarais, however, who had an excellent record at Power Corporation and to whom ownership of the Davie shipyard had once been a source of pride, was losing patience. The battle with Veliotis and the unabated militancy of the union following Veliotis's departure had tempered that pride. He was finally convinced that as long as Power owned Davie, the union would continue to make unrealistic demands, presuming on the financial strength of the parent company. Warnings about productivity had had no effect. The general feeling was that Power would not let the shipyard disappear.

But Power Corporation was in business to make, not lose, money. Moreover, the parent company was decidedly uncomfortable with the publicity (mostly bad) emanating from the shipyard and its struggles with the unions. Louis Desmarais recommended in 1976, therefore, that Power dispose of Davie and that, if no purchaser were found, the shipyard be closed after the existing contracts had been completed. Fortunately for Davie's employees, a purchaser was found. In February 1976, Power Corporation announced that it had sold its shares in Davie Shipbuilding to a group of Quebec businessmen who had set up the holding company Soconav (Société de construction navale) for the purpose.

And so the fifty-six-year close association between Canada Steamship Lines and the Davie shipyard came to an end. For the first five years of that association (from 1920 to 1925), CSL had managed the yard without acquiring it. It had kept George D. Davie at the helm. He had known, as had his father before him, how to keep the loyalty of the employees. He had chosen his key men well. Later, with McLagan and Lowery in charge at CSL, the Davie family credo had been continued. The Davie shipyard had become Canada's top shipyard and a source of immense pride to its parent company. Naturally, the men who worked at the yard had been equally proud to be part of the CSL group. The family yard had become what Dick Lowery liked to call a "world-class shipyard." It had paid a heavy price to reach the top, however, for in the process, management and workers had lost touch. Well aware of the situation, the new owners were nevertheless convinced that, under their own hands-on management, goodwill and co-operation would again prevail.

Drill rig undergoing jack-up test.

21

HEAD OFFICE, LAUZON

1976-81

SOCONAV LTÉE HAD been set up by four men in the shipbuilding business: Louis Rochette, William H. White, Maurice Provencher, and Marcel Lafrance, all of whom were employed by Marine Industries Limited at Tracy at the time of the sale. Power had twice formally offered the Davie shipyard to the Société générale de financement or General Investment Corporation (GIC), the Quebec government corporation that owned the Sorel shipyard, and each time its president, Louis Rochette, had recommended that MIL purchase it, but the GIC, Marine Industries Limited's main shareholder, had decided that its involvement in one shipyard was enough. Louis Desmarais had then offered the yard to Louis Rochette himself. When Rochette replied that he lacked the means, Desmarais assured him that the financing could be arranged. Thus encouraged, Rochette sought to set up a partnership with the three men in whose abilities he had confidence. White, like Rochette, a former Davie employee, had faith in the company, its workers, and its potential for success. Together they had no trouble convincing Provencher and Lafrance to join them.

Colleagues in the shipbuilding industry could not understand why the four men would leave a secure situation at Marine Industries Limited to take over the Lauzon shipyard. Many observers were convinced that the

Louis Rochette

William White

challenge was too great and that they would fail. This widespread doubt made the partners more determined to succeed. Their confidence was well-founded. They were the team whose varied and valuable shipbuilding and business experience had turned MIL's $10-million loss in 1973 into a $2.4-million profit in 1974, and a $7.4-million profit in 1975.

After sixty-two years during which all important decisions concerning Davie had either originated in or been sanctioned by owners in Montreal, the partners in Soconav Ltée brought its head office and direction back to Lauzon. Partly because of the move and partly because three out of the four were French Canadians, they felt sure that the men would respond positively to the change. As a first step, they renamed the shipyard Les Chantiers Davie Ltée/Davie Shipbuilding Limited and adopted a new company logo.

Louis Rochette, the president, was the former Davie treasurer and comptroller who had left CSL in 1965 following disagreements with Veliotis. He had spent five years as vice-president of the Marine Industries

Marcel Lafrance *Maurice Provencher*

Limited shipyard at Tracy, Quebec, and had held the position of executive vice-president and general manager there since 1971.

Bill White became the new senior vice-president. He had learned his profession at the naval dockyard at Bermuda and formed part of the British Admiralty Technical Mission in North America in 1944. Engaged as a ship draftsman at Davie in 1945, he rose to the position of naval architect, then assistant to the general manager, and then technical manager. Returning to Bermuda in 1960, he set up his own boatyard, Bermuda Marine Services, but returned to Montreal two years later to take up the position of marine superintendent in Hall Corporation in Montreal, where he was subsequently appointed manager of operations. In 1963, he was named vice-president and general manager of St. John Shipbuilding & Dry Dock, a position he held until 1969, when he was struck down by a heart ailment that had dogged him since 1953. He was still recuperating when he joined MIL's Shipbuilding Division at Sorel as general manager in 1970, rising to be named vice-president, Shipbuilding, in 1974.

Marcel Lafrance, the new vice-president, Production, a native of Baie-Saint-Paul, had graduated as a mechanical engineer and then studied to become an engineer in production control and planning, while taking public relations courses. Following his training, he joined MIL Tracy in 1960 as the general foreman of the mechanical department and rose to become senior superintendent of production in 1973 and production manager of the shipbuilding division from 1974 to 1976. In the latter capacity, he had visited shipyards in North America, Europe, and Japan to learn from their methods.

Maurice Provencher had been on the staff of Domtar Ltd. for eighteen years, during which time his various financial responsibilities had included helping to set up their new plant at Quevillon in the Abitibi region. He left Domtar to become comptroller at Sorel and was named vice-president, Finance, of MIL in 1973. He held the same position at Davie.

The purchase of the Davie shipyard by these four executives could not have occurred had Paul Desmarais not been prepared to cut Power's losses. He bent over backwards to put an acceptable deal on the table. The partners were unable, however, to raise the additional $2 million at which Davie's fleet of tugs was valued, and it was agreed that they would remain under the Canada Steamship Lines flag. This arrangement was accepted with regret by the new owners: it meant that for the first time in its history the shipyard did not have its own tug.

During more than half a century of ownership, Canada Steamship Lines had taken great pride in maintaining and upgrading the Davie shipyard. The insurance settlement for the fire of 1955 had given its modernization program a boost, and other improvements had been made under various government programs. Physically, the yard was in good condition. Its manufacturing capacity had recently been increased. And its workers knew their trade well. Many were second-, third-, or even fourth-generation employees and, despite their loyalty to the union, they shared a deep underlying affection for the yard.

A few months after their arrival, the new owners brought in several new men from MIL Tracy, particularly from the production side. These included Jean-Claude Houle, Richard Deshaies, Richard Côté, and Jean-Yves Rhéaume. The last-mentioned individual was a British-trained former George T. Davie and MIL employee, who joined Davie in June 1976, replacing Tom Pickersgill as yard manager. Pickersgill was named technical director following the departure of Bill Farish, Davie's long-time naval architect.[1] Michael Ayre kept the responsibility for quality assurance, and test and trials but, as contracts manager, was asked to form a new contracts department to handle their administration, including post-delivery warranty work.

The first task for the new team was to complete the delivery of the Ogden and Athel ships. Steinar Draegebo had been recruited from the Norwegian company SRS, a subsidiary of the Aker Group, as planning manager but he served successively as project manager for the second Ogden Marine ship and then as technical manager.[2]

But all was not plain sailing in the yard. Unfortunately, over the years the militancy of the union had increased, weakening management's control of the shop floor, so that, at all levels of the organization, morale was low. To make matters worse, in spite of the orders on the books, the yard was losing money. At the end of the first year under new ownership, Davie had a deficit of more than $3 million.[3] The owners were seriously concerned. They had gambled on the union's demands becoming more reasonable once Power Corporation's vast resources were no longer behind the shipyard. At first it seemed as if they would, but Louis Rochette does not hesitate to speak of his disappointment on realizing how the attitude of the men had changed over the years. He remembered his previous stint at Davie when the men arrived early and chatted as they changed into their working clothes and prepared their tools, so that when the whistle blew they were ready to begin work. Now, he discovered, a multitude of customs had grown up that reduced productive time. In spite of this, however, the change in administration and a full order book did produce results: in 1977 the yard broke even.

NEW CHALLENGES

Above: Ogden Ottawa, *39,000 d.w.t., built for Ogden Marine of New York.* Left: Athel Monarch, *39,000 d.w.t., built for the Athel Line in 1978.* Below: *Executive secretaries Louise Ferland and Diane Beaubien act as hostesses at the launching of the* Athel Monarch.

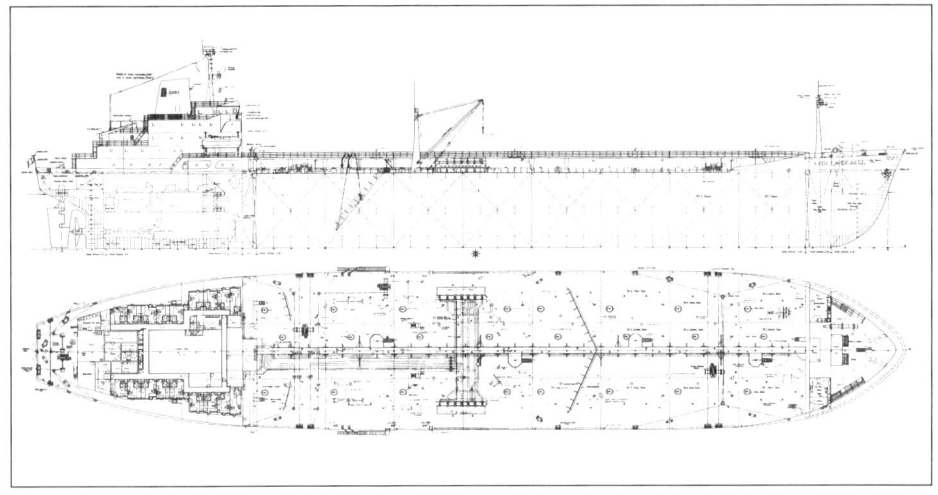

General arrangement profile and upper deck of MV Athel Monarch, *one of two 39,000-ton d.w.t. tankers built in 1978 for Tate & Lyle's Athel Line.* Designed by Dr. Laski of CAMAT INTERNATIONAL

Between April 1977 and May 1978, the shipyard completed the contracts the new owners had assumed for the 39,000-ton d.w.t. tankers *Athel Monarch* and *Athel Queen* for Tate & Lyle's Athel Line,[4] as well as CSL's 33,860-ton self-unloader *Jean Parisien*. In addition, in just 368 days, three 18,000-ton German-built ships that had been bought by Hall Corporation were converted to Great Lakes bulk carriers. The hulls of these eighteen-year-old ships were in poor condition as a result of their ore-carrying operations between Venezuela and Germany, but their engine rooms were still sound. Rebuilt with new hulls and the midship accommodations moved aft, they would sail as the *Cartiercliffe Hall*, *Montcliffe Hall*, and *Steelcliffe Hall* until 1987, when they were bought by N.M. Paterson and renamed *Winnipeg*, *Cartierdoc*, and *Windoc*.[5]

They were followed down the ways by the *Youpwe*, an 1,800-m³ suction hopper dredger built under a Canadian international aid program for the Office National des Ports du Cameroun. She was designed by IHC of Holland. Modular in construction, the largest of her twenty-two prefabricated sections weighed 90 tons. German & Milne of Montreal, represent-

NEW CHALLENGES

Overhead view of the Davie shipyard in 1977, with the Jean Parisien *on the right-hand berth beyond the plate shop, the* Cartiercliffe Hall *beside her, and the* Athel Monarch *on the inside of the outfitting wharf.*

Right: *Great Lakes bulk carrier* Steelcliffe Hall *(later the* Windoc*) converted from a German bulk carrier for Hall Corporation in 1978.* Below: *The self-unloader* Jean Parisien, *22,772 gross tons, built for Canada Steamship Lines in 1977.*

ing the owners, conducted the bidding and contract-award process and supervised construction. Following her dredging trials in the St. Lawrence River and a somewhat rough journey across the Atlantic, with a Davie-hired crew from the United Kingdom, the *Youpwe* was delivered to her owners, the Cameroun government, in Douala.

By the late 1970s, it was becoming increasingly evident that after two decades of growth, the overall world demand for new ships had dropped sharply and would continue to drop. The shipbuilding subsidy was on its way down from 20 per cent to 12 per cent; the tonnage ordered for the world fleets was 20 per cent less than in the two previous years; and an overall reduction of at least another 35 per cent was forecast for 1978. Moreover, the contracts for the new Canadian patrol frigates that the partners had been counting on appeared still to be a long way off. Nor were there any other immediate prospects for government work. The solution, the partners felt, was to diversify, and Louis Rochette's bold plan to do so paid off.

In 1978, Soconav made an offer to buy Branch Lines, a shipping company that owned seven tankers and controlled at least 20 per cent of the Canadian market for the marine transportation of bulk liquids. Founded in 1938 by Joseph Simard, the founder of the MIL shipyard at Sorel, and his brothers, it was still under the ownership of the Simard family. Rochette had first-hand knowledge of the company from his days in Sorel and knew exactly what Soconav was getting into. He had maintained good relations with the Simards, and a deal was made.[6] Ownership of Branch Lines had a couple of positive results. The shipyard could count on getting the maintenance work and any new construction the fleet needed,[7] and the positive cash flow the fleet generated changed Davie's financial position.

While orders for ships were drying up, the partners noted (and market research confirmed) that there was an increasing demand for oil rigs. The yard had some experience in this line: in 1969 Davie had delivered to the Petrolia Oil Well Drilling company a 1,142-ton oil rig with three jack-up

NEW CHALLENGES

Above: *Marcel Lafrance, Raynald Guay, Liberal Member of Parliament for Levis, and Jean Chrétien, Minister of Industry, Trade and Commerce, announce the signing of the contract to build the* Youpwe. Below: *Dredger* Youpwe *built for and delivered to the Port of Douala, Cameroon, in 1978.*

legs for service in Lake Erie. With the knowledge that the subsidy program and export financing would be available, Davie entered into negotiations with Marathon-Letourneau of Houston, Texas, the world's largest manufacturer of jack-up oil rigs. In the spring of 1978, Don Johnson, their agent in Texas, helped them conclude a licensing agreement for the design and construction of an 82-SD-C jack-up drilling rig. It would be the first of nine rigs built at the shipyard to the Marathon-Letourneau design, re-engineered to suit conditions at Davie where a great deal of the rig would be prefabricated under cover. These rigs were followed by three larger 116-C jack-ups built under a separate licence agreement.[8]

The smaller rigs, which could operate in 250 feet of water, rested on three 360-foot-long legs of triangular-truss with K-brace design. Their 207-by-176-foot platforms were of modular construction, had a hull depth of 20 feet, could be elevated at a speed of 90 feet per hour, and contained customized accommodation for a crew of up to ninety men. The larger rigs, which were designed to operate in 300 feet of water and to withstand wind velocities of up to 125 mph, had four legs and measured 243 feet by 200 feet 6 inches, with a 26-foot deep hull.

The first rig-building contract in the series was signed in June 1978 with the Global Marine Drilling Company of Houston, Texas, for the *Glomar Jackup I*. Its launching in May 1979 promised to be spectacular, and the press was advised to bring high-speed film! By that time there were already two more orders in the books, one for Global Marine and the other, *Salenergy IV*, for Salen Offshore Drilling Company also based in Houston.[9] Each of these rigs was worth approximately $25 million and was built with the support of Canada's Export Development Corporation. Gary Kott, of Global Marine, and his technical team led by Marvin Schindler, were impressed by Davie's workmanship and missed no opportunity to speak about its quality and the record-breaking almost non-existent "downtime."[10] Gary Kott put his money where his mouth was, and by December 1980, contracts had been signed for Global's sixth and seventh rigs. A larger 116-C rig was ordered at about the same time, by Petrobas, Brazil's national

NEW CHALLENGES

Keel-laying of a drilling rig built for Global Marine in 1983. Graham Reynolds, Georges Berberi, George Neal, Steve Kack, Gerry Giroux, Evelyn LaRoche, Paul Rininger, Pierre Méthot, Claude Ouellet, Monique Gagnon Lassiter, an unidentified visitor, Jean-Yves Rhéaume, Marty Knapp, Esther Normand.

petroleum company, for use off the Brazilian east coast. Perforadora Mexico S/A ordered another of the same size after examining and comparing the quality of rigs that they had previously had built in the United States, Japan, and Brazil with those built by Davie. The value of the larger rigs varied from $35 to $40 million, and Davie now had orders totalling more than $240 million on its books. Under the momentum of the program, the level of employment at the yard reached 2,350. It was a time when there was a great deal that was new and exciting. Davie's engineers, especially, were facing new challenges.

The rigs usually were towed to their destinations on barges, but Davie's fifth jack-up rig, *Glomar Jackup IV*, left for the Gulf of Mexico under a different form of transport: she was taken on board the *Sea Serpent*, a

Glomar High Island IX 82-SDC, jack-up drilling rig under construction on the launch ways.

Dutch submersible vessel with ballast chambers especially designed for transporting offshore rigs. Before they became operational, many of the rigs paid a visit to the Marathon-Letourneau yard in Brownsville, Texas, to have their legs extended as necessary and any painting or other finishing work done. *Salenergy IV* which, like the Glomar rigs, was intended ultimately to operate in the Gulf of Mexico, became the first Canadian-built jack-up rig to be used in Canadian waters. It commenced operations under charter to Conoco by drilling two exploratory wells on leases owned by the Hudson's Bay Oil and Gas Company off Prince Edward Island.

A newly restructured executive guided the shipyard through these unfamiliar waters. Louis Rochette relinquished the presidency to Bill White and assumed the office of chairman and chief executive officer; Marcel Lafrance

Petrobas VI 116-C drilling rig for Petroleo Brasileiro, with square-section legs is carried piggy-back on the MV Divi Swan on its way to the Gulf of Mexico in August 1982.

and Maurice Provencher became executive vice-presidents. Michael Ayre became vice-president in charge of engineering and contracts, and Jean-Yves Rhéaume, who had joined Davie from Sorel on June 14, 1976, vice-president, Production.

It was not only management that was new. With Davie's entry into the oil industry, a change came over the entire yard. Even casual conversation revolved around oil – exploration, its dangers, the lifestyles of the men who lived on the rigs, and so on. New terms entered the employees' vocabulary. People spoke of "shale shakers," "Schlumberger units," "high-pressure cement systems," "mud pumps," and so forth. It was not only conversation that was different; there was also a large influx of new people in the yard. For the most part they were Texans, whose easy-going yet go-ahead attitude earned them the goodwill of the French-Canadian workers.

As it proceeded with its new line of production, the shipyard became better known in the oil industry and increasingly involved in Canadian petro-engineering projects. As Canada's only offshore drilling-rig manufacturer at the time, Davie was frequently solicited to bid on projects both because of its expertise and because its participation provided "Canadian" content. In order to participate in the new Hibernia development off Newfoundland, Davie joined with Aker Engineering A/S, of Oslo, Norway, and Crosbie Offshore Services Ltd. in October 1980 to form the DAC group.[11] The group's first objective was to establish a permanent supply and maintenance facility in Newfoundland for offshore platforms and supply vessels.

The rigs themselves fascinated staff, workers, and local townspeople, and attracted visitors from far and wide. Engineers and schoolchildren alike stood and stared in awe. With giant legs that could be raised and lowered by their own hoisting mechanisms, and a platform that was both factory and hotel, they had the appearance of robot insects from another planet. They became even more impressive at night when they were illuminated by lights strung along their girders. "We didn't need to travel to Paris to see the Eiffel Tower when we had these in our back yard," an old man told me.

Unlike the ships built at the yard, many of which came back for refits or repairs, the oil rigs never returned. Their silhouettes remained strongly imprinted in the minds of the people of Lauzon, however, and any reference to them by the media was a source of pride. The thrill was even greater on the rare occasions when a rig was encountered in operation. Mary Jane Perkins, one of a group of Lauzonite touring the United States, remembered seeing three Davie-built rigs in action while crossing the Pontchartrain Bridge in Louisiana. When the guide announced that they were built at the Davie Shipbuilding yard in Lauzon, Quebec, she said, it was all they could do not to stand up and cheer.

Another special project of this period was the construction in 1980 of the steel barge *Polaris* for Bechtel of Canada. This vessel, because it was so nearly unique, also attracted many foreign visitors to the yard, particularly from countries with an Arctic frontier. Four hundred feet long and one

The barge Polaris *under construction in the Champlain Dry Dock before leaving for Trois-Rivières, where she was outfitted with a complete mining complex for Cominco Ltd. by Dominion Bridge-Sulzer.*

After completion, the Polaris, *whose size was almost that of a football field, travelled all the way to the Arctic, where a permanent foundation had been prepared for her on Little Cornwallis Island.* Courtesy Cominco Ltd.

hundred wide, almost the size of a football field, it was designed to be the base for a floating concentrator plant that was to be operated at Cominco Ltd.'s zinc-lead mine on Little Cornwallis Island in the Northwest Territories, less than seventy miles from the magnetic North Pole. The barge had to be strong enough not only to resist Arctic weather conditions, but also to withstand the journey there. Because of its size, there was a danger that its back might be broken in the heavy seas that it was bound to encounter on the way. Completed in September 1980, *Polaris* was handed over to its owners in a ceremony during which a commemorative plaque was fixed to it. It then left for Trois-Rivières, Quebec, where a consortium made up of Comstock Quebec Limitée and Dominium Bridge Sulzer installed the mining complex – power plant, concentrator, warehouse, office, and maintenance shops – on its deck. A year later workers cheered as the outfitted barge passed the shipyard again on its passage to Little Cornwallis Island. Once there, a rock cutaway that had been blasted and levelled in preparation for its arrival served as its permanent foundation. *Polaris* had predecessors in other remote parts of the world but was the first "floating plant" in Arctic resource development in Canada. Approximately 500 miles north of the Arctic Circle, Cominco's Polaris mine was, and still is, the world's most northerly base-metal mining operation.

Polaris *installed in the Arctic.* Courtesy Cominco Ltd.

NEW CHALLENGES

During these years the river took its customary toll on visiting merchantmen, keeping the Repair Division busy. In addition, the major rebuilding and conversion of a former Italian trawler produced a brand-new fleet diving support ship, HMCS *Cormorant*, which was delivered to the Canadian Navy in 1978, while the operational support vessel HMCS *Protecteur* underwent a major reconditioning and modification in 1980. On its fourth attempt and in competition with Bethlehem Steel, Todd Shipbuilding, and the Norfolk Shipbuilding & Drydock Company, Davie was successful in obtaining the first planned repair contract won by a Canadian shipyard for a U.S. military vessel since the Second World War. The vessel in question was the 644-foot underway replenishment vessel USNS *Waccamaw* of U.S. Military Sealift Command. Subsequently, some U.S. naval repairs were awarded to Canadian west coast shipyards, but after the contract for a major refit of the USNS *Algol*, the largest ship to enter the Champlain Dry Dock, was given to Davie in 1985, legislation was passed in the United States to prevent future contracts of this kind from being given to Canadian or other foreign yards.

Because they were qualified to work to higher tolerances, the welders of the General Engineering Division built the legs of the oil rigs. Among other equipment manufactured by the division at this time were personnel and equipment air-locks for CANDU nuclear reactors under construction for New Brunswick and Korea, and hydro-electric gates for the Baie James power project. Davie also subcontracted to build assemblies for American shipyards involved in U.S. naval programs. These included hull and deck units for dock landing ships, replenishment posts for fleet support ships, and aluminum elevator platforms for Nimitz-class aircraft carriers. The division also cut titanium components for Canadair's new Challenger twin-engine jet.

Towards the end of the 1970s, Davie's operations caught the eye of Dome Petroleum, Canada's largest domestically owned oil company, with assets of $842 million and four drill vessels exploring in the Beaufort Sea. Dome's executives were convinced that it was only a matter of time before

The former Aspa Quarto *was converted by Davie in 1978 to serve as the diving tender* HMCS Cormorant. *She is the mother ship to an SDL-1 submersible.*

the firm made a major find in the Arctic and that a period of intense activity lay ahead. They envisaged a tripling of Canada's current $750-million-a-year shipbuilding capability during the following ten years. In order to be sure of obtaining the vessels the program would require, they planned to build their own shipyard. They also decided to buy Davie, which not only had experience in building oil rigs, but was considered the foremost shipyard in Canada. According to Dome's calculations, the size of the Beaufort Sea program was such that the higher cost of building ships in Canadian shipyards could be offset by an increase of one cent a gallon on the price of oil at the pump.

An offer made in the fall of 1980 for equity participation or outright purchase of the shipyard was turned down by Soconav. Not to be thwarted, Dome raised its purchase offer to $38.6 million in 1981, and this time the offer was accepted. The partners knew the shipbuilding business well and had first-hand knowledge of the financial setbacks that can easily arise. After all, they had seen MIL suffer a multi-million-dollar loss on a single contract for seven cargo ships built for French owners.[12] They had been well aware of the risk they were taking when they bought the Davie yard, and all had not been plain sailing since they had taken it on. Though they had made money on the smaller rigs, they had not done so well on the large ones. Indeed, they were about to go to court to claim ownership of a rig nearing completion from a customer who had defaulted on progress payments even though $20 million had already been spent on her construction. They had neither established the climate of confidence with the union, nor brought about the improvement in productivity that they had expected. The market for oil, which had been selling at $40 a barrel, had begun to soften, and the market for oil rigs could be expected to soften with it. Their good fortune could easily disappear. The decision to sell was understandable.

The Branch Lines fleet of six tankers, which were used to ship petroleum products on the Atlantic seaboard and the St. Lawrence, was included in the deal. As Dome was not interested in operating a shipping line and Henri Tellier, the Branch Lines president, was, the fleet was leased to him on a bareboat charter basis, and he continued to manage it under the name Ligne Branche (1981).

The four owners were now in a position to retire as wealthy men, but as a condition of the sale they agreed to continue to manage the yard for at least three years. That the decision to make the sale was the right one would soon be demonstrated, yet it was not without regret that they gave up their ownership of the Davie yard.

Bill White, who had been dogged by a serious heart condition since 1953, would not have a long association with Dome. He died on April 16, 1982. I asked his son Ed for the word that best described his father, and he shot back, "Integrity." Business, Bill White believed, should be based on goodwill. Whether it required a simple or complex written agreement, it should benefit both parties and be sealed with a handshake. Bill White was a courageous man who had always given more than a full measure. He believed also in giving men a chance to prove themselves, as Desmarais had with him and his partners. Canadian shipyards, he maintained, had shown prejudice over the years by recruiting almost all their draftsmen in Britain: at Davie's, he saw to it that local French Canadians were given a chance. He helped several promising young men at the start of their careers by teaching them himself at his home in the evenings. Bill White had many friends throughout the industry.[13]

    I learned more about the four partners when I interviewed the surviving three. They are men who, in Maurice Provencher's words, "lived a fantastic experience together." Yet they were not then, nor are the three now, close friends. In fact, both Marcel Lafrance and Maurice Provencher told me that there was no love lost between them and Bill White when they were at Tracy and during their first years at Davie, although, in the end, dislike was replaced by admiration and affection. Why, I asked, did Rochette put together a team knowing that such strong feelings existed, and what kept the partnership from falling apart? The answer to your first question lies in Rochette's character, Provencher replied. He had confidence that we would act professionally, and he knew that Bill had the greatest marketing and negotiating sense. What held us together was our absolute determination to prove those who had scoffed at our taking over Davie were wrong. For that reason alone, we *had* to succeed, and we did.

Gulfspan class ferry Caribou, *179 m by 25 m by 8.4 m, 2,7212.69 gross tonnage, built in 1986 for* CN *Marine's service between Nova Scotia and Newfoundland. Built from 180 modules, she is seen here undergoing evacuation trials.*

22

DOME AND VERSATILE DAVIE

1981-87

Dome's purchase of the Davie shipyard was supposed to usher in an era of prosperity.¹ A planned $100-million expansion would have increased the work force from 2,300 to 3,000, and to more than 4,500 within three or four years, expanded engineering by 400 per cent, doubled the steel capacity to 35,000 tons a year, and greatly extended the existing 400,000 square feet of shop space. New facilities on the land immediately to the east of the yard would perhaps have included a third dry dock.² The world's most powerful icebreaker was to have been the first ship on the stocks, with 68,000 s.h.p. engines enabling her to cut through ten-foot-thick ice.³ Twenty-five to thirty other vessels would have followed within ten years. The Industrial Division was to have shared in the bonanza, building semi-submersible drilling equipment and components for super tankers and specialized LNG vessels for petroleum exploration and production. An extremely rosy future for Dome and the Davie shipyard was forecast.⁴

In order to carry out this program, an outstanding engineering team was needed. A whirlwind recruiting drive, first in Canada, then in England, resulted in the hiring of nineteen top designers, who were quickly settled into their offices in Lauzon. Teams of employees flew back and forth

NEW CHALLENGES

between Lauzon and Dome's head office in Calgary for technical and management meetings. A group from Davie was among the 1,000 Dome employees who attended a Christmas barbecue at the Saddledome – the largest party ever given in Calgary.

Within months, however, a serious downswing in Dome's financial situation occurred. The labyrinth of deals that was put together to pay for its takeover of the Hudson's Bay Oil and Gas Company proved to be far more expensive than was anticipated, and the whopping $3.4-billion bill put Dome in an extremely vulnerable position.[5] Though the shipyard was a relatively minor investment, it was one more source of worry at a particularly bad time. Plans for Davie's development were put aside while Dome's principals scrambled to meet their payment deadlines.[6] Nevertheless, Dome worked hard to remain a good and supportive owner. The search for the shipbuilding contracts continued, but bidding on them was often made impossible by Dome's inability to post the required performance bonds. Employees could only hope that Dome president Jack Gallagher's dream of opening up the Beaufort oil fields would eventually be realized.

But it was not to be. Far from heralding a brilliant future, Dome's acquisition of the Davie shipyard was the beginning of a fifteen-year period of instability and concern. The extra designers who had been hired in Britain, many of whom had sold their homes to begin a new life in Canada, were the first to find themselves without work. Davie was willing to pay for their repatriation, and some availed themselves of the offer, but others had burned their bridges or had some other reason not to return. Soon, employees in every department were affected.

In the course of trimming its assets, Dome decided to sell the Branch Lines fleet and Louis Rochette was asked to find a buyer. Michel Gaucher of Montreal was interested in acquiring part of the fleet, which prompted Rochette to make a proposal that was acceptable to both Gaucher and Dome. Accordingly, Dome released Rochette from his contract as president of the shipyard,[7] and he and Gaucher each bought a number of the Branch Lines ships, which they operated together under the name Sofati-Soconav Inc.[8]

Left: *Jack Gallagher, chairman and* CEO *of Dome Petroleum.* Right: *W.E. Richards, president of Dome Petroleum.*

The Rochette–Gaucher partnership would last from 1982 until 1986, when it became a public company under the name Socanav Inc.[9]

Graham Day, a talented man with considerable experience in the field of shipping and shipbuilding, was appointed Davie's new president. Seven years of private law practice at the outset of his career, followed by eight years on the staff of Canadian Pacific, had led to his appointment in 1971 as chief executive officer of Cammell Laird Shipbuilders in Birkenhead, England. At the time, however, Britain's shipbuilding, ship-repairing, and marine-engine building industries were struggling for survival, and in 1975, Day accepted responsibility for planning their public ownership. That job accomplished, he spent the next four years as the director of the Canadian Marine Transportation Centre at Dalhousie University, Halifax, and as a professor in the School of Business Administration.[10] In 1981, he returned to the industry as Dome's vice-president of shipyards and marine development, responsible for planning and organizing the shipbuilding facilities that the Beaufort development would require. On the west coast, a major shipyard was to be built on a "greenfield" site, and on the east coast, either Davie or Saint John Shipbuilding would be acquired. Davie was chosen, partly because of the successful rig program, partly because of its better facilities, and partly because it had room to expand. Day's appointment as president of Davie on September 29, 1982, was a natural outcome.

But Day would have just seven months to put his stamp on the shipyard: long enough to deliver two oil rigs, to lay the keel of *Glomar High Island IX*, and to sign the contract for a new ferry for CN Marine (later called Marine Atlantic). He was not there for the delivery to Branch Lines of the ship that was on the stocks when he took office, *L'Erable No. 1* (later renamed *Hubert Gaucher* in memory of Michel Gaucher's father), but played an active role in the early stages of the contract definition phase of the frigate program, for whose prime contract the Pratt & Whitney–Davie team (known as SCAN Marine) would later vie with the Sperry–Saint John Shipbuilding team.

When Day was offered the prestigious but thankless position of chairman and chief executive of British Shipbuilders in 1983, he accepted the

At the keel-laying ceremony in February 1981 for the Branch Lines tanker. Maurice Provencher, Bill White, and Louis Rochette, three of the four owners of the yard, Guy Bazinet of Branch Lines, Jean-Yves Rhéaume, Michael Ayre, Joe Bewick, Project Manager.

Graham Day, president and CEO of Davie 1982–83.

challenge. Half of the thirty-two shipbuilding yards, six marine works, and six general engineering shops that British Shipbuilders had comprised in 1977 had already been closed, and the state conglomerate had an accumulated trading loss of £338 million.[11] It was Day's task to oversee the rationalization of the British industry by closing most of the remaining yards.[12]

Meanwhile, with the fall in oil prices, costly exploration was no longer viable, and the demand for oil rigs had dried up. Davie delivered four rigs in 1982 and laid down two others, but the last one on order was cancelled, and another order that was being negotiated did not materialize, bringing an end to the program and increasing Davie's unemployment figure to 1,500. With the order book empty, the announcement in January 1983 that, in competition with Saint John Shipbuilding, Davie had won the prestigious $121-million contract for a Gulfspan class ferry, MV *Caribou*, for service between Nova Scotia and Newfoundland was good news indeed. However, it did not prevent another 300 temporary layoffs, leaving an overall total of 550 employed.

The ferry contract was for a single ship but, it was understood, it might lead to a second. What Davie's employees were hoping to hear, however, was that the consortium led by SCAN Marine of Longueuil, and to which Davie belonged, had been awarded the prestigious prime contract for the six new

Canadian Patrol Frigates (CPF) of the *Halifax* class.[13] The winner would design and build the ships, arrange for the necessary training and the life-cycle services required to maintain them during their operational service, implement the whole project, and deliver the ships to the navy under a turn-key arrangement. To Davie's great disappointment, it was announced in July 1983 that the prime contract had been given to the consortium led by Saint John Shipbuilding. The Saint John shipyard itself was to build three of the ships, while Marine Industries and Versatile Vickers would share the construction of the other three – Marine would build the hulls, and Vickers would do the outfitting. It appeared that Davie had been shut out, though the contract for the second six frigates was still to be awarded.

Marcel Lafrance, one of the group of four owners who had sold Davie to Dome, took over the presidency of the shipyard from Graham Day on April 7, 1983. Work on the last of the oil rigs Davie would build, *Glomar High Island IX*, was nearing completion. It had been chartered to Chevron/Irving, and was to drill off Prince Edward Island. Beverley Henderson, wife of Gerry Henderson, president of Chevron, broke the traditional bottle of champagne, while K.C. Irving and his two sons attended

Ferry *Joseph Savard*, 62.7m by 21m by 5.7m, 1,800 gross tons, built for service between Saint-Joseph-de-la-rive and the Ile aux Coudres, and delivered in December 1985.

the commissioning ceremonies. The father did not hesitate to walk every inch of the rig as it lay in the shipyard and, despite his well-known abhorrence of alcohol, attended the cocktail party and the cruise on the river boat *Louis Jolliet*, greeting and talking with the guests with obvious pleasure.

By August, the plans for the ferry *Caribou*[14] had been drawn and accepted, and the first plates were cut at a plate-cutting ceremony attended by the Minister of Industry, Michel Côté. The first completed section of her hull was laid on the ways in December. The ferry was to be the largest of her class in the world. Her bow visor alone would weigh 110 tons. She would have a carrying capacity of 1,200 passengers and space for 350 automobiles or 88 tractor trailers. Her installed horsepower of 28,000 and maximum speed of 22 knots would enable her to make two round trips daily between her terminal ports, Port aux Basques, Newfoundland, and North Sydney, Nova Scotia. Special care was accorded to planning the accommodation: most services for travellers were on the main passenger deck, including the facilities for the handicapped, a video theatre, a games room, playroom, first-aid station, a combined gift shop and newsstand, and baggage lockers.

Those who had a hand in her construction, including Rupert Tingley, president of CN Marine, and the technical team of Alec Lawrence, were justifiably proud of the fine-looking ship that was launched in October

Jean Garon, former provincial cabinet minister, strong supporter and good friend of the shipyard, with Caroline Gagnon, the young sponsor of the Joseph Savard's *sister ferry* Catherine Legardeur. *She had won the honour of christening the ferry in a competition to choose her name. The* Catherine Legardeur *was built for the Société des traversiers de Quebec's service between Sorel and Saint-Ignace de Loyola in 1985.*

Left: MV Caribou *wins the magazine* The Marine Engineering/Log's *Distinctive Oceangoing Ship award in 1985.* Right: *Bridge of* MV Caribou *showing the large expansive layout and the modern controls.* Courtesy CN Marine.

1984. But early in 1985, as her final outfitting got under way, Dome's financial position became critical, and it was soon apparent that Dome would not be there to deliver the ferry to her owners. A search for a new owner for the Davie shipyard was once again under way and, with help from the federal government, a new owner was found.

The new owner, the Versatile Corporation, was a British Columbia conglomerate that had a near monopoly of shipbuilding and repairs on the west coast. Its other interests included farm equipment, gas and cold storage, and financial services. In 1972, the group had bought the two shipyards owned by the Burrard Dry Docks, in Esquimalt and Vancouver, renaming them Burrard-Yarrows.[15] More recently it had turned its sights on eastern Canada. In 1981, it acquired Vickers Canada Ltd., together with its engineering subsidiary, Vickers Stanwick Systems Inc. (VSSI), the former Naval Central Drawing Office.[16] The incentives that the Canadian government was offering made the acquisition of the Davie shipyard an attractive proposition. In 1985, Versatile acquired Davie from Dome, taking over all of Davie's guarantees on contracts and receiving a commitment from the federal government to cover short-term capital needs up to the amount of $15 million. Versatile thus became the largest shipbuilding conglomerate in Canada. Burrard-Yarrows was renamed

Versatile Pacific Shipyards Inc.; Vickers became Versatile Vickers Inc.; and Vickers Systems Inc., or VSI, became Versatile Systems Engineering Inc. (VSEI). It was Versatile's intention to name Davie Shipbuilding "Versatile Quebec," but Davie's management successfully argued against losing the continuity, reputation, and image of the Davie name, and so it became Versatile Davie Inc.

Though Versatile had suffered operating losses of $9.8 million in 1984, and Davie had lost $2 million, there were several contracts on the horizon and Peter Paul Saunders, its self-reliant president, was optimistic about Davie's future. Davie was still feeling the sting of losing the frigate program to Saint John Shipbuilding and was waiting anxiously for the Tribal Class

The Irving Eskimo *in the Champlain Dry Dock for steelwork and electrical repairs in 1983.*

NEW CHALLENGES

Peter Paul Saunders, president and CEO of Versatile Corporation.

Update, Refit and Modernization Program (TRUMP) for Canada's four Tribal class destroyers to be awarded. It was expected to provide 1,100 jobs over a period of four years from the fall of 1986. The Lauzon shipyard was also counting on obtaining a contract for a second ferry from CN Marine as soon as the *Caribou* was completed and expected, furthermore, to win the prestigious contract for the Polar 8 icebreaker, for which bids were being finalized. As Versatile owned both Vickers and Davie, Saunders planned to transfer Vickers' share of the CPF contract (half of three frigates) to Davie, and at the same time split the work with MIL in a more efficient manner.

Versatile Pacific, Davie, and Saint John Shipbuilding were the only qualified bidders for the polar icebreaker, and Davie felt it had the advantage due to the depth of its engineering capability and facilities. The launch of the mammoth ship would stretch even its own capacity and was almost certainly beyond the capability of Versatile's Burrard-Yarrows yard. But, because the military contracts had been awarded to eastern shipyards, Versatile felt sure that the icebreaker would be built in the west. Moreover, Versatile had the luxury of vetting and approving both Davie's and Versatile Pacific's bids. One way or another, Saunders felt he could count on the contract.[17]

While Davie could look to the government for at least some military contracts, there was no owner on whom it could rely for private work. In the domestic shipping market, the declining production of U.S. steel mills, combined with the revival of U.S. iron ore mines, had drastically cut down U.S. demand for iron ore from Quebec, while the heavily subsidized movement of grain westward from the prairies had reduced its movement eastward. As a result, seaway shipping was falling off in both directions. Consequently, in the early 1980s Canada Steamship Lines alone laid up more than thirty of its ships. The likelihood of an increase in the demand for Canadian shipping in the near future was virtually nil. Internationally, the rapid expansion in trade, fuelled by the growth in the fuel-oil trades during the early 1970s, had led to the overproduction of ships, particularly tankers. Much of the construction had been speculative, and this had led to a severe overcapacity during the 1980s followed by a worldwide slump in shipbuilding. Davie, like other Canadian shipyards, simply could not compete with far eastern yards. The 9 per cent government Shipbuilding Industry Assistance Program subsidy came to an end in 1985, just at a time when many foreign competitors were receiving larger government subsidies. Taking all these factors into account, the timing of the naval and second ferry contracts, which had still not been awarded, became critical. Instead of new jobs, delays in the implementation of both programs brought layoffs. Soon, only 1,350 of Davie's 2,300 union members were still on the payroll.

By that time Marcel Lafrance had resigned as president and CEO of the shipyard to pursue other interests,[18] and Maurice Provencher had taken over the presidency, reporting to Versatile's executive vice-president, Bernie Charbonneau. In 1986, it was time for the bargaining to begin for a new collective agreement and Versatile, which had a history of good labour relations, confidently expected that the workers would understand that an increase in productivity was essential if Davie were to tender successfully for new contracts. A softening of demarcations among trades was one of the ways in which Maurice Provencher expected to achieve it. And these negotiations did become a turning point. The number of metal trades was reduced slightly, and stagers were merged with carpenters. There still remained a long way to go in this regard. And the concessions were achieved only after Versatile's board of directors took a firm stand, passing a resolution that Davie could take on no new contracts until a satisfactory agreement had been signed.[19]

Following an impressive commissioning ceremony attended by Governor-General Jeanne Sauvé and Lieutenant-Governor Gilles Lamontagne, the *Caribou* had her sea trials in March and April 1986 and came through with flying colours. Diverted to free a Russian ship that was stuck in the Gulf, she showed herself to be more powerful than any Canadian icebreaker. She made her maiden voyage to Port aux Basques on May 12, 1986, and subsequently paid a courtesy call to St. John's for a gala reception attended by John Crosbie, Don Mazankowski, and the mayor of St. John's. Placed in service, she performed beautifully and won the hearts of the Newfoundlanders. Her owners were delighted with her performance and quality.[20]

At about this time, there was another change at the Davie shipyard. Disagreements had arisen between Maurice Provencher and head office, as a result of which Provencher resigned. Following a number of other senior management changes and a management review in the winter of 1985–86, Versatile named Don Challinor president and chief executive officer, effective July 7, 1986. Challinor was born in Australia and trained at Sydney Technical College and Poplar Technical College, London. He served for many years as a chief engineer and had obtained certification as an extra-first marine engineer. He came to Canada in 1960 to take up his appointment as ship inspector with the Department of Transport, Ship Safety Branch, and later became senior inspector for the Canadian Coast Guard in New Brunswick. He joined Burrard-Yarrows Corporation in 1966 as chief engineer in their Vancouver shipyard, and was then general manager of its Victoria Division for eight years before returning to Vancouver as senior vice-president of the corporation. In 1982, he was appointed president and chief executive officer. By effectively introducing efficient methods to build 1100 and 1200 class icebreakers, he was widely credited

Governor-General Jeanne Sauvé meets some of the shipyard workers after the christening of the Caribou. *Here, she shakes the hand of Paul-Henri Leclerc, a welder.*

with having turned the ailing Burrard shipyard around. All in all, he had enjoyed an outstanding career in the Versatile Pacific shipyards.

His credentials were impressive, but Davie was much bigger than the Burrard shipyard, and Challinor was seriously handicapped, as John Shepherd had been before him, by his inability to speak French. Well-liked and widely respected throughout the industry, he would undoubtedly have made greater progress in changing attitudes and increasing productivity had he been able to communicate better with the men. Moreover, his lack of knowledge of the Quebec scene put him at a distinct disadvantage in dealing with the provincial government. Nevertheless, with the full confidence of Versatile management, Challinor proceeded with his plan to upgrade the facilities and building methods.

To back him up, he had four vice-presidents. Michael Ayre, a vice-president since 1979 and the longest-serving member of the management team, was now in charge of Marketing, Estimating, Quality Assurance, and Tests and Trials. British-trained, Ayre had served his apprenticeship at the Vickers-Armstrong Naval Yard in Newcastle-upon-Tyne, and was an Honours graduate in Applied Science (Naval Architecture) from the University of Durham. He came to Canada in 1967 to become a ship manager at the Canadian Vickers shipyard in Montreal, leaving less than a year later to join the more dynamic Davie shipyard. He had occupied various positions at Davie since 1967, and had been senior vice-president in charge of Engineering and Contract Administration since 1983.

Jean-Yves Rhéaume continued as vice-president in charge of Operations, a position he had held since 1979. A graduate of the Institut Technologique of Québec and former apprentice draftsman at the George T. Davie yard at Lauzon, Rhéaume had won a scholarship to study shipbuilding in Britain and, like Michael Ayre, trained at the Vickers-Armstrong shipyard in Newcastle. While there, he studied naval architecture at the Rutherford Institute of Technology and spent some time in every department of Palmers, the Vickers' ship-repair yard, at the Vickers experimental tanks at St. Alban's, and took courses in computer programming. Visits to English, Scottish, and continental European shipyards rounded out a busy and fruitful two years. On his return, he worked at the George T. Davie yard in Lauzon until it was closed in 1968 and then at MIL in Sorel. He had joined Davie as yard manager in 1976.

As his vice-president in charge of Naval Projects, Challinor brought in Richard M. Bertrand. Bertrand had earned his master's degree in naval architecture and marine engineering at the Massachusetts Institute of Technology and had served afloat as an engineer in the Canadian Navy prior to holding several appointments in the Department of National Defence and the Transportation Centre, Montreal. He also earned an M.B.A. In the course of his duties at DND, he had participated in the development of the specifications for the frigates and the estimate of the project, and thus brought inside knowledge to the job. Bertrand's arrival at Davie coincided with the commencement of the fabrication of the first frigate module at Tracy on May 25, 1987.

Challinor completed his roster with Sami Roubil, who replaced Pierre Letourneau as vice-president, Finance, in June 1986. (Letourneau had joined Davie as vice-president and comptroller in 1981 and held the position of vice-president, Finance, as well as that of assistant secretary of the company since 1984.) With these as his senior men, Challinor tackled the problem of runaway production costs, while preparing for the two navy programs.

It was apparent to all, however, including the Canadian government, that the time had come to rationalize the Canadian shipbuilding

Robert Monette, the CSN president from 1982 to 1992, entered the shipyard as a helper to his father, a stager, in 1971. He is seen here in the shipyard's Salon Rouge, at the time the construction of the Joseph and Clara Smallwood *was announced, with his vice-presidents and two political visitors to the yard. Denis Tardif; Jules Morin, who was secretary of the union for twenty years; Nelson Roy; Robert Monette; Michel Coté, Minister for Industry; Gabriel Fontaine, Conservative MP for Levis; Maurice Carrier; Denis Plante; and Jean-Paul Therrien.*

capacity. In March 1986, a letter of intent was signed between the Minister of Regional Industrial Expansion, on the one hand, and Versatile Corporation, Ltd. and Versatile Davie Inc. on the other, according to which Versatile agreed "to start a process of negotiation with owners of other shipyards in the Province of Quebec to formulate a strategic plan regarding the reduction of its shipbuilding capacity." It was also confirmed that Davie would build a second passenger ferry for Marine Atlantic, which would be based on the *Caribou* and would enter into service on the Sydney–Argentia run by June 1990. The design of the *Caribou* was to be revised by the Davie engineers in conjunction with the Department of Transport and CN Marine, to improve its cost effectiveness. In return Versatile had to give up "any claims it might have regarding the allocation of part or all of the last two TRUMP contracts," and to agree that they, as well as the contract for a Polar icebreaker Class 8, would be awarded following the normal competitive process.[21]

Peter Paul Saunders tried to find a way for Versatile to buy Marine Industries and to rationalize the river yards of Vickers, Tracy, and Davie. He did not succeed. Versatile had reached the end of its financial tether due to the intense pressure it was undergoing on several fronts: the losses of its farm machinery division, on account of the fall in wheat prices; the drop in oil and gas prices; the delay in the signing of the promised destroyer conversion contracts (TRUMP);[22] the concurrent delay in the start of fabrication of the first frigate (CPF 03) at Marine Industries and Versatile Vickers; and finally, a several-million-dollar overrun in the construction of the *Caribou*.[23] The difficult financial situation of the corporation was exacerbated in September 1986 when, after Versatile succeeded in negotiating the sale of its farm division to the U.S. firm, Deere & Co., which would certainly have helped to relieve the pressure, the U.S. Justice Department failed to give its approval within the time period that Versatile had been given to settle its loans, and the loans were called by the banks.

The process of rationalization, when it occurred, was the reverse of what Saunders had envisioned: MIL would acquire Versatile, not the other way round. Negotiations began. At the end of 1986, however, the final agreements had still not been signed and Versatile's situation had deteriorated. Operations at the Davie shipyard were grinding to a standstill. Some of the yard's creditors had not been paid for more than 200 days, and the unionized and supervisory staff payroll, as of the end of December, had not been met. The withholding of credit for air travel was preventing Davie from meeting contractual obligations on the TRUMP program and from finalizing important contract negotiations that were under way with U.S. Military Sealift Command. Refusal by suppliers to deliver steel halted work on the ferry; court suits were threatened; and settlement of electric, telephone, and heating-oil bills had become a matter of extreme urgency. So bad was the situation that oil was being transferred between reservoirs, so that the parts of the shipyard most in need of heat could be kept warm.[24] When Hydro-Québec sent their man to cut off power, in Don Challinor's absence, Jean-Yves Rhéaume and Michael Ayre took it on themselves to refuse him entry to the yard, thus preventing the dire, possibly irreversible, consequences of closing down operations. Meanwhile, a group consisting of local businessmen and officials, and a representative of the shipyard workers, had been set up by Marcel Gosselin, president of the Corporation du développement économique Pointe-Lévy to lobby for the shipyard. With himself as president and André Lemieux, president of the Chambre de Commerce of the South Shore as vice-president, the comité de survie du chantier Davie worked tirelessly contacting those in authority who might influence a decision; giving news conferences; pressuring municipalities to write letters of support; and generally promoting the shipyard.

Negotiations crept forward. According to a second letter of intent, signed by the parties on January 16, 1987, Marine Industries Limited would acquire from Versatile Corporation all the outstanding shares of its three eastern Canadian subsidiaries, Versatile Vickers Inc., Versatile Davie, and Versatile Systems Engineering Inc. This was followed on January 30, 1987, by the signing of the Ferry Contribution Agreement, by which the Canadian government agreed to provide working capital for the construction of the second Newfoundland ferry in the amount of $125 million. On February 3, 1987, Davie learned that agreement had been reached and that MIL, its former rival, had become its new owner.[25]

For Versatile it was a bitter defeat. Two years after buying the Davie shipyard, it had debts totalling more than $200 million and the company had not succeeded in signing a single contract for a new ship. It had lobbied hard to obtain the ferry contract for Davie, and that of the world's largest icebreaker, the Polar 8, for its Vancouver yard, while waiting impatiently for the frigate and destroyer programs to start. But finally, Versatile had to trade in whatever assurances it had been given of obtaining contracts and, reeling from the accumulation of setbacks, it limped back to its home base in British Columbia to regroup and recoup.[26]

The ferry Joseph and Clara Smallwood, *179 m by 25 m by 8.4 m, 27,229.25 gross tonnage, delivered in 1989 to Marine Atlantic Inc. (the new name for* CN *Marine). She was built for the fifteen-hour summer service between Sydney, Nova Scotia, and Argentia, Newfoundland, and is seen here approaching North Sydney at the completion of her sea trials.*

23

MIL – DONALD CHALLINOR

1987-89

NEWS OF MARINE Industries Limited's acquisition of the Davie shipyard was received with relief by Davie employees, but the relief was accompanied by resolve rather than rejoicing. Barely accustomed to the change of name to Versatile Davie Inc., they now had to adjust to being MIL Davie Inc.[1] and to learn the ways of the MIL Group whose bureaucratic approach contrasted sharply with the entrepreneurial attitudes of Soconav, Dome, and Versatile. Nevertheless, they had survived: Don Challinor was still in charge at Lauzon – and had MIL's full support; Jean-Roch Brisson was president and chief executive officer of the MIL Group, whose head office was in Montreal;[2] and the Quebec government's Société générale de financement (SGF) was the MIL Group's major shareholder.

All the Upper St. Lawrence shipyards had been brought together in the MIL Group as the first step towards their rationalization; the reduction of their combined overcapacity was the next. Governments, managements, and unions alike knew that painful decisions would have to be made and their consequences faced, but Davie's order book was not empty, and it hoped to escape the axe. Fortunately it did.

Challinor's priorities were to prepare the shipyard for the military contracts, to see that it reach an acceptable level of productivity, and to build the second ferry and deliver it on schedule. He moved ahead quickly with his program of improvements. To accommodate the large influx of staff that the naval projects would require,[3] a new four-storey office building was built, immediately to the west of the Lorne Dry Dock, while a large empty supermarket in the vicinity became a temporary extra drawing office. To enhance fabrication performance, a plasma cutting machine was ordered. Then, following an environmental impact study, work began on the refurbishment of the Murphy outfitting wharf. By December 1988, the 260-metre-long Murphy Wharf had been rebuilt and two new tower cranes installed. Major improvements were made to the Lorne Dry Dock, including the addition of new cranage[4] and power facilities in anticipation of four years of TRUMP destroyer work in the dock; a new 40,000-square-foot stores with handling systems was erected; and the old stores building became an up-to-date electrical shop. Finally, a brand-new pipe shop, with gravity-fed conveyor systems and two new hydraulic pipe bending machines, was built. Despite the two rapid changes of ownership, the latest five-year program of improvements had been carried through.

Turning the sod for the new office building beside the Lorne Dry Dock. Jean-Guy L'Hébreux, plant engineer; Sami Roubil, vice-president, Finance; Don Challinor, president; Michael Ayre, vice-president; and René Hallé, marketing representative, General Engineering Division.

While these new facilities were being built, Challinor tackled the problem of productivity. This required both the introduction of state-of-the-art technology and a complete change of attitude towards shipbuilding on the part of all employees. Resisting strong pressure from traditionalists who wanted work on the second ferry to begin immediately, Challinor convinced the MIL board that improved shipbuilding methods should be introduced first. He looked to Japanese shipyards as the model to emulate. It was their efficient methods he had successfully introduced in the Burrard-Yarrows shipyard. The Japanese, suffering at that time from overcapacity and a surplus of engineers, were only too willing to earn valuable dollars teaching their western counterparts the new technology.

Six teams made up of management, engineers, production staff, and union representatives each spent ten days studying the advanced techniques of modular construction employed at the Tokyo and Kure shipyards of Ishikawajima-Harima Heavy Industries (IHI), one of Japan's largest and most modern shipbuilders.[5] They saw for themselves the giant strides that had been made in shipbuilding over the previous twenty years and were quick to realize that the Davie shipyard could, and must, be made far more efficient.

Don Challinor, president of MIL Davie, exchanging gifts with senior IHI representatives.

On their return, Richard Gauvin, a union vice-president, now the president, spoke of the immensity of the Japanese shipyards' shops, the "state-of-the-art" facilities, the advanced building methods, and careful planning procedures. He was impressed, he said, by the general attitude of the workers, whom he found to be punctual and respectful towards their fellow employees. He learned in Japan that when a steelworker was hired, he was trained to carry out any steel-working task that might be required. He was surprised to discover that though the Japanese worker earned ten to fifteen thousand dollars more than an equivalent Quebec worker, the cost of living was three times higher in Japan. He was particularly interested in health and safety issues. Gauvin learned that the supply of protective equipment to the individual Japanese worker was a strong point of their program. He and others on the union executive, and even senior members of management, also met with Japanese union officials to discuss common issues and were amazed at their knowledge of the industry generally and by their understanding of worldwide economics and currency issues. As Challinor had expected, Robert Monette, who was then president of the union, and the union executive came away from Japan with a clear understanding that without changes, Davie would not survive.[6] Monette stressed, though, that it would be neither possible nor desirable to embrace all the aspects of the Japanese employer-to-employee relationship, many of which sprang from centuries of Japanese culture.

According to Michael Ayre, who headed one of the teams, these visits marked the beginning of a new relationship between union and management, based on the realization that the shipyard's future prosperity was their shared concern and responsibility. As a result of the time they spent travelling, eating, and socializing together, the company's management, supervisors, technicians, and union representatives developed greater mutual respect and trust and a common resolve to succeed.

The visits were followed by a determined effort to improve productivity under the guidance of the IHI engineers who had arrived at Lauzon even before the Davie teams left for Japan. The engineering drawings originally

Davie employees at the Kure shipyard. Back row, *Michael Donnison, Roger Carpentier.* Standing, *Claude Bélanger, Michel Tessier, Daniel Landry, Robert Monette, Roger Fortier, Donald Breton, Denis Tardif, Denis Breton, Marc Samson, Larry Wilkins, Richard Gauvin, Victor Lai, Jose Galvez, Robert Demers.* Front, *Michael Ayre.*

IHI *engineers take leave of Davie staff members (back row): Larry Wilkins, Michael Ayre, Don Challinor, Jean-Yves Rhéaume, and Richard Bertrand.*

prepared for the *Caribou* were redrawn, maximizing the pre-outfitting of modules, for which a new module shop was built. The plasma cutting equipment was installed. Directed by a computer, it allowed the thinnest sheets of steel to be cut under water extremely accurately, without any distortion and at high speed. (This would have particular benefits later in the cutting of the thin plates for the frigates.) Line heating was introduced in the plate shop for plate forming, which did away with handling and congestion at the plate rolls, greatly improved accuracy of fit-up, and eliminated distortion and locked-in stresses. The information system for pipe fabrication was completely overhauled. Gravity welding was adopted, and all existing welding procedures were rewritten, integrating the latest technology from IHI, including one-side welding. The material control and planning system was changed. Palletization or work packaging, the preparation of separate pallets containing the components required for each job, became standard practice. Finally, new accuracy-control technology was introduced into the steel departments following special training under an accuracy-control supervisor.

At the same time, courses in modular construction were given, and the newly acquired knowledge was immediately applied to the construction of the ferry. By the spring of 1989, between the investments for the Navy and the technology program, a total of $40 million had been spent on new equipment and facilities at the yard, and a further investment of $25 million was planned.

IHI engineers were surprised by the enthusiasm with which their technology was accepted, adopted, and further developed. In fact, Davie's efforts made it an industry leader in North America. When the yard began to receive the frigate drawings from Saint John Shipbuilding, Davie's engineers revised them to suit the newly learnt technologies. They modelled the hull using 3-D CAD software, integrating the outfit and steelwork, and optimizing the design for modular construction to the maximum extent possible within the limits of the contract as follow yard. The Saint John yard, as lead yard, later integrated these concepts into the design of its follow ships.

While the new technology was being introduced, Challinor took on the thorny problem of the accumulation of restrictive practices that had crept into the union agreements over the years. As part of a carefully prepared program called "Crossroads," he made sure that the employees, and indeed the entire community, understood the issues on which the long-term survival of the shipyard depended. He stressed the bright prospects that might be achieved through increased competitiveness, the harmful effects of rigorous demarcation, and the inevitability of oblivion if the yard's productivity did not improve. Challinor established a new public affairs service as a cornerstone of his program,[7] and named as vice-president in charge of it Terry Liston, a retired major general who had served as the public relations officer to the Chief of Defence Staff. Liston was a graduate of the Canadian Army Staff College, the National Defence College, Queen's University, and the École nationale d'administration publique. He described his responsibilities in the shipyard's newspaper, *MIL Davie Info*, of February 1989, as covering the company's external relations, including governments, the news media, and the Quebec community; and internal communications, including the newsletter.[8] Liston soon became known as a "hands-on P.R. guy" who made it his business to be active in meeting all levels of government and to be always accessible to the media. He arranged for employees to get together and to understand one another's needs, and he brought to the job a co-operative attitude towards the union, to which the leaders responded.

The eighty shipyard employees, including the union president and other union officials, who had visited Japan did their part to convince others that there had to be a change. So, after the initial customary posturing when bargaining began on a new three-year contract in April 1989, management succeeded in obtaining more flexible work rules that allowed it to regain some measure of efficiency on the shop floor. Seven of the twenty-nine trades were brought together in larger groupings that encouraged teamwork through the use of common and related skills, while many restrictions on the assignment of personnel between work areas were removed to cut down on wasted time and to improve quality.

And if some workers opposed giving up their "acquired rights," they had only to look around to see how fortunate they were. At other major shipyards in the province of Quebec, the story had been very different. Following the MIL Group's disastrous financial results in 1987, rationalization of the St. Lawrence shipyards proceeded apace. MIL Vickers stopped ship repairing in January 1988 and the principal work at the plant became the fabrication of components for U.S. warships and CANDU nuclear reactors. Of the two shipbuilding yards that remained, MIL Tracy was to carry out offshore, modular construction and power generation, and MIL Davie would do shipbuilding and repair. By the end of 1988, however, MIL Tracy had completed a number of frigate modules, and the contracts had not yet been awarded for the Hibernia Program, so it was decided that it would leave the marine field and specialize in the construction of hydro-electric machinery. In July 1989, MIL Tracy was sold to a newly formed corporation, GEC Alsthom Electromécanique, and GEC Alsthom (in Europe) became its sole owner.

When the MIL Vickers union refused to agree to far-reaching changes in their contract that might have made the company competitive, the shipyard's fate was effectively sealed. Following an aborted attempt to sell the company to private interests, MIL announced that it would be shut down at the end of 1989. The firm wound up its business and the whole plant was levelled, thus irrevocably ending the eighty-year history of what had once been Canada's premier shipyard.[9] Shocking though it was, the disappearance of Vickers was by no means unique. All over Europe and North America, shipyards both big and small had suffered and continued to suffer the same fate.

An important part of Challinor's policy was to rekindle the strong community support that had previously existed, spearheaded by the lobby

> ## ᘰ CANADIAN VICKERS LIMITED ᘱ
>
> ESTABLISHED IN 1911 by Vickers of England, at the express invitation of Sir Wilfrid Laurier, the Canadian Vickers shipyard had been equipped from its inception so as to be able to engine and outfit the ships it built. From 1916, when it launched its first ship, Vickers had built a wide variety of commercial and naval vessels for customers around the world, among them submarines for the Allied navies during World War I. It also provided the engines for ships that were built in other Canadian yards, such as Davie. At its peak during World War II it employed 12,000 men and women in its Marine, Engineering and Aircraft Divisions. After the war, it maintained its leading position and, in 1949, at the outset of the Destroyer Escort Program, it was chosen by the Canadian government to develop the "Naval Central Drawing Office." Originally British owned and directed, by 1927 all Canadian Vickers' owners and directors were Canadian. Following World War II, however, Vickers repurchased a controlling interest in Canadian Vickers, but in 1978, it was bought from them by a group of Canadians and became Vickers Canada Ltd. Purchased by Versatile Corporation in 1981, it became renowned for its work on multi-ship refits, which also gave it the volume it required to survive. When these contracts dried up, the facility was no longer profitable and it was sold to the MIL group in 1987.[10]

group, the Committée de survie. He wanted the South Shore to be proud of the shipyard, to understand the causes of its problems, to feel that it could influence its future, and to work actively to do so. With this in mind, a new lobby group known as the Committée d'Appui was formed whose members included representatives of the local Chamber of Commerce,

NEW CHALLENGES

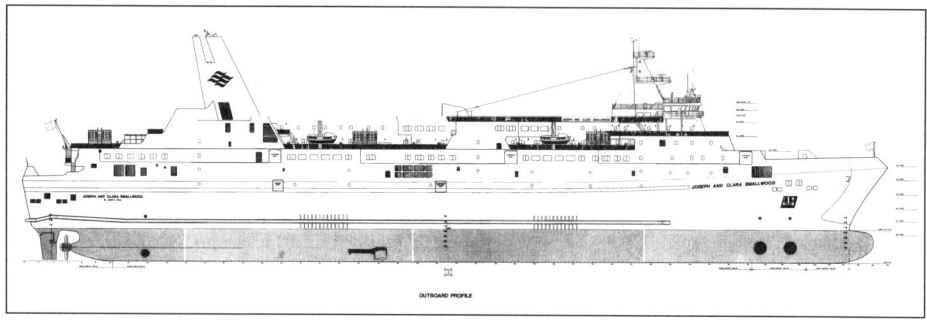

Outboard profile of the ferry MV Joseph and Clara Smallwood, *built for Marine Atlantic in 1989. A sister ship to the* Caribou *with certain modifications to enable her to undertake the longer, fifteen-hour summer service from Sydney to Argentia.*

various South Shore municipalities and local business support organizations, members of Davie's Public Affairs Division, and the presidents of its shipyard and office workers' union.[11] The group met frequently and kept abreast of what was going on at the yard, which at that time consisted mostly of the construction of the new ferry for Marine Atlantic, now nearing her launching date.

The ferry *Joseph and Clara Smallwood* was launched early on a Saturday morning in May 1989. Ten thousand spectators turned out, despite driving rain, to celebrate the occasion with the guest of honour, the Honourable Joseph R. Smallwood. Every man, woman, and child on the South Shore seemed to be there. They had tramped down to the yard, the littlest perched on their father's shoulders, others clasping older hands, and all hurrying purposefully towards the same point, the slip on which the great blue and white ferry waited. And as she began to move slowly down the ways, the crowd gave a tremendous cheer – as it had so often on similar occasions before – for the ship and for their menfolk, to whose skills she was now a "living" tribute.

Later, those who had gathered at the Château Frontenac for the reception hosted by Marine Atlantic gave the guest of honour several long standing ovations. For a while, thoughts of the handsome ferry faded into the background, as they showed their appreciation for the only surviving Father

452

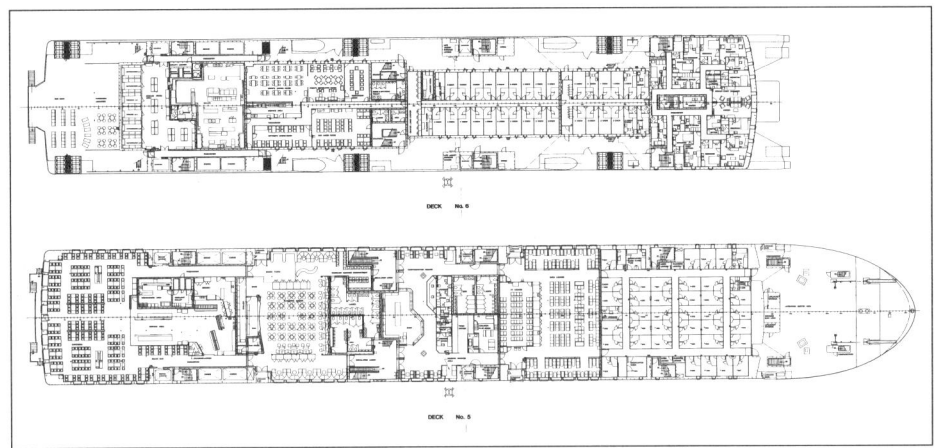

Decks numbers 5 and 6 of the MV Joseph and Clara Smallwood. *Like* Caribou, *she could carry 1,200 passengers and 350 vehicles, but she was given more cabins and sleeping berths on account of her longer run.*

of Confederation. Joey Smallwood, who had brought Newfoundland into Confederation forty years earlier, died two years later, on December 17, 1991. A splendid ship helps to keep his memory alive.

The outfitting of the *Smallwood* continued through the summer. Though she was a sister ship to the *Caribou*, certain modifications were made, since she was to undertake the longer, fifteen-hour summer service from Sydney to Argentia. Like *Caribou*, she could carry 1,200 passengers and 350 vehicles, but she was given more cabins and sleeping berths on account of her longer run, and comfortable aircraft-type seats were fitted in the side casings of decks 3 and 4. Another innovation was the large area on the seventh deck that was completely enclosed in thick Plexiglass to serve as a sheltered observation deck. This area was found to be too cold, and therefore unpopular, even during the summer, and was replaced by an attractive, heated steel-enclosed lounge during a refit in 1991. As in the case of *Caribou*, her owners' investment of $2 million in Sperry (of England) stabilizers was very much appreciated both by her passengers and her crew.

After successfully submitting to 121 different tests and formalities, the *Smallwood* left the shipyard on October 15 to undergo her sea trials. These

NEW CHALLENGES

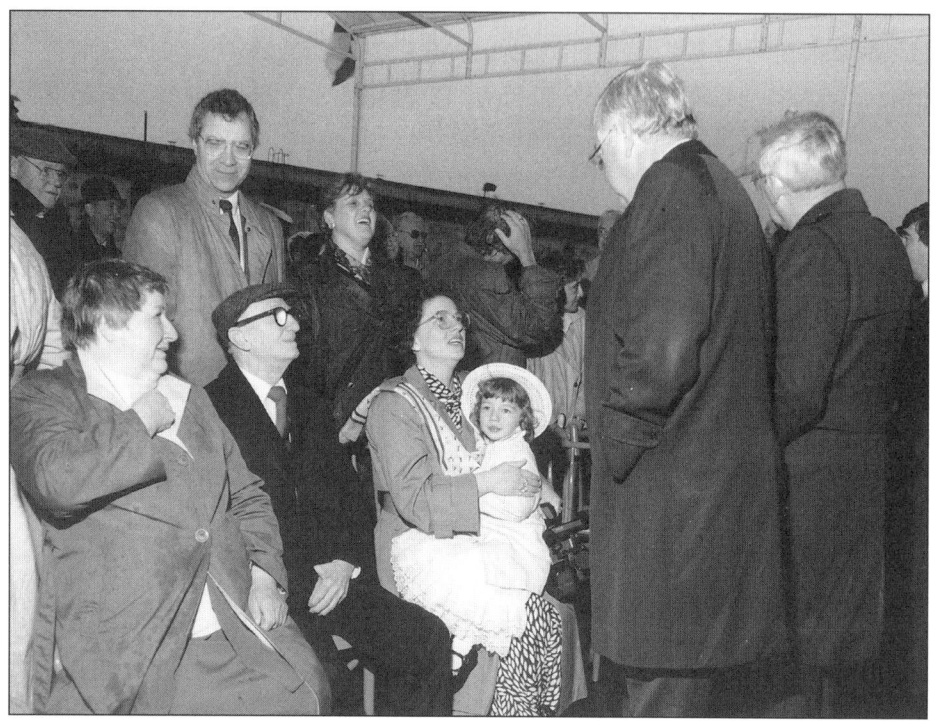

The former premier of Newfoundland, Joey Smallwood; his daughter, Clara Smallwood Russell, the sponsor; his granddaughter, Mrs. Russell Fitzpatrick; and great-granddaughter Ashley Russell Fitzpatrick; with Jean-Marc Lessard, mayor of Lauzon, behind, are seen here speaking to International Trade Minister and Newfoundland's representative in the federal Cabinet, John Crosbie.

Lounge of the ferry MV Joseph and Clara Smallwood. Courtesy CN Marine.

entailed routine navigation, communications, and manoeuvrability tests, and the excitement of sailing flat out at 20.888 knots on the measured mile, followed by an eight-hour endurance trial, and finally sailing full astern for half an hour.

Following her delivery in November 1989, Captain John Taylor, one of her two captains, took over. As he berthed her in Sydney, a broad grin broke over his face. "It's like parking a Volkswagen on the Main Street in Sydney," he commented to Steve Kack, the Davie contracts administrator who was standing beside him on the bridge. In June 1990, the *Joseph and Clara Smallwood* boarded her first passengers for her maiden trip between North Sydney and Argentia.

The client was well satisfied,[12] and a significant modernization of Davie's facilities had been accomplished. But in building the *Joseph and Clara Smallwood*, the shipyard had been learning to use the new modular technology, and though this technology resulted in a 25 per cent reduction in production costs over the *Caribou*, the cost of the engineering (preparing the plans and planning the construction) was three times as great. The high learning expense, which was charged against the building, was not counted in the price of the ship and appeared, therefore, as an overrun. This, added to Challinor's inability to communicate in French and his inexperience regarding large military programs, tipped the scale. Though his work in the introduction of advanced outfitting and the success of the *Smallwood* project had earned him the Society of Naval Architects and Marine Engineers' prestigious William M. Kennedy award,[13] the time had come for another to take over. It was up to Robert Tessier, the president of the MIL Group, who until then had given him his full support, to handle the situation. On October 20, 1989, Don Challinor resigned the presidency.[14]

The first module of the Ville de Quebec *arrives from* MIL *Tracy by barge.*

24

MIL – GUY VÉRONNEAU

1989-96

ON OCTOBER 20, 1989, Guy Véronneau took up his appointment as Davie's new president. A graduate of the École des hautes études commerciales in Montreal, Véronneau was well-known to Marine Industries Limited, where his first appointment was as manager of systems and data processing in 1973 and his subsequent positions included those of project manager and production manager of shipbuilding and ship repairing operations. In 1987, he had been named vice-president of MIL's Naval Division at Sorel. In that capacity he played a leading role in the CPF contract negotiations with Saint John and Versatile. Following two years as vice-president of Bombardier Inc.'s International Marketing Division, he returned to the MIL Group as vice-president, Operations, and shortly after was named president and CEO of MIL Davie. When questioned about his mandate, he strongly denied that he was there to close the yard. He was there to ensure the efficiency of operations, he said, to see that contract obligations were respected, to develop good customer relations, and to seek new contracts to ensure the survival of the shipyard. The naval contracts now underway would soon fill the shipyard. Seeing that the obligations attached to them were respected would be a major concern.

Though there were frequent complaints in shipping circles that the

Guy Véronneau. President and CEO of Davie from 1989 to 1996, and president of the MIL Group from 1991 to 1996.

Canadian government lacked a comprehensive shipping policy, the government was not entirely insensitive to the problems facing the industry. In November 1987, as a preliminary step, a marine outlook conference was held under the auspices of the Department of Supply and Services, at which various government departments discussed their future shipping requirements and came up with the following list:

- four-ship TRUMP project (already under way)
- second six-ship frigate project
- Polar 8 icebreaker
- ten- to twelve-ship nuclear-powered submarine project
- NATO frigate project (NFR-90)
- small fleet of mine counter-measure vessels and minor war vessel replacements for DND Auxiliary fleet and training vessels for Naval Reserve
- nine or ten new medium to small ships for Coast Guard
- up to ten mid-life modernizations (some in process)
- six medium to small vessels for Fisheries and Oceans, plus periodic refits and dockings of ships of all three departments

It was noted that various ships and other equipment would be needed by private interests for offshore hydrocarbon exploration and production in the Arctic and off the east coast, and that there would be a demand for the replacement of the ships in the coasting trade that were aging.[1]

The list was well-received by shipbuilders, but soon after that meeting, the world changed. *Perestroïka*, the destruction of the Berlin Wall, the breakup of the Warsaw Pact, and the collapse of the Soviet Union itself led to a fundamental re-evaluation of National Defence requirements. The RCN suddenly found itself hard pressed to justify its expensive shopping list.

The Canadian multi-billion-dollar nuclear-propelled submarine program, which many had considered essential because of the Soviet naval buildup, was shelved. The program had been debated in 1958 and again in 1964, and on both occasions dropped because of its high cost and relatively new technology. The decision to proceed had been finally announced by the federal government in 1987, and it led to the most intensive lobbying and preparatory homework ever done by the Canadian marine industries.[2]

The choice of submarine design had been narrowed down to two: the British (Vickers) Trafalgar Class, 85.4 metres in length, of larger size and greater power; and the French (DCN DCAN Shipyard, Cherbourg) Rubis-Améthyste, 79.65 metres, which was smaller and less expensive, so more units could be purchased. The MIL Group had joined with the SNC Group, Litton Systems Canada Limited, Lavalin and Halifax-Dartmouth Industries Limited to form the Canadian Submarine Consortium, or CSC, in order to bid for the prime contract, and like the other two groups in contention, it had passed the Source Qualification Proposal.[3] Between them the members of the CSC had a wealth of experience: MIL Davie, for instance, offered its skill in building surface warships; MIL Tracy was engaged in a research contract it had won from DND for the development of Canadian steel for submarine construction;[4] MIL Vickers was an experienced subcontractor to the U.S. submarine builders, Newport News and Electric Boat, to whom it had supplied pressure-hull cylinders, torpedo tubes, and many other components for their nuclear-powered attack submarines; MIL Systems

Engineering was Canada's premier naval engineering design house; the SNC Group was internationally recognized for its leadership in the management of large and complex programs, and particularly for its engineering and procurement capabilities; Litton Systems Canada Limited, a division of Litton Industries, had a long and successful history of designing and manufacturing sophisticated electronics equipment for naval and commercial use, which, together with its recognized combat systems integration skills, had earned it the prime contract for TRUMP; Lavalin, like SNC, offered engineering, procurement, construction, and management skills; and Halifax-Dartmouth Industries Limited (HDI) had a background of warship building and was the only private shipyard to have undertaken refits of the current fleet of Canadian Oberon Class diesel electric submarines. Moreover, HDI was strategically located near the Halifax Naval Base and the Atlantic where a great many tests and trials would be carried out.

The choice between the French and the British submarine was never made. The cancellation of the project put an end to the argument about their respective merits, as well as to the intense lobbying by both the European designers and the Canadian consortia. Most Canadians, wary of all that is nuclear, accepted the news of the project's withdrawal with relief, but not the shipyard workers, for whom it would have meant years of work. Submarine acquisition was put on the back burner, with attention focused on the diesel-electric alternative, and on a much smaller scale. This made it almost certain that the final decision would be in favour of foreign-built and, perhaps, second-hand boats. A great deal of time, effort, and money was spent by all contenders for the submarine contracts. The MIL Group, which had considered itself well-placed to win the competition, found the cancellation particularly difficult to accept.

Shelved, too, as a result of the federal government's budget of February 1990, was construction of the Polar 8 super icebreaker. This struck a hard blow at a west coast shipbuilding consortium, which included Versatile Pacific.[5] The budget also signalled a reduction and restructuring of the Coast Guard fleet, which culminated in the plan to privatize some of its services in 1996. Canadian shipbuilders could no longer expect to use their specialized ice technology and expertise for icebreaker construction.

The Hibernia Program was another disappointment. Despite the Canadian government's insistence that a full and fair opportunity to provide goods, services, and employment be given to Canadians, with first consideration for Newfoundlanders, the most lucrative contracts went to foreign companies. MIL and Davie had spent several million dollars on the project since 1979, yet Davie's share of the sole contract obtained by the consortium of Davie, MIL Offshore Inc., and M. & M. Manufacturing of Dartmouth amounted only to $13.5 million, roughly a year's work for 100 Davie employees.[6] Moreover, the utility shaft's nine structural decks, four mezzanine decks, elevator shaft and control room module, which Davie fabricated, had to be sent on to M. & M. Manufacturing at Dartmouth, Nova Scotia, to be assembled in modules and outfitted,[7] because the Hibernia Management Development Corporation (HMDC) had been concerned that Davie's ability to deliver the modules on schedule would be hampered by ice in the St. Lawrence. The final assembly at the Bull Arm site was done by MIL's offshore partner, Peter Kiewit Sons & Co.

Davie was fortunate that both the Canadian Patrol Frigate (CPF) program and the Tribal class refit, update, and modernization (TRUMP) program survived. Davie initially had no part of the CPF contract but, because of Versatile's and MIL's successive acquisition of Davie, and the subsequent closing of the Vickers' shipyard, it inherited the complete subcontract for three frigates originally awarded to Vickers and MIL Tracy. Changes in the subcontract, or "building plan," reflected the corporate transformations, which in the end allowed a more practical division of labour to be worked out: originally Vickers was to have outfitted the three empty hulls built by MIL Tracy; then it was proposed that Tracy and Davie each build one complete ship and half of the third, which would be joined together at Lauzon; in the end, it was agreed that Tracy would build the modules of the stern section of all three ships and ship them to Davie.

It soon became apparent that, despite the lengthy contract definition phase, the contract terms did not adequately cover the design development. Saint John[8] was having to make a great many alterations to the lead ship, so many, in fact, that in May 1987, it advised MIL that it could no longer supply validated plans. The inordinate number of changes and frequent delays in delivery of materials and equipment that resulted made the already challenging task of building these frigates many times more difficult.

Tracy, as a subcontractor on the project, wanted to stop work until the plans were sorted out. Davie could not stop without breaching its contract. So the work continued at both shipyards despite the difficulties. Although they had to follow the work instructions received from Saint John about such things as where the ships were to be cut into modules, Davie planned and did as much pre-outfitting as possible. This, together with the radical change in the building strategy, enabled them to make significant savings on their first ship.

The modules had to be specially strengthened in order to withstand the journey from Tracy to Lauzon, which sometimes took place under extreme winter conditions. The first to arrive was the keel block module of the frigate HMCS *Ville de Québec*. It was laid at Davie in sub-zero temperatures in December 1988, in the presence of the Honourable Perrin Beatty, the former Minister of Defence, and Vice-Admiral C.M. Thomas, Commander of the Maritime Command, who placed the traditional silver dollar under the keel. By October 1989, fabrication of the other modules was well under way, and it was the turn of Thomas's successor, Vice-Admiral Robert E. George to lay the keel of HMCS *Regina*. Vice-Admiral J.R. Anderson, Chief Maritime Doctrine and Operations, Department of Defence, performed the honours for HMCS *Calgary* in June, 1991.

The construction of all three frigates advanced steadily, but there was no slowdown in the number of requests for changes, so it was impossible for Davie to adhere to its schedule either in regard to time or cost. Relations between Saint John Shipbuilding Limited (SJSL) and Davie worsened continually until finally, on June 29, 1990, SJSL sued Davie for non-compliance in the amount of $1.7 billion, and MIL counter-sued in July for $200 million,

Left: *The outfitted module, number 3130, ready for the keel-laying ceremony.* Right: *Keel laying of the City-class Canadian patrol frigate* HMCS Ville de Quebec *in December 1988. Vice-Admiral C.M. Thomas, Commander Maritime Command, places the silver dollar under the keel, accompanied by Perrin Beatty, Minister of National Defence, and Don Challinor.*

alleging non-respect of contractual obligations.[9] SJSL went to the courts again in June 1991 in an attempt to take the contract away from Davie, alleging that Davie was in default of certain clauses of the contract, and that it lacked the financial means to carry out the entire contract. If Saint John had been successful, it would have been entitled to lay its hands on Davie's performance bonds in the amount of $30 million. Davie obtained an injunction to prevent this. SJSL then stopped all payments to Davie.

It was apparent that, whatever blame might be found elsewhere, the underlying problems lay in the original contract. Negotiations between the federal government, the Quebec government, as shareholder, and the two shipyards eventually brought an agreement in December 1992. Davie received a total settlement for the CPF and TRUMP programs of approximately $363 million, of which $100 million was put forward by the provincial government and $263 million by the federal government. Davie regarded it as a justifiable contract adjustment, but many called it a bailout, and because of the media coverage, considerable damage was caused unfairly to Davie's reputation. It is interesting to note that a similar contract settlement was made by the federal government and SJSL at a later

NEW CHALLENGES

date. SJSL eventually settled with Davie as well, bringing to an end a difficult period and restoring some contractual harmony.

All of this did not prevent the work from going forward. On September 23, 1993, HMCS *Ville de Québec* was handed over to the Navy by David Christopher, director of Tests and Trials. The ship had performed beautifully and the Navy was delighted. Following her commissioning, members of the crew were surprised to find themselves hurrying down such familiar Quebec streets as *Grande Allée* and *rue du Trésor* as they went about their daily duties. Thanks to David Christopher (whose idea it was) and Quebec mayor Jean-Paul L'Allier (who provided the information) not only were the street names posted in the passages aboard ship, but so also was a brief history of each name. It was a special touch indicative of the warm relationship that has always existed between Davie and the Navy. The same attention would be accorded to each of her sister ships that Davie built, with the full support of the mayors of Regina and Calgary.

A short two months later, HMCS *Regina* left for her sea trials with a crew of 200 on board: 100 from the Davie shipyard, and the rest from the Navy, SJSL, and its various suppliers. Virtually no defects were uncovered and the report regarding quality assurance and tests was perfect. It was in every way a triumph. One who especially appreciated the results was her captain, Captain Jellineck. "I am particularly proud," he said, "to have the command of the best ship of the fleet." Work on the third frigate, HMCS *Calgary*, continued. She set sail on her sea trials in June 1994.

Every Davie employee was aware of the contractual disputes. Perhaps partly because of them, everyone who took part in building the CPFs was determined that the Davie-built frigates would be the best, and their pride in the job was matched by their achievement. A letter from Captain (Navy) Bert Blattmann summed up the sentiments of many others whose letters were pinned on the notice board at the shipyard: "The Navy was very pleased with the exceptional cleanliness and the excellent workmanship displayed in the finishing of the vessel," he wrote. "*Regina* achieved high

The CPF Ville de Quebec *salutes the City of Quebec before leaving for Halifax. The* Ville de Quebéc *measures 134.1 by 16.4 by 11.1 metres, has a 4,750-ton deep displacement, and is driven by two gas turbines of 23,000 s.h.p. She can achieve a speed of more than 27 knots over a range of 4,500 nautical miles.*

standards of performance at sea and was delivered in a highly polished state, reflecting MIL Davie's pride in workmanship and commitment to meeting the customers' requirements." . . . "I feel very strongly that your fine ship has given the Commanding Officer the best possible head start toward bringing HMCS *Regina* into operational service." He added, "The building of *Regina* was an enormous team effort, and I would be grateful if you would pass along my congratulations to your team, the superb professional shipbuilders of MIL Davie. I certainly look forward to the delivery of *Calgary* next summer, and I feel confident that MDI will equal or exceed the fine results achieved for *Regina*."

In parallel with the CPF program, Davie managed the TRUMP program, which kept a large number of workers occupied for the best part of seven years, and provided more than 21 million man-hours of labour in all. Though state of the art when they left the shipyard in 1972 and 1973 respectively, HMCS *Athabaskan* and *Algonquin*, like their sisters *Iroquois* and *Huron*, built at MIL Tracy, were extremely vulnerable to the newer weapons

of war. They had been designed with a strong anti-submarine capability, but the Falkland Islands War had underlined the fact that they were virtually defenceless against air and particularly missile attack. It was both to correct this deficiency and to provide for a task force command capability that their extensive refits were ordered.

The four destroyers were to be given new propulsion and auxiliary systems to improve their speed, power, operability, and energy efficiency. Their maintenance was to be made easier and their detection more difficult. Though they were to be fitted with the latest in long-range anti-air missile technology, they would keep their strong anti-submarine capability. As a consequence, their hulls had to be strengthened to offset an extra 800 tons' displacement, which the new equipment would add to their original 4,300 tons.[10]

Litton Systems Canada Limited was responsible for defining the contract, for the design, and for the fulfilment of the entire project. Davie, Pratt

Left: *At the cutting of the first plate for the* CPF *program, June 20, 1988. Donald Breton, Davie's director of Planning, who was director of the* CPF *program 1986 to 1991, with Lieutenant Commander Victor Chan,* DND, *Quality Control; Brian Hodgson, senior representative of Saint John Shipbuilding; and Lieutenant Commander Ed. Paquette, senior naval officer for the* CPF *program at Davie.* Right: HMCS Algonquin *undergoing sea trials following her modernization as lead ship in the* TRUMP *program.*

& Whitney, Versatile Systems, and, in the initial stages, the naval architects German & Milne, all worked together in a team effort with Litton and the Navy. It was up to Litton to supply the technical data to Davie, and to provide strip-out and working drawings, as well as most of the equipment needed to complete the work efficiently and on time. Davie, the shipyard subcontractor,[11] had to carry out all of the fabrication, modernization, and refit work.

Initially, Litton and Davie worked well together and a warm relationship developed – Davie employees still compete for a trophy presented by Litton for an annual golf tournament – but somewhere along the line things started to go very wrong. Once again, the contract definition was inadequate. The integration of modern systems with those already in place and the refit itself were far more complex than expected, and a massive field engineering effort was needed to overcome the difficulties. Delays and cost overruns soon led to bitter disputes. Eventually Litton, whose contract allowed the government to step in under certain circumstances, commenced legal proceedings against Her Majesty, MIL, et al. The Minister of Supply and Services' ultimate response was to withdraw Litton's contract as prime contractor on July 14, 1991, and to take over the management itself. This left Litton responsible only for integrating the combat systems, an area of the work in which they excelled. The significant losses experienced by Davie due to the delays, changes, and rework were eventually made good in the omnibus government settlement referred to above.

The settlement, however, came later. In the meantime, with *Algonquin*, the first ship, beset by technical and contractual problems and *Iroquois* having to wait, while holding costs mounted, for her work to begin, and cost overruns for the whole program increasing steadily, Davie made the decision to force the program forward. The company risked its contractual position by going ahead. The worse prospect, however, was the possible loss of credibility if the program remained stalled. This would be disastrous, both for the industry and the Navy. The situation had already deteriorated to the point that DND was seriously considering cancelling the program, and this might well have happened if Davie had not completed the work on *Algonquin*. A close working understanding had grown up between the senior Davie team of Guy Véronneau, Michael Ayre,[12] and Jean-Yves Rhéaume, who directed Operations, and the senior government team of Commander Denis Reilly, TRUMP program manager, and Jean Roy of DSS, both of whom never ceased to believe in Davie's capabilities. As a result of their efforts the program was saved. *Algonquin* was delivered on October 1, 1991, and *Iroquois* on July 3, 1992.

In spite of all the problems, Davie won the contract for the second part of the TRUMP program, that is, for the destroyers HMCS *Athabaskan* and *Huron*, for which it had had to bid in competition against the Halifax shipyard and Versatile Pacific (now "divorced" from Davie).[13] *Athabaskan* arrived at the shipyard in 1991, fresh from her tour of duty in the Persian Gulf War. She was followed by *Huron*, a year later. In a spirit of co-opera-

Staff members enjoy a joke with DND project manager on a TRUMP vessel. Maryse Langevin, Trials Group, electronic systems manager; Captain (N) R. De Blois, project manager, TRUMP; Jean-Yves Rhéaume, vice-president, Operations; David Christopher, director, tests and trials; Guy Véronneau.

tion and mutual respect, and with a lot of hard work by many other people, the program was gradually brought back into line. It ended with the delivery of *Huron* in December 1994.

All the ships of the CPF and TRUMP programs were delivered out of Halifax in order to avoid exposure to winter conditions in Quebec. In order to get offshore work contracts, MIL had bought shares in a fabricating company, M. & M. Manufacturing, situated alongside a large public wharf in Dartmouth. Bolstered when necessary with Davie employees, it became invaluable for the naval programs, serving from 1992 to 1995 for finishing the work and as a base for tests and trials. For a long time, an almost permanent "trailer city" accommodated the more than 100 Davie, Litton, and Navy/DSS people. Many warm friendships developed between local Nova Scotians and Davie's managers, supervisors, and trials and quality assurance personnel during the tours of duty in the maritime province.

The simultaneous implementation of both major military programs put an enormous strain on the contractors and subcontractors who were hard put to find enough qualified people to handle them. This was true for the Navy also, which had to man the new ships and train the crews. For Davie, it meant increasing the workforce to 3,500 people, of which more than 1,000 were white-collar workers. That Davie was able to take this in its

NEW CHALLENGES

Davie shipyard in May 1992. HMCS Algonquin *in foreground, with* HMCS Ville de Quebec *and* HMCS Regina *alongside wharf beyond.* CTMA Voyageur *and tug* Leonard W. *in floating dock.* MV Caribou *can be seen at the mouth of the Champlain Dry Dock,* centre top.

stride and deliver seven quality warships despite all the contractual problems is remarkable. In fact, in one year, 1994, four warships left the shipyard, two new frigates and two newly outfitted destroyers.

Increased productivity at the shipyard, which was essential if the naval program was to be a success, remained Véronneau's top preoccupation throughout. A major challenge was the handling of negotiations for the renewal of the shipyard collective agreement in the summer of 1991. The most important single clause (because government contract settlement depended on it) was the one stipulating that there would be neither strikes nor lockouts before December 31, 1994, or later, if the naval contracts had not been completed. Besides the "no strike" clause, agreements with all four unions included an across-the-board increase in wages of 3½ per cent on the July 1, 1992, 3 per cent on January 1, 1993, and 2 per cent on January 1, 1994. In addition, various committees and other mechanisms to improve productivity and competitiveness were agreed upon.

One such committee was the study group, Groupe témoin. Its members consisted of eight employees representing the unions and the association of draftsmen, four representing management, Marcel Gosselin, president of the committee Action/MIL Davie representing regional commerce, and Gilles Lehouiller, councillor for the City of Levis. The president was lawyer André Lemieux of the firm Poissant Thibault-Peat Marwick Thorne. Its mandate was to familiarize itself with Davie's standing in the marketplace – its relative productivity and competitiveness; to identify and direct any studies of productivity that were needed; and to comment on the results. According to their final report, presented in May 1992, there would be a strong future demand for ships, but Davie would get no further contracts unless it reduced costs by 30 per cent by 1994. The committee recommended that Davie build ships on an assembly-line basis (which was what management had already concluded) and that management and unions work together to find ways to improve productivity. The Groupe témoin was dissolved, to be succeeded by an action committee, or "Comité d'entreprise." Made up of members of management and the unions, it was to meet regularly and ensure that the recommendations of the Groupe témoin were carried out.

Véronneau was able to report in his year-end message to employees in December 1991 that the year had been an excellent one. All delivery dates had been met. There had been as many as ten ships at one time in various stages of construction and repair at the yard. Shipyard strength had peaked at 3,400 employees, 300 more than the previous year.

More significantly, a new relationship between management and workers at Davie augured well for the future. Confrontation had finally given way to co-operation. Total Quality Management (Processus d'amélioration continue, or PAC) had been introduced in 1991. A study group made up of six members of the staff, headed by Guy Véronneau, and six union representatives, three from the shipyard workers' union, and one each from the office workers', security force, and designers' unions, held its first meeting in June 1992. Twenty-four subcommittees were then set up to

NEW CHALLENGES

AQAP-1 *award presentation, March 1992. David Christopher, director, Quality Assurance Operations and Tests and Trials; Captain D.V. Jacobson, project manager,* TRUMP, DND; *Graham Reynolds, manager, Quality Systems; Jim Williams, president,* MSEI; *Ken McCormick, vice-president, Quality,* MIL *Davie and the* MIL *Group; Commander N. Blatchford,* CPF *Detachment; Don Wilson, director general, Quality Assurance,* DND; *D.A. Vandevenne,* CO, *2nd Canadian Forces Technical Services Agency; Guy Véronneau; W. Doering, director, Quality Assurance Operations,* DND; *André Roy, technical inspector, 203* CFTS *Detachment; Commander R. Payne, Commander,* TRUMP *program; Lieutenant (N) R. Nahhas, manager, Quality Assurance,* TRUMP *Detachment; Major P. Bérubé,* CO, *203* CFTS *Detachment; Michael Ayre, vice-president, Business Development; Lieutenant Commander D. Bernier, production manager,* TRUMP *Detachment at* MIL *Davie; Bernard Giguère, assistant to the president.*

scrutinize all manufacturing processes and management procedures and to make recommendations leading to their increased efficiency to "benchmark" international standards. Every other aspect of the shipbuilding process was also to be reviewed. Estimating, design, procurement, planning and control, as well as the plant, would be considered in the light of their future conversion from naval to commercial building. The Department of National Defence had awarded Davie NATO standard AQAP-1 qualification, the equivalent of ISO-9001, for its military program. The goal was to obtain the ISO qualification itself.

"Openness" or "transparency," meaning easy, unrestricted communication between management, unions and staff, received a lot of attention. In addition, management's goal of a 50 per cent increase in productivity in four years, 1990–93, was well on its way to being realized. Productivity rose 16.4 per cent in the second year, and a target of 25 per cent was set for 1992. No one had had any illusions about the effort that was required to meet this target but neither, for the most part, were there doubts about the consequences of failure. Véronneau was tireless in his crusade to change Davie's corporate culture, to instil in its employees a strong sense of mission, and to inspire them with a vision and confidence in a strong future. He asked that every employee make a personal commitment to excellence. The common will to increase productivity led to an increase in the number of labour-saving ideas that were suggested and rewarded. Some were simple, but nonetheless effective. When one man took his bicycle to the yard to save time when he moved from one part of the yard to another, the idea was seized upon, and heavy-duty bicycles were made available at various locations so that others could do the same.

Unfortunately, despite the size and success of the two naval programs, and despite the fact that Davie had produced first-class ships, the programs did not provide the financial boost that Davie had counted on to pay for the improvements that the shipyard required. The company did gain experience in working with new technologies, however, and the programs kept the yard fully occupied when there was little else but repair work to be had. And the strong performance by both workers and management allowed Davie to make overall profits in the years 1991 to 1994 and thus to show that the yard could have a future.

1987-1996

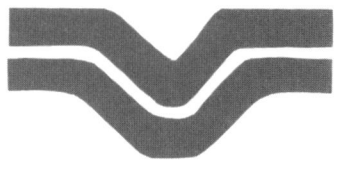
1985-1987

1958-1976

1976-1979

1979-1985

1996-

Davie logos over the years.

25

LOOKING AHEAD

1991-96

BY THE BEGINNING of the 1990s, the MIL Group had been reduced to the parent company and three subsidiaries: MIL Davie Inc., MIL Systems Engineering Inc., and MIL Offshore Inc., the last-named company created to organize and co-ordinate the group's participation in the Hibernia and other Atlantic Canada oil-field projects.[1] Following a decision to streamline the group's structure, Guy Véronneau took over the presidency of the MIL Group from Robert Tessier in October 1991, while keeping his position as president of Davie.[2] Three months later, the Group left Montreal and joined MIL Davie's top management on the third floor of the administrative office building at the shipyard, thus consolidating the two corporate bodies under one president and one roof. New appointments accompanied this move: Réal Auclair, MSC and CA, formerly of Bombardier, became treasurer and vice-president, Finance, of both; Denys Lamarre was named legal counsel and also vice-president of both; and Ken McCormick was appointed vice-president, Quality. The government of Quebec through SGF still had a 65 per cent interest in the MIL Group, and the Franco-British company, GEC Alsthom, the other 35 per cent.

As a result of these changes, a heavy workload fell on Guy Véronneau's shoulders, for in addition to his new duties as president of the group, and

NEW CHALLENGES

Robert Tessier, president of the MIL *Group from 1988 to 1991.*

his overall responsibility for the Davie shipyard, the yard's long-term survival remained a major concern.

Though the naval program was by far the most important focus of activity, there were others. The Repairs Division was also busy. Back in 1973, Canada Steamship Lines had approached the federal government with a proposal that Davie purchase the Champlain Dry Dock, but the discussions had not led to action. More recently, the government tried to persuade Davie, which had been the Lauzon docks' sole user for many years, to buy both dry docks, but following a feasibility study, Davie demurred. Instead, management decided that it could better afford to increase the shipyard's dry-docking capacity by making use of the Vickers' floating dock *Général Georges P. Vanier*. A suitable space was dredged alongside the finger-jetty, and the dock was towed to the shipyard in the summer of 1989. History thus repeated itself, for a century earlier George T. Davie had brought down the larger of two wooden dry docks from the Davie shipyard at Levis to save on the docking fees of the recently built Lorne Dry Dock.

As the employees set to work to put the dock in good order, Davie's marketing and repairs divisions organized a team of representatives and agents to contact European shipowners and advise them of the new repair facility at the Lauzon yard. But, as far as the U.S. market was concerned, those who had hoped that the U.S.–Canada Free Trade Agreement would in some way alter the terms of the Jones Act, which has for so long effectively prevented Canadian shipyards from undertaking shipbuilding or repair for U.S. owners, were disappointed. A proposed Transportation Annex to the Free Trade Agreement, which would have required each country to treat the other as domestic with respect to maritime legislation and regulations, was withdrawn at the last minute by U.S. negotiators.

The floating dock soon justified itself. It proved particularly useful during the first half of the 1990s when, because of the naval programs, it was often the only dry-docking facility available for other work. Even

Réal Auclair, vice-president of finance, is presented with a plaque from R. Maze, CD, commanding officer of HMCS Huron. Standing at left is Max Groslouis, chief of the Huron Nation Wendat.

Arrival of the floating dock Général Georges P. Vanier *at the shipyard in June 1989. Built in 1964, the dock is 585 feet by 143 feet by 58 feet high, and can lift a vessel of 25,000 tons. The side walls contain offices, machine shops, storage rooms, a dining room, and toilets. She was towed down from Montreal following* MIL *Vickers' closure.*

though naval vessels occupied the Champlain Dry Dock for much of the time, the Repairs Division still handled some 300 ships in seven years. The year 1992 was especially busy. At one time there were ten large ships in the shipyard either building or under repair, including the 177-metre-long *Canmar Victory*, the longest ship that the division had yet handled in the Vanier Floating Dock, which was in for the repair of major hull damage.

Paul Vandal, who came to Davie from Sorel in 1988, and is manager of the Repairs Division, appreciates the far greater capacity of Davie's facilities. A 5,400-GRT was the biggest ship that MIL Tracy could handle, whereas Davie can take on any ship that will fit into the 1,100-foot-long Champlain Dock. Its main restriction is the 120-foot gate that permits vessels of up to so-called Panamax size to use it.

Few eastern Canadian shipyards remain to compete with Davie for ship repairs. Mainly, they are the Halifax Shipyard for larger jobs, and the Les Méchin shipyard downriver, which can take ships of up to 540 feet in length.

LOOKING AHEAD

Regulars that are brought in for maintenance and upkeep include the Canadian Coast Guard ships that are stationed at Quebec. They are seen regularly for rudder inspections and for the special "coatings" with Inerta 160 that are often applied to ships working in ice.[3] Some CSL ships, also, have their maintenance, tailshaft inspection, and so forth done by Davie, and sometimes larger jobs. For instance, in 1995, Davie got the contract to replace the five steel holds of the fifteen-year-old *Nanticoke*. It took 500 tons of steel. Another large job was the lengthening of the MV *Cabot* by 125 feet for Oceanex (a Fed Nav subsidiary), while the Société des traversiers du Quebec's two ferries, *Joseph Deschênes* and *Armand Imbeau*, which operate between Tadoussac and Sainte-Catherine, were both lengthened by 60 feet.

Other ships brought in as a result of accidents and fitted in among the scheduled work included the *OOCL Challenger*, whose 22-foot diameter propeller was repaired in 1989. More recently, the Polish ship *Reduta Ordona* hit an iceberg in Hudson Strait and came to Davie to have a gaping

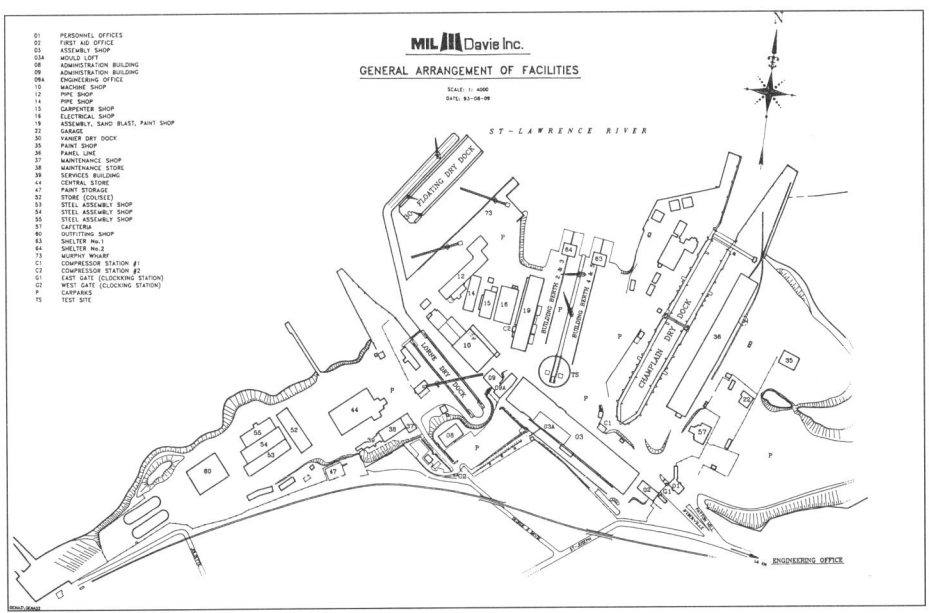

The MIL Davie shipyard in 1992.

NEW CHALLENGES

These rocks were lodged in the hulls of the following ships when they were brought in for repair. From left to right: Iberian, *docked November 3, 1902 (she had gone aground at Isle-aux-Grues);* ss Franconia, *docked July 16, 1950 (she had gone aground on the Isle of Orleans); and* ss Samaria, *docked October 16, 1951 (she had gone aground on Ile Vert). Standing among the rocks are the Repair team: Roch Dufour, Marc Aussant, Marielle Couture, and Paul Vandal.*

100-by-30-foot hole made good. Each repair job is different. Paul Vandal says that he enjoys the challenge of the custom-tailored work.

Ship repair technology has been updated along with shipbuilding technology. The Tribon computer programs, for instance, are used in ship repair both for controlling plate cutting and for prefabrication. The welding processes have also changed. Plates that were formerly joined together with double-sided welding can now be welded from one side only, with a ceramic backing strip fixed under the seam. Another innovation is a "miracle" putty called Chockfast that becomes as tough as steel when it cures. It is used for chocking, or securing, the main engines, steering gears, and other equipment in their final position.

The ships in for repair bring Davie employees into contact with men, and sometimes women, from distant countries. Their culture – the way the food is prepared, their religious practices, the language they speak, and a host of other details – makes an impression. Vandal vividly remembers how in 1992, sailors energetically painted the blue, white, and red livery of their new country over the hammer and sickle on the funnel of the *Khudozhnik Pakhomov*, and then changed the name of the home port on her stern from Leningrad to St. Petersburg.

The Industrial Division also continued to bring work to the shipyard. Georges Berberi has been its manager since 1974. Directing the department, he says, has not been easy. When the shipyard was busy, shop space would be taken up with marine work, and little left for industrial work. He was often unable to make firm delivery commitments because of these space limitations, and no effective marketing could be done. But, when shipbuilding fell off, the Industrial Division was asked to take up the slack, and he had to hustle to land new contracts. The remarkable variety of contracts that the Industrial Division has handled over the years has been described in other chapters. It also has often acted as a subcontractor to Davie's own Marine Division, fabricating the more complicated steelwork, because of its specialized skills and expertise in maintaining tight tolerances. It built the stem and stern of the ferry *Joseph and Clara Smallwood*, for example. This capability has enabled it to continue to build the complex sonar domes for the USN and U.S. shipyards, seventy-eight of which have been delivered since 1971. Improved productivity of more than 30 per cent, achieved through its Continuous Improvement Program, has allowed Davie to slash $500,000 off the unit contract price and maintain its edge in the market.

An interesting project, begun in 1994, is the manufacture of special bogies and motorized units for transporting truck trailers on existing railways. Their operation over medium distances is expected to increase trucking companies' efficiency by reducing fuel consumption, wear and tear, accidents, and manpower requirements. The system was designed, planned,

NEW CHALLENGES

Testing the intermodal train unit on the railway tracks outside the shipyard. It is now running a regular service between Drummondville and Mississauga.

and developed by Innotermodal Inc. of Brossard, and was funded partly by the SGF and CN Rail. The MIL Group set up a subsidiary for its manufacture, MIL Intermodal Inc., which passed on a subcontract for two trains with twenty bogies each, as a pilot program. These are being manufactured on a production line set up for the purpose in the steel shops in Davie's West Yard, under the direction of Michel Gendron. The prototype is already running daily between Drummondville, Quebec, and Mississauga, Ontario. It is hoped that the project will generate a revenue of up to $20 million a year for the next five years.

Michael Ayre and his marketing team of Brian Smith and Mark DeRoche have worked hard to identify new markets and bring contracts to the shipyard. They were encouraged by the fact that some major European yards began to recapture their share of the market after years of losing out

American-owned, and carrying 9,000 tons of liquid asphalt, the 12,000 ton Rio Orinoco *went aground off Anticosti Island in October 1990 and was abandoned by both her owners and crew. When a first attempt by salvage experts to refloat her failed, the Desgagnés Group made the winning bid to salvage her on a no cure, no pay basis, succeeded in her salvage and ended up buying her. After five months of repairs in Davie's floating dock, she left the dock to join the rest of the Desgagnés fleet under her new name* Thalassa Desgagnés.

in competition with far eastern shipyards. There was a renewed optimism, a feeling that "if they can do it, so can we."

Though domestic demand in the short term appeared unlikely to rise, by the end of 1992, a new worldwide shipbuilding cycle appeared to be starting. There were signs that there would be a steady increase in the movement of products by sea. Given that the effective life of a ship was normally less than twenty-five years, it was to be expected that half of the world's 3,150 tankers and bulk carriers would have to be replaced within the next ten years in order to maintain the size of the fleet. Moreover, many countries were becoming alarmed by the large number of bulk car-

NEW CHALLENGES

Davie's exhibition booth at the Canadian Marine Industries Association meeting in Ottawa in 1993. Steve Kack and Brian Smith receiving clients.

riers that had been lost at sea with commensurate loss of life, ecological damage, and economic hardship. In many cases, they were instituting new regulations that would force owners to phase out vessels that were unsafe. These factors[4] together clearly promised a significant increase in the shipbuilding market from 1994 to 2005.

In 1992, therefore, Davie carried out studies of market opportunities in conjunction with consultants such as A & P Appledore International, experts in the shipbuilding field. The options that were considered included maintaining the status quo, diversification, penetration of the international market, and even closing the shipyard in an orderly manner. From among these options, it was decided that Davie would engage in the well-organized construction, in series, of tankers and bulk carriers, beginning with ships of 40,000 d.w.t., or Handymax size, and perhaps going on to build 70,000 d.w.t., or Panamax size.

It was also decided that Davie could best implement this program by teaming up with another world-class shipyard and, following a systematic review,[5] Burmeister & Wain (BWS) of Denmark was selected. BWS had built up an international reputation as a leader in building standard ships in series and had been one of the few European yards to compete successfully against far eastern yards for more than twenty years. During that time it had developed a shipbuilding strategy that enhanced its competitiveness, particularly by using designs that were simple, minimized the number of parts, and kept production costs low. These, together with innovative and efficient facilities and processes, and a strong procurement capability due to its many associations, had helped it to maintain its leading position. Burmeister's experienced marketing department placed special emphasis on market intelligence to select effective market segments and innovative financing plans. The high quality of its designs was internationally recognized. Consequently, its ships commanded a high price and retained a high second-hand value. All these attributes made BWS a valuable strategic partner.

Davie's management team drew up a detailed business plan that identified the target market and outlined the strategy needed to penetrate it. Certain prerequisites were identified: an alliance with BWS allowing for benchmarking of all aspects of the shipbuilding process; an investment of some $60 million to upgrade the yard's facilities to allow for the construction of large modules and their erection in the Champlain Dry Dock; and a totally new union agreement compatible with an internationally competitive yard. The market was to be tested with owners and brokers during the last half of 1993; a sales effort would follow; and, it was hoped, the first contracts would be signed during the early part of 1994.

A number of factors appeared to favour Davie's initiative. Rising demand had driven ship prices significantly higher than they had been in the mid-1980s. Exchange rates had forced up the relative value of the currencies of most formerly low-cost competitors. Inflation and rising expectations in competing countries had further increased their wage rates. And, finally, in many countries subsidies to shipbuilders and ship operators had been substantially reduced. In Europe, for example, they had dropped from well over 20 per cent to 9 per cent, and there were great hopes that an international agreement at OECD (Organization for Economic Co-operation and Development) in Paris would be reached to eliminate subsidies globally. This would have the effect of "levelling the playing field" for Davie and other Canadian yards, which had had no subsidy support since 1985.

Economic and trade analyses had led BWS to conclude that freight rates and second-hand ship values would increase dramatically in the mid-1990s. Acting on this expectation, by mid-1994 BWS had either acquired or taken majority ownership in thirty-one vessels, mostly, but not all, built by themselves.

Unhappily for BWS, unforeseen developments were about to have a catastrophic effect on the company's plans. The value of the Danish Kroner measured against the U.S. dollar increased by 30 per cent in one year. Just as significantly, the fight for shipbuilding supremacy between Japanese and Korean shipyards drove down the price of their next selected ship series, the Panamax Bulk Carrier, and invalidated the predictions of increased freight rates and second-hand values, creating a crisis of significant proportions[6] leading eventually to the bankruptcy of the Burmeister & Wain shipyard.

Even though the design development, production, and facility studies Davie conducted with BWS were completed before the collapse, the agreement with BWS for continuing support remains in force. Ironically, Davie put in a successful bid on equipment that was being sold off from the BWS yard by its Trustee.

In view of the fact that Korean shipbuilders had driven prices for both tankers and bulk carriers out of reach, a review of Davie's business strategy was made in 1994. This led to the conclusion that the container ship market was far stronger than that of the tanker or bulk carrier, and it was on this type of ship that Davie should concentrate. Early in 1995, a team visited the major European builders of container ships to find a strategic partner. The well-known Thyssen Nordseewerke shipyard of Emden, Germany, had focused from an early date on merchant ship construction, and now specialized in building sophisticated container vessels, advanced gas or chemical carriers, and icebreaking vessels. Its excellent container ship designs and efficient organization made it Davie's first choice. An agreement was reached to market and build container ships of 1,500, 1,700 and 2,200 teu (20-foot equivalent unit containers) to their designs.[7]

LOOKING AHEAD

༄ SHIPBUILDING IN THE 1990s ༄

CLOCKWISE FROM upper left: Architects and draftsmen use Tribon software to design the ships on computer. A steel plater cuts the plates using computer guided machinery. Also using computer guided equipment, pipes are cut and bent to the precise size and shape required. A side shell unit, completely pre-outfitted, is positioned on the slipway.

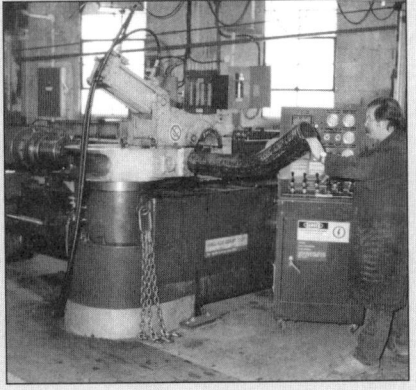

When the time came to renew the collective agreement in 1994, negotiations were slow and the atmosphere tense. So much had to change. The majority of workers now accepted the need for change, but it took time to find acceptable terms. It was not until January 1995 that an agreement was reached with the union executive, and only in March, at an extremely vocal meeting, that union leaders succeeded in persuading their members to ratify the far-reaching changes. The union had refused to accept the 15 per cent wage roll-back that Véronneau had told them was essential, but a compromise had been found that blended wage reductions with cuts to other benefits such as premiums and vacations to achieve the equivalent of the 15 per cent reduction. A 5 per cent wage reduction in 1995 was to be followed by a freeze for 1996 and 1997, and a 2 per cent rise in each of the years 1998, 1999, and 2000. There is provision, however, for all employees to share in the future profits of the company.

The most important change was the reduction in the number of designated trades by more than a third, from twenty-two to fourteen, of which only six were lead production trades, and their regrouping in broadened categories. Work was to be done by teams, which would be given a great deal of autonomy in carrying out a job, the members of each team deciding among them who would do what. Employees were allowed to move from one type of job to another as the need arose. By further reducing restrictive labour practices, the new contract helped to make the company more competitive. It also gave the individual worker far more responsibility and the opportunity to contribute more fully than ever before.

The market had been tested and the design perfected. It was understood that no more than 280 office staff and about 1,200 workers would be employed in the building program, with an expected output of some 2 million direct man-hours per year. Now that the matter of the union agreement had been satisfactorily solved, the remaining unfinished item in Davie's business plan was a complete reorganization of the facilities to allow four merchant ships of standard size to be built economically in series, annually. To do this, it would be necessary to build complete pre-outfitted "rings" (vertical slices of the hull) of up to 2,000 tons, under cover, transport them to the Champlain Dry Dock, and weld the rings together before floating the completed hull off.

An injection of some $130 million of new capital would be required to put the program into operation. Davie's owner, SGF, was willing to provide part of that investment on two conditions. First, a private partner must be found for the venture. Second, the Canadian government should assure a smooth transition from the employment peak of the naval programs to the relative trough of its aftermath by awarding Davie a "transition contract." This would provide a base from which to launch Davie's international program. Several possibilities were considered. Among them was a proposal to build a replacement for the thirty-year-old MV *Lucy Maud Montgomery*, a ferryboat connecting the Magdalen Islands and Souris, Prince Edward Island, which would create work for 750 workers for a year. No agreement could be reached with the owner, CTMA, and the federal Department of Transport, however, so the Quebec government stepped in with its own plan. In need of expanding its service at Tadoussac and having available a backup ferry to serve all of its different routes from Sorel to Tadoussac, the Société des traversiers du Quebec placed orders for lengthening the two Tadoussac ferries and for the construction of a new multi-purpose ferry for delivery in 1998.

Meanwhile, SGF was unable to find a suitable partner and decided to solve the problem differently. In May 1994, it announced that it was prepared to sell the yard to the right buyer, one who was willing to make a sufficiently large investment to turn it into a going concern.[8]

Thus, MIL Davie was put out for tender, and, after the bids had been evaluated, there remained two possible purchasers: Groupe Maritime Verreault, a consortium led by Verreault Navigation Inc., of Les Méchin, Quebec, who were dredgers, shipbuilders, and repairers; and the Cedar Group, of Montreal, a group of engineering firms. On January 15, 1996,

SGF announced that Cedar's bid had been accepted, and that after a period of "due diligence" (or verification) and final negotiations, the terms of the contract would be announced. To the employees who were anxious to turn over a new leaf, the period of waiting seemed endless, but in April it was announced that all was in order and the deal would go through.

On April 30, Guy Véronneau's seven-year presidency of MIL Davie came to an end. He had reason to be pleased with what he had accomplished, but he had to leave his ultimate goal, Davie's return to the international market as a competitive force, to others.

The sale of the Davie shipyard to the Dominion Bridge Corporation, as the Cedar Group is now known, was ratified on May 15. At a news conference held in the Panel Line Shop, presided over by the deputy premier, Bernard Landry, and attended by Michel Branchaud of the SGF, and Jean Garon, member of the Legislative Assembly for Levis, the keys to the yard were handed over to Dominion Bridge's president and CEO, Michel L. Marengère, who spoke of the Group's plans for the future. Davie, he assured the workers would continue to be a shipbuilder, while broadening its industrial base by developing its offshore oil platform capability and building such heavy equipment as the large cranes used to handle containers. In this way, it would fit in well with the other companies in the Group. He praised the high standard of the workers and looked forward to the day when the current work force of 500 would be more than doubled. He was confident, he said, that the end of shipbuilding subsidies worldwide would open up the shipbuilding market.

Dominion Bridge Corporation has three other subsidiaries: Dominion Bridge Inc., of Montreal, founded in 1882, a company originally set up to build the bridges for Canadian Pacific Limited's transcontinental railway, and now a major industrial fabrication company with plants across Canada involved in major construction projects of all types from coast to coast. Steen Contractors Limited of Toronto (also known as Steen Becker) is a civil and mechanical engineering contractor that operates throughout North America. Finally, McConnell Dowell, an Australian-based engineer-

J.-Arthur Gélinas, flanked by Robert Mezzana and Louis Caron, winners of the contest to choose a new name for the company.

ing and construction company, is active in Australia, New Zealand, and Southeast Asia. Davie thus became a member of a major international engineering, project management, and construction team.

On May 17, J. Arthur Gélinas took office as Davie's new president and chief executive officer. In keeping with its new status, he announced, Davie would be given a new name. A contest was organized among the employees, as a result of which MIL Davie Inc. became Industries Davie Inc. or Davie Industries Inc. as of October 11, 1996. "The firm is known around the world by the family name of the founder," he said, "and we felt that it should be perpetuated."

Open House in 1988, when workers are proud to show off the shipyard to their families and friends.

EPILOGUE

IN 1887, WHEN George T. Davie gave the contract for the machine shop at the Lauzon shipyard, the Taylor Davie family had been in the shipbuilding and repair business in the port of Quebec for close to eighty years. Had he been able to foresee that the yard would still be operating a century later he would not have been surprised, though he might have been disappointed to learn that only a small part of the machine shop had survived. He knew that he was fortunate to secure the ideal spot for his yard immediately beside the Lorne Dry Dock. And he knew that he could count on his employees, as they could on him. His foreman, Pierre Duclos, had been with him since he took over the upper yard in Levis from his mother. Davie and Duclos, and probably many others, made the transition from wooden to metal shipbuilding. He kept up, then, with his shipbuilding competitors. And, with his brother's expertise on the river, the Davie yard stayed on top of the salvage business. Above all, George T. Davie had four sons who would follow in his footsteps, though he could hardly have guessed that it would be George Duncan Davie, the youngest, who would carry on what he had begun.

In this past century, the trades and the technology have changed to an even greater degree. The computer technician intent on his screen has

EPILOGUE

replaced the loftsman kneeling on the mould loft floor. Plasma cutting equipment cuts through steel plates under water far more efficiently than any shears did before. Even the welder, who took over from the riveter, sees the development of the welding robot. Trucks and transporters have long since done away with the need for horses.

The new generation of workers has kept up with the profound recent changes, mastering the computer technology as their great-grandfathers mastered the change to building in steel a century ago. They can be counted on to carry on the Davie tradition of excellence, and to display the same passion and determination that has enabled the shipyard to survive the many setbacks it has encountered in its long history and to celebrate the one hundredth anniversary of the construction of the first ship at the Lauzon shipyards.

Who are the individual men and women who together make up Davie's history? Besides those who have been mentioned, there are countless others who must, unfortunately, remain anonymous because of limitations of space. In the following pages, however, you will find a representative sample of the many thousands who have worked on the ships, in the sheds, and in the offices. They not only worked together. They played on the shipyard's baseball, bowling, and hockey teams, took part in company-sponsored golf tournaments, and enthusiastically attended the events that their social club, the Club des Mousaillons, organized. Fiercely loyal to their unions, they responded in strength when they were asked to show their solidarity. They attended the Red Cross blood donor clinics that were set up at the shipyard, and organized and gave generously to charity drives. In many cases they lived side by side, worshipped side by side, sent their children to the same schools, patronized the same stores, and spent a part of their social lives together. When they retired, the strong bonds formed by their common pride in the success of their company remained intact and the friendships formed at the shipyard continued to fill an important part of their lives.

Invariably, when I have asked a Davie retiree why he chose to work at

EPILOGUE

the shipyard, he has answered that his father and his older brothers were Davie employees, that one or both of his grandfathers and many other relatives were, too. He took it for granted from the time he was a boy that one day he would work there. He could not imagine working anywhere else. Starting to work at the shipyard was synonymous with growing up – it was real man's work. There was the thrill of building ships, but above all, there was the feeling of belonging, the companionship.

Members of the Sénéchal family who had worked at the Davie shipyard a total of 391 years. This photograph was taken in 1988. They are: back row, 3rd to 6th, *the four brothers André, Arsène, Wilbrod, and Gérard,* 1st, 2nd, and 7th, *André's sons René, Jean-Louis, and Claude.* Front row, *Gérard's son Guy, Arsène's sons Roland, Richard, Marcel, and Jean Marie. André's sons Paul, Lionel, Henri Yvon, and Denis, and Gérard's son Gérard, who were not present, had also worked there – a total of 26 years.*

EPILOGUE

Above: *The Pelletier family, with 242 years of service.* Front row, *Ghislain, Alain, Claude, Nancy, and Bertrand.* Second row, *Michel, Stéphane, Benoit, Clément, and Gilles.* Back row, *Roland, Norbert, Jean-Marie, and Jean-Louis.* Below: *Davie's canoe team at the 1976 Quebec Winter Carnival. Left, Paul Brulotte, Fernand Brulotte, Bertrand Geoffroy; right, Henri Bourassa, Claude Duquet, and Claude Royer.*

EPILOGUE

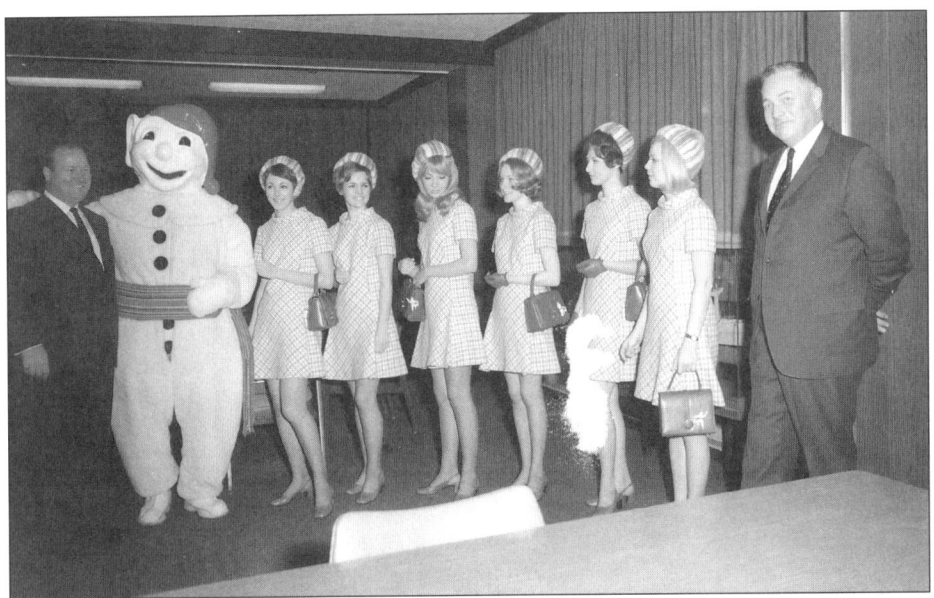

Above: *Bonhomme Carnaval and the Duchesses visit the Davie Shipyard during the winter carnival in the early 1970s. Left, Jacques Regnaud, treasurer; right, Don Page, yard manager.* Below: *On an outing of the company's social club, Club des Moussaillons.*

EPILOGUE

Girls will be girls. When Anne Quigley brought in her young son a few days before Christmas 1996, the secretaries deserted their computers for the time it took to take a commemorative snapshot. Seen here are Ann Quigley (lawyer), Diane Beaubien, Maryse Prince, Suzanne Dupont, Suzanne Guay, Gina Perreault (public relations officer), and Denise Labbé.

Baseball team in the 1940s. Standing, W. Belleau, A. Gosselin, F. Bérubé, J.-P. Théberge, A. Laperrière, G. Bilodeau, L. Viger, M. Morency, E. Blais, R. Cantin, W. Blais, and A. Leblond. Seated, G. Isabelle, J.-C. Sauvageau, F. A. Morley, J. Gagnon, W. Scallen, Roland Bourget, Robert Sweeney, André Ruel, mascot. Jean-Paul Gagnon was absent.

EPILOGUE

Davie's Bowling League trophy winners in 1996. Marcel Saint-Amand, Gisèle Giguère, Louise Bilodeau, Michel Tessier, Jean-Marc Boisvert, and Glen Fielding.

The Shipyard workers have always been generous to the less fortunate, and their committee was proud to hand over their donation of $26,093.72 in October 1985. They are: Front row, Lionel Barthe, three Centraide representatives, Frank A. Betts, France Bérubé, Gisèle Giguère, and Suzanne Dupont. Second row, Jean Cauchy, Jean-Paul Blouin, Richard Leblanc, Marc-André Bouffard, Raymond Berrigan, Christian Boudreault, Raymond Gagné, Raymond Labrie, Pauline Demers, Réal Robitaille, Roger Dionne, Sarto Descoteaux. Third row, Guy Rousseau, Léopold Guay, Marcel Poirier, Alain Bédard, Robert Alain, Marcel Cantin, Jacques Cantin, Paul-Arthur Roy, Serge Tiremarche. Fourth row, Armand Aubé, Ronald Baller, Jean-Guy L'Hebreux.

EPILOGUE

When the Hotel Dieu hospital in Levis made a special appeal for funds, MIL Davie responded with a $10,000 donation. Receiving the cheque from Guy Véronneau, Marcel Lacroix, president of the Fondation Hotel Dieu de Levis. At left is Richard Gauvin, president of the Shipyard Workers Union, and at right, Georges Berberi, Davie's manager of the Industrial Division, president of the campaign.

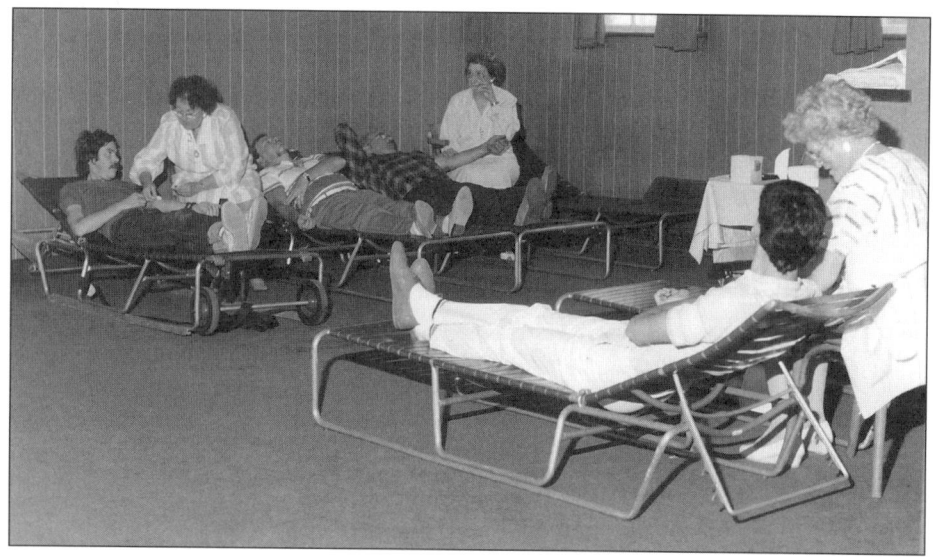

A Red Cross blood donor clinic at the shipyard. Recognized in the photo are Louis Leclerc, Raymond Lemelin, and, with his back to the camera, Pierre Audet.

EPILOGUE

Plaques presented to Davie's retirees in 1985. Seated, Clement Brulotte, Gabriel Martineau, Armand Morency, Adjutor Gendreau, Marthe Huot, Maurice Provencher, president, Marc Levesque, Robert Berrigan, Charles Bussières, Roger Alain. Second row, Maurice Vallières, George Wilson, ?, Philippe Castonguay, Léo Boulé, Reggie Johnston, Lucien Lord, Dan Power, Maurice Coté, Léonce Dionne, Alcide Demers. Third row, Luc Jolicoeur, Roland Guay, Bob Branion, ?, Robert Guay, ? Nadeau, ?, Edgar Dionne, Ernest Saint-Onge. Top row, Honorius Parent, Julien Turgeon, Rosaire Beaulieu, Roger Picard, Paul Prémont, Théo Migneault, Charles Carrier, Roger Dumont, Auguste Rivard, Marcel Lamontagne.

EPILOGUE

Following the presentation of a plaque to Roland Lévesque, steel plater, on his retirement in 1986: front row, Michel Marotte, Gilles Pagé, Richard Tremblay, Roland Lévesque, Richard Labrecque, Gaston Couture, Walter Park, Bertrand Thibault, Robert Plamondon. Second row, Willy Goulet, Michel Garant, Marcel Jolicoeur, Alain Bédard, Wilbrod Sénéchal, Jules Samson, Léonce Beaudoin, Léopold Roberge, Léon Labonté, René Audet. Top row, Gilles Gagné, Richard Laflamme, François Michaud, Norbert Asselin, Yves Samson, André Dupont.

EPILOGUE

The tinsmiths Richard Langlois and Albert Cantin reached retirement age in 1986. They are seen here after a send-off party given to them by their fellow workers: Joseph Giguère, Rosaire Catellier, Denis Turgeon, Denis Goulet, Jacques Cantin, Paul Arsenault, Raynald Guay, Jean Marie Gaudreault, Pierre Drouin, André Leveillé, René Vezina, Jean Paul Beaumont, Bertrand Arguin, Michel Germain, Raymond Gilbert, Marc Gilbert, Claude Labrie, Marcel Cantin, Robert Alain, S. Coté, Noël Duchesneau, Roger Guay, Jean Yves Lacroix, R. Fournier, Raymond Leclerc, R. Gaumond, Gérard Anctil, L. Gosselin, Clément Couture, Rodrigue Beaumont, Jean Wellman, Camilien Montminy.

EPILOGUE

The Executive of the Retirees Club at their soirée in 1991. René Hallé, Maurice Chouinard, Aurore Nadeau, Georges Brousseau, Paul Mercier, Charles Guay, Julien Turgeon, and Robert Carrier, and wives.

One hundred years after the launching of the paddle steamer *Champion*, Davie stands poised at the beginning of another era of its history, its cranes once again circling slowly over the workshops and building berths, another generation of workers eager to take on the challenges that lie ahead.

APPENDIX A: South Shore Jurisdiction

1628 The south shore of the St. Lawrence opposite Quebec named "Lévy" by Champlain, after Henry de Lévy, Duke of Ventadour, Vice-Roy or Governor of New France.

1636 The large tract of land on the south shore of the St. Lawrence that stretched for 6 leagues, or 18.6 miles, along the coast line, from a point 3 leagues above to 3 leagues below the mouth of the Chaudière River, and to a depth of 6 leagues, granted to Jean de Lauson (alias Simon Le Maistre) one of the 100 Associates and a Member of the Parliament in Paris, a future governor of New France, "*en fief et seigneurie, avec haute, moyenne et basse justice*," and given the name "la Seigneurie de Lauson."

1651 The Seigneury of Lauson given by Jean de Lauson to his son Jean.

1673 Lévy given the name "Saint-Joseph-de-la-Pointe-Lévy."

1675 Mother church of the parish of Saint-Joseph-de-la-Pointe-Lévy erected.

1851 Breakaway parish of Notre-Dame-de-la-Victoire founded by Curé Déziel. Municipal "Corporation de la Paroisse de Notre-Dame-de-la-Victoire" formed.

1853 An area of 272 square miles bordering on the St. Lawrence River and reaching from Saint-Antoine-de-Tilly on the southwest to Beaumont, Saint Charles, and Saint Gervais to the north, detached from the "Comté de Dorchester" to form the "Comté de Levis." It was named Levis after the Chevalier de Levis, hero of the Battle of Saint Foy.

1861 Corporation de la Paroisse de Notre-Dame-de-la-Victoire incorporated as the "Ville de Lévis." Louis Carrier first mayor.

1910 "Ville de Lauzon" incorporated November 9. Telesphore Charland first mayor.

1916 The Ville de Lévis became the "Cité de Levis" on March 16, and annexed Villeray nine months later.

1989 Fusion of Lévis and Lauzon to form Lévis-Lauzon, September 1.

1990 Levis-Lauzon renamed "Lévis."

APPENDIX B: Davie Family Genealogy

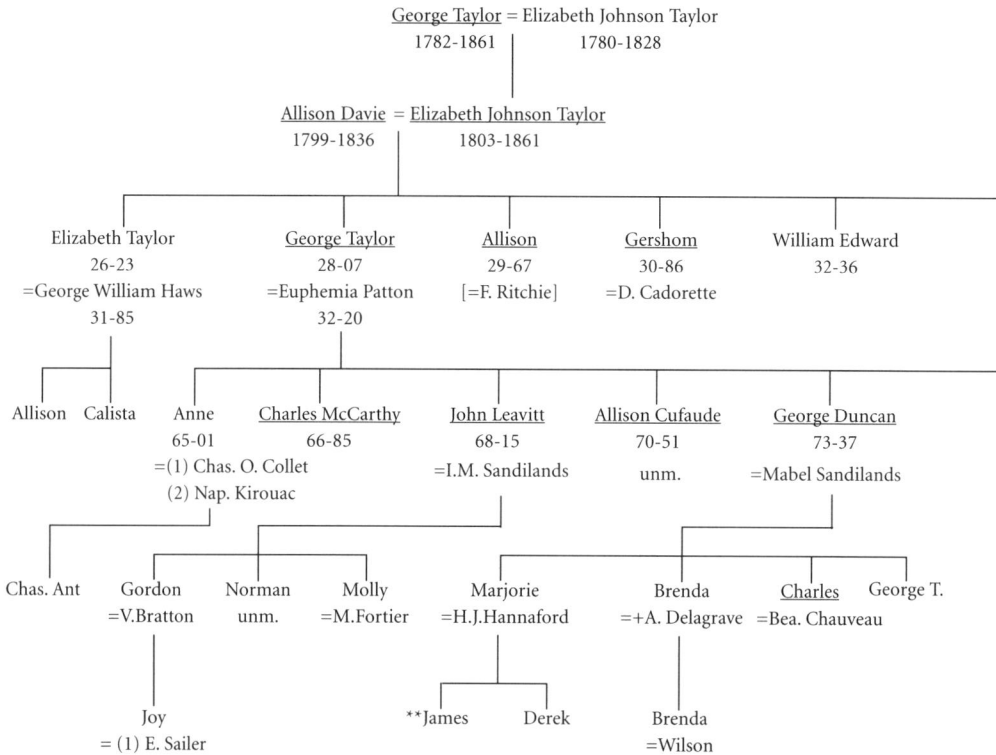

Shipbuilders names are underlined
* Worked in shipyard
** Worked in yard during holidays
# Inherited Davie Brothers from A.C. Davie and sold it
+ President of Geo. T. Davie Ltd. following Charles Davie's death
§ Went to sea and settled in United States

APPENDIX

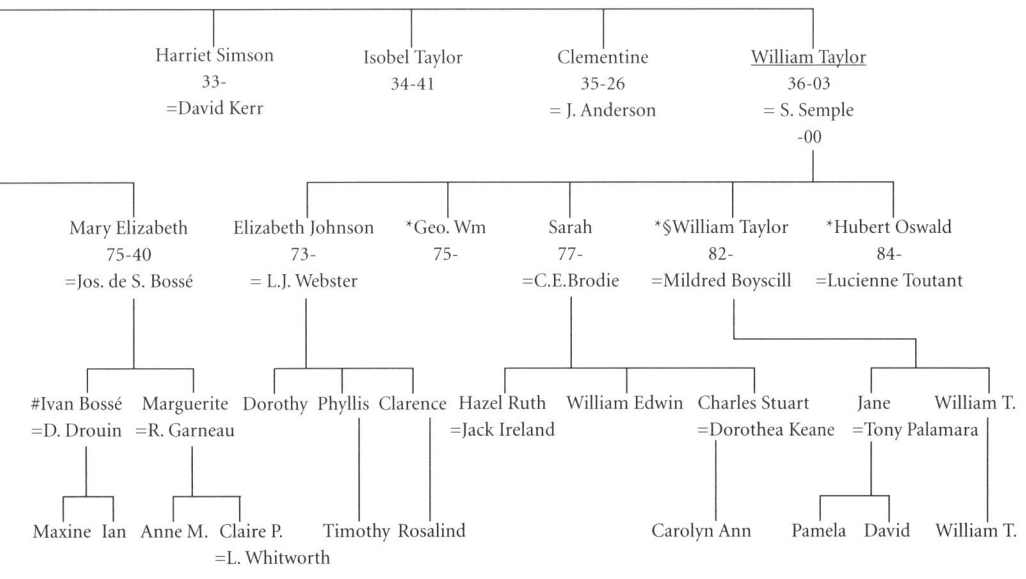

APPENDIX C: Presidents of the Shipyards

DAVIE SHIPYARD AT LAUZON
 1886-1897 Owner manager – George T. Davie

GEORGE T. DAVIE AND SONS
 1897-1914 Partners and managers – John, Allison, and George D. Davie

DAVIE SHIPBUILDING AND REPAIRING COMPANY
 Presidents
 1914 George D. Davie
 1916 Charles A. Barnard (chairman, with powers normally conferred on the president)
 1920 Horace Smith

DAVIE SHIPBUILDING & REPAIRING CO. LTD.
 1925 William H. Coverdale
 1950 K.R. Marshall

DAVIE SHIPBUILDING LIMITED
 1952 Richard Lowery
 1972 Takis Veliotis
 1972 George L. Cole
 1973 Arthur Nightingale

LES CHANTIERS DAVIE LTEE – DAVIE SHIPBUILDING LIMITED
 1976 Louis Rochette
 1979 William White
 1982 J. Graham Day
 1983 Marcel Lafrance

VERSATILE DAVIE INC.
 1984 Maurice Provencher

VERSATILE DAVIE INC. and MIL DAVIE INC.
 1986 Don Challinor

MIL DAVIE INC.
 1989 Guy Véronneau

INDUSTRIES DAVIE INC. – DAVIE INDUSTRIES INC.
 1996 J. Arthur Gélinas

APPENDIX D: Presidents of the Shipyard Workers' Unions, 1949–97

LE SYNDICAT DES TRAVAILLEURS DU CHANTIER NAVAL DE LAUZON INC.

Raymond Doré	1949 to 1951
Paul Côté	1951 to 1953
Armand Pouliot	1953
Louis-Philippe Ouellet	1953 to 1955
Rolland Labrecque	1955 to 1959
Maurice Boucher	1959 to 1961
Hervé Demers	1961 to 1962
Hugues Pérusse	1962 to 1965
Robert Rouillard	1965 to 1968
Clément Fleury	1968 to 1976
Yves Deschênes	1976 to 1978
Clément Fleury	1978 to 1980
Yves Deschênes	1980 to 1982
Robert Monette	1982 to 1992
Richard Gauvin	1992 to present

CURRENT PRESIDENTS OF UNIONS:

SYNDICAT DES EMPLOYÉS DU BUREAU
  Dominique Savard

SYNDICAT DES EMPLOYÉS DU CORPS DE SÉCURITÉ
  Pierre Nadeau

ASSOCIATION DES DESSINATEURS MARITIMES
  Alain Theriault

APPENDIX E: Yard Lists

Abbreviations: ba-barque; bg-barge; br-brig; ps-paddle steamer; sc-schooner; sh-ship; ss-screw steamer

GEORGE TAYLOR
CANOTERIE

Port No.	Name	Rig	Tonnage	Length	Owner
3/1819	HENRY	sh	385	107	Patterson, Dyke, Usborne, Benson
4/1819	MONTMORENCY	sh	381	106	Patterson, Dyke, Usborne, Benson
32/1825	GEORGE CANNING	sh	424	112	Wm. Atkinson

GEORGE TAYLOR AND ALLISON DAVIE
CANOTERIE

Port No.	Name	Rig	Tonnage	Length	Owner
22/1825	LORD MELVILLE	sh	425	111	Wm. Atkinson
94/1826	BRANCHES	sh	452	116	Morisson, Usborne, Benson, Dyke
166/1826	HOPE	sh	455	116	Huddart, Branton, Cotton
188/1826	JAMAICA	br	111	64	Moffat, Stephens, Jameson, Mtl, Gillespie, Ldn
25/1827	KINGFISHER	br	221	91	Geo. Douglas, Thos Harby, Lndn, shipownrs
32/1828	GULNARE	sc	146	75	Wm. Stevenson
46/1829	CORRIB	br	198	84	Wm. & H. Pemberton, Que, Geo. Pemberton, Ldn
2/1830	GRENADA	br	224	89	Jeremiah Leaycraft & Co – Nfd, W.I. etc

APPENDIX

GEORGE T. DAVIE AND ALLISON DAVIE
LEVIS

Port No.	Name	Rig	Tonnage	Length	Owner
6/1855	RAMBLER	ps	0	116	Elizabeth Johnson Davie

GEORGE T. DAVIE
LEVIS

Port No.	Name	Rig	Tonnage	Length	Owner
13/1857	COMET	ba	337	122	G.T. Davie
83/1857	GANANOQUE	sh	785	158	G.T. Davie
5/1859	ROVER	bg	195	122	Geo. T. Davie
28/1859	LORD SEAFORTH	ps	173	133	Chas McKenzie
68/1864	ONDINE	ba	383	123	Geo. T. Davie
34/1865	BONNITON	sh	1064	174	James G. Ross
16/1877	CHAMPION	sc	323	131	Augustin Beaulieu
1/1878	RAMBLER	ss	59	76	Geo. T. Davie
1/1880	KATE	ss	23	49	Geo. T. Davie
5/1883	GTD	sc	196	95	G.T. Davie
3/1886	NORTH	ps	30	132	Quebec & Levis Ferry Co Ltd
0/1886	CHALLENGER	ss	86	89	Wm. T. Davie

APPENDIX

YARD LIST
of
GEO. T. DAVIE & SONS (1897)
ST. JOSEPH (LAUZON)

Abbreviations (propulsion): de-diesel; gt-gas turbine; m-motor; mv-motor; n-none; s-steam; w-wind

Hull No.	Name		Vessel Type	Tonnage	Launch Date	Delivery Date	Owner
1	CHAMPION	s	side-wheeler – iron frame	481.83	May 1897	May 1897	Cie maritime & indus. de Levis
2	GEORGE T. DAVIE	s	river barge – composite	680.00	May 1897	Jun 1898	J.L., A.C. and G.D. Davie
3	LAUZON	s	ferry – steel frame	419.00	Apr 1910	Spr 1910	Levis Ferry Company
4	LEVIS	s	ferry – steel frame	419.00	Apr 1910	Apr 1910	Levis Ferry Company
5	COLOMB	s	ferry – steel frame	559.00	Fall 1910	Nov 1910	Levis Ferry Company
6	PLESSIS	s	ferry – steel frame	559.00	Fall 1910	Nov 1910	Levis Ferry Company
7	HOPPER BARGE NO. 1	s	hopper barge – steel	785.00	May 1913	Sep 1913	Department of Marine
8	PWD NO. 51	n	scow		Apr 1914	May 1914	Department of Public Works
9	PWD NO. 52	n	scow		Apr 1914	May 1914	Department of Public Works
10	PWD NO. 53	n	scow		May 1914	Jun 1914	Department of Public Works
11	PWD NO. 54	n	scow		May 1914	Jun 1914	Department of Public Works
12	PWD NO. 55	n	scow		May 1914	Jun 1914	Department of Public Works
13	PWD NO. 56	n	scow		May 1914	Jun 1914	Department of Public Works
14	LE PROGRES	s	ferry – steel frame	465.00	Aug 1914	Sep 1914	City of Three Rivers

DAVIE SHIPBUILDING AND REPAIRING CO LTD.

Hull No.	Name		Vessel Type	Tonnage	Launch Date	Delivery Date	Owner
15	LOUIS-PHILIPPE	s	ferry – steel frame	600.00	Sep 1914	Oct 1914	Canada Steamship Lines
16	WOBURN		vessel – composite		Apr 1915	Jun 1915	Paradis, Levis
17-56	ML 261 – ML 300	m	submarine chasers – wood	292.91		Oct 1915	British Admiralty
57-306	ML 301 – ML 550	m	submarine chasers – wood	292.91		Nov 1916	British Admiralty
307	CANORA	s	ferry – railway car	2383.00	Jun 1918	Jul 1918	Canadian Northern Rlys

APPENDIX

Hull No.	Name		Vessel Type	Tonnage	Launch Date	Delivery Date	Owner
308-357	B 426 – B 476		barges – steel			Sep 1917	Imperial Royal Enginee
358-407	CD 1 – CD 50	s	drifters – wood	90.78		Jun 1919	Naval Service Canada
408	TR NO. 35	s	trawler – steel	136.00	Apr 1918	May 1918	Naval Service Canada
409	TR NO. 36	s	trawler – steel	136.00	May 1918	May 1918	Naval Service Canada
410-439	ML 551 – ML 580	m	submarine chasers – wood	292.91		Jul 1918	British Admiralty
440	LABRADOR (TR 45)	s	passenger ship	316.95	Apr 1919	Apr 1919	Clarke Steamships
441	TR 46	s	trawler – steel	316.95	Apr 1919	Apr 1919	Naval Service Canada
442	TR 47	s	trawler – steel	316.97	May 1919	May 1919	Naval Service Canada
443	TR 48	s	trawler – steel	316.95	May 1919	May 1919	Naval Service Canada
444	TR 49	s	trawler – steel	316.95	Jun 1919	Jun 1919	Naval Service Canada
445	TR 50	s	trawler – steel	316.95	Jun 1919	Jul 1919	Naval Service Canada
446-457	V.62 – V.73	m	submarine chasers – wood			Jul 1919	French Admiralty
458	JUMBO 1		repair scow		Spr 1919	Spr 1919	Davie Shipbuilding
459	CANADIAN TRAPPER	s	cargo ship	3599.94	Oct 1919	Jun 1920	Department of Marine
460	CANADIAN HUNTER	s	cargo ship	3609.84	May 1920	Aug 1920	Department of Marine
461	GORZE	s	steamer – wood	1152.87	Jul 1919	Jun 1920	French Government
462	METZWISSE	s	steamer – wood	1153.79	May 1919	Nov 1919	French Government
463	HAGUENEAU	s	steamer – wood	1159.32	Jun 1919	Jun 1920	French Government
464	HUNNINGUE	s	steamer – wood	1165.92	Jun 1919	Jun 1920	French Government
465	LORQUIN	s	steamer – wood	1167.63	Jun 1919	Jun 1920	French Government
466	MARMOUTIERS	s	steamer – wood	1143.93	Aug 1919	Jul 1920	French Government
467	MASSEVEAU	s	steamer – wood	1158.28	Sep 1919	Jul 1920	French Government
468	METZ	s	steamer – wood	1155.55	Sep 1919	Jul 1920	French Government
469	MULHOUSE	s	steamer – wood	1158.13	May 1920	Jul 1920	French Government
470	NEUF BRISACH	s	steamer – wood	1162.45	May 1920	Jul 1920	French Government
471	AUBERNALE	s	steamer – wood (approx.)	1160.00	Jun 1920	Aug 1920	French Government
472	PANGE	s	steamer – wood (approx.)	1160.00	Jun 1920	Aug 1920	French Government
473	MAPLEDENE	s	package freighter	1444.94	Oct 1919	Aug 1920	Canada Steamship Lines
474	BUSY BEE	s	tug	115.00	Jun 1919	Oct 1919	Davie Shipbuilding
475	CSL NO. 3	n	pontoon – wood		Apr 1920	Apr 1920	Canada Steamship Lines

APPENDIX

Hull No.	Name	Vessel Type		Tonnage	Launch Date	Delivery Date	Owner
476	CANADIAN CHALLENGER	cargo ship	s	5439.00	Jul 1920	Oct 1921	Department of Marine
477	KITTY	scow – wood	n		Apr 1920	Apr 1920	Davie Shipbuilding
478	PERREAULT	vessel – composite				Apr 1920	Andre Donaldson
479	W.A. BOWDEN	tug	s	112.96	Apr 1924	Apr 1924	Dept of Railways & Canals
480	CSL NO. 2	pontoon	n	577.28	Apr 1924	May 1924	Canada Steamship Lines
481	CSL NO. 4	pontoon	n	649.44	May 1924	May 1924	Canada Steamship Lines
482	NIBROC	scow	m			May 1924	Brown Corporation
483	JACQUES CARTIER	ferry – car	m	228.00	May 1924	May 1924	La traverse de Lachine
484	PONTOON NO. 3	pontoon	n	334.09	Apr 1925	Apr 1925	Levis Ferry Company
485	PONTOON NO. 4	pontoon	n	334.09	Apr 1925	Apr 1925	Levis Ferry Company
486	WILLIAM PRICE	tug	s	225.24	Jun 1925	Jun 1925	Price Brothers
487	L'ILE D'ORLEANS	ferry	m	795.27	Jun 1925	Jul 1925	Trav. l'Ile d'Orléans
488	COOSIE	tug	m	47.54	May 1925	May 1925	Price Brothers
489	CITY OF TORONTO	package freighter	s	1687.62	Nov 1925	Apr 1926	Canada Steamship Lines
490	CITY OF KINGSTON	package freighter	s	1689.81	Nov 1925	Apr 1926	Canada Steamship Lines
491		scow – wood	n		May 1925	May 1925	Davie Shipbuilding
492		pontoon	n		May 1925	May 1925	Department of Public Works
493	WINNIPEG	package freighter	s	2382.51	Jul 1926	Aug 1926	Canada Steamship Lines
494	SELKIRK	package freighter	s	2384.38	Aug 1926	Sep 1926	Canada Steamship Lines
495	ST-LAWRENCE	passenger ship	s	6328.00	Jun 1927	Jun 1927	Canada Steamship Lines
496	TADOUSSAC	passenger ship	s	7012.51	Oct 1927	May 1928	Canada Steamship Lines
497	QUEBEC	passenger ship	s	7015.59	Apr 1928	May 1928	Canada Steamship Lines
498	GEO. MCKEE	tug	m	220.94	May 1928	May 1928	Anticosti Corporation
499	FOUNDATION FAFNIR	dump scow	n	331.00	Jun 1928	Jun 1928	Foundation Company
500	FOUNDATION FASOLT	dump scow	n	331.00	Jun 1928	Jun 1928	Foundation Company
501	CITY OF WINDSOR	package freighter	s	1905.11	Apr 1929	May 1929	Canada Steamship Lines
502	DONNACONA NO. 3	barge	de	345.69	May 1929	May 1929	Donnacona Paper Company
503	GRAIN MOTOR	bulk carrier	s	1829.13	Aug 1929	Sep 1929	Canada Steamship Lines
504	GRAHAM BELL	tug	s	249.77	Jun 1929	Jul 1929	Dept of Railways & Canals

APPENDIX

Hull No.	Name		Vessel Type	Tonnage	Launch Date	Delivery Date	Owner
505	HOPPER BARGE NO. 5	s	hopper barge	842.67	May 1930	Jun 1930	Department of Marine
506	MANOIR	s	tug	250.45	May 1930	Jun 1930	Davie Shipbuilding
507	CHARLOTTETOWN	s	ferry – car	5889.36	May 1931	Jul 1931	Canadian National Railways
508	PRESCOTONT	de	tug	302.25	Sep 1930	Oct 1930	Canadian Pacific Railways
509	CITADEL	s	fire tug	430.68	Sep 1932	Oct 1932	Department of Marine
510	DARTMOUTH	s	ferry	531.11	Nov 1934	Nov 1934	Dartmouth Ferry Commission
511	NORTH GASPE	m	passenger/cargo ship	888.30	May 1938	Jun 1938	Clarke Steamships
512	RCMP FRENCH	m	patrol cruiser	225.88	Jul 1938	Aug 1938	Dept. of Justice (RCMP)
513	LOUIS JOLLIET	s	ferry	949.71	May 1938	May 1938	Levis Ferry Co.
514	ERNEST LAPOINTE	s	icebreaker	1179.16	Nov 1939	Feb 1941	Department of Transport
515	HMCS WINDFLOWER K155	s	corvette	728.11	Jul 1940	Nov 1940	Naval Service Canada
516	HMCS HEPATICA K159	s	corvette	717.44	Jul 1940	Nov 1940	Naval Service Canada
517	HMCS SNOWBERRY K166	s	corvette	717.44	Aug 1940	Nov 1940	Naval Service Canada
518	HMCS SPIKENARD K198	s	corvette	717.44	Aug 1940	Dec 1940	Naval Service Canada
519	HMCS RIMOUSKI K121	s	corvette	711.35	Oct 1940	Apr 1941	Naval Service Canada
520	HMCS PICTOU K146	s	corvette	711.35	Oct 1940	Apr 1941	Naval Service Canada
521	HMCS BADDECK K147	s	corvette	711.35	Nov 1940	May 1941	Naval Service Canada
522	HMCS BUCTOUCHE K179	s	corvette	711.35	Nov 1940	May 1941	Naval Service Canada
523	HMCS SHEDIAC K110	s	corvette	711.35	Apr 1941	Jul 1941	Naval Service Canada
524	HMCS BRANDON K149	s	corvette	711.35	Apr 1941	Jul 1941	Naval Service Canada
525	HMCS MELVILLE	de	minesweeper	566.50	Jun 1941	Dec 1941	Naval Service Canada
526	HMCS GRANBY	de	minesweeper	566.50	Jun 1941	Apr 1942	Naval Service Canada
527	HMCS NORANDA	de	minesweeper	566.50	Jun 1941	May 1942	Naval Service Canada
528	HMCS LACHINE	de	minesweeper	566.50	Jun 1941	Jun 1942	Naval Service Canada
529	HMCS DIGBY	de	minesweeper	566.50	Jun 1941	Jun 1942	Naval Service Canada
530	HMCS TRURO	de	minesweeper	566.50	Jun 1941	Aug 1942	Naval Service Canada
531	FORT TADOUSSAC	s	cargo ship	7128.86	Nov 1941	Apr 1942	War Supplies
532	FORT LA MAULNE	s	cargo ship	7129.65	Apr 1942	May 1942	War Supplies
533	FORT CHAMBLY	s	cargo ship	7130.17	Nov 1941	Apr 1942	War Supplies

APPENDIX

Hull No.	Name	Vessel Type		Tonnage	Launch Date	Delivery Date	Owner
534	PRINCE ALBERT PARK	s	cargo ship	7133.47	May 1942	Jun 1942	Canadian Government
535	GATINEAU PARK	s	cargo ship	7127.53	Jun 1942	Jul 1942	Canadian Government
536	BANFF PARK	s	cargo ship	7132.60	Jul 1942	Sep 1942	Canadian Government
537	JASPER PARK	s	cargo ship	7128.56	Aug 1942	Sep 1942	Canadian Government
538	FORT CATARAQUI	s	cargo ship	7130.35	Sep 1942	Oct 1942	War Supplies
539	FORT CONCORD	s	cargo ship	7130.31	Oct 1942	Nov 1942	War Supplies
540	FORT ST-FRANCOIS	s	cargo ship	7124.84	Nov 1942	Dec 1942	War Supplies
541	FORT MINGAN	s	cargo ship	7130.00	Dec 1942	May 1943	War Supplies
542	FORT CARILLON	s	cargo ship	7129.23	Apr 1943	May 1943	War Supplies
543	RIVERVIEW PARK	s	cargo ship	7130.12	May 1943	May 1943	War Supplies
544	FORT ALBANY	s	cargo ship	7131.15	May 1943	May 1943	War Supplies
545	HIGH PARK	s	cargo ship	7134.75	Jun 1943	Jul 1943	Canadian Government
546	CHIPENA PARK	s	cargo ship	7137.64	Jun 1943	Aug 1943	Canadian Government
547	RIVERDALE PARK	s	cargo ship	7131.95	Aug 1943	Sep 1943	Canadian Government
548	POINT PLEASANT PARK	s	cargo ship	7135.54	Oct 1943	Nov 1943	Canadian Government
549	FORT BRUNSWICK	s	cargo ship	7140.89	Dec 1943	Dec 1943	Canadian Government
550	HMCS TORONTO K538	s	frigate		Sep 1943	May 1944	Naval Service Canada
551	HMCS STE-THERESE K366		frigate		Oct 1943	May 1944	Naval Service Canada
552	HMCS LASALLE K519	s	frigate		Nov 1943	Jun 1944	Naval Service Canada
553	HMCS COATICOOK K410	s	frigate		Nov 1943	Jul 1944	Naval Service Canada
554	HMCS ST-PIERRE K680	s	frigate		Dec 1943	Aug 1944	Naval Service Canada
555	HMCS PRESTONIAN K662	s	frigate		Jun 1943	Sep 1944	Naval Service Canada
556	HMCS SEA CLIFF K394	s	frigate		Jul 1943	Sep 1944	Naval Service Canada
557	HMCS PENETANG K676	s	frigate		Jun 1943	Oct 1944	Naval Service Canada
558	HMCS BUCKINGHAM K685	s	frigate		Apr 1944	Nov 1944	Naval Service Canada
559	HMCS INCH ARRAN K667	s	frigate		Jun 1944	Nov 1944	Naval Service Canada
560	HMCS SUSSEX VALE K683	s	frigate		Jul 1944	Nov 1944	Naval Service Canada
561	HMCS CARLPLACE K664	s	frigate		Jul 1944	Dec 1944	Naval Service Canada
562	HMLST 3507		landing craft	4290.74	Oct 1944	May 1945	British Admiralty

APPENDIX

Hull No.	Name	Vessel Type		Tonnage	Launch Date	Delivery Date	Owner
563	HMLST 3508	s	landing craft	4290.74	Oct 1944	Jun 1945	British Admiralty
564	HMLST 3509	s	landing craft	4290.74	Nov 1944	Jun 1945	British Admiralty
565	HMLST 3510	s	landing craft	4290.74	Nov 1944	Jul 1945	British Admiralty
566	HMLST 3511	s	landing craft	4290.74	Nov 1944	SOR 1945	British Admiralty
567	HMLST 3512	s	landing craft	4290.74	Apr 1944	Aug 1945	British Admiralty
568	HMLST 3513	s	landing craft	4290.74	Apr 1945	Sep 1945	British Admiralty
569	HMLST 3522	s	landing craft	4290.74	Jun 1945	Oct 1945	British Admiralty
570	HMLST 3523	s	landing craft	4290.74	Jul 1945	Oct 1945	British Admiralty
571	HMLST 3524	s	landing craft	4290.74	Jul 1945	Nov 1945	British Admiralty
572	HMLST 3525	s	landing craft	4290.74	Aug 1945	Nov 1945	British Admiralty
573	BEYLA	m	cargo ship	4512.85	Dec 1946	Aug 1947	Chargeurs Réunis – France
574	BILMA	m	cargo ship	4512.98	May 1947	Sep 1947	Chargeurs Réunis – France
575	BOFFA	m	cargo ship	4512.85	Jun 1947	Oct 1947	Chargeurs Réunis – France
576	BOUGA	m	cargo ship	4513.18	Oct 1947	Dec 1947	Chargeurs Réunis – France
577	PONTOON NO. 5		pontoon		Apr 1945	Apr 1945	Canada Steamship Lines
578	CANADIAN CHALLENGER	m	cargo ship	7500.00	Jun 1946	Dec 1946	Canadian National Steamshps
579	DAKAR	s	collier	3656.71	Oct 1947	Jan 1948	French Government
580	PHRYNE	s	collier	3657.15	Oct 1947	Apr 1948	French Government
581	SNA 1	s	collier	3658.00	Nov 1947	May 1948	French Government
582	KAOLACK	s	collier	3658.00	Dec 1947	May 1948	French Government
583	THESEE	s	collier	3658.00	Apr 1948	Jun 1949	French Government
584	CROISSET	m	cargo ship	4061.00	Apr 1949	Jun 1949	Co. France – Navigation
585	CANTELEU	m	cargo ship	4061.00	May 1949	Jul 1949	Co. France – Navigation
586	GAUMONT	m	cargo ship	4061.00	May 1949	Jul 1949	Co. France – Navigation
587	QUEBEC	s	collier	3660.00	May 1948	Jul 1948	French Government
588	CCGS C.D. HOWE	s	arctic patrol ship	3628.00	Sep 1949	Jun 1950	Canadian Government
589	GASPE AMC143	m	minesweeper	478.59	Nov 1951	Nov 1953	Canadian Government
590	CCGS D'IBERVILLE	s	icebreaker	5677.76	Jun 1952	Jun 1953	Canadian Government
591	OTIS WACK	m	tug	237.38	Nov 1950	Dec 1950	Gypsum Packet Co.

APPENDIX

DAVIE SHIPBUILDING, LTD.

Hull No.	Name	Vessel Type		Tonnage	Launch Date	Delivery Date	Owner
592	HMCS COWICHAN AMC 147	m	minesweeper	478.00	Nov 1951	Dec 1953	Canadian Government
593	HMCS UNGAVA AMC 148	m	minesweeper	478.00	May 1953	Jun 1954	Canadian Government
594	HMCS GATINEAU DE 236	s	destroyer escort	3248.51	Jun 1957	Jun 1959	Canadian Government
595	ANDROS VENTURE	s	oil tanker	17844.98	Jul 1953	Nov 1953	Andros Shipping
596	ANDROS FORTUNE	s	oil tanker	17846.66	May 1954	Aug 1954	Andros Shipping
597	SUNRIP	s	bulk carrier	9541.41	Jun 1954	Nov 1954	Sun Shipping
598	BLUENOSE	m	ferry – passenger/car	6419.18	May 1955	Dec 1955	Department of Transport
599	HMCS FUNDY MCB 159	m	minesweeper	484.19	Jun 1956	Nov 1956	Canadian Government
600	RADISSON	m	ferry passenger/car	1148.75	Jun 1954	Jun 1954	Cité de Trois-Rivières
601	CHARLIE S	m	tug	224.88	Aug 1954	Sep 1954	Davie Shipbuilding
602	FLEUR DE LYS NO. 1		dredge	498.58	Oct 1954	Oct 1954	Const Agg Corporation
603		n	pontoons (3)			Nov 1954	Const Agg Corporation
604	LANDING BARGES A,B	n	scows (2)	27.00		Jul 1955	Department of Transport
605	LANDING BARGES A–F	n	scows (6)	18.00		Aug 1955	Department of Transport
605	LANDING BARGES G, H	n	self-propelled scows (2)	15.00		Aug 1955	Department of Transport
606	LANDING BARGES A–F	n	scows (6)	18.00		Sep 1955	Department of Transport
607	CCGS MONTMORENCY	m	buoy tender	750.58	Jul 1957	Aug 1957	Department of Transport
608	ROBERT B	m	tug	196.59	May 1956	Jun 1956	Davie Shipbuilding
609	METIS	m	canaller	2332.13	Jun 1956	Jul 1956	Canada Steamship Lines
610	CCGS MONTCALM	s	icebreaker	2017.23	Oct 1956	Mar 1957	Department of Transport
611	CONISCLIFFE HALL	m	lake canaller	2129.40	Jun 1957	Jul 1957	Hall Corporation
612	FOUNDATION VICTOR	m	tug	244.33	Nov 1956	Jan 1957	Foundation Maritime
613	SUNRHEA	s	bulk carrier	11813.38	May 1958	Dec 1958	Sun Shipping
614	CCGS SIR HUMPHREY GILBERT	de	icebreaker	1930.57	Oct 1958	Jun 1959	Canadian Government
615	ROCKCLIFFE HALL	m	canaller	2261.79	Apr 1958	May 1958	Hall Corporation

APPENDIX

Hull No.	Name	Vessel Type		Tonnage	Launch Date	Delivery Date	Owner
616	FEDERAL MONARCH	s	oil tanker	26909.38	Jun 1959	Sep 1959	Federal Commerce
617	ESKIMO		general cargo vessel	4462.42	Apr 1959	May 1959	Canada Steamship Lines
618	SAGUENAY	m	ferry passenger/car	428.54	Apr 1958	May 1958	Clarke Steamships
619	EMERILLON	s	oil tanker	26967.52	Apr 1960	Jul 1960	Papachristidis
620	CCGS JOHN A. MACDONALD	m	icebreaker	6186.36	Oct 1959	Sep 1960	Canadian Government
621	FOUNDATION VALOUR	m	tug	246.78	Jun 1958	Jul 1958	Foundation Maritime
622	HMCS QU'APPELLE DDE 264	s	destroyer escort	3263.49	May 1962	Sep 1963	Canadian Government
623	SLS NO. 3		sounding sweep	179.28	May 1959	May 1959	St. Lawrence Seaway
624	NEW QUEDOC	s	bulk carrier	9957.33	Jun 1960	Aug 1960	N.M. Paterson & Sons
625	WHITEFISH BAY	s	bulk carrier	17349.54	Nov 1960	Apr 1961	Canada Steamship Lines
626	JERRY G.	m	tug	201.99	Jun 1960	Jul 1960	Davie Shipbuilding
627	CANADOC	m	bulk carrier	10060.61	Apr 1961	Jul 1961	N.M. Paterson & Sons
628	HMCS PROVIDER	s	fleet support ship	14054.70	Nov 1962	Dec 1963	Canadian Government
629	HUDSON TRANSPORT	m	oil tanker	14076.31	Apr 1962	Jun 1962	Hall Corporation
630	MENIER CONSOL	m	pulpwood carrier	2575.25	Apr 1962	Jun 1962	Anticosti Shipping
631	FOUNDATION VISCOUNT	m	tug	207.11	Oct 1962	Apr 1963	Foundation Maritime
632	FOUNDATION VIM	m	tug	207.21	Oct 1962	Dec 1962	Foundation Maritime
633	FOUNDATION VIGOUR	m	tug	207.20	Oct 1962	Apr 1963	Foundation Maritime
634	FOUNDATION VIKING	m	tug	207.24	Oct 1962	Dec 1962	Foundation Maritime
635	FOUNDATION VICEROY	m	tug	207.22	Nov 1962	Apr 1963	Foundation Maritime
636	FOUNDATION VANGUARD	m	tug	207.12	Nov 1962	Mar 1963	Foundation Maritime
637	FOUNDATION VALIANT	m	tug	316.64	Apr 1963	Jun 1963	Foundation Maritime
638	FRANKCLIFFE HALL	s	bulk carrier	17888.60	Dec 1962	May 1963	Hall Corporation
639	BAIE ST. PAUL	s	bulk carrier	17809.66	Nov 1962	Jun 1963	Canada Steamship Lines
640	CCGS RALLY	m	coast guard cutter	140.09	Apr 1963	Jun 1963	Department of Transport
641	FORT ST. LOUIS	m	package freighter	5346.80	May 1963	Aug 1963	Steel Company of Canada
642	HAMILDOC	m	bulk carrier	3357.07	Jul 1963	Aug 1963	N.M. Paterson & Sons
643	KINGDOC	m	bulk carrier	3357.93	Aug 1963	Sep 1963	N.M. Paterson & Sons

APPENDIX

Hull No.	Name	Vessel Type		Tonnage	Launch Date	Delivery Date	Owner
644	CCGC ARCTICA	m	bait vessel	702.27	Jun 1964	Jul 1964	Department of Fisheries
645	BLUE PETER II	m	frozen fish carrier	1126.28	Apr 1964	May 1964	Blue Peter Steamships
646	BLUE CLOUD	m	frozen fish carrier	1126.29	Apr 1964	Jun 1964	Blue Peter Steamships
647	SAGUENAY	m	bulk carrier	18058.49	Jun 1964	Aug 1964	Canada Steamship Lines
648	ACADIA ALBATROS	m	stern trawler	661.44	Nov 1964	Dec 1964	Acadia Fisheries
649	CABOT	m	package freighter	6016.82	May 1965	Jul 1965	Gulf Ports Steamships
650	MANITOULIN	m	bulk carrier	19281.76	May 1966	Jul 1966	Canada Steamship Lines
651	LAWRENCECLIFFE HALL	m	bulk carrier	17916.67	Apr 1965	Jul 1965	Hall Corporation
652	FORT WILLIAM	m	package freighter	6792.75	Apr 1965	May 1965	Canada Steamship Lines
653	JAMES TRANSPORT	m	oil tanker	4699.60	Dec 1966	Jun 1967	Hall Corporation
654	RICHELIEU	m	bulk carrier	17822.16	Nov 1966	Apr 1967	Canada Steamship Lines
655	BEAVERCLIFFE HALL	bu	bulk carrier	17895.08	Sep 1965	Oct 1965	Hall Corporation
656	LABRADOC	m	bulk carrier	3610.00	Nov 1965	Apr 1966	N.M. Paterson & Sons
657	PRINDOC	m	bulk carrier	3610.00	Nov 1965	Mar 1966	N.M. Paterson & Sons
658	A.S GROSSBRENNER	m	bulk carrier	17955.45	May 1966	Jul 1966	Labrador Steamships
659	CCGS J.E. BERNIER	de	icebreaker	2457.25	Apr 1967	Nov 1967	Department of Transport
660	FREDERIC CARTER	m	ferry – train & truck	12220.98	Jun 1967	Jan 1968	Department of Transport
661	FRONTENAC	m	bulk carrier	17820.77	Dec 1967	May 1968	Canada Steamship Lines
662	CHIMO	m	package freighter	6025.93	Jun 1967	Oct 1967	Gulf Ports Steamships
663	CCGS ALERT	m	search & rescue vessel	1751.63	Jul 1969	Dec 1969	Department of Transport
664	CCGS GRIFFON	de	supply & buoy vessel	2211.87	Sep 1969	Apr 1970	Department of Transport
665	LAKE MANITOBA	m	bulk carrier	17820.20	May 1968	Jul 1968	Nipigon Transport
666	IMPERIAL BEDFORD	m	oil tanker	9499.73	Dec 1968	Aug 1969	Imperial Oil
667	OTTERCLIFFE HALL	m	bulk carrier	17907.57	Dec 1968	May 1969	Hall Corporation
668	CHEMICAL TRANSPORT	m	oil tanker	4981.33	Jun 1969	Jul 1969	Hall Corporation
669	INDUSTRIAL TRANSPORT	m	oil tanker	4981.63	Jun 1969	Aug 1969	Hall Corporation
670	HMCS ATHABASKAN DDH 287	gt	destroyer escort	5641.50	Nov 1970	Sep 1972	Canadian Government
671	HMCS ALGONQUIN DDH 283	gt	destroyer escort	5641.50	Apr 1971	Nov 1973	Canadian Government

APPENDIX

Hull No.	Name	Vessel Type	Tonnage	Launch Date	Delivery Date	Owner
672	KENTING NO. 1	jack up drilling rig	1142.54	May 1969	May 1969	Petrolia Oil Well Drill
673	DONALD P	m tug	320.40	May 1970	Jul 1970	Davie Shipbuilding
674	LOMER GOUIN	m ferry – passenger/car	1741.15	Apr 1971	Jun 1971	Quebec Government
675	ALPHONSE DESJARDINS	m ferry – passenger/car	1741.20	Apr 1971	Jun 1971	Quebec Government
676	KRITI STAR	m oil tanker	42469.78	Aug 1972	Apr 1973	Varnicos Primero Corp.
677	KRITI LAND	m oil tanker	42469.78	Aug 1973	Dec 1973	Varnicos Segundo Corp.
678	KRITI WAVE	m oil tanker	42469.78	Nov 1973	Apr 1974	Varnicos Tercero Corp.
679	LEONARD W	m tug	447.98	Mar 1973	Sep 1973	Davie Shipbuilding
680	BASSIN	m stern trawler	446.29	Nov 1972	Apr 1973	General Mills Canada
681	FATIMA	m stern trawler	445.66	Nov 1972	Apr 1973	General Mills Canada
682	GRANDE ENTREE	m stern trawler	447.81	Nov 1973	Dec 1973	General Mills Canada
683	GROSSE ILE	m stern trawler	437.19	Nov 1973	Dec 1973	General Mills Canada
684	JEAN PARISIEN	m bulk carrier (su)	22772.09	Jul 1977	Dec 1977	Canada Steamship Lines
685	LUCELLUM	m oil tanker	23736.23	Dec 1974	Jul 1975	Cunard Steamships
686	LUCERNA	m oil tanker	23736.23	May 1975	Nov 1975	Cunard Steamships
687	OGDEN SAGUENAY	m oil tanker	23462.92	Sep 1975	Mar 1976	Ogden Marine

LES CHANTIERS DAVIE LIMITEE – DAVIE SHIPBUILDING LIMITED

Hull No.	Name	Vessel Type	Tonnage	Launch Date	Delivery Date	Owner
688	OGDEN OTTAWA	m oil tanker	23462.92	Dec 1975	Oct 1976	Ogden Marine
689	ATHELMONARCH	m oil tanker	24131.56	Oct 1976	May 1978	Athel Line
690	ATHELQUEEN	m oil tanker	24131.56	Apr 1977	Sep 1977	Athel Line
691	POLARIS	m barge	4166.97	Jul 1980	Sep 1980	Bechtel Canada
692	CARTIERCLIFFE HALL	m bulk carrier	18531.24	Aug 1977	Nov 1977	Hall Corporation
693	MONTCLIFFE HALL	m bulk carrier	18531.24	Dec 1977	Apr 1978	Hall Corporation
694	STEELCLIFFE HALL	m bulk carrier	18531.24	Dec 1977	Apr 1978	Hall Corporation
695	YOUPWE	suction hopper dredger	1808.12	May 1978	Sep 1978	Cameroun Government
696	GLOMAR HIGH ISLAND I	drilling platform 82sd	4818.22	May 1979	Jun 1979	Global Marine Drilling
697	GLOMAR HIGH ISLAND II	drilling platform 82sd	4825.81	Nov 1979	Nov 1979	Global Marine Drilling
698	SALENERGY IV	drilling platform 82sd	4828.38	Apr 1980	May 1980	Salen Offshore Drilling

521

APPENDIX

Hull No.	Name	Vessel Type	Tonnage	Launch Date	Delivery Date	Owner
699	GLOMAR HIGH ISLAND III	drilling platform 82sd	4832.12	Aug 1980	Sep 1980	Global Marine Drilling
700	GLOMAR HIGH ISLAND IV	drilling platform 82sd	4483.00	Nov 1980	Dec 1980	Global Marine Drilling
701	GLOMAR HIGH ISLAND VI	drilling platform 82sd	4831.00	Jun 1981	Jul 1981	Global Marine Drilling
702	GLOMAR HIGH ISLAND VII	drilling platform 82sd	4825.00	Apr 1982	Apr 1982	Global Marine Drilling
703	PETROBAS – VI – 116	drilling platform 116c	4298.84	Nov 1981	Aug 1981	Petro Brasileiro
704	L'ERABLE NO. 1	m oil tanker	7743.00	Nov 1981	Aug 1982	Branch Lines
705	CARIBOU	m ferry – passenger/car	27213.00	Oct 1984	Aug 1986	C.N. Marine
706	GLOMAR HIGH ISLAND VIII	drilling platform 825sd	4827.00	Nov 1982	Nov 1982	Global Marine Drilling
707	GLOMAR ADRIATIC III	drilling platform 116c	4625.47	Jul 1982	Sep 1982	Global Marine Drilling
708	MEXICO II	drilling platform 116c	4647.57	Nov 1982	Nov 1983	Perforadora Mexico
709	GLOMAR HIGH ISLAND IX	drilling platform 82sd	4821.00	May 1983	Jun 1983	Global Marine Drilling

VERSATILE DAVIE INC.

Hull No.	Name	Vessel Type	Tonnage	Launch Date	Delivery Date	Owner
710	JOSEPH SAVARD	m ferry – passenger/car	1800.00	Jul 1985	Dec 1985	Soc des Traversiers Qué
711	CATHERINE LEGARDEUR	m ferry – passenger/car	1750.00	Jun 1985	Nov 1985	Soc des Traversiers Qué

MIL DAVIE INC.

Hull No.	Name	Vessel Type	Tonnage	Launch Date	Delivery Date	Owner
712	HMCS VILLE DE QUEBEC	patrol frigate	4750.00	May 1991	Sep 1993	Canadian Government
713	HMCS REGINA	patrol frigate	4750.00	Oct 1991	Mar 1994	Canadian Government
714	JOSEPH & CLARA SMALLWOOD	ferry – passenger/car	27229.00	May 1989	Nov 1989	Marine Atlantic
715	HMCS CALGARY	patrol frigate	4750.00	Aug 1992	Aug 1994	Canadian Government

APPENDIX

GEO. T. DAVIE & SONS, LAUZON, 1928

Hull No.	Name		Vessel Type	Tonnage	Delivery Date	Owner
1	DONPACO	d	cargo vessel	241.00	1935	Donnaconna Paper Co. Ltd.
2	NEWSCARRIER	d	cargo vessel	243.00	1936	Donnaconna Paper Co. Ltd.
3	INTERNATIONAL NO. 1	d	cargo vessel	245.00	1936	Donnaconna Paper Co. Ltd.
4	G.T.D.	d	barge	244.00	1936	Davie Transportation Co.
5	KERMIC	d	cargo vessel	247.00	1937	Donnaconna Paper Co. Ltd.
6	A.C.D.	d	barge	247.00	1937	Davie Transportation Co.
7	G.D.D.	d	barge	246.00	1937	Davie Transportation Co.
8	HMCS LEVIS K-115	s	corvette	950.00	1941	Naval Service Canada
9	HMCS SHAWINIGAN K-136	s	corvette	950.00	1941	Naval Service Canada
10	HMCS LUNENBURG K-151	s	corvette	950.00	1941	Naval Service Canada
11	HMCS KITCHENER K-225	s	corvette	950.00	1941	Naval Service Canada

GEO. T. DAVIE & SONS LTD.

Hull No.	Name		Vessel Type	Tonnage	Delivery Date	Owner
12	HMS DOCHET T-286	s	trawler	545.00	1942	Royal Navy
14	LANSDOWNE PARK	s	cargo vessel	2965.00	1943	Park Steamship Co.
15	MAYFAIR PARK	s	cargo vessel	2965.00	1943	Park Steamship Co.
16	DUFFERIN PARK	s	cargo vessel	2965.00	1943	Park Steamship Co.
17	FLINT T-287	s	trawler	545.00	1943	Royal Navy
18	GATESHEAD T-288	s	trawler	545.00	1943	Royal Navy
19	HERSCHELL T-289	s	trawler	545.00	1943	Royal Navy
20	(cancelled)		(4700 ton freighter)			
21	(cancelled)		(4700 ton freighter)			
22	(cancelled)		(4700 ton freighter)			
23	HMCS CHARLOTTETOWN K-244	s	frigate	1445.00	1943	Naval Service Canada
24	HMCS JONQUIERE K-318	s	frigate	1445.00	1943	Naval Service Canada
25	HMCS LEVIS K-400	s	frigate	1445.00	1944	Naval Service Canada
26	HMCS LAUZON K-671	s	frigate	1445.00	1944	Naval Service Canada

APPENDIX

Hull No.	Name	Vessel Type		Tonnage	Delivery Date	Owner
27	HMCS GLACE BAY K-414	s	frigate	1445.00	1944	Naval Service Canada
28	HMCS FORT ERIE K-670	s	frigate	1445.00	1944	Naval Service Canada
29	HMCS VICTORIAVILLE K-684	s	frigate	1445.00	1944	Naval Service Canada
30	BALDWIN PARK	s	cargo vessel	2965.00	1944	Park Steamship Co.
31	WILLOW PARK	s	cargo vessel	2965.00	1944	Park Steamship Co.
32	BELL PARK	s	cargo vessel	2965.00	1945	Park Steamship Co.
33	CANADIAN VICTOR	s	cargo vessel	2965.00	1945	Park Steamship Co.
34	SAULT AU MOUTON	de	pulpwood carrier	450.00	1945	Donnaconna Paper Co.
35	OTTAWA MAY CREST	s	coaster	521.00	1946	B.M.O.W.T.
36	OTTAWA MAY FALL	s	coaster	521.00	1946	B.M.O.W.T.
37	OTTAWA MAY HAVEN	s	coaster	521.00	1946	B.M.O.W.T.
38	OTTAWA MAY SPRING	s	coaster	521.00	1946	B.M.O.W.T.
39	OTTAWA MAY THORN	s	coaster	521.00	1946	B.M.O.W.T.
40	CHING MEN	de	river boat	909.00	1948	Ming Sung Ind. Corp.
41	SHIH MEN	de	river boat	909.00	1948	Ming Sung Ind. Corp.
42	(cancelled)		(de river boat)			
43	(cancelled)		(de river boat)			
44	SAUTAURISKI (CAP DE L'ISLE)	de	pulpwood carrier	450.00	1947	Donnaconna Paper Co.
45	HU MEN	de	river boat	3079.00	1948	Ming Sung Ind. Corp.
46	YU MEN	de	river boat	3079.00	1948	Ming Sung Ind. Corp.
47	YEN MEN	de	river boat	3079.00	1949	Ming Sung Ind. Corp.
48	PORTE SAINT JEAN YMG-180	de	gate vessel	429.00	1951	Naval Service Canada
49	PWD NO. 70	s	scow – dump barge	48.00	1950	D.P.W.
50	PWD NO. 71	s	scow – dump barge	48.00	1950	D.P.W.
51	PORTE SAINT LOUIS YMG-183	de	gate vessel	429.00	1952	Naval Service Canada
52	HMCS TRINITY AMC 157	de	minesweeper	412.00	1954	Naval Service Canada
53	ONT. ST. LAW. DS NO. 21	n	scow – dump barge	48.00	1951	D.O.T.
54	IRVINGWOOD	de	canaller	2491.00	1952	Kent Line Ltd.
55	HMCS BLUETHROAT AGH-114	de	minelayer	785.00	1955	Naval Service Canada
56	PWD NO. 72	n	scow	48.00	1951	D.P.W.

APPENDIX

Hull No.	Name	Vessel Type		Tonnage	Delivery Date	Owner
57	PWD NO. 73	n	scow	48.00	1951	D.P.W.
58	ST. JOHN	de	salvage tug	840.00	1955	Naval Service Canada
59	PWD 401	n	drill boat	512.00	1954	D.P.W.
60	HMCS CHIGNECTO AMC-160	de	minesweeper	412.00	1956	Naval Service Canada
61	PWD 23	n	dredge	127.00	1955	D.P.W.
62	PWD 24	n	dredge	127.00	1955	D.P.W.
63	PWD 187	n	scow	48.00	1955	D.P.W.
64	PWD 188	n	scow	48.00	1955	D.P.W.
65	PWD 189	n	scow	48.00	1955	D.P.W.
66	PWD 190	n	scow	48.00	1955	D.P.W.
67	LIGHTSHIP NO. 1	de	lightship	527.00	1956	D.O.T.
68	RCMP WOOD	de	patrol boat	657.00	1957	R.C.M.P.
69	MONT SAINT MARTIN	de	coaster	493.00	1957	Transport Desgagnés Inc.
70	FUNDY	n	dredge	894.00	1957	J.P. Porter Co. Ltd.
71	BEAUPORT	de	sounding vessel	813.00	1959	D.O.T.
72	VERENDRYE	de	buoy tender	297.00	1958	D.O.T.
73	NORTH VOYAGEUR	de	coaster	895.00	1958	Orleans Navigation
74	FLEUR DE LYS	n	dredge	251.00	1960	D.P.W.
75	YBZ 60	s	naval tank cleaner	164.00	1961	Naval Service Canada
76	W.N.TWOLAN	de	tug	299.00	1962	N.H.B. for Churchill
77	JOHN A. FRANCE (bow)	n	lake boat	5250.00	1961	Canadian Vickers
78	POLARIS EXPLORER	de	coaster	605.00	1962	Polaris Shipping Ltd.
79	TRANS SAINT LAURENT	de	vehicular ferry	2173.00	1963	Gulf Ports Steamship Co.
80	CAPE RACE	de	trawler	291.00	1963	National Sea Products
81	CAPE ASPY	de	trawler	291.00	1963	National Sea Products
82	CAPE MIRA	de	trawler	291.00	1963	National Sea Products
83	ANN C. SPENCER	de	trawler	310.00	1963	Booth Fisheries Ltd.
84	ROSE J. GORDON	de	trawler	310.00	1963	Booth Fisheries Ltd.
85	ELLEN N. FLETCHER	de	trawler	310.00	1963	Booth Fisheries Ltd.
86	RUPERT BRAND VI	de	trawler	310.00	1963	B.C. Packers Ltd.

APPENDIX

Hull No.	Name	Vessel Type	Tonnage	Delivery Date	Owner
87	RUPERT BRAND VII	de trawler	310.00	1963	B.C. Packers Ltd.
88	PRIMO	de trawler	310.00	1963	St. Lawrence Sea Products
89	EXCEL-O	de trawler	310.00	1963	St. Lawrence Sea Products
90	SILLERY	de coaster	1091.00	1964	Polaris Shipping Ltd.
91	CACOUNA	de coaster	1091.00	1964	La cie. navigation Golfe
92	GOLDEN SCARAB	de trawler (tuna seiner)	981.00	1964	Scarab Fishing Ventures
93	RUPERT BRAND VIII	de trawler	308.00	1964	B.C. Packers Ltd.
94	DON DE DIEU (bow)	n lake boat	5250.00	1964	Canadian Vickers Ltd.
95	GEORGE KENTNER	de trawler	312.00	1965	Booth Fisheries Ltd.
96	SIEUR DAMOURS	de vehicular ferry	2558.00	1965	Traverse Matane Godbout
97	MAPLECLIFFE HALL (bow)	n laker	5250.00	1965	Canadian Vickers Ltd.
98	PATRICIA G. LINDER	de trawler	311.00	1965	Booth Fisheries Ltd.
99	TRIANO	de trawler	380.00	1968	St. Lawrence Sea Products
100	DAWSON	de survey vessel	1311.00	1967	Dept. of Mines & Fisheries
101	ATLANTIC MARIE	de trawler	624.00	1966	Atlantic Sugar Refineries
102	ATLANTIC JANE	de trawler	624.00	1966	Atlantic Sugar Refineries
103	ATLANTIC PEGGY	de trawler	624.00	1967	Atlantic Sugar Refineries
104	ATLANTIC ELLEN	de trawler	624.00	1967	Atlantic Sugar Refineries
105	ATLANTIC BEATRICE	de trawler	624.00	1967	Atlantic Sugar Refineries
106	ATLANTIC RUTHAN	de trawler	624.00	1967	Atlantic Sugar Refineries
107	ATLANTIC TONI	de trawler	624.00	1968	Atlantic Sugar Refineries
108	ATLANTIC NORMA	de trawler	624.00	1968	Atlantic Sugar Refineries

APPENDIX

DAVIE BROTHERS, LTEE (1951)

Hull No.	Year		Name	ft	Type
1	1953	m/v	ASTRID	48	trawler (rebuilt)
2	1953	m/v	SERCONA	54	wood trawler
3	1954	m/v	KERRCARPOUI	54	wood trawler
4	1955	m/v	MARCEL JOCELYNE	60	wood trawler
5	1955	m/v	TABATIÈRE	60	wood trawler
6	1956	m/v	LA GASPÉSIENNE	45	wood longliner
7	1956	m/v	LA GASPÉSIENNE NO 2	45	wood longliner
8	1956	m/v	LA GASPÉSIENNE NO 3	45	wood longliner
9	1956	m/v	LA GASPÉSIENNE NO 4	45	wood longliner
10	1956	m/v	LA GASPÉSIENNE NO 5	45	wood longliner
11	1956	m/v	LA GASPÉSIENNE NO 6	45	wood longliner
12	1956	m/v	LA GASPÉSIENNE NO 7	45	wood longliner
13	1956	m/v	LA GASPÉSIENNE NO 8	45	wood longliner
14	1956	m	for RCN	27	sea motorboat
15	1956	m	for RCN	27	sea motorboat
16	1956	m	for RCN	27	sea motorboat
17	1956	m	for RCN	27	sea motorboat
18	1957	m/v	LA GASPÉSIENNE NO 9	45	wood longliner
19	1957	m/v	LA GASPÉSIENNE NO 10	45	wood longliner
20	1957	m/v	LA GASPÉSIENNE NO 11	45	wood longliner
21	1957	m/v	LA GASPÉSIENNE NO 12	45	wood longliner
22	1957	m/v	LA GASPÉSIENNE NO 13	45	wood longliner
23	1957	m/v	LA GASPÉSIENNE NO 14	45	wood longliner
24	1957	m/v	LA GASPÉSIENNE NO 15	45	wood longliner
25	1957	m/v	LA GASPÉSIENNE NO 16	45	wood longliner
26	1958	m/v	LA GASPÉSIENNE NO 17	45	wood longliner
27	1958	m/v	LA GASPÉSIENNE NO 18	45	wood longliner

APPENDIX

Hull No.	Year		Name		ft	Type
28	1958	m/v	LA GASPÉSIENNE NO 19		45	wood longliner
29	1958	m/v	LA GASPÉSIENNE NO 20		45	wood longliner
30	1958	m/v	LA GASPÉSIENNE NO 21		45	wood longliner
31	1958	m/v	LA GASPÉSIENNE NO 22		45	wood longliner
32	1958	m/v	LA GASPÉSIENNE NO 23		45	wood longliner
33	1958	m/v	LA GASPÉSIENNE NO 24		45	wood longliner
34	1958	m/v	LA GASPÉSIENNE NO 25		45	wood longliner
35	1958	m/v	LA GASPÉSIENNE NO 26		45	wood longliner
36	1958	m/v	LA GASPÉSIENNE NO 27		45	wood longliner
37	1958	m/v	LA GASPÉSIENNE NO 28		45	wood longliner
38	1958		FOUNDATION CO.		30	workboat
39	1959	m/	LA GASPÉSIENNE NO 29		45	wood longliner
40	1959	m/v	LA GASPÉSIENNE NO 30		45	wood longliner
41	1959	m/v	LA GASPÉSIENNE NO 31		45	wood longliner
42	1959	m/v	LA GASPÉSIENNE NO 32		45	wood longliner
43	1959	m/v	LA GASPÉSIENNE NO 33		45	wood longliner
44	1959	m/v	LA GASPÉSIENNE NO 34		45	wood longliner
45	1959	m/v	LA GASPÉSIENNE NO 35		45	wood longliner
46	1959	m/v	LA GASPÉSIENNE NO 36		45	wood longliner
47	1959	m/v	LA GASPÉSIENNE NO 37		45	wood longliner
48	1959	m/v	LA GASPÉSIENNE NO 38		45	wood longliner
49	1959	m/v	LA GASPÉSIENNE NO 39		45	wood longliner
50	1959	m/v	LA GASPÉSIENNE NO 40		45	wood longliner
51	1959	m/v	LA GASPÉSIENNE NO 41		45	wood longliner
52	1959	m/v	LA GASPÉSIENNE NO 42		45	wood longliner
53	1959	m/v	LA GASPÉSIENNE NO 43		45	wood longliner
54	1959	m/v	LA GASPÉSIENNE NO 44		45	wood longliner
55	1960	m/v	LA GASPÉSIENNE NO 45		45	wood longliner
56	1960	m/v	LA GASPÉSIENNE NO 46		45	wood longliner
57	1960	m/v	LA GASPÉSIENNE NO 47		45	wood longliner

APPENDIX

Hull No.	Year		Name		ft	Type
58	1960	m/v	LA GASPÉSIENNE NO 48		45	wood longliner
59	1960	m/v	LA GASPÉSIENNE NO 49		45	wood longliner
60	1960	m/v	LA GASPÉSIENNE NO 50		45	wood longliner
61	1960	m/v	LINE C.		60	wood trawler
62	1960	m/v	PLEASANT BAY		60	wood trawler
63	1960	m/v	MARIE ELIZABETH		60	wood trawler
64	1961	m/v	LA COMÈTE		60	wood trawler
65	1961	m/v	GHISLAIN M.		60	wood trawler
66	1961	m/v	RÉNALD YVON		65	wood trawler
67	1962	m/v	FLAMINGO		60	wood trawler
68	1962	m/v	LE YVES B.		60	wood trawler
69	1962	m/v	JEAN RENE		60	wood trawler
70	1962	m/v	FLEUR DU GOLFE		65	wood trawler
71	1962	m/v	DUNE DU SUD		65	wood trawler
72	1962	m/v	GILLES ODETTE		65	wood trawler
73	1963	m/v	SAPHIR		65	wood trawler
74	1963	m/v	TOPAZ II		65	wood trawler
75	1963	m/v	JOCELIN B.N.		65	wood trawler
76	1963	m/v	MARIE-HELENE		65	wood trawler
77	1964	m/v	RÉNALD YVON		65	wood trawler
78	1964	m/v	ROMA L.		60	wood trawler
79	1965	m/v	MARIE JOSEPH		65	wood trawler
80	1965	m/v	SANCY		60	wood trawler
81	1966	m/v	MBV BELLE ILE		45	wood patrol boat
82	1966	m/v	FPV LA PINASSE		37	multi-purpose fishing boat
83	1966	m/v	FPV CAP DAUPHIN		37	multi-purpose fishing boat
84	1966	w	LA GRANDE HERMINE		79	historic replica
85	1966	w	INTRÉPIDE		30	steel sloop
86	1967	m/v	MARIE CLAUDE		87	wood trawler
87	1967	m/v	FPV JACQUES CARTIER		45	wood patrol boat

APPENDIX

Hull No.	Year		Name	ft	Type
88	1968	m/v	MARIE PAUL	87	wood trawler
89	1968	m/v	S.P. BONAVENTURE	52	wood patrol boat
90	1968	m/v	G.K. AUBERT	30	hydrographic survey boat
91	1968	m/v	VÉZINA NO. 2	37	steel pilot boat
92	1969	w	SOLITAIRE II	33	steel sloop
93	1969	w	MASCARET	33	steel sloop
94	1969	w	CHANTERELLE	33	steel sloop
95	1970	w	AQUARIUS	33	steel sloop
96	1970	w	CONQUISTADOR	33	steel sloop

LES INDUSTRIES A.C. DAVIE, INC.

Hull No.	Year		Name	ft	Type
97	1971	w	yacht	33	steel sloop
98	1971	w	yacht	33	steel sloop
99	1971	w	yacht	33	steel sloop
100	1971	w	yacht	33	steel sloop
101	1972	m/v	PILOUP	65	wood shrimper
102	1973	m/v	HESPERUS	60	wood longliner
103	1973	m/v	RENARDVILLE	60	wood longliner
104	1973	m/v	VÉZINA NO. 3	65	port supply boat
105	1974	m/v	LEADER B.	60	wood longliner
106	1976	m/v	SAINT MALO NO. 1	60	wood trawler
107	1977	m/v	FPV SAINT LAURENT	55	fibreglass patrol boat
108	1979	m/v	PILOUP	65	wood trawler
109	1979	m/v	EAGLE SEA	60	wood longliner
110	1980	m/v	ALDO M.	65	wood trawler
111	1980	m/v	JOCELYN LUC	65	wood trawler
112	1980	m/v	REED	24	steel tug
113	1981	m/v	FRÉDÉRIC C.	60	steel crabber
114	1982	m/v	KARINE II	60	steel shrimper

APPENDIX

Hull No.	Year		Name	ft	Type
115	1982	m/v	MONIKAROLINE S.	60	steel shrimper
116	1982	m/v	ANNIE CLAUDE	60	steel shrimper
117	1983	m/v	DOMEGA	65	steel shrimper
118	1984	m/v	CT/52	52	aluminium sail boat
119	1985	m/v	MANIC V	65	steel shrimper
120	1986	m/v	YOHAN MIRJA	65	steel shrimper
121	1986	m/v	JEAN MATHIEU	65	steel crabber
122	1987	m/v	ANTICOSTI	65	steel shrimper
123	1987	m/v	MANON YVON	65	steel trawler
124	1988	m/v	SAMOURAI	65	steel shrimper
125	1988	m/v	L'HORIZON I	60	steel trawler
126	1988	m/v	CAP DES VENTS	65	steel shrimper

APPENDIX

MORTON ENGINEERING AND DRY DOCK CO., LTD.

Hull No.	Name	Vessel Type		Tonnage	Delivery Date	Owner
1	BERMICO	steel winding			1926	Brown Corp.
2	?					
3	JOAN	composite yacht	n		1928	H.H. Wilson
4	PB NO. 7	wood barge	n	197	1930	Price Navigation Co.
5	PB NO. 8	wood barge	n	196	1930	Price Navigation Co.
6	RCMP LAURIER	patrol vessel	de	201	1936	Dept. of Justice (RCMP)
7	RCMP MACDONALD	patrol vessel	de	201	1936	Dept. of Justice (RCMP)
8	HMCS GASPE	minesweeper	s	460	1938	RCN
9	?					
10	HMCS MATAPEDIA K-112	corvette	s	950	1941	RCN
11	HMCS ARVIDA K-113	corvette	s	950	1941	RCN
12	HMCS SUMMERSIDE K-141	corvette	s	950	1941	RCN
13	HMCS LOUISBOURG K-143	corvette	s	950	1941	RCN
14	HMCS VILLE DE Q K-242	corvette	s	1015	1942	RCN
15	)	(a/s trawler)				
16	)	(a/s trawler)				
17	) cancelled	(a/s trawler)				
18	)	(freighter – Gray type)				
19	)	(freighter – Gray type)				
20	HMS MUSK CN-310	corvette	s	980	1942	RN
21	HMS MILFOIL CN-311	corvette	s	980	1942	RN
22	HMS MANDRAKE CN-312	corvette	s	980	1942	RN
23	HMS NEPATA CN-313	corvette	s	980	1942	RN
24	HMS PRIVET CN-314	corvette	s	980	1942	RN
25	HMCS DUNVER K-03	frigate	s	1370	1943	RCN
26	HMCS CAPE BRETON K-350	frigate	s	1370	1943	RCN
27	HMCS OUTREMONT K-322	frigate	s	1370	1943	RCN

APPENDIX

Hull No.	Name	Vessel Type		Tonnage	Delivery Date	Owner
28	HMCS VALLEYFIELD K-329	s	frigate	1370	1943	RCN
29	HMCS THETFORD MINES K-459	s	frigate	1370	1944	RCN
30	HMCS JOLIETTE K-418	s	frigate	1370	1944	RCN
31	HMCS CAP DE LA MAD K-663	s	frigate	1370	1944	RCN
32	HMCS ATHOLL K-15	s	corvette	980	1943	RCN
33	HMCS RIVIERE DU LOUP K-537	s	corvette	980	1943	RCN
34	HMCS LOUISBOURG II K-401	s	corvette	980	1943	RCN
35	HMCS NORSYD K-520	s	corvette	980	1943	RCN
36	HMCS ST. LAMBERT K-343	s	corvette	980	1944	RCN
37	HMCS HAWKESBURY K-415	s	corvette	980	1944	RCN
38	HMCS ASBESTOS K-358	s	corvette	980	1944	RCN
39	HMCS BEAUHARNOIS K-540	s	corvette	980	1944	RCN
40	HMCS STELLARTON K-457	s	corvette	980	1944	RCN
41	HMCS LACHUTE K-440	s	corvette	980	1944	RCN
42	HMCS MERRITONIA K-688	s	corvette	980	1944	RCN
43	HMCS KIRKLAND LAKE K-337	s	frigate	1370	1944	RCN
44	)		(frigate)			
45	)		(frigate)			
46	)		(frigate)			
47	)		(frigate)			
48	)		(corvette)			
49	)		(corvette)			
50	)		(corvette)			
51	)		(corvette)			
52	) cancelled		(corvette)			
53	)		(corvette)			
54	)		(corvette)			
55	)		(corvette)			
56	)		(corvette)			
57	)		(corvette)			

533

APPENDIX

Hull No.	Name	Vessel Type		Tonnage	Delivery Date	Owner
58	)	(corvette)				
59	)	(corvette)				
60	)	(corvette)				
61	ROCKLAND PARK	s	freighter – revised Gray	2905	1945	Park Steamship Co.
62	HAMILTON PARK	s	freighter – revised Gray	2905	1945	Park Steamship Co.
63	WESTDALE PARK	s	freighter – Dominion	2967	1945	Park Steamship Co.
64	MAISONNEUVE PARK	s	freighter – Dominion	2960	1945	Park Steamship Co.
65	OTTAWA MAYBANK	s	coaster – C type	526	1946	BMOWT
66	OTTAWA MAYCLIFF	s	coaster – C type	525	1946	BMOWT

ST. LAWRENCE METAL AND MARINE WORKS INC.

67	OTTAWA MAYGLEN	de	coaster – C type	302	1946	BMOWT
68	OTTAWA MAYMORE	de	coaster – C type	528	1946	BMOWT
69	OTTAWA MAYSTAR	de	coaster – C type	392	1946	BMOWT
70	KUEI MEN	de	cargo vessel	903	1948	Ming Sung Ind. Co.
71	CHI MEN	de	cargo vessel	904	1948	Ming Sung Ind. Co.
72	LANG MEN	de	cargo vessel	901	1948	Ming Sung Ind. Co.
73	CHIEN MEN	de	cargo vessel	901	1948	Ming Sung Ind. Co.
74	CARTAXO	de	coaster	1157	1948	Portugal
75	COLARES	de	coaster	1158	1948	Portugal
76	CORUCHE	de	coaster	1154	1949	Portugal
77	COVITHA	de	coaster	1154	1949	Portugal
78	PWD NO. 69	n	scow	212	1949	DPW

534

ABBREVIATIONS USED IN NOTES AND BIBLIOGRAPHY

ACQ	Archives civiles de Québec
ADM	Admiralty records
ANQ	Archives nationales du Québec à Québec
ANQM	Archives nationales du Québec à Montréal
APQ	Archives du Port de Québec
AVQ	Archives de la Ville de Québec
CGMM	Canadian Government Merchant Marine
CPF	Canadian Patrol Frigate
CS&MEN	*Canadian Shipping and Marine Engineering News*
DCB	*Dictionary of Canadian Biography*
DDP	Department of Defence Production
DND	Department of National Defence
GED	General Engineering Division
gr	Greffe of the notary – (at ANQ, unless otherwise indicated)
L.S.	Lloyd's Survey Report
MG	Manuscript Group, National Archives, Ottawa
MMGLK	Marine Museum of the Great Lakes at Kingston
NA	National Archives of Canada
NCDO	Naval Central Drawing Office
NMC	National Museums of Canada
PR	Parish Register
PRO	Public Record Office, Kew, England
RG	Record Group
RPQ	Register of the Port of Quebec (originals at PRO and NA)
RSC	Revised Statutes of Canada
SC	Statutes of Canada
SRO	Scottish Record Office, Edinburgh
TRUMP	Tribal class refit, update and modernization program
UL	Université Laval

NOTES

INTRODUCTION

1. The seigneury was in fact granted to Simon Le Maistre, an alias used by Lauson, who was Intendant of the 100 Associates, and a Member of the Parliament in Paris. The Seigneury at that time had a frontage of eleven miles, five and a half miles on either side of the mouth of the Chaudière River. Through its acquisition, the Lauson family became by far the biggest landholders in New France. Marcel Trudel, *Le terrier du Saint-Laurent en 1663*, 485-86.
2. 15 May 1647, gr Guillaume Audouart.
3. A.J.H. Richardson, *Quebec City: Architects, Artisans and Builders*, 185.
4. Talon decreed, for example, that the army's shoes must be made in the colony. Régis de Roquefeuil, "Byssot (Bissot) de la Rivière, François," *DCB*, I:145-46.
5. Réal Brisson, *La charpenterie navale à Quebec sous le régime français*, 217-43.
6. Marcel Trudel, *Le terrier du Saint-Laurent en 1663*, 504.
7. Jacques Mathieu, *La construction navale royale à Quebec*, 101-103.
8. It was leased in 1774 and sold in 1801. Andrée Héroux, "Caldwell, Sir John," *DCB*, vol.7, 133.
9. It would later be discovered, however, that John Caldwell had abused his position as receiver general of the colony by borrowing heavily from public funds, which was not in itself illegal had he been able to reimburse the amount.
10. Besides the Seigneury of Lauson, Gaspé, Foucault, and St. Etienne. Marcel Caya, "Caldwell, Henry," *DCB*, vol.5., 130-33.
11. William Oviatt was agent for Christopher Idle, John Idle, and Thomas Coates, of London, until 1815 when he returned to England for reasons of health and William Price took over. Price bought out their interest in the business in 1837, and in the property in 1840. Release, Idle to Price, 2 January 1837, and sale, 30 January 1840, gr L. McPherson (notary Lauchlan Macpherson, as spelled on the family tombstone at Mount Hermon Cemetery, Sillery, generally used the spelling McPherson on notarial documents). The Cove was named after Hadlow, Kent, England, the home of Idle.
12. Eileen Marcil, "Square-Rigged Rafts and the Export of Quebec Timber," *The American Neptune*, Spring 1988, XLVIII:2, 77-86.
13. Pierre-Georges Roy, *Profils lévisiens*, 1:104-7.

NOTES

14. The town was named after the Chevalier François de Levis, hero of the Battle of Saint Foy of 1760. In 1853, the new Comté de Levis, which reached as far as Saint Antoine de Tilly to the southwest and Beaumont, Saint Charles, and Saint Gervais to the north, and covered 272 square miles, was detached from the Comté de Dorchester.
15. Pierre-Georges Roy, *Dates lévisiennes*, vol.I 1848-1869 passim.
16. Edmund W. Sewell was both a designer and a builder of steamboats, who counted among his achievements the screw steamer *Northern Light*, a winter ferry contracted for by the Dominion government and put into service in 1876; it was built for winter navigation of the Northumberland Strait and the Gulf of St. Lawrence.
17. Frederick William Wallace, *Wooden Ships and Iron Men*, 92.
18. Pierre-Georges Roy, "James Tibbitts [sic]," *Profils lévisiens*, 1:104.
19. Georges-Etienne Proulx, "Déziel, Joseph-David," *DCB*, XI:283-84. Originally awarded to the stonemason David Dussault, the contract for the stonework of the church of Notre-Dame-de-la-Victoire was subcontracted by him to Augustin Trepanier fils, while the general building and carpentry were carried out by Joseph Nadeau for the sculptor André Paquet. 16 August 1850, no. 11765, gr Louis Panet.

CHAPTER 1

1. Herbert Heaton, *Economic History of Europe*, 317; A.J. Holland, *Ships of British Oak*, 30. A load was "the amount that could be drawn by a horse, or the equivalent of forty cubic feet or one ton weight."
2. Marcil, "Shipbuilding at Quebec, 1763 to 1893: The Square-Rigger Trade," Ph.D. thesis, 1987, UL, 28-35.
3. Typical contracts with shipwrights, 27 July 1811 and 13 February and 26 May 1812, gr J. Bélanger.
4. Davie family Bible.
5. Agreement, George Taylor with Patterson, Dyke and Company, 27 November 1811, gr J. Bélanger, ANQ.
6. The *Mary*, *Wolfe's Cove*, and *Thomas Henry*, registered at Quebec 20/1812, 22/1812, and 28/1812.
7. Lease, Brehaut to Taylor, 10 October 1817, gr L. McPherson.

CHAPTER 2

1. The brig *Findlay* arrived in Quebec on 9 November 1821.
2. The crew included Henry Quill, first mate, Allen Corrie, carpenter, and Edward McGilvray, seaman. Protest, 15 November 1821, gr L. McPherson.
3. The brig *Findlay* was built in Yarmouth in 1810.
4. Registered at the Port of Quebec (RPQ) 6/1822 on May 27.
5. See for example, Contract between J. Munn and H. Atkinson, 16 November 1821, gr A. Campbell.
6. *Quebec Gazette*, 11 April to 23 May 1822 passim.

NOTES

7. Launching, *Quebec Gazette*, 23 May 1822.
8. Protest, Forsyth *et al.*, 7 May 1822, gr L. McPherson.
9. George W. Haws, *The Haws Family and Their Seafaring Kin*, 150.
10. Built at the Campbell and Sheppard shipyard at Cape Cove, and registered 21/1822, 23 September, RPQ.
11. Register of St. Andrew's Church, Quebec, 16 April 1825; inventory of Allison Davie 19 July 1836, in which it is stated that the partnership began then.
12. Register of St. Andrew's Church, Quebec, 14 August 1826.
13. Register of St. Andrew's Church, Quebec, 10 March 1828, 6 July 1829, and 17 September 1830.
14. RPQ 3 and 4/1819.
15. *Quebec Official Gazette*, 17 May 1827.
16. Contract to build brig, Taylor with Douglas, 18 November 1826, gr L. McPherson; Report of launching, *Quebec Official Gazette*, 17 May 1827.
17. Contract to build schooner, Stewart, for Trinity House, with Taylor, 7 February 1828, gr E.B.L. Lindsay.
18. E.g., Survey, J. Munn and George Taylor, 28 May 1816, and G. Taylor and Sam Finch, 27 June 1816, gr A. Campbell.
19. *Montreal Gazette*, 21 and 24 May 1827.

CHAPTER 3

1. Register of Metropolitan Church, Quebec, 15 July 1828.
2. Sale, Carrier to Davie, 2 December 1829, gr L. McPherson; Sale, Thomson to Davie, 28 December 1830, gr L. Panet.
3. Petition, 5 July 1831, ff. 35411-35441, Lower Canada Land Papers, reel C-2520, NA. In the years ahead, Trinity House would also support Allison financially, granting him a loan to help him meet his heavy building costs. Allison Davie, inventory, 19 July 1836, gr L. McPherson.
4. RPQ 46/1829 and 2/1830.
5. *Quebec Gazette*, 5 March 1832.
6. Contract, Wiseman with Davie, 28 March 1832, gr L. McPherson.
7. Inventory, Allison Davie, 19 July 1836, gr L. McPherson.
8. Lease, Bégin to Davie, 2 March 1832, gr L. McPherson.
9. *Quebec Gazette*, 29 October 1832.
10. *Ibid.*, 3 May 1833.
11. *Ibid.*, 3 June and 3 July 1833.
12. *Le Canadien*, 10 June 1836; Account for coffin among bills outstanding in inventory, 19 July 1836, gr L. McPherson.
13. Born on 20 December and baptized 21 March 1937. Register of St. Andrew's Church.
14. Allison Davie, inventory, 19 July 1836, gr L. McPherson.

NOTES

CHAPTER 4
1. Report, Black and Munn, 15 September and Lease, 17 September 1836, gr L. McPherson.
2. Eric R. Axelson, "A Shipbuilding Dynasty," *Canadian Shipping and Marine Engineering News*, January 1953.
3. Simon Temple built for both the Admiralty and the Honourable East India Company between 1795 and 1809, and his Admiralty contracts, which invariably did not meet their deadlines, are said to have been a factor in his bankruptcy in 1811. A.C. Flage, *History of Shipbuilding*, Section IX "Simon Temple and His Son," 121-34.
4. Petition for patent, 9 February 1837, ff. 35411-35441, Lower Canada Land Papers, NA.
5. Quittance, government to Davie, 31 August 1883, gr Austin, ACQ.
6. Contract to build yacht, Trinity House between Trinity House and Taylor, 3 March 1841, gr E.B. Lindsay.
7. Report of launching, *Quebec Mercury*, 16 September 1841.
8. Haws, 150-51; "George Taylor Davie," *The Canadian Album: Men of Canada*, V: 224.
9. He inherited half the yard and bought the other half from his stepmother.
10. Marcil, "Munn, John," *DCB*, VIII: 646-49.
11. RPQs.
12. In 1813 and 1814 respectively.
13. Marcil, "Shipbuilding at Quebec," 59-66.
14. *The Canadian Magazine and Literary Repository*, II:477.
15. *Report of the Secretary of State of Canada for the Year ended 31st December 1894.* Appendix G, 63.
16. H. Philip Spratt, *Transatlantic Paddle Steamers*, 26-28.

CHAPTER 5
1. The merchant George Grant Allan.
2. George MacBeath and Donald F. Taylor, *Steamboat Days on the St. John 1816-1946*, 50.
3. The origin of the dock is unknown. It may have been built by the Davies or acquired elsewhere, but it may also have been the former Tibbits dock handed over in settlement of the Davie claim.
4. Agreement, James Tibbits, George Davie, Allison Davie, and George Grant Allan, gr A. Campbell, 1 October 1851; Sale, Allan to Davie, gr W.D. Campbell, 17 April 1852; Sale and resiliation [annulment], Taylor to Jamieson, gr W.D. Campbell, 16 August 1852 and 16 August 1853; gr Hossack, 13 October 1852, 26 May(2) and 26 November 1853.
5. Agreement, Davie with Price, 26 April 1853, gr A. Campbell.

NOTES

6. Agreement, Davie with Price, 26 April 1853, gr A. Campbell; RPQ, 97/1853; Lloyd's Survey, 77/1853. Menzies, who had taken up his appointment in 1852, was the first Lloyd's Surveyor named outside of Great Britain.
7. Partnership agreement, 6 April 1854, gr D. McPherson; Lease of yard, Taylor and Davie to Davie, 11 May 1853, gr L. McPherson.
8. Reg. London 306/1847, Captain John Brown, Master.
9. Sale, Captain John Barron, Master of the *Elizabeth*, to G. and A. Davie, 21 June 1854, gr A. Campbell.
10. RPQ 6/1855 of 20 April.
11. Contract to build, 15 December 1854, gr Bowen.
12. See, for example, Obligations for £1,000 on 28 November 1854, gr Bowen, for £500 on 24 May 1855, gr Bignell, and for £1,200 on 20 January 1863.
13. Built in Rotherhithe, Kent, England.
14. Sale, Roberts to Davie, 2 July 1856; RPQ 5/1856 of 5 July.
15. Dissolution of partnership, 1 April 1856, gr J. Hossack.
16. Agreement Symes with Davie, 23 March 1857 and Obligation 21 December 1857, gr D. McPherson.
17. *Lloyd's Register of 1866. Lloyd's Register of 1901.*
18. Lloyd's Register of Casualties and Port Warden's Register, ANQ.
19. St. Andrew's Church, Levis, 3 September 1860.
20. Notre Dame de Victoire, Levis.
21. *Quebec Mercury*, 12 October 1860.
22. Agreements, 30 January 1856, gr D. McPherson; 11 July 1863, gr F. Langlois.
23. Aubigny Church, Levis, 7 February 1861.

CHAPTER 6

1. Some of the "Port salvage associations [in Britain] were organized by local Lloyd's marine insurance underwriters and owners of ships and cargoes, as a means of minimizing their losses. They made arrangements with reputable [tug] owners, in order to ensure efficient, reliable salvage at economic rates. Such contracts were to the advantage of the tug owners, too, for they were a source of steady income – the elusive ideal of all operators." Tim Nicholson, *Take the Strain*, 45.
2. Incorporation of St. Lawrence Tow Boat Company, 29 Vic., c.59. The associates were Edward, Edward Henry and James Baker, Édouard and Pierre Barras, J.-B. and Themolaus Beaulieu, Isidore, Odule, Joseph and Ferdinand Begin, Charles and Pierre Bourget, Julien Chabot, sr. and jr., Thédore and F.-X. Chabot, George T., Gershom and William T. Davie, Mathieu and Robert Dickey, William Dinning, John Flanagan, Théodule Foisy, Denis and James Gaherty, Edouard Gingras, Felix Georges Harbour, Antoine Lemieux, Archange Labadie, veuve de Poiré, veuve Rosalie Bacquet dit Lamontagne, Charles and François Samson, and William Dinning. Agreement, 27 January 1863, gr S. Glackemeyer.

NOTES

3. Lease signed by J. Beaulieu, president, and Allison Davie, Manager, gr Fisher Langlois, 19 March 1863.
4. Sale Withall & Ross to St. Lawrence Tow Boat Company, 19 August 1863, gr S. Glackemeyer; Benson to Davie, 17 December 1863, gr W.D. Campbell.
5. Bond in the amount of $8,000 signed by G.T. Davie, Allison Davie, A. Falkenberg and H. McBlain on appointment of W.T. Davie as manager, gr F. Langlois, 31 July 1866; Protest, William T. Davie, manager of St. Lawrence Tow Boat Company vs. the Quebec Harbour Commissioners, gr Fisher Langlois, 31 July 1867. Allison had signed a marriage contract with Fannie Ritchie, daughter of the late John Ritchie and Margared Colclough on 21 August, 1866. The inventory taken following his death makes no mention of this union. Fanny Ritchie herself died soon after Allison.
6. Foundation of Levis Tow Boat Co. Inc., 11 February 1871, gr S. Glackemeyer.
7. According to endorsements on the certificates of the steamboats in Port Registers.
8. Agreement Davie with Ross, 22 October 1864, gr W.D. Campbell.
9. Agreement between Davie brothers, 30 September 1870, gr Austin.
10. J.E. Bernier, *Master Mariner and Arctic Explorer: A Narrative of Sixty Years at Sea from the Logs and Yarns of Captain J.E. Bernier*, 261.
11. RPQ 23/1872, which is endorsed with instructions that she was not to be sold for less than $4,000.
12. Sale of dock, Henry to Davie, 6 November 1872, gr W.D. Campbell.
13. The Traverse is that part of the North Channel that crosses the St. Lawrence obliquely to the north of the Isle of Orleans to its juncture with the South Channel at St. Jean.
14. Contract, Davie with Gillon, 25 September 1878, gr W.D. Campbell.
15. RPQ 1/1878 of 24 April.
16. RPQ 1/1880 of 11 May.
17. RPQ 5/1883 of 21 May.
18. P.-G. Roy, *Dates lévisiennes*, 24 December 1883, 107; "Les Bateaux traversiers," 156.
19. P.-G. Roy, *Les dates lévisiennes*, 28 October 1885, 177, and "Les Bateaux Traversiers," 156.
20. RPQ 14/1886 of 7 September.
21. Department of Railways & Canals, RG43, vol. 366, file 674, part 1, 28 April 1887, NA.
22. Department of Railways & Canals, RG43 vol. 366, file 674 part 1, Federal Archives Division, NA. Deed of expropriation, gr J. Edmond Roy, 28 April 1887.
23. Deed of expropriation, gr J. Edmond Roy, 28 April 1887.
24. Sale Hanbury to Davie, 20 December 1882, gr Austin, ACQ.

CHAPTER 7

1. In addition, there were two schooners that carried their builders' names, the 185-ton *A.D. Boucher*, laid down in Saint-Romuald in 1881 and the 196-ton *G.T.D.*, launched from the Davies' shipyard at Levis in 1883.

NOTES

2. Dimensions of the five remaining floating docks in the port in 1890 were given by their owners in letters to Trinity House as:

Davie	180 x 48 feet	1,065 tons
"	236 x 54 feet	2,175 "
Russell	160 feet	1,000 "
"	225 feet	2,500 "
Roche	212 feet	2,200 "

3. The Quebec Harbour Commissioners and the Quebec Board of Trade could not come to an agreement on the choice of site. *L'Evènement*, 22 October 1874, *Courrier du Canada*, 5 June 1877, 16 May 1878, and 25 July 1878. See also Kenneth S. McKenzie, "Steam Operations on the Lower St. Lawrence to 1914," *Seaports and the Shipping World*, January 1987.
4. Before the Notary John Strang.
5. Son-in-law of Queen Victoria.
6. *Courrier du Canada*, 5 November 1879 and 8 July 1880.
7. Sale, Patton to Davie, 22 December 1882, H. Austin, ACQ.
8. Leases, Patton to McLaren, 16 October 1866, 22 July 1869, and 15 October 1873, gr W.D. Campbell.
9. Lease, Davie to Patton, 1 May 1883, gr W.D. Campbell.
10. Original sale 20 January 1887 before notary Jacques Auger. Lot "4" on the plan was bought back by George T. Davie at the sale following J. Murphy & Co.'s bankruptcy 2 March 1897, and a large beach lot at the east end of the property, sale Judge Belleau *et al.* to Davie Ship 6 May 1943, reg. Levis 86597. The lots marked "1" and "3" that appear to be wharves were not in fact wharves, though Davie had letters patent for the two lots and could have built them.
11. Contract, Michaud and Couture with Davie, 17 June 1887, gr J. Auger, ACQ.
12. Lorne Dry Dock register, and Bernier, *Master Mariner*, 263.
13. "Profile of Patent Slip to be constructed at Lauzon near Levis by George T. Davie." From location survey by Ashe & Morency, Surveyors and Engineers, Quebec, January 1890. ANQ.
14. *Le Quotidien*, 11 April 1889.
15. A comparison of the weight of marine machinery at various times shows that the total weight per indicated horsepower in early screw ships was about 600 pounds, in early compound-engined ships about 400 pounds, and in ships with triple-expansion engines, 200 to 300 pounds. Major P.J. Cowan, *A Short History of Naval and Marine Engineering*, 255.
16. They had existed in the United States since 1869.
17. *Courrier du Canada*, 27 September 1990.
18. Register of Mount Hermon Cemetery.
19. Partnership agreement, 9 April 1897, gr Meredith; Agreement, *ibid*.

NOTES

CHAPTER 8
1. RPQ, 7/1897.
2. RPQ, 5/1898.
3. The *Manitoba*, of 2,616 gross tons, was built for the Canadian Pacific Railway, at the new Polson Iron Works at Owen Sound. She replaced the wrecked *Algoma*, whose engines she was given, and was the largest vessel then afloat on fresh water. Dana Ashdown, *Railway Steamships of Ontario*, 246.
4. The situation was different on the Great Lakes where competition in the construction of large steel ships came only from United States yards until much later, and the Collingwood shipyard built steel ships successfully from 1901 on. See Skip Gillham, *The Ships of Collingwood*, cited by Garth Wilson in *A History of Shipbuilding and Naval Architecture in Canada*, 48.
5. Protest Davie v. Powers, 7 February 1900, gr E. Meredith.
6. Contract, Department of Public Works to Thomas Powers, contractor.
7. *Quebec Chronicle*, 5 May 1902.
8. Various Montreal and Quebec newspaper clippings.
9. *Morning Chronicle*, 16 October 1901.
10. *Morning Chronicle*, 15 May and 13 September 1902; Register of Lorne Dry Dock, 22 February and 15 May 1902.
11. Obituary, *Le Quotidien*, 4 April 1903.
12. *In the Wake of the Windships*, 120.
13. Lease, Ryarson to Sample and Davie, 25 January 1873; Copartnership, Sample and Davie, 5 April 1873; Assignment under Insolvency Act, Sample and Davie to Murphy, 29 August 1878.
14. It is through William's son, William Taylor, and his descendants who live in the United States, that the family name "Taylor" has survived.
15. Roy, *Dates lévisiennes*, V:138; *Le Soleil*, 23 and 25 May 1903.
16. Roy, *Dates lévisiennes*, V:221.
17. Translated from Pierre-Georges Roy, *Profils lévisiens*, 77-78.

CHAPTER 9
1. Letters from owners of floating docks. Trinity House Records, II.9 1890, APQ; Port Wardens' and Lloyd's Casualties Registers in the Port of Quebec Collection, ANQ.
2. Sale Russell to Ross to cover $48,000 mortgage, 11 September 1900, gr Austin (Russell's yard, including his 2,500-ton floating dock and 200-foot gridiron, would later be taken over by the Quebec and Levis Ferry Company); *Lloyd's Register 1908-1909*, II:543; Report Book, 1900-1908, Port of Quebec, F0002-9, ANQ.
3. *Le Soleil*, 23 and 27 April 1910.
4. Davie bought it from Bernier in 1903.
5. For earlier attempts to set up a Canadian Navy, see Richard H. Gimblett, "Reassessing the Dreadnought Crisis of 1909 and the Origins of the Royal

Canadian Navy," *The Northern Mariner/ Le Marin du nord*, IV, No. 1 (January 1994), 35-53.
6. Correspondence between Department of Naval Service and various shipyards, RG24 5604 N SS 29-6-1, NA; correspondence between Tyne & Wear Archives Service and author, December 1992.
7. Graham D. Taylor, "Vickers in Canada, 1911-1927; The Reluctant Multinational," 6-8.
8. Quebec and Montreal newspaper reports, October and November, 1912; *Beeson's Marine Directory of the Northwestern Lakes: Season of Navigation 1913.*
9. Daniel McCarthy was godfather of the Davie's first son, Charles McCarthy Davie, while John and Catherine McCarthy were godparents of John Leavitt Davie. Notre Dame de Levis Parish Registers, 30 July 1866 and 11 November 1868. Moreover, Catherine E. McCarthy was one of the witnesses at George and Euphemia's wedding.
10. Gillham, *The Ships of Collingwood.*
11. Incorporated under letters patent of 19 April 1914, and Charter surrendered 21 March 1956, the company having been sold to the Foundation Company of Canada, 30 September 1944. George Musk, *Canadian Pacific Afloat, 1883-1968: A Short History and Fleet List*, 57.
12. The first steel hull built in Canada was that of the *Manitoba*, built in 1889 at Owen Sound by the Polson Iron Works. Maurice Smith.
13. When the construction of wooden ships came to an end in Quebec, its place was taken by shoe manufacturing. As Carrier, Lainé had failed, the important works became a factory that made shoe-making machines.
14. The first hopper dredge was built in Britain in 1861, and the first hydraulic suction dredge was suggested in France in 1867. Dredge design had been in full evolution since the 1890s, with advances made on both sides of the Atlantic. See "The History of Dredges and Dredging," *Sessional Paper No. 21*, Appendix No. 3, 3 Geo. V., A. 1913.
15. According to a staff article in *Canadian Machinery and Plant Manufacturing News*, "The Shipbuilding Plant of G.T. Davie and Sons, Levis, P.Q.," 10:9 215, 28 August 1913.
16. The proof being that when the river was full of ice and there was an appearance of an ice bridge being formed, the winter ferries ran down there for safety and always found it free of ice. Ships had been docked in 10 degrees (Fahrenheit) below zero weather without any trouble. Letter from Alf. Samson, Dock Master, to George T. Davie & Sons, 10 January 1912. Borden Papers, 26HI(C) 230:128819, reel C-4408, NA.
17. Borden Papers MG26 H1 (C) vol. 230, pp 128807(6 pages), microfilm C 4408, NA.
18. "Champlain Dry Dock for Quebec Harbor," *Canadian Railway and Marine World*, June 1918, 269-73.
19. Charles Barnard was apparently the owner "in Trust" since December 1913.

Minutes of the Board of Directors, DSRCL, 26 October 1914; Mentioned also in Sale, Davie to Barnard, 29 April 1914.
20. The Levis yard was not included in the sale.
21. The company stock book.
22. Cf. Ralph Linwood Snow, "The Trust Pied Piper," *Bath Iron Works: The First Hundred Years*, 133-12.
23. At this time, Vickers was the largest of Britain's four important armament shipbuilding complexes, with a capitalisation of £5.2 million. Anthony Slaven, "Modern British Shipbuilding, 1800-1990," *The Shipbuilding Industry: A Guide to Historical Records*, L.A. Ritchie (ed.), 9; see also, J.D. Scott, *Vickers*, 82.
24. Board Minutes, Swan, Hunter, 1903-5, Tyne & Wear Archives, with thanks to Bruce Jackson, Chief Archivist.
25. G.W. Taylor, *The Shipyards of British Columbia*, 68.

CHAPTER 10
1. RPQS.
2. Michael Moss and John R. Hume, *Shipbuilders to the World*, 325.
3. Acting on behalf of Winston Churchill, Britain's First Sea Lord of the Admiralty. Bill Swanson, "Elco," *Nautical Quarterly*, 1985, 30:23-24.
4. The same guns were used in some instances on M.L.s in the Second World War.
5. "Solving the Problem of the Power," *Motor Boat*, 1919, 28.
6. Lease for one year and a half with an option for another year at the same price, i.e., $3,000 p.a., 8 August 1915, gr Ed. Cholette, ACQM.
7. Letter, G.D. Davie to Robert Borden, Borden Papers, MG26HI(C) 201:112234, NA. The Canadian government sent strong representations to Vickers Limited regarding the placing of the order through the American firm, but it was explained that no Canadian yard had the necessary experience in the construction of such boats and that instructions had been given to the Electric Boat Company that the maximum amount of work possible was to be given to Canadian firms. Reply from A.T. Dawson, of Vickers Limited, to Sir George Perley, M.P., acting on behalf of the Canadian government, 10 November 1915. Microfilm C-4379, 96291-2, NA.
8. Yard list.
9. Henry R. Sutphen, "The Problem – The Plan – The Achievement," *Motor Boat*, 1919; Minutes of a meeting of the Board of Directors of DSRCL, April 1916.
10. The other being the construction of P.T. boats in the Second World War. Bill Swanson, "Elco," *Nautical Quarterly*, 1985, 30:20.
11. Bill Swanson, *ibid.*, 24; Archibald Hurd, *The Merchant Navy*, II, 266-67.
12. A difference of opinion exists surrounding their overall value, however. John Lambert writes rather disparagingly of them in *The Fairmile 'D' Motor Torpedo Boat*, 7, but in view of the repeat orders that were received, Archibald Hurd's appreciation of them in *The Merchant Navy*, II: 266-7, would seem to be justified.

See also, F.J. Dittmar and J.J. Colledge, *British Warships 1914-1919*, 136, London: Ian Allan Ltd., 1972.
13. In August 1921, A.A. Wright was vice-president and managing director of Davie Shipbuilding and Repairing Company Limited.
14. Cdr J.W. Skentelbery, RNVR, was sent over by the Admiralty and acted as expert adviser throughout the program.
15. Telegram, Admiralty to Canadian Naval Service, 14 February 1917. RG24 vol.5604, file NSS. 29-16-1, 1:24.
16. RG24, vol. 5604, NSS 29-16-1, vol.1, 19 October 1917.
17. Wooden ships were also built for the Department of Naval Service at the four shipyards at Sorel and by Vickers at Montreal. RG 24, 5601, 29-2-1, vol.1, p.51, NA. Shipyards on the Great Lakes, as well as Vickers and the government yard at Sorel, supplied the other trawlers. Gilbert Tucker, I:234.
18. John G.B. Hutchins, *The American Maritime Industries and Public Policy 1789-1914*, I:246-260.
19. January 1988.
20. For the Entrerios Railways Co.
21. J.P. Andrieux, *East Coast Panorama*, 127-31; Ivan Brookes, *The Lower Saint Lawrence*, 44-45, 167, 178.
22. At Quebec, Quinlan and Robertson built four vessels and Quebec Shipbuilding and Repairing Co. Ltd. built two. David Carnegie, *The History of Munitions Supply in Canada*, 204-14; W.H. Mitchell and L.A. Sawyer, *British Standard Ships of World War I*, vol.3 of *Wartime Standard Ships*, ix-xi, 141-56.
23. Minutes of the meeting of the Board of Directors, 18 February.
24. Appraisal by Canadian Appraisal Co. Limited, Montreal, 19 February 1920.
25. Letter from George D. Davie to Minister of Railways and Canals making application for discarded rails, 11 May 1915; Letter from Assistant Deputy Minister of Railways and Canals regarding supply of rails, 10 March 1917. RG43, vol. 572, file 18253.
26. Letter from Lafleur, MacDouggall *et al.*, Montreal, to Blake, Lash *et al.*, Toronto, 17 September 1923.
27. Letter to the *Gazette*, 12 March 1914.
28. He even signed his correspondence to his family that way.
29. Request made at meeting of the directors of the company on 19 October 1916.
30. An estimate of $187,108.66 for the War Profits Tax that Davie expected to be assessed for the years 1916 to 1918 is given in the company's annual report for 1919.

CHAPTER 11
1. "The Growth of a Giant," *Canadian Shipping and Marine Engineering News*.
2. Meeting of Directors, 19 August 1918, DSRCL Minute Book.
3. CSL gave up its first venture into shipbuilding, Tidewater, in the mid-1920s,

NOTES

(Collard, *Passage to the Sea*, 123), but kept the property. In 1935-37, most of the buildings had been demolished; new shops were built in 1940.
4. *Canadian Railway and Marine World* (henceforth *CR&MW*), December 1918, 570-71 and May 1919, 281-82.
5. *Montreal Star*, 14 March 1917, RG24 5604: 29-16-1.
6. Of which three were ordered from the British American Shipbuilding Co. at Welland, Ontario, five from Canadian Vickers, Montreal, three from Canadian Allis Chalmers, Ltd., Bridgeburg, Ontario, four from Collingwood Shipbuilding Co., Collingwood, Ontario, four from Davie (only three were built), two from Midland Shipbuilding Co., Midland, Ontario, two from Nova Scotia Steel & Coal Co., New Glasgow, Nova Scotia, four from Polson Iron Works, Ltd., Toronto, four from Port Arthur Shipbuilding Co., five from Thor Iron Works, Ltd., Toronto, two from Tidewater Shipbuilders, Ltd., three from Wallace Shipyards, Ltd., Vancouver, two from Victoria Machinery Depot, two from Prince Rupert Drydock.
7. There is some lack of clarity as to what became of the buildings and equipment of Plant number 3 that was erected to fulfil the Electric Boat Company contract.
8. Legal opinion, Fred Markey to DSRCL, 18 March 1920.
9. Case 389, Superior Court for the Province of Quebec District of Montreal, 1920.
10. Contract dated 4 October 1918, cancelled on 14 March 1919.
11. Letter, Royal Trust to the Toronto legal firm of Blake, Lash, Anglin & Cassels, 17 September 1923.
12. Davie Shipbuilding Co. Ltd. (Liabilities Canada S.S. Lines Ltd.) 8. 375-6 29/9/21 and 9.95 1179 27/4/22. Vickers Archives. Courtesy Hugh Scrope.
13. Original contract of 4 October 1918 between Davie Shipbuilding and Repairing Company Limited and Livanos in the amount of $335,000 was cancelled on 14 March 1919 in consideration of a fee of $70,000.
14. *CR&MW* October 1919, p.567. Five years later, the *Maplecourt* was cut in two at the Canadian Vickers shipyard and towed to Buffalo in two sections, which were rejoined by the Buffalo Drydock Company. *CR&MW*, May 1924, p. 254.
15. Contract, Minister of Marine and Fisheries and DSRCL, 2 February 1920; Letter re insurance, G.U. Price to CSL, 14 March 1921.
16. Information given by Martial Tremblay, her owner.
17. Collard, *Passage*, Chapter 3, passim.
18. *Marine Engineering and Canadian Merchant Service Guild Review*, X: April 1920.
19. With thanks to Steve Salmon.
20. Collard, *Passage*, 101-2.
21. William L. Tazewell, *Newport News Shipbuilding: The First Century*, 114; Ralph Linwood Snow, *Bath Iron Works: The First Hundred Years*, 199.
22. *Le Soleil*, 3 May 1921.
23. Opinion re reconstruction work given by Smith, Markey as advisers to CSL, 14 February 1922.

NOTES

24. From Auditor's Report:

Management Commission	$184,915.34
Special Distribution to Shareholders	132,000.00
Commission re French Barge Contract	360,000.00
Payments on account of repairs to SS *Maplecourt* (formerly SS *Northwest*) transferred to credit of personal account on instructions of Mr. Barnard	<u>330,057.74</u>

25. "Report of Proceedings in London – December 1920 to April 1921 – relating to a Claim by Canada Steamship Lines against Colonel Grant Morden and others," prepared by Brown, Quayle and Bentley Turner.
26. Letter from Norcross to Sir Trevor Dawson with copy to Grant Morden, 16 December 1919.
27. Collard, *Passage*, 89, 90, 94.
28. Barnard had also had interests in Halifax Shipyards with Mercantile Securities and others, which he had transferred to the Home Bank, *ibid.*, 4-970, vol. 28.
29. The King v. Charles Barnard, C.C. 112/1924, Home Bank, MG28 II 11 vol. 124, Agreements, and vol. 125, A. Barnard and Prudential Trust Co., NA. See also, *The Canadian Annual Review 1924-1925*, 582-587.
30. *Ibid.*
31. It should be pointed out, however, that conflict of interest in business was widespread in the frontier days of Canada's business economy at the beginning of the twentieth century. Duncan McDowall's *The Light*, the history of the growth of one of Canada's largest companies, the Brazilian Traction Light and Power Company Limited, shows this up well. Some was self-interest, some in the company's interest, and some both. Men will continue to press to the boundary, and government to pass laws to restrain them.
32. Collard, *Passage*, 95-113.
33. Notice sent by P.S. Ross & Sons, Liquidator, to the Creditors and Shareholders of the Davie Shipbuilding and Repairing Company Limited, 31 July 1925.
34. Minutes of the Meeting of Directors held that day; *CR&MW*, July 1925, 371.

CHAPTER 12

1. He also sold Davie's derrick scow *Jumbo No. 1* to William Noble for $7,500. Minutes of a Meeting of the Directors of Davie Shipbuilding and Repairing Company Limited, 22 May 1925.
2. See Donald Page, "Canada Steamship Lines: The Fleet Develops, 1913 to the 1980's," *Freshwater: A Journal of Great Lakes Marine History*, vol. 3:2, Winter 1988, 5-12.

NOTES

3. As had at least two other large pleasure cruisers on the St. Lawrence, the *Saguenay* in 1884 and the *Montreal* in 1926.
4. For information on St. Lawrence River cruises, see Philippe Dubé, *Deux cents ans de villégiature dans Charlevoix*, 62-84.
5. Written by A.C. Hardy and referred to in *CR&MW*, November 1929, 723.
6. Of which 20 per cent was to be paid when the keel plate and vertical keel and Hopper Keelson were completed and laid on keel blocks; another 20 per cent when the vessel was in frame; 20 per cent when the vessel and its boilers were plated and the cylinders bored; 20 per cent when launched and docked ready for the boilers and engine to be placed on board; and the last 20 per cent after satisfactory trials. The barge was to be classed with the British Corporation BS (River Service) with freeboard certificate, and to be built under their Special Survey and government inspection and to the requirements of the Canadian Board of Steamship Inspection. Contract, Davie with the Minister of Marine and Fisheries, October 1929.
7. It was estimated that the new tug would cost $75,000 to build and would earn $13,000 annually. Average earnings over the previous three years for the *Chateau* and the *Busy Bee* after depreciation had been $15,554 and $13,263 respectively. Minutes of the Board of Directors, 22 November 1929.
8. Horace German, who was brought to Canada by Vickers in 1913, had joined Walter Lambert, who had been brought over by the IMB in 1922, to form Lambert & German. Harold Milne joined the firm when Lambert retired prior to the Second World War and it became German & Milne. In 1945 the name changed again to Milne, Gilmore & German with the addition of James Gilmore, and eventually it became German & Milne. Sons Gordon and Bill German and Bill Milne joined the firm at various times later. Maurice Smith, "German & Milne: Its Role in the History of Ship Design in Canada," 11-12, *Fresh Water*, 9:1, 1994, and "German & Milne: Its Role in the History of Ship Design in Canada," *A History of Canadian Marine Technology*, Westwood, Farrell and Fyfe (eds.). Ottawa, (Eastern Canadian Section of the Society of Naval Architects & Marine Engineers, 1995).
9. In which a 50 per cent share was bought by the New York Central & Hudson Railroad Co. in May 1930. Dana Ashdown, *Railway Steamships of Ontario*, 97.
10. Built for the purpose by the American Shipbuilding Company of Lorrain, Ohio. They replaced the steam ferry *Charles Lyons*. Lambert & German, *Floating Equipment Designed by Lambert & German*.
11. Dana Ashdown, *Railway*, 97.
12. An entirely Canadian company since 1927.
13. Silver Donald Cameron, "The P.E.I. and Fundy Services," *Iceboats to Superferries: An Illustrated History of Marine Atlantic*, 71-73.
14. Collard, *Passage*, 121-23, 422-24.

15. Contract between Department of Marine and DSRCL, 16 March 1932, for tug at $216,250 and fire equipment at $13,420.
16. David Dougan, *The History of North East Shipbuilding*, chapters 5 and 6, passim. Ian Johnston, *Beardmore Built: The Rise and Fall of a Clydeside Shipyard*, 144-47. Tom Gibson recounts from personal experience that his father was naval architect of William Beardmore at Dalmuir on the Clyde, which was one of the country's leading yards in warship construction and had reinforced building berths for the construction and launching of battleships with steel armour belts of up to 12 inches. He lost his job and was unemployed for two years when Beardmore was bought by National Shipbuilders Security Limited in 1930 as part of the rationalization of the Clyde shipyards.
17. There is some contradiction as to this. Most sources refer to his having been manager until his death in 1937.
18. Sale, Charland to Klein, 13 October 1927, gr Antonio Benoit; Klein to Davie, 21 October 1927, ratified 21 October 1930, gr Jos. Sirois; private sale, G.D. and A.C. Davie to C. Davie, 1 May 1929, ratified 5 November 1933, gr R. Meredith.
19. Partnership agreement, Allison Davie and George D. Davie, gr R. Meredith, 13949, 21 November 1933.
20. Bernier, *Master Mariner and Arctic Explorer: A Narrative of Sixty Years at Sea from the Logs and Yarns of Captain J. E. Bernier*, 408.

CHAPTER 13

1. Tucker, *Naval Service*, I:304.
2. The proposal was made to Britain by Earl Jellicoe in the course of a visit to Canada. Tucker, *Naval Service*, I:318-19.
3. Because Laurier's Naval Act had been shelved by his successor, Robert Borden, who did not succeed in persuading the Senate to pass his own Naval Aid Bill in its place, Canada had had neither her own fleet nor any ships representing her in the Royal Navy when the First World War broke out. The entire RCN Fleet consisted then of two old British cruisers HMS *Rainbow* and *Niobe*, which Laurier had bought from the Admiralty in 1910 to serve as training ships. They were stationed on the west and east coasts respectively, but by 1914 only the *Rainbow*, at Victoria, was operational. However, hearing that two submarines had been built at a Seattle shipyard for the Chilean government, which had defaulted in its payments, the governor of British Columbia had stepped in and bought them using provincial funds without waiting for federal approval or any other formalities that might delay and perhaps prevent the sale. Slipping their berths on August 4, 1914, they arrived at Victoria the following morning and joined the Canadian Navy as *CC1* and *CC2*, thus beating the American embargo on the sale of warships. To serve as a tender for the two submarines, the old RN ship HMS *Shearwater*, a 980-ton sloop built in 1899, was commissioned into the RCN, and HMS *Algerine*, a 1,050-ton sail

NOTES

and steam gunboat built in 1894 was also secured. *CH14* and *CH15* were commissioned into the RCN in 1919 and were paid off in 1922 and disposed of in 1927. MacPherson and Burgess, *The Ships of Canada's Naval Forces*, 14.
4. The former HMS *Torbay* and *Toreador*.
5. Minute No.3, Meeting of the Defence Council, August 29, 1930. RG24, vol.3840:1017-10-17.
6. Memorandum Percy Nelles to Minister of Naval Defence, February 12, 1935, RG24 vol. 3840, 1017-10-17, 39-40, NA.
7. Memorandum, Percy Nelles to Minister of Naval Defence, March 19, 1935, October 30, 1935, and November 23, 1936. RG24 vol.3840, 1017-10-17, 50-51,56-57, 13-17, NA.
8. The *Kempenfelt* had been the flotilla leader of the destroyers when they were in the RN.
9. Tucker, *Naval Service*, II:22-23.
10. Tucker, *Naval Service*, II:23.
11. In addition to those already mentioned, there was a training schooner on the east coast and a training motor vessel on the west coast.
12. Tucker, *Naval Service*, vol.II:11 and Appendix II, "The Machinery of Port Defence," 523.
13. See Fraser McKee, *Armed Yachts of Canada*.

CHAPTER 14
1. Which it was later decided to omit.
2. Tucker, *Naval Service*, II:34. Four destroyers were eventually built at the Halifax Shipyard, but were not ready for action during the war.
3. At the same time three corvettes were ordered from the George T. Davie shipyard at Lauzon, while Morton's was given a contract for four.
4. "... the 1936 whalecatcher *Southern Pride* ([yard building number] 1018)." Ian Macdonald and Len Tabner, *Smith's Dock: Shipbuilders 1908-1987*. Thomas G. Lynch, *Canada's Flowers: History of the Corvettes of Canada 1939-1945*.
5. Moss and Hume, *Shipbuilders to the World*, 325.
6. "Castle class" corvettes were built in 1943 and 1944, but not in Canada.
7. Later versions of the corvette, known as the Revised Flower class, had a displacement of 1,015 tons and measured 208 feet 4 inches overall in length, while their draft was 11 feet 5 inches forward and 16 feet aft. The sheer and flare of their bows was greater than those of the earlier boats, and their forecastles were longer.
8. Tucker, *Naval Service*, II:38,39; Lynch, *Canada's Flowers*, 10-14.
9. Tucker, *Naval Service*, II:39; Lynch, *Canada's Flowers*, 10-14; correspondence, Tony Price and Tony German.
10. In June the following year, the shortage of steel was so severe that plans had to be made to lay off some of the men despite the full order book.

NOTES

11. Tucker, *Naval Service*, II:41-42.
12. December 7. Lynch, *Canada's Flowers*, 25-26.
13. Alec Douglas, "Grant Macdonald's Navy," *Freshwater*, 6:1, 1991, 38; Lynch, *Canada's Flowers*, 28-29.
14. Lynch, *Canada's Flowers*, 10.
15. Macpherson and Burgess, *The Ships of Canada's Naval Forces*, 85, 156-57.
16. With the exception of *Noranda*, which had a 20-mm gun.
17. Ken Macpherson, *Minesweepers of the Royal Canadian Navy 1938-1945*, 58-69.
18. Tucker, *Naval Service*, II:363.
19. Fairplay, "Characteristics of American, Canadian and Australian War-Built Tonnage," 1947.
20. Marine Industries Limited was founded by Joseph Simard in 1937. It grew from a dredging company which Joseph, with his brothers Ludger and J. Edouard Simard, had been operating at the former Chantiers Manseau at Sorel.
21. Memo to C.D. Howe from F.H. Brown, 23 March 1943. RG28 B-2, vol.663, 204-D-1, NA.
22. Memorandum, Engineer Captain G.L. Stephens, RCN, to C.N.S., 2 February 1942. RG24 vol. 5604, NSS 29-1-31 vol.12, 29-44-1, M12640, NA.
23. Of these, eight went to the RN and two to the USN. F.M. Smith, "History of the British Admiralty Technical Mission [BATM] in Canada," p.66.
24. Memo of Meeting at Naval Shipbuilding Branch of Department of Munitions and Supply, Ottawa. RG24 vol.5619, N-5-529-72-1, 1698.
25. Ken Macpherson, *Frigates of the Royal Canadian Navy, 1943-1974*, 57-89.
26. Agreement, Minister of Munitions and Supply and DSRCL, 1 February 1944, RG28 vol.566, 200-612.
27. Her original contract price was $670,000, with penalties for late delivery, insufficient horsepower, too great a draft, and so forth.
28. The assets of the Morton Engineering and Dry Dock Company were bought by Hervé Baribeau on 28 June 1946, at which time its name was changed to St. Lawrence Metal & Marine Works Inc. Information received from James N. Morton.
29. Exceptionally, George T. Davie built and outfitted HMCS *Lauzon*.
30. Diane Bélanger, *La construction navale à Saint-Laurent, Ile d'Orléans*.
31. Approximately 254,681 displacement tons in all. Six Bangor minesweepers and eight Western Isles anti-submarine trawlers were built for RN but loaned to RCN.

CHAPTER 15

1. Thomas Steven, ed., "Shipbuilders of the St. Lawrence," *CS&MEN*, January 1944.
2. A horse lover, Morley would have the yard horse brought up to the office building each morning for a treat of sugar, and when the horse died, he had one of the hoofs mounted and kept it on his desk.
3. Collard, *Passage*, 166.

4. Leonard Winslade.
5. *L'Écho Maritime*, September 1943, 5.
6. At the premises of the Union nationale ouvrière de la Rive Sud, at 12, rue Sainte-Catherine, Lauzon.
7. Emery Roy, *Centenaire de Levis 1861-1961*.
8. Allan C. MacNeish, "Training of Shipbuilders in Quebec," *CS&MEN*, February, 1942, 19-22.
9. Though not always without problems. In speaking of his shipyard years, Alphonse Desjardins, who later became the steel stockyard manager, recalls his frustration and that of his fellow travellers from Saint Romuald when their tram was held up at the ferry landing on its way to the yard, because the special trams that met the ferry had left before them and were using up all the electricity. Arriving late at the yard through no fault of their own, they nevertheless had a quarter of an hour docked from their day's pay. Though the situation was eventually remedied by the construction of another electrical substation, the unfairness of the practice while it lasted still rankles.
10. The buses were subsidized by the two shipyards. Agreement between Levis Tramways Co., DSRCL, and Quebec Shipyards Ltd.(Geo. T. Davie), 15 January 1944.
11. Senator Leon Mercier Gouin was chairman, with Edouard G. Rinfret and Walter F. Schroeder, K.C., as counsel to the commission.
12. These did not cover the amount paid to foremen or assistant foremen.
13. Special Records, RG 28 B2 vol:860.
14. "History of the British Admiralty Technical Mission in Canada," appendix 6, 1.
15. Under D.W. Ambridge, the former director general of naval shipbuilding. *CS&MEN*, December 1943.
16. The BATM arrived in Canada in July 1940 and carried on until 1946.
17. The siren has recently (June 1995) given way to individual alarm bells in the sheds as a result of pressure from neighbours who were disturbed by it.
18. According to the terms of the contract, Campbell was to prepare all plans, sketches, and specifications for conversions, replacements, and alterations to CSL vessels and floating equipment, and to compile related technical information and data. For Davie, he would supply all the information needed for the drydocking of any vessels, make the sketches for replacements on repairs or alterations to vessels undergoing repairs, prepare all data, calculations, etc., for ordering material, castings, forgings, etc., and provide plans showing the repairs that were carried out. He further undertook to compile estimates of material for new construction being tendered on, and to prepare estimates on the cost of labour, dealing with all technical correspondence relative to the tenders and supplying detailed weights and calculations on them, this for Davie exclusively. Finally, he agreed to prepare all the plans and information that might be required in connection with the shipyard plant, including the layout plans of shops with

NOTES

locations of machines, and other equipment, and to furnish recommendations and data for any proposed improvements or additions to the plant.

He would prepare, also, the plans, sketches, and specifications for repairs, conversions, replacements and/or alterations to the Marine Industries Limited fleet, compile technical information, give advice or instructions to the Drawing Office in connection with them, and render any assistance that might be required on new construction already on hand. As with Davie, he would prepare plans and information required on the shipyard plant and furnish recommendations and data relative to proposed improvements or additions. He would also perform the services of naval architect for new construction contracted for by either of the shipyards. The shipyards agreed to lend any services of their technical staff that were needed, and Campbell agreed not to take on additional outside work that would interfere with his work to the three parties.

19. He was given a contract for the duration of the war at $675 per annum, a portion of which was to be paid by CSL. Minutes of the Meeting of the Board of Directors, 14 April 1941.
20. The architects in each case were Hutchison & Wood, and the builders Komo Construction. CSL/Davie agreements 522 and 528.
21. The Foundation Company were the contractors for this new work and the dismantling of existing buildings, together with road repairs and alterations to the railroad track. Contract, Foundation Company with DSRCL, Hutchison & Wood, architects, 11 May 1942, CSL agreement 542.
22. CSL agreement 557, see also RG28 vol.501, 51-D-20 for contracts between government and Davie.
23. The offer held good during the war or within three years of its end. Letter, Department of Munitions and Supply to Davie, 27 March 1943. Memo from F.H. Brown to C.D. Howe, 23 March 1943. RG28 B-2, 663:204-D-1.
24. Morton's extension of its operations across the river was not a success. The first ship handled in Lauzon was the government icebreaker *Mikula*, which it docked for general repairs in the Champlain Dry Dock in June 1932.
25. Though there was resentment and resistance to the introduction of welding on the part of some of the more conservative shipbuilders. In order to help the shipyards make the change, a Mr. Gooderham was hired by the Department of Munitions and Supply to encourage and assist them. RG24 vol.5601, 29-1-1, NA. Davie, however, was already committed to the new technology – welding had been introduced there before the war – and was only too pleased to be able to benefit from the government financial assistance that was forthcoming for the job.
26. Electrical work March 1943 for building berths 6 and 7 by Bedard-Girard, $13,792, for RCN T.S. corvette programme, CSL agreement 555, 28 April 1943. 5 July 1944. Additional welder receptacles and wiring, berths 1 to 5, $15,766. Done by Bedard-Girard Ltée, contract 5 July 1944, CSL agreement 567.

NOTES

27. Contracts between DSRCL and Quebec Power Company, 8 August 1939, 6 August 1940, 20 September 1943.
28. Operations, which had been suspended at the Midland yard in 1930 (Collard, 123), were renewed during the war.

CHAPTER 16

1. Department of Reconstruction Act, secs. 4 and 5.
2. "Canada's Industrial War Effort," typescript, RG28 vol. 862.
3. CSL took an active part in the commission set up on shipbuilding, because Canadian shipbuilders could not compete with the low wages of British yards, and British ships were allowed to trade freely in Canada. After lengthy hearings, the commission advised the government to leave things as they were, one of their points being that if the coasts were restricted, freight rates would go up.
4. The Canadian Vessel Construction Assistance Act of 1948.
5. Felicity Hannington, *The Lady Boats*, 122, 134, 151, 170.
6. Interview with Jean-Paul Zizka.
7. "France Gets Three More," *Canadian Shipping*, July 1949, 13-14.
8. Information given by Gilles Fortin.
9. He later became president of the company.
10. O'Neill moved on to the Kingston shipyard with Kenneth King soon after. Information supplied by Robert McGilvray.
11. Information supplied by Bill McCloy and by the Ship Registry Department of the Department of Transport.
12. Many of the facts in this chapter come from "Davie Shipbuilding Limited: An Outline of Its History...," a typescript graciously furnished by Robert McGilvray that has been of great help to the author.
13. Ordered by the Ming Sung Industrial Co. Typescript history of Geo. T. Davie supplied by Vickers Limited.
14. Undoubtedly technological advancement in the use of aluminum in shipbuilding in Canadian shipyards fitted in with the developments that were going on elsewhere. The P. & O. Line's 45,270-ton *Canberra*, which was launched from the Harland & Wolff shipyard at Belfast in 1960, is said to have had 1,200 tons of aluminum in her superstructure. Moss and Hume, *Shipbuilders to the World*, 378.
15. CSN, *35 ans de lutte au chantier*, 9.
16. Joel J. Sokolsky, "Canada and the Cold War at Sea, 1945-1968," *The RCN in Transition*, W.A.B. Douglas (ed.), 214.
17. Dan W. Middlemiss, "Economic Considerations in the Development of the Canadian Navy since 1945," *The RCN in Transition*, Douglas (ed.), 261.
18. *Ibid.*, 273-74.
19. Kelloch Report.
20. Collard, *Passage*, 236-43.

NOTES

21. Although Stubbs had no formal job interview with Delagrave, he found out afterwards that he had checked him out very thoroughly before hiring him.

CHAPTER 17
1. Collard, *Passage*, 250.
2. McLagan made Brock Thomson company secretary of CSL. When he reached retirement age, he made him a director of the company. Collard, *Passage*, 298.
3. That is, Davie, Kingston, Collingwood, Midland, and Port Arthur.
4. Louis Rochette, for example, who was alerted by one of his staff and remembers seeing the glow of the fire in the evening sky from his home in Sainte-Foy, ten miles away.
5. Messrs. Johnson & Higgins, insurance brokers.
6. Another two would be added in 1964.
7. At cost plus 7½ per cent. Purchase order, government to Davie, 3 March 1954.
8. The first destroyer to wear this name, she was launched in September 1943 as the British "V" Class Fleet Destroyer, HMS *Valentine*, and was commissioned into the RCN as HMCS *Algonquin* in February 1944.
9. After administering the contracts for HMCS *Gatineau* DDH 282, Gibson did the same for the supply Ship HMCS *Provider* and the second DDH escort vessel, *Qu'Appelle* DDH 283, for the overhaul and updating of the aircraft carrier *Bonaventure*, as well as the DDH 280 Tribal Class destroyers, and for many other contracts for maintenance and repair of DDE and DDH ships, including the conversion of a second-hand Italian fishing trawler to a diving support vessel, HMCS *Cormorant*, which was commissioned in 1978.
10. Originally set up in the summer of 1949 under NCC (Naval Constructor in Chief) Constructor Captain (later Commodore) R. Baker, who was on loan from the Admiralty's Royal Corps of Naval Constructors. Its original purpose was to produce the designs for a class of Canadian ASW vessels, the *St. Laurent* class of destroyers, of which seven were built with Vickers as the lead yard. S. Mathwin Davis, "The St. Laurent Decision: Genesis of a Canadian Fleet," *The RCN in Transition 1910-1985*, W.A.B. Douglas (ed.), 195-202; Macpherson and Burgess, *The Ships of Canada's Naval Forces 1910-1985*, 163.
11. S. Mathwin Davis, "The Defence Supply Naval Shipbuilding Panel, 1955-1965," *The Northern Mariner*, II: 4 October 1992.
12. *Ibid.*, 12-13.
13. The *d'Iberville* was broken up in Taiwan in 1988.
14. Built at Canadian Vickers.
15. Gilbert took possession of the territory in the name of Queen Elizabeth in 1583, thus establishing the first English colony in North America.
16. As a result over many years Canada Steamship's account with the Château Frontenac Hotel was their single biggest.

NOTES

17. They were handsome ships, with curved raked stems and cruiser sterns, of the three-island type, with forecastle, bridge, and poop deck. Their cargo tank space was divided into thirty compartments, and they would carry a crew of eleven officers and thirty-three men. George T. Campbell, of Montreal, acted as consulting naval architect for the owner.
18. Supplementary letters patent, Libro 211, Folio 310, Department of Financial Institutions, Companies and Cooperatives.
19. *The Alcan Ingot*, December 1954, XIII:12, 4-5. Richard Lowery described her before the Institute of Marine Engineers in London in 1957 as "a most exciting ship to build." "Shipbuilders," he said, "built many vessels which they merely produced and virtually forgot about afterwards. The *Sunrip* was a stimulating job and a very exacting job for the shipyard and staff.... Apart from the basic dimensions and the preliminary investigations into the choice of machinery almost all the investigations ... were actually undertaken after the order was placed and while the vessel was under construction."
20. Photo and full description. *CS&MEN*, January 1955.
21. The *Sunrip* was sold to Companea de Navegacia of Panama in June 1967.
22. She spent most of her time after that on Lake Ontario, a frequent loader at the cement dock in Toronto. Skip Gillham and Alfred Sagon-King, *Canadian Fleets Along the Seaway*, 17, 46.
23. She was sold to Underwater Gas Developers in 1973 and rebuilt and renamed *Telesis* in 1975. She later became a gas drill barge on Lake Erie. Gillham and Sagon-King, *Canadian Fleets along the Seaway*, 46.
24. They were two of eight diesel-powered canallers acquired by the line between 1952 and 1958, the remaining six being built in other shipyards. Hall Corporation was wound up in 1988.
25. Christening her with a forty-seven-year-old bottle of champagne, given by Yarmouth's George MacInnis, that had been taken from a wreck on Seal Island in 1907. John Belliveau, Silver Donald Cameron, and Michael Harrington, *Iceboats to Superferries: An Illustrated History of Marine Atlantic*, 111-12.
26. Ibid., 113-14, 122. See also, Robert H. Worthen, *For Love of the Sea*.
27. Tovar, who had a degree in Business Administration, as well as Engineering, moved on the following year to the General American Transportation Corporation in Pennsylvania, and was later manager of the Quonset Point Facility of Electric Boat where he is credited with having been the driving force behind the modular method of submarine construction. He became general manager and then corporate vice-president of Electric Boat.
28. Nathan Keyfitz, *Canada and the Colombo Plan*, 3. Toronto: Canadian Institute of International Affairs, 1961. For more on the seaway, see next chapter.
29. The order from the Union Tank Car Company in Chicago was obtained by Veliotis and John Gorman, his senior draftsman.

NOTES

30. Mrs. Hemsley of the St. Lawrence Seaway Corporation; Lowell Thomas, *The St. Lawrence Seaway Story*; R.S. Misener, *The Great Lakes/Seaway: Setting a Course for the 80s*. Toronto, Ontario government, 1981.

CHAPTER 18
1. Under the command of Captain Norman Donaldson, an old friend of Davie, since he was the master of choice for many of the trial trips of ships built by Davie.
2. Collard, *Passage*, 287-88.
3. The date was June 26, and President and Mrs. Eisenhower did not complete the journey, returning to the United States shortly after the ribbon-breaking ceremony.
4. In 1853, when the St. Lawrence Channel between Montreal and Quebec was completed, Montreal became Canada's Atlantic terminal and a port of transshipment, because the locks above Montreal could not accommodate large carriers. Between 1853 and 1900, various programs of lock construction between Montreal and Lake Erie were undertaken which increased the standard size of lock between the two points to 270 x 45 x 14 feet, and also increased the maximum-size vessel that was able to travel from the Gulf to Lake Erie to 259 feet.
5. Donald Page, "Canada Steamship Lines," *Freshwater*, Winter 1988, 11.
6. P. Papachristidis's long and successful career in shipping began with the purchase of a 10,000-ton ocean-going Park vessel in 1943 that was soon joined by eight others. All these ships were sold in 1953 when the market declined. Following the opening of the seaway in 1959, Papachristidis acquired another fleet, this time of seaway vessels, which he sold in 1972. Since his death in 1981, his son and daughter, Basil and Niky, have followed in their father's footsteps and have built up a large internationally renowned shipping company. Gillham and Sagon-King, *Canadian Fleets along the Seaway*; Desmond Allard, "The Man and His Fleet," *Canadian Shipping and Marine Engineering*, January 1972.
7. Converted by Captain Norman Rogers of the Toronto Drydock Corporation in 1990.
8. Andrieux, *East Coast Panorama*, 107.
9. "Hydroconic Design Impact Grows," April 1962, Harry Chapin Plummer, "Diesel Tugs for Foundation Maritime," January 1963 and December 18-19, 1962, *CS&MEN*.
10. *CS&MEN*, December 1965, 66.
11. It would be Pullen's last seagoing naval appointment, and in the course of it he directed the first 20-knot night refuelling of a Mackenzie-class destroyer escort. He is better known and remembered, however, as an Arctic explorer who lobbied to protect its environment, and whom the Geographical Society ranked with Larsden and Amundsen when they awarded him their Massey Medal in 1984. W.A.B. Douglas, "In Memoriam: Thomas Charles Pullen, 1918-1990," *Argonauta*, VII:4, 1-2 October, 1990; and W.A.B.Douglas (comp.), "Captain T.C. Pullen,

RCN: An Arctic Bibliography," *The Northern Mariner/Le Marin du Nord*, II:2, 51-54, April 1992.
12. *Huron* was built by Vickers-Armstrong Ltd. at the Walker Naval Yard at Newcastle-on-Tyne, and commissioned in 1943; *Sioux*, at the J. Samuel White & Co. Ltd. yard Cowes, Isle of Wight, during the Second World War. Macpherson and Burgess, 209. They were paid off in Halifax in 1963 and sent to Italy to be broken up two years later.
13. Built by Burrard's at Vancouver in 1957. Macpherson and Burgess, 209.
14. Lt. Peter Ward, RCNR, "DEs Get Long-Range A/S Punch," *CS&MEN* March 1964.
15. The White Ensign was replaced by the Canadian flag on 15 February 1965.
16. The actual final figure for her refit was $12,629,000 – $10,290,090 paid to Davie Shipbuilding plus $2,750,000 for the equipment that the government provided. Inevitably, the increased cost made headlines; for more about this see Chapter 19.
17. Later Admiral Falls, Chief of Defence Staff.
18. George Hees, Minister of Transport, "New Icebreaker Is launched," *CS&MEN*, November 1959.
19. She was bought by Americans in 1993 to be broken up.
20. "'New Look' in Coast Guard Fleet," *CS&MEN*, August 1962.
21. "Keel-laying to Launch: 15 Days!," *CS&MEN*, July 1968, 15, 39; "Keel-laying to Launch: 13 Days!," *CS&MEN*, August 1968, 60-61.
22. Yolande Dorion-Robitaille, *Le capitaine J.-E. Bernier et la souveraineté du Canada dans l'Arctique*. Ottawa: Department of Indian & Northern Affairs, 1978.
23. Page, "Canada Steamship Lines," *Freshwater*, Winter 1988, 7.
24. Collard, *Passage*, 335-6.
25. Terry MacCormack, "Are the Ferry's Days Numbered?" *CS&MEN*, August 1971. See also, Michael F. Harrington, "The Gulf and Coastal Services," *Iceboats to Superferries: An Illustrated History of Marine Atlantic*, 150-152, 156.
26. There were two such barges. They dragged a bar at a certain level under the surface that pinged when it touched the bottom to warn that some dredging was required.
27. *CS&MEN*, September 1964.
28. How long it would last, however, was a matter of conjecture, for by 1966, at least one Canadian shipowner had ordered a large upper laker from a Japanese shipyard.
29. Not including the sixteen 15- to 27-ton scows that were built in 1955 for the Department of Works.

CHAPTER 19

1. *CS&MEN*, August 1962, 86.
2. Interview, author with Rochette, September 1993.
3. Mainly for Union Tanker, Ltd. Also, CGTX and ATX tank-car tanks for propane and ammonia.

NOTES

4. The foundation for the warehouse was built by the Foundation Company of Canada.
5. Davie received enquiries through an agent, but did not tender.
6. The project consisted of creating storage on the Emerald Avalanche and Upper Bharani rivers to develop a gross head of 1,185 feet.
7. John Gorman went to Pittsburgh and spent a week with Leon Bidder, inventor of T1 steel, learning how it was created and how to weld it.
8. It was necessary to build the right facilities, a vault in the side of the huge rock in front of the Champlain Dry Dock to keep the cobalt source Iridium 192, a potent radioactive material for very heavy castings and X-ray equipment. Interview with John Gorman.
9. Louis Desmarais interview with author, 1 November 1991.
10. Collard, *Passage*, 353.
11. According to Wilbrod Bherer, former president of George T. Davie and a director of Canadian Vickers, since the Canadian government had no new work available and as improved navigational aids on the St. Lawrence had greatly cut down on the number of ship being damaged and in need of repairs, it was evident that one of the two shipyards would have to go.
12. A group of Gaspé university students, who felt that as Jacques Cartier had first set foot in Gaspé the *Grand Hermine* should be berthed there instead, took the opportunity to make their point at her christening. Quebec had Champlain, they chanted, Cartier belonged to Gaspé. And though their suggestion had not been without merit, by then the intervention was far too late.
13. Information given by Ladrière Samson, former manager.

CHAPTER 20
1. Collard, *Passage*, 356, 362.
2. "New Bulk Carrier Is Commissioned," *CS&MEN*, May 1966, 24.
3. *Lake Manitoba* changed owners when Nipigon Transport Limited was sold to Algoma Central Marine in 1986; renamed *Algomarine* in 1987; converted to self-unloader 1988-89. Gilham and Sagon-King, *Canadian Fleets along the Seaway*, 72.
4. The *Imperial Bedford* was 40 per cent larger than her consort, *Imperial Acadia*, designed by E.E. "Ernie" Bustard, designer of all Imperial Oil's new tankers, powered by 6,600-h.p. diesel.
5. Though procurement procedures had changed considerably with the passing of the Government Organization Act in 1968. S.C. 1968/69 Chap. 28.
6. The failure of Canadian Vickers to win any of the work, either in its customary role of lead yard or even as follow yard, was a shattering blow to Canada's primary naval shipbuilder and heralded the beginning of the end for the Montreal yard. Soon after, Eric Harrington, president of Canadian Vickers, announced that his company was withdrawing from new construction, to concentrate on sophisticated industrial and nuclear fabrication, including submarine subcontracts for

NOTES

the U.S. Navy, besides which it would undertake only refits and repairs. Two other shipyards, the Halifax Shipyards Division of DOSCO and the Burrard Dry Dock Co. Ltd., had also submitted tenders as follow yards.

7. Although still referred to as the keel-laying ceremony, in fact a module with a part of the keel is laid.
8. They were built in ring units up to the Number 1 Deck.
9. A modified Fort-type cargo ship built in Vancouver in 1944 as HMS *Beachy Head*; she served in the Royal Netherlands Navy as the repair ship *Vulkaan* from 1947-50, was back in the RN 1950-52; transferred to the RCN and was renamed HMCS *Cape Scott* in 1953. Macpherson and Burgess, *Ships of Canada's Naval Forces*, 181.
10. Built at the Halifax Shipyards and commissioned in 1957. Macpherson and Burgess, *Ships of Canada's Naval Forces*, 163.
11. Formed by the merging of the Department of Industry with that of Trade and Commerce in 1969 (RSC 1970, c.1-11).
12. Established in 1969 (RSC 1970, c.R-4).
13. Countries that made the most enquiries were the United Kingdom (25), followed by the United States (13) and then Canada (10) in 1970; and Canada (16), followed by the United Kingdom (10)and then the United States (6) in 1971.
14. Internal DSL report "Considerations of Optimum Future Shipbuilding Programme."
15. The Export Development Corporation of the federal government had pledged financing to the extent of $43.5 million, or 80 per cent, to the owners, repayable over eight years at an annual interest rate of 7½ per cent, as per OECD terms. Davie was to receive a 14 per cent subsidy on the audited costs of each vessel.
16. *CS&MEN*, April 1971; memos, Lowery to Regnaud, 18 February, and 12 May 1970.
17. One cannot use the word "floor" when speaking of a metal ship, as this term is used for what is generally known as a wall.
18. Georges Berberi spent two weeks in Vicksburg, Mississippi, learning how the legs were to be built. The gears, racks, and electric motors were supplied by Marathon-Letourneau.
19. When the rig was unable to find a solid bottom in Lake Erie, and almost turned over as she continued to settle into the mud, she was sent to the Gulf of Aqaba. She was strafed there by Egyptian fighter aircraft during the Arab-Israeli war!
20. R.S. (Bob) Faulkner, the former manager of the GED, had become manager of Dosco and eventually chairman of Hawker-Siddley. He had knowledge of Davie's costs, profit margins, and so forth, and was able to consistently underquote Davie.
21. Interview between Louis Desmarais and the author, 1 November 1991.
22. If Takis Veliotis's departure from Davie was dramatic, his rupture with General Dynamics ten years later would be even more so, though in the meantime his performance there was impressive. Under his management, the General Dynamics

Corporation's shipyard in Quincy turned a profit after years of operating in the red. He was then offered the challenging position of general manager of the Electric Boat shipyard, and with it the direction of the Trident submarine program. He became executive vice-president, Marine, of General Dynamics Corp., and was awarded the Admiral Jerry Land Medal in 1980 by the Society of Naval Architects of New York. But Takis Veliotis was playing a losing game, for while carrying out what was considered a brilliant job at the Quincy and the Electric Boat yards, allegations were made that his business arrangements had not always been above reproach. In 1982, Takis Veliotis chose to return to his native Greece and exile, rather than face the inevitable enquiry and possible court proceedings.

23. In fact, this was not the first dispute with Varnima. According to the contract, Davie agreed to build three large tankers on the basis of the plans for M.T. *Sylvania*, but they were to be three transverse spaces shorter, a Sulzer 8 RND 90 main engine was to be substituted, and classification was to be changed from Det Norske Veritas to Lloyd's. Shortly after the commencement of construction, however, the owners protested that Davie had reduced the thickness of the steel on account of the vessels being smaller, though Lloyd's classification standards were met. They demanded a reduction in price of some $18 million as their "only available remedy at the present time," the builder having proceeded with the construction of the ships. The arbitration hearings before a panel of arbitrators under the presidency of the retired Judge Choquette took more than two years to complete and involved a Rogatory Commission headed by Quebec judge Alan Gold for special hearings in Athens, Oslo, and London. Finally it was the decision of the arbitrators that Davie had acted in accordance with the contract and the claim was refused. However, the case had taken its toll, requiring almost the full time and attention of Michael Ayre and some of his staff, and no doubt contributed to distracting management's attention from the deteriorating performance. Varnicos Primero Corporation S.A., Varnicos Segundo Corporation S.A., Varnicos Tercero Corporation S.A. v. Davie Shipbuilding Limited, and covering memorandum to Gordon Black from P.W. Gauthier, October 1972.
24. Both Nightingale and Shepherd were former Davie employees. Appointed on 16 April 1973, Winslade in fact left the company five weeks later.
25. He had previously been employed as a hull designer at Davie from 1956 to 1967.
26. Because of the high cost of buying a panel line, i.e., $1 million or more, it was designed and built at the shipyard with an eye to the state-of-the-art European panel lines, but for the modest outlay of $150,000 besides material that was available at the yard.
27. John O'Keefe, "Welding: The Changing Scene in Canada's Yards," part 2, *CS&ME*, June 1974; Davie Shipbuilding Limited, "Shipbuilding Facility Modernization: Summary," May 1974.

NOTES

28. *CS&MEN*, January 1974, 22-23.
29. Paul Martin is (in 1997) Minister of Finance in the Liberal government of Canada. Though he resigned his positions on the Board of CSL on joining the government, he still owns CSL through a blind trust.
30. "Report on the Proposed Merger of Canadian Shipbuilding and Engineering Limited, Davie Shipbuilding Limited, Marine Industries Limited, March 1973."

CHAPTER 21

1. Pickersgill held this position until September 1979, when he left to join John Shepherd in Saint John.
2. Later managing director of the Kvaerner Govan shipyard on the Clyde.
3. Management reckoned that an important part of this was attributable to labour disruption and poor productivity.
4. Because of the lateness in the year when the *Athel Monarch* was completed, she sailed for Tampa to have the epoxy coating applied to her tanks, a job that had to be done in mild weather. The co-operation of the owners' representatives, John Hicks and Harry Kay, and their professional approach, which contributed to the overall quality of the ships, are long remembered.
5. A fire with loss of life on the *Cartiercliffe Hall* in 1979, coupled with another fire on board the *Hudson Transport*, contributed to the downfall of Hall Corporation and to a major change in the Canadian Coast Guard approach to safety regulations and inspections.
6. Socanav, "Cap sur l'avenir: Steady on Future 1938-1988," *La revue maritime l'Escale*, No. 26, November 1988.
7. Davie's own Drawing Office being extremely busy, Rochette gave a contract to make the detailed design and working drawings for a new Branch Lines tanker *l'Erable No. 1* to MIL Sorel, which had done those of the rest of the Branch Lines fleet.
8. The numbers 82 and 116 in the designation of the rigs refer to the depth of water in which they were originally designed to dig, i.e., 82 metres (269 feet) and 116 metres (381 feet). However, these figures are not those given in their specifications, which are 250 and 300 feet respectively.
9. Member of the Saleninvest Group of Stockholm, Sweden.
10. Apparently Davie's rigs were rarely non-operational due to breakdown.
11. DAC's shares were owned 51 per cent by Crosbie, and the balance equally by the other two partners, Aker and Davie. Later, with the addition of Keyes Drilling, the company became DACK.
12. Marine Industries, "Document d'information pour la commission parlementaire de l'industrie et du commerce," dated 30 November 1978, 4.
13. He was a director and past president of the Canadian Shipbuilding and Repairing Association, a Fellow of the Royal Institute of Naval Architects, a Member of the

NOTES

Society of Naval Architects and Marine Engineers, of the Standards Council of Canada, the Bureau Veritas International Committee, and the American Bureau of Shipping Committee.

CHAPTER 22

1. Declarations made by Jack Gallagher and Bill Richards during their visit to take over the yard.
2. For the construction of semi-submersibles.
3. Designated AML 10 (Arctic) Marine Locomotive Class 10.
4. Jim Lyon, *Dome: The Rise and Fall of the House that Jack Built*, 1983, 4, 128.
5. It had accumulated $1.5 billion in tax credits for exploration, far more than it could itself benefit from, but the original plan was that they would cash them in against the high taxes that the Hudson's Bay company was required to pay on its productive oil fields.
6. For the four partners the sale at the top of the market had seemed optimal, but their payment, substantially in Dome shares, now put a slightly different face on the deal.
7. As of 13 August 1982.
8. He did this by taking over all the outstanding shares in Soconav, under which name he bought part of the Branch Lines Fleet, while Sofati of Montreal, the Gaucher family firm, acquired the rest.
9. Société de construction navale (SOCONAV); Société canadienne de navigation (SOCONAV).
10. *Who's Who*, 1987.
11. Anthony Slaven, "Modern British Shipbuilding, 1800-1990," *The Shipbuilding Industry: A Guide to Historical Records*, L.A. Ritchie (ed.), Manchester: Manchester University Press, 1992.
12. His work was appreciated, and in 1986 Day was made chairman and chief executive officer of the British Leyland Group by the British prime minister, Margaret Thatcher, with a mandate to make it profitable and privatize it. His skill in doing so earned him a knighthood and another challenge as chairman of troubled Cadbury-Schweppes and British Aerospace.
13. The requirements had initially been circulated to the industry in 1978 with a request for pre-qualification proposals. This was followed by a funded contract definition phase.
14. An earlier *Caribou* was torpedoed and sunk in the Gulf of St. Lawrence with the loss of 137 lives in 1942, one of several that fell prey to the U-boats. She had served on the same run for seventeen years. Michael F. Harrington, "The Gulf and Coastal Services," *Iceboats to Superferries*, 142.
15. Taylor, *Shipyards of British Columbia*, 205.
16. Founded in 1949 as the Naval Central Drawing Office (NCDO), it became the Naval Ship Design Agency in 1972. In 1978, its name was changed once more to

NOTES

Marine Design and Drawing Office. One year later it took the name Vickers Stanwick Systems Inc.
17. Saint John Shipbuilding's bid was double either Davie's or Versatile Pacific's. The latter eventually won the contract and entered into an extensive design-to-cost phase, but the cost kept rising, and the whole project collapsed for lack of funding and pessimism about Arctic development.
18. Among them history and lecturing.
19. Inter-Office memo, 16 May 1986 from Peter Paul Saunders to M. Provencher.
20. Harrington, "From Small Fry to Superferries," *Iceboats to Superferries*, 172-73.
21. ???
22. Which was delayed twelve months due to the inability of Litton and the Crown to conclude a prime contract that gave the desired scope of work at a price within the ceiling laid down by the Treasury board.
23. A contract to build three frigates had been signed with Saint John Shipbuilding on 29 July 1983. The contract for the first two destroyers of the TRUMP program, HMCS *Algonquin* and *Iroquois*, was finally signed on 31 July 1986.
24. Letter Don Challinor to Guy Véronneau, 6 January 1987.
25. A fax from Versatile Corporation to Don Challinor, 2 February 1987, announced that the sale had been completed. Peter Paul Saunders's resignation as chairman, president and CEO of Versatile Corporation was announced on 17 June 1987 in the *Wall Street Journal*.
26. Following Peter Paul Saunders's retirement, Bruce McKay, Brian Kenning, and Terry Lyons restructured the Versatile Group. The eastern shipyards were sold to MIL, another buyer was found for the cold-storage division, and Ford bought the farm machinery division. After the sale of its Australian interests, Versatile still owned its western shipyards, and its debt amounted to $90 million. With Edper of Toronto's help, the corporation re-financed and in June 1989 sold the western shipyards to Shieldings. The name Versatile has disappeared, but the corporation lives on under the name British Columbia Pacific Capital. Telephone conversation, Terry Lyons with author, 20 December 1996; Roland H. Webb, "Burrard Drydock Co. Ltd.: The Rise and Demise of Vancouver's Biggest Shipyard," *The Northern Mariner/Le Marin du nord*, VI:3, July 1996, 9.

CHAPTER 23

1. As of January 30, Versatile Vickers and Versatile Vickers Systems Inc. were MIL Vickers and MIL Systems Engineering Inc.
2. Robert Tessier, the executive vice president of the SGF and former deputy minister of Energy and Resources, would replace him at the beginning of 1988.
3. It was not only Davie employees that had to be accommodated. Office space for the military project was required for a large contingent from Litton (approximately eighty), SJSL (twenty), MIL Systems (fifteen to twenty), Pratt & Whitney (three), and the Navy (ninety-five). It is interesting to note the tremendous

difference in the work required to manage this contract and the original DDH 280 contract in 1970-73, which was handled by two or three of Davie's staff, Tom Gibson, Michael Ayre, and subsequently, Bob House.
4. The crane installed beside the dock had previously been used by MILTHOM to erect the tower at the Olympic Stadium in Montreal.
5. Others were sent from MIL Tracy and MSEI.
6. From an interview with and a report written by Richard Gauvin on his return, with thanks.
7. As of 6 December 1988.
8. It was run then, as it is today, by Gina Perreault, the company's Public Affairs officer.
9. Its nuclear technology was passed to Tracy, but the submarine work for Newport News ceased.
10. Vickers, "History of Canadian Vickers Limited, Montreal, P.Q., Canada," typescript dated 30 November 1956. See also, Graham D. Taylor, "Vickers in Canada, 1911-1927: The Reluctant Multinational." Paper presented to the Second Canadian Business History Conference, Victoria, British Columbia, March 3, 1988. *Annual Report 1986*, Marine Industries Limited.
11. They were: Robert Monette, president of the shipyard workers' union; Raynald Leclerc, president of the union of office workers; Pierre Nadeau, president of the security force's union; and Alain Thériault, president of the association of maritime draftsmen. Early in 1990, the committee set a publicity campaign in the media in motion explaining the situation. It circularized Davie's suppliers and major local industries and socio-economic groups asking them to write supporting letters to the governments and called upon the federal and provincial governments to take the necessary steps to save "the last shipyard in Quebec."
12. Moreover the *Caribou* was named one of the Distinctive Ships of the Year by Marine Engineering/Log.
13. Presented to him by the president, Arthur J. Haskell, on 14 April 1989 at New Orleans.
14. Don Challinor suffered a fatal heart attack on 23 June 1991. He was sixty-three years old.

CHAPTER 24

1. J.Y. Clarke, Cdr. RCN (Retd.), "Yesterday, Today and – Will There Be a Tomorrow?" *The Navy League of Canada Maritime Affairs Bulletin No. 1/88*, passim.
2. Diesel-electric submarines had been planned and a change to nuclear-powered boats was made in June 1987.
3. The other groups were the CSE (Canadian Shipbuilding and Engineering Ltd.) Submarine Group Inc., and Saint John Shipbuilding Limited.
4. In 1991, this contract was transferred to Davie together with the extensive metallurgical laboratory facilities and installed at one end of the Machine Shop.

Subsequently, the scope of the contract was extended to include development of robotic welding procedures, of which use was made in the MIL Intermodal production line.
5. The extensive design phase had shown there would be a major price increase from the original figures.
6. The MIL Group had bought an interest in M. & M. in 1988. The work was done at Davie between 3 August and 2 September 1994.
7. *MIL Davie Info.*, vol. 6: 3 August 1993.
8. The company had undergone a change of name from St. John Shipbuilding and Dry Dock Limited on 1 September 1984.
9. Groupe MIL Inc. vs. Saint John Shipbuilding Limited *et al.*, C.S. BR 0122 ND MC6322/02.
10. The TRUMP program was announced by the government in July 1983. Contract Definition Contract between Litton Systems Canada Ltd. and Davie signed July 1984. Prime Contract executed by Litton and government on 6 June 1986 and dated 9 May 1986. Implementation Contract between Litton and Davie signed 1 August 1986. New equipment was to include a single funnel, a vertical launch standard missile system, an integrated machinery control system to constitute the BRAIN of the ship, long-range and medium-range radars and a water displacement fuel system. A 76-mm Oto Molara gun was to replace the 5-inch 54-calibre radar-controlled gun, and a PHalanx close-in weapon system, the Canadian Sea Sparrow system. For propulsion there were Allison 570KF 6,400-h.p. gas turbines. Electronic warfare equipment was updated through the new CANEWS system and shields. DND, *Backgrounder Documentation*, "Tribal Class Update and Modernization Project (TRUMP)," May 1989; Litton Systems Canada Limited, *Tribal Class Update and Modernization Project*, Executive Summary, February 1985; Martin Shadwick, "Tribal Update and Modernization Program," *A Salute to Canada's Navy*, 69; "Shipbuilding and Defence," *Seaports and the Shipping World*, May 1989, 39.
11. Though it had the expertise, Davie had not been able to bid as Prime Contractor due to Dome's weak financial position.
12. Véronneau released Ayre from Marketing and put him in charge of the TRUMP program for eighteen months, specifically to help solve the problems.
13. Contract signed in March 1989.

CHAPTER 25
1. Prior to 1987, it had operated out of Tracy, as Marine Industries' Offshore Sector.
2. Tessier became president of GEC Alsthom, Electromécanique, at Tracy.
3. Manufactured by the International Paint Company, Inerta hardens like glass and stands up as no other coating does to the ice conditions that the ships encounter.
4. OPA 90 regulations (Oil Pollution Act 1990, U.S. Government) impose severe pollution liabilities on owners and require that all tankers entering U.S. waters have

double-hulls and segregated ballast. International Maritime Organization (IMO) has introduced similar regulations which, when enacted and adopted by members, will require all the world's tanker fleet to be double-hulled or have equal design characteristics.
5. Of nine potential Asian and European partners.
6. BWS tried to maintain liquidity by raising funds in Denmark and the United States, while selling off its shipholdings at a loss. On 3 October 1994, in a general shakeup, Cato Sverdrup resigned as managing director and board member of B & W Holding A/S. Unable to come to a restructuring agreement with its creditors, BWS went into voluntary liquidation in June 1995. In October 1995, Burmeister & Wain Ship Design A/S, the consulting arm of BWS, was separated from the shipyard. Its new senior management acquired all of its shares in collaboration with Cato Sverdrup, the former president of BWS.
7. A member of the Thyssen Group, one of Germany's major industrial and trading corporations, with 135,000 employees in its more than 300 companies in West Germany, the United States, and many other countries.
8. SGF press release, 5 May 1994.

BIBLIOGRAPHY

PRINCIPAL MANUSCRIPT SOURCES

1. CANADA
Archives civiles du Québec à Québec(ACQ)
    Notarial records (1838-1933)
    Parish records (1875-1910)
Archives nationales du Québec à Montréal (ANQM)
    Notarial records CN 601
Archives nationales du Québec à Québec (ANQ)
    Court records – Superior Court (1811-80) T 0011
    Notarial records (1811-94) CN 301
    Parish registers (1811-75) CEO 301
    Port of Quebec
        Bureau Veritas Letter Book (1883-1905) F0002 16
        Lloyd's Agency Registers (1856-89) F0002
        Register of Ship Mortgages (1857-76)
        Port Wardens' Report Books (1872-1907) F0002 1-5, 7, 13
        Quebec Exchange Daily Reports (1832-33) F0002 14, 21
        Trinity House Meetings Book (1818-21) F0002 21
        Surveyors' records (1760-1917) CA 301
Archives du Port de Québec (APQ)
    Trinity House Letter Books, 1 and 2 (1804-16)
    Trinity House Minute Books (1804-12)
    Maps
Archives de la Ville de Québec (AVQ)
    Chemins Surveyor's reports and plans QD4
    Juges de Paix – Sessions of the Peace (1814-33; 1836-40) B4
Canada Steamship Lines – Internal records and correspondence
Marine Museum of the Great Lakes at Kingston (MMGLK) – Canada Steamship Lines Collection
Mount Hermon Cemetery Records, Sillery, Quebec

BIBLIOGRAPHY

National Archives of Canada, Ottawa (NA)
    Admiralty papers MG 12
    Census returns for Quebec RG 31
    Lower Canada Land Papers RG 1, L 3L
    Lower Canada Marriage Bonds RG 4, B 28
    Military C-series RG8
    Public Works Department RG 11
    Department of Transport RG 12
    Registers of the Port of Quebec RG 12
    Shipbuilding Policy RG 19
    Borden Papers Home Bank MG 28
    National Defence – Navy RG 24
    Munitions and Supply RG 28
    Statistics – Census RG 31
    Marine Branch RG 42
    Railways and Canals RG 43
    St. Lawrence Seaway Authority RG 52
Queen's University, Kingston – Canada Steamship Lines Collection
Registrar for Shipping, Quebec – Registers of the Port of Quebec
Registry Office, Levis – Registered land deeds
Rowan, Frank – Personal papers

2. UNITED KINGDOM
National Maritime Museum, Greenwich
    Lloyd's Survey Reports for Quebec (1852-80)
Public Record Office, Kew, England
    ADMIRALTY
    Records of Naval Yards (1813-16):
    Lake Champlain ADM 37/5000-5001, 42/2167, 2170, 2174, 38/2294
    Lake Erie ADM 42/2167, 2170, 2173-4, 2177-78, 2180-81
    Lake Ontario ADM 37/5000-5002, 32/254, 42/2167, 2169-70, 2172, 2174-2175, 2177-2181
    Letters to and from Admiralty ADM 106/1997, 106/3179 (1814-1816)

REFERENCE WORKS

Beeson's Marine Directory of the Northwestern Lakes: Season of Navigation 1913. Chicago: Harvey C. Beeson, 1913.

Cochrane, William. *The Canadian Album: Men of Canada 1831-1898*, 5 vols. Brantford, Ontario: Ganetson Bradley, 1891-96.

The Canadian Annual Review of Public Affairs. Toronto; [1902-1925].

The Dictionary of Canadian Biography, vols. I-XIII. Toronto: University of Toronto Press, 1967-94.

Lloyd's Register of British and Foreign Shipping 1834 to 1920. London: Lloyd's Register of British and Foreign Shipping. London: J.L. Cox and Son, J. & H. Cox, brothers, Cox & Wyman, [and probably others].

Muir, Allan Thomas (ed.) Originally compiled by the late Frederick William Wallace. *The Canadian Ports and Shipping Directory, including the St. Lawrence Seaway System and United States Ports on the Great Lakes.* Gardenvale, Quebec: National Business Publications Limited, 1960.

The Register of Shipping for the year 18.. (1821-1833). London: Society for the Registry of Shipping.

Trudel, Marcel. *Le terrier du Saint-Laurent en 1663.* Ottawa: Editions de l'Université d'Ottawa, 1973.

Who's Who in Canada, Including the British Possessions in the Western Hemisphere. Toronto: International Press, 1922.

ROYAL CANADIAN NAVY/ROYAL NAVY

Bélanger, Diane. *La construction navale à Saint-Laurent, Ile d'Orléans.* Saint-Laurent, Ile d'Orléans: Bibliothèque David Gosselin, 1984.

British Admiralty Technical Mission (Smith, F.M.). "History of the British Admiralty Technical Mission in Canada." BATM: Ottawa, 1946.

Douglas, W.A.B. "Grant Macdonald's Navy." *Freshwater*, 6:1, 1991.

—— *Gunfire on the Lakes.* Ottawa: National Museum of Man, 1977.

—— (ed.) *The RCN in Transition 1910-1985.* Vancouver: University of British Columbia, 1988.

Lambert, John. *The Fairmile "D" Motor Torpedo Boat.* London: Conway Maritime Press, 1985.

Lawrence, Hal. *Victory at Sea.* Toronto: McClelland & Stewart, 1989.

Lynch, Thomas G. *Canada's Flowers: History of the Corvettes of Canada 1939-1945.* Halifax: Nimbus, 1981.

MacDonald, Ian, and Len Tabner. *Smith's Dock: Shipbuilders 1908-1987.* Great Britain: Seaworks (Limited Edition), 1986.

McKee, Fraser. *The Armed Yachts of Canada.* Erin, Ontario: Boston Mills, 1983.

Macpherson, Ken. *Frigates of the Royal Canadian Navy 1943-1974.* St. Catharines, Ontario: Vanwell, 1988.

—— *Minesweepers of the Royal Canadian Navy 1938-1945.* St. Catharines, Ontario: Vanwell, 1990.

—— *River Class Destroyers of the Royal Canadian Navy.* Toronto: Charles J. Musson, 1985.

Macpherson, Ken, and John Burgess. *The Ships of Canada's Naval Forces 1910-1985*, 2nd edition. Toronto: Collins, 1985.

Niven, John, Courtlandt Canby, and Vernon Welsh. *Dynamic America.* New York: Doubleday, 1958.

Perkins, Dave. *Canada's Submariners 1914-1923.* Boston Mills, Ontario: Erin, 1989.

Shadwick, Martin. "Tribal Update and Modernization Programme," *A Salute to Canada's Navy, Canadian Defence Quarterly*, December 1985-January 1986, 69.
Smith, F.M. "History of the British Admiralty Technical Mission in Canada."
Swanson, Bill. "Elco," *Nautical Quarterly*, (Essex, Connecticut), Summer 1985, 19-29.
Tucker, Gilbert Norman. *The Naval Service of Canada*, 2 vols. Ottawa: King's Printer, 1952.
Vat, Dan van der. *The Atlantic Campaign: The Great Struggle at Sea 1939-1945*. London: Hodder & Stoughton, 1988.
Ward, Peter. "DEs Get Long Range A/S Punch," *Canadian Shipping and Marine Engineering News*, March 1964, 79-80.

DEPARTMENT OF TRANSPORT/COAST GUARD

Appleton, Thomas. "Early Marine Services in Canada," *Canadian Shipping and Marine Engineering News*, August 1969, 64-67.
—— "The Growing Role of Our Coast Guard," *Canadian Shipping and Marine Engineering News*, August 1972, 19-21.
—— "Lifeboats: How Search-and-Rescue Began in Canada," *Canadian Shipping and Marine Engineering News*, August 1974, 16-18.
Canadian Shipping. "DOT Operates Vast Fleet: Marine Superintendent's Branch Handles Floating Equipment Which Makes It Country's Most Diversified Single Owner," *Canadian Shipping*, August 1954, 48-49, 68.
—— "Nascopie's Successor Is Sturdy Ship," *Canadian Shipping*, January, 1948, 20-21, 32.
Canadian Shipping and Marine Engineering News. "Another Summer – Another Arctic Tour," *Canadian Shipping and Marine Engineering News*, August 1965, 68-69.
—— "Arctic Test Voyage," *Canadian Shipping and Marine Engineering News*, August 1969, 48-9.
—— "Arctic Undertakings Since 1953," and "Davieship Gets Order for New Icebreaker," *Canadian Shipping and Marine Engineering News*, August 1965, 70.
—— "The CGS *Arctica* Is Completed," *Canadian Shipping and Marine Engineering News*, September 1964, 24-25.
—— "Chaperones to 2,400 Vessels," *Canadian Shipping and Marine Engineering News*, August 1972, 29.
—— "Davie Shipbuilding Gets $5.2 Mill Order," *Canadian Shipping and Marine Engineering News*, April 1965, 39.
—— "DOT and Coast Guard Vessels as of August 1962," *Canadian Shipping and Marine Engineering News*, August 1962, 72-75.
—— "DOT's Expo '67 Exhibit Will Show Coast Guard's Role in Ice Breaking," *Canadian Shipping and Marine Engineering News*, August 1965, 103.
—— "Farthest North Record Is Set," *Canadian Shipping and Marine Engineering News*, January 1962, 22-25.
—— "How the Icebreakers Are Built," *Canadian Shipping and Marine Engineering News*, August 1966, 74-75.

BIBLIOGRAPHY

——— "Icebreaker Fleet Works Around the Clock," *Canadian Shipping and Marine Engineering News*, March 1965, 93.
——— "Ice Problems Were Few," *Canadian Shipping and Marine Engineering News*, August 1964, 72-73."
——— "In all Canada's Waters – There Is the CCG," *Canadian Shipping and Marine Engineering News*, August 1964, 52-53.
——— "Is the St. Lawrence a Graveyard?" *Canadian Shipping and Marine Engineering News*, December 1965, 168-169.
——— "New Coast Guard Ship Is Launched by Allied Shipbuilders Ltd." *Canadian Shipping and Marine Engineering News*, March 1964, 57.
——— "New Icebreaker Is Launched: Powerful Addition to Canada's Arctic Service Fleet Will Be Able to Stay Full Season in Arctic Without New Supplies," *Canadian Shipping and Marine Engineering News*, November 1959, 29, 46.
——— "'New Look' in Coast Guard Fleet," *Canadian Shipping and Marine Engineering News*, August 1962, 50-53.
——— "Saurel Retirement Stirs Memories of Early Exploits of Coast Guard," *Canadian Shipping and Marine Engineering News*, August 1967, 63.
——— "Shipbuilding Program Moves Ahead," *Canadian Shipping and Marine Engineering News*, August 1967, 62-63.
——— "Ship Registration Fees are Upped by D.O.T.," *Canadian Shipping and Marine Engineering News*, January 1969, 25.
——— "Thomas Appleton, *Usque ad Mare*," *Canadian Shipping and Marine Engineering News*, August, 1969, 67.
——— "Triple Screw Icebreaker in Service," *Canadian Shipping and Marine Engineering News*, August 1969, 50-52.
——— "Two Centuries of Lights at Sea," *Canadian Shipping and Marine Engineering News*, August 1965, 56-57.
——— "Vital Statistics of the Coast Guard Fleet," *Canadian Shipping and Marine Engineering News*, August 1972, 22-28.
Cutler, Maurice. "Arctic Operations," *Canadian Shipping and Marine Engineering News*, August 1971, 31-2.
Department of Transport. "SS *C.D. Howe*, Eastern Arctic Patrol Ship." Typewritten Brochure
Franck, Alain. *Le Ernest Lapointe: Brise-Glace du Saint-Laurent.* L'Islet-sur-mer, Musée Maritime Bernier, 1995.
Haglund, M.G. "Shipping and the Mysterious Arctic," *Canadian Shipping and Marine Engineering News*, August, 1974, 31-32.
Massue, Huet. "All-winter Navigation Is Predicted," *Canadian Shipping and Marine Engineering News*, April 1962, 30-1, 49.
Plummer, Harry C. "Maiden Voyage in North: SS *C.D. Howe* Is Latest Addition to D.O.T. Service Fleet – Superpowerful, Multipurpose Vessel Carries Arctic Supplies," *Canadian Shipping*, August 1950, 21-22.

Snider, Rob (co-ordinator). "The Canadian Coast Guard," *A History of Canadian Marine Technology*. Ottawa: Eastern Canadian Section of the Society of Naval Architects and Marine Engineers, 1995.

Wade, George. "Ice Breaking," *Canadian Shipping and Marine Engineering News*, August 1974, 19-20.

GENERAL

Alcan. "All-welded Superstructure," *The Alcan Ingot*. December 1954, XIII:4-5.

Andrieux, J.P. *East Coast Panorama: The History of Shipping Companies on Canada's East Coast from 1900 Onward*. Lincoln, Ontario: W.F. Rannie, 1984.

Ashdown, Dana. *Railway Steamships of Ontario*. Erin, Ontario: Boston Mills, 1988.

Bernier, J.E. *Master Mariner and Arctic Explorer*. Ottawa: Le Droit, 1939.

Brisson, Réal. *La charpenterie navale à Quebec sous le régime français*. Quebec: Institut québécois de recherche sur la culture, 1983, 217-43.

Brookes, Ivan. *The Lower Saint Lawrence*. Cleveland: Freshwater Press, 1974.

Burton, Anthony. *The Rise and Fall of British Shipbuilding*. London: Constable, 1994.

Cameron, Silver Donald. *Iceboats to Superferries: An Illustrated History of Marine Atlantic*. St. John's, Newfoundland: Breakwater, 1992.

Campbell, Duncan. *The Story of ALCAN*. Montreal: ALCAN, 1990.

Canada. "The History of Dredges and Dredging." *Sessional Paper No. 21, Appendix No. 3, 3 Geo. V., A. 1913*.

Canadian Machinery and Plant Manufacturing News. "The Shipbuilding Plant of G.T. Davie and Sons, Levis, P.Q.," *Canadian Machinery and Plant Manufacturing News*, 10:9 215, 28 August 1913, 215.

Canadian Railway and Marine World. "Marine Department: Steel Cargo Building for Dominion Governments," *Canadian Railway and Marine World*, October 1918, 562-63.

Canadian Shipping. "France Gets Three More," *Canadian Shipping*, July 1949, 13-14.

Carnegie, David. *The History of Munitions Supply in Canada*. London: 1925.

Caya, Marcel. "Henry Caldwell," *Dictionary of Canadian Biography*, vol. 5. Toronto: University of Toronto Press, 1983.

Collard, Edgar Andrew. *Passage to the Sea: The Story of Canada Steamship Lines*. Toronto: Doubleday, 1991.

CSN. *35 ans de lutte au chantier*.

de Rocquefeuil, "Byssot (Bissot) de la Rivière, François," *Dictionary of Canadian Biography*, vol.1. Toronto and Quebec: University of Toronto Press, 1967.

Dougan, David. *The History of North East Shipbuilding*. London: George Allen & Unwin, 1968.

Dubé, Philippe. *Charlevoix: Two Centuries at Murray Bay*. Montreal: McGill-Queen's University Press, 1990.

Flage, A.C. *History of Shipbuilding*, Section IX "Simon Temple and His Son."

Gillham, Skip. *The Ships of Collingwood: Over One Hundred Years of Shipbuilding Excellence*. St. Catharines, Ontario: Riverbank Traders, 1992.
—— *The Ships of Port Weller*. St. Catharines, Ontario: Riverbank Traders, 1992.
Gillham, Skip, and Alfred Sagon-King. *Canadian Fleets Along the Seaway*. St. Catharines, Ontario: Stonehouse, 1989.
Hamilton, George. *A History of the House of Hamilton*.
Hannington, Felicity. *The Lady Boats*. Halifax: Canadian Marine Transportation Centre, 1980.
Harrington, Michael F. "The Gulf and Coastal Service," *Iceboats to Superferries: An Illustrated History of Marine Atlantic*. St. John's: Breakwater, 1992.
Haws, George W. *The Haws Family and Their Seafaring Kin*. Dunfermline: N.P., 1932.
Heaton, Herbert. *Economic History of Europe*. New York: Harper & Row, 1948.
Héroux, Andrée. "Caldwell, Sir John," *Dictionary of Canadian Biography*, vol. 7. Toronto: University of Toronto Press, 1988.
Hill, John C.G. *Shipshape and Bristol Fashion*. Bristol: Redcliffe, 1951.
Holland, A.J. *Ships of British Oak*. Newton Abbot: David & Charles, 1971.
Huot, L.H. *Annuaire du commerce et de l'industrie de Quebec, contenant l'histoire de Quebec, un essai sur la vallée de l'Outaouais, le commerce du Canada et beaucoup d'autres renseignements, pour 1873*. Quebec: L.H. Huot, 1873.
Hurd, Archibald. *The Merchant Navy*, II. London: John Murray, 1924.
Hutchins, John G.B. *The American Maritime Industries and Public Policy 1789-1914*. Cambridge, Massachussets: Harvard University Press, 1941.
Johnston, Ian. *Beardmore Built: The Rise and Fall of a Clydeside Shipyard*. Clydebank, Scotland: Clydebank District Libraries & Museum Department, 1993.
Lambert, Walter, and Horace German. *Floating Equipment Designed by Lambert and German*. Montreal: Lambert & German, 1932.
Lesstrang, Jacques. *Cargo Carriers of the Great Lakes*. Boyne City, Michigan: Harbor House Publishers, 1985.
Lyon, Jim. *Dome: The Rise and Fall of the House that Jack Built*. Toronto: Macmillan of Canada, 1983.
Marcil, Eileen Reid. *The Charley-Man: A History of Wooden Shipbuilding at Quebec 1763-1893*. Kingston, Ontario: Quarry Press, 1995.
—— "Goudie, John," vol. VI, 1987; "Munn, John," vol. VIII, 1985; "Wood, Charles," vol. VII, 1988; "Davie, George Taylor," vol. XIII, 1994. *Dictionary of Canadian Biography*. Toronto: University of Toronto Press.
—— "Ship-Rigged Rafts and the Export of Quebec Timber," *The American Neptune*, Spring 1988, XLVIII:2, 77-86.
—— "Wooden Floating Docks in the Port of Quebec from 1827 until the 1930s," *Mariner's Mirror*, 81:4 (November 1995), 448-56.
Mathieu, Jacques. *La construction navale royale à Quebec 1739-1759*. Cahiers d'histoire 23. Quebec: Société historique de Quebec, 1971.

BIBLIOGRAPHY

―― "Levasseur, René Nicolas." *Dictionary of Canadian Biography*, vol. IV. Toronto: University of Toronto Press, 1979.

McBeath, George, and Donald F. Taylor. *Steamboat Days on the St. John 1816-1946*. St. Stephen, New Brunswick: Print N'Press, 1982.

McDougall, J. Lorne. *Canadian Pacific: A Brief History*. Montreal: McGill University Press, 1968.

McDowall, Duncan. *The Light*. Toronto: University of Toronto Press, 1988.

McKenzie, Kenneth. "Steam Operations on the St. Lawrence to 1914 – The Quebec City Graving Dock," *Seaports and the Shipping World*, January 1987.

Mills, John M. *Canadian Coastal and Inland Steam Vessels 1809-1930*. Providence, R.I.: Steamship Historical Society of America, 1979.

Misener, *The Great Lakes/Seaway: Setting a Course for the 80s*. Toronto: Ontario Government, 1981.

Mitchell, W.H., and L.A. Sawyer. *British Standard Ships of World War I, Wartime Standard Ships*, 3:ix-xi, 141-156. Liverpool: Sea Breezes, 1968.

Moss, Michael, and John R. Hume. *Shipbuilders to the World: 125 Years of Harland and Wolff, Belfast 1861-1986*. Belfast: Blackstaff, 1986.

Musk, George. *Canadian Pacific Afloat, 1883-1968: A Short History and Fleet List 1883-1968*. London: Canadian Pacific, 1968.

Nicholson, Tim. *Take the Strain: Alexandra Towing*. Liverpool: The Alexandra Towing Co., Ltd., 1990.

Pilkington, Woodford. *On Methods Adopted in Carrying out Dock and Harbour Works at Quebec with Descriptions of Plant Employed*. London: Institution of Civil Engineers, 1899.

Proulx, Georges-Etienne. "Déziel, Joseph-David," *Dictionary of Canadian Biography*, vol. XI. Toronto: University of Toronto Press.

Richardson, A.J.H. *Quebec City: Architects, Artisans and Builders*. Ottawa: History Division, National Museum of Man, 1984.

Ritchie, L.A. (ed.) *The Shipbuilding Industry: A Guide to Historical Records*. Manchester: Manchester University Press, 1992.

Roy, Emery. *Centenaire de Levis 1861-1961*. Levis, Quebec: The author, 1961.

Roy, J. Edmond. *Histoire de la Seigneurie de Lauzon*. 5 vols. Levis: The author, 1904.

Roy, Pierre-Georges. *Les Bateaux Traversiers*.

―― *La Chambre de Commerce de Levis 1872-1947*. Levis: Le Quotidien, 1947.

―― *Dates lévisiennes*. 6 volumes. Levis: 1932-1934.

―― *Profils lévisiens*. 2 volumes. Levis: 1948.

Samson, Roch (dir.), Andrée Héroux, Diane Saint-Pierre, and Martine Côté. *Histoire de Levis-Lotbinière*. Quebec: Les presses de l'université Laval, 1996.

Scott, John Dick. *Vickers*. London: Weidenfeld and Nicolson, 1963.

Skelton, Jim. *Speybuilt: The Story of a Forgotten Industry*. Mrs. W. Skelton [Moray, Innes Road, Garmouth, Morayshire. IV32 7NL], 1994.

Slaven, Anthony. "A Guide to Modern British Shipbuilding, 1800-1990," *The Shipbuilding Industry: A Guide to Historical Records*, L.A. Ritchie (ed.). Manchester: Manchester University Press, 1992.

Smith, Edgar C. *A Short History of Naval and Marine Engineering.* Cambridge: University Press, 1937.

Snow, Ralph Linwood. *Bath Iron Works: The First Hundred Years.* Portland, Maine: Anthoesen Press, 1987.

Spratt, H. Philip. *Transatlantic Paddle Steamers.* Glasgow: Brown, Son & Ferguson, 1967 (2nd edition).

Sykes, Al, and Skip Gillham. *Pulp and Paper Fleet: A History of the Quebec and Ontario Transportation Company.* St. Catharines, Ontario: Stonehouse, 1988.

Talbot, Allen (ed.) *Five Years Residence in the Canadas.* London: Longman, Hurst, Rees, Orme, Brown and Creen, 1824.

Taylor, G.W. *The Shipyards of British Columbia.* Victoria, British Columbia: Morriss, 1986.

Taylor, Graham D. *Vickers in Canada 1911-1927: The Reluctant Multinational.*

Tazewell, William L. *Newport News Shipbuilding: The First Century.* Newport News, Virginia: Mariners' Museum, 1986.

Terrien, Paul. *Quebec à l'âge de la voile.* Hull, Quebec: Éditions Asticou, 1985.

Thomas, Lowell. *The St. Lawrence Seaway Story.* Buffalo: H. Stewart, 1957.

Valiquet, U. "Champlain Dry Dock for Quebec Harbor," *Canadian Railway and Marine World*, June 1918, 269-73.

Walker, Fred M. *Steel Shipbuilding.* Aylesbury, Bucks.: Shire Publications Ltd., 1981.

Wallace, Frederick William. *In the Wake of the Windships.* Toronto: Musson, 1927.

—— *Record of Canadian Shipping.* Toronto: Musson, 1929.

—— *Wooden Ships and Iron Men.* London: Hodder and Stoughton, 1924.

Weeks, Ezra. *A Statement in Relation to the Concerns of the New-York Dry Dock Company.* New York: N.P., 1825.

Westwood, Roger, Keith Farrell, and Abigail Fyfe (eds.). *A History of Canadian Marine Technology.* Ottawa: The Eastern Canadian Section, the Society of Naval Architects and Marine Engineers, 1995.

Wilson, Garth. *A History of Shipbuilding and Naval Architecture in Canada.* Ottawa: National Museum of Science and Technology, 1994.

Woodcock, Robert. *Side Launch: The Collingwood Shipyard Spectacle.* Toronto: Summerhill Press, 1983.

Wright, Esther Clark. *Saint John Ships and Their Builders.* Wolfville, Nova Scotia: The Author, 1976.

NEWSPAPERS

Le Canadien, Courrier du Canada, L'Evènement, Montreal Gazette, Montreal Star, Morning Chronicle, Quebec Chronicle, Quebec Gazette, Quebec Mercury, Quebec Official Gazette, Le Quotidien

GLOSSARY

barque a three-masted sailing ship that is square-rigged on the foremast and the mainmast, and fore-and-aft rigged on the mizzen

barquentine a three-masted sailing ship that is square-rigged only on the foremast

beam 1) the breadth of a ship; 2) a heavy timber fixed across the width of a ship to strengthen the frame, which generally supports a deck

block-maker a craftsman who makes sheaves and pulleys

boiler maker the worker who built, assembled and/or repaired boilers, and in later times formed the steelwork of a ship

bolter the worker who laid up the structural members and placed the bolts when ships were riveted

bow the forward end of the ship

bridge the superstructure on a ship from which it is steered or controlled

brig a two-masted sailing ship that is square-rigged on both masts

bulwark a safety wall at the sides of exposed decks

burner the mechanism that delivers oil and air in a furnace or boiler for combustion

capstan a machine for moving or raising heavy weights that consists of a vertical drum which can be rotated, usually manually, and around which cable or rope is turned

careen to heel a ship over on her side so that her bottom can be cleaned or repaired

caulk to force oakum (made from old rope) between the planks of a ship and seal it with pitch so as to make it watertight

chain plate the metal plates attached to the side of a sailing ship, to which the dead eyes holding the shrouds are attached

chipper a man or boy who chips the scale off the inside of a boiler

clinker built with overlapping planks fixed like the clapboard of a house

craneman the operator of a crane

deck the decks of a ship are the equivalent of the floors in a house

dock a basin with facilities for loading and unloading where ships can lie afloat at wharf or quay

drogher a large cumbersome cargo ship

dry dock a usually artificial basin or enclosure for the reception of ships that is equipped with means for controlling the water height

erector a worker who puts the parts of a ship together and secures them in their place

GLOSSARY

floor a vertical plate extending from side to side at the bottom of an iron or steel ship

fore foot foremost piece of a keel, also known as the gripe

forecastle the short deckhouse above the upper deck at the bow

furnaceman the worker who heats handles and bevels frame bars and fashion plates when they come out of the furnace

futtocks the timbers of the frame between the floor timbers and the top timbers

gate vessel vessel designed to tend the anti-submarine barriers in a harbour

graving dock a dry dock used for repairing vessels

grid iron heavy timber grid fixed on a beach

hawser a heavy rope made either from fibre, nylon, polypropylene, or steel

horsepower:
   h.p. (Horsepower) the unit of measurement for the power of motors or engines – 1 h.p. is required to raise 33,000 pounds one foot per minute
   b.h.p. (Brake horsepower) the effective horsepower given out by an engine
   i.h.p. (Indicated horsepower) the power developed by the cylinders of an engine
   s.h.p. (Shaft horsepower) power at the propeller

iron caulker a worker who caulks riveted seams on steel ships

jackstay a rope or rod that runs up and down a ship's mast, or along a yard

joiner a carpenter who takes over from the framer after the ship is in frame and does the rest of the carpentry

keel the backbone of a ship at the bottom

keelson a vertical structure above the keel providing further strength

knee an L-shaped timber, often taken from the trunk and root of a tree used as a bracket to join timbers lying in different planes

loftsman a craftsman who lays down the lines of a vessel in a mould loft, and makes templates from them

loop layer a small naval vessel used for laying submarine nets

marine railway the equipment used to haul a ship out of the water on rails up an inclined plane, and on which it slides back into the water

master shipbuilder a master shipwright who owns and operates his own shipyard, or in certain cases someone else's

mould loft a large clear space used for laying down the full-size lines of a vessel and for making templates from them

pattern maker a craftsman who makes a full-size model of a part for making a mould into which molten metal is poured to form a casting

pier a heavy structure that juts into the water for ships to come alongside for mooring

pipefitter one who installs pipes or fits them together

planking wooden covering on the outside of a ship's frame

plate erector (same as bolter) see also erector

platform (in ship repair) a temporary floor in a hold that seals off a damaged area

plating external layer of steel plates on a hull

GLOSSARY

poop a short superstructure above the afterpart of the weather deck

poppet a wooden support structure used in launching, fitted between the launchway and the ship

rail the safety rail at the sides and ends of exposed decks; tracks for cranes or trains, such as in the ferry MV *Frederick Carter*, Hull 660

rigger the man who assembles and installs a ship's rigging

riveter the man, or the machine, that flattens rivets

rudder the steering device of a boat or ship

schooner (or goëlette) a fore-and-aft rigged sailing ship with two or more masts

ship carpenter formerly: one who could build the hull of a ship, now: the man who sets the blocks, shores, etc. on the berth prior to launch

ship's carpenter a carpenter employed aboard ship

ship railway see marine railway

shipwright a skilled all-round ship carpenter

slinger a longshoreman who fastens the sling around the load and attaches it to the winch fall

slip an incline between two wharves

slipway (building slip or berth) an inclined space in a shipyard used for building and launching a ship

square-rigged 1) a ship with sails that are set from yards that lie square to one or more of its masts; 2) a mast that is rigged that way

stager a scaffolder

stanchion upright wood or iron support under a deck beam

steam-box house a shed in which a fire is used to produce steam for the steam box

steam box a box in which planks are steamed to make them pliable

steamer steamboat or steamship

steel plater one who works with steel plates

stem the curved piece of timber at the foremost part of a ship's hull, also the fore end of a ship

stern the straight piece of timber at the aftermost part of the ship's hull, also the after end of a ship

timber cove a beach property which serves for sorting, storing, and unloading and loading timber

tramp steamer a steamer that does not operate on a fixed schedule

transom the upper part of the stern of a ship which has a square stern

transom stern the vertical or almost vertical transverse timbers in a square-sterned ship connected to and placed square with the sternpost

tug a small but sturdy mechanically propelled vessel for towing or assisting other vessels

ways (to slide down the) to slide down a heavily-greased frame (the launching ways) leading into the water

wharf a landing platform for cargos

windlass used aboard ship for hoisting the anchor

INDEX OF SHIPS

Numbers in italics refer to photograph captions.

A.C.D., barge, *204*
A.S. Glossbrenner, bulk freighter, 321
Acadia Albatross, trawler, 327
Accommodation, paddle steamer, 60
Alert, search and rescue vessel, *341*, 342, 360
Algol, U.S. naval ship, 420
Algonquin, destroyer, 300, *301*, 395, 465-66, *467*, 468
Alphonse Desjardins, ferry, 381, *382*
Andros Fortune, tanker, 305
Andros Venture, tanker, 305, *306*
Anomia, sailing ship, 10
Arctic, winter ferry, 129, 178
Arctica, bait-boat, 344
Armand Imbeau, ferry, 479
Aspa Quarto, see Cormorant
Assiniboia, steamer, 119
Assiniboine, destroyer, 222
Athabaskan, destroyer, 379, *380*, 465-66, 468
Athel Monarch, tanker, *408*, *409*, 410
Athel Queen, tanker, 409
Aurora, cruiser, 218
Aviso Bouvet, steamer, 102

Baddeck, corvette, 229-30
Baie Saint Paul, bulk freighter, 321-22
Banff Park, merchant steamer, 232
Baron of Renfrew, sailing ship, 6
Bassin, trawler, 395

Batavian, steamer, 121
Bavarian, steamer, 113
Beavercliffe Hall, bulk freighter, 321
Beyla, cargo carrier, 271, *272*
Bilma, cargo carrier, 271
Biscayne Freeze, see Blue Cloud
Blue Cloud, fish carrier, 327, *329*
Blue Peter II, fish carrier, 327
Bluenose, car ferry, 298, 309-10, *311*
Boffa, cargo carrier, 271
Bonaventure, aircraft carrier, 336, *337*, 361, 363-64
Bonniton, sailing ship, 80
Bouga, cargo carrier, 271
Brandon, corvette, 229
Bratsberg, sailing ship, *76*
Britannia, royal yacht, 319
Brockville, minesweeper, 231
Brunelle, sailing ship, 10
Buckingham, frigate, 236
Buctouche, corvette, 229
Bulk Gold, see Grainmotor
Busy Bee, tugboat, 175, *176*, 310-11

C.D. Howe, arctic patrol ship, 275, *276*, 277, 279, 302
Cabot, package freighter, 324, *325*, 479
Caledonia, steamboat, 60
Calgary, frigate, 462, 464-65
Calista Haws, sailing ship, 73
Canadian Challenger, steamer, 174, 178

INDEX OF SHIPS

Canadian Challenger, motor cargo vessel, 242, 269, *270*, *271*, 306
Canadian Hunter, steamer, *166*, 169-70, 174
Canadian Trapper, steamer, 169-70, *170*, 174
Canmar Victory, 478
Canopus, steamer, 103
Canora, ferry, 154, *157*
Canteleu, cargo carrier, 272-73
Cap de la Madeleine, frigate, 300
Cape Scott, destroyer escort, 379
Car of Commerce, steamboat, 60
Caribou, ferry, *424*, 429, 431, *432*, 434, 436, 439-40, 448, 453, 455
Carl Vinson, aircraft carrier, *391*
Carlplace, frigate, 236-38
Carolina, steamer, 113, *116*
Cartier, 178
Cartiercliffe Hall, freighter, 409, *410*
Cartierdoc, see Montcliffe Hall
Catherine Legardeur, ferry, *431*
Cathie McAllister, see Charlie S.
Caumont, cargo carrier, 272-73
CC1, submarine, 219
CC2, submarine, 219
Challenger, tugboat, 86-87, 104, *106*
Champion, paddle steamer, *110*, 111
Champlain, 159
Champlain, destroyer, 220-21
Charlie S., tugboat, 311, 327
Charlottetown, car ferry, 195-96, *197*, *198*, 200
Chateau, tugboat, 310-11, 327, 329, *331*
Chemical Transport, tanker, 376, *377*
Chesterfield, buoy tender, 343
Chimo, package freighter, 324-25
Chippewa Park, merchant steamer, 233
Citadel, screw tug and fire boat, 197
Cité, paddle steamer, 84
Cité des Trois Rivières, see Lauzon, summer ferry

City of Kingston, freighter, 188, *190*
City of Toronto, freighter, 188
City of Windsor, package freighter, 191
Ciudad de Habana, see Canadian Challenger
Coaticook, frigate, 236, 238
Collingwood, corvette, 228
Colomb, winter ferry, 128, *129*, 200
Columbus, timber drogher, 6, *7*, 61, 504
Comet, barque, 72
Comet, destroyer, 221
Coniscliffe Hall, freighter, 308
Constantia, barque, 32
Coosie, steel winding tug, 187, *189*
Cormorant, diving tender, 420, *421*
Corrib, brig, 43
Covadonga, see Sea Cliff
Cowichan, minesweeper, 279, 300
Crescent, destroyer, 221
Croisset, cargo carrier, 272-73, *274*
Crusader, destroyer, 221
Cygnet, destroyer, 221
Cygnus, see Melville
Cynthia, steamer, 102-3, *104*

Dakar, collier, 272
Daluarnic, steamer, *239*
Dartmouth, ferry, 197, 199
David K. Gardiner, see Lawrencecliffe Hall
Daylesford, 68-69, *70*
De Vallier, steamer, *239*
Deddington, tramp steamer, 103
d'Iberville, icebreaker, 280, 302-4, 319, 340
Digby, minesweeper, 230-31
Donald P. tugboat, 393
Donpaco No. 4, barge, 204
Draug, see Penetang
Dunver, steamer, 240

Efthalia, see Baddeck

Elizabeth, barque, 70
Emerillon, tanker, 323-24
Empress of Britain, liner, 113
Empress of France, liner, *176*
Empress of Ireland, liner, 113
Erable No.1, 428
Ernest Lapointe, icebreaker, 200, 240
Eskimo, coaster, 343, 356
Ethelred, sailing ship, 71
Evi, see Baddeck
Explorer II, see Busy Bee

Fatima, trawler, 395
Federal Monarch, tanker, 323, *324*
Findlay, brig, 27-29
Fort Albany, merchant steamer, 233
Fort Brunswick, merchant steamer, 233
Fort Carillon, merchant steamer, 233
Fort Cataraqui, merchant steamer, 233
Fort Chambly, merchant steamer, 232
Fort Concord, merchant steamer, 233
Fort LaMaulne, merchant steamer, 232
Fort Mingan, merchant steamer, 233
Fort Saint-François, merchant steamer, 233
Fort Saint Louis, package freighter, 324, *326*
Fort Tadoussac, merchant steamer, 232
Fort William, package freighter, 330, 332
Foundation Valiant, tugboat, 327
Foundation Valor, tugboat, 311
Foundation Vanguard, tugboat, 327
Foundation Viceroy, tugboat, 327
Foundation Victor, tugboat, 311
Foundation Vigour, tugboat, 327
Foundation Viking, tugboat, 327
Foundation Vim, tugboat, 327
Foundation Viscount, tugboat, 327
Franconia, 480
Frankcliffe Hall, bulk freighter, 321-22, *323*
Frederic C., crabbing boat, 371

Frederick Carter, railway car ferry, 343, 344
Fremona, steamer, *159*
French, patrol cruiser, 199
Frontenac, bulk freighter, 321, 376
Frontenac, steamer, 179
Fundy, minesweeper, *290*, 298, 300

G.D.D., barge, 204, *211*
G.T.D., barge, 204
G.T.D., original salvage schooner, 85, 89, 104, *115*, *118*, 121
G.T.D., replacement salvage schooner, 122
Gananoque, sailing ship, 72
Garm, see Toronto
Gaspé, minesweeper, 278-79, 300
Gatineau, destroyer escort, 298, *300*, 301, 332
Gatineau Park, merchant steamer, 232
George Canning, sailing ship, 33
George M. McKee, tugboat, 194
George T. Davie, barge, 111
Glacier, icebreaker, 338
Gladiolus, corvette, 226
Glomar High Island IX, oil rig, *415*, 428, 430
Glomar Jackup I, oil rig, 413-14
Gopher, see Chateau
Graham Bell, tugboat, 194
Grainmotor, bulk freighter, 191, 330
Granby, minesweeper, *224*, 230-31, 239
Grand Hermine, replica galleon, *370*, 371
Grande Entrée, trawler, 395
Grenada, brig, *35*, 43
Griffon, icebreaker, 380, *381*
Grosse Ile, trawler, 395
Gulf Mariner, see Truro
Gulfport, freighter, *325*

Hamilton, steamer, 179
Hamiltonian, see Champion

583

INDEX OF SHIPS

Hector, steamboat, 79
Hella, see Carlplace
Henderson, brig, *31*
Hepatica, corvette, 227, *228*, 230
Herchmer, see Truro
Hercules, paddle steamer, 37
Hercules, towboat, 60-61
High Park, merchant steamer, 233
Highlander, freighter, *325*
Hilda Marjanne, freighter, 325
HMLST 3508, transport ferry, 239, *240*
Hopper Barge No. 5, 191
Horten, see Prestonian
Hubert Gaucher, see Erable No. 1
Huron, destroyer, 336, 465-66, 468-69, 477

Iberian, steamer, 115-16, *480*
Illex, bait-boat, 344
Imperial Bedford, tanker, 376, *377*
Inch Arran, frigate, 236
Industrial Transport, tanker, 376, *377*
International No. 1, barge, 204
Intrépide, yacht, 371
Iroquois, destroyer, 378, 465-66, 468
Irvine, see Noranda
Irving Eskimo, tanker, *433*
Isabela Segunda, see Royal William

J.E. Bernier, icebreaker, *342*, 343, 380
Jacques Cartier, 184
Jalobert, tugboat, 197
Jasper Park, merchant steamer, 233
Jean Parisien, self-unloader, 409, *410*
Jerry G., tugboat, *318*, 327
John A. Macdonald, icebreaker, 338, *339*, 340
John Munn, paddle steamer, 64
Jonquière, frigate, 300
Jooske W. Vinke, see Shediac
Joseph Savard, ferry, *430*

Joseph Deschênes, ferry, 479
Joseph and Clara Smallwood, ferry, *439*, 442, *452*, *453*, *454*, 455, 481

Kaolack, collier, 272, *273*
Kate, tugboat, 85, 89
Keewatin, barque, 97
Keewatin, steamer, 119
Kempenfelt, see Assiniboine, destroyer
Kenting No. 1, drilling rig, 386-87
Kermic, barge, *204*
Khudozhnik Pakhomov, 481
Kingfisher, brig, 34
Kingston, steamer, 283
Kitchener, corvette, 226
Kitty, wooden scow, 188
Knørrur, charter sailing vessel, 154
Kriti Land, tanker, 395
Kriti Star, tanker, 393, *395*, *397*
Kriti Wave, tanker, *396*, 397

Labradoc, bulk freighter, *326*
Labrador, freight steamer, 154
Lachine, minesweeper, *224*, 230
Lady Grey, *159*
Lady Laurier, *159*
Lady Sherbrooke, steamboat, 60
La Hulloise, frigate, 300
Lake Huron, steamer, 102, *103*
Lake Manitoba, bulk freighter, 321, 376
Lasalle, frigate, 236, 238
Lauderdale, sailing ship, 10
Laurentian, see Polynesian
Lauzon, side-wheeler, 5
Lauzon, summer ferry, *126*, 128
Lawrencecliffe Hall, bulk freighter, 321, 332
Lenin, icebreaker, 338
Leonard W., tugboat, 395
Le Progrès, paddle steamer, 143
L'Erable No. 1, tanker, 428

INDEX OF SHIPS

Lethbridge, corvette, 226
Levis, summer ferry, 128
L'Ile d'Orléans, ferry steamer, 188, *189*
Listowel, tugboat, 241
Lomer Gouin, ferry, 381, *382*
Lord Seaforth, paddle steamer, 71
Lord Stanley, tugboat, *83*, 105, *106*, 113, 114, 120, 122
Lord Strathcona, tugboat, 113-15, *115*, 119, 122, 135, 312
Louis Jolliet, ferry, 200, 431
Louis Philippe, ferry, 143, *144*
Louis Saint Laurent, icebreaker, 368
LST 3507–3525, landing ship tanks, 239-40
Lucellum, tanker, 400
Lucy Maud Montgomery, ferry, 489
Lumber Merchant, towboat, 68

M.P. Connolly, *142*
Madelon II, see *L'Ile d'Orléans*
Malsham, steamboat, 60
Manitoba, steamer, 111
Manitoulin, bulk freighter, 321, *323*
Manoir, tugboat, 195, 310
Manola, steamer, *179*
Maplecliffe Hall, freighter, 376
Maplecourt, steamer, 174
Mapledene, steamer, 174, *175*
Margaree, destroyer escort, 379
Margaret, sailing ship, *31*, 61
Marie Louise, steamer, 105
Marine Bluenose, see *Bluenose*
Marloch, liner, 329
Mary, sailing ship, 21
Maureen, steamer, *238*
McLeod, see *Brockville*
Mechins, steamer, *238*
Medicine Hat, minesweeper, 300
Melville, minesweeper, *224*, 230
Menier Consol, freighter, 325, *328*

Metis, lake canaller, 308
Minnetonka, steamer, 118-19
Minnewaska, steamer, 119
Miriana, see *Noranda*
Montcalm, icebreaker, 240, 304, 319
Montcliffe Hall, freighter, 409
Montmorency, icebreaker, 240, 304
Montreal, steamboat, 60
Mulhouse, twin-screw steam barge, *171*
Murray Bay, bulk freighter, 321

Nanticoke, freighter, 479
Narragansett, steamer, 179
Newscarrier, barge, 204
Nicolette, barque, 80
Niobe, cruiser, *216*, 218
No. 3, sound sweeping barge, 344
Noranda, minesweeper, *224*, 230-31
Noronic, steamer, 283
North, ferryboat, 85, *86*, 128l
North Gaspé, passenger and cargo vessel, 199
Northern Light, steam ferry, *11*
Northern Venture, freighter, 325
Northwest, see *Maplecourt*

Ocean King, see *Chateau*
Ogden Ottawa, tanker, 400, *408*
Ogden Saguenay, tanker, 400
Ogdensburg, railway car float, 195
Olympic Catcher, see *Pictou*
Ondine, barque, 79
OOCL *Challenger*, 479
Otis Wack, tugboat, 279
Otori Maru, see *Pictou*
Ottercliffe Hall, bulk freighter, 321, 376

Palacios, see *St. Pierre*
Panama, steamer, 102
Papoonge, 182
Patrician, destroyer, 218-19

INDEX OF SHIPS

Patriot, destroyer, 218-19
Penetang, frigate, 236-38
Phryne, collier, 272
Pictou, corvette, 229-30
Pilot, paddle steamer, 85
Plessis, winter ferry, 128, *129*, 200
Point Pleasant Park, merchant steamer, 233
Polaris, steel barge, 417, *418*, *419*
Polynesian, steamer, 102-3, *104*
Powerful, tugboat, 6
Prescotont, tugboat, *194*, 195, *196*
Presidente Trujillo, see *Carlplace*
Prestonian, frigate, 236, 238
Prince Edouard, passenger ferry, 85
Prince Albert Park, merchant steamer, 232
Prince Edward Island, ferry, 196
Prince Regent, frigate, 23
Princess Charlotte, frigate, 23
Prindoc, bulk freighter, *326*
Protecteur, operational support vessel, 420
Provider, replenishment tanker, 334, *335*

Qu'Appelle, destroyer escort, *334*
Quebec, steamer, 60, 103
Quebec, passenger steamer, 190
Quebec, cargo carrier, 272, 283

Radisson, car ferry, 312
Rainbow, cruiser, *216*, 218
Rally, cutter, 340, 342
Rambler, side wheeler, 71-72, 85
Rambler, tugboat, 84-86
Redfern, steamer, 278
Redriver, steamer, 278
Reduta Ordona, 479
Regina, frigate, 462, 464-65
Richelieu, steamer, 190, 366
Richelieu, bulk freighter, 321
Rimouski, corvette, 226, 229

Rio Orinoco, tanker, *483*
Riverdale Park, merchant steamer, 233
Riverview Park, merchant steamer, 233
Rivière du Loup, see *L'Ile d'Orléans*
Robert B. No. 1, tugboat, 311, 327
Rockcliffe Hall, freighter, 308
Rosalind, brig, 44
Rowland Hill, side wheeler, 60, 64
Royal William, side wheeler, 63-64

Saguenay, bulk freighter, 321-22
Saguenay, car ferry, 308, *309*
Saguenay, destroyer, 220
Saguenay Trader, steamer, 238
St. Charles, sailing ship, 29
St. Lawrence, sailing ship, 23, *24*
St. Lawrence, passenger steamer, *186*, 190, *192*, 366
St. Pierre, frigate, 236, 238
Saint-Thérèse, frigate, 236
Salenergy IV, oil rig, 413, 415
Samaria, *480*
Sardhana, iron barque, *116*
Saurel, icebreaker, 343
Scotland, barque, 33
Scotland, sailing ship, 60
Sea Cliff, frigate, 236, *237*, 238
Sea Serpent, submersible vessel, 414-15
Selkirk, package freighter, 191
Shediac, corvette, *229*, 230
Simcoe, canaller, 319
Sioux, destroyer, 336
Sir Humphrey Gilbert, icebreaker, 304-5
Sir John A. Macdonald, *304*, 305
Sir Watkin, barque, 33
Skeena, destroyer, 220
Skeena, destroyer escort, 336
Sna-1, collier, 272
Snowberry, corvette, 227, *228*
South, ferryboat, 85, 128
Southern Pride, whaling ship, 226
Spikenard, corvette, 227, *228*, 230

586

INDEX OF SHIPS

Steelcliffe Hall, freighter, 409, *410*
Steelton, steamer, *161*
Stena Jutlandia, car ferry, 310
Strathardle, barque, 82
Summerside, corvette, 226
Sunek, freighter, 332
Sunrhea, frieghter, 308
Sunrip, freighter, 306, *307*, 308-9
Sussexvale, frigate, 236
Swiftsure, steamboat, 60

Tadoussac, passenger steamer, 190, *192*, 310, 366
Takis V., tugboat, 393
Telegraph, steamboat, 60
Teniente Palacios, see St. Pierre
Thalassa Desgagnes, see Rio Orinoco
Thesee, collier, 272
Thomas Henry, sailing ship, 21
Three Brothers, sailing ship, 19
Thunder Bay, steamer, 179
Titania, steamer, *96*, 99-102
Toronto, frigate, 236, 238
TR 35, steel trawler, *155*
Triano, fishing trawler, 369
Troll, see Prestonian
Truro, minesweeper, 230-31
Tyree, schooner, 122

Ungava, minesweeper, 279
Union, schooner, 34, *36*
Union Yacht, schooner, 55-56

Valkyrien, see Toronto
Vancouver, corvette, 226
Vancouver, destroyer, 220-21
Vaudreuil, 182
Venus, brig, 45
Victoriaville, frigate, 238-39
Victory, sailing ship, 23-24
Ville de Québec, frigate, *456*, 462, *463*, 464, *465*
Vincennes, destroyer, 389
Vindolana, steamer, 83-84, *85*

W.A. Bowden, tugboat, 184
Wabana, 137
Waccamaw, replenishment vessel, 420
White Wings, barquentine, *11*, 97
Whitefish Bay, bulk freighter, 321, *322*
William Price, steam tug, 187, *189*
Windflower, corvette, *227*, *228*, 229
Windoc, see Steelcliffe Hall
Winnipeg, package freighter (1925), 191
Winnipeg, freighter (1978), see Cartiercliffe Hall
Wolfe, icebreaker, 304
Wolfe's Cove, sailing ship, 21
Wyle, barque, *98*

Youpwe, suction hopper dredger, 409, 411, *412*

Zypenberg, freighter, 229

GENERAL INDEX

Numbers in italics refer to photograph captions.

A & P Appledore International, 484
Acadia Fisheries Ltd., 327
Acraman, William, 32
Aker Engineering A/S, 385, 407, 417
Alain, Robert, *499, 503*
Alain, Roger, *501*
Algoma Steel Company, 283, 291
Allan, Commodore Andy, *322*
Allan Line, *104*, 113, 121
Aluminum Company of Canada, 278
Aluminum construction, 278-79
American Ship Company, 201
American Shipbuilding Company, 118
American Welding Bureau, 359
Anctil, Gérard, *503*
Anderson Company, 169
Anderson, Vice-Admiral J.R., 462
"Angel Plan," 269-70, 320
Anglo Pulp and Paper Mills, Limited, 240
Angstrom, A., *126*, 128, 154
Annapolis River dam, 356
Anticosti Corporation, 194
Anticosti Shipping Company, 325, *328*
Apprenticeship system, 57-60
Arguin, Bertrand, *503*
Armstrong Whitworth and Company, 133, 247
Armstrong, Sir W.G., 133
Arsenault, Paul, *503*

Asselin, Benoit, Boucher, Ducharme, Lapointe consultants, 399-400
Asselin, Norbert, *502*
Association des rémorquers de Levis, 79
Astor, John Jacob, 144
Athel Line, 398, 400, 407
Atomic Energy Commission of Canada, 314
Aubé, Armand, *499*
Auclair, Réal, 475, *477*
Audet, Pierre, *500*
Audet, René, *502*
Aussant, Marc, *480*
Ayre, Michael, ix, 351, 394, 407, 416, *428*, 437-38, 441, *444*, 446, *447*, 468, *472*, 482

Baker, Neil, *142*, 152, 245
Balcer, Leon, 320
Baldwin, Peter, 97
Ballantyne, C.C., 170
Baller, Ronald, *499*
Baribeau, Hervé, 283
Barnard, Charles A., 139-40, 160-63, 167, 169, 172, 177-83
Barthe, Lionel, *499*
Bartleman, Peter, 252
Battle of the Atlantic, 229-30, 237
Bazinet, Guy, *428*
Beardmore, William, 133, 177

Beatty, Perrin, 462, *463*
Beaubien, Diane, *408*, *498*
Beaudoin, A., 250
Beaudoin, Gilles, *294*
Beaudoin, Léonce, *502*
Beaulieu, Jean-Baptiste, 10, *78*
Beaulieu, Rosaire, *501*
Beaumont, Jean Paul, *503*
Beaumont, Rodrigue, *503*
Bechtel of Canada, 417
Bédard, Alain, *499*, *502*
Bégin, Jean-Baptiste, 44
Bélanger, Claude, *447*
Bélanger, Édouard, *262*
Belleau, W., *498*
Bell's Shipyard, Quebec, 27, 29, *63*
Berberi, Georges, 355, 361, *414*, 481, *500*
Bernier, Commander D., *472*
Bernier, Johnny, 249
Bernier, Joseph-Elzéar, 129, *209*, 211
Berrigan, Édouard, 250
Berrigan, R., *281*
Berrigan, Raymond, *499*
Berrigan, Robert, *501*
Bertram Shipyard, Toronto, 245
Bertrand, Richard M., 438, *447*
Bérubé, F., *498*
Bérubé, France, *499*
Bérubé, Major P., *472*
Bethlehem Steel, 420
Betts, Frank A., *499*
Bewick, Joe, 428
Bilodeau, G., *498*
Bilodeau, Henri, 250
Bilodeau, Louise, *499*
Bilodeau, Willie, 249
Bishop, Commander J.M., 334
Bissonet, Achille, 124
Bissonette, Roméo, 295
Bissot de la Rivière, François, 1-2, 15

Bjornstad, Sue, 247
Black, George, 64
Black, Gordon, 393
Black, Robert (Bert), *268*, 293-94, 311-12, 347
Black, Mrs. Robert, 311
Blacksmiths, 50
Blais, E., *498*
Blais, Jacqueline, 352
Blais, Roméo, 250
Blais, W., *498*
Blatchford, Commander N., *472*
Blattman, Captain Bert, 464
Blouin, Jean-Paul, *499*
Blue Peter Steamship Co., 327
Boissinot, J.T., 162, 184-85
Boisvert, Jean-Marc, *499*
Bolduc, Alphonse, 249
Borden, Sir Robert, 132, 134, 137, *208*, 217, *218*
Bossé, Yvon, 316
Boudreault, Christine, *499*
Bouffard, Marc-André, *499*
Boulé, Léo, *501*
Bourassa, Henri (politician), 132
Bourassa, Henri (Davie employee), *496*
Bourget, Roland, *498*
Boutin, Johnny, 158, 250
Branch Lines, 411, 422, 426, 428
Branchaud, Michel, 490
Branion, Bob, *501*
Brer, Raymond, 358
Breton, Denis, *447*
Breton, Donald, *447*, *467*
Brisson, Jean-Roch, 443
British Admiralty Technical Mission (BATM), 257, 274
British Columbia Salvage Company, 135
British Empire Steel Company (Besco), 178

British Maritime Trust Limited, 139-40, 167
British Merchant Shipbuilding Advisory Committee, 156
British Navy, *see* Royal Navy
Brousseau, Georges, *504*
Brulotte, Clement, *501*
Brulotte, Fernand, *496*
Brulotte, Paul, *496*
Brunelle, Pierre, 9, 64, 77, *79*, 99
Brunet, Ovide, 251
Bryan, Claude, 139
Bull, Gerald, *357*, 358-59
Bullen shipyard, Esquimalt, 140
Bureau, Madeleine, *294*
Burmeister & Wain (BWS), 484-86
Burrard Dry Dock, 231, 334, 359, 432
Burrard-Yarrows, 432, 434, 436, 445
Bussières, Charles, *501*

Caldwell, Henry, 4, 9
Caldwell, John, 4-5, 9
Calgary Power, 356
Camat Transportation Consultants, 398
Cammell Laird and Co., 133, 427
Campbell, Alex, C. *147*, 185, 190, *212*, 213, 236, 247, *248*, 258, 261, *268*, 286, 344
Campbell and Black shipyard, Cape Cove, 37, 63
Campbell, E.D., *202*
Campbell, Kitty, 247
Campbell, William 190
Canada Floating Dock, 37
Canada Steamship Lines, 140, 143, *144*, 152, 167, 169, 172-74, *175*, 177-80, 183-84, *186*, 187-88, 190-91, 196-97, 199-200, 203, 233, 241, 246, 258, 261, 263, 282-83, 291-93, 305, 315, 321, *326*, 329, 343, 347-48, 356, 363-64, 366-67, 375, 399-401, 404, 406, 435, 476

Canadair, 420
Canadian Army Research and Development Establishment, 356, 358
Canadian Coast Guard, 200, 276, 302, 338, 340-43; *see also* Canadian Marine Service
Canadian General and Shoe Machinery Company, 128, 136
Canadian Government Merchant Marine (CGMM), *166*, 169-74, 178
Canadian International Paper, 388
Canadian Marine Industries Association, *484*
Canadian Marine Service, 200, 302, 332, 337, 340, 345; *see also* Canadian Coast Guard
Canadian Marine Transportation Centre, 427
Canadian Maritime Commission, 269
Canadian National Railway, 154, 225, 317; *see also* CN Marine
Canadian National Steamship Company, 242, 270
Canadian National West Indies Steamship Line, 271
Canadian Navy, *see* Royal Canadian Navy
Canadian Northern Steamships Limited, 154
Canadian Pacific, 113, 119, 130, 135, *194*, *354*, 329, 427
Canadian Pacific Car and Passenger Transport Company, 195, *196*
Canadian Patrol Frigate (CPF) program, 430, 434, 440, 458, 461-63, 465
Canadian Shipbuilding and Engineering Limited, 263, 359, 399
Canadian Shipbuilding and Ship Repairing Association, 353
Canadian Shipping Federation, 137

GENERAL INDEX

Canadian Skinner Uniflow, 272, 276
Canadian Submarine Consortium, 459
Canadian Vessel Capital Assistance Plan, 344-45
Canadian Vessel Construction Assistance Act (CVCAA), 269-70
Canadian Vickers Limited, 134-35, 136, 138, 140, 144-46, 149, 152-53, 167, 177, 195, 231, 233, 235-36, 255, 270, 291-94, 316, 334, 336, 353, 359, 368, 378, 387, 432-33, 451; Versatile Vickers, 430, 433, 440-41; Vickers Stanwick Systems Inc., 432; MIL Vickers, 450, 461
Canadian Welding Bureau, 359
CANDU nuclear reactors, 420
Cantin, Albert, *503*
Cantin, Jacques, *499*
Cantin, Laurent, *294*
Cantin, Marcel, *499, 503*
Cantin, R., *498*
Cargill Grain Company, 314, 356
Caron, Albert, *294*
Caron, Louis, *491*
Carpentier, Roger, *447*
Carrier, Charles, *501*
Carrier, Charles William, 12, 109
Carrier, Georges, *294*
Carrier, Lainé et Cie, 12-13, 15, 82, 86, *106*, 108, 128, 250
Carrier, Maurice, *439*
Carrier, Robert, *504*
Carruthers, James, 180
Casgrain, T.C., *208*
Castonguay, Philippe, *501*
Catellier, Rosaire, *503*
Cauchy, Jean, *499*
Cedar Group, 489-90; *see also* Dominion Bridge Corporation
Challenger jet, 420
Challinor, Don, ix, 436-38, 441, 443-44, *445, 447,* 449, 455, *463*

Champlain Dry Dock, 138, 156-58, *192, 272,* 293, 314, 332, 395, *418,* 475, 478, 485, 489
Chan, Commander Victor, *467*
Chantier Maritime de St. Laurent, Limitée, 241, 287
Charbonneau, Bernie, 435
Chargeurs Réunis, 242, 272
Charland, Guillaume (William), Sr., 9-10, *79,* 97, 181-82
Charland, Guillaume (William), Jr., 9, *79,* 97
Chart, George Edward, 181
Chevron, 430
Cholera epidemic (1832), 44, 63
Chouinard, Maurice, *504*
Chrétien, Jean, *412*
Christopher, David, 464, *469, 472*
Christopher Idle & Company, 5
Churchill, Winston, 226
Clarke, George, 154
Clarke, John, 154
Clarke Steamship Company, 199, 308
Clarke's Gulf Ports Steamship Co. Ltd., 324, *325*
Clarkson, G.T., 182
Clicher, Fernand, 358
Club des Moussaillons, 494, *497*
CN Marine, 428, 431, 434, *442*
Coker, William, 10
Cole, George, 393
Coleman, R.D., (Bob), 351
Collingwood shipyard, 135, 177, 221, 306, 321, 347, 359
Colombo Plan, 313-14
Compagnie France Navigation, 272
Compagnie Générale d'Entreprises Publiques, 87
Compagnie Maritime et Industrielle de Lévis, *110*
Compagnie Traverse Rivière du Loup-Tadoussac Ltée, 188

Comstock Quebec Ltée, 419
Confédération des travailleurs catholiques du Canada (C.T.C.C.), 280
Conoco, 415
Conseil des Arts et Manufacturiers, 250
Continental Construction Company, Limited, 181-82
Coopérative de Transport Maritime et Aérien (CTMA), 489
Corrie, Allen, *28*
Corriveau, Albert, 250
Corriveau, Philias, *244*, 249-50, *257*
Corvettes, 225-30
Côté, Mrs. Joseph, 129
Coté, Maurice, *501*
Côté, Michel, 431, *439*
Côté, Richard, 407
Coté, S., *503*
Couture, Clément, *503*
Couture, Gaston, *502*
Couture, Georges, 10
Couture, Guillaume, 1-3, 15
Couture, Ignace, 10
Couture, Joseph, 102
Couture, Marielle, *480*
Coverdale and Colpitts, 183
Coverdale, Mary, 188, *190*
Coverdale, William H., *183*, 184, 188, 196, 203, 282
Cowie, Captain, 343
Cox and Stephens, 270
Craig, Cyril (Sonny), 350
Craig, David, 185, 199, *212*, 213, 245-46, *246*, 261, 293, 350
Craig, Mrs. L.T., *326*
Crandall marine railway, 103, 203
Cresswell, H.A., 246
Crosbie, John, 436, *454*
Crosbie Offshore Services Ltd., 417
Crump, Captain Kenneth, 310

Cunard Steamship Company, 156, 398
Currie, Ronald J., 250
Cuthbert, Captain James L., 338

DAC Group, 417
Dalhousie, George Ramsay, 34
Davie: corporate history: George Taylor establishes Canoterie shipyard (1817), 25; Allison Davie enters partnership (1825), 33; Shipyard moved to Levis (1829), 41; G. & A. Davie partnership formed (1854), 69; Lauzon shipyard established (1887), 93; George T. Davie and Sons formed (1897), 109; bought by Charles Barnard (1914), 139; management assumed by Canadian Steamship Lines (1920), 169, 174, 177; becomes subsidiary of Canada Steamship Lines (1925), 184-85; bought by Soconav (1976), 401, 404, 406; bought by Dome Petroleum (1981), 421-22, 425; bought by Versatile Corporation (1985), 432-33; bought by Maritime Industries Limited (1987), 440-41; bought by Dominion Bridge Corporation (1996), 489-90
Davie: operations, labour, and management: drawing office, 294, 352; general engineering/industrial operations, 295, 312-15, 355-61, 386-88, 390, 420, 481; military shipbuilding, 433-34, 440, 444, 458, 460-61, 463, 465-69; plant engineering, 384; quality management, 387-88, 471-73, 481; repair work, 35-37, 136, 203, 329-30, 420, 479-81; salvage operations, 70-71, 79-80, 82, 97, 100-3, 115-17, 135-36, *483*; steamboat operations, 77-79; strikes, 107, 285, 294, 301, 315; training, 250-52; unions, 106-7, 280-81, 295, 315, 363, 383,

592

390, 407, 446, 449-50, 471, 488; wages, 255-56, 280-81, 315, 390, 470; wartime shipbuilding (First World War), 143-59, 163, 217-19, (Second World War), 222-23, 225-43; *see also* Aluminum construction, Corvettes, Destroyers, Frigates, Icebreakers, Minesweepers, Oil rigs, Sonar domes, Tugboats, Tankers

Davie: shipyards: at Levis, 7, 15, *32, 42* 43-45, 48-50, 55, 87-89; fire (1845), 63; expropriated, *88,* 89, 91, 93; at Lauzon, 99, 102, *112,* 127, *193;* fire (1906), 122; "Little Davie" yard (Davie west), 203, *383,* 386, 395; Davie Brothers shipyard, 203, *239,* 241, *242,* 369, *370;* fire (1955), 295-96, *297, 298;* improvements (1960s), 360-61, 382-3; improvements (1970s), 398-99; improvements (1980s), 444

Davie, Captain Allison, 1, 7, 10, *26,* 27-30, 32-37, 41-47, 50-52, 55, 75, *81,* 285

Davie, Allison (Jr.), 34, 67-72, 78

Davie, Allison Cufaude, (Foddie), 47, 73, *81, 101,* 108, 125, 135, 139-40, 203, 241, 283, 285-87, 315-16

Davie, Anne, 73

Davie, Brenda (Kitty), 129, 188, *207*

Davie, Charles Gordon (Charlie), 201, *202,* 203-4, *212,* 213, 283-85, 315-16

Davie, Charles McCarthy, 73, 108

Davie, Clementine, 45

Davie, Elizabeth Johnson (née Taylor), 1, 19, 29-30, 32-34, 41, 44-46, 50-51, *52,* 53-57, 62, 67, 72-73, *81,* 121, 285

Davie, George Duncan, 15, 73, *101,* 105, *108,* 109, 117, 124, 129-30, 135-40, *142, 148,* 157-63, 172, 180, 184, 188, 200, *201,* 203-5, *206,* 207, *208,* 209-13, 245, 247, 249, 254, 349, 401, 493

Davie, George Taylor, viii, 9-10, 15, 34, 47, *48,* 55, 57, 59, 65, 67-75, 77, 79-80, *81,* 82-89, 91, 100-2, 104, 107-9, 113, *117,* 117-18, 121-25, 127, 476, 493

Davie, George W., 120

Davie, Gershom, 10, 34, 72, 78, 80, 108

Davie, Harriet, 45, 67

Davie, Isobel, 45

Davie, John (Jack) Leavitt, 73, *101,* 108-9, 135, 139-40

Davie, Mary Elizabeth, 73

Davie, Mary Euphemia (née Patton), 73, 87, 108, *117*

Davie, Oswald, 120

Davie, William (Willie), 120

Davie, William Edward, 44-45

Davie, William Taylor, 10, 53, 57, 72, 78, 80, 82, 86, *106,* 109, 119-21, *120,* 124

Davis, Rhea, 308

Davis, Rear Admiral S. Mathwin, 302

Dawson, Sir Trevor, 144-45, 177

Day, Graham, 427-28, *429*

De Blois, Captain R., *469*

Deere & Co., 440

Defence Purchasing Board, 222, 256

Delagrave, André, *207,* 285-86, 316-17

Delagrave, Brenda, 285

Delisle, Ernest, 250-51

Demers, Alcide, *501*

Demers, Pauline, *499*

Demers, Robert, *447*

Department of Defence Production, 282, 301-2, 376

Department of Fisheries, 344

Department of Industry, Trade and Commerce, 384

Department of Munitions and Supply, 225, 231-32, 256, 275

Department of National Defence, 285, 302

Department of Public Works, 283, 312, 316, 330

Department of Supply and Services, 376, 458
Department of Transport, 302-5, 309, 341, 343, 376
DeRoche, Mark, 482
Descoteaux, Sarto, *499*
Desgagnés Group, *483*
Deshaies, Richard, 407
Desjardins, Alphonse, 381
Desmarais, Louis, 363, 375-76, 392, *396*, 399-401, 403, 421
Desmarais, Paul, 375, 406
Després, Gérard, 241
Destroyer escorts, 300-1, 332, 336, 379
Destroyers, 218-22, 336, 378-79
Déziel, Joseph-David, *13*, 14
Diefenbaker, Olive, 338
Dinning, Henry, 127
Dionne, Edgar, *501*
Dionne, Léonce, *501*
Dionne, Roger, *499*
Distant Early Warning (DEW) Line, 343
Divers, 136
Doering, W., *472*
Dome Petroleum, 420-21, 425-27, 432, 443
Dominion Bridge Corporation, viii-ix, xi, 490
Dominion Bridge-Sulzer, *418*, 419
Dominion Coal Company, 135
Dominion Steel Corporation, 177
Domtar Ltd., 406
Donaldson Line, *96*, 99
Donnacona Paper Company, 204
Donnison, Michael, 351, *352*, *447*
Dosco, 387
Draegebo, Steinar, 407
Drifters, 152-54
Drouin, Pierre, *503*
Drury, C.M., 376
Dry Dock Subsidies Act, 133-34, 137
Duchesneau, Hector, 124, 249

Duchesneau, Noël, *503*
Duclos, Jean, 10
Duclos, Pierre, 91, *121*, 124, 493
Dufour, Roch, *480*
Dugas, Rita, *294*
Duguid, Charles, *197*
Duke of Connaught Dry Dock, 134
Dumont, Joseph, 250
Dumont, Roger, *501*
Dunn, Sir James, 283, 291, 298-99
Dunn, Thomas, 9
Duplessis, Maurice, 305
Dupont, André, *502*
Dupont, Suzanne, *498*, *499*
Duquet, Claude, *496*
Dussault, Jean-Baptiste, 10

East India Company, 54
East India Dock, 82-83
École des Arts et Métiers, 251
École technique, 251
Eisenhower, Dwight, 319
Elco (Electric Launch Company), 144-45, 149, 152, 158, 163
Electric Boat Company, 144, 181
Elizabeth II, Queen, 303, 319
Empire Parliamentary Association, 177
Export Development Corporation, 413

Fairbanks Morse, 204, 327
Fall, Captain R.H., 337
Farish, Bill, 351, 407
Faulkner, Bob, 313
Federal Petroleum Carriers, 323
Federal Shipping Company, 308
Federal S.N. Company, 156
Ferland, Alexis, 45
Ferland, Louise, *408*
Ferry Contribution Agreement, 441
Ferry service across St. Lawrence, *40*, 85, 128-30
Fielding, Glen, *499*

GENERAL INDEX

Fillion, Roméo, 287
Findlay, Archibald, 28-29
Fitzpatrick, Ashley Russell, *454*
Fitzpatrick, Mrs. Russell, *454*
Fleury, Clement, 363
Fontaine, Gabriel, *439*
Forbes, Lewis J.-B., 316
Fore River Shipbuilding Company, 247
Fortier, Roger, *447*
Fortin, Gilles, *294*, 340-41
Foundation Maritime Company, 312, *330*, 327, 332
Fournier, R., *503*
Free Trade Agreement, 477
French Merchant Marine, 169-70
Frigates, 235-36
Fulcher, Jimmy, 351
Furness Withy, 156, 177
Furois, Charles, 247

Gaboury, Fernand, *294*
Gagné, Gilles, *502*
Gagné, Raymond, *499*
Gagnon, Caroline, *431*
Gagnon, J., *498*
Gagnon, Joe, *294*
Gagnon, Joseph, 350
Gagnon, Jean-Paul, *498*
Gagnon, Jérémie, 248-49, *269*, *294*, 327, 349-50
Gagnon, Jérémie Jr., 350
Gagnon, Wilfrid, 241
Gale, Sue, *254*
Gallagher, Jack, 426, *427*
Garant, Alfred, *262*
Garant, Michel, *502*
Garant, Napoléon, *262*
Garon, Jean, *431*, 490
Gaucher, Michel, 426-27
Gaudreault, Jean Marie, *503*
Gaumond, R., *503*
Gaumont, Roger, 358

Gauvin, Richard, 446, *447*
GEC Alsthom, 450, 475
Gélinas, J. Arthur, *vii*, 491
Gendreau, Adjutor, *501*
Gendron, Michel, 482
General Dynamics Corporation, 310, 392
Général Georges P. Vanier floating dock, 476-77, *478*
General Investment Corporation, 403
General Mills of Canada, 395
Geoffroy, Bertrand, *496*
George, Vice-Admiral Robert E., 462
Germain, Michel, *503*
German & Milne, 409, 411, 467
Gibson, Tom, 277, 300, *301*
Giguère, Bernard, *472*
Giguère, Gisèle, *499*
Giguère, Joseph, *503*
Gilbert, Marc, *503*
Gilbert, P., engine works, 71, 85
Gilbert, Raymond, *503*
Gilliland, Jimmy, 351, 392
Gillon, Robert Robertson, 83
Gilmore, J., 236
Giroux, Gerry, *414*
Glavez, Jose, *447*
Global Marine Drilling Company, 413, *414*
Godbout, Louis, 254
Gorman, Ernest, 274, *382*
Gorman, John, 313, 350, 358-59
Gosselin, A., *498*
Gosselin, Gustave, 274, 351, *382*
Gosselin, L., *503*
Gosselin, Marcel, 441, 471
Goudie, James, 63
Goudie, John, 5, 23, *24*
Gouin, Lomer, 251, 381
Goulet, Denis, *503*
Goulet, Willy, *502*
Gourdeau, Paul, *242*, 316

GENERAL INDEX

Gravel, Joseph, 139-40
Great Lakes and St. Lawrence Transportation Company, 118
Great Lakes Transportation Company, 188, 196
Groslouis, Max, *477*
Groupe Maritime Verreault, 489
Guay, Charles, 351, *504*
Guay, Léopold, *499*
Guay, Raynald, *503*
Guay, Robert, 248, 275, *294*, *501*
Guay, Roger, *503*
Guay, Roland, *501*
Guay, Ronald, *412*
Guay, Suzanne, *498*
Guérin, Joseph, 124
Guttridge, John, 149
Gwyn, Peter, 351, 392
Gypsum Packet Company, 280

H. & C. Grayson shipyard, Garston, 327, *331*
Halifax Shipbuilding Co. Ltd., 133, 140, 177, 334
Halifax-Dartmouth Industries Limited, 459-60
Hall Corporation, 308, 324, 332, 376, 405, 409
Hallé, Dénary, 251
Hallé, René, *444*, *504*
Hamelin, Joseph, 249
Hamilton, Emily, 255
Hanbury, Mary, *92*, 93, 99
Haney, M.J., 180-82
Hanlon, Ronald, *301*
Harland & Wolff shipyard, Belfast, 144, 226
Harrington, J., *294*
Hart, Kathleen, 211
Hart, Thomas, 211, 255
Havens, Warren, 277, *294*
Haws, Allison Davie, 89

Haws, Elizabeth Taylor (née Davie), 34, 73, *74*, 82, 89
Haws, George William, 73, *74*, 82
Haws, John, *73*
Haws, Richard, 82, 101
Hébert, Louis-Philippe, *13*, 14
Hellyer, Paul, 336
Henderson, Beverley, 430
Henderson, D. & W., 106
Henderson, Gerry, 430
Henderson shipyard, Glasgow, 101, 104
Herdman, Lorne Clayton, 181-82
Hibernia Management Development Corporation, 461
Hibernia Program, 417, 461
High Altitude Research Project (HARP), 358
"Hire Purchase" Plan, 269-70
Hodgson, Brian, *467*
Hogan, Gerry, *294*
Holderness and Chilton, 72
Home Bank, 182-83
Homestead (Davie house), 44, 46, *47*, *48*, *56*, 73, 125
Hose, Commodore Walter, *220*, 221
Houle, Jean-Claude, 407
Howe, C.D., 232-33, *266*, 282, 291
Howe, Mrs. W.H., 276
Hudson's Bay Oil and Gas Company, 415, 426
Hunt, William, 120
Huot, Adolphe, 250
Huot, Marthe, *501*
Huot, Norman, 358
Huot dit Saint Laurent, Benjamin, 7, 12
"Hydroconic" hull design, 327
Hydro-Quebec, 356, 387

Iacurto, Francesco, *244*
Icebreakers, 200, 240, 302-5, 338-40, 342-43, 380
Imperial Conference (1918), 217

GENERAL INDEX

Imperial Munitions Board, 156
Imperial Oil, 356, 376
Ingalls Shipbuilding, *374*, 387
Inland Navigation Company, 167
Innotermodal Inc., 482
Institut des Ouvriers, 250
Institution of Naval Architects of Great Britain, 205
Intercolonial Railway, 13, 89
International Brotherhood of Electrical Workers, 280
International Moulders and Foundry Workers Union of North America, 280
International Nickel, 388
Irving, James, 248
Irving, K.C., 430-31
Isabelle, G., *498*
Ishikawajima-Harima Heavy Industries (IHI), 445-48

Jacobson, Captain D.V., *472*
Jacques Cartier bridge, 317
Jellicoe, Lord, 217
Jellineck, Captain, 464
Jeune, Edmond, 249
John Inglis Company, 154, 194
Johnson, Daniel, ix
Johnson, Don, 413
Johnston, Reggie, *501*
Jolicoeur, Luc, *501*
Jolicoeur, Marcel, *502*
Joyce, Ernest, 274-75

Kack, Steve, *414*, 455
Kerr, A. McLean (Archie), 294
Kilpatrick, Commander A.G., 334
King, Kenneth, 248
Kissel, Kennicot and Company, 183
Knapp, Marty, *414*
Knights of Labour, 106-7
Knipple and Morris engineers, 98

Korean War, 282
Kott, Gary, 413
Kundah Hydro-Electric Project, 314

Labbé, Denise, *498*
Labelle, J. Edouard, 316
Labonté, Léon, *502*
Labrecque, Richard, *502*
Labrie, Claude, *503*
Labrie, Raymond, *499*
Lachine Ferry Company Ltd., 184
Lacroix, Jean Yves, *503*
Lacroix, Marcel, *500*
Laflamme, Jacques, 249
Laflamme, Léon, 249
Laflamme, Lucien, 50, 249
Laflamme, Richard, *502*
Lafrance, Marcel, 403, *405*, 406, *412*, 415, 423, 430, 435
Lai, Victor, *447*
L'Allier, Jean-Paul, 464
Lamarre, Denys, 475
Lamb, Eddie, *294*
Lambert & German, *194*, 195, *196*, 212
Lambert, Walter, 188
Lamontagne, Gilles, 436
Lamontagne, Harry, 124, *142*
Lamontagne, Marcel, *501*
Landry, Bernard, 490
Landry, Daniel, *447*
Langevin, Hector, 99
Langevin, Maryse, *469*
Langlois, Richard, *503*
Laperrière, A., *498*
Larkin & Connolly, builders, 98
LaRoche, Evelyn, *414*
Laskey, Norman, 398
Lassiter, Monique Gagnon, *414*
Latremouille, Lorne, 284-85
Latulippe, Adélard, 249
Laurier, Sir Wilfrid, 132, 134, *218*, 451
Lauson, Seigneurie de, 1, 4

GENERAL INDEX

Lavalin, 459-60
Lavery, James, 101, 124
Lavoie, Mgr. Raymond, 383
Lawrence, Alec, 431
Leblanc, Richard, *499*
Leblanc, Zéphrin, 7, 13
Leblond, A., *498*
Leclerc, Louis, *500*
Leclerc, Raymond, *503*
Leclerc, Rosaire, 249, 261
Lecours dit Barras, Michel, 5
Lecours dit Barras, Pierre, 10
Lehouiller, Gilles, 471
Lemelin, J.B., 283
Lemelin, Raymond, *500*
Lemieux, André, 441, 471
Lennox, Joseph (Joe), 350, 392
Lepage, Joseph, 249
Lépine, A.T., 106-7
Lessard, Jean-Marc, *454*
Letarte, Louis, 251
Letarte, Raymond, 275, *294*
Letourneau, Pierre, 438
Leveillé, André, *503*
Lévesque, Joseph, 249
Lévesque, Marc, *501*
Lévesque, Mark, *301*
Lévesque, Ovide, 209
Lévesque, Roland, *502*
Levis Tow Boat Company, 79
Levis Tramway Company, 252
Lévy, Henry de, 1
L'Hébreux, Jean-Guy, 384, *444*, *499*
Ligne Branche, 422
Liston, Terry, 449
Litton Systems Canada, 459-60, 466-68
Livanos, 172, 174, *175*
Lloyd's of London, *70*, 114, *175*, 257, 332
Lord, Lucien, *501*
Lorne Dry Dock, viii, 13, 14, *96*, 203, 98-99, *100*, *101*, 102-3, 113, 118, 127, 136-37, 146, 157-58, *168*, 169, 179, 211, 240, 260, *270*, 293, 310, 368, 316, 444, 476, 493
Lorne, Marquess of, 98
Lowery, Richard, *292*, 293, 295, 298, 300, 303, 305, 313, 315, 319, 347, 351, 353, 355, 364, 366, 376, 390, 392, 401
Lynn McLeod, 388

M. & M. Manufacturing, 461, 469
Mair, Commander C.J., 336
Manic II dam, *355*, *356*
Manitoba Hydro, 356
Manning, Mrs. W.J., 341
Marathon-Letourneau, 387, 413, 415
Marchand, Mrs. Jean, 342, 370
Marengère, Michel L., *ix*, 490
Marine Atlantic, 428, *442*, 452
Marine Railway Cradle, *331*
Marine Industries Limited (MIL), 233, 255, 258, 332, 334, 349, 359, 378, 399, 403-7, 411, 421, 430, 434, 440-41, 443, 445, 449, 457, 459-60, 475; *see also* MIL Tracy
Marotte, Michel, *502*
Marquis, F.-X., 10, *79*, 127
Marshall, Colonel K.R., 283
Martin, Paul, 399
Martineau, Gabriel, *501*
Matossian, Nicholas, *vii*
Mazankowski, Don, 436
Maze, R., *477*
McAllister Towing & Salvage Ltd., 311
McCarthy shipyard, Sorel, 134-35
McClean, Commodore Ralph, *301*
McCloy, Bill, 338
McConnell Dowell, 490
McCormick, Ken, *472*, 475
McDonald, Pat, 295
McGiffin, John, 367, 375
McGill University, 310, 358
McGilvray, Robert W. (Bob), 271, 274, 294, 351, *382*

McGregor, Ian, 294, 314
McKenzie, James, 10, 71, 93
McLagan, T. Rodgie, 291, *292*, 293-95, 298-300, 305, 308, 315, 319, 343, 345, 347-48, 351, 360, 366-68, 375-76, 386, 392, 401
McLaren, James, 99
McPherson, Lauchlan, 27, 29
Menzies, Thomas, 69, *70*
Mercier, Paul, *504*
Mercure, Fernand, *294*
Méthot, Pierre, *414*
Mezzana, Robert, *491*
Michaud, François, *502*
Michaud, Olivier, 102
Migneault, Théo, *501*
MIL Intermodal Inc., 482
MIL Offshore, 461, 475
MIL Systems Engineering, 475
MIL Tracy, 399, 403, 404-5, 407, 450, 459, 461-62, 465, 478
Milne, Gilmore & German, 276, 302, *339*
Minesweepers, 230-31, 277-78
Molson, John, 60, 68
Monette, Robert, *439*, 446, *447*
Monk, Frederick, 132-33
Montminy, Camilien, *503*
Montreal Harbour Commission, 134
Montreal Transportation Company, 111
Morden, W. Grant, 139, 167, 177-78, 180
Morency, Armand, *501*
Morency, M., *498*
Morency, Napoléon, 249
Morgan, Thomas, 68
Morin, Jules, *439*
Morin, Henri, 250
Morley, Al, 246, 293
Morley, F.A., *498*
Morrell, Robert W., 280

Morris, Hollis, 275
Morris, William, 275
Morritt, Thomas, 124
Morse Dry Dock and Repair Company, 201
Morton, Bruce, 275
Morton Engineering and Dry Dock Company, 221, 228, 235, 240, 245, 251, *259*, 260-61, 274, 283
Morton Patent Slip, *42*
Morton, Thomas, 43
Moses-Saunders Hydro-electric Station, 317
Motor launches (M.L.s), 143, 145-46, 149-50
Mulrooney, Captain Edward, 344
Munn, John, 57, 59-60, 62, 64-65
Murphy, John Simon, *92*, 99

N.M. Paterson & Sons, 324, *326*
Nadeau, Aurore, *504*
Nahhas, Lieutenant R., *472*
Napoleonic Wars, 19-20, 30
National Research Council, 271, 356, 387
National Shipbuilders Security Limited, 199
Naval Central Drawing Office, 302, 378, 432, 451
Naval Central Procurement Agency, 302
Naval Engineering Test Establishment, 302
Naval Service Act, 133
Navy, *see* Royal Canadian Navy, Royal Navy
Neal, George, *414*
Nelles, Captain Percy, 221
Nesbitt, Thomson and Company, 183
New York Central Railway, 195
Nicholson, John, 7-8
Nightingale, Arthur, 314, *394*, *396*, 397-99
Nipigon Transport, 376

GENERAL INDEX

Norcross, Joseph W., 152, 167, 170-74, 178, 180-81, 183-84, 188
Norfolk Shipbuilding & Drydock Company, 420
Normand, Esther, *414*
Normand, Jacques, 10
Northern Navigation Company, 167
Northern Steamship Company, 174
Notre-Dame-de-la-Victoire, 8, 9, *13*
Nova Scotia Steel and Coal Co., 177

O'Grady, Donald, *294*
O'Neil, Roméo, 250
O'Neill, John, 274
O'Neill, Thomas, 124, 139-40
Ogden Marine, 398, 407
Oil rigs, 413-17
Oliver, Thomas H., 82
Orkney, Captain, 10
Ouellet, Claude, *414*
Ouellet, Évariste, 249

P.S. Ross and Sons, 184
Page, Donald, 347, *350*, 361, 393, 397, *497*
Pagé, Gilles, *502*
Pageau, Marcel, *294*
Palmers shipyard, Jarrow, 247
Papachristidis Co. Ltd., 323, 343
Papachristidis, Phrixos, 308, 323
Paquet, J. Arthur, 316
Paquet, Maurice, 283, *284*, 285, 316
Paquette, Lieutenant Commander Ed, 467
Parent, Honorius, *501*
Park Steamship Company, 232
Park, Walter, *502*
Patterson, Dyke and Company, 21
Patton, Duncan, 73, *79*, 93, 99, *117*
Patton, William, 99
Payne, Commander R., *472*
Pelletier family, *496*

Peltier, Lambert, 358
People's Line of Steamers, 64
Perforadora Mexico S/A, 414
Perkins, Mary Jane, 254, 417
Perreault, Gina, *498*
Pérusse, A., 249
Pérusse, Alfred, *126*
Pérusse, P.G., 249
Peter Kiewit Sons & Co., 461
Petrobas, 413-14
Petrolia Oil Well Drilling Ltd., 387, 411
Philip, Prince, 319
Picard, Roger, *501*
Pickersgill, Tom, 394, 407
Pippy, Mrs. C.A., 344
Plamondon, Robert, *502*
Plante, Denis, *439*
Playfair, James, 167, 196
Poirier, Marcel, *499*
Polar 8 icebreaker, 434, 440-41, 458, 460
Pollock, Jim, 248
Polson Iron Works, 245
Pontoon No. 2, 242
Porter, John, 249-50
Pottinger, James, 154
Powell, R.E. (Rip), 307
Power Corporation, 375, 406, 399-401, 403, 407
Power, Dan, *501*
Pratt & Whitney, 467
Préfontaine, Pierre, ix
Prémont, Paul, 275, *294*, *501*
Price Brothers, 187
Price, William, 50, 68, *69*, 72
Prince, Maryse, *498*
Program for the Advancement of Industrial Technology, 386
Provencher, Maurice, 403, *405*, 406, 416, 423, *428*, 435-36, *501*
Prudential Trust Company, 174
Pullen, Captain Thomas C., 335
Pullin, Alec, 308

GENERAL INDEX

Quebec and Halifax Steam Navigation Company, 62-63
Quebec and Levis Ferry Company, 85, 130
Quebec Bridge, 205, *206*, 207
Quebec Paper Sales and Transportation Company, 204
Quebec Salvage and Wrecking Company, 135, 312, 329
Quebec Shipyards Limited, 241
Quebec Steamship Company, 113
Quigley, Anne, *498*
Quinn, Captain H.L., 332

Ray, John, 22
Read, Captain John, 196
Reed, William, 225, 235
Regnaud, Jacques, 350, 394, *497*
Reilly, Denis, 468
Rennoldson and Sons, 113
Reynolds, Graham, *414*, *472*
Rhéaume, Jean-Yves, 407, *414*, 416, *428*, 438, 441, *447*, 468, *469*
Rhodes, Cecil, 177
Richards, W.E., *427*
Richelieu and Ontario Navigation Company, 128
Ringuet, Emile, 249-50
Rinninger, Paul, *414*
Rivard, Auguste, *501*
River St. Lawrence Ship Channel Service, 136
Riverside Steel Works, 317
Robb, Thomas, 162
Roberge, Léopold, *502*
Robertson, John F., 274
Robinson, Emile, *357*, 358
Robitaille, Aurèle, 249
Robitaille, Réal, *499*
Roche, John, 127
Rochette, Louis, 311, 348-49, 403, *404*, 407, 411, 415, 423, 426-27, *428*

Rogers, Captain Norman, 325
Rosa, Narcisse, 89
Ross, James G., 80
Roubil, Sami, 438, *444*
Rousseau, Guy, *499*
Routhier, A., 249
Rowe, John H., 101
Roy, Pierre-Georges, 123
Roy, André, *472*
Roy, Jean, 468
Roy, Nelson, *439*
Roy, Paul-Arthur, *499*
Royal Air Force, 217
Royal Arcanum Society, 205
Royal Canadian Navy, 132-33, 141, 150, *216*, 217-23, 226, 228, 231, 235, 237-38, 241, 277, 282, 284, 300-2, 332, 335-36, 345, 360, 420
Royal Canadian Mounted Police, 199, 303
Royal Engineers, 150, *151*, 152
Royal Naval Reserve, 150
Royal Navy, 131-34, 145, 149-50, 217, 223, 226-27, 235, 241
Royer, Claude, *496*
Ruel, André, *498*
Ruel, Ronaldo, 249
Russell, Alexander, 14-15, 85, 127-28, *128*
Russell, William G., 7

Saguenay Shipping Limited, 307
Saint John Dry Dock and Shipbuilding Co., 329, *331*, 336, 405
Saint John Shipbuilding Limited (SJSL), 336, 429-30, 433-34, 448-49, 462-64
Saint-Amand, Marcel, *499*
Saint-Onge, Ernest, *501*
Salen Offshore Drilling Company, 413
Sample, Robert George, 10, 85, 120
Samson, Edouard, 124
Samson, Emile, 249

Samson, Etienne, 10, 14, 97
Samson, Isaie, 124
Samson, J.A.D., 283
Samson, José, 249
Samson, Jules, *502*
Samson, Lauréat, 249
Samson, Marc, *447*
Samson, Omer, 250
Samson, Yves, *502*
Saunders, Peter Paul, 433, *434*, 440
Sauvageau, J.-C., *498*
Sauvageau, Charles (Charlie), 246-47, *268*, 294, 311, *312*, 348
Sauvé, Jeanne, 436, *437*
Scallen, J.W., 250
Scallen, W., *498*
SCAN Marine, 428-29
Schindler, Marvin, 413
Scott, George W., 184
Scotts shipyard, Greenock, 247
Scully, Mrs. V.W., *322*
Sea King helicopters, 336, 378
Seaworks Ltd., 327
Sénéchal family, *495*
Sénéchal, Wilbrod, *502*
Seton, George, *56*
Sewell, Edmund, 8, 10, 11
Sharples, Charles, 80
Shell Oil, 324
Shepherd, John, *394*, 398, 437
Shipbuilding Industry Assistance Program, 435
Ship Carpenters' Society, 107
Simard, Joseph, 411
Simons, William, 89
Small, Vera, *294*
Smallwood, Joseph, 452-53, *454*
Smallwood, Mrs. J.R., *325*
Smith, Brian, 482
Smith, Lieutenant Commander Jim, *301*
SNC Group, 459-60

Société de construction navale, *see* Soconav
Société des traversiers de Quebec, *431*, 489
Société générale de financement (SGF), 403, 443, 475, 482, 489
Society of Mechanical Engineers, 359
Society of Naval Architects and Marine Engineers, 353
Soconav, 401, 403-4, 411, 421, 443
Sofati-Soconav Inc., 426
Soles, William E., 241
Sonar domes, *374*, 387-88, *389*, 481
Space Research Institute Incorporated, 358
Spithead Review, 303
St. Andrew's Wharf, 77
St. Lawrence Metal and Marine Works Inc., 283
St. Lawrence Seaway, 293, 313, 317, 319-21, 327, 330, 345
St. Lawrence Steam Navigation Company, 79
St. Lawrence Tow Boat Company, 77-79
St. Laurent, Louis, 293
St. Laurent, Mme Louis, 310
Staveley, Harry, 102
Steel Company of Canada (Stelco), 177, *322*, *326*, 356, 388
Steen Contractors Limited (Steen Becker), 490
Stephens, Captain G.L., 234
Stubbs, John, 286
Stylidiadis, Captain John, 105
Submarine chasers, *see* Motor launches
Submarines, 143, 459-60
Suez Canal crisis, 308
Swan Hunter, 133
Swan, Hunter & Wigham Richardson, 140

GENERAL INDEX

Sweeney, Robert, *498*
Symes, George Burns, 72
Syndicat des Travailleurs des Chantiers Maritimes, 280

Talon, Jean, 2
Tams, Lemoine and Crane, 169
Tankers, 305-6, 323-24, 334-35, 393, 395, 397, 400, 409
Tardif, Denis, *439*, *447*
Tate & Lyle, 409
Taylor, Edward, 25
Taylor, George, *xii*, 1, *18*, 19, 21-23, 25, 29-36, 41, 46, *48*, 51-56, *58*, 62, 75
Taylor, (Simon) Temple, 23, 30, 41, 53
Taylor, Captain John, 455
Taylor shipyard (Canoterie), 8, 25, *32*, 33, 43-44, *63*, 75
Tellier, Henri, 422
Temple, Simon, 23-24, 53-54
Tennet, Jack, 250
Tessier, Michel, *447*, *499*
Tessier, Réal, 275
Tessier, Robert, 455, 475, *476*
Thames Ironworks, Shipbuilding and Engineering, 133
Théberge, J.-P., *498*
Théberge, Jérôme, 250
Therrien, Jean-Paul, *439*
Thibault, Bertrand, *502*
Thomas, Vice-Admiral C.M., 462, *463*
Thompson, J.L., 231
Thomson, Andrew, 139-40
Thomson, R. Brock, 184, 246, 283, 291
Thornycroft, John I., 220
Thousand Island Navigation Company, *110*
Thyssen Nordseewerke shipyard, Emden, 486
Tibbets, Benjamin, 68
Tibbits shipyard, 109

Tibbits, James, 7, 10, 12, 67-68, 129
Tidewater Shipbuilders, Trois-Rivières, 169, 172-74, 246
Tingley, Rupert, 431
Tiremarche, Serge, *499*
Tobin, J., 185
Todd Shipbuilding, 420
Torrance, John, 60
Tovar, Fritz, 313
Tow boats, 61-62; *see also* Tugboats
Trades & Labour Congress of Canada, 108
Traverse de l'Ile d'Orléans Limitée, 188
Traverse de Lévis Limitée, 128, 130
Trawlers, 150-54
Tremblay, Laurent, *294*
Tremblay, Maurice, *294*
Tremblay, Nilus, 250
Tremblay, Paul, 248
Tremblay, Richard, *502*
Tribal Class Update, Refit and Modernization (TRUMP) program, 433-34, 440, 444, 458, 460-61, 463, 465-69
Tri-University Meson Facility (TRIUMF), 387, *388*
Trinity House, *36*, 43, 50, 55
Tugboats, 84-87, 104-5, 113-15, 122, 175, 187, 194-97, 310-12, 327, 329; *see also* Tow boats
Turcotte, Pierre, 275
Turgeon, Denis, *503*
Turgeon, Julien, *501*, *504*
Tweddell, Thomas, 44
Tweddle, Arthur, 91

U.S. Military Sealift Command, 420, 440
Union Carbide, *354*
Union Steamship Company of New Zealand, 154

GENERAL INDEX

Union Tank Car Corporation, 314
United Association of Journeymen, 280
United States Navy, 235, 241, 387
United States Shipping Board, 178
University of Alberta, 387
University of British Columbia, 387, *388*

Valiquet, U., 138
Vallières, Joseph, 286
Vallières, Maurice, *501*
Vandal, Paul, 478, *480*, 481
Vandevenne, D.A., *472*
Variable Depth Sonar, 336
Varnima Group, 385-86, 392-93, 397
Veliotis, Takis, 313-14, 330, 342, 347, *348*, 355-56, 359-60, 362-64, 366, 368, 375-76, 379, 386, 390, 392-93, 400, 404
Véronneau, Guy, 457, *458*, 468, *469*, 470-71, *472*, 473, 475-76, 488, 490, *500*
Verrault, Édouard, 10
Verrault, François, 10
Verrault Navigation, 204, 489
Versatile Corporation, 432-36, 439-41, 443
Versatile Pacific Shipyards Inc., 433-34, 468
Versatile Systems Engineering Inc., 433, 441
Vestgron Mines, 277
Vezina, René, *503*
Vickers, Sons and Maxim, 133-34; *see also* Canadian Vickers Limited
Victoria Machinery, 334
Vidal, Aymerick, *59*
Vien, Roméo, 249
Viger, L., *498*

Walker, E., *202*

Wallace, Frederick William, 119
War of 1812, 22-23
War Supply Board, 222, 256
Wartime Merchant Shipping Limited, 232, 256
Wartime Shipbuilding Limited, 257, 269-70
Wears, K.M. (Ken), 248-49, *269*
Weir, Mr., 248
Wellman, Jean, *503*
Weston & Galbraith, 44
White, Ed, 422
White, William (Bill), 274, 294, 347, *382*, 403, *404*, 405, 415, 422-23, *428*
Wildes, Thomas, 44
Wilkins, Larry, *447*
William Gardner & Co., 154
Williams, Jim, *472*
Wilson, Don, *472*
Wilson, George, *501*
Wilson, John, 65
Wind tunnels, 387
Winslade, Leonard (Len), 275, 350, *382*, 393-95
Wiseman, Francis, 43
Wiseman, James, 43
Wolvin, Roy M., 177, 263
Wood, Ken, 368
Wright, A.A., 152
Wright, Rear Admiral R., 335
Wright, Mrs. R., 335

Yarrow, Commander R.D., 379
Yarrows shipyard, Esquimalt, 140, 219, 235
Yarrows, Sir Alfred, 140-41
Yarrows, Norman, 141
Yeo, Sir James, *24*

Zizka, Jean-Paul, 274, *275*, 294, 351, *382*